16.2

2004 02 18

Dimensions of Anticipatory Mourning

Clinical Dimensions of Anticipatory Mourning

THEORY AND PRACTICE
IN WORKING WITH THE DYING,
THEIR LOVED ONES,
AND THEIR CAREGIVERS

THERESE A. RANDO, Editor

Research Press
2612 North Mattis Avenue   Champaign, Illinois 61822
www.researchpress.com

Composition by Jeff Helgesen
Printed by Malloy Lithographing
Cover design by Publication Services, Inc.

ISBN 0–87822–380–0

Library of Congress Catalog Number 99–74472

This book is lovingly dedicated . . .

In celebration of Tommy

With both thanksgiving and hope for Devon,
and continued missing of Berkeley

In memory of attorney Gary Yesser,
one of the "good guys" who was the exception
that proved the rule

In memory of Fay Carr Ashmore,
who lived living and dying
with generosity, dignity, and an indomitable spirit
that continues to enrich all those she touched

With deepest appreciation
for the unique wit, wisdom, and thanatological contributions
—particularly regarding anticipatory mourning—
of Robert Fulton, Ph.D.

Contents

Part II

Anticipatory Mourning from Different Perspectives

Part III

Applied Cases

Figures and Tables

Figures

Tables

Acknowledgments

A number of individuals have personally and/or professionally left their imprint upon this book via their impact upon me. Vast numbers of them cannot be named due to restrictions of confidentiality or anonymity. The former are those I have been privileged to work with in various clinical capacities for the past 30 years; the latter are those who have participated in educational programs in which I was involved. Together, these persons have educated me formally and informally about loss, grief, and mourning; disability, coping, and illness; trauma, victimization, and transcendence; dying, death, and bereavement. I sincerely hope that I have given to them at least a small proportion of what they have given to me.

During the preparation of this book, the life-threatening or terminal illnesses of three persons in my life were particularly, if not quite painfully, instructive about numerous aspects of anticipatory mourning. Among many other lessons, including those stimulated by personal courage and honesty, each one has highlighted a specific issue. Attorney Gary Yesser's illness taught me about being a "concerned other" in the anticipatory mourning scenario and how to contend with its often frustrating and painful disenfranchisement. Fay Ashmore's dying reminded me that even in fairly dire circumstances, character, love, determination, and autonomy are powerful allies that can enable real differences in quality of life. The struggle with cancer experienced even now by my dear aunt, Dorothy Morris, illustrates that, on occasion, the will to live—especially in order to care for a beloved other—can marshal the most effective resources and temporarily stay even death.

Professionally, I am particularly indebted to my colleagues at the Association for Death Education and Counseling, who continue to support, educate, and uplift me as they have for the past quarter century. In recent times, my appointment to the American Psychological Association's Working Group on Assisted Suicide and End-of-Life Decisions has exposed me to a cadre of psychologists who have greatly expanded my awareness in a number of areas associated with anticipatory mourning. In this regard, I want to acknowledge Drs. John Anderson, Silvia Canetto, Delores Gallagher-Thompson, Judith Gordon, Judy Stillion, and Jim Werth.

My association with two experts in traumatology has been especially instructive as I continue to discover clinically, theoretically, and empirically the interweaving of loss and trauma in both anticipatory and postdeath grief and mourning. I consider myself exceptionally fortunate for the opportunity to collaborate with Drs. Charles R. Figley and Roger M. Solomon, with both individuals' influence upon me being clearly evident at various points in this book as well as in aspects of my clinical practice.

Last, I could not fail to mention at this point the extent of my indebtedness to the chapter contributors. Without a doubt, these professionals are among the best of the best, and I cannot thank them enough for all the time and effort put into developing these chapters into clinical and academic resources that will directly translate into making anticipatory mourning be the most positive experience possible for all of the parties involved.

Sitting in both the professional and personal corners of my life, Ann Wendel of Research Press deserves distinct recognition. Her compassion and her wisdom, as both friend and publisher, are astounding. I cannot thank her enough for all she has done for me in both realms. Others at Research Press also must be acknowledged for their assistance and expertise. Russ Pence, Gail Salyards, and Dennis Wiziecki truly spoil me for working with others in publishing. In her role as editor, Karen Steiner has once again risen to a series of challenges that would overwhelm someone else. I am in awe of her ability not only to write, but to conceptualize, synthesize, and cut to the heart of the matter. I hope that by a kind of psychological osmosis some of her skill can rub off on me.

Several other persons merit specific mention because of what they have done for and meant to me. Lena DeQuattro helped to hold down the fort at Therese A. Rando Associates, Ltd., and The Institute for the Study and Treatment of Loss when it was required. She embodies loyalty. I owe a member of our extended family, Holly Blythe Stephenson, for all the time she enabled me to have to work on this book. She is among the relatively few people in this world who truly acts on her values. I will always remember how she kept her commitments when there were incentives not to do so. As always, no book of mine could ever fail to acknowledge the importance of Marion A. Humphrey and Lawrence C. Grebstein, two mainstays in my life.

My relatives must be identified once again as pivotal to my being who I am and able to do what I do. Deep affection and gratitude go to Miss Rita E. Rando, Mr. and Mrs. Joseph Morris, and Mr. and Mrs. Joseph Franco. I thank them for all their support. So, too, must I publically recognize my siblings, Beth and Randy, for their critically significant roles in my life. The attachments to them are among the strongest I shall ever have. My love and admiration belong to them in unique ways, and on behalf of our parents I note with extreme pride all that they have become and have accomplished.

The penultimate acknowledgment must go to Luann S. Gallant. Without her, this book really would not exist. As administrative assistant, she enabled me to juggle the myriad demands placed upon me as a private practitioner in the age of managed care who also happens to want to write. As friend and confidante, she supported me in coping with the immense challenges that the juggling entailed. I have never worked with anyone as skilled as she. I will remain forever grateful that I decided to listen to my intuition and "take the chance" on her.

Finally, the very most important and special acknowledgment of all necessarily goes to my family—Elizabeth-Ann, Tommy, Devon, Berkeley (in absentia), and my best friend, Anthony—because, along with my deceased parents, Thomas A. and Letitia G. Rando, they know and they love; they provide the joy and the meaning.

INTRODUCTION
Anticipatory Mourning: What It Is and Why We Need to Study It

I was three-quarters through my workshop on anticipatory grief, delineating specific processes occurring therein, when I came to the point in my notes about particular actions that a family member of a dying person might undertake. It pertained to the family member's striving to take in, through all of the senses, everything about the terminally ill loved one in order to construct a mental and sensory composite image of that person to endure after the death. I had just mentioned the attempt to try to emblazon upon one's memory the loved one's image as precisely as possible when the thought hit me: *In this day and age of home video cameras, people don't have to rely on memory to conjure up their deceased loved one's image anymore. They can put in a videotape and see and hear the real thing!*

This realization led to my thinking about the myriad other changes that had occurred since I originally edited the book *Loss and Anticipatory Grief* in 1986. There were now new diseases with unusual patient populations, different clinical and time courses, unique characteristics, and novel dilemmas about end-of-life decision making. These illnesses transpired amidst a context characterized by the proliferation of biomedical technology, quagmires posed by dementing disorders, and Oregon's controversial legalization of physician-assisted suicide. The topics of dying and death had received unparalleled media attention: The television program *60 Minutes* had shown "Dr. Death" Jack Kevorkian administering a lethal injection; *How We Die* (Nuland, 1993) had become a bestseller; and extensive psychological commentary on trauma and bereavement were being routinely provided after virtually all disasters. Organizations in the field were having broad impacts, with the

---

To Simon Chan, Chinese healer, who enabled control and hope
when there was none

multifocal "Project on Death in America" spending millions of dollars in its mission to transform the culture and experience of dying and bereavement in the United States, while the Hospice Foundation of America's annual teleconference was becoming the most visible and accessible source of professional education for tens of thousands in fields associated with thanatology. It had become rare to encounter someone who didn't know at least one person who had died in a hospice program. Serious calls were made for improving care at the end of life through such investigations as the SUPPORT study (The SUPPORT Principal Investigators, 1995) and the Institute of Medicine's exploration of extant practices in and experiences with dying and death in America (Field & Cassel, 1997). Heightened focus was being trained on the potential for growth and even transcendence during illness and dying (e.g., Byock, 1997).

Certainly, contemporary experiences of, attitudes toward, and conflicts around life-threatening and terminal illness—the distinction between these two entities being one of the many changes occurring since 1986—had been influenced by a host of sociocultural and technological trends, with the result that the anticipatory mourning phenomenon was at once vastly different than ever before while it retained many of its age-old elements. Although I had been considering putting forth a revised edition of *Loss and Anticipatory Grief*, it became clear that revision was not a real option. Far too many major changes had taken place in the medical, technological, psychosocial, legal, sociocultural, and sociopolitical contexts for anticipatory mourning—and clinical conceptions related to it had been transformed in consequence. Only a new volume could adequately address contemporary issues and concerns. *Clinical Dimensions of Anticipatory Mourning: Theory and Practice in Working with the Dying, Their Loved Ones, and Their Caregivers* aims to do just that.

To capture the best and most current thinking on the topic, this entirely new volume includes chapters by clinicians at the forefront of issues in anticipatory mourning. Topics range broadly, from clinical knowledge and theory to the specifics of anticipatory mourning from the perspectives of the different parties involved to a host of applied cases. Part I, "Knowledge and Theory," commences with my own extensive review and critique of the literature in chapter 1. In chapter 2, I define and discuss the six dimensions of anticipatory mourning. Kenneth J. Doka writes in chapter 3 of issues in anticipatory mourning associated with re-creating meaning in the face of illness. Chapter 4, by Thomas Attig, investigates the phenomenon of anticipatory mourning and the transition to loving in absence, and chapter 5, by Betty Davies, focuses on the phenomenon and the transition of fading away. Traumatic stress in anticipatory mourning is the subject of my own contribution in chapter 6. Charles A. Corr and Donna M. Corr delineate similarities, differences, and helper guidelines for anticipatory mourning and coping with dying in chapter 7, and Stephen R. Connor takes on the topic of denial and the limits of anticipatory mourning in chapter 8. Chapter 9, J. William Worden's look at anticipatory mourning and appropriate death, concludes the section.

The chapters in Part II, "Anticipatory Mourning from Different Perspectives" are small in number but potent in clinical information. Grief in dying persons is the subject of chapter 10, by William M. Lamers, Jr. In chapter 11, I outline strategies for promoting healthy anticipatory mourning in intimates of the life-threatened or dying person. The section comes to a close with chapter 12, Dale G. Larson's inquiry into the challenges in anticipatory mourning for professional and volunteer caregivers.

Part III, "Applied Cases," begins with chapter 13, Donna Jeane Hitchcock Pappas' examination of anticipatory mourning associated with prenatal diagnosis. Chapter 14, by Joyce Ashton and Dennis Ashton, continues the focus on the child-parent relationship by considering the dynamics of anticipatory mourning in dealing with the chronic/terminal illness or disability of a child. The phenomenon as witnessed in HIV/AIDS is the topic of chapter 15, by Sandra Jacoby Klein. In chapter 16, the second contribution by Kenneth J. Doka, the topic is anticipatory mourning and psychosocial loss brought about by Alzheimer's disease, ALS, and irreversible coma. David K. Meagher and Marsha (Max) Quinn take on the topic of anticipatory mourning and advance directives in chapter 17. Issues of anticipatory mourning in organ donation are the subject of chapter 18, by Sue C. Holtkamp. Finally, in chapter 19, Barbara Meyers delves into issues of anticipatory mourning as relating to the human-animal bond.

Readers will note that contributors to this book approach the subject from different viewpoints, may define the terms and the experience in various ways, and often focus on divergent aspects of it. What our differences reflect is the currency of the debate about nomenclature and, in fact, the topic itself. The reality that there are arguments about terminology or selected elements of anticipatory mourning is irrelevant to the existence of the phenomenon. Regardless of interpretations, as caregivers we must offer assistance with it.

As detailed in my review and critique of the literature in this volume's first chapter, anticipatory mourning, as variously conceptualized, appears to be a "double-edged sword," with the potential for both benefit and harm. Despite a lack of consistency across the research, it is a clinical reality that what happens before a person's anticipated death has a profound influence upon both that person's dying experience and the pre- and postdeath bereavement of survivors. The point upon which we all appear to agree is that before an anticipated death a critically important experience takes place both in the life-threatened or dying individual and in the family, intimates, and caregivers of that person.

ANTICIPATORY MOURNING VERSUS ANTICIPATORY GRIEF

Perhaps most central to the ongoing discussion of anticipatory mourning is the definition of the phenomenon and its discrimination from anticipatory grief. In the past, as well as currently, the term *anticipatory grief* has been most often used to describe what in this volume is referred to as *anticipatory mourning*. My recent use of the term had not been without a "force fit," however, given my earlier discriminations between grief and mourning (Rando, 1993, 1995), in which I defined grief as the reactions to the perception of loss, and mourning—which incorporates grief as its beginning processes—as going further to include actions undertaken to cope with, adapt suitably to, and accommodate that loss and its ramifications.

A number of early writers identified grief as only one component of several in the anticipatory mourning experience (e.g., see Futterman, Hoffman, & Sabshin, 1972; Lebow, 1976). Later authors (see Levy, 1991), including chapter authors in this book (see especially Corr & Corr, chapter 7), also have pointed out this distinction, precisely why it was necessary, and what implications it carries. With these resources to bolster my already deep conviction of the theoretical and clinical importance of distinguishing between grief and mourning, it became impossible for me to retain the term *anticipatory grief*, even though changing the terminology might be "bucking the tide" of conventional usage. Consequently, during the preparation of this book, I communicated with each contributor and addressed my concerns about the need for more precision in the language. As a result, *anticipatory mourning* became the chosen term. The specific definition that informs the present discussion, along with my four other chapters in this book, is as follows:

> Anticipatory mourning is the phenomenon encompassing
> seven generic operations (grief and mourning, coping,
> interaction, psychosocial reorganization, planning, balancing
> conflicting demands, and facilitating an appropriate death)
> that, within a context of adaptational demands caused by
> experiences of loss and trauma, is stimulated in response to
> the awareness of life-threatening or terminal illness in oneself
> or a significant other and the recognition of associated losses
> in the past, present, and future.

Consequently, the term *anticipatory grief* is employed in this work only (a) when it refers specifically to reactive responses to a loss without denoting any type of actions undertaken to cope with or accommodate to that loss or (b) on its first appearance, when the term is historically accurate because it describes the usage of an author or authors whose work is under discussion. In subsequent mentions, unless specifically noted, the term *anticipatory mourning* is employed.

As the proposed definition implies, anticipatory mourning is not a unitary concept that remains unaffected by person, place, time, and experience. Rather, it is multidimensional, occurring across four perspectives (the life-threatened or dying individual, intimates, concerned others, and caregivers) and three time foci (past, present, and future). Its content and course are determined by three classes of influencing factors (psychological, social, and physical) and are subject to two major sources of adaptational demands (experiences of loss and experiences of trauma). The phenomenon involves seven generic operations (grief and mourning, coping, interaction, psychosocial reorganization, planning, balancing conflicting demands, and facilitating an appropriate death), which are played out on three contextual levels (intrapsychic, interpersonal, and systemic).

WHY STUDY ANTICIPATORY MOURNING?

There are two main reasons for studying anticipatory mourning. One pertains to the life-threatened or dying person; the other concerns his or her intimates. In terms of the life-threatened or dying person, healthy anticipatory mourning is critical on two accounts. First, it offers that person the opportunity to have the best possible experiences in his or her living with illness, dying, and death. Second, to the extent that healthy anticipatory mourning can be promoted in the ill person's intimates, those intimates are subsequently better able to relate to the ill person and enable him or her to realize whatever would personally constitute a better life with the illness and a more appropriate death (Weisman, 1972).

As regards intimates, it is well known that the experience of a loved one's life-threatening or terminal illness has a profound influence upon the postdeath bereavement of survivors. When an individual presents for treatment after the death of a loved one, what he or she brings to the caregiver is a fait accompli (i.e., nothing can be done after the fact to alter the dying of the loved one and one's experiences with it). Failures in anticipatory mourning—as evidenced in unfinished business, unrecognized grief, complicated mourning, dysfunctional coping, premature detachment, poor communication, negative interactions with the ill person, inadequate psychosocial reorganization, and lack of appropriate planning and anticipation, among others—all predispose survivors to poorer bereavement outcomes (Rando, 1986). However, before the death, the caregiver has the golden opportunity to utilize primary prevention strategies to facilitate healthy anticipatory mourning. To the extent that healthy behavior, interaction, and processes can be promoted during the time before the loved one's death, the intimates' postdeath mourning can be made relatively better than it would be if the predeath experience had lacked these therapeutic experiences, made possible by anticipatory mourning.

MISCONCEPTIONS ABOUT ANTICIPATORY MOURNING

A precise definition of anticipatory mourning is essential to us as caregivers. However, before we can effectively enable anticipatory mourning, we also must address some long-held misconceptions about the phenomenon. Analyzing the assumptions underlying these misconceptions and setting the latter aside will better permit us to work toward a consistent operationalization of anticipatory mourning.

A number of these assumptions are present in the works of three learned thanatology pioneers, whose work has undeniably influenced our conceptualization of the anticipatory mourning phenomenon: Colin Murray Parkes, Robert Weiss, and Phyllis Silverman (see Glick, Weiss, & Parkes, 1974; Parkes & Weiss, 1983; Silverman, 1974; Weiss, 1988). Although each of these individuals believes that a period of anticipation can be useful, he or she does not feel that the benefits derive from what traditionally has been termed anticipatory grief. In fact, they appear variously to feel that anticipatory mourning is impossible, only partially possible, limited in value, or actually inappropriate and ill advised.

Many writers have erroneously interpreted anticipatory mourning as being a process that fully reconciles the survivors with what they will have to contend with subsequent to the death. In attempts to clarify this mistaken idea, both Silverman (1974) and Weiss (1988) are absolutely correct in noting that a rehearsal is not the real thing. However, rehearsal does give time to see a glimmer of what the future will be like, enabling such operations as psychosocial reorganization and planning, which are, by definition, aspects of anticipatory mourning. Parkes and Weiss (1983) are equally correct when they assert that there is rarely the same acceptance and recovery witnessed in anticipatory mourning as in postdeath mourning. Why should there be? Many losses are still in the process of being experienced, so they cannot yet be accommodated. However, this lack of resolution or accommodation, obviously precluded by the fact that hope still exists and the final irreversible separation has not yet occurred, does not mean that mourning is not taking place. In point of fact, some of the losses attendant to the life-threatening or terminal illness may indeed already have been accepted and accommodation may have been attained for them, even though the major loss of the actual death of the loved one has been neither accepted nor accommodated. Along with Silverman, Parkes and Weiss are once more on point in their observation that anticipation of loss frequently increases attachment. Again, attachment does not obviate mourning processes because anticipatory mourning need not mean withdrawal from the dying loved one. Finally, Parkes and Weiss are quite accurate in their assertion that as a result of omissions or commissions, thoughts, and feelings during this time period, the survivors are vulnerable to later self-accusation. These last realities are part and parcel of the anticipatory mourning experience, illustrating some of its limitations and possible dangers. They are not reasons that discount or invalidate anticipatory mourning.

I contend that most of the erroneous conclusions about anticipatory mourning are based on three underlying misconceptions, next discussed: (a) the overfocus on the ultimate loss of death (given that death is the major loss and that "anticipatory" suggests that one is mourning solely for anticipated as opposed to past and current losses as well); (b) the misinterpretation that "mourning" implies, at least to some, a necessity for a complete decathexis or letting go of the dying person (as opposed to a letting go of one's hopes for and with that person in the future, along with relevant elements in the assumptive world); and (c) the fallacious belief that since both predeath and postdeath mourning involve mourning, predeath mourning is necessarily the same in character and substance as postdeath mourning. Earlier, these misconceptions prompted me to suggest that, strictly speaking, the term *anticipatory mourning* is a misnomer (Rando, 1988).

Overfocus on the Ultimate Loss of Death

Overfocus on the ultimate loss of death influences and is influenced by disregard for, or at the very least a lack of sufficient appreciation of, the numerous other losses inherent in life-threatening or terminal illness. Although when compared with the major loss of death itself, these losses may seem minor, they are nonetheless real and of great impact. They include, among many others, the losses of previous functioning, health, abilities, and body parts; the loss of the future that had been planned with and for the loved one; the losses of the hopes, dreams, and expectations that had been invested in the relationship and in the loved one; the losses of security, predictability, and control; and the loss of notions of personal invulnerability.

These last four sets of losses represent elements of the assumptive world that require revision in light of the reality of the loved one's life-threatened status. The assumptive world is the mental schema containing everything a person assumes to be true about the world and the self on the basis of previous experience (e.g., assumptions, expectations, and beliefs; see chapter 2 in this volume). It is the person's internal model against which he or she constantly matches incoming sensory data in order to orient the self, recognize what is happening, and plan behavior (Parkes, 1988). Parkes has noted how readjustment of one's assumptive world is mandated after psychosocial transitions or psychological changes, and such transitions or changes certainly are witnessed in life-threatening or terminal illness. These readjustments are in themselves losses (being, at the very least, departures from the status quo) and cause further secondary losses (Rando, 1984), requiring their own mourning. Thus, anticipatory mourning is not solely relegated to the major loss of death, which has yet to occur, but in fact pertains to losses throughout the illness experience, in the past, present, and future.

Decathexis

The second misconception centers on the assumption that anticipatory mourning necessarily involves a major decathexis or detachment from the dying individual. Although it certainly can result in decathexis, anticipatory mourning need not automatically result in this outcome. Unfortunately, presumption of decathexis has been incorrectly derived from Lindemann's (1944) original example of a soldier's wife, who so effectively mourned in anticipation of the potential death of her husband that she demanded a divorce from him when he returned home alive. She had effectively worked through all of her ties to him and no longer loved him. This situation was viewed by many as illustrating the dangers of anticipatory mourning—premature detachment, letting go, or withdrawal from one not yet dead.

There was a failure on the part of many of Lindemann's readers to appreciate that this was an extreme case and not necessarily an inevitable one. Premature detachment is a dramatic example of a misdirected component of anticipatory mourning. Indeed, some loosening of ties with the ill or dying person must occur. However, what actually is let go in anticipatory mourning is not the actual person, but the hopes, dreams, and expectations of a long-term future with that person and for that person. The future can be mourned without relinquishing the present. Precisely because the target of the mourning is the anticipatory mourner's internal assumptive world, not the dying loved one, there is no need to abandon the here-and-now relationship as in Lindemann's famous example.

Students of anticipatory mourning also must realize that this example is not readily generalizable to anticipatory mourning in contemporary life-threatening or terminal illnesses. Lindemann's case involved total physical separation of the loved one from the mourner. It was impossible for the wife to have continued interaction with her soldier husband. Under the psychosocial circumstances of today's illnesses, this is not typical. Most seriously ill or dying persons are not totally separated from family and friends. On the contrary, usually there is contact and the opportunity to have ongoing, if not increased, involvement and interaction. To avoid confounding the issues, Lindemann's cautions must be reserved for situations with similar conditions (i.e., total physical separation from the loved one and significant threat to that person's life) and not inappropriately applied to dissimilar experiences.

It may be that the operative factor in premature detachment is total physical separation under conditions of severe life threat as opposed to life threat alone. Absences were more complete earlier in this century during hospitalizations of dying children, when there was relatively more separation of the child from the parent and less rooming-in. Since studies of and clinical discussions about parents of dying children at that time (e.g., Friedman, 1967; Friedman, Chodoff, Mason, & Hamburg, 1963; Levitz, 1977; Natterson & Knudson, 1960; Travis, 1976, among others) showed elements of premature detachment more often than did later writings, this may constitute further proof that in today's illness scenarios, premature detachment may be moderated by ongoing involvement. Rosenblatt's (1983) work also seems to bolster this notion. He found that, in contrast to the situation in which the anticipatory mourner and loved one live apart, co-residence with the dying person appears to interfere with anticipatory grief work and the disconnecting that can occur when one does not live with that individual.

Plainly, continued involvement with the dying person, and the goal of maximizing the possibility for whatever living is possible, is not inconsistent with or precluded by the experience of anticipatory mourning. This fact is evident in the observations of Futterman et al. (1972), who reported on the mourning of bereaved parents during the terminal illness and after the death of their child. These researchers observed that although anticipatory mourning had been engaged in prior to the death, at the time of the child's actual death mourning was rarely completed, and significant work remained to be accomplished. They also reported that although some signs of detachment were evident, parents had maintained care of their child's physical and emotional needs. Because parents were able to integrate both anticipatory mourning and the care of their child, the authors perceived detachment and provision of care and love as not being mutually exclusive.

More recent evidence that anticipatory mourning processes do not invariably result in detachment is found in Kramer's (1996–1997) research on women's relationships with terminally ill husbands and their subsequent adjustment to bereavement. In terms of the women's relationships with their ill partners, Kramer studied affiliation (defined as remaining physically and emotionally close to a dying husband, perhaps denying that he will die), separation (meaning facing the reality that he is, indeed, dying, and beginning the process of separating from him in preparation for life without him), and communication (implying that the members of the couple are open and honest with each other, discussing the husband's illness and impending death). Her results suggest that the kinds of behavior people think of in terms of "separation" are in no way inconsistent with "affiliation." She writes:

> A woman who has separated from her husband during this process has not necessarily done so at the expense of affiliating. To be quite frank about it, it suggests that a woman whose husband is dying can do something to provide for a better adjustment for herself later on without in any way detracting from her or her husband's sense of affiliation in the present.

> *Had the data shown that affiliation and separation were negatively related to one another, or mutually exclusive, there would have been cause for concern. Expectant widows would be forced to choose one mode of relating exclusively. Either choice they make carries a penalty.* To stay too close is to bury one's self prematurely; to withdraw completely is to bury one's husband prematurely. What a dilemma! Based upon this study's findings, however, women do not have to make this difficult choice. *Separation does not preclude a woman's affiliating with her dying husband. . . . It does not imply emotional detachment from the dying loved one, as has heretofore been believed.* (Kramer, 1996–1997, pp. 102–103, emphasis added)

Several other arguments against anticipatory mourning also were refuted in Kramer's interesting study. She found that the ability to separate from a dying husband bodes well for postdeath adjustment; that it is possible for the wife to be honest with herself and face the reality of her husband's death, but not to feel the pressure to talk to him about it; and that as the wife communicates with her husband about his illness and possible death, she is, in essence, affiliating as well as separating—remaining close while accepting the fact that he eventually will die.

In 1976, Lebow had come to a similar conclusion in her articulation of the six adaptational tasks in anticipatory mourning. The first two tasks were remaining involved with the dying loved one and remaining separate from him or her. The first means participating in the reality of the other, such as responding to what the loved one is going through, sharing with him or her some of the family members' experiences, with the goal of treatment being to maintain the relationship between the ill person and the family by encouraging open communication to the extent the family style permits. Remaining separate is a task of individuation, requiring that the family member appreciate his or her own sense of self as an individual apart from the ill person. The family member must be able to tolerate the awareness that the loved one will die and recognize his or her own ongoing existence. The treatment goals are to support the family member's own unique identity and capabilities, assist him or her in differentiating individual needs from those of the dying person, and encourage him or her to begin to circumscribe future life. Lebow writes: "Families often become blocked in the adaptational process, particularly in the first two tasks of remaining involved and remaining separate. These opposite movements must be blended so that there will be neither an untimely pulling away nor such overinvolvement that separation can not be accepted" (1976, p. 461). She clarifies: "*The goal of casework with the family prior to death is not to loosen emotional bonds,* as is appropriate later, on the contrary, *it aims at increased involvement balanced with individuation*" (Lebow, 1976, p. 465, emphasis added).

Similarity to Postdeath Grief and Mourning

The third major misconception about anticipatory mourning concerns the fallacy that to be legitimate mourning, anticipatory mourning must resemble postdeath grief and mourning in character and substance. As the literature reviewed in chapter 2 shows, it is clear that despite some similarities there are significant differences between the two. The reader is referred there for specifics. (In particular, see Aldrich, 1974; Glick et al., 1974; Hofer, Wolff, Friedman, & Mason, 1972; Parkes & Weiss, 1983; and Wolff, Friedman, Hofer, & Mason, 1964.) Just because anticipatory mourning is not exactly like postdeath mourning—which it never could be since the death has not yet transpired and different psychosocial and physical realities and reactions prevail—does not mean it is not mourning.

CONCLUSION

Significant discrepancies in thought about anticipatory mourning are, I believe, the result of definitional differences, failure to appreciate sufficiently the complexity of the phenomenon, misconceptions, or any combination of these. Anticipatory mourning is a real phenomenon, and as caregivers we are obliged to observe well and respond to the best of our abilities when it occurs. There is a need to capitalize on the opportunity for intervention and use it to the individual's advantage. Interventions made at this point can prevent problems in postdeath mourning from developing; later interventions can only attempt to remedy difficulties that already have occurred. Further observation and discussion are needed to clarify terminology, underlying concepts, and the exact character of anticipatory mourning across different individuals in different circumstances. The chapters collected in this book will, I hope, give wise clinical guidance and stimulate further inquiry to refine both our understanding and practice.

REFERENCES

Aldrich, C. (1974). Some dynamics of anticipatory grief. In B. Schoenberg, A. Carr, A. H. Kutscher, D. Peretz, & I. Goldberg (Eds.), *Anticipatory grief.* New York: Columbia University Press.

Byock, I.R. (1997). *Dying well: The prospect for growth at the end of life.* New York: Riverhead Books.

Field, M., & Cassel, C. (Eds.). (1997). *Approaching death: Improving care at the end of life.* Washington, DC: National Academy Press.

Friedman, S. (1967). Care of the family of the child with cancer. *Pediatrics, 40,* 498–504.

Friedman, S., Chodoff, P., Mason, J., & Hamburg, D. (1963). Behavioral observations on parents anticipating the death of a child. *Pediatrics, 32,* 610–625.

Futterman, E., Hoffman, I., & Sabshin, M. (1972). Parental anticipatory mourning. In B. Schoenberg, A. Carr, D. Peretz, & A. H. Kutscher (Eds.), *Psychosocial aspects of terminal care.* New York: Columbia University Press.

Glick, I., Weiss, R. S., & Parkes, C. M. (1974). *The first year of bereavement.* New York: Wiley.

Hofer, M., Wolff, C., Friedman, S., & Mason, J. (1972). A psychoendocrine study of bereavement. *Psychosomatic Medicine, 34,* 481–504.

Kramer, D. (1996–1997). How women relate to terminally ill husbands and their subsequent adjustment to bereavement. *Omega, 34,* 93–106.

Lebow, G. (1976). Facilitating adaptation in anticipatory mourning. *Social Casework, 57*, 458–465.

Levitz, I. (1977). Comment in section on "The Parents." In N. Linzer (Ed.), *Understanding bereavement and grief.* New York: Yeshiva University Press.

Levy, L. (1991). Anticipatory grief: Its measurement and proposed reconceptualization. *The Hospice Journal, 7*(4), 1–28.

Lindemann, E. (1944). Symptomatology and management of acute grief. *American Journal of Psychiatry, 101*, 141–148.

Natterson, J., & Knudson, A. (1960). Observations concerning fear of death in fatally ill children and their mothers. *Psychosomatic Medicine, 22*, 456–465.

Nuland, S. (1993). *How we die: Reflections on life's final chapter.* New York: Knopf.

Parkes, C. M. (1988). Bereavement as a psychosocial transition: Processes of adaptation to change. *Journal of Social Issues, 44*(3), 53–65.

Parkes, C. M., & Weiss, R. S. (1983). *Recovery from bereavement.* New York: Basic.

Rando, T. A. (1984). *Grief, dying, and death: Clinical interventions for caregivers.* Champaign, IL: Research Press.

Rando, T. A. (Ed.). (1986). *Loss and anticipatory grief.* Lexington, MA: Lexington Books.

Rando, T. A. (1988). Anticipatory grief: The term is a misnomer but the phenomenon exists. *Journal of Palliative Care, 4*(1/2), 70–73.

Rando, T. A. (1993). *Treatment of complicated mourning.* Champaign, IL: Research Press.

Rando, T. A. (1995). Grief and mourning: Accommodating to loss. In H. Wass & R. Neimeyer (Eds.), *Dying: Facing the facts* (3rd ed.). Washington, DC: Taylor & Francis.

Rosenblatt, P. (1983). *Bitter, bitter tears: Nineteenth-century diarists and twentieth-century grief theories.* Minneapolis: University of Minnesota Press.

Silverman, P. (1974). Anticipatory grief from the perspective of widowhood. In B. Schoenberg, A. Carr, A. H. Kutscher, D. Peretz, & I. Goldberg (Eds.), *Anticipatory grief.* New York: Columbia University Press.

SUPPORT Principal Investigators. (1995). A controlled trial to improve care for seriously ill hospitalized patients: The Study to Understand Prognoses and Preferences for Outcomes and Risks of Treatment (SUPPORT). *Journal of the American Medical Association, 274*, 1591–1598.

Travis, G. (1976). *The experience of chronic illness in childhood.* Stanford, CA: Stanford University Press.

Weisman, A. D. (1972). *On dying and denying: A psychiatric study of terminality.* New York: Behavioral Publications.

Weiss, R. S. (1988). Is it possible to prepare for trauma? *Journal of Palliative Care, 4*(1/2), 74–76.

Wolff, C., Friedman, S., Hofer, M., & Mason, J. (1964). Relationship between psychological defenses and mean urinary 17-hydroxycorticosteroid excretion rates: I. A predictive study of parents of fatally ill children. *Psychosomatic Medicine, 26*, 576–591.

PART I

Knowledge and Theory

CHAPTER 1

Anticipatory Mourning: A Review and Critique of the Literature

Therese A. Rando

There are few, if any, topics in thanatology more debated, less clear-cut, and quite as subject to misconception as the phenomenon of anticipatory mourning. Previously termed *anticipatory grief,* and introduced almost as an afterthought in the final paragraph of Erich Lindemann's classic 1944 article, "Symptomatology and Management of Acute Grief," anticipatory mourning occupies the interesting position of being an arena of significant controversy as well as one in which relatively minimal research exists. This is the case despite encompassing experiences for life-threatened patients, their loved ones, concerned others, and caregivers—a reality about which very few would disagree.

The purposes of this chapter are fourfold. I intend to (a) trace the relevant literature contributing to current understanding of anticipatory mourning; (b) identify germane research studies and delineate their contradictory findings; (c) address the reasons for discrepancies in the literature; and (d) specify the costs of anticipatory mourning. To my knowledge, no other resource has compiled all of this information in the fashion done here, incorporating literature from a variety of specializations and disciplines in order to substantiate the complex experience of anticipatory mourning.

It is difficult, if not impossible, to differentiate the topic of anticipatory mourning from writings about the life-threatened or terminally ill patient and that patient's loved ones. Depending upon one's definition of anticipatory mourning, it would not be technically inaccurate to consider every source that addresses dying, death, and issues of loss, grief, mourning, or bereavement as also addressing some aspect of the phenomenon. To provide an exhaustive review of literature pertinent to anticipatory mourning, one would need to

---

To my aunt and uncle, Florence and Joseph Franco, for all their love and support

incorporate the lion's share of all thanatology publications and many that address aspects of traumatic stress related to medical illness and disability. The following review will be restricted to publications that focus specifically on anticipatory mourning or that in my determination have an important contribution to make to the topic. These materials are most represented in the content domains of dying (life-threatened or terminally ill) persons and their loved ones, sudden death (which by definition permits little to no anticipatory mourning), and coping with physical illness and disability.

When reporting the work of a particular author, I have used his or her terminology (with the exceptions noted) and assumed that underlying philosophy and approaches are valid. The focus is restricted to adults, although certainly numerous extrapolations, with proper cautions, could be made to children.

CHRONOLOGICAL REVIEW OF THE LITERATURE

Lindemann, His Peers, and His Predecessors

In 1944, Lindemann observed that in some cases of wartime separation, individuals were so concerned about their adjustment following the potential death of a loved one that they underwent all the phases of grief, specifically "depression, heightened preoccupation with the departed, a review of all the forms of death which might befall him, and anticipation of the modes of readjustment which might be necessitated by it" (pp. 147–148). In essence, in an attempt to protect against future distress, the person mourned the death of the loved one before it actually occurred.

While such a practice might be adaptive in preparing the mourner should the death in fact transpire, it can be problematic if the loved one does not die and is reunited with the mourner. Lindemann illustrated this by describing a wife who had grieved so effectively the possible death of her soldier husband that when he returned home from battle alive she no longer loved him and demanded an immediate divorce. She had completed her grief work so well that she had emotionally detached herself from the person she previously had loved and was oriented toward a life that no longer included him. Clearly, the seeds of concern about the problems that could be associated with anticipatory mourning were sown at the same time the phenomenon was recognized.

The duality inherent in anticipatory mourning—that is, the presence of a downside as well as an upside—has fueled much of the controversy around the topic since the publication of Lindemann's article. However, the issue is not solely the presence or absence of anticipatory mourning, but also the amount, quality, and components of the phenomenon, as well as the manner in which it is perceived, experienced, and responded to.

Despite the fact that Lindemann is the person most often cited as introducing the concept of anticipatory mourning into the literature, earlier writings, as well as some that were relatively contemporaneous, also grappled with the topic, although under different terms. Fulton and Gottesman (1980) note that Freud addressed the topic in two early essays. In "Premonitory Dreams Fulfilled" (1899/1953) and "On Transcience" (1916/1957), Freud raised the possibility that mourning could be unconscious and considered that certain premonitory fantasies involving separation or loss might obscure libidinal ties and serve as a mode of displacement. He concluded that the death of a significant person could be anticipated and mourned in advance with less psychic pain.

In the same year as Lindemann's article, Rosenbaum (1944) noted the depressive effects of separation on the families of soldiers. Shortly thereafter, Eliot (1946) discussed the possibly benign effects of anticipation, or what he termed *forewarning*, on potential survivors as a partial defense against the shock of the actual occurrence of death. He proposed that "pre-bereavements" such as leaving home, partings at furloughs, and leave takings before overseas duty might serve as rehearsals for what would come should death actually transpire.

The 1950s and 1960s: Early Research

In the 1950s and 1960s, a number of research investigations examined forewarning of loss or length of illness, with anticipatory mourning as an important inference. In these two decades, the bulk of the research was conducted prospectively with parents of terminally ill children. (Bereaved spouses were the subjects of most of the studies in the late 1960s and 1970s.)

In 1956, in his exposition "Reactions to Untimely Death," Lehrman appears to have been the first to offer an in-depth elucidation of the significance of anticipation, timing, and expectation as critical factors influencing mourning. Like myriad others who followed, Lehrman's case for the harmful consequences of an unanticipated and unexpected death implies the benign effects of forewarning and mourning prior to the actual death. In fact, where death has been expected, he writes, "The work of mourning is done quickly, because a certain amount of this work (detaching the libido from the object) has already preceded the event of death" (p. 565). Therefore, just as the literature about the dying person and his or her loved ones contains information pertinent to anticipatory mourning, so does the sudden and traumatic death literature enlighten about the subject, either explicitly or implicitly.

In 1958, Janis published a study on patients coping with the stress of surgery. Findings revealed that patients who carried out the "work of worry" prior to their surgeries had better psychological and physical outcomes, experienced less distress postsurgically, and adjusted better than those who did not. This pivotal piece of research demonstrated the potential relationship between rehearsing a stressful event and subsequent coping; as such, it provided empirical and clinical underpinning for the adaptive potential of anticipatory mourning.

Major and unparalleled medical, psychosocial, and cultural changes relevant to anticipatory mourning were sparked by two women in the 1960s. Formalizing humankind's concern for the dying, in 1967, Dr. Cicely Saunders founded St. Christopher's Hospice in London. This is typically noted as the beginning of the modern hospice movement. Since Saunders' founding of St. Christopher's, rather than designating an actual place offering rest, support, and shelter, *hospice* has come to refer to a philosophy and approach to care of the terminally ill (or those who have no reasonable hope of benefit from cure-oriented intervention) and their loved ones. The movement embodying this philosophy and approach articulates a number of central principles (Corr, Nabe, & Corr, 1997) and defining components (Lattanzi-Licht & Connor, 1995). Those most applicable to anticipatory mourning are as follows: (a) hospice philosophy affirms life, not death; (b) the focus of care is on improving the quality of remaining life—that is, on palliative, not curative, measures; (c) the patient and family are the unit of care; (d) hospice is holistic care addressing physical, psychological/emotional, social, and spiritual needs, and includes giving major attention to effective symptom control and pain management; (e) care is provided by an interdisciplinary team; and (f) the patient is kept at home or in an inpatient setting with a homelike environment where there is coordination and continuity of care, with services available 24 hours a day, 7 days a week.

Providing a rallying cry for numerous professionals already in the field, as well as an introduction to the topic for the general public, in 1969 Elisabeth Kübler-Ross's *On Death and Dying* broke through personal and institutional silence and identified some of what the dying could teach. Although the book later would be the subject of much debate, it delineated five different stages people experience when faced with the tragic news of their own impending death: denial and isolation, anger, bargaining, depression, and acceptance. Terming them at once "defense" but also "coping" mechanisms, Kübler-Ross contended that the stages lasted for different periods of time, replacing each other or existing at times side by side, with hope usually persisting throughout all stages.

While Kübler-Ross's widespread acclaim in the popular arena contrasted with sharp criticism in the scholarly world, the fact remains that her underlying lessons were important (Corr et al., 1997). Of particular consequence were her drawing attention to the human aspects of living with dying; her highlighting the concept of "unfinished business"; her illustrating our fear and avoidance of death and the dying, along with the consequences to the dying individual; her underscoring the need to listen actively to the dying and to identify with them their own needs; her fleshing out of the five coping mechanisms; her documenting the importance to the patient of some amount of hope; her mandating us to "refocus on the patient as a human being, to include him in dialogues, to learn from him" (p. xi) and to incorporate the patient as the central party in the dying scenario; and her explicating the effects of the loved one's dying upon the family, the coping demanded from them, and the family's experience after the death.

The 1970s and 1980s: Years of Expansion

In 1971, Fulton and Fulton spoke directly about the phenomenon of anticipatory mourning. Along with Lindemann's (1944) first discussion of the topic, their article "A Psychosocial Aspect of Terminal Care: Anticipatory Grief" is the most often cited resource on the subject, although the clinical concerns raised by these two authors frequently are overlooked.

Purposefully and explicitly, Fulton and Fulton delineated what they termed the "two-edged effect" of anticipatory grief, which they saw to be increasing in presence and importance in society: "It possesses the capacity to enhance our lives and secure our well-being, while possessing at the same time the power to undermine our fragile existence and rupture our tenuous social bonds" (p. 99). Amplifying Lindemann's position, they believed that anticipatory grief operated in such a fashion that over an extended period of time family members may experience depression, feel a heightened concern for the ill member, rehearse the death, and attempt to adjust to the various consequences of it. Additionally, they thought that by the time the death occurred, the family members would, to the extent that they had anticipated the death or dissipated their grief, display little or no emotion. It was this last point, and what led up to it during the person's illness, that was of primary concern to these observers.

Specifically, Fulton and Fulton identified three areas of social and psychological ramifications that can develop when loved ones have undergone anticipatory grief:

1. It may result in a lack of expected response at the time of actual death that can precipitate undeserved critical judgment by others, as well as the critical judgment of one's self accompanied by feelings of guilt and shame.

2. It may result in a turning away of the family from the dying patient and a blocking of support needed at that time from the family, possibly compelling the patient to grieve not only for his or her own death but also for the seeming loss of the family's love.

3. It may result in the family's deeming that a traditional funeral is unnecessary, thus depriving the family and other members of the extended social group of experiences afforded by rituals that historically have served critical psychological, social, and religious functions.

The next authors to operationalize and clinically examine anticipatory processes were Futterman, Hoffman, and Sabshin (1972). They appear to have been the first to discriminate between the terms *anticipatory mourning* and *anticipatory grief*. Futterman et al. wrote that, in contrast to their own and others' previous work, in which the terms had been used interchangeably, anticipatory mourning is the overall process, distinct from grieving, which is one of its component processes.

In this excellent study on parental anticipatory mourning, the findings of which are applicable to anticipatory mourning in general, Futterman et al. define anticipatory mourning as "a set of processes that are directly related to the awareness of the impending loss, to its emotional impact, and to the adaptive mechanisms whereby emotional attachment to the dying [patient] is relinquished over time" (p. 251). They found it useful to differentiate anticipatory mourning from other related tasks of equal importance in the total adaptation of families (e.g., maintaining family life-style and integrity, maintaining a sense of mastery and confidence—including dealing with helplessness, anger, and guilt—and caring for the patient's needs and promoting his or her development).

Based on the clinical data from this study, the authors posit the sequential emergence of five interdependent and continually interacting part-processes: Together, these processes comprise anticipatory mourning:

1. Acknowledgment: Becoming progressively convinced that the child's death is inevitable.

2. Grieving: Experiencing and expressing the emotional impact of the anticipated loss and the physical, psychological, and interpersonal turmoil associated with it.

3. Reconciliation: Developing perspectives on the child's expected death which preserve a sense of confidence in the worth of the child's life and in the worth of life in general.

4. Detachment: Withdrawing emotional investment from the child as a growing being with a real future.

5. Memorialization: Developing a relatively fixed conscious mental representation of the dying child which will endure beyond his death. (p. 252)

Another delineation of anticipatory mourning was provided in 1972 by McCollum and Schwartz. In "Social Work and the Mourning Parent," they offered a conceptual framework to facilitate examination of the four component aspects of the anticipatory mourning experience: (a) defensive processes, (b) affective states, (c) issues presented, and (d) adaptive behavior. Like the Futterman et al. (1972) research, findings, while written specifically about parents of dying children, can be extrapolated for other populations.

McCollum and Schwartz identified four *defensive processes* utilized by parents to ward off acknowledging the unendurable reality of the child's illness and to protect themselves from being engulfed by anguish. When the illness was prolonged, intermittent remobilization of these defenses was essential to keep the parents from continuous despair. The processes most frequently observed included denial, repression, isolation of affect, and avoidance. A number of intense *affective states* were stimulated by the parents' acknowledgment of the reality of the child's danger. These included sorrow (the central emotion aroused), anger, guilt, and anxiety. *Issues* parents faced included management of the ill child, contending with the influence of the illness upon the family's life-style and psychological relationships, and addressing emotionally charged questions around further reproduction. The *adaptive behavior* that enabled the parents to assimilate reality, master affective states, and resolve issues included information seeking, invoking emotional support, partialization (i.e., separation of the mourning experience into component parts that could be assimilated and mastered), and rehearsal of the death.

Further dimensions of anticipatory mourning were added by Weisman (1972a) in his clinical opus *On Dying and Denying: A Psy-*

chiatric *Study of Terminality* and elaborated upon in other writings (see Weisman, 1972b, 1977, 1979). Among his numerous contributions are three clinical concepts that are particularly relevant to the topic of anticipatory mourning. These concepts constitute goals for therapeutic intervention with dying persons: safe conduct for the dying, significant survival and dignified dying, and appropriate death.

The dimension beyond diagnosis, treatment, and relief, *safe conduct for the dying* pertains both to the caregiver's behavior and to the patient's experience because of it. The caregiver must behave cautiously and prudently when providing guidance through the maze of uncertain, perplexing, and distressing events of the patient's dying. The patient is helped to cope psychologically and socially. Anguish, loneliness, and other types of emotional suffering secondary to the personal crisis of dying are minimized by the caregiver, who behaves compassionately, prevents dehumanization of the patient, and enables significant survival.

Significant survival and dignified dying are facilitated by and are measurements of safe conduct. *Significant survival* means realizing the value in what we are and do. The caregiver attempts to help the dying person find significance in the last phases of living—not just relieving suffering, but enabling the person to look back to earlier and healthier days to recall a sense of well-being and self-esteem. Although these events may not be experienced as they were previously, their remembrance, along with the experience of dignity in dying and the maintenance of as much self-control as possible, makes survival significant to the dying person. *Dignified dying* is afforded to the patient when that person is continually regarded as a responsible individual capable of clear perceptions, honest relationships, and purposeful behavior despite physical decline and disability. Dignity, relief, and privacy are provided, while demoralization, emotional neglect, and infantilization are avoided. The individual is treated as a living person, despite the fact that he or she is dying.

An *appropriate death* is a death one might choose for oneself. It is not necessarily an ideal death, but it is experienced as being consistent with the person's ego-ideal. Facilitation of an appropriate death, one of Rando's seven generic operations in anticipatory mourning, is discussed in detail in chapter 2.

In 1974, Schoenberg, Carr, Kutscher, Peretz, and Goldberg edited a landmark book in a series produced by the Foundation of Thanatology. *Anticipatory Grief* was the first book devoted specifically to the phenomenon of anticipatory processes. Among its 41 interdisciplinary chapters analyzing the topic from a wide variety of perspectives, several are important to highlight here. In one of these, Aldrich (1974) specified the dynamics of anticipatory grief. Using the term *anticipatory grief* to distinguish grief occurring prior to a loss from grief occurring at or after loss, Aldrich noted some parallels between the two types of grief but also pointed out important dissimilarities in ambivalence, denial, hope, endpoints, and acceleration.

Aldrich viewed ambivalence as having a special impact on anticipatory grief because the target of the ambivalent feelings (i.e., the dying patient) was not only still alive but was also particularly vulnerable, balanced between life and death. This vulnerability makes any hostility or death wish seem especially potent and dangerous. The fact that this is so may contribute to the clinical impression that anticipatory grief is more readily denied than conventional postdeath grief. On the dying patient's part, anticipatory grief also may tend to be denied, not only because of the extent of the anticipated losses but also because of the normal ambivalence the patient may feel about the fact that he or she, and not someone else, is dying.

According to Aldrich, hope is present as long as there is some life left: Conceivably, some action could always delay the loss or prevent death's occurrence. By definition, this hope is missing in conventional postdeath grief, where the loss has irreversibly occurred. The potential for action can be both positive and negative in anticipatory grief. For the mourner with unacceptable ambivalence, guilt about that ambivalence can be increased by committing what may be interpreted as errors of omission or commission in patient care. Concerns about one's behavior's influencing the timing or extent of the loss are absent for the individual whose loved one has already died.

Aldrich also noted that the endpoints of anticipatory and conventional postdeath grief are markedly different. Anticipatory grief has a definite end. It ceases with the death of the patient and, although grief will continue thereafter, it will no longer be anticipatory grief. Theoretically, conventional postdeath grief may continue indefinitely, as is best illustrated by chronic mourners. The acceleration of both types of grief differs as well. Conventional grief ordinarily diminishes as time passes. Although one might expect anticipatory grief to accelerate as the loss approaches, clinical observation reveals that it does not. Probably the balance between denial (which presumably forestalls grief work) and acceptance (which presumably facilitates it) helps to explain the discrepancy between the theoretical expectation and the clinical reality that anticipatory grief does not consistently increase as the loss grows nearer.

In conclusion, Aldrich's work suggests that a period of anticipation can provide a positive opportunity to grieve in advance of the loss; however, that very same period also can complicate the working-through process by giving the hostile component of ambivalence a more realistically destructive potential. As others before him found, anticipatory mourning is a double-edged sword.

A second particularly important chapter in *Anticipatory Grief* is Gerber's (1974) "Anticipatory Bereavement." Gerber astutely pointed out that what is generally missing in the various descriptions of anticipatory grief is the social component. To address this, Gerber introduced the term *anticipatory bereavement,* which he saw as less restrictive than *anticipatory grief* because it takes into account both emotional and social preparations for the death. Gerber clearly saw that the experience of anticipatory bereavement had both potentially positive and negative ramifications.

The same year that *Anticipatory Grief* was published, Glick, Weiss, and Parkes published their groundbreaking study, *The First Year of Bereavement* (1974). This book and a subsequent one entitled *Recovery from Bereavement,* by Parkes and Weiss (1983), generated a number of significant empirical and clinical findings. The 1974 title was particularly important in documenting that grief following unanticipated bereavement differs from anticipated grief in both form and duration. This is not because a period of anticipation necessarily lessens the grief. Rather, it is because unanticipated loss so overwhelms adaptive capacities and so seriously affects functioning that uncomplicated recovery can no longer be expected. Because the adaptive capacities are enormously and severely assaulted, mourners are often unable to grasp the full implications of their loss. They frequently suffer extreme feelings of bewilderment, anxiety, self-reproach, and depression that render them unable to function normally. They are stunned and cannot fully comprehend what has happened. Because they are struck without warning, they lose their security and confidence, with many never being able to regain it and instead always waiting for another major loss to befall. Despite intellectual recognition of the death, there is difficulty in accepting the loss, which may continue to seem inexplicable. The world is without order and, like the loss, does not make sense. Grief symptomatology persists longer than usual.

Glick et al. (1974) and Parkes and Weiss (1983) concluded that because grief is as deep among those who anticipated the death of their loved ones as among those who did not, in unanticipated loss grief is not augmented, but the capacity to cope is diminished. In this regard, the value of a period of anticipation is that it allows an opportunity for emotional preparation. In contrast to the unanticipated loss, when expected death comes it will make sense because it can be understood as the result of a predicted process.

In 1976, Lebow contributed to the anticipatory mourning literature by delineating a set of adaptational tasks for family members in anticipatory mourning, which she defined as "the total set of cognitive, affective, cultural, and social reactions to expected death felt by the patient and family" (p. 459). She also designated that portion of anticipatory mourning involving the affective responses as "anticipatory grieving." Lebow wrote that the goal of intervention with the family prior to the death was "not to loosen emotional bonds, as is appropriate later [i.e., after the death], on the contrary, it aims at increased involvement balanced with individuation" (p. 465). Her adaptational tasks for family members in anticipatory mourning included (a) remaining involved with the patient, (b) remaining separate from the patient, (c) adapting suitably to role changes, (d) bearing the affects of grief (i.e., anticipatory grieving), (e) coming to some terms with the reality of the impending loss, and (f) saying good-bye to the dying person.

Pattison (1977) presented a most useful conceptualization of the dying process, with an identification of the corresponding tasks presented to the caregiver. It is quite helpful in refining crucial aspects of the anticipatory mourning experience and in delineating specific crises, coping mechanisms, fears, and developmental concerns. Pattison termed the period of time between the crisis of knowledge of death (stimulated by receipt of a life-threatening or terminal diagnosis) and the point of death the *living-dying interval* and divided it into three clinical phases, each requiring a different style and set of phase-appropriate responses from the caregiver.

The *acute crisis phase* is characterized by acute crisis anxiety stemming from the knowledge that one's life has been foreshortened. Many primitive and immature (i.e., pathological) defenses are temporarily employed to deal with this intense stress and its anxiety. The caregiver's task is to prevent this crisis anxiety from causing a chaotic disintegration of the person's life during the rest of the living-dying interval.

In the *chronic living-dying phase,* the patient—still living although on a dying trajectory—struggles to cope with the illness and its problems, along with the psychosocial responses to the illness and the impending death, interpersonal relationships, and problems in daily living. The individual must contend with a number of fears: the unknown, loneliness, sorrow, loss of family and friends, loss of body, loss of self-control, suffering and pain, loss of identity, and regression. Coping mechanisms tend to be those normally appropriate for the patient's developmental stage of life. The caregiver's task is to respond to the adaptive issues of this phase.

The onset of the *terminal phase* is thought to commence when the dying individual begins to pull back and respond to internal body signals indicating that he or she now must conserve energies. There appears to be a psychic as well as physical turning away from the outside world into the self, and the coping mechanisms of the previous phase are replaced by isolating mechanisms, withdrawal, and increasing detachment. The caregiver's task is not to draw the person back into life, but to allow the patient to withdraw appropriately from it.

In 1978, the International Work Group on Death, Dying, and Bereavement disseminated the document "Assumptions and Principles Underlying Standards of Care for the Terminally Ill." Prior to that time, there were no explicit, recognized standards of treatment for the dying and their families. Assumptions and principles promoting good terminal care indirectly spoke to issues of promoting healthy anticipatory mourning and the dying process.

In explicating behavioral family systems intervention in terminal care, Cohen and Cohen (1981) delineated seven coping tasks, inherent in the death crisis itself, that all families must negotiate. These reveal the multifocused psychosocial demands placed upon family members during the anticipatory mourning experience. They include (a) denial versus acceptance of the illness, (b) establishing a relationship with health caretakers, (c) meeting the needs of the dying person, (d) maintaining a functional equilibrium, (e) regulation of affect, (f) negotiating extrafamilial relationships, and (g) coping with the postdeath phase.

In 1983, Rando conducted a research investigation on the grief and adaptation of parents whose children had died from cancer. Previous investigators had assumed the existence of anticipatory grief, based on the length of the terminal illness. Rando's study was the first to operationalize anticipatory grief. A parent's anticipatory grief score was determined by the numerical sum of the behaviors he or she reported to have engaged in during the child's terminal illness. These behaviors included (a) discussing with someone the possibility that the child would die, (b) grieving in anticipation of the loss of the child, (c) thinking what the future would be like without the child, (d) acknowledging the fact that the child was going to die, (e) discussing the child's dying with the child, (f) planning the type of death they wanted for the child, (g) making funeral preparations, and (h) starting partially to disengage emotionally from the child.

Two associations were found to be statistically significant. Anticipatory grief was found to be positively associated with preparedness at death, with parental preparation increasing directly as the amount of anticipatory grief increased. A stronger level of statistical significance described the association between anticipatory grief and abnormal grief after the death. The more anticipatory grief behaviors engaged in prior to the death, the less abnormal grief was present following the death.

Several findings argued for the therapeutic effects of avoiding too little or too much anticipatory grief. There appeared to be a medium amount of anticipatory grief that was optimum as related to facilitating appropriate participation with the child during the illness and to lower indicies of anger and hostility and loss of emotional control after the death. The study also concluded that there seems to be an optimum length of illness as it relates to the survivors' at-death and postdeath experiences. Those illnesses that were too brief or too lengthy were associated with compromised preparedness at death and adjustment thereafter, with the longest illnesses appearing to cause the most difficulty in these two areas and also to be associated with greater anger and hostility and more abnormal grief.

Several other patterns implied the relative importance of anticipatory grief. Although not statistically significant, findings strongly suggested that psychosocial support during the child's terminal illness was related to the experience of anticipatory grief. Parents who were low on support during the child's illness tended to have engaged in fewer anticipatory grief behaviors, suggesting that anticipatory grief may be assisted by, or possibly requires, the support of others. Additionally, individuals who were low in subsequent adjustment after the death tended to have engaged in fewer anticipatory grief behaviors prior to the death. As the amount of anticipatory grief behaviors increased, so did the percentages of parents with high subsequent adjustment. This finding provides more evidence for the assertion that anticipatory grief may facilitate postdeath grief, and that the absence of it predisposes one to poorer bereavement outcomes.

Following Schoenberg et al. (1974), *Loss and Anticipatory Grief*, edited by Rando in 1986(b), was the second book ever to be devoted exclusively to the topic of anticipatory mourning. In addition to examining clinical issues and treatment strategies, differential concerns for diverse parties in the dying experience, developmental issues, and practical considerations, the work was noted for proposing a broader definition of anticipatory grief and for delineating three categories of interrelated processes that operationalized it (Rando, 1986a). Perceiving anticipatory grief as a complex and multidimensional set of processes that could be called up during the terminal illness of a loved one, Rando offered the following definition:

> Anticipatory grief is the phenomenon encompassing the
> processes of mourning, coping, interaction, planning, and
> psychosocial reorganization that are stimulated and begun
> in part in response to the awareness of the impending loss of
> a loved one and the recognition of associated losses in the
> past, present, and future. It is seldom explicitly recognized,
> but the truly therapeutic experience of anticipatory grief

mandates a delicate balance among the mutually conflicting demands of simultaneously holding onto, letting go of, and drawing closer to the dying patient. (Rando, 1986a, p. 24)

Additionally, Rando provided arguments asserting that the term *anticipatory grief* was a misnomer, primarily because "anticipatory" suggests that one is grieving solely anticipated losses, as opposed to both past and current losses as well, and because "grief" implies (to some) the necessity for complete detachment from the dying person as opposed to from one's hopes for and with that person in the future. Rando also made clear that continued involvement with the dying person and maximizing the possibility for that individual's living are not inconsistent with nor precluded by the experience of anticipatory grief. Rando labeled Lindemann's (1944) case of the soldier's wife who had totally detached emotionally as a result of anticipatory grief work anticipatory grief gone awry because it had not facilitated the finishing of unfinished business between the two parties and had not promoted whatever continued involvement remained possible—two of the primary objectives of anticipatory grief. Finally, Rando advanced that therapeutic anticipatory grief prompts appropriate engagement in each of three sets of interrelated processes (incorporating 50 subprocesses) that facilitate one another during the dying of a loved one.

The 1990s: Refining Concepts

Part of a larger investigation of effects of hospice care and mutual support interventions on the course and outcome of bereavement among surviving spouses of cancer patients, Levy (1991) and colleagues developed a measure of conjugal anticipatory grief. Statistical analysis of their instrument, the Anticipatory Grief Inventory (AGI), yielded three factors, identified as conjugal coping, anticipatory grief, and cognitive coping.

Conjugal coping involved activities that seemed to deepen the couple's relationship and strengthened their ability to face the spouse's death. The items on this factor seemed to pertain to the couple's summing up of their life together; their joint acknowledgment of, and preparation for, the spouse's impending death; and their sharing of thoughts and feelings stemming from this acknowledgment. *Anticipatory grief* items focused on the impending loss and its consequences; several involved various strong emotional responses to the prospect of the spouse's death. The final factor, *cognitive coping,* represented items that reflected the prospective survivor's dispassionate, cognitive acknowledgment of the spouse's impending death and cognitive preparations for the death and life thereafter.

A number of interesting findings were generated from subjects responding within the first 2 to 3 months after the death of their spouse. Along with the AGI, they were administered two measures of depression (one for depressive symptoms and one for depressed mood) and one measure of subjective distress. Although acknowledging that it may have been too soon in the bereavement process for some effects to be manifested, Levy reported, among other findings, that (a) women scored significantly higher than men on anticipatory grief; (b) conjugal coping scores were significantly lower than scores on the other two factors; (c) length of terminal illness (differentiated from total duration of illness) correlated significantly with conjugal coping, cognitive coping, and total AGI, but not with anticipatory grief; (d) high scores on anticipatory grief were associated with increased depressive symptomatology and increased levels of subjective stress, suggesting that high levels of anticipatory grief may be a potential risk factor for poor early bereavement adjustment and that caution should be exercised in attempting to facilitate anticipatory grief in the loved ones of the dying; (e) no correlation occurred between length of terminal illness and any of the depression and stress measures, suggesting that anticipatory grief cannot be inferred from the length of the forewarning of loss itself; and (f) no correlation between anticipatory grief scores and length of terminal illness existed, perhaps reflecting that, in contrast to the coping variables, anticipatory grief may be more dependent on the individual's customary level of emotional adjustment and ability to cope with stress. In light of these and other findings, Levy recommended that anticipatory grief be regarded as one component of anticipatory bereavement (as termed by Gerber, 1974), which also includes, among other yet-to-be determined processes, conjugal and cognitive coping.

Charles Corr (1992) proposed a task-based approach to understanding and interpreting dying, in which efforts involved in coping with dying are interpreted as "tasks" or "task work." Reacting to what he felt had been the overly passive qualities in stage and phase models, Corr argued that dying individuals selected which tasks they wished to pursue, as well as how and when they did so. Such choice empowers the individual and rests the emphasis, at least in principle, squarely upon that person's efforts. Corr identified four areas of task work in coping with dying: *Physical tasks* center on the satisfaction of bodily needs and the minimization of physical distress; *psychological tasks* emphasize security, autonomy, and richness in living; *social tasks* involve interpersonal attachments to particular individuals and social groups; and *spiritual tasks* center on the identification, development, or reaffirmation of sources of spiritual energy and the fostering of hope.

Around the same time Corr was struggling with a task-based approach, so, too, was Kenneth Doka. In 1993, a book based on Doka's own task-based model was published. *Living with Life-Threatening Illness: A Guide for Patients, Their Families, and Caregivers* brilliantly elucidated a number of phenomena related to anticipatory mourning. Doka expanded upon Pattison's (1977) model. He differentiated between "life-threatening illness"—any illness that endangers life or that has significant risk of death with which one may live for an extended period of time—and "terminal phase" or "terminal illness"—when the patient has progressed to a point that recovery or remission is highly improbable, health has declined, and death is likely to occur within a specific time frame. He constructed a task-based model of living with life-threatening illness that posits different coping tasks within each of five phases of living with the illness: prediagnostic phase, acute phase, chronic phase, recovery phase (for some), and terminal phase.

Doka asserted that in any experience with life-threatening illness one is faced with four major tasks: (a) responding to the physical fact of the disease, (b) taking steps to cope with the reality of the disease, (c) preserving self-concept and relationships with others in the face of the disease, and (d) dealing with the affective and existential/spiritual issues created or reactivated by the disease. At each phase of the illness, these basic tasks may raise different issues, concerns, and challenges.

In 1994, the International Work Group on Death, Dying, and Bereavement published "A Statement of Assumptions and Principles Concerning Psychosocial Care of Dying Persons and Their Families." This document delineates the needs of dying persons, families, and caregivers, and outlines courses of actions best to meet them. Although anticipatory mourning is not directly mentioned, many guidelines are relevant.

In that same year, Nuland (1993) explored issues relevant to anticipatory mourning in the bestseller *How We Die: Reflections on Life's Final Chapter*. By presenting the biological and clinical realities of different types of death, he illustrated what is undergone by those who witness or experience a certain way of dying, the goal being for frank discussion and truth to enable better coping, more effective preparation, and freedom from the fear of death that leads to self-deception and disillusionment.

Rolland (1994) added to the anticipatory mourning literature with his clinically useful resource, *Families, Illness, and Disability: An Integrative Treatment Model*. Taking the family or caregiving system rather than the ill person as the central unit of care, Rolland presented a framework to address the full range of experience and treatment issues faced by couples and families where one or more members suffered a serious illness or disability. His Family Systems–Illness Model highlights the interactive processes between the psychosocial demands of different disorders over time and key components of family functioning. According to Rolland, to create a functional family–illness system to meet the demands of chronic disorders, families need (a) psychosocial understanding of the condition in systems terms, particularly the expected patterns of practical and emotional demands of the disorder over its course and a time line for disease-related developmental tasks associated with different phases of the disorder; (b) an understanding of themselves as a functional unit in systems terms; (c) an appreciation of individual and family life cycles to help them stay attuned to the changing fit between demands of a chronic disorder and new developmental issues for the family unit and individual members; and (d) an understanding of the values, beliefs, and multigenerational legacies that underlie health problems and the types of caregiving systems they establish.

Of special interest is Rolland's discussion of anticipated loss in relation to future life cycle nodal points in personal and family lives. Expanding the concept of anticipatory grief, which he feels has been limited to the terminal phase of an illness, Rolland addresses issues for families dealing with anticipated loss over the entire course of a chronic or life-threatening condition. Writing that anticipation of loss in physical illness can be "as challenging and painful for families as the actual death of a family member" (p. 165), Rolland poignantly describes the interweaving of family efforts simultaneously to sustain hope, cope with uncertainty, and prepare for loss over the course of an illness:

> The experience of anticipatory loss involves a range of intensified emotional and interactional responses over the course of an illness, including separation anxiety, existential aloneness, denial, sadness, disappointment, anger, resentment, guilt, exhaustion, and desperation. There may be intense ambivalence toward the ill member, vacillating wishes for closeness and distance, and fantasies of escape from an unbearable situation. Especially in chronic illnesses involving long-term threats of loss, families often become hypervigilant and overprotective. They may repeatedly rehearse the process of loss and imagined scenarios of family suffering and hardship. These complex emotions can powerfully influence families' dynamics as they try to adapt to threatened loss. Family members' emotions often fluctuate between these painful feelings and more positive states such as a heightened sense

of being alive, of life's preciousness, intimacy, and
appreciation of routine daily events, and hope. . . . The
meaning of possible loss evolves over time with changing
life-cycle demands. . . . Also, the salience of anticipatory
loss varies according to members' multigenerational
experience with actual and threatened loss: with the kind
of illness, its psychosocial demands over time, and the
degree of undertainty about prognosis. (p. 166)

Rolland stresses the important influence of the meanings family
members ascribe to disability and death and their sense of competence to influence the outcome of events. As well, Rolland focuses
upon unresolved issues of blame, shame, and guilt, which can
strongly affect family members' views of the cause of an illness and
the meanings they attach to threatened loss, and which can seriously impede adaptation (Rolland & Walsh, 1988).

In 1997, in its Fourth Annual National Bereavement Teleconference, the Hospice Foundation of America focused its attention
upon the topic "Living with Grief: When Illness Is Prolonged." The
teleconference was accompanied by an edited book by the same
name (Doka, 1997). Anticipatory mourning, referred to frequently
in both the teleconference and the book, was examined in detail as
having both potentially positive and negative influences upon the
dying of the life-threatened person and the postdeath bereavement
of his or her survivors. In the context of contemporary long-term
illness, the dual nature of anticipatory mourning has never been
more apparent.

Making it quite evident that there is a better way to care for the
dying, Byock's (1997) critically acclaimed *Dying Well: The Prospect for
Growth at the End of Life* has illuminated the human potential in the
dying experience. It is particularly important in terms of anticipatory
mourning because it makes plain that being with people who are
dying in conscious and caring ways is of value to them and to us.
Asserting the positive gains that can be made in what would be
viewed in this work as healthy anticipatory mourning, Byock
observes, "[Dying persons'] reminiscences, our care, and the time we
spend together all contribute to a legacy that enriches our lives. . . .
[People can live] in the shadow of death while growing within
themselves and becoming closer with the ones they love" (p. xv).
Byock contributes greatly by showing that dying has the capability
of being so much more than merely a series of losses.

In 1998, Gilliland and Fleming reported on their empirical
investigation comparing spouses of terminally ill patients prior to
the death ("anticipatory grief") and following the death ("conventional grief"). The two phenomena were found to be statistically

similar in terms of emotional, physical, and social dynamics, as measured by the majority of subscales on the Grief Experience Inventory (Sanders, Mauger, & Strong, 1977). However, when compared to conventional grief, anticipatory grief was associated with higher intensities of anger, loss of emotional control, and atypical grief responses. Among numerous other findings, the authors write that the anticipatory grief responses of spouses of terminally ill patients did not change significantly following the death with regard to such subscales as despair, somatization, death anxiety, social isolation, and denial, suggesting a continuum of grief responses characterized by similar levels of emotional distress, as well as personal death awareness and concern. Similarities were found between both anticipatory and conventional grief in degree of somatic symptoms and with regard to social withdrawal and feelings of social abandonment. The two factors identified to influence levels of anticipatory grief significantly were gender (with men more inclined to defend themselves against experiencing or reporting their grief to the same degree as women) and perceived stress and difficulty coping.

CONTRADICTORY RESEARCH

Positive, Neutral, Minimal/Transitory, and Negative Findings

Much of the clinical research points to the adaptational value and positive effects on postdeath grief and mourning of having some advanced warning and the opportunity to experience a moderate amount of anticipatory mourning (Ball, 1976–1977; Binger, Ablin, Feuerstein, Kushner, Zoger, & Mikkelsen, 1969; Burton, 1974; Chodoff, Friedman, & Hamburg, 1964; Friedman, 1967; Friedman, Chodoff, Mason, & Hamburg, 1963; Fulton & Fulton, 1971; Futterman et al., 1972; Gass, 1989; Glick et al., 1974; Goldberg, 1973; Hegge, 1991; Huber & Gibson, 1990; Kramer, 1996–1997; Lehrman, 1956; Lundin, 1984; Natterson & Knudson, 1960; O'Bryant, 1990–1991; Parkes, 1972, 1975; Parkes & Weiss, 1983; Rando, 1983; Raphael, 1983; Raphael & Maddison, 1976; Rees & Lutkins, 1967; Richmond & Waisman, 1955; Sanders 1982–1983; Shanfield, Swain, & Benjamin, 1986–1987; Vachon, Formo, Freedman, Lyall, Rogers, & Freeman, 1976; Vachon, Rogers, Lyall, Lancee, Sheldon, & Freeman, 1982; Wiener, 1970; Zisook, Shuchter, & Lyons, 1987).

However, other studies have suggested a period of anticipation is unrelated to the postdeath grief and mourning experience (Benfield, Leib, & Reuter, 1976; Bornstein, Clayton, Halikas, Maurice, & Robbins, 1973; Clayton, Desmarais, & Winokur, 1968; Gerber, Rusalem,

Hannon, Battin, & Arkin, 1975; Hill, Thompson, & Gallagher, 1988; Kennell, Slyter, & Klaus, 1970; Maddison & Viola, 1968; Maddison & Walker, 1967; Parkes, 1970; Schwab, Chalmers, Conroy, Farris, & Markush, 1975; Wolff, Friedman, Hofer, & Mason, 1964). Some writers have found a period of anticipation to have at most only minimal or transitory impact (Lund, 1989; Roach & Kitson, 1989).

Finally, some writings speak to the negative effects of anticipatory mourning. There are those who caution more specifically than others that a period of anticipatory mourning can lead to premature detachment, which can deprive the patient and family of the possibilities still remaining in the relationship and may end in the patient's emotional or actual abandonment (Levitz, 1977; Lindemann, 1944; Peretz, 1970; Rosenbaum, 1944; Travis, 1976).

A Combination of Positive and Negative Findings: Mixed Results

A number of studies of anticipatory processes have netted mixed results. For instance, in a study on rehearsal for widowhood, Remondet, Hansson, Rule, and Winfrey (1987) found that certain dimensions of rehearsal are associated with positive long-term adjustment (e.g., "behavioral" rehearsal, such as social comparison, planning, and making changes) but that others are associated with increased emotional disruption after the death (e.g., "cognitive" rehearsal, such as ruminating). In another study, forewarning of death was found to be a significant factor in good adjustment to widowhood only for those who had undergone some period of unhappiness in their marriage (Carey, 1977).

In their Tübingen longitudinal study of bereavement of younger widows and widowers, Stroebe and Stroebe (1993) determined that unexpectedness seemed to increase the immediate vulnerability to the loss experience but that the effect weakened over time as those whose spouses died suddenly had a chance to adjust. Unexpected loss, by definition precluding a period of forewarning, had a differential impact upon the widowed and was a very powerful risk factor for certain mourners. Compared to those with high levels of belief in their own personal control, those with low internal control experienced higher levels of depression and somatic complaints at 4 to 7 months after their loss and improved very little over the 2-year period of the study.

In examining differences in grief intensity among bereaved parents, Fish (1986) found that scores for mothers were consistently higher in anticipated deaths than in sudden deaths but that scores for fathers were the reverse. In each of three time periods since the child's death (less than 2 years, 2 to 4 years, or 5 or more years), sig-nificantly greater incongruence existed between marital partners after an anticipated death than after a sudden death, with the peri-ods after 2 years reflecting differences of more than a standard devi-ation. Thus, couples who suffered the anticipated death of a child tended to be more incongruent in general intensity of grief than couples who suffered sudden death losses of children.

Cleiren, van der Wal, and Diekstra (1988a, 1988b) found that the length of time the bereaved had been aware of the loved one's impending death only feebly predicted their outcome in terms of health and posttraumatic stress. These investigators identified a much more potent predictor: the extent to which the bereaved had given up hope for the dying person's recovery during the last month of life. When the factor of hope was partialled out, duration of fore-warning of loss did not predict adaptation to the loss at all. Cleiren et al. observed that giving up hope may be seen as a cognitive prepa-ration for the loss.

From his outstanding study of 19th century diaries, Rosenblatt (1983) concluded that anticipatory grief has mixed impacts when associated with the dying of a loved one. He asserted that cases could be made for greater anticipation's being associated with less postdeath grief as well as greater postdeath grief. To support the for-mer, he noted that anticipation permits the commencement of grief work that can reduce the amount of grief necessary after the death. However, he also observed that long-term anticipation may only appear to reduce grief; the emotional exhaustion it engenders can lead to temporary numbness, transient suppression of grief work, and even to relief that such a long and excruciating struggle has ceased. In other words, a transitory, artificial deflation of symptoms may lead one to erroneous conclusions about the impact of antici-pation upon subsequent grief.

Rosenblatt also noted that long-term anticipation can increase one's involvement in the care of the dying person. This caring involvement may make the loss more painful when the death actu-ally occurs or may leave the survivor with additional memories and emotional involvement that then would require disengagement. Further, he found that when survivor and decedent did not live together, anticipation tended to be associated with less grief in the first 2 years, whereas co-residence with the dying person limited or prevented anticipatory grief work. If such grief work did occur, it may have been offset by the acquisition of additional memories, ideas, and behavior links. Rosenblatt observed that

> even if one has done some anticipatory grief work, after long
> hope (or uncertainty) and struggle in support of that hope

(or uncertainty), one's efforts may seem to be invalidated by the death, which may increase grief. Moreover, a daily routine that centers on nursing the sick person would be ended by the death, and a new pattern would have to be developed. Such a change in routine and role may augment grief. (pp. 50–51)

Rosenblatt concluded, then, that postdeath grief work is facilitated by anticipation of a death when one does not live with—and hence has no involvement in the care of—the dying person. He hypothesizes that this is the case because one is able to disconnect from the dying person, something that is impossible when one lives with the individual. Living with and caring for the dying person during the terminal illness may actually add "a rich store of additional memories and hopes to deal with during grief work" (p. 157).

Observing that there indeed can be "too much of a good thing," Rando (1983) found that there were optimum amounts of anticipatory grief, participation during the dying person's hospitalizations, and lengths of illness. Below and above these optimal ranges, postdeath bereavement and adjustment were compromised for survivors. Sanders (1982–1983) also found that both the shortest and longest periods of anticipation were associated with poorer outcomes, as compared with a medium length of time of anticipation. Although Gerber et al. (1975) and Schwab et al. (1975) did not find an overall correlation between anticipation and postdeath grief, they did corroborate some of Rando's and Sanders' findings. In their respective populations, the longest illnesses were related to the poorest adjustment subsequent to the death. These findings are supported by Hamovitch (1964) and Maddison (1968).

Several notable researchers believe a period of anticipation can be useful but do not feel that the benefits derive from anticipatory mourning per se (e.g., Glick et al., 1974; Parkes & Weiss, 1983; Silverman, 1974; Weiss, 1988). They agree that forewarning of loss allows for certain kinds of therapeutic preparations: learning to live with the prospect of loss so that when it occurs it is at least not unexpected, nor conducive to the deleterious experience of unanticipated bereavement; making plans for the future to the extent that such plans are not felt as betrayals of the dying loved one; and readying the assumptions regarding one's reality for examination and change. Parkes and Weiss (1983) point out that these preparations all help the survivor make sense of the loss as the end result of an understood, although hated, process. Weiss (1988) further clarifies that preparation is not entirely without value, but that its value is severely limited because the pain engendered by the death is in no way reduced by preparation, nor are the recovery processes any different. He makes plain that it is not that forewarning makes for anticipatory grieving; it is, rather, that the absence of forewarning makes for impeded recovery.

These same researchers believe that anticipatory grief per se rarely happens, and they maintain that this is only proper. They support this conviction by noting that (a) periods of acceptance and recovery usually witnessed after the period of searching in early postdeath grief are rarely found before actual death, no matter how early the forewarning; (b) grief implies that there has been a loss and that to accept a loved one's loss while he or she is still alive leaves the bereaved-to-be vulnerable to later self-accusation for having partially abandoned the dying person; (c) grief presupposes decathexis, which is quite difficult no matter what the understanding of the future might be, with the bonds of attachment and love not being so tractable to the demands of expediency and, in fact, resisting detachment; and (d) anticipation of loss frequently intensifies attachment.

Like Parkes and Weiss, Silverman (1974) emphasizes the fact that widows usually remain involved with their terminally ill husbands until the time of death. Her data suggest that for these women it would have been dysfunctional to have commenced grieving in advance of their husbands' deaths and that mourning could begin only after death took place. According to Silverman, any efforts to have helped the widows and their husbands cope with the problems of illness and ultimate death, to grieve in advance, or to aim for open discussion about the impending death would have been inappropriate. The appropriate goal in this situation is instead to maximize the possibilities for whatever living is possible. Further, Silverman asserts that shock, emptiness, reluctance to face widowhood, and loneliness are parts of a process that cannot truly be encountered until the husband is no longer there. Anything prior to this is a rehearsal and not the real thing: "Some people even talk about the coming death, but this is not grieving in advance. Engagements are not marriages" (p. 330).

REASONS FOR DISCREPANCIES IN THE ANTICIPATORY MOURNING LITERATURE

A number of reasons account for the discrepant information that has been put forth by those attempting to articulate the costs and benefits of anticipatory mourning. A main reason for inconsistency in the writings and research devoted to this topic concerns the practice of conceptually confusing forewarning of loss with anticipatory mourning (Fulton & Gottesman, 1980; Siegel & Weinstein, 1983).

This occurs despite there being no certainty as to the course, complexion, or even existence of anticipatory mourning after warning of impending death. For instance Friedman (1967) observed great variety in anticipatory grief among prospective survivors, with some never evidencing any anticipatory grief at all. Clayton, Halikas, Maurice, and Robbins (1973) demonstrated that individuals may be well aware of an impending loss but not mourn in anticipation. Other research has indicated that there may be even earlier problems: Some may have been explicitly informed of a fatal diagnosis but refused to believe it, ignored it, or misunderstood the warnings (Parkes, 1970; Vachon, Freedman, Formo, Rogers, Lyall, & and Freeman, 1977). Thus, the perception that death is likely to occur says nothing about whether anticipatory mourning will necessarily follow; in fact, the provision of warnings says nothing about whether the person has even grasped them in a fashion to develop a perception of impending death that would stimulate healthy anticipatory mourning.

Consequently, in research where sudden death is construed to operationalize a lack of anticipatory mourning and an illness death to operationalize its presence (with length of terminal status, if not entire illness, inferred as operationalizing the amount of anticipatory mourning), significant contradictions in the literature can be accounted for by the difference between forewarning and actual anticipatory mourning. In other words, if researchers look solely at length of illness and not at anticipatory mourning behaviors therein, they may draw the mistaken conclusion that anticipatory mourning has no impact upon postdeath adjustment when they have measured only impact of forewarning and not the presence of anticipatory mourning. Relatively few studies actually operationalize anticipatory mourning (see Levy, 1991; Rando, 1983), and only a few more attempt either to operationalize related aspects of it (e.g., affiliation, separation, and communication with the terminally ill loved one; Kramer, 1996–1997) or to concretize survivors' assessments regarding aspects of it (e.g., measurement of the impact of hospice experiences upon anticipatory bereavement through the 10-Mile Mourning Bridge; Huber & Gibson, 1990). Very simply, the majority of studies have failed to focus sufficiently upon anticipatory mourning's intrinsic elements to warrant acceptable conclusions about the phenomenon. What legitimately can be concluded is that neither anticipatory mourning nor awareness of impending death can be assumed to exist merely based upon the length of time the loved one was ill prior to the death or on the delivery of a fatal diagnosis by a physician.

In a particularly insightful article, Siegel and Weinstein (1983) delineate other explanations for contradictory research findings.

They note that the many factors associated with protracted illness—such as potentially destructive ambivalence, guilt, anxiety-prompted defenses of denial or reversal, social isolation, physical exhaustion, emotional anguish, and depletion of emotional and financial resources—may artificially inflate or actually create postdeath symptoms and be so strongly associated with poor bereavement outcome that they overshadow or cancel out gains provided by a period of anticipation. Additionally, these observers note that poor research designs, often predicated on popular but untested assumptions, contribute to diverse findings.

Lack of sophistication and oversimplification of factors also mark most of the studies in this area. For instance, the Stroebe and Stroebe (1993) study revealed differential impacts of unexpected, unforewarned loss upon mourners. Those with low internal control were more adversely affected than those with high internal control. This means that for some mourners sudden, unexpected death constitutes a very powerful risk factor, whereas for others it may be less potent. As studies are able to account for personality factors such as these, control for other relevant variables, and better regulate subject populations, the inconsistency in findings may diminish.

Several untested assumptions also have played parts in fostering incongruity within the anticipatory mourning literature. Fulton and Gottesman (1980) identified two such assumptions arising from the traditional psychoanalytic perspective on grief: (a) All those in a particular state of bereavement experience a comparable volume of grief, and (b) Once grief work is begun, the grief reaction is dissipated in a continuous and irreversible path toward resolution. Agreeing with Glick et al. (1974) that anticipatory grief is not simply grief begun in advance but different from postdeath grief in both duration and form, Fulton and Gottesman suggest that failure to analyze anticipatory grief on three levels—psychological, interpersonal, and sociocultural—and to understand how individuals experience and respond to the phenomenon leaves undetermined whether anticipatory grief is benign or harmful in any given situation.

Still other issues obfuscate the anticipatory mourning literature. Differences in methodologies and significant variations among subject populations preclude important comparisons. Both Raphael (1983) and Bowlby (1980) point out that in numerous studies severe reactions occurring after a sudden bereavement were generated not only because the deaths were sudden, but also because they were untimely (i.e., the deceased were younger than in studies where sudden death had a less traumatic impact) or traumatic (i.e., involving violence, mutilation, accidents, etc.). For example, in the Gerber et al. (1975) study, in which the deaths were of elderly persons who succumbed to illness, sudden death was found to be unrelated to an increase in postdeath bereavement symptomatology. In contrast, in the Glick et al. (1974) study, which investigated reactions to the deaths of younger individuals, many of whom died in traumatic circumstances, sudden death was associated with an overwhelming of the survivor's adaptive capacities; postdeath grief might not be augmented per se, but the capacity to cope appeared diminished, and there was less likelihood of regaining full capacity for functioning and happiness. While it seems only natural that the sudden death of an elderly individual under natural circumstances would elicit different reactions than the sudden death of a younger person in violent circumstances, such important variations have been insufficiently accounted for in the literature.

A related issue concerns the intersection of methodological inconsistency and clinical phenomena of anticipatory mourning. For instance, while Siegel and Weinstein (1983) note that a protracted illness has the potential to inflate postdeath symptomatology artificially, the reverse also must be considered. An artificial deflation of symptoms may be observed after a death from protracted illness, secondary to the exhaustion and depletion that has occurred during it. Especially in cases of overly lengthy illness (identified elsewhere as being a high-risk factor for complicated mourning; Rando, 1993), the survivor may be drained following the death of the loved one, toward which so much time and effort has been directed for such a prolonged period. Assessment of the survivor's phenomenological experience or measurement of his or her bereavement symptomatology may reflect temporary relief, not indicate the nature of the loss experience once that person has recouped enough to address it. Not unlike posttraumatic stress symptomatology, which often obscures loss and grief following circumstances of traumatic bereavement (Rando, 1993), the clinical picture immediately after an overly lengthy illness often fails to reflect accurately the underlying grief and loss issues. To the extent that research studies have measured postdeath bereavement symptoms at different points in time, inconsistencies in findings about long-term illness should be expected secondary to the symptom fluctuations known to occur. Follow-up studies often reveal changes that recast original results in a different light (cf. Sanders, 1982–1983).

In some studies the data on length of illness are dichotomized or the variable of time is continuous but no overly lengthy illnesses are included. In either case, the statistics may be unable to reveal the true impact of length of illness and time available for anticipatory mourning because there is a failure to capture those patterns that can be found when discriminating among short, medium, and lengthy illnesses. As well, conclusions based on the collapsing of data into just two categories (i.e., short- and long-term illness) can be quite misleading if some of the short-term illnesses are too short and some of those in the long-term illnesses are too lengthy. In such cases, positive benefits of optimum time for anticipatory mourning may be obscured, if not cancelled out, by the negative effects of too little or too much time for anticipatory mourning. Similar issues could be raised for other variables that sustain a curvilinear rather than linear relationship with the anticipatory mourner's healthy adjustment.

Clinically and empirically, anticipatory mourning is a multi-dimensional concept. However, when studies focus on only one or a few dimensions and call this anticipatory mourning in its entirety, results could be expected to diverge depending upon the dimensions chosen. Both Fulton and Gottesman (1980) and Siegel and Weinstein (1983) identify as problems the lack of a precise and consistent operational definition of anticipatory mourning and the narrowness of its conceptualization, which typically overlooks sociological dimensions. These factors, they point out, have impaired the generalizability of findings in the literature and limited the validity of the studies.

COSTS OF ANTICIPATORY MOURNING

Although anticipatory mourning may offer therapeutic benefits to all parties in the experience, it is not without its problems. Some of the research discussed here has been described earlier in this chapter; it is readdressed not only to provide a balanced perspective, but also to identify areas in which anticipatory mourning may cause increased vulnerability.

As noted earlier in this chapter, anticipatory mourning can serve to bring people together and to heighten emotional attachment; however, too much of it or inappropriate application of its processes may result in premature detachment from the dying person. It is also possible for immoderate amounts of anticipatory mourning to compromise the mourner's participation during the dying person's hospitalizations (and, by implication, possibly during home care) and to exacerbate his or her anger and hostility and loss of emotional control following the death (Rando, 1983). Rosenblatt (1983) has suggested that long-term anticipation of loss may appear at times to lead to less postdeath grief because the emotional exhaustion following the loved one's prolonged illness may involve temporary numbness, transient suppression of grief after the loss, or even relief that the long and excruciating struggle is over. This latter point is reminiscent of the concern articulated by Aldrich (1974) that anticipatory mourning may possibly complicate the working-through process by giving the hostile component of ambivalence a more realistically destructive potential, despite offering an opportunity for the survivor to experience some grief in advance of the loss.

Rosenblatt (1983) clearly describes how anticipatory mourning can make postdeath mourning more problematic. He notes that anticipation can lead to enhancement of postdeath grief if it increases one's involvement in the care of the dying person: That care can make the loss hurt more or leave one with more memories and emotional involvement to disengage from after the loss. He also found that co-residence affects anticipatory mourning and that home care for the dying may make anticipatory mourning more difficult. In such cases, where the survivors-to-be are living with the dying person, anticipatory mourning work may not occur. If it does, it may be offset by the acquisition of additional memories, hopes, ideas, and behavior links, all of which will require decathexis after the death. Rosenblatt points out that, even if one has experienced some anticipatory mourning, following long periods of hope and uncertainty and the struggle that ensues in support of that hope, one's efforts may seem invalidated by the actual death, thus intensifying the grief experience. Also, a daily routine that centers on the dying person and then is shattered by the death mandates a new pattern of life, with such changes in routine and roles possibly augmenting the grief experienced following the death. In contrast, when the survivor-to-be and the dying person do not live together and the survivor-to-be has no involvement in the care of the dying person, the longer the period of anticipation the less the grief after the death, at least within the first year of bereavement. Obviously, these findings have profound implications for families of home-care hospice patients and for those who make their living caring for the dying.

Despite asserting the benefits of anticipatory mourning and a period of anticipatory socialization into the bereaved role, Gerber (1974) cautions that the period of anticipatory mourning may contain the seeds of future problems because of the emotional strain of waiting for the death to occur, the poorly defined set of bereaved-role expectations, and the drastic change in life-style brought about by the permanent loss. More specific concerns have been delineated by Fulton and Fulton (1971), who observe that a period of anticipation may reduce the amount of public mourning survivors display, putting them in the difficult situation of being expected by others, as well as themselves, to show emotions that already have been worked through. This can cause mourners guilt or shame. A period of anticipatory mourning also may make survivors feel that funeral rituals are unnecessary, taking away the opportunity to experience the social confirmation and support such rituals afford. And, very important, Fulton and Fulton see anticipatory mourning as possibly being less than therapeutic in its impact on the dying person, insofar as the responses of survivors-to-be who already have decathected may be negative toward that person. These observers perceptively underscore the two-edged effects of anticipatory mourning, noting that while it has the potential "to enhance our lives and secure our well-being," at the same time it has sufficient power "to undermine our fragile existence and rupture our tenuous social bonds" (Fulton & Fulton, 1971, p. 99).

Involvement with a loved one dying from a long-term chronic illness can result in a host of problems secondary to that chronicity (Rando, 1993). These problems include psychological conflict, emotional exhaustion, physical debilitation, compromised development, social isolation, and familial discord. Illness-generated emotional reactions such as anxiety, sorrow, depression, anger, and guilt take their toll on anticipatory mourners, as do the stresses inherent in attempting to manage clashing responsibilities, discordant roles, and antagonistic tasks.

Chapter 6 in this volume presents arguments to demonstrate that anticipatory mourning is a form of traumatic stress. If, as suggested, healthy engagement involves the survivor-to-be in the care of and ongoing interaction with the dying person, then the chances are increased for exposure to any traumatic experiences that are a part of the loved one's illness and dying. Essentially, healthy anticipatory mourning tends to leave the mourner vulnerable to psychological, perceptual, behavioral, social, and physical experiences that are not without significant expense and traumatization.

Yet, in terms of long-term impact on the mourner, a death permitting healthy anticipatory mourning appears to be better than an unanticipated death. Benefits may include precluding the malignant sequelae of a sudden death and eliminating or minimizing unfinished business, premature detachment, poor communication and interaction with the dying person, and lack of appropriate participation—all of which are known to predispose to poor bereavement outcomes (Rando, 1986a). Additionally, healthy anticipatory mourning can enable a more appropriate death for the dying person, and thus promote better adjustment for the survivor after the death.

Put very simply, one conclusion is apparent: Anticipatory mourning may facilitate the postdeath bereavement process, but it does not assure a problem-free course.

REFERENCES

Aldrich, C. (1974). Some dynamics of anticipatory grief. In B. Schoenberg, A. Carr, A. H. Kutscher, D. Peretz, & I. Goldberg (Eds.), *Anticipatory grief*. New York: Columbia University Press.

Ball, J. (1976–1977). Widow's grief: The impact of age and mode of death. *Omega, 7*, 307–333.

Benfield, D., Leib, S., & Reuter, J. (1976). Grief response of parents after referral of the critically ill newborn to a regional center. *New England Journal of Medicine, 294*, 975–978.

Binger, C., Ablin, A., Feuerstein, R., Kushner, J., Zoger, S. & Mikkelsen, C. (1969). Childhood leukemia: Emotional impact on patient and family. *New England Journal of Medicine, 280*, 414–418.

Bornstein, P., Clayton, P., Halikas, J., Maurice, W., & Robbins, E. (1973). The depression of widowhood at 13 months. *British Journal of Psychiatry, 122*, 561–566.

Bowlby, J. (1980). *Attachment and loss: Vol. 3. Loss: Sadness and depression*. New York: Basic.

Burton, L. (1974). Tolerating the intolerable—The problems facing parents and children following diagnosis. In L. Burton (Ed.), *Care of the child facing death*. London: Routledge and Kegan Paul.

Byock, I. R. (1997). *Dying well: The prospect for growth at the end of life*. New York: Riverhead Books.

Carey, R. (1977). The widowed: A year later. *Journal of Counseling Psychology, 24*, 125–131.

Chodoff, P., Friedman, S., & Hamburg, D. (1964). Stress, defenses and coping behavior: Observations in parents of children with malignant disease. *American Journal of Psychiatry, 120*, 743–749.

Clayton, P., Desmarais, L., & Winokur, G. (1968). A study of normal bereavement. *American Journal of Psychiatry, 125*, 64–74.

Clayton, P., Halikas, J., Maurice, W., & Robbins, E. (1973). Anticipatory grief and widowhood. *British Journal of Psychiatry, 122*, 47–51.

Cleiren, M., van der Wal, J., & Diekstra, R. (1988a). Death after a long term disease: Anticipation and outcome in the bereaved: Part I. *Pharos International, 54*(3), 112–114.

Cleiren, M., van der Wal, J., & Diekstra, R. (1988b). Death after a long term disease: Anticipation and outcome in the bereaved: Part II. *Pharos International, 54*(4), 136–139.

Cohen, M., & Cohen, E. (1981). Behavioral family systems intervention in terminal care. In H. Sobel (Ed.), *Behavior therapy in terminal care: A humanistic approach*. Cambridge, MA: Ballinger.

Corr, C. A. (1992). A task-based approach to coping with dying. *Omega, 24*, 81–94.

Corr, C. A., Nabe, C., & Corr, D. M. (1997). *Death and dying, life and living* (2nd ed.). Pacific Grove, CA: Brooks/Cole.

Doka, K. J. (1993). *Living with life-threatening illness: A guide for patients, their families, and caregivers*. Lexington, MA: Lexington Books.

Doka, K. J. (Ed.) with Davidson, J. (1997). *Living with grief: When illness is prolonged*. Washington, DC: Taylor & Francis.

Eliot, T. (1946). War bereavements and their recovery. *Marriage and Family Living, 8,* 1–6.

Fish, W. (1986). Differences of grief intensity in bereaved parents. In T. A. Rando (Ed.), *Parental loss of a child.* Champaign, IL: Research Press.

Freud, S. (1953). Premonitory dreams fulfilled. In J. Strachey (Ed. and Trans.), *The standard edition of the complete psychological works of Sigmund Freud* (Vol. 5). London: Hogarth. (Original work published 1899)

Freud, S. (1957). On transience. In J. Strachey (Ed. and Trans.), *The standard edition of the complete psychological works of Sigmund Freud* (Vol. 14). London: Hogarth. (Original work published 1916)

Friedman, S. (1967). Care of the family of the child with cancer. *Pediatrics, 40,* 498–504.

Friedman, S., Chodoff, P., Mason, J., & Hamburg, D. (1963). Behavioral observations on parents anticipating the death of a child. *Pediatrics, 32,* 610–625.

Fulton, R., & Fulton, J. (1971). A psychosocial aspect of terminal care: Anticipatory grief. *Omega, 2,* 91–100.

Fulton, R., & Gottesman, D. (1980). Anticipatory grief: A psychosocial concept reconsidered. *British Journal of Psychiatry, 137,* 45–54.

Futterman, E., Hoffman, I., & Sabshin, M. (1972). Parental anticipatory mourning. In B. Schoenberg, A. Carr, D. Peretz, & A. H. Kutscher (Eds.), *Psychosocial aspects of terminal care.* New York: Columbia University Press.

Gass, K. (1989). Health of older widowers: Role of appraisal, coping, resources, and type of spouse's death. In D. Lund (Ed.), *Older bereaved spouses: Research with practical applications.* New York: Hemisphere.

Gerber, I. (1974). Anticipatory bereavement. In B. Schoenberg, A. Carr, A. H. Kutscher, D. Peretz, & I. Goldberg (Eds.), *Anticipatory grief.* New York: Columbia University Press.

Gerber, I., Rusalem, R., Hannon, N., Battin, D., & Arkin, A. (1975). Anticipatory grief and aged widows and widowers. *Journal of Gerontology, 30,* 225–229.

Gilliland, G., & Fleming, S. (1998). A comparison of spousal anticipatory grief and conventional grief. *Death Studies, 22,* 541–569.

Glick, I., Weiss, R. S., & Parkes, C. M. (1974). *The first year of bereavement.* New York: Wiley.

Goldberg, S. (1973). Family tasks and reactions in the crisis of death. *Social Casework, 54,* 398–405.

Hamovitch, M. (1964). *The parent and the fatally ill child.* Los Angeles: Delmar.

Hegge, M. (1991). A qualitative retrospective study of coping strategies of newly widowed elderly: Effects of anticipatory grieving on the caregiver. *The American Journal of Hospice and Palliative Care, 8*(4), 28–34.

Hill, C., Thompson, L., & Gallagher, D. (1988). The role of anticipatory bereavement in the adjustment to widowhood in older women. *The Gerontologist, 28,* 792–796.

Huber, R., & Gibson, J. (1990). New evidence for anticipatory grief. *The Hospice Journal, 6*(1), 49–67.

International Work Group on Death, Dying, and Bereavement. (1978). Assumptions and principles underlying standards of care for the terminally ill. In C. A. Corr, J. Morgan, & H. Wass (Eds.), *International Work Group on Death, Dying, and Bereavement statements on death, dying, and bereavement.* London, Ontario: King's College.

International Work Group on Death, Dying, and Bereavement. (1994). A statement of assumptions and principles concerning psychosocial care of dying persons and their families. In C. A. Corr, J. Morgan, & H. Wass (Eds.), *International Work Group on Death, Dying, and Bereavement statements on death, dying, and bereavement.* London, Ontario: King's College.

Janis, I. (1958). *Psychological stress: Psychoanalytic and behavioral studies of surgical patients.* New York: Wiley.

Kennell, J., Slyter, H., & Klaus, M. (1970). The mourning response of parents to the death of a newborn infant. *New England Journal of Medicine, 283,* 344–349.

Kramer, D. (1996–1997). How women relate to terminally ill husbands and their subsequent adjustment to bereavement. *Omega, 34,* 93–106.

Kübler-Ross, E. (1969). *On death and dying.* New York: Macmillan.

Lattanzi-Licht, M., & Connor, S. (1995). Care of the dying: The hospice approach. In H. Wass & R. Neimeyer (Eds.), *Dying: Facing the facts* (3rd ed.). Washington, DC: Taylor & Francis.

Lebow, G. (1976). Facilitating adaptation in anticipatory mourning. *Social Casework, 57*(7), 458–465.

Lehrman, S. (1956). Reactions to untimely death. *Psychiatric Quarterly, 30,* 564–578.

Levitz, I. (1977). [Comments in section on "The Parents."] In N. Linzer (Ed.), *Understanding bereavement and grief.* New York: Yeshiva University Press.

Levy, L. (1991). Anticipatory grief: Its measurement and proposed reconceptualization. *The Hospice Journal, 7*(4), 1–28.

Lindemann, E. (1944). Symptomatology and management of acute grief. *American Journal of Psychiatry, 101,* 141–148.

Lund, D. (1989). Conclusions about bereavement in later life and implications for interventions and future research. In D. Lund (Ed.), *Older bereaved spouses: Research with practical applications.* New York: Hemisphere.

Lundin, T. (1984). Morbidity following sudden and unexpected bereavement. *British Journal of Psychiatry, 144,* 84–88.

Maddison, D. (1968). The relevance of conjugal bereavement for preventive psychiatry. *British Journal of Medical Psychology, 41,* 223–233.

Maddison, D., & Viola, A. (1968). The health of widows in the year following bereavement. *Journal of Psychosomatic Research, 12,* 297–306.

Maddison, D., & Walker, W. (1967). Factors affecting the outcome of conjugal bereavement. *British Journal of Psychiatry, 113,* 1057–1067.

McCollum, A., & Schwartz, A. (1972). Social work and the mourning parent. *Social Work, 17,* 25–36.

Natterson, J., & Knudson, A. (1960). Observations concerning fear of death in fatally ill children and their mothers. *Psychosomatic Medicine, 22,* 456–465.

Nuland, S. (1993). *How we die: Reflections on life's final chapter.* New York: Knopf.

O'Bryant, S. (1990–1991). Forewarning of a husband's death: Does it make a difference for older widows? *Omega, 22,* 227–239.

Parkes, C. M. (1970). The first year of bereavement. *Psychiatry, 33,* 444–467.

Parkes, C. M. (1972). *Bereavement: Studies of grief in adult life.* New York: International Universities Press.

Parkes, C. M. (1975). Determinants of outcome following bereavement. *Omega, 6,* 303–323.

Parkes, C. M., & Weiss, R. S. (1983). *Recovery from bereavement*. New York: Basic.

Pattison, E. M. (Ed.). (1977). *The experience of dying*. Englewood Cliffs, NJ: Prentice Hall.

Peretz, D. (1970). Reaction to loss. In B. Schoenberg, A. Carr, D. Peretz, & A. H. Kutscher (Eds.), *Loss and grief: Psychological management in medical practice*. New York: Columbia University Press.

Rando, T. A. (1983). An investigation of grief and adaptation in parents whose children have died from cancer. *Journal of Pediatric Psychology, 8*, 3–20.

Rando, T. A. (1986a). A comprehensive analysis of anticipatory grief: Perspectives, processes, promises, and problems. In T. A. Rando (Ed.), *Loss and anticipatory grief*. Lexington, MA: Lexington Books.

Rando, T. A. (Ed.). (1986b). *Loss and anticipatory grief*. Lexington, MA: Lexington Books.

Rando, T. A. (1993). *Treatment of complicated mourning*. Champaign, IL: Research Press.

Raphael, B. (1983). *The anatomy of bereavement*. New York: Basic.

Raphael, B., & Maddison, D. (1976). The care of bereaved adults. In O. Hill (Ed.), *Modern trends in psychosomatic medicine*. London: Butterworth.

Remondet, J., Hansson, R., Rule, B., & Winfrey, G. (1987). Rehearsal for widowhood. *Journal of Social and Clinical Psychology, 5*, 285–297.

Rees, W., & Lutkins, S. (1967). Mortality of bereavement. *British Medical Journal, 4*, 13–16.

Richmond, J., & Waisman, H. (1955). Psychologic aspects of management of children with malignant diseases. *American Journal of Diseases in Children, 89*, 42–47.

Roach, M., & Kitson, G. (1989). Impact of forewarning on adjustment to widowhood and divorce. In D. Lund (Ed.), *Older bereaved spouses: Research with practical applications*. New York: Hemisphere.

Rolland, J. (1994). *Families, illness, and disability: An integrative treatment model*. New York: Basic.

Rolland, J., & Walsh, F. (1988). *Blame, shame and guilt: Family belief systems in chronic and life-threatening disorders*. Paper presented at the 46th annual conference of the American Association for Marriage and Family Therapy.

Rosenbaum, M. (1944). Emotional aspects of wartime separations. *The Family, 24*, 337–341.

Rosenblatt, P. (1983). *Bitter, bitter tears: Nineteenth-century diarists and twentieth-century grief theories*. Minneapolis: University of Minnesota Press.

Sanders, C. M. (1982–1983). Effects of sudden versus chronic illness death on bereavement outcome. *Omega, 13*, 227–241.

Sanders, C. M., Mauger, P., & Strong, P. (1977). *A manual for the Grief Experience Inventory*. Tampa: University of Florida.

Schoenberg, B., Carr, A., Kutscher, A. H., Peretz, D., & Goldberg, I. (Eds.). (1974). *Anticipatory grief*. New York: Columbia University Press.

Schwab, J., Chalmers, J., Conroy, S., Farris, P., & Markush, R. (1975). Studies in grief: A preliminary report. In B. Schoenberg, I. Gerber, A. Wiener, A. H. Kutscher, D. Peretz, & A. Carr (Eds.), *Bereavement: Its psychosocial aspects*. New York: Columbia University Press.

Shanfield, S., Swain, B., & Benjamin, G. (1986–1987). Parents' responses to the death of adult children from accidents and cancer: A comparison. *Omega, 17*, 289–297.

Siegel, K., & Weinstein, L. (1983). Anticipatory grief reconsidered. *Journal of Psychosocial Oncology, 1,* 61–73.

Silverman, P. (1974). Anticipatory grief from the perspective of widowhood. In B. Schoenberg, A. Carr, A. H. Kutscher, D. Peretz, & I. Goldberg (Eds.), *Anticipatory grief.* New York: Columbia University Press.

Stroebe, W., & Stroebe, M. (1993). Determinants of adjustment to bereavement in younger widows and widowers. In M. Stroebe, W. Stroebe, & R. Hansson (Eds.), *Handbook of bereavement: Theory, research, and intervention.* Cambridge, England: Cambridge University Press.

Travis, G. (1976). *The experience of chronic illness in childhood.* Stanford, CA: Stanford University Press.

Vachon, M., Formo, A., Freedman, K., Lyall, W., Rogers, J., & Freeman, S. (1976). Stress reactions to bereavement. *Essence, 1,* 23–33.

Vachon, M., Freedman, K., Formo, A., Rogers, J., Lyall, W., & Freeman, S. (1977). The final illness in cancer: The widow's perspective. *Canadian Medical Association Journal, 117,* 1151–1154.

Vachon, M., Rogers, J., Lyall, W., Lancee, W., Sheldon, A., & Freeman, S. (1982). Predictors and correlates of high distress in adaptation to conjugal bereavement. *American Journal of Psychiatry, 139,* 998–1002.

Weisman, A. D. (1972a). *On dying and denying: A psychiatric study of terminality.* New York: Behavioral Publications.

Weisman, A. D. (1972b). Psychosocial considerations in terminal care. In B. Schoenberg, A. Carr, D. Peretz, & A. H. Kutscher (Eds.), *Psychosocial aspects of terminal care.* New York: Columbia University Press.

Weisman, A. D. (1977). The psychiatrist and the inexorable. In H. Feifel (Ed.), *New meanings of death.* New York: McGraw-Hill.

Weisman, A. D. (1979). *Coping with cancer.* New York: McGraw-Hill.

Weiss, R. S. (1988). Is it possible to prepare for trauma? *Journal of Palliative Care, 4*(1 & 2), 74–76.

Wiener, J. (1970). Reaction of the family to the fatal illness of a child. In B. Schoenberg, A. Carr, D. Peretz, & A. H. Kutscher (Eds.), *Loss and grief: Psychological management in medical practice.* New York: Columbia University Press.

Wolff, C., Friedman, S., Hofer, M., & Mason, J. (1964). Relationship between psychological defenses and mean urinary 17-hydroxycorticosteroid excretion rates: I. A predictive study of parents of fatally ill children. *Psychosomatic Medicine, 26,* 576–591.

Zisook, S., Shuchter, S., & Lyons, L. (1987). Predictors of psychological reactions during the early stages of widowhood. *Psychiatry Clinics of North America, 10*(3), 355–368.

CHAPTER 2
The Six Dimensions
of Anticipatory Mourning

Therese A. Rando

Anticipatory mourning defines itself across six dimensions. The first three dimensions determine the experience. These include (a) perspective, (b) time focus, and (c) influencing factors. The second three are experiential dimensions that constitute areas of intervention. These include (d) major sources of adaptational demands, (e) generic operations, and (f) contextual levels. To understand and intervene effectively with an anticipatory mourner, a caregiver must specifically consider the mourner's position relative to each of these areas. This chapter describes these six dimensions and delineates the central issues in each. Table 2.1 outlines the dimensions and their components.

As discussed here, *anticipatory mourning* is defined as the phenomenon encompassing seven generic operations (grief and mourning, coping, interaction, psychosocial reorganization, planning, balancing conflicting demands, and facilitating an appropriate death) that, within a context of adaptational demands caused by experiences of loss and trauma, is stimulated in response to the awareness of life-threatening or terminal illness in oneself or a significant other and the recognition of associated losses in the past, present, and future. Note that there is a distinction made between life-threatening and terminal illness. As suggested by Doka (1993), a *life-threatening illness* is any illness that endangers life or has a significant risk of death. The final, dying phase of such an illness is a *terminal illness*. This term signifies that recovery or remission is highly improbable and that the ill person's health has declined to a point that death is likely to occur within a specific time frame.

The present discussion assumes a healthy, positive relationship between the mourner and the ill or dying person. To the extent that a particular relationship is not so characterized, this material will need to be extrapolated.

❋

To my dear friends Ken Doka and Edie Stark, who occupy such very cherished places in my heart

TABLE 2.1

The Six Dimensions of Anticipatory Mourning

1. Perspective
   - Patient
   - Intimate
   - Concerned other
   - Caregiver

2. Time focus
   - Past
   - Present
   - Future

3. Influencing factors
   - Psychological factors
   - Social factors
   - Physiological factors

4. Major sources of adaptational demands
   - Loss
   - Trauma

5. Generic operations
   - Grief and mourning
   - Coping
   - Interaction
   - Psychosocial reorganization
   - Planning
   - Balancing conflicting demands
   - Facilitating an appropriate death

6. Contextual levels
   - Intrapsychic-level processes
   - Interpersonal-level processes
     with the life-threatened or dying person
   - Systemic-level processes

PERSPECTIVE

Anticipatory mourning may be viewed, experienced, and understood from four distinct perspectives. Each viewpoint belongs to one of the main parties in the anticipatory mourning experience. The first perspective is that of the life-threatened or dying person. Hereafter, this will be referred to as *patient anticipatory mourning* to reflect that the illness, among other things, has given the person a new role to play—that is, the patient role in the context of a life-threatening or terminal illness. Use of this term distinguishes this perspective from the others but does not imply passivity, absence of control, or any other attribute except the ill or dying individual's being the central figure in the drama of his or her own living-dying process. In this perspective, the affected individual is simultaneously the anticipatory mourner and the ill or dying loved one.

A second perspective from which anticipatory mourning can be experienced is that of family member, close friend, or other associate in the ill or dying person's intimate network. *Intimate anticipatory mourning* is a term reserved for those who are intimates of the afflicted person—that is, those who have relatively close association, contact, familiarity, and interaction with the ill or dying individual and to whom that person feels strongly and reciprocally connected. Biological or kin ties are not necessary to be an intimate.

A third perspective of anticipatory mourning is *concerned other anticipatory mourning.* This refers to the mourning of individuals who have some interest in the ill person's dying, but who do not sustain an intimate relationship with him or her. The relationship, if there is one, is not as close as that of an intimate. A concerned other may be an extended family member or a neighbor down the street, or someone in touch with the ill person but not too closely, such as a business associate or, even more distant, a mail carrier. In many cases, the mourner knows the ill person only from a distance or through the media, yet sustains feelings and concerns about the welfare of the individual and is impacted by his or her illness or dying. Examples include the fans of an actor, the citizens in a politician's district, the readers of a novelist, or any of a group of other persons who feel connected to the ill person despite a lack of personal relationship. Because these individuals do not sustain a relationship with the life-threatened or dying person that is socially recognized and/or validated, they are particularly susceptible to being disenfranchised in their mourning and may require intervention to address this problem and those that develop from it.

The last perspective from which anticipatory mourning may be experienced is the caregiver's. Discussed in depth in chapter 12, by Dale Larson, *caregiver anticipatory mourning* can vary greatly depending on the factors involved, particularly the nature and meaning of the relationship with the ill person, illness-related variables, and the contemporaneous psychology of the mourning caregiver.

Each of these four perspectives has its own issues, concerns, needs, demands, and intervention implications. These require address by the caregiver if healthy anticipatory mourning is to be enabled.

TIME FOCUS

The term *anticipatory mourning* suggests that it is solely a future loss that is being mourned. There are, however, three time foci involved: past, present, and future. After receipt of a life-threatening or fatal diagnosis, the experience of mourning is stimulated by losses that have occurred in the past, and those currently occurring, as well by those to come.

Even in the face of an ongoing terminal illness, losses that already have transpired will need to be mourned. For example, in nursing her husband during his final bout with cancer, it is not uncommon for a wife to mourn the vibrant and healthy man she *already has lost* to cancer and to mourn their altered relationship, life-style, and dreams for the future, which will never be realized. It is not unusual for her to remember the activities they shared when he was well; to recall how, in contrast to his current status, he was strong and independent; to grieve over the fact that so many limitations have been placed on their lives and have interfered with their plans; and to mourn for all that already has been taken away by the illness. This past may be recent, as in the case of altered life-style, or more distant, as in lost opportunities, regretted now in light of the limited time left. In both cases, the wife's attention to these past losses does not mean she is not still fully involved with her husband in his present state. In fact, because of her concern for her remaining time with him and out of her desire to protect him, the wife may not even explicitly address these losses. She may work to keep them out of her own conscious awareness or put them aside to deal with after the death. If she does mourn these losses, it might not be evident, just as mourning after a death might not be visibly manifested, or it, too, may be denied or put aside. Despite the response, the situation calls for some mourning because losses have transpired. This is true even though the content of the loss may pertain to the future (i.e., hopes, dreams, plans, beliefs, expectations, and assumptions). Whether or not these losses actually are mourned or even acknowledged is not the issue. The issue is that, even in the shadow of the ultimate loss of death, other losses that necessitate mourning already have occurred.

In addition to past losses, the woman in this scenario will experience conditions that stimulate mourning in the present. She witnesses the ongoing losses of progressive debilitation, increasing dependence, continual uncertainty, decreasing control, and so forth. A fundamental part of her mourning is grief for *what is currently being lost* and for the future, which is being eroded. This is different from mourning about what will happen in the future. Rather, it pertains to mourning over what is slipping away from her right now, for the sense of having her loved one being taken from her, and for what the increasing awareness of her husband's impending death means at this very moment in time.

This woman also mourns for future losses, yet to come. She mourns not only her husband's ultimate death, but also the *losses that will arise* before his death. This may entail mourning in advance for such things as the fact that she and her husband will not be able to take their annual vacation to the Bahamas this year or that he will lose his mobility and become bedridden. Such mourning is not limited to losses that happen prior to the death. It also may focus on those losses that will or might ensue in the future after the death, as a consequence of it. Examples include loneliness, insecurity, social discomfort, assaulted identity, economic uncertainty, life-style alterations, even the fact that her husband will not be present to walk their daughter down the aisle on her wedding day, among countless others.

Although the reality of the loved one's absence cannot completely be realized until the death has occurred and the person is no longer available for interaction, small but important indications foreshadow the permanent future absence. During the illness, the wife may be forced to attend a social function alone, the children to accommodate to their father's missing their award ceremonies, or the family to readjust to a reduced income. In some ways these kinds of alterations can help the family prepare for the new world that will exist after the father's death. These changes do not mean there is not a continued relationship with and investment in the father in the present, only that precursors suggest that the ultimate loss is drawing closer. The detachment in healthy anticipatory mourning is not from the dying loved one in the present but is undertaken on the intrapsychic level in the assumptive world, where the illness invalidates and the mourner relinquishes elements pertinent to the present and future of and with the ill loved one.

INFLUENCING FACTORS

Anticipatory mourning has myriad hues. Like conventional post-death mourning, an individual's anticipatory mourning experience is idiosyncratic, determined by a unique combination of psychological, social, and physiological factors.* The factors influencing anticipatory mourning, adapted and synthesized from Rando (1984, 1986a, 1993), are next described. All mourning, whether anticipatory or postdeath, can be understood and evaluated only in light of its influencing variables.

Psychological Factors

Psychological factors influencing a person's anticipatory mourning fall into three categories. First are those *characteristics pertaining to the nature and meaning of the person and relationship to be lost.* These include (a) the unique nature and meaning of the specific losses to be experienced; (b) the qualities of the relationship to be lost; (c) the roles that the life-threatened or dying person has occupied in the family, intimate, or social system of the mourner; (d) the psychological characteristics of the ill person; (e) the amount of unfinished business between the mourner and the ill person; (f) the mourner's perception of the ill person's fulfillment in life; and (g) the number, type, and quality of secondary losses that result from the illness and that will occur after the death.

In the second category are the personal *characteristics of the mourner.* These include (a) the mourner's coping behaviors, personality, and mental health; (b) the mourner's level of maturity and intelligence; (c) the mourner's past experience with loss, illness, disability, dying, and death; (d) the mourner's social, cultural, ethnic, and religious-philosophical backgrounds; (e) the mourner's gender conditioning; (f) the mourner's age; (g) the presence of concurrent stresses or crises in the mourner's life; (h) the mourner's life-style; (i) the mourner's sense of fulfillment in life; (j) elements of the mourner's assumptive world and the needs, emotions, cognitions, conations, and behaviors to which these elements give rise; and (k) the mourner's personal criteria for an appropriate death.

The final category of psychological factors are those *characteristics that pertain to the illness and type of death* with which the mourner must contend. These include (a) the mourner's specific fears about loss, illness, disability, dying, and death; (b) the mourner's previous experiences with and personal expectations about loss, illness, disability, dying, and death; (c) the mourner's knowledge about the illness; (d) the personal meaning of the specific illness to the mourner; (e) the type, frequency, and intensity of the mourner's involvement in the ill person's care and treatment; (f) the mourner's

---

*As used throughout, the term *psychological* includes emotion, cognition, philosophy/spirituality, conation, perception, defenses, and attempts at coping.

perception of the timeliness of the illness and impending death; (g) the mourner's perception of the preventability of the illness; (h) the length of the illness; (i) the nature of the illness (e.g., death trajectory, problems of the particular illness, location in the body, treatment regimen and side effects, amount of pain, degree of deterioration, rate of progression, number and rate of secondary losses); (j) the quality of the ill person's life after the diagnosis; (k) the location of the ill person (e.g., home, hospital, extended care facility, nursing home, hospice, relative's house); and (l) the mourner's evaluation of the ill person's experiences and the care, treatment, and resources that the ill person is provided and to which he or she has access.

Social Factors

Social factors that influence a person's anticipatory mourning also fall into three categories. These social dimensions encourage or discourage anticipatory mourning, help define the psychosocial context in which it takes place, and create some of the secondary losses that will be sustained. In the first category are the *characteristics of the ill person's knowledge of and response to the illness and ultimate death*. These affect the mourner because they determine the experience to which he or she must react. They include (a) the ill person's subjective experience of the illness (e.g., course of illness, treatment regimen and side effects, amount of pain, degree of deterioration, rate of progression, number and rate of secondary losses, proximity to death); (b) the ill person's attitude and responses toward, and coping with, the illness and its ramifications (psychologically, behaviorally, socially, and physically); (c) the personal meaning to the ill person of the specific illness and its bodily location; (d) the ill person's feelings, fears, and expectations about the loss, illness, disability, dying, and death; (e) the degree and accuracy of the ill person's knowledge of the illness and its ramifications; (f) the ill person's comfort in expressing thoughts, feelings, needs, impulses, wishes, and behaviors, and the style and extent of that communication; (g) the ill person's feelings of being supported, understood, and helped by others; (h) the ill person's satisfaction with treatment; (i) the degree of the ill person's acceptance of or resignation to impending death; (j) the ill person's will to live; and (k) the ill person's personal criteria for an appropriate death.

The second category of social factors are *characteristics of the family and its members' responses to the illness and impending death*. The term *family* as used here extends to the entire intimate network. These factors include (a) the family constellation (e.g., makeup of

family, developmental stage within the life cycle, familial sub-
systems, specific roles of family members and appropriateness of
roles and how they are assigned); (b) the specific characteristics of
this family system (e.g., degree of flexibility and adaptability, cohesion, boundaries, differentiation, communication style and patterns,
rules, norms, expectations, values, beliefs, assumptions, type and
quality of interrelationships, behavior and socialization patterns,
family strengths and vulnerabilities, family resources, established
patterns of transaction and interaction, system alliances and coalitions, habitual methods of problem resolution and coping strategies, anticipated immediate and long-range needs of the family,
quality of communication with caregivers); (c) generic premorbid
family history and specific history in terms of loss, illness, disability,
dying, and death, along with expectations therefrom; (d) current
family awareness and understanding of the illness and its implications; (e) family members' specific feelings, thoughts, and fears
about the ill person's particular losses, illness, disability, dying, and
death; (f) the number and type of roles the ill person filled in the
family and the degree of role reorganization required to ensure that
roles are fulfilled; (g) the role changes and psychosocial transitions
undergone by the mourner as a result of family reorganization in
the face of the ill person's illness and impending death; (h) the
degree of strain the illness and the family members' responses to it
puts on the family system; (i) the family's participation in the ill
person's care; (j) the extent and quality of the family's communication about the illness and its sequelae; (k) the relationship of each
family member with the ill person since the diagnosis; (l) the presence of family rules, norms, values, styles, and past experiences that
might inhibit mourning or interfere with a therapeutic relationship
with the ill or dying person; and (m) the total impact on the family
system of each family member's unique constellation of anticipatory
mourning–influencing variables.

The third category of social factors influencing a person's anticipatory mourning experience are *general socioeconomic and environmental
factors*. These include (a) types of relationships and communication
with caregivers; (b) quality and quantity of the mourner's social support system (e.g., degree of acceptance, support, security, and assistance of its members; quality of communication with its members;
degree of access the mourner has to it during the illness); (c) the
mourner's social, cultural, ethnic, and religious/philosophical backgrounds; (d) the mourner's and ill person's financial resources and
their expected stability; (e) the educational, economic, and occupational status of the mourner; (f) the degree of access to quality medical treatment and caregiving intervention for the ill person and

mourner; and (g) family and community rituals for loss, illness, disability, dying, and death.

Physiological Factors

The third class of variables influencing an individual's anticipatory mourning experience are the physiological factors. These include (a) the mourner's physical health; (b) the amount of the mourner's energy depletion; (c) the amount of rest, sleep, and exercise available to and engaged in by the mourner; (d) the mourner's use of drugs, alcohol, nicotine, food, and caffeine; and (e) the mourner's nutrition.

MAJOR SOURCES OF ADAPTATIONAL DEMANDS

Two major, ongoing experiences associated with life-threatening or terminal illness pose weighty demands for adaptation upon the anticipatory mourner. These are the experiences of loss and of trauma. Loss is the overarching process taking place in dying. It is punctuated by a series of discrete physical and psychosocial losses (see the section in this chapter on grief and mourning under the heading "Generic Operations") that often can end up blending together at times. Dying inherently involves loss, and it is this experience—occurring in itself and in the specific fashions in which it may transpire during the illness—that brings some of the experience of trauma to the anticipatory mourner. Trauma tends to be created as well by the separation anxiety associated with a loved one's dying, the characteristics of the anticipatory mourning situation, and the exposure of and demands placed upon the anticipatory mourner—including exposure to horrific stimuli, the multiplicity and chronicity of illness-induced losses and trauma, the creation of secondary traumatic stress, the inherent generation of helplessness, and the confrontation with overwhelming emotions and conflicting demands during times of strained resources. (See chapter 6 for more on these topics.)

Suffice it to say here that loss is always found in trauma, and elements of trauma are present in most major losses. They can add to as well as potentiate each other. Loss and its ensuing grief and mourning, and trauma and its resulting traumatic stress, are fundamental experiences to which the anticipatory mourner is significantly and repeatedly exposed and with which he or she must contend. These two experiences—alone, in combination, and in their sequelae—are the major origins of the adaptational demands placed on the anticipatory mourner. They shape the context within which anticipatory mourning takes place.

GENERIC OPERATIONS

Seven generic operations constitute healthy anticipatory mourning. At a given point in time, an individual may be engaged in any one or combination of these. Each has its attendant issues, concerns, needs, demands, and implications for intervention. The caregiver must assess and intervene in each of these operations as required.

Traditionally, the focus when thinking or writing about anticipatory mourning has been on the experience of grieving. While this is a central issue, it must not be construed to be the only one. As noted in the introduction to this book, recognition that the anticipatory mourning experience involves more dimensions than merely grief has prompted a number of writers in addition to myself to suggest use of the expanded term *anticipatory mourning* (e.g., Corr & Corr, chapter 7 in this volume; Futterman, Hoffman, & Sabshin, 1972; Lebow, 1976; Levy, 1991). The generic operations integral to the anticipatory mourning experience are (a) grief and mourning, (b) coping, (c) interaction, (d) psychosocial reorganization, (e) planning, (f) balancing conflicting demands, and (g) facilitating an appropriate death. In practice, these processes enable and facilitate one another. For the purpose of discussion, I attempt to separate them here.

Grief and Mourning

It is clinically useful to differentiate between grief and mourning. *Grief* refers to the process of experiencing the psychological, behavioral, social, and physical reactions to the perception of loss. Any grief response represents one or a combination of four things (Rando, 1993): the mourner's feelings about the loss and the deprivation it causes, the mourner's protest at the loss and wish to undo it and have it not be true, the effects caused by the assault on the mourner as a result of the loss, and the mourner's personal actions stimulated by these first three.

Any loss may be categorized in one of two ways. A *physical loss* is the loss of something tangible. Examples include a leg that is amputated or the loss of hair after chemotherapy. A *psychosocial loss*— sometimes called a *symbolic loss*—is the loss of something intangible and abstract. Examples include loss of one's health with the development of a chronic illness or the shattering of a dream. A physical loss is generally easily recognized and socially validated because it entails the absence of what was once concretely present. Consequently, such a loss is more perceptible. However, a psychosocial loss is no less of a loss for its being abstract and physically imperceptible. Each type of loss results in the demand for some amount of grief and mourning, depending on the unique and idiosyncratic constellation of factors circumscribing the mourner and his or her particular loss (see Rando 1984, 1993).

A *secondary loss* is a physical or psychosocial loss that coincides with or develops as a consequence of an initial loss (Rando, 1984). For example, if a mourner has to move to a new home because having a leg amputated makes negotiating stairs impossible, the loss of that home is a secondary physical loss.

A mourner experiences secondary psychosocial losses as well. Roles lost consequent to the death of a loved one, the body image devastated after an amputation, and the sense of order and predictability violated when a child contracts a life-threatening illness are all examples of secondary psychosocial losses. While a mourner can sustain a psychosocial loss without a secondary physical loss, it is impossible to experience a physical loss without a secondary psychosocial loss. At the very least, the meaning the mourner assigned to the physical object is lost when that object is lost.

One type of secondary psychosocial loss is known as "assumptive world violation." The *assumptive world* is the mental schema that contains all a person assumes to be true about the self, the world, and everything and everyone in it. Previous experiences in life form the basis for the person's assumptive world elements. These elements represent all of that person's assumptions, expectations, and beliefs, with most of these becoming virtually automatic habits of cognition and behavior. In large part, the assumptive world determines the individual's needs, emotions, and behavior, and gives rise to hopes, wishes, fantasies, dreams, and other conations. The assumptive world is the internal model against which the individual constantly matches incoming sensory data in order to orient the self, recognize what is happening, and plan behavior (Parkes, 1988). Two categories of elements in the assumptive world pertain to pre- or postdeath loss. *Global elements* concern the self, others, life, the world in general, or matters spiritual. *Specific elements* are associated with precisely what is being or has been lost to the mourner (e.g., the loved one, the life-style, the leg) and its usual and continued interactive presence in the individual's world. Any type of illness or death-related loss brings violations of those assumptive world elements predicated specifically upon the existence of the lost person or object. Depending upon the nature of that loss and its sequelae, global assumptive world elements may be violated as well. Those violations that cause particularly significant problems to and traumatization of the mourner are the fundamental assumptions that the world is benevolent, the world (and life) is meaningful, and the self is worthy (Janoff-Bulman, 1992). These are frequently shattered by and during life-threatening or terminal illness and constitute a main area of loss and major targets for intervention.

In contrast to grief, the term *mourning*, as used here, refers to the conscious and unconscious processes and courses of action that promote three operations, each with its own particular focus: (a) undoing of the psychosocial ties binding the mourner to the loved one/object, with the eventual facilitation of the development of new ties appropriate to the now altered relationship—here the focus is on the deceased/lost object; (b) personally adapting to the loss— here the focus is on the mourner and his or her assumptive world and identity; and (c) learning how to live in a healthy way in the new world without the deceased/lost object—here the focus is on the external world. These three broad operations give rise to the *six "R" processes of mourning*, which must be completed in order to accommodate a loss in a healthy way (Rando, 1993). They are listed in Table 2.2.

The ultimate functions of grief and mourning are to assist the mourner in recognizing that the deceased/lost object truly is gone and then in making the necessary internal (psychological) and external (behavioral and social) changes to accommodate this reality. Grief helps the mourner recognize the loss and prepare for the later processes of mourning by providing the experiences and learning necessary to initiate those processes. Grief is actually the beginning of mourning. In and of itself, grief is insufficient for healthy loss accommodation because it involves only the mourner's reactions to the perceptions of loss and not the active work of readjustment, adaptation, and integration.

Any mourner's bereavement experience represents the accumulation of all the courses of grief and mourning initiated by the original loss and all the secondary losses associated with it.

Coping

Dovetailing with the central processes of grief and mourning, *coping* is what parties involved in anticipatory mourning do, both internally and externally, to deal with loss. Anticipatory grief as a phenomenon can justifiably be placed within the conceptual domain of coping; as a clinical reality, coping constitutes one of the primary elements of anticipatory mourning.

Coping implies the individual's active encountering of a stressor (i.e., the life-threatening or terminal illness and its sequelae) in a dynamic attempt to contend with it in one of three different ways:

TABLE 2.2

The Six "R" Processes of Mourning

1. Recognize the loss
    *   Acknowledge the loss
    *   Understand the loss

2. React to the separation
    *   Experience the pain
    *   Feel, identify, accept, and give some form of expression to all the psychological reactions to the loss
    *   Identify and mourn secondary losses

3. Recollect and reexperience the deceased/lost object and the relationship
    *   Review and remember realistically
    *   Revive and reexperience the feelings

4. Relinquish the old attachments to the deceased/lost object and the old assumptive world

5. Readjust to move adaptively into the new world without forgetting the old
    *   Revise the assumptive world
    *   Develop a new relationship with the deceased/lost object
    *   Adopt new ways of being in the world
    *   Form a new identity

6. Reinvest

to withstand it (i.e., simply not be vanquished by it); to manage it (i.e., have some control over it in order to minimize its impact, although not to eliminate it); or to surmount it (i.e., prevail over it). At any given point, coping can be directed toward disease-related issues and dying processes, and/or toward ongoing life independent of these issues and processes.

The clinical definition of coping that appears to have attracted the most adherents is that proposed by Lazarus and Folkman (1984) in their classic work *Stress, Appraisal, and Coping,* upon which the present discussion of coping rests heavily. They define coping as "constantly changing cognitive and behavioral efforts to manage specific external and/or internal demands that are appraised as tax-ing or exceeding the resources of the person" (p. 141). They further clarify that coping is a meaning-centered, active process through which the person manages not only these demands but also the emotions they generate. Coping involves efforts to deal with demands independent of outcome; coping is still coping whether or not these efforts are successful. The focus of the definition is on the person's active attempts to handle what is perceived as stressful. The significance for the person's well-being is appraised differently at different points and mandates different modes of coping depending on that appraisal. The caregiver must continually evaluate and accu-rately assess where the anticipatory mourner is in his or her processes and what that mourner needs at a given point in time.

Coping can be categorized according to function (problem focused, emotion focused, appraisal focused) and type (e.g., avoid-ance, information seeking, seeking emotional support). *Problem-focused coping* is directed at managing or altering the situation or factors causing distress and is most likely to be undertaken when conditions are appraised as amenable to change. Problem-focused coping strategies are similar to those for problem solving: defining the problem, generating alternative solutions, weighing alternatives, choosing among them, and acting. Although the term *problem solv-ing* implies an objective, analytic process focused primarily on the environment, problem-solving coping also includes strategies directed inward, toward the self. Such strategies involve motiva-tional or cognitive changes, such as shifting one's level of aspiration, reducing ego involvement, finding alternative channels of gratifica-tion, developing new standards of behavior, or learning new skills and procedures (Kahn, Wolfe, Quinn, Snoek, & Rosenthal, 1964).

In contrast, *emotion-focused coping* aims to regulate the person's emotional response to the problem and is more likely to occur when appraisal suggests that nothing can be done to modify harm-ful, threatening, or challenging environmental conditions. A wider range of emotion-focused forms of coping than problem-focused forms exists, and the former have been studied more. One category of emotion-focused coping strategies consists of cognitive processes directed toward decreasing emotional distress (e.g., avoidance, mini-mization, distancing, selective attention, positive comparisons, and wresting positive value from negative events; Lazarus & Folkman, 1984). Many of these strategies derive from theory and research on defensive processes and are used in virtually every type of stressful encounter. In addition to cognitive forms of emotion-focused cop-ing, behavioral forms exist. These do not change the meaning of an event directly, as does cognitive reappraisal, but their use can lead to reappraisal. Examples include engaging in physical exercise, meditating, having a drink, venting anger, or seeking emotional support.

According to Lazarus and Folkman (1984), problem-focused coping and emotion-focused coping can impede or facilitate each other. To give an instance of how these two types of coping may be at cross purposes, sometimes seriously ill medical patients employ emotion-focused coping strategies (i.e., minimization and avoidance) to soften realities that might prove overwhelming if directly confronted. Unfortunately, these emotion-focused strategies can interfere with their treatment regimen, in effect compromising a problem-focused function. Yet emotion- and problem-focused strategies can also facilitate each other. For example, Hay and Oken (1972) observed that emotion-focused strategies such as distancing and avoidance seemed to decrease the distress of nurses in an intensive care unit. This in turn enabled them to pursue their patient care tasks more effectively (i.e., to be more problem focused).

Problem- and emotion-focused coping also can occur concurrently. Folkman and Lazarus (1980) conclude that people use both problem- and emotion-focused coping strategies to deal with the internal and/or external demands posed by real-life stressful situations. Caregivers working with those experiencing anticipatory mourning will need to pay attention to both the expression of feelings and other emotion-focused coping strategies, and problem-focused approaches.

It should be noted that certain cognitive forms of emotion-focused coping lead to a change in the way an encounter is construed without changing the objective situation. Some theorists further differentiate these cognitive forms, which deal with coping via reappraisals, into a third type of coping, termed *appraisal-focused coping* (Moos & Billings, 1982). In this form, the coping involves attempts to understand and find a pattern of meaning in the crisis. This is often witnessed in anticipatory mourning and in coping with major loss in general.

In anticipatory mourning, as in other contexts in which coping is necessitated, the cognitive appraisal process is critical and must be understood by caregivers if they want to comprehend the anticipatory mourner's experience. The appraisal provides the evaluation of meaning on which the person's emotion depends. Appraisal-related processes shape the reactions of people to any encounter by characterizing it and its various facets with respect to its meaning or significance for the person's well-being. Any appraisal reflects the unique and changing relationship taking place between a person with certain distinctive characteristics (values, commitments, styles of perceiving and thinking) and an environment whose characteristics must be predicted and interpreted (Lazarus & Folkman, 1984). This is what gives every appraisal its own idiosyncratic flavor.

According to Lazarus and Folkman (1984) there are three forms of cognitive appraisal. All of these can be witnessed in anticipatory mourning. *Primary appraisal* focuses on whether one is involved in an event and, if so, what is at stake in the encounter; *secondary appraisal* concerns what might and can be done, and involves the person's evaluation of coping options and the assessment of their potential effectiveness. *Reappraisal* refers to changing an earlier appraisal in the same encounter on the basis of new information. One form of reappraisal is quite pertinent to anticipatory mourning. *Defensive reappraisal* consists of any effort made to reinterpret the past more positively or to deal with present harms and threats by viewing them in less damaging and/or threatening ways. These defensive reappraisals differ from other reappraisals in that they are self-generated, originating specifically from needs within the person rather than from environmental or internal feedback. In themselves, they are coping efforts.

Many factors influence cognitive appraisal and, therefore, the emotions a person experiences. These factors can be broken down into two groups: person factors and situation factors. Person factors tend to confer meaning on an event. Among the most important person factors influencing cognitive appraisal are one's commitments and beliefs, especially about personal control and existential concerns. These influence appraisal by determining what is salient for well-being, shaping the person's understanding of the event and consequent emotions and coping efforts, and providing the basis for evaluating outcomes.

Situation factors tend to have the potential for creating threat. Eight situation factors are known, as formal properties of situations, to create the potential for a stress appraisal of harm, threat, or challenge. As identified by Lazarus and Folkman (1984), they include novelty, predictability, event uncertainty, imminence, duration, temporal uncertainty, ambiguity, and timing of stressful events in relation to life cycle.

It behooves the caregiver to be aware of how each of these two groups of factors play out in the anticipatory mourner's particular situation. The caregiver will need to evaluate these areas in order to be best able to appreciate the subjective experience of the anticipatory mourner and then choose the most effective interventions to enable healthy coping.

Interaction

The third of the seven generic operations in anticipatory mourning, *interaction* refers to a transactional relating to or engagement with another person in which there is mutual or reciprocal action or influence. Interaction may occur as an independent act or as part of a process; in any event, it implies some amount of cross-contact, cross-connection, and interface.

At any given time, interaction may center on issues related to the illness or on previous or ongoing life independent of the illness. Typically, for all parties (with the possible exception of concerned others), healthy anticipatory mourning is predicated upon involvement with the life-threatened or dying person. Levels of involvement are heavily influenced not only by personalities but also by circumstances. For instance, sometimes intimates are geographically separated and inter-action is not in person, face-to-face, but via telephone, computer, tele-conference, videotape, audiotape, e-mail, facsimile, or standard mail. Sometimes concerned others do have close interaction with the ill person. Depending on the party, the types and degrees of interaction necessary for healthy anticipatory mourning will differ.

Interactional processes with the ill or dying loved one are con-strued in this model of anticipatory mourning as fundamental. (The reader is referred to subsequent discussion in this chapter under the heading "Contextual Levels" for a delineation of interpersonal-level processes with the life-threatened or dying person.) These processes include (a) directing attention, energy, and behavior toward the life-threatened or dying person; (b) resolution of personal relationship with the life-threatened or dying person; and (c) helping the life-threatened or dying person.

The central relationship within the anticipatory mourning con-text is between a particular party and the life-threatened or dying person. The literature has focused on psychosocial aspects of dying as they relate to interrelationships between the ill individual and his or her intimates. It is no coincidence that virtually all authors' delin-eations of coping tasks for the dying person relate in one way or another to the need to preserve and maintain that person's relation-ships with significant others. Social isolation is universally identified in Western society as something to be avoided and perceived as a characteristic indicative of a "bad dying experience." It is also no coincidence that, consistently in studies both of coping in general and of illness adaptation and grief and mourning specifically, social support is a key factor in influencing outcome.

Interaction with significant others, the preservation of key rela-tionships, and the support of those most meaningful to the ill per-son are so critical that their absence is almost always a target for intervention. The exception to this rule is during the natural points in the illness when social relationships are gradually relinquished. This occurs as the seriously ill or dying person's world necessarily becomes more restricted, culminating eventually in the end stage of terminal illness, when the dying person often withdraws into the self. Peripheral relationships are let go initially, and there may be a steady decrease in involvement with others until at the end only those closest to the ill person remain, if he or she is still able to maintain connection. Across this time, involvement and interaction with those most important to the ill person must be enabled. At the end, some dying persons turn away from even those closest loved ones, as detachment from the outside world and those in it prepares the person for a final exit from life. The letting go and total self-involvement seen in many individuals at this time is not a lack of love but a natural part of the process of dying. Nevertheless, even at the very end and even if the dying person is totally withdrawn, it appears that it is meaningful and comforting to have the sense that loved ones are still present: One of the worst fears an individual can have is to be left to die alone.

Awareness Contexts and Types of Death

Two conceptualizations have direct bearing on interaction with the life-threatened or dying person. Despite the fact that each was introduced over 30 years ago, they continue to have impressive applicability today. One concerns the different types of awareness contexts that can exist between the ill person and others; the second pertains to the types of death the person may undergo.

In 1965, Glaser and Strauss described four types of interactional and awareness contexts that could exist between dying persons and their intimates and caregivers. In a *closed awareness context*, intimates and caregivers are aware of the dying person's condition but keep this information from the person. This information usually cannot be hidden for too long because illness-related changes in the ill person's body and the verbal and nonverbal communications of intimates and caregivers usually signal that something is wrong.

A *suspicion awareness context* is present when others know the truth and the ill person suspects it. This situation can undermine trust and complicate future communication. In this context, the dying individual simultaneously wants to discover the truth and desires to avoid it.

The *mutual awareness context* is one in which all involved are aware of the illness and its implications but pretend that they are not. This is a very emotionally and physically draining situation that demands constant vigilance and the acting out of roles in a shared drama of silence.

Finally, an *open awareness context* is one in which there is shared knowledge, information, and communication about the person's dying. While this does not mean that all parties are always equally able to and interested in addressing the reality and its implications, it does mean that when they are, they can communicate about it honestly and without pretense. This is considered the ideal context within which to operate. Like the others, this context has pluses and minuses. While it permits honest communication and healthy relating, enables the finishing of unfinished business, and eliminates problems stemming from suspicion and pretense, it does expose the parties to painful feelings (e.g., sadness, anger, perhaps guilt) and recognized facts (e.g., choices unmade, paths not taken). These issues can be quite difficult, yet for many the costs are preferable to those associated with the lack of openness (Corr, Nabe, & Corr, 1997).

The second conceptualization concerns types of death. In 1967, Sudnow delineated four types of death that each individual undergoes: social death, psychological death, biological death, and physiological death. *Social death* represents the symbolic death of the person in the world he or she has known. Socially, the world begins to shrink. This occurs naturally when the illness forces a change in life-style or the individual is hospitalized and removed from the familiar environments of work, home, and neighborhood. This, plus illness-related changes in function and ability to carry out previous roles, can cause the ill person's social contacts to diminish accordingly. In some cases, however, social death occurs much earlier than necessary. In these situations, dying individuals may be deserted and placed in nursing homes by families who already consider them dead. This is the premature detachment that some critics of anticipatory mourning fear. Social death may be a natural part of the dying process, but it should result from the natural course of the person's dying trajectory and not from the defensiveness or lack of concern of those around that individual.

Psychological death refers to the death of aspects of the dying individual's personality. The nature of terminal illness demands some degree of regression and dependency because the individual is no longer capable of the same degree of autonomous functioning as before. Grief and mourning over physical and psychosocial losses resulting from the illness affect the personality. The disease process itself often fosters personality changes biochemically, as do medication and pain. Coinciding with this, ill persons may experience changes in their relationships with others, changes that all too frequently can lead to isolation and invalidation. Regardless of what has occurred before, as the end draws closer most dying individuals begin to let go of the world, naturally decathecting from it and most, if not all, of the people they know. In essence, the individual, as others know that person, dies.

When psychological death transpires at the proper time and under the appropriate conditions, it is part of "healthy dying" (Pattison, 1969) and paves the way for the person's exit from human life. Where it becomes problematic is when the psychological death of the person too prematurely precedes the biological and physiological deaths of the person. Situations like Alzheimer's disease and irreversible coma, among others, place great and painful burdens on all parties (see Doka, chapter 16 in this volume). To the extent that the dying person is aware of these social and/or psychological deaths, he or she must contend with yet other losses. Some of these losses (e.g., alterations of aspects of the individual's personality or cognitive functioning secondary to the illness process) may play into that individual's largest fears, particularly of losses of self-control and identity, disability, and regression (see Pattison, 1977).

Even if the dying person is unaware of psychological death, the intimates usually are not. In recent years, interest has increased about the dilemmas and burdens of family caregivers and other intimates who are put in difficult psychosocial situations by the psychological deaths of their loved ones, who then survive physically for protracted periods of time. Such a circumstance leaves the intimates in a type of limbo; the person they knew as their loved one essentially is dead, but the physical shell lives on. This creates the image of the loved one's continued survival, despite the actual loss of the essence of that person. This image often carries with it obligations and expectations that are psychologically untenable (e.g., to relate as if the person were the same as before, even though he or she is not).

Another poignant set of issues associated with psychological death is found in circumstances where there is intermittent or fluctuating awareness of the psychological death on the part of the ill person or intimate. For example, the affected individual may be aware of the "slipping away" of cognitive capacities and of the social reactions of others to this. Similarly, the intimate may be excruciatingly cognizant of the "slipping away" of the loved one, who is being slowly but inexorably overtaken by a disease process that robs that person of defining personality, capacities, and identity-composing attributes. Witnessing this but being powerless to stop it, the intimate is forced to attend the psychological deterioration of the loved one and to confront—whether successfully or not—the myriad emotional reactions and psychosocial dilemmas that arise.

As well, the intimate may be saddled with difficulties posed by the instability of the condition. Difficult, guilt-provoking questions can arise under these circumstances, such as "Should I go to visit my mother today? It may be one of the days when she recognizes me." The ill person's being "in touch" periodically and unpredictably can intermittently reinforce the intimate's behaviors and prevent the closure or mourning-related reconstruction that would permit the intimate to redefine his or her relationship with the patient (e.g., to revise assumptive world elements pertaining to the patient as a sentient, consistently mentally competent person).

Biological death refers to death in which the organism as a human entity no long exists. Artificial supports may keep certain organs functioning, but the human traits of consciousness and awareness in a self-sustaining mind-body connection are gone. *Physiological death* occurs when there is a cessation of the operation of all vital organs.

Ideally, these four types of death occur in order, succeeding and facilitating one another. Therapeutic intervention in anticipatory mourning attempts to structure the environment so that these first two types of death do not occur too far in advance of these last two. When biological death precedes physiological death by too great an interval, crucial questions of bioethical concern arise around such legal and moral issues as euthanasia, "pulling the plug," organ donation and transplantation (see Holtkamp, chapter 18 in this book), and so forth. The goals of intervention will include, among others, promoting circumstances in which all four types of death coincide as closely as possible. In the anticipatory mourning context of terminal illness, these four types of death can be made more proximate by minimizing premature detachment from the ill person, socially and psychologically. Continued interaction with important others is crucial in affirming the social and psychological existence of the dying person right up until actual physiological death or until such time that the dying individual's appropriate withdrawal suggests involvement be modified. While the circumstances are unique in each situation, the dying person should be accompanied and supported throughout the illness and permitted to die in a context including whatever amount of sustaining interaction is required. Healthy anticipatory mourning encourages and capacitates this.

Psychosocial Reorganization

One of the relative "pluses" of healthy anticipatory mourning is that it affords the opportunity to commence the psychosocial reorganization necessary to permit the life-threatened or terminally ill person to live—physically and psychosocially—as well as possible for as long as possible. Psychosocial reorganization then enables that person to die appropriately, in an environment surrounded by intimates and caregivers who have made the readjustments necessary to "hold" the dying person's experience as well as their own: within themselves (intrapsychically); between that dying person and themselves, as well as among themselves (interpersonally); and as a familial, organizational, or social group (systemically).

Like other aspects of anticipatory mourning, psychosocial reorganization is multifaceted. For instance, it can occur on all contextual levels—that is, within the person on the intrapsychic level; among the parties on an interpersonal level; and/or on a systemic level within such entities as the intimate network, the extended social group of concerned others, and other pertinent organizations and systems. Its domain also encompasses all dimensions of the individual person: psychological, behavioral, social, and physical.

As used here, the term *psychosocial reorganization* refers to the psychosocial changes that are undertaken in any of the aforementioned realms in order to respond to the reality of the situation— specifically, the demands of the illness and its sequelae. There are four main ways psychosocial reorganization is achieved: (a) cognitive processing, (b) adaptive readjustment, (c) role redistribution and reassignment, and (c) rehearsal and socialization.

Cognitive Processing

Cognitive processing must be addressed first in terms of psychosocial reorganization because conclusions brought about by the cognitive processing of information are what stimulate the remaining psychosocial adjustments. Cognitive processes and illness experiences facilitate each other—that is, one learns from the illness experience to know what must be reorganized, and reorganization itself stimulates learning.

Healthy adaptation to illness and loss is predicated upon two pivotal sets of processes of cognitive adjustment to loss that have received insufficient attention in thanatology (Rando, 1995b). As pertains to bereavement, whether anticipatory or postdeath, the first set relates to the individual's learning about the reality of the loved one's impending or actual death and developing an appreciation of its implications. The second set, contingent upon the success of the first, pertains specifically to the stimulation of necessary internal and external changes necessary to adjust to that reality and accommodate subsequent losses. These processes include (a) the revision of the assumptive world (insofar as the transformation, deterioration, or death of the loved one has violated any global or specific assumptions); (b) developing a new relationship with the loved one (to reflect the changes in his or her status); (c) adopting new ways of being in the external world (to compensate for the changes in or loss of the loved one); (d) the formation of a new identity (incorporating the adjustments brought about by the alterations in or loss of the loved one); and (e) selected reinvestment (of emotional energy once invested in that which has been or is being lost—now redirected toward rewarding new people, objects, hopes, goals, pursuits, and so forth). (See Rando, 1993, for a full discussion of these changes.)

The first set of cognitive processes:
Learning about the reality of a loved one's dying

When one is informed that a loved one is dying, whether that loved one is the self or another person, the reality and its full implications cannot be comprehended at once. Coupled with the temporary inability to fathom the information, the traumatic stress reactions experienced in the acute crisis of diagnosis interfere with the cognitive processing of whatever information is grasped. In essence, the individual is overloaded and, consequently, overwhelmed. It remains for the individual to learn about the reality of the loved one's dying via the gradual erosion of disbelief that occurs through the experiences in the illness.

Historically, the defensive processes of denial have been cited as interfering with the acquisition and processing of information at this time. Yet what traditionally has been viewed as denial is often less active contradiction of reality than disbelief occasioned by inadequate information (Bowlby, 1980). It is such disbelief, and by extension the lack of evidence that gives rise to it, that operates to prevent the person from apprehending the current situation and its violation of what he or she has come to know and expect in life. In other words, it is not that one is able to grasp the reality of the loved one's dying and then on some level chooses not to do so. Rather, one simply is unable to grasp that reality for some period of time. If someone has been an integral part of one's physical, emotional, and social existence, it will take considerable effort to realize that he or she will not be there anymore. Only over time, as one is gradually taught through the experiences of the terminal illness (and ideally through healthy anticipatory mourning processes), will one truly learn the reality that the loved one is dying.

Cognitive processing and education take place throughout the entire illness. The anticipatory mourner learns through confrontation with the loved one's illness, and through the experience of repeated frustration of the need to see the loved one not be sick, to be as he or she used to be, or at least to improve. A progressively deepening awareness develops of the seriousness of the illness and its implications as the realization occurs that certain hopes about recovery or stabilization are not being actualized. New information gradually starts to supplant the old assumptions, expectations, and beliefs about the ill person, such as the person's being healthy, having a long-term future, and being able to be with the anticipatory mourner in the fashion that he or she needs and wants. When the loved one relies more on medication for symptom control, when there is yet another social occasion that must be missed because of the fatigue, as the anticipatory mourner witnesses increasing disability, as another remission is cut short by a relapse, as the mourner continues to be frustrated in his or her desires to have the loved one back as before—these are all experiences that teach the anticipatory mourner that the dying loved one is truly seriously ill, that this is not a nightmare but a reality that must be dealt with despite intense needs and wishes otherwise.

Each of these lessons erodes the mourner's disbelief a little bit more, at the same time providing additional information about the seriousness of the situation, until at some point he or she truly believes and comprehends the reality of the loved one's dying and appreciates its implications. The information that the mourner may have intellectually acknowledged initially at the time of diagnosis now has been internalized at a gut level, the journey from head to heart fueled by repeated confrontations with the illness and the consequent demands for changes in the anticipatory mourner's assumptive world, ways of relating to the loved one and being in the external world, and sense of self.

The mourner now operates in the world with the awareness of the reality of the loved one's dying (at first intermittently and then gradually more constantly) and in some amount of accordance with that fact. Whether the reality that mourner has been taught through the experiences of witnessing the illness and its impacts upon the patient sinks in permanently, whether it is responded to in a healthy way (if at all), or whether it eventuates in appropriate anticipatory mourning are not the issues here. The central point is that the individual can only absorb the reality of a loved one's dying—whether that loved one be the self or another person—after having had experiences of sufficient kind and number to teach this reality. Otherwise, the gravity and traumatic nature of the situation, as well as the assumptive world violations it inherently contains, are so significant that it simply cannot be comprehended. To reiterate, this is not necessarily a result of denial but the consequence of understandable incredulity and disbelief.

The second set of cognitive processes: Adjusting to the reality of a loved one's dying

It takes hundreds if not thousands of experiences with the loved one's life-threatening or terminal illness before the anticipatory mourner really learns that the loved one is dying. Even before these lessons are completely understood, changes are initiated. Perhaps subtle at first, these changes reflect the anticipatory mourner's beginning adjustment to the new reality. The awareness that the world is no longer the same leads to the anticipatory mourner's ultimate revision of his or her assumptive world and relinquishment, modification of, or additions to previous expectations, assumptions, and beliefs predicated upon the continued existence of the loved one as before. For instance, insofar as the illness has adversely affected the loved one's health, mobility, or productivity, the mourner is called upon to change his or her relevant assumptive world elements to reflect the current reality. Thus, the expectation that "My mother will always be there to take care of me, as a strong and independent person" must be revised to accommodate the dependency shift caused by the illness: "My mother is always my mother, but she is ill and frail, and it is my turn to care for her." The same thing occurs with global assumptions (e.g., belief in God, justice, invulnerability to personal tragedy) affected by the intrusion of severe threat, illness-related symptomatology, and the various losses and limitations brought about by the illness.

This process of assumptive world revision and its often consequent learning not to need the ill loved one in the same ways anymore, plus observations of the illness's impact upon the person, typically leads the anticipatory mourner to redefine his or her relationship with the dying individual to be consistent with the new reality (i.e., the loved one is now perceived to be life-threatened, and the anticipatory mourner may shift priorities to reflect this fact). At this point, the cognitive processes stimulate the need for change in order to incorporate the new reality now reflected in the revised assumptive world.

Five theories of cognitive adaptation to threatening or traumatic events can be helpful in understanding the cognitive processes in anticipatory mourning that pertain to the readjustments required. These theories address a number of cardinal issues associated with both trauma and the dying of a loved one. They include (a) Parkes' (1988) revision of the assumptive world following psychosocial transitions and Woodfield and Viney's (1984–1985) work on personal construct dislocation and adaptation in bereavement; (b) Horowitz's (1986) cognitive processing aspects of the stress response syndrome and integration of memories and responses, meanings, new assumptive world, and new sense of self; (c) Taylor's (1983) theory of cognitive adjustment to threatening events centering on the search for meaning in the experience, the attempt to regain mastery over the event in particular and over one's life in general, and the effort to restore self-esteem through self-enhancing evaluations; (d) Janoff-Bulman's (1992) theory of the necessity to rebuild shattered assumptive worlds following victimization and the loss of the sense of personal invulnerability subsequent to the violation of fundamental assumptions of the world as benevolent, the world (life) as meaningful, and/or the self as worthy; and (e) Neimeyer's (1997) constructivist theory, which identifies personal meaning reconstruction as the central dynamic of mourning.

Adaptive Readjustment

Once the anticipatory mourner learns the reality of the loved one's illness and makes the necessary cognitive changes in his or her assumptive world (including redefinition of the relationship with the ill or dying loved one), certain modifications are required. For instance, the mourner is called upon to make adaptations in the external world to accommodate the altered—and, in many cases, continually altering—status of the loved one. The mourner must find other people or ways to meet the needs the loved one filled when well, change his or her desire for what was previously needed, or learn to tolerate doing without. The relationship with the dying loved one may be transformed by the anticipatory mourner's directing of attention, energy, and behavior toward that person; working to achieve resolution of their personal relationship; and performing assorted acts designed to assist the loved one therapeutically in his or her illness or dying. Roles, skills, behaviors, and relationships may have to be taken on, modified, or relinquished to compensate for what has already been, and is being, lost with the loved one's illness, dying, or death. In this regard, the mourner may adopt myriad new ways of being in the world that now exists. For some, there may be limited or selected reinvestment of the emotional energy once invested in that which has been or is being lost.

Thus, adjustments are called for in oneself in relation to the loved one, as well as to one's identity and to life in general. There is an incorporation of changes into one's sense of self and ways of being necessitated by illness in the life-threatened or dying loved one and by one's relationships with that person, oneself, and various others—in fact, often the whole world—given how anticipatory mourning can result in revision of global elements of the assumptive world as well as specific ones. The "R" process readjustments necessary to accommodate any major loss (see the fifth "R" process in Table 2.2) translate directly to the anticipatory mourning experience and what is required when losses occur therein.

Role Redistribution and Reassignment

Like the adjustments made in the cognitive spheres, other aspects on the intrapsychic, interpersonal, and systemic contextual levels become reorganized over time to accommodate the loved one's life-threatening or terminal illness. Given that human beings are notoriously resistant to change, we can assume that the parties undertake these adjustments only because they perceive no possibility for recourse, a better outcome, or less pain. It is not true that these adjustments and reorganizations are always consciously undertaken. What is true is that they are enacted in response to the confrontation with the vicissitudes and physical and psychosocial sequelae of the illness, to the demands this encounter necessitates, and to whatever amount of increasing awareness and knowledge it precipitates.

We know from the family systems literature that illness in a family or intimate network can be expected to result in the reassignment of power, responsibility, roles, and functions within that system to regain the homeostatic balance lost consequent to the ill member's inability to fulfill roles or obligations as he or she did previously. Many theorists view negotiating and adapting to such role changes as primary aspects of anticipatory mourning (e.g., Cohen & Cohen, 1981; Lebow, 1976; Rando, 1986a).

Several factors affect the suitability of the role for the person assigned it. Healthy reassignments are made with consideration for such issues as appropriateness of a given role responsibility for a specific family member, the member's preparation for and probable rewards in assuming the role, and the congruence of the new responsibilities with existing roles (Arndt & Gruber, 1977). Role reassignments can constitute either secondary losses or secondary gains for individual family members. The degree of role reorganization that will be necessary in the family depends on the number of roles held by the life-threatened or terminally ill member and the types of roles he or she fulfilled (Vollman, Ganzert, Picher, & Williams, 1971), along with that member's degree of inability to fulfill them.

This last factor is especially salient for individuals during the chronic living-dying interval, given that their dysfunction in a particular role may only be partial and a complete reassignment of it may be premature. For instance, while an ill father may be unable to shoot baskets with his 8-year-old son, and this need may be reassigned to the child's older brother, this specific inability does not mean other paternal role responsibilities must be reassigned at this point. There may be no reason this man still cannot engage in the less strenuous sport of fishing or continue in other roles, such as reviewing his son's homework. One of the main agendas in healthy anticipatory mourning is to promote as much normalcy and appropriate interpersonal engagement among intimates as is possible. Premature role reassignment violates this agenda and contributes substantially to the suffering and losses experienced by the ill person. Also, it often can create a precipitous impression of social death.

Rehearsal and Socialization

Rehearsal

Two of the four elements originally identified by Lindemann in 1944 as primary components of anticipatory mourning are "a review of all the forms of death which might befall [the individual], and anticipation of the modes of readjustment which might be necessitated by it" (p. 148). In extending Lindemann's work, Fulton and Fulton (1971) employed the following phrases to restate the third and fourth features delineated by Lindemann: "rehearse [the] death" and "attempt to adjust to the various consequences of it" (p. 93). With their introduction of the term *rehearse* into the anticipatory mourning situation and their acknowledgment of the mourner's attempts to adjust contingent upon the rehearsal, Fulton and Fulton clarify the salience of this generic operation in anticipatory mourning.

In essence, the cognitive-behavioral process of rehearsal (a) serves as a vehicle to anticipate, identify, and ultimately help problem solve relevant issues and concerns; (b) promotes a relative level of mastery via in vivo and/or abstract practice in new areas occasioned by current or forthcoming circumstances; and (c) as a result of practice, inoculation, and/or preparation, reduces traumatization secondary to difficult illness and/or loss-related experiences. Cognitive-behavioral rehearsal has a long history in the realms of psychotherapy, counseling, and education as an intervention for confronting novel situations or those perceived as problematic.

Janis's (1958) demonstration of the facilitative impact of the "work of worry" is often cited as evidence of the relationship between rehearsing a stressful event and subsequent coping. Siegel and Weinstein (1983) utilize Janis's concept to illustrate that anticipatory mourning is potentially adaptive because it permits the future survivor to practice the bereaved role and begin working through the complex emotional reactions associated with the death. Janis's "work of worry" also has implications for the planning component of anticipatory mourning, the next generic operation.

Rehearsal of the bereaved role is not necessarily actively sought out by the dying person or the survivors-to-be, but it frequently is inherent in the illness experience. In the case of the ill or dying person, rehearsal would involve anticipating what it would be like to be bereaved from some expected future loss—for instance, loss of a breast or drastically reduced mobility. When the ill person's fatigue forces his or her spouse to attend a child's music recital alone, when a parent misses a child's eighth-grade graduation because the child has had a relapse and is too ill to participate, or when an adult child has only one parent over for Sunday dinner because the other one is hospitalized—all of these experiences give glimpses of what it will be like for survivors after the death occurs.

These precursors of what the world will be like later on in the illness or after the death—small but important indications of what is to come—afford opportunities to practice the bereaved role, although they are not often perceived by anticipatory mourners as having such a positive value. These experiences teach about the current situation, inform about the future, and provide a vehicle for coping and adaptation. In these regards, the vicissitudes of the illness both bring home reality and prompt some ways of responding to it.

Rehearsal in anticipatory mourning also may take place in other than practical behavioral or social ways. Emotionally, the anticipatory mourner may extrapolate from a current feeling to anticipate what that emotion may be like in all its dimensions and intensities further on in the illness or after the death (e.g., "If this is how lonely I feel now and he's only in the hospital for 2 days, it must be going to be excruciating when he's gone permanently"). Alternatively, emotional experiences may signal that one will get through the death and the adjustment it will entail (e.g., "As distressing as this is, I'm still managing to hold on emotionally and do what must be done. I guess I will be able to survive this ordeal after all").

Rehearsal can occur cognitively, as when the assumptive world is readied for revision by one's thoughts about what the world will be like in the future (e.g., "I'll be a single parent. I'll be the one totally responsible for the kids"). Perceptually, one might rehearse during the latter stages of the loved one's illness, when the ill person's verbalizations decline and one begins to become accustomed to not hearing that person's voice. Physically, the new behaviors, roles, and responsibilities taken on to compensate for the loved one's illness can help one rehearse for the physical demands and effects to be expected after the death. However, these rehearsals may lend a somewhat distorted picture because the stress of the experience already may have compromised the anticipatory mourner's health or physical functioning.

Rehearsal in each of the various realms can facilitate and enable anticipation and gradual change in one or more of the others. For instance, acting alone as a parent because of the illness of one's spouse can pave the way for some of the cognitive rehearsal of being a single parent and help ready some of the relevant assumptive world elements for change.

Rehearsal need not always focus on unpleasant aspects; positive ones may be rehearsed as well (e.g., cognitively rehearsing how one will undertake specific behaviors to care for the patient when he or she returns home after hospitalization). Nevertheless, much of the rehearsal in anticipatory mourning is focused on preparing for the world later on in the illness or after the loss, a world the survivor-to-be typically construes as less than desirable, given that that he or she would prefer to have the loved one healthy and alive.

Rehearsal is not inherently positive or facilitative of good outcome, as the work of Remondet, Hansson, Rule, and Winfrey (1987) shows. These investigators conducted a retrospective study that looked directly at the impact of certain dimensions of rehearsal on adjustment to widowhood. They found that whereas "behavioral" rehearsal (that is, social comparison, planning, and making changes) was associated with better adjustment, "cognitive" rehearsal (that is, ruminating) was associated with increased emotional disruption. These findings coincide with others that indicate that mere rumination about a loss does not help individuals cope with it; in fact, it is associated with increased health problems (Pennebaker & O'Heeron, 1984). To be successful as a cognitive strategy, the intellectual work of coping with threatening events must depart from the passive process of ruminating by involving a search for meaning in the experience, an attempt to gain mastery over one's life, and an effort to enhance self-esteem (Taylor, 1983).

Socialization

It has been observed frequently that, for those in anticipatory mourning, role expectations are poorly defined or nonexistent. For example, Fulton and Gottesman (1980) note that "the role of anticipatory griever is even more confused and problematical for it has never been an institutionalized role, being void of norms for appropriate behaviour" (p. 51). Along with many others, Gerber (1974) writes about "the poorly defined set of bereaved role expectations." Describing one particular pattern of response, Davidson (1975) identifies the awkward, ill-defined, and emotionally conflicted "waiting vulture syndrome." Rando (1986b) observes that "already present confusion is magnified by situations in the [life-threatening and] terminal illness that breed inconsistency, resentment, and ambivalence. The lack of norms and clearly specified expectations and responsibilities . . . contribute to the psychological conflicts, emotional exhaustion, physical debilitation, social isolation, and family discord so routinely reported by those whose loved one is dying" (p. 99).

Weisman (1979) finds it odd that anticipatory mourners are left without definitions and structures to help them cope and, with regard to preterminal and terminal cancer, conjectures why this might be so. Weisman's comments, although specific to cancer, apply equally well to other medical situations—and to anticipatory mourning in general:

This stage of cancer is a grave plight, not just for the patient, but for survivors-to-be. It is strange that we have no widely accepted, commonly used term for people who are soon to be widows, widowers, or orphans, even though it is a lonely death, indeed, that arouses no grief in anyone. Surely, before-death survivors have a set of attributes and roles, just as they have after death, when someone closely related dies. But the complicated rituals and taboos that follow death are less evident before death, possibly because inevitability is so difficult to accept, until it happens. (p. 95)

The conceptualization of rehearsal as a component of the phenomenon of anticipatory mourning, and the lack of appropriate norms and guidelines for anticipatory mourners, inevitably brings up the issue of socialization in the anticipatory mourner role. As used here *socialization* refers to the psychosocial education, indoctrination, or acculturation processes through which an individual becomes a competent member of a group. Numerous observers have called for a broadening of anticipatory mourning's emphasis to include more social dimensions. This is exemplified by Gerber's (1974) proposal of the term *anticipatory bereavement*. Feeling that grief, as an emotional state, could not be considered the sole aspect of preparing for the death of a loved one and believing that what generally had been missing in descriptions of anticipatory grief and mourning is the consideration of a social component, Gerber interpreted anticipatory bereavement as being akin to what sociologists and social psychologists have labeled *anticipatory socialization* (Brim & Wheeler, 1966). As such, he perceived anticipatory mourning as a period of deliberation about and preparation for role functioning after the death, essentially providing socialization into the bereaved role.

Dovetailing with this view, Fulton and Gottesman (1980) put forth the notion that a social network including persons who had previously experienced bereavements, such as the elderly, "might encourage and assist prospective survivors to deal realistically with their anticipatory grief and pre-bereavement planning—adult socialization as described by Mortimer and Simmons (1978)" (p. 52).

While the general public may more readily understand rehearsal as an element contributing to successful adaptation during anticipatory mourning and after a loved one's death, it is unclear whether they would see socialization per se in the same light. Nevertheless, the importance of mutual support groups for many dying persons and/or their loved ones does suggest that socialization might be one of the elements that may have substantial merit (see Spiegel & Yalom, 1978; Taylor & Aspinwall, 1990; and Taylor, Falke, Shoptaw, & Lichtman, 1986).

Planning

As a generic operation in anticipatory mourning, planning relates to all dimensions of the person (i.e., psychological, behavioral, social, physical). In terms of the individual's psychology, planning is quite cognitive in nature, but it certainly has emotional aspects and is related to attempts at coping. Planning can occur at each contextual level (i.e., intrapsychic, interpersonal, systemic); it may be relatively casual or formal and recorded. The focus of the planning may range from immediate future events (e.g., deciding who will accompany the ill loved one to the doctor's appointment this afternoon), to those later on in the illness (e.g., discussing how to respond when the hospice nurse makes her initial visit), to those in the postdeath future (e.g., weighing whether or not to consider relocation after things stabilize). Planning may focus on negative or expected crisis events (e.g., how to rearrange the living room to accommodate the hospital bed when the loved one's health declines further) or positive or expected developmental events (e.g., how best to present the dying person when the eldest son brings home his new fiancée). Planning may be conducted within oneself or among different combinations of the various parties (i.e., life-threatened or dying person, intimates, concerned others, caregivers).

Planning is intimately related to psychosocial reorganization, most particularly with its component of rehearsal. Sometimes planning flows from the psychosocial reorganization; sometimes planning precipitates it. As just noted, planning is a central action on each of the three contextual levels of anticipatory mourning. Within the intrapsychic-level processes, it is one of the four identified component subprocesses. The generic operation of planning is also implicit within a number of other subprocess categories. Actually, in the anticipatory mourning experience, anything that entails future anticipation involves some amount of planning, whether explicitly recognized or not. Indeed, it is the opportunity to plan that distinguishes the phenomenon of anticipatory mourning as having the potential to influence both the ill person's living and dying and the survivor's postdeath adjustment. Planning permits parties the opportunities to avoid the harmful sequelae of sudden and unanticipated loss and to reap therapeutic benefits from the experiences of healthy anticipatory mourning.

The operation of planning may be one instigator of the important readjustment processes of assumptive world revision, development of a new relationship with the ill person, adoption of new behaviors and roles, formation of a new identity, and selected reinvestment. However, because of the particular conditions under which planning occurs in anticipatory mourning—that is, in the context of the loss-filled and emotionally charged life-threatening or terminal illness of a loved one—planning may not always be conducted in an ideal fashion. For instance, Gerber (1974) has observed that too much time to think and plan under the expectation of permanent loss can be self-defeating. He also observes that anticipatory bereavement can lead to false promises based on unrealistic assessments of what lies ahead and may cause future problems when the person cannot or does not deliver in the promise (e.g., the person reneges on keeping the ill person at home when the medical condition becomes too demanding).

In a discussion of prevention of defective coping patterns in decision making under stress, Janis (1993) has delineated techniques to prevent or minimize such patterns in threatening situations. One of these techniques, stress inoculation via preparatory communications, is directly relevant to anticipatory mourning, where many of the parties involved are expected to make decisions about future events both pre- and postdeath. Janis feels that stress inoculation fosters a vigilant approach to potentially disruptive and demoralizing recurrent threats, precisely like those found in life-threatening illness. Planning is an implicit aspect of the process:

> *The underlying principle is that accurate preparatory information about an impending crisis gives people the opportunity to anticipate the loss, to start working through their anxiety or grief, and to make plans that will enable them to cope more adequately.* The psychological processes stimulated by preparatory information include correcting faulty beliefs, reconceptualizing the threat, and engaging in realistic self-persuasion about the value of protective action, as well as developing concepts and self-instructions that enable the person to deal more effectively with setbacks. (Janis, 1993, p. 69, emphasis added)

> All of these findings support the conclusion that many people will display higher stress tolerance in response to undesirable consequences if they have been given advance warnings about what to expect, together with sufficient reassurance, so that fear does not mount to an intolerably high level. (Janis, 1993, p. 70)

Two other points must be raised regarding planning in anticipatory mourning. First, both the efficacy and therapeutic value of planning depend on the amount, type, quality, accuracy, and timeliness of the information upon which that planning is based. It follows, therefore, that to the extent information conveyed to or received by the anticipatory mourner is not appropriate for optimal planning, that planning will be compromised. Communication problems interfere with this process.

A final point about planning is that caregivers may underestimate its importance when it comes to practicalities. While anticipatory mourners have impressive amounts of abstract, higher level psychosocial planning to undertake during a loved one's life-threatening or terminal illness, they also must contend with more mundane matters. The focus of planning may shift repeatedly given the exigencies of the illness, but at a given point a mourner's concern may be more for arranging transportation for a child from an after-school activity than for planning for that child's being told that the loved one's health status has declined.

Balancing Conflicting Demands

Part of the anticipatory mourning experience necessarily involves struggling to withstand, respond to, and create some order out of the chaos caused by opposing needs, discordant roles, incompatible obligations, and a seemingly endless list of other conflicting demands. Although relatively unacknowledged in the literature, efforts to balance oneself and what one is expected (by self and others) to do can be exhausting psychologically, behaviorally, socially, and physically. In fact, such efforts are a primary source of stress.

As next addressed, conflicts arise on each of the three contextual levels. Incompatible or conflicting demands create great tension, not only from the actual experience of being pulled in different directions, but also from anxiety over being in the position of having to identify, prioritize, and then pick from these divergent demands. Having to choose is an additional burden that can bring other emotional reactions in its wake, such as guilt over the unmet demand, anger over having to elect between two or more legitimate needs, sorrow at being in the situation, and so forth. Constantly being put in the position of having to triage what often are the emergent concerns of others can wear a person down, causing that person to feel overwhelmed, less than optimally effective, and burned out.

Intrapsychic Level

On the intrapsychic level, conflict comes from competing demands in anticipatory mourning itself. By definition, the mourner is pulled in opposing directions. The mourner moves toward the life-threatened or dying person, directing increased attention, energy, and behavior toward that person. At the same time, the mourner works to sustain some normalcy and maintain the status quo by continuing ongoing involvement with the person. Directly coinciding with these efforts, however, the mourner moves away from the seriously ill or dying loved one in terms of beginning to decathect or detach from the image of that person as someone who will be present as before in the postdeath future as well as from previously held assumptive world elements that have been or will be invalidated by the illness, dying, and death of that individual.

A critical task in anticipatory mourning is to juggle and balance (which actually are two separate processes, with differing results) incompatible demands and cope with the stress generated by that incongruence. No wonder many mourners feel immobilized. They are simultaneously pulled in different directions: moving closer, remaining the same, moving away. It is easy to see how they can get stuck in the middle. Fortunately, conflicting demands can be responded to in different ways, so that moving toward the ill loved one can occur psychologically, behaviorally, and socially, and moving away—in terms of detachment from former assumptive world elements—can occur intrapsychically and not be evidenced as premature detachment from the ill person.

The following list specifies some of the many conflicting demands that can occur intrapsychically. While some do involve overt behaviors or social interaction (thereby encompassing some interpersonal elements), they are included because they originate in the intrapsychic realm. The actual stress of trying to decide how to proceed with regard to any one or combination of these demands only exacerbates the quandary and heightens the normal emotional responses that accompany the experience of anticipatory mourning as one is losing a loved one.

- Holding on to versus letting go of the ill person
- Planning for life after the death of the loved one versus not wanting to betray the loved one by considering life in his or her absence
- Experiencing the full intensity of the feelings involved in anticipatory mourning versus trying to avoid becoming overwhelmed
- Acknowledging the terrible reality and its implications versus trying to maintain some hope
- Paying sufficient attention to and thinking about what is transpiring and how to cope with it versus wanting to avoid nonproductive ruminating or obsessing
- Balancing support for the ill person's increased dependency versus supporting the ill person's continued need for autonomy
- Redistributing family roles and responsibilities versus not wanting to do anything that would call attention to or cause more losses for the ill loved one

- Focusing on the ill person as a living person versus remembering that the ill individual is dying

- Identifying a loss so it can be mourned by the ill person versus focusing more positively on remaining potential

In addition to the competing demands of anticipatory mourning, in the intrapsychic realm conflict can arise as a function of any of the usual influencing factors, but particularly because of (a) psychological struggles and meaning-related issues within the individual mourner; (b) fluctuations in ability to realize, acknowledge, and then deal with the reality of the loved one's illness and the implications it has for that mourner; and (c) time, stress appraisal–related, support, resource, and contextual factors (e.g., the mourner can admit to and deal with anticipatory mourning pressures when the loved one is ill and confined to bed, but not when he or she is a little stronger and plays with the children).

Interpersonal Level

On the interpersonal contextual level, conflicts can transpire between the individual mourner and the ill person, between the ill person and the family/intimate network, between the mourner and the rest of the family/intimate network, and among other family members/intimates as well as with and among concerned others and caregivers. If one or more of the parties are disenfranchised (Doka, 1989) in their anticipatory mourning, conflict can escalate in the present or fester until it erupts in the future. Frequently, the most problematic conflicts on the interpersonal level boil down to differences in demands for tending to the needs of the ill person or the individual mourner versus the needs of various portions of the rest of the family/intimate network. The most common conflict is the situation in which a mourner is torn between wanting to minister to the needs of the ill loved one as well as to the simultaneous needs of others.

Family members must strike a delicate balance: They must cope with the life-threatening or terminal illness of the loved one while continuing to take care of the family unit. Competing demands in these two areas often leave individuals feeling guilty because frequently time or energy is insufficient to attend completely to both sets of needs. When visiting at the hospital, they may be concerned about the children at home; when at home, they may constantly wonder what is happening at the hospital in their absence. Although this problem may be slightly attenuated when the loved one is dying at home, other conflicts can stimulate the tug-of-war between attending to the needs of the dying and those of the survivors-to-be. Where the anticipatory mourner is a family member taking care of the ill person at home, fewer chances for respite may exist and more guilt when respite is taken can occur. Some family members or intimates may feel discomfort or guilt when they know that the dying loved one has observed them in situations of levity or heard them talk about an enjoyable few hours out of the house, almost as if there is a sense of betrayal with the momentary putting aside of pain and grief.

While providing care for the dying person and being immersed in the context of death, the family must continue to meet its members' needs, function as a social unit, and provide a structure for the growth and development of its members (Barton, 1977b). As noted by Fleck (1975), the family must struggle to continue to perform nurturant functions (i.e., caring for both physical and psychological needs); relational functions (i.e., developing interpersonal abilities); communicative functions (i.e., educating family members in verbal and nonverbal skills); emancipative functions (i.e., equipping family members to attain physical, emotional, and economic independence, along with the desire and ability to begin their own families); and recuperative functions (i.e., providing family members with a setting allowing them rest, relaxation, and reconstitution of energies for continued participation in society).

When the family members perceived to be getting "the short end of the stick" are children, this can increase distress. Concerns that illness-related interference in a child's normal development could have long-term sequelae are compounded by legitimate apprehension about the child's inability to appreciate why his or her needs are so often in conflict with those of the ill person's and why he or she frequently gets second priority. It is difficult for most children to understand that they are not the center of the universe when serious illness is not a part of the picture. The situation is even more problematic when illness is a component. Grave illness has the potential to produce guilt and magical thinking on both the child's and everyone else's parts. Many times these negative effects can be ameliorated when the child is appropriately included as an anticipatory mourner in the care of the dying person (see Rando, 1995a); at other times, such reactions continue to be an issue.

Systemic Level

On the systemic level, we find conflicts between the family and caregivers; the family/intimate network and other social and organizational groups; the family/intimate network and the health care system; and, sometimes, caregivers and the health care system. Typically, such conflicts are most relevant when they involve some or all of the family/intimate network versus the caregivers. Sometimes caregivers' advocacy for the ill person pits them against the expressed wishes of the family/intimate network (e.g., the dying individual has expressed the desire to forego further treatment, and the family wants to persevere). When this happens, caregivers can be put in an awkward and ethically confusing situation. A similar dilemma occurs when the family directs caregivers not to inform affected individuals about various aspects of their illness or not to include children in the care of a dying loved one. In such circumstances, caregivers can have hard decisions to make about to whom they are legally, morally, and ethically responsible, and whether they can continue to provide care under conditions as they are. Here is where good supervision, professional consultation, institutional backing, and peer support are enormously valuable.

Facilitating an Appropriate Death

The last of the generic operations, facilitating an appropriate death, is also the goal of many of the previous operations. The discussion here is presented to make the connection between anticipatory mourning and appropriate death explicitly clear. The unparalleled work of Avery Weisman elucidates this. In one of his classic books, *Coping with Cancer* (1979), Weisman has a chapter entitled "Coping and Anticipatory Grief." In this brief but brilliant gem he describes the fundamental linkage between anticipatory mourning and appropriate death. Translated into the terminology used in the present work and simply stated: If an appropriate death can be enabled by a survivor-to-be for his or her dying loved one, then that same individual's anticipatory mourning will be more positive and, in turn, postdeath adaptation will be facilitated. This is the case because those criteria identified to promote an appropriate death for a dying person also nurture healthy anticipatory mourning in survivors-to-be. Correspondingly, individuals engaged in healthy anticipatory mourning are better able to foster appropriate deaths for their loved ones.

Along with safe conduct for the dying, and significant survival and dignified dying, an appropriate death is one of Weisman's (1972) three objectives for intervention with dying persons. Briefly, Weisman describes an appropriate death as a death one might choose for oneself if choice were possible. In other words, the death is idiosyncratically appropriate for that particular individual given his or her own phenomenology. What will be appropriate for one may be unsuitable for another, and what seems inappropriate from the caregiver's viewpoint may be desirable from the ill person's frame of reference. An appropriate death is not necessarily an ideal death, but it is experienced as being consistent with the person's ego ideal. Weisman clarifies:

> It means dying in the best possible way, not only retaining vestiges of what made life important and valuable, but surviving with personal significance and self-esteem, along with minimal distress and few intractable symptoms, as long as possible. In effect, an appropriate death is one we can "live with." (1988, p. 67).

According to Weisman, an appropriate death is marked by four characteristics: awareness, acceptability, propriety, and timeliness. To achieve such a death, there are six prerequisites (Weisman, 1979, 1988), each of which is ideally enabled by the intimates.

- Care: This refers both to adequate physical symptom relief and comfort, and to the psychosocial support of significant others.

- Control: This refers to the extent to which the dying person is able to participate in management, self-care, and decisions, even if the last consists of yielding control to respected and trusted others. Exercising choices, even limited ones, maintains morale and a sense of self-definition.

- Composure: This means that mood and emotionality are kept within bounds. It does not mean emotional unreponsiveness nor signal serenity. Wide swings of emotions are checked and kept within whatever constraints are deemed personally and environmentally acceptable. While mildness is the key quality, there is still ample room for feelings.

- Communication: Verbal and nonverbal communication that provides support and identifies needs transpires between the dying person, intimates, and caregivers. When needs cannot be met, reasons this is so are clear and compassionate, and compromises can usually be reached. Given that the essence of mutuality is communication and that positive support implicitly requires good communication, a well-informed dying individual with whom communication is open generally does better.

- Continuity: The main purpose of continuity is to protect authentic self-identity during the last stages of life. Bringing the past into functional relation with the present can strengthen positive support through reminders of past struggles successfully addressed, recollection of outstanding accomplishments, interaction with people and tokens associated with preterminal activities—anything that establishes a link between then and now.

• Closure: Residual problems are resolved or redefined. Unfinished business is finished.

Describing the person who achieves an appropriate death, Weisman (1972) delineates targets that the anticipatory mourner ideally addresses:

> Someone who dies an appropriate death must be helped in the following ways. He should be relatively pain-free, his suffering reduced, and emotional and social impoverishments kept to a minimum. Within the limits of disability, he should operate on as high and effective a level as possible, even though only tokens of former fulfillments can be offered. He should also recognize and resolve residual conflicts, and satisfy whatever remaining wishes are consistent with his present plight and with his ego ideal. Finally, among his choices, he should be able to yield control to others in whom he has confidence. He also has the option of seeking or relinquishing significant key people. (pp. 39–40)

Because of what goes into helping a loved one achieve an appropriate death, a person is helped in his or her own anticipatory mourning. A more appropriate death for the loved one promotes better postdeath bereavement for survivors.

CONTEXTUAL LEVELS

Anticipatory mourning can occur on three contextual levels: the intrapsychic (i.e., the personal or internal world of the individual mourner), the interpersonal (i.e., between two or more of the parties in anticipatory mourning), and the systemic (i.e., on the level of the family or intimate network, social group, organization, or larger system, such as the health care system). These three levels are interrelated.

Healthy anticipatory mourning is experienced on all three contextual levels. Following is a list of selected components on each level. These are grouped according to the particular subprocesses occurring at each level. Note that these components essentially are specific applications of the seven generic operations of anticipatory mourning.

For the purpose of discussion, these components are presented as would be relevant to the intimate anticipatory mourner. Most of the discussion may be extrapolated to the other three parties. For instance, actions pertaining to the life-threatened or dying person necessarily are experienced differently by the anticipatory mourner if that individual is the dying person him- or herself. The processes next delineated focus specifically on interactions with the life-threatened or dying person. Application to other parties can be made with appropriate extrapolation. The systemic-level processes are delineated from the perspective of the family and intimate network but also can be extrapolated to broader groups.

Ideally, anticipatory mourning that is therapeutic will prompt appropriate engagement on each of these three levels. As always, the appropriateness is determined by the unique constellation of factors pertaining to the specific anticipatory mourner and situation. Four of particular importance are (a) the point where the ill person is in the illness trajectory; (b) the amount of time since the diagnosis; (c) the circumstances that have transpired since the diagnosis, especially the nature of the illness experience and its sequelae; the affected individual's attitude, disposition, and approach to life after diagnosis, and his or her quality of life; and (d) the meaning of the disease to the anticipatory mourner and his or her perceptions of the ill person's suffering.

The following discussion of components—which are representative but not exhaustive of all possibilities—is based in part on the writings of Cohen and Cohen (1981), Doka (1993), Fulton and Fulton (1971), Futterman and Hoffman (1973), Futterman et al., (1972), Gerber (1974), Lebow (1976), McCollum and Schwartz (1972), Parkes and Weiss (1983), Pattison (1969, 1977), Rando (1984, 1986a, 1986b, 1993), and Weisman (1972, 1979, 1988). The components are those that *ideally* occur in anticipatory mourning. Departure from these by any party in the anticipatory mourning experience reflects the fact that human beings do not always approximate the ideal, as well as the fact that idiosyncratic variables potently effect one's experience of anticipatory mourning and what needs to be done therein. All components are not equally pertinent to all mourners, nor do they all necessarily have to occur, mean the same things, or warrant the same responses over the course of an illness. The amount and type of components vary in each mourner. Consequently, for example, it would be inappropriate to expect that the anticipatory mourning of one whose loved one is imminently dying would mirror that of one whose loved one is life-threatened but in remission.

Intrapsychic-Level Processes

On the intrapsychic level, the anticipatory mourner ideally experiences four interrelated categories of subprocesses: awareness of and gradual accommodation to the threat, affective processes, cognitive processes, and planning for the future. These categories of sub-processes are not mutually exclusive. Each is presented along with a listing of its own components.

Awareness of and Gradual Accommodation to the Threat

- Experiencing assumptive world violations and other losses that teach that the world is different from before and that psychosocial reorganization is mandated

- Acquiring a realistic understanding of the disease, its sequelae, and its treatment

- Developing a progressively deepening awareness of the seriousness of the illness and its implications through the growing realization that certain hopes about recovery or stabilization are not being actualized

- Gradually absorbing and coming to terms with the reality of the oncoming death over time

- Rehearsing the death and its consequences, with attempts to adjust in part

- Becoming partially socialized into the bereaved role through this time of anticipatory bereavement (Gerber, 1974)

- Developing strategies and undertaking coping to deal with the issues brought about by the illness, losses, disability, dying, and death of the loved one, and their impacts upon loved others

Affective Processes

- Confronting the need to cope with and manage the stress of and emotional reactions to the experience of the loved one's illness, its sequelae and implications, and the conflicting demands inherent in life-threatening or terminal illness

- Mourning past, present, and future losses attendant to the life-threatening or terminal illness and death and the unrelated losses that have been revived in this loss situation. This also means experiencing, managing, and coping with associated emotions, fears, and reactions such as shock, traumatic stress, denial, sadness, depression, anguish, sorrow, anxiety, fear, anger, cognitive dysfunction, frustration, resentment, ambivalence, jealousy, despair, guilt, shame, helplessness, hopelessness, confusion, violation, regression, uncertainty, numbness, alienation, inadequacy, vulnerability, hypervigilance, insecurity, exhaustion, and depletion, along with their social, behavioral, and physiological counterparts.

- Experiencing and coping with the separation anxiety and fear elicited by the threat of permanent loss

- Gradually decathecting or detaching from the previously held image of the ill or dying person in the pre- or postdeath future and from the needs, emotions, hopes, wishes, fantasies, dreams, plans, beliefs, expectations, assumptions, and behaviors that were associated with this image

- Recognizing one's separateness from the ill or dying person and learning to tolerate the awareness that the individual will die while the mourner continues to exist

- Maintaining some confidence in the face of the profound threat, which includes mastery operations such as information seeking and participation in care, as well as strategies for maintenance of emotional and interpersonal equilibrium, affirmation of life and its meaning, and processes of reorganization, such as revising values, goals, and philosophy of life in light of the loved one's illness and death (Futterman & Hoffman, 1973)

Cognitive Processes

- Experiencing heightened preoccupation with and concern for the ill or dying person

- Psychosocially reorganizing by incorporating appropriate changes into one's assumptive world, identity, and ways of being in the external world that reflect the current reality and begin to prepare the mourner for the reality that will exist in the future

- Searching for personally effective ways of coping to contend with the demands of anticipatory mourning

- Attempting to make sense of and find personal meaning (spiritually, existentially, religiously, philosophically) in the experience

- Striving, through all the senses, to take in the ill or dying person in order to emblazon these perceptions in the mind and senses, for the purpose of constructing a mental and sensory composite image of that person that will endure after death

- Reviewing the past and attending carefully to the present in order to crystallize memories to keep after the death

- Bargaining with God, some other supreme power, or fate for a reprieve, for more time, or for a different illness experience

- Recollecting previous losses, griefs, mourning, periods of vulnerability, and other experiences that have been revived by the loved one's illness and its sequelae

- Contemplating one's own death
- Developing a philosophy about how to cope with the ill or dying person's remaining time. For example, should pressure be exerted to experience and squeeze as much out of remaining life as possible? Or should a more natural and passive attitude be undertaken in which one takes what comes without the burden of rushing to make all the last times memorable and meaningful?

Planning for the Future

- Considering what the future will be like without the ill or dying person and experiencing associated reactions
- Anticipating, planning, and, as necessary, rehearsing future losses and changes that will occur, both before and after the death
- Anticipating and planning for emotional, practical, social, behavioral, and physical concerns that need to be addressed both before and after the death

Interpersonal-Level Processes with the Life-Threatened or Dying Person

As noted at the beginning of this section on contextual levels, discussion focuses on the intimate anticipatory mourner's interpersonal interaction with the life-threatened or dying person. Other interpersonal relationships (i.e., with concerned others or caregivers) can be extrapolated. If the anticipatory mourner is simultaneously the life-threatened or dying person, even more extrapolation will be required. This extrapolation demands knowledge about the experiences, issues, concerns, and tasks of the ill individual, as well as familiarity with the particular intrapsychic, social, physical, and pragmatic demands placed upon that person. (See Barton, 1977a; Byock, 1997; Corr, Morgan, & Wass, 1994; Corr et al., 1997; Costa & VandenBos, 1990; Doka, 1993; Garfield, 1978; Glaser & Strauss, 1965; Kalish, 1970; Kübler-Ross, 1969; Pattison, 1969, 1977; Rando, 1984; Rolland, 1994; Verwoerdt, 1996; Weisman, 1972, 1979.) In terms of the interpersonal-level processes, the ill person does direct attention, energy, and behavior toward the self. Although strictly speaking he or she cannot have an interpersonal relationship with the self, one may witness numerous processes that reflect the ill individual's attempts to resolve personal relationships. Most of the components delineated under "Resolving the Personal Relationship with the Life-Threatened or Dying Person" can be extended to speak to issues between the ill person and significant others. Finally, the components described under "Helping the Life-Threatened or Dying Person" reveal the issues with which the ill anticipatory mourner must contend and for which he or she will probably need to permit and accept assistance from others.

For anticipatory mourners besides the ill person, anticipatory mourning also engenders numerous interpersonal and interactional processes. This fact, critical to the concept of anticipatory mourning, invalidates the belief that anticipatory mourning necessarily leads to premature detachment from the ill or dying loved one, causes the relationship with him or her to deteriorate, or predisposes the survivor to guilt after the death. In fact, all of the processes described here imply continued involvement with the ill person, with some actually serving to intensify the attachment and improve the relationship as compared to what existed before the awareness of limited time. Thus, although some persons may construe anticipatory mourning and continued involvement as seemingly opposite processes, this is quite untrue. By preparing for the ultimate loss of their loved one through healthy anticipatory mourning, intimates can become aware of any unfinished business remaining with the ill person. Correspondingly, the healthy interacting with the ill person found in therapeutic anticipatory mourning enables intimates to finish any unfinished business with the loved one, itself a crucial part of anticipatory mourning. In this regard, anticipatory mourning facilitates both the identification of unfinished business and the development of ways to achieve closure. Three interrelated categories of subprocesses are subsumed under interpersonal-level processes: directing attention, energy, and behavior toward the life-threatened or dying person; resolving the personal relationship with the life-threatened or dying person; and helping the life-threatened or dying person.

Directing Attention, Energy, and Behavior toward the Life-Threatened or Dying Person

- Remaining as involved as possible with the person; avoiding withdrawal and promoting whatever communication, interaction, dignity, control, living, and meaning remains available
- Directing increased attention to the person and being hyperalert to cues pertinent to him or her
- Focusing energy (physical and emotional), behavior, thought, and resources (emotional, physical, time, financial, social) on caring for the person
- Balancing the incompatible and conflicting demands of simultaneously holding onto, letting go of, and drawing closer to the person

- Assigning the person a high priority in terms of giving consideration, fulfilling wants and needs, planning activities, and so forth
- Readjusting the relationship with the ill person to accommodate the losses, assumptive world violations, and new realities
- Possibly doing painful things (e.g., taking the ill person for an uncomfortable medical procedure) or omitting pleasurable ones (e.g., refusing to buy the person's cigarettes) that are for the person's own good and that signal debilitation and/or the terminality of the illness
- Responding to the ill person in ways that make allowances for deterioration, loss, and disability without supporting inappropriate or prematurely regressive defenses

Resolving the Personal Relationship with the Life-Threatened or Dying Person

- Finishing unfinished business with the person. Although the term *unfinished business* can refer to practical, financial, and business matters, as used here it primarily concerns psychosocial issues that have never been addressed or that lack successful closure in the relationship between the life-threatened or dying person and the mourner. It can incorporate such behaviors as expressing feelings, resolving past conflicts, saying good-bye, explaining past omissions or commissions, articulating important messages, tying up loose emotional ends, and manifesting or ceasing behaviors in accordance with the loved one's preferences, values, needs, or desires.
- Specifically informing or reinforcing what the person means and has meant to the mourner, providing other pieces of personal feedback, and stating promises and intentions for the future
- Recollecting the mutual relationship and shared memories from common experiences
- Planning the future with the person so that such plans will not be felt as betrayals after the death
- At the appropriate time, saying good-bye to the person and providing permission to die

Helping the Life-Threatened or Dying Person

- Working to minimize pain, stress, and suffering; promote comfort; maintain as much as possible and comfortable a sense of competence, mastery, and control; preserve satisfactory self-image and identity; and enable effective coping

- Identifying, anticipating, and meeting the needs of the person
- Maximizing the life that is possible, while preserving its normalcy and optimizing its quality to the extent possible, and maintaining realistic hope
- Promoting an open awareness context (Glaser & Strauss, 1965) to the fullest extent possible
- Acting to facilitate an appropriate death for the dying person (Weisman, 1972) and to ensure accompanying safe conduct, significant survival, and dignified dying
- Assisting the person with his or her own anticipatory mourning; problem solving of specific fears and concerns; completion of life-threatening and terminal illness tasks (e.g., Doka, 1993; Kalish, 1970); finding of meaning in living, dying, and death; management of stress; and finishing of unfinished business with others in order to provide the person with closure and the ability to let go when the time is appropriate
- Acting to minimize the psychological, behavioral, social, and physical suffering and losses of the person
- Providing the acceptance and psychosocial, instrumental, and logistical support necessary for the person to cope with, express, and manage the feelings, thoughts, fears, concerns, needs, and discomfort generated by the illness; its sequelae, treatment, and caregivers; and the ultimate death it will bring
- Assuming necessary body and ego functions for the person without fostering shame, depreciation, or unnecessary loss (Pattison, 1969)
- Joining the person in an appropriate and constructive process of life review (Butler, 1963)
- Enabling appropriate discussion, decision making, and action around end-of-life decisions, if the person desires
- Working with the person to determine how he or she wants to be remembered and attempting to bring this to pass
- Tending to the last wishes of the person
- If desired by the person, preplanning the type of postdeath rituals preferred

Systemic-Level Processes

Finally, anticipatory mourning stimulates a series of social processes on the familial, intimate network, concerned other, institutional, community, and/or societal levels. These illustrate that the illness and dying of the loved one take place in a social context, which in itself is affected. Some of these processes are as follows:

- The family and intimate network's starting to reorganize itself to regain a functional equilibrium without the ill member's fulfilling the same roles in the same manner as before
- Individual mourners in the family and intimate network's beginning to assume and adapt to new roles and responsibilities because of the incapacitation and future absence of the ill person
- Making plans with other survivors-to-be for what will happen later in the illness and after the death
- Negotiating needed or desired relationships with those outside of the intimate network
- Networking with other people, institutions, and organizations to secure the best services and to provide the ill person with the best treatment and quality of life possible
- Working with clergy and funeral service personnel to arrange for postdeath rituals to honor the ill person's preferences

The six dimensions of anticipatory mourning provide the caregiver with a schema for understanding the experience of an anticipatory mourner and for identifying specific targets for intervention. The schema highlights the importance of recognizing the multidimensionality of the phenomenon and the necessity of integrating strategies to address issues beyond mere anticipation of future loss.

REFERENCES

Arndt, H., & Gruber, M. (1977). Helping families cope with acute and anticipatory grief. In E. Prichard, J. Collard, B. Orcutt, A. H. Kutscher, I. Seeland, & N. Lefkowitz (Eds.), *Social work with the dying patient and the family.* New York: Columbia University Press.

Barton, D. (Ed.). (1997a). *Dying and death: A clinical guide for caregivers.* Baltimore: Williams & Wilkins.

Barton, D. (1977b). The family of the dying person. In D. Barton (Ed.), *Dying and death: A clinical guide for caregivers.* Baltimore: Williams & Wilkins.

Bowlby, J. (1980). *Attachment and loss: Vol. 3. Loss: Sadness and depression.* New York: Basic.

Brim, O., & Wheeler, S. (1966). *Socialization after childhood.* New York: Wiley.

Butler, R. (1963). The life review: An interpretation of reminiscence in the aged. *Psychiatry, 26,* 65–76.

Byock, I. R. (1997). *Dying well: The prospect for growth at the end of life.* New York: Riverhead Books.

Cohen, M., & Cohen, E. (1981). Behavioral family systems intervention in terminal care. In H. Sobel (Ed.), *Behavior therapy in terminal care: A humanistic approach.* Cambridge, MA: Ballinger.

Corr, C. A., Morgan, J. D., & Wass, H. (Eds.). (1994). *International work group on death, dying, and bereavement statements on death, dying, and bereavement.* London, Ontario: International Work Group on on Death, Dying, and Bereavement.

Corr, C. A., Nabe, C., & Corr, D. M. (1997). *Death and dying, life and living* (2nd ed.). Pacific Grove, CA: Brooks/Cole.

Costa, P., & VandenBos, G. (Eds.). (1990). *Psychosocial aspects of serious illness: Chronic conditions, fatal diseases, and clinical care.* Washington, DC: American Psychological Association.

Davidson, G. (1975). The "waiting vulture syndrome." In B. Schoenberg, I. Gerber, A. Wiener, A. H. Kutscher, D. Peretz, & A. Carr (Eds.), *Bereavement: Its psychosocial aspects.* New York: Columbia University Press.

Doka, K. J. (Ed.). (1989). *Disenfranchised grief: Recognizing hidden sorrow.* Lexington, MA: Lexington Books.

Doka, K. J. (1993). *Living with life-threatening illness: A guide for patients, their families, and caregivers.* Lexington, MA: Lexington Books.

Fleck, S. (1975). The family and psychiatry. In A. Freedman, H. Kaplan, & B. Sadock (Eds.), *The comprehensive textbook of psychiatry* (Vol. 1, 2nd ed.). Baltimore: Williams & Wilkins.

Folkman, S., & Lazarus, R. (1980). An analysis of coping in a middle-aged community sample. *Journal of Health and Social Behavior, 21,* 219–239.

Fulton, R., & Fulton, J. (1971). A psychosocial aspect of terminal care: Anticipatory grief. *Omega, 2,* 91–100.

Fulton, R., & Gottesman, D. (1980). Anticipatory grief: A psychosocial concept reconsidered. *British Journal of Psychiatry, 137,* 45–54.

Futterman, E., & Hoffman, I. (1973). Crisis and adaptation in the families of fatally ill children. In E. Anthony & C. Koupernik (Eds.), *The child in his family: The impact of disease and death* (Vol. 2). New York: Wiley.

Futterman, E., Hoffman, I., & Sabshin, M. (1972). Parental anticipatory mourning. In B. Schoenberg, A. Carr, D. Peretz, & A. H. Kutscher (Eds.), *Psychosocial aspects of terminal care.* New York: Columbia University Press.

Garfield, C. (Ed.). (1978). *Psychosocial care of the dying patient.* New York: McGraw-Hill.

Gerber, I. (1974). Anticipatory bereavement. In B. Schoenberg, A. Carr, A. H. Kutscher, D. Peretz, & I. Goldberg (Eds.), *Anticipatory grief.* New York: Columbia University Press.

Glaser, B., & Strauss, A. (1965). *Awareness of dying.* Chicago: Aldine.

Hay, D., & Oken, S. (1972). The psychological stresses of intensive care unit nursing. *Psychosomatic Medicine, 34,* 109–118.

Horowitz, M. (1986). *Stress response syndromes* (2nd ed.). Northvale, NJ: Jason Aronson.

Janis, I. (1958). *Psychological stress: Psychoanalytic and behavioral studies of surgical patients*. New York: Wiley.

Janis, I. (1993). Decisionmaking under stress. In L. Goldberger & S. Breznitz (Eds.), *Handbook of stress: Theoretical and clinical aspects*. (2nd ed.). New York: The Free Press.

Janoff-Bulman, R. (1992). *Shattered assumptions: Towards a new psychology of trauma*. New York: The Free Press.

Kahn, R., Wolfe, D., Quinn, R., Snoek, J., & Rosenthal, R. (1964). *Organizational stress: Studies in role conflict and ambiguity*. New York: Wiley.

Kalish, R. (1970). The onset of the dying process. *Omega, 1*, 57–69.

Kübler-Ross, E. (1969). *On death and dying*. New York: Macmillan.

Lazarus, R., & Folkman, S. (1984). *Stress, appraisal, and coping*. New York: Springer.

Lebow, G. (1976). Facilitating adaptation in anticipatory mourning. *Social Casework, 57*(7), 458–465.

Levy, L. (1991). Anticipatory grief: Its measurement and proposed reconceptualization. *The Hospice Journal, 7*(4), 1–28.

Lindemann, E. (1944). Symptomatology and management of acute grief. *American Journal of Psychiatry, 101*, 141–148.

McCollum, A., & Schwartz, A. (1972). Social work and the mourning parent. *Social Work, 17*, 25–36.

Moos, R., & Billings, A. (1982). Conceptualizing and measuring coping resources and processes. In L. Goldberger & S. Breznitz (Eds.), *Handbook of stress: Theoretical and clinical aspects*. New York: Macmillan.

Mortimer, J., & Simmons, R. (1978). Adult socialization. *Annual Review of Sociology, 4*, 421–454.

Neimeyer, R. (1997). Meaning reconstruction and the experience of chronic loss. In K. J. Doka (Ed.) with J. Davidson, *Living with grief: When illness is prolonged*. Washington, DC: Taylor & Francis.

Parkes, C. M. (1988). Bereavement as a psychosocial transition: Processes of adaptation to change. *Journal of Social Issues, 44*(3), 53–65.

Parkes, C. M., & Weiss, R. S. (1983). *Recovery from bereavement*. New York: Basic.

Pattison, E. M. (1969). Help in the dying process. *Voices: The Art and Science of Psychotherapy, 5*, 6–14.

Pattison, E. M. (Ed.). (1977). *The experience of dying*. Englewood Cliffs, NJ: Prentice Hall.

Pennebaker, J., & O'Heeron, R. (1984). Confiding in others and illness rate among spouses of suicide and accidental-death victims. *Journal of Abnormal Psychology, 93*, 473–476.

Rando, T. A. (1984). *Grief, dying, and death: Clinical interventions for caregivers*. Champaign, IL: Research Press.

Rando, T. A. (1986a). A comprehensive analysis of anticipatory grief: Perspectives, processes, promises, and problems. In T. A. Rando (Ed.), *Loss and anticipatory grief*. Lexington, MA: Lexington Books.

Rando, T. A. (1986b). Understanding and facilitating anticipatory grief in the loved ones of the dying. In T. A. Rando (Ed.), *Loss and anticipatory grief*. Lexington, MA: Lexington Books.

Rando, T. A. (1993). *Treatment of complicated mourning*. Champaign, IL: Research Press.

Rando, T. A. (1995a). Anticipatory grief and the child mourner. In D. Adams & E. Deveau (Eds.), *Beyond the innocence of childhood: Vol. 3. Helping children and adolescents cope with death and bereavement*. Amityville, NY: Baywood.

Rando, T. A. (1995b). Grief and mourning: Accommodating to loss. In H. Wass & R. Neimeyer (Eds.), *Dying: Facing the facts* (3rd ed.). Washington, DC: Tayor & Francis.

Remondet, J., Hansson, R., Rule, B., & Winfrey, G. (1987). Rehearsal for widowhood. *Journal of Social and Clinical Psychology, 5,* 285–297.

Rolland, J. (1994). *Families, illness, and disability: An integrative treatment model*. New York: Basic.

Siegel, K., & Weinstein, L. (1983). Anticipatory grief reconsidered. *Journal of Psychosocial Oncology, 1*(2), 61–73.

Spiegel, D., & Yalom, I. (1978). A support group for dying patients. *International Journal of Group Psychotherapy, 28,* 233–245.

Sudnow, D. (1967). *Passing on: The social organization of dying*. Englewood Cliffs, NJ: Prentice Hall.

Taylor, S. (1983). Adjustment to threatening events: A theory of cognitive adaptation. *American Psychologist, 38,* 1161–1173.

Taylor, S., & Aspinwall, L. (1990). Psychosocial aspects of chronic illness. In P. Costa & G. VandenBos (Eds.), *Psychological aspects of serious illness: Chronic conditions, fatal diseases, and clinical care*. Washington, DC: American Psychological Association.

Taylor, S., Falke, R., Shoptaw, S., & Lichtman, R. (1986). Social support, support groups, and the cancer patient. *Journal of Consulting and Clinical Psychology, 54*(5), 608–615.

Verwoerdt, A. (1966). *Communication with the fatally ill*. Springfield, IL: Charles C. Thomas.

Vollman, R., Ganzert, A., Picher, L., & Williams, W. (1971). The reactions of family systems to sudden and unexpected death. *Omega, 2,* 101–106.

Weisman, A. D. (1972). *On dying and denying: A psychiatric study of terminality*. New York: Behavioral Publications.

Weisman, A. D. (1979). *Coping with cancer*. New York: McGraw-Hill.

Weisman, A. D. (1988). Appropriate death and the hospice program. *The Hospice Journal, 4*(1), 65–77.

Woodfield, R., & Viney, L. (1984–1985). A personal construct approach to the conjugally bereaved woman. *Omega, 15,* 1–13.

CHAPTER 3

Re-Creating Meaning in the Face of Illness

Kenneth J. Doka

Mark is astounded at the diagnosis of lung cancer. He has never smoked a day in his life. It seems so wrong and unfair that of all the diseases, this should be the one he gets. Conversely, his hospital roommate, Paul, is not surprised by his diagnosis of the same disease. He has smoked two, sometimes three packs a day since adolescence. But, as he told his daughter, you have to die of something. After all, he muses, he is 90.

Each day Marian watches her once-handsome son slowly waste away from AIDS. She has never understood why he used drugs or how he could die of a disease that she barely even knew existed a decade ago. He recovered from his adolescent drug habit three years before he even knew he had the disease. It seems so unfair to Marian.

It seems unfair to Tom, too, as he tends his dying wife. Jenny has so much to live for: three young children, a new master's degree. She watched her health so carefully—exercise, diet, regular checkups. His once-strong faith is shaken as he watches her cry out in pain.

Gwen grieves her dying mother as well. For the past 2 weeks she has come home to care for her. But she feels comfort in the way her mother is dying. She is close to 90. She was fine until a few months ago. Her mind and her warm humor are intact. The hospice team has been able to keep her comfortable and alert.

The individuals in these case vignettes are grieving the loss of themselves or people they love. Each one is not only anticipating a future death but also grieving the daily losses that occur as the illness progresses. But Tom, Marian, and Mark mourn an additional loss that is not shared by Gwen or Paul. That loss is spiritual. They mourn the loss of meaning as they struggle to understand why this has occurred. Their assumptions about how the world works, about the expectations for their own lives and the lives of others, have been shattered. Theirs is a spiritual pain.

In all cases, they are left with the task of reconstructing meaning, a task that some see as one of the central issues of mourning (e.g., Neimeyer, 1997). Not every loss challenges meaning; some losses reinforce a sense of meaning, as exemplified by Gwen's response to the loss of her mother. In Gwen's case, it was not her mother's age alone that made the death acceptable. Had her mother died in a traumatic incident, Gwen might have felt that same senselessness. Here, all the circumstances of death reinforce Gwen's notions of how and when someone should die. This is not to imply that Gwen will not experience mourning. But in her mourning, the issue of rebuilding a faith challenged by the loss (Doka, 1993a) will not loom large. For Tom and Marian, however, that task is—and will continue to be—a central issue.

This chapter addresses the task of re-creating meaning in the face of illness. Its goal is to explore the spiritual components of anticipatory mourning. In order to do so, it is critical first to review spirituality and to discuss the ways in which it affects the search for meaning. Within that context, the discussion concerns how that spiritual struggle is experienced throughout the illness by patients, families, and caregivers. Finally, the chapter concludes with a discussion of strategies that caregivers can use to assist in the spiritual struggle.

SPIRITUALITY AND MEANING

Spirituality is a concept that we understand and acknowledge but find hard to define. Part of the trouble lies in the fact that spirituality is distinct from religion. The latter can be more readily recognized as an institutionalized set of beliefs or dogma shared by a defined group. Spirituality, though, is broader than that. Though religion certainly may be part of spirituality, it does not encompass spirituality. Miller (1994) explains this distinction well:

> While spirituality is necessarily very personal, religion is more communal. In fact, if you take the word back to its origins, religion means that which binds together, that which ties things into a package. Religion has to do with collecting and consolidating and unifying. Religion says, "Here is a set of beliefs that forms a coherent whole. Take it as your own." Religion says, "Here are people for you to revere and historical events for you to recall. Remember them." Religion says, "Here's a way for you to act when you

come together as a group, and here's a way for you to
behave when you're apart." (p. 314)

Yet even Miller has a difficult time defining spirituality:

Spirituality relates to our souls. It involves that deep inner
essence of who we are. It is an openness to the possibility
that the soul within each of us is somehow related to the
Soul of all that is. Spirituality is what happens to us that is
so memorable we cannot forget it. (p. 3)

To Morgan (1988), the essence of spirituality lies in specialness.
He emphasizes that spirit refers to the aspects of the person that
define uniqueness: thinking, willing, deciding. This pushes
humans—as they seek to think, feel, and decide to engage in a perpetual quest to make sense of life—to find meaning. Knowledge,
philosophy, ethics, and religion all emerge from this quest for
meaning.

Understanding the relationship between spirituality and meaning is critical for two reasons: First, it reminds one of the existential
challenge that death itself presents. Humans can transcend the
immediacy of the present. They can acknowledge and plan for the
future. Yet this ability symbolically to transcend time and space
paradoxically compels one to recognize one's own mortality. One
faces, then, the challenge of constructing meaning even in the face
of death. That struggle, Becker (1973) reminds us, lies at the heart of
much philosophy and religion.

Second, for many this struggle can remain remote and avoid-
able as one engages in the everyday realities and diversions of life.
However, a diagnosis of life-threatening illness is a time of existential plight (Weisman, 1980), when all assumptions and expectations
about one's world and one's future place in it are challenged (see
Rando, 1993; Kelley, 1955). This, then, is the core of the spiritual
pain that one experiences in life-threatening illness. One's systems
of meaning may be challenged. The constructs of beliefs by which
one has led life are now secondary losses that—along with physical,
social, psychological, or financial losses—must be mourned.

THE SPIRITUAL STRUGGLE
THROUGHOUT THE ILLNESS

As with other facets of anticipatory mourning, the spiritual aspects
continue to unfold as the illness progresses. At different points in
the illness, distinct spiritual issues arise. Building on the work of Pattison (1969, 1978) and Weisman (1980), I earlier proposed a

model of life-threatening illness as a series of phases (Doka, 1993a). It would be helpful to delineate these phases as a way of illuminating the distinct spiritual issues, or struggles with meaning, that may arise at different points in the illness experience.

First is the prediagnostic phase: the time prior to the individual's attempt to seek the formal medical assistance that leads to the diagnosis. In many cases, it is the time between the recognition or suspicion of illness and the decision to seek medical diagnosis. But it can refer as well to the time before the individual decides to undergo medical tests, such as HIV testing, or even to seek a routine physical examination. Exploring this period can provide excellent opportunities to gain insights into a patient's expectations, knowledge, coping mechanisms, and social support (Doka, 1993a). For example, in one case a woman whose lover had died of AIDS resisted HIV testing for herself or her children, despite the fact that she and her older son both evidenced compromised immune systems. Her prediagnostic behavior presaged the strong use of denial, a pattern she would continue as the illness progressed.

In this prediagnostic period, an individual may struggle with the possibility of disease. A key question may be "Am I the type of person who gets this disease?" With questions such as this, individuals struggle to interpret and make sense of their experience. Such questions often imply both a sense of biography and personal beliefs. For example, a person who has experienced cancer or has a family history of the disease would likely respond to pain or other symptoms differently than someone who has no such history. Similarly, a person who is sexually active and at risk for HIV infection may interpret a night sweat differently from someone who does not seem at risk. But beyond biography, this attempt to interpret symptoms may reveal other constructs of meaning—perhaps even a belief that the symptom is a warning or punishment or that God will protect the individual.

These questions reverberate through the acute or diagnostic phase, which centers around the crisis of diagnosis. Weisman (1980) has referred to this period as one of existential plight, emphasizing the very spiritual dimension of the encounter with possible death. This encounter raises questions of past, present, and future. Questions of "Why me?" or "Why now?" may indicate a review of the past—life-styles and perhaps questions of morality. "I am a good person." "I have been so careful with my health." But they may raise questions about present time lines: "My life is going so well now. My kids have just moved out. This was supposed to be my time."

There is a future dimension as well: "How will my life change?" To some, this questioning may lead to reprioritizing time and relationships, perhaps even as they search for meaning, rediscovering aspects of their own spirituality. But fundamentally, in this phase, the spiritual task remains to incorporate the present reality or diagnosis into one's sense of past and future. For some, as for Paul in the first case vignette, this may not present significant difficulty. In his case, a diagnosis of lung cancer is not unexpected. He even takes joy in recounting that he has outlived the first physician who urged him to stop smoking. But to Mark, who has never smoked, the diagnosis is both shocking and manifestly unfair. His spiritual outrage, his inability to incorporate that diagnosis into his own sense of meaning, becomes the focal point of counseling.

The immediacy of these issues may recede somewhat as the individual begins treatment. In this period—the chronic phase—the individual continues to cope with the disease, the treatment, and its side effects as well as the continuing demands of everyday life. Often, questions of meaning center on the suffering and struggle experienced in this phase, where individuals have to find meaning in suffering, chronicity, uncertainty, and decline. It is critical to understand that suffering is more than simply physical pain. It is a subjective response to the varieties of pain—physical, social, psychological, spiritual, even financial—that people experience as they continue to struggle with illness.

This suffering may raise anew the question of "Why me?" Some may experience a sense of spiritual abandonment, feeling a loss of their beliefs about God or other constructs of meaning. For example, C. S. Lewis, the great Christian apologist, experienced this as his beloved wife suffered with cancer:

> Not that I am (I think) in much danger of ceasing to believe
> in God. The real danger is of coming to believe such
> dreadful things about Him. The conclusion I dread is not So
> there's no God after all, but So this is what God is really
> like. Deceive yourself no longer. (1961, p. 5)

The following expresses another nuance of Lewis's spiritual loss:

> Meanwhile, where is God? . . . A door slammed in your face,
> and a sound of bolting and double bolting on the inside.
> (1961, p. 4)

These questions of finding meaning or purpose in suffering are even more difficult in an era when suffering itself is devalued, as it is in many Western societies. Aries (1987) contrasts this modern devaluation with medieval times, when suffering was seen as atonement for sins, sparing time in purgatory. For some, the inability to find meaning in suffering may yield conclusions that the struggle is not worthwhile, leading perhaps to premature termination of treatment, suicide, or even a seeming passive unwillingness to live (see Sudnow, 1967).

In the terminal phase, the goal of treatment ceases to be cure or extension of life. Instead it is now palliation. Now, spiritual questions such as "Why me?"—perhaps diverted earlier—may come to the fore again. In this terminal phase, I have suggested (Doka, 1993a, 1993b), individuals struggle with three spiritual needs. Those who manage effectively to meet these needs can find meaning in their lives and deaths and retain hope even as they die.

The first need is to die an appropriate death. This means to die in a way consistent with self. To some, this may mean gently accepting death; to others, it may mean avoiding or fighting it. Appropriateness also involves the ways in which individuals approach death. Some may wish to put affairs in order, finish business, or give advice.

A second spiritual need is to find meaning in one's life. Developmental psychologists and sociologists (Butler, 1963; Erikson, 1950; Marshall, 1980) have emphasized that awareness of one's finitude can lead to an intense review of one's life in order to find meaning and purpose in one's very existence. To fail in that task would, to Erikson, lead to a state of "ego despair," in which one views one's life as meaningless and wasted. One of the reasons that the death of a child can be such a high-risk factor for complicated mourning (see Rando, 1993) is that it challenges these constructs of meaning. Not only do these notions seem inappropriate and unfair, it may be hard to find meaning in the life of one who died in such an untimely way. As one parent of a 10-year-old girl who died of cancer once expressed, "She had so much promise. We never got to see how the story ended."

The spiritual need to find meaning in life is related to a third need: to find hope that exists beyond the grave. As humans, aware of the paradox of transcendence and mortality, we like to believe that the story does not stop—even at death. In some cases, belief in an afterlife, a cycle of nature, or constructs such as transcendence or reincarnation can provide that hope. In addition, other factors such as the continued survival of one's family, community, or progeny may continue to provide comfort, as might one's accomplishments or legacies (see Doka, 1993b; Lifton & Olsen, 1974).

Not every life-threatening illness leads to death. Sometimes a recovery phase follows a diagnostic or chronic phase. People who recover from life-threatening illness experience a wide range of aftereffects (see Doka, 1993a; Koocher & O'Malley, 1981). These can be physical, emotional, social, even financial. There may be spiritual effects as well. Individuals who have recovered from life-threatening illness may struggle still with questions of meaning. Earlier questions such as "Why did this happen to me?" may continue to be probed. Again, prior systems of meaning may be challenged. Some may experience crises of belief.

New meanings or values may emerge from the experience. Some people may see their faith strengthened or see enhanced value in their own strengths or the support of family or friends. Others may experience different priorities or new personal insights concerning self, others, or life itself. In any case, individuals may have to redefine who they are now that they have experienced and recovered from life-threatening illness.

In some cases, a recurrence of disease may follow a recovery. Here, the cycle replays itself, and many of the same issues arise once again. The very fact that the illness is a recurrence can either facilitate or complicate the inner quest. To some, the fact that the disease has been faced before may give hope and confidence. To others, it can lead to renewed questions of "Why me? Why do I have to go through this again?"

In summary, throughout the struggle with life-threatening illness, individuals must constantly wrestle with questions of meaning. For some, their constructs of meaning may prove sufficient to the struggle: That is, their systems of meaning allow interpretation of both their lives and their illness, as well as provide comfort and hope as they face death. For others, though, spiritual beliefs may offer neither interpretation nor hope; they are forced to simultaneously rebuild their faith and philosophical systems—reconstructing systems of meaning—as they struggle with illness.

Some points remain to be made concerning this spiritual struggle. First, the struggles for meaning may affect the behavior and decisions of both the patient and the family. A decision, for example, to donate one's body or to participate in medical experiments that might offer little hope and perhaps even negatively affect the quality of life may allow an individual to feel that he or she is leaving a legacy.

Second, the spiritual struggle is shared by the family. It is critical to remember that all family members, as well as other members of the patient's network, may have their own distinct spiritual beliefs, which may support or complicate their respective struggles to find meaning in the illness experience. Moreover, the degree to which they share systems of meaning with the patient may affect their ability to offer spiritual support. In cases where family members do not share the same systems of meaning or where they resist having their beliefs challenged, the spiritual struggle may be protracted. In addition, in cases where the patient's effort to find meaning is intense and unsuccessful, the subsequent grief of survivors may be complicated (Doka & Morgan, 1993).

Finally, it is not just patients and their families and intimate networks who may struggle with meaning. Health professionals and other caregivers, too, may struggle similarly. Questions of meaning—of fairness and purpose—inevitably occur in the caregiving experience. And as Vachon (1987) found, health care professionals whose spiritual constructs of meaning do not allow them to account for or accept the unfairness of life are more likely to experience higher levels of occupational stress.

ASSISTING IN THE SPIRITUAL STRUGGLE

As patients and their families struggle with spiritual issues, caregivers can provide critical assistance. It is important to acknowledge that while clergy, chaplains, and pastoral care workers may be able to offer valued counsel in this area, other caregivers may be called upon as well. A client, whether the patient or a member of the patient's intimate network, will sometimes choose to share spiritual concerns with a clergy member or other religious worker, but often it will be someone else—perhaps because that person is trusted, perhaps because the client's own sense of spirituality does not identify with clergy, or perhaps simply because the person is available at the moment when spiritual issues and questions arise. The point is that the responsibility for spiritual care is shared throughout the caregiving team. The option of waiting for clergy to arrive may not be viable.

This responsibility is less intimidating when one acknowledges that the role of the caregiver is not to impose his or her own religious or spiritual beliefs but rather to assist clients in utilizing their own spiritual resources. Although this is an appropriate role in any counseling, it is even more compelling in situations of life-threatening illness. In these cases, challenging beliefs may deprive clients of utilizing whatever spiritual resources they do possess in periods when they may have neither the time nor the energy to explore fully and to reconstruct their belief systems. Instead they may be left stripped of any effective systems of meaning.

The caregiver's role will be to witness, empower, and validate the spiritual quest. Sometimes just legitimizing or interpreting that struggle can be critical. For instance, in a support group for parents of children with cancer, one woman railed against God and was then upset by what she perceived as her disbelief. The support group leader assisted her in reaffirming that anger was part of any relationship and that her anger toward God was, in fact, a reaffirmation of belief.

Throughout this process of constructing or reconstructing meaning, reminiscence and life review remain powerful tools. Activities that prompt these processes, such as reviewing photographs, watching movies, or listening to music from particular periods, can encourage clients to review their lives, allowing them to rediscover legacies, meaning, and spiritual strengths.

Such techniques may also assist caregivers in assessing clients' spirituality, for life review can allow a caregiver to understand a client's spiritual journey. Tracing a client's religious and spiritual beliefs from childhood can reveal both spiritual roots and the ways in which earlier challenges led the client to discard, modify, or reconstruct his or her systems of meaning. Once spirituality is assessed, the caregiver can assist the client in utilizing his or her spiritual resources—beliefs, rituals, and faith communities.

A key element of assessment may be to discern how resilient the client's belief system is. The biblical story of Job provides examples of spiritual resilience, as well as a rigidity that may complicate coping. Job is a good man, richly blessed. Yet within a short time his family and fortune are wiped out, and he is struck with painful illness. He can find no meaning in this sudden turn of events. Job's friends arrive to comfort him, but because for them the world has to be a logical place, they believe that Job must have, even inadvertently, angered God or perhaps that God is testing him. Job rejects these understandings and demands an explanation from God. At the climax of the story, Job finally has his confrontation with his God. Poetically, God challenges him—"Were you there when I laid the foundations of the world?"—reminding Job that all is not open to explanation. Yet Job is comforted by God's presence, no longer feeling abandoned.

Job provides a paradigm of spiritual resilience. A rigid system of meaning may provide logical explanation for an event, yet some experiences defy ready interpretation. Believing, for example, that God or the universe will return good acts with blessing offers little meaning for catastrophic illness. Job's spirituality allows him to accept and to acknowledge mystery while finding comfort in presence. Moreover, Job's spirituality allows him to hold and to express all his spiritual anger and other feelings toward his deity. At the conclusion, Job's God commends him for his honesty.

Job's story also provides a model of how clients may be assisted to find more resilient sources of meaning. Caregivers can review pericopes or stories from their clients' own spiritual traditions, asking the clients to interpret what these stories mean. This can assist clients in finding new, more resilient sources of meaning.

Moreover, rituals and faith communities can also be critical tools. Rituals allow people to mark moments as sacred. They can be used to acknowledge moments of transition as well as to affirm continuity. They can empower both reconciliation and affirmation. For example, the Catholic sacrament of anointing the sick reaffirms, in the face of illness, both the presence of God and the support of the religious community. Although the topic of ritual is rich enough for yet another chapter, caregivers should be reminded that clients may not only utilize rituals from their own traditions but also may create rituals continuous with their spirituality that allow them to express and to reaffirm meaning.

Caregivers do not need to shoulder these responsibilities alone. One of their most effective roles is helping clients identify other resources that might assist in the spiritual struggle. For some care-givers, members of their own spiritual communities may provide not only counsel but very practical support as well.

Lest the task still seem daunting, caregivers may be reminded that sometimes all that is required is to be there—to listen, to wit-ness, to validate that spiritual quest. The ministry of presence is, in and of itself, a great gift.

CONCLUSION

Being present at moments in the spiritual struggle is both an honor for caregivers and of value to clients, but it has the potential to take a toll on caregivers. Therefore, they may need to be sensitive to their own spiritual needs. Spiritual resilience becomes as essential as any other aspect of life-style management (see Vachon, 1987). Care-givers are wise to replenish their own spirituality by whatever means—worship, prayer, meditation, reading, communion with nature. Unless caregivers attend to their own spirituality, they will have little to offer those whose struggles they share.

REFERENCES

Aries, P. (1987). *The hour of our death*. New York: Knopf.

Becker, E. (1973). *The denial of death*. New York: Free Press.

Butler, R. (1963). The life review: An interpretation of reminiscence in the aged. *Psychiatry, 26*, 65–76.

Doka, K. J. (1993a). *Living with life-threatening illness: A guide for patients, their families and caregivers*. Lexington, MA: Lexington Books.

Doka, K. J. (1993b). The spiritual needs of the dying. In K. J. Doka and J. Mor-gan (Eds.), *Death and spirituality*. Amityville, NY: Baywood.

Doka, K. J., & Morgan, J. (1993.) *Death and spirituality*. Amityville, NY: Baywood.

Erikson, E. (1950). *Childhood and society*. New York: Norton.

Kelley, G. (1955). *The psychology of personal constructs* (Vol. 2). New York: Norton.

Koocher, G., & O'Malley, J. E. (1981). *The Damocles syndrome: Psychological conse-quences of surviving childhood cancer*. New York: McGraw-Hill.

Lewis, C. S. (1961). *A grief observed.* New York: Barton.

Lifton, J., & Olsen, G. (1974). *Living and dying.* New York: Bantam.

Marshall, V. (1980). *Last chapters: A sociology of aging and dying.* Monterey, CA: Brooks/Cole.

Miller, J. (1994, November). *Spirituality.* Presentation at a conference on transformative grief, Burnsville, NC.

Morgan, J. (1988). Death and bereavement: Spiritual, ethical and pastoral issues. *Death Studies, 12,* 85–90.

Neimeyer, R. (1997). Meaning construction and the experience of chronic loss. In K. J. Doka and J. Davidson (Eds.), *Living with grief: When illness is prolonged.* Washington, DC: Taylor & Francis.

Pattison, E. M. (1969). Help in the dying process. *Voices, 5,* 6–14.

Pattison, E. M. (1978). The living-dying process. In C. Garfield (Ed.), *Psychological care of the dying patient.* New York: McGraw-Hill.

Rando, T. A. (1993). *Treatment of complicated mourning.* Champaign, IL: Research Press.

Sudnow, D. (1967). *Passing on: The social organization of dying.* Englewood Cliffs, NJ: Prentice Hall.

Vachon, M. (1987). *Occupational stress in the care of the critically ill, the dying and the bereaved.* New York: Hemisphere.

Weisman, A. D. (1980). Thanatology. In O. Kaplan (Ed.), *Comprehensive textbook of psychiatry.* Baltimore: Williams and Wilkins.

CHAPTER 4
Anticipatory Mourning and the Transition to Loving in Absence

Thomas Attig

When we mourn, we relearn the worlds of our experience (Attig, 1996). Loss transforms everything in the worlds we inhabit. Mourning requires that we relearn our physical surroundings, our relationships with others, our selves, and our relationships with the deceased. We relearn our worlds not only as individuals but also as families and communities. As we mourn, we find and make individual and collective ways of going on in these worlds in the absence of those who have died. We find our ways within our new realities and learn how to be ourselves in them. We do this as we combine still viable patterns of give and take with new ones in our daily life patterns. We regain our bearings in our life stories. We secure new self-, family, and community identities. These emerge as we develop new perspectives on or reinterpret our past relationships and the lives built around them; pursue new meanings and purposes in present living; and redefine expectations, hopes, and dreams for the future. We recover or find places as parts of larger wholes in our families, with friends and associates, in the broader community, and with God or with the greater powers and larger histories of the world. As we reconnect in these ways, we seek acceptance, a sense of belonging, forgiveness, peace, solace, and ultimate meaning and purpose. Effectively relearning the world mitigates our pain and anguish, restores much of what is still viable in our lives, and transforms us and the ways we inhabit the worlds we experience.

This chapter first focuses on relearning our relationships with the deceased as a central theme in mourning, a process that involves a transition from loving in presence to loving in absence. Then, it shows anticipatory mourning as less tension ridden than has been supposed: It does not entail a premature "letting go" of the dying in anticipation of ultimate emotional separation. Rather, anticipatory mourning in part entails taking first steps in learning to balance the pain of missing those who die with holding and cherishing their legacies in lasting love. The chapter examines these steps and discusses ways for caregivers to support others as they take them.

RELEARNING OUR RELATIONSHIPS
WITH THE DECEASED

Death ends the lives of those we love; it does not put an end to our loving them. A long history of writing about mourning, beginning with Freud on the necessity of decathexis, or emotional separation, insists that we must break virtually all ties to the deceased to avoid morbidity (Klass, 1988). I have urged for over a decade that this view is mistaken, first in print in an essay on love in separation (Attig, 1987) and most recently in an expanded treatment of relearning the relationship with the deceased (Attig, 1996). Only lately have empirical researchers begun to explore the limitations of the view (Klass, Silverman, & Nickman, 1996). Not all counselors or therapists hold the traditional view, but many still hold some variation of it. Mourning, properly understood, is not a process of severing ties with those we love. Rather, it is, centrally, a transition from loving in presence to loving in absence. Counselors and therapists who are following the shift in the literature, and others who have been listening well to their clients all along, have begun to support mourners in making this transition and finding paths to lasting love and enduring connections with those who have died. My most recent writing encourages and supports mourners in making this transition and guides their caregivers (Attig, in press).

What, then, does relearning our relationships with the deceased entail? Or, to put it another way, what does the transition from loving in presence to loving in absence involve? Of course, it involves acknowledging—and coming to terms with—the pain of missing the deceased, the ache of separation. And it involves modifying patterns of give and take between those who die and those who survive and still love them.

The Pain of Missing the Deceased

We ache when we experience the deaths of people we love. Our feelings, desires, motivations, habits, dispositions, expectations, and hopes aim in their direction as before. It is as if our love for them is suspended in midair with no place to land. Their absence frustrates us constantly. We have lived as if they would always be with us. Our pain and anguish derive in part from reminders of how we took their presence for granted in the intimate corners and public places where we knew them. Those feelings also derive from our sense that even the small part of the world that we know best is not ours to control. We realize helplessly that our daily lives can never be as they were. We will no longer see and be seen by, hear and be heard by, touch or be touched by, or hold and be held by our loved ones.

Nor will we share a room or a view, converse or wrangle, laugh or cry, break bread, walk or dance, hope or plan with them. We will no longer give to or receive from them in person. We will not know them as they grow older, and they will not know us. We will no longer be party to their joys and sorrows, their successes or failures; nor will they be party to ours. Central characters in our life dramas and comedies no longer share the stage with us. Our biographies and the stories of our families and other circles of intimacy veer from their expected courses. We are powerless to connect in the usual ways with those we love. We are repeatedly caught up short by a reality transformed by loss. When we lose those who are closest to us, their absence spreads like dense clouds over our lives. We are easily tempted to conclude that our pain and anguish will never relent and that we have lost everything of those who died.

What, exactly, do we lose when a loved one dies? We lose his or her physical presence and all that it means to us. We lose the fulfillment of the desires, expectations, and hopes centered on the deceased that we still carry within. We lose our abilities to interact daily and to continue into the future with the deceased as our habits, dispositions, and motivations still incline us. We begin the days of our lives as individuals and in our families and other circles of intimacy without the deceased, postured as if he or she were still with us. We cannot hold the posture, try as we might. In losing someone, we have lost the possibility of going on as we would have had he or she lived. A possibility is intangible, yet we feel the reality of the loss in the deepest recesses of our being.

We should never allow ourselves or others to underestimate or dismiss the significance of the loss of another's presence. Presence is one of the most precious things we can give one another. We sometimes learn most poignantly the value of that presence when we lose someone. Some of us believe that reunion will come in another life; some do not. For both groups this is certain: In this, the only life we know, separation is palpable and will last as long as we survive. We simply cannot have things as they were before death intervened. Momentous change alters permanently the worlds we experience as individuals, families, and communities. Our familiar life patterns are irretrievable. Whatever story captures the unfolding of the days to come for any of us, it cannot be a story of a return to life just as it was. Our hearts, souls, and spirits ache with a kind of homesickness. We are acutely aware that we are far from what brings value, meaning, and hope in our lives, distant from consolation and comfort.

We hurt most where absence frustrates our abiding feelings, desires, motivations, habits, dispositions, expectations, and hopes aimed in the direction of one who has died. If we do not modify or let go of any of these, we will not move through suffering. Any story of the journey through suffering will be one of emergence from chaos where hurt prevails to new order in life where it does not. We will search for new patterns of living and courses into the future without the presence of the deceased. We will seek ways to let go of the intensity of our longing for that presence and to carry some inevitable continuing frustration in separation. We will seek ways to recover what is still viable in our ways of living. And we will seek ways to transform our lives and even ourselves.

Early in the journey, our pain and anguish are constant companions. They permeate every waking moment and cast the world around us in dark shades. Sometimes our early agony is so great and our pain and anguish so preoccupying that we seem to be nothing but the hurt that we feel. No wonder we fear that hurt will not end. When escape seems impossible, what is the point of moving?

But hurt following loss moderates with time. Early preoccupying hurt becomes more episodic. Loss transforms our experiences of the intimate corners and public places of our worlds. Early in mourning, virtually all of our physical surroundings, social surroundings, and daily routines arouse pain and anguish as we meet them for the first time. First encounters tend to be the most difficult, but, fortunately, we have them only once. Gradually, some of our life circumstances and living patterns become familiar again as we encounter them repeatedly. We grow accustomed to the light and shadow that our loss casts upon them. Later, some of their colorful aspects return, and new ones appear. Over time, moments, then hours, even days of relative happiness penetrate the pervasive darkness. A balance between sorrow and joy begins to emerge in our lives. Even the most familiar parts of our worlds may at times still arouse pain and anguish as fresh memories and associations surface, but the intensity is rarely as great or as long lasting. We can and do relearn how to be and act at home and at ease, in ways old and new, in the worlds we experience.

Because we do not meet the world around us all at once, there will always be first encounters with people, places, and things. The paths we walk following loss extend throughout our lifetimes. We do not one day revert to old paths that existed before the loss. We can expect many first encounters later along the way: We visit places half forgotten. We find ourselves in spots where we had expected or hoped to go with the deceased. We are surprised by objects that surface unexpectedly or that remind us of some who are long lost. We hear music once shared, see paintings or sculptures, or hear beloved stories that take us back. We meet or hear from people who knew our lost loved ones. Others tell us they wish they had known them. We recognize something of the deceased in others. First encounters like these can provoke fresh, sometimes powerfully intense episodes of pain and anguish. Even the most familiar corners of our lives can arouse fresh hurt. We see something there that we had missed before, or we see things in the light of later experience. We lose other people, and the earlier loss surfaces again. But the specters of early, preoccupying intensity need not frighten us: They are precisely specters. The intensity is real, but it does not last. We are not again at the beginning of the journey through suffering. Rather, we have come a long way. We carry the possibility of hurt with us for the remainder of our lives, but it no longer permeates every corner. Hurt becomes companion to whatever joy and happiness we find.

Paths through Suffering

The desire to avoid dwelling in intense suffering can motivate us powerfully—*if* we can see some way out of it. The "*if*" here is huge. Many of us fear changing the feelings, desires, motivations, habits, dispositions, expectations, and hopes that held us close to the deceased while the loved one was alive. We fear that if we change these things, we may forget or stop loving the person; two things we most fervently want not to do. Because we resist these changes, we strongly resist facile advice to "move on" and "get over" what has happened. We desperately want to find paths that allow us to keep our love alive. The paths are there for us to walk with our fellow survivors. Along those paths we transform our loving in presence to loving in absence.

As we reshape our feelings, desires, motivations, habits, dispositions, expectations, and hopes, we need not disconnect completely from the deceased. We can change our feelings of love in presence to feelings of love in absence. We can transform our desires for their presence into desires for enduring connections where our love abides. We can change the forces that move us toward our loved ones into motivations to be and become all that we can be in the light of having known them. We can transform habits of face-to-face interaction into habits that sustain enduring connections. We can let go of dispositions to act as if the deceased were still with us and dispose ourselves to act in ways that are consonant with the values and meanings we found with them when they were alive. We can transform the expectations and hopes we felt when they were literally by our sides to expectations and hopes that they can and will abide with us in soul and spirit. If we move in these directions, we pass through our pain and anguish, beyond suffering to life with new shape and new direction.

Earlier, I stressed how necessary it is not to underestimate the importance of the loss. Presence *is* precious. However, paradoxically, we gain a vital perspective on our suffering when we remember this:

We should not overestimate what we have lost. The lives of our loved ones were, and remain, real for us. We retain our unique acquaintance with those who lived them. Their deaths do not cancel the days they walked with us. The times spent together are not erased from history. We still hold memories that we can share with fellow survivors and others. We still hold much of what our loved ones have given. We still feel the imprints of their lives upon us. We still hold the legacies of their lives, the differences they made in our individual, family, and community lives. We retain our capacity to love, and to sense abiding love from, those who died. When we realize these things, we begin to sense how we may "let go" of what we have lost (their presence) and begin to move toward cherishing what we still have of them.

New Patterns of Give and Take

Reciprocity in give and take changes when someone dies. Still, we continue to give and receive. For example, we still give our attention, interest, admiration, understanding, respect, acceptance, forgiveness, loyalty, affection, praise, and gratitude to those who have died, and we can sense that they reciprocate or that what they have given of these things is still with us. We also continue to receive and benefit from, for example, their material assistance, advice and counsel, instruction, intellectual stimulation, perspective, direction, honesty and candor, moral and spiritual guidance and support, modeling of how to be and act, encouragement, expressions of confidence, enthusiasm, sense of belonging, and inspiration. We may believe that they literally watch over us or walk with us, sharing our joys and sorrows, or we may sense that they are with us in spirit and remain our life companions. Those who die continue to give us their legacies, the fruits of their lives. For our part, we give them places in our hearts—that is, at the vital centers of our individual, family, and community lives.

Legacies are various. Family members, companions, and friends leave us inheritances or shares of estates or businesses, grand and modest, accumulated over their lifetimes. Wills provide for us or leave us prized possessions, sometimes things from the hands of the deceased. Within families, we inherit biologically in physical resemblances, the genes of our forbears, and the very being of other family members. From living with family members, companions, and friends, we inherit similarities in gestures, speech patterns, behaviors, habits, dispositions, and temperaments. Those we love, however, leave us much to treasure that is less tangible; we inherit more than their material, physical, or biological legacies. In the time we have known them, they have touched our hearts, souls, and spirits.

They have influenced the ways we live, shaped our characters, and inspired us. They retain the power to do these things after they die. It remains only for us to acknowledge, accept gratefully, and cultivate what their lives still have to offer.

We continue to love those who have died when we give them and their legacies places in our lives. When we love living family members, companions, or friends, we care about what they care about. What matters to them matters to us *because* we see how much it matters to them. Sometimes we identify with them as we make their cares our own. We come to share some of their interests, concerns, values, hopes, and dreams. We can continue this caring and sharing after they die. When we do, we thrive in activities, experiences, and ways of being ourselves and with others that derive from having known and loved them. As we still care about what they cared about, we continue loving them.

As we come to know and love others, we also come to know and value the stories of their lives. Often, their life stories are intimately interwoven with our own life stories. As we cherish the stories of those who have died, we continue the interweaving process. Our love for them deepens as we allow the values and meanings in their stories to permeate our lives. When we share the stories with others, we enrich our family and community lives. We can explore the stories endlessly as objects of our fascination. We can allow the stories to influence the interests and preferences that shape our daily lives or the directions we take into the future. In the stories we can find and use lessons about dealing with the world and with one another. We can become like the stories' central characters because we have known and loved them and been known and loved in return. We can walk in the world as their representatives as we continue to value and care for the things they once treasured and the places they once inhabited (often with us) or held sacred. We can take inspiration from the stories to fulfill our potential; meet life's challenges; and transform ourselves, our families, and our communities. As we remember and cherish the stories of our loved ones, we sustain connection with them. We hold them dear as we welcome differences they still make in our lives. We retain and appreciate the gifts that were their lives. We give their legacies places in our memories, practical lives, souls, and spirits. We become their living legacies.

We remain true to ourselves as well as to those who have died as we continue to care about what they cared about and as we cherish the stories of their lives in these ways. As we make new places for the deceased in our memories, our practical lives, and the lives of our souls and spirits, we relearn our relationships with them.

Making the transition to loving in absence mitigates, or balances, the pain of missing those who have died. We can love them still without longing intensely for their return or attempting to freeze the world in place at the moment of death. We can avoid the frustrations of these dangerous paths. Loving in absence helps us to carry our pain. It reassures us that our loved ones did not live in vain. It brings comfort and solace as it gives them new, enriching, dynamic, and enduring presence in our lives. It makes missing them more like loving them while we were apart when they lived. The motivation to loving in absence draws upon the best that is in us. It sets us on hopeful paths into futures where we feel powerfully and intimately connected to the deceased. When we cherish their legacies, we connect with the best life has to offer.

Loving in absence makes us whole again as individuals, families, and communities. When we mourn and relearn our relationships with the deceased, we put our shattered lives back together. We reweave threads of caring, first woven into the fabrics of our lives while the deceased lived, into newly integrated daily life patterns. When we mourn, we redirect and reshape the stories of our lives that were disrupted by death. We reintegrate the values and meanings of the stories of the lives now ended into our own life stories as well as those of our families and communities. We reinterpret our past lives with the deceased, alter how we live in the present, and project new hopes and purposes into the future. And, when we mourn, we find and make ourselves newly at home in the larger contexts of our lives. We join our changed and enduring connections with the deceased with modified connections with our family, friends, the larger community, and God. As we find or achieve wholeness in each of these ways, we partially define who we are in terms of our continuing relationships with those we love in absence. We grow in understanding of how much our relationships matter to us, including relationships with those who have gone before us. As we give places in our lives to loving in absence, we become whole again—but differently so—as selves, families, and communities.

ANTICIPATORY MOURNING AND LETTING GO

From the time the concept of anticipatory mourning was first introduced as "anticipatory grief" (Lindemann, 1944), theorists and clinicians have worried that advance preparation for the death of another could bring about potentially destructive, premature emotional separation. Lindemann cited the famous example of a soldier who returned from the battlefront to a wife who had thought him dead, no longer loved him, was now involved elsewhere, and insisted on an immediate divorce. According to Lindemann's reading of the example, the wife had done anticipatory mourning too well and freed herself from all emotional ties to her husband. Of course, Lindemann's example is a bit off the mark because it centers on the case of a person who had changed her life in response to what she believed to be a death that had already occurred. Still, he roused other theorists and clinicians to hesitate to support or encourage anticipatory mourning where someone is dying of a lingering illness.

The central worry is that premature detachment can deprive the dying, or us as family members, companions, or friends, of realizing the possibilities that remain in the time before death, and it may even result in abandonment of the dying. Some give great weight to this worry and caution us against all anticipatory mourning. Others simply urge moderation in anticipatory mourning so that we may avoid this danger. Still others argue that we rarely engage in anticipatory mourning because mourning presupposes emotional separation that rarely happens prior to death and because anticipation of loss often intensifies attachment.

But, as I discussed earlier, mourning does not entail emotional separation or detachment from another person. Rather, it requires that we adjust emotionally in separation, that we make a transition from loving in presence to loving in absence. There is a world of difference here. Surely, no one should encourage us to detach ourselves emotionally from, or abandon, the dying while they still live. However, this is problematic not solely for the reason that it encourages us to do something prematurely, before death occurs. It is equally a mistake to encourage us to sever all, or even most, emotional ties with the dead. Anticipatory mourning, as properly understood, has nothing to do with such detachment.

Mourning does involve coming to terms with loss. As I showed earlier, when death occurs, we must mourn the loss of the physical presence of the deceased. We must come to terms with missing our loved one. It should be clear by now that this letting go of presence is not the same as letting go of the person who dies. Furthermore, mourning not only means letting go of what is lost. It also requires that we learn new ways of going on in the world and living with what is not lost. Centrally, it involves making a transition to loving in new ways, learning how to have, hold, and cherish the legacies of a life now ended. Mourning, then, is a process that combines learning to carry the pain of missing the deceased and balancing that pain with continued loving of the deceased in his or her absence.

Anticipatory mourning may be defined as the mourning that we and the dying do while death is anticipated. Before death comes, and as terminal illness takes its toll, the dying and we who love them suffer many losses. We mourn over what we have already lost, losses in process, and expectations for the future that we can no longer realize. We already miss much of the usual shapes of our daily lives and experience major disruptions in the unfolding of our life stories. We, as survivors-to-be, anticipate missing the presence of the dying when death comes. However, anticipatory mourning is not only letting go of what is lost or will be lost. It also involves anticipating the transition from loving in presence to loving in absence. Continuing engagement enables the dying and us to take steps to address unfinished business, live out as well as possible the time that we still have together, and look toward the future in ways that will promote loving in absence. On this understanding, anticipatory mourning is in part a process of taking first steps in learning to balance the pain of missing those who die with holding and cherishing their legacies.

There should be no hesitation to encourage anticipatory mourning when this is understood to be its character and shape. Tensions that would arise if mourning involved severing emotional ties with the dying should either not arise or be greatly diminished. We can remain involved with the dying, increase attachment to them during their illnesses, or sustain engagement with them through remissions and relapses without fear that it will make later severing of ties more difficult, though it may intensify the early pain of missing their presence. Holding on to the dying will be problematic only when it involves withholding our permission to die or denies them timely release from suffering through death. Holding on will not be problematic because it is incompatible with letting go in the sense of separating emotionally from the dying. We can plan for life after the death and consider life in the absence of the dying without our planning's being experienced as a betrayal. Rather, planning can be experienced as integral to furthering the interests of the dying and enabling us to love them still. We can understand remembering the past with the dying as a process of recovering and enriching their legacies, and we can see anticipating the future as leading to cherishing of those legacies and the memories of those who leave them.

ANTICIPATING THE PAIN OF MISSING THE DECEASED

We cannot know the full implications of missing others until they have died. Presence is so powerful and so precious. However, we can anticipate that pain and see aspects of the paths we will walk when our loved ones are gone. Caregivers can support us as we anticipate these things.

Missing the Dying though They Are Still with Us

We typically experience loss of presence to some extent even before death occurs. We have some of our first encounters with absence in public and private corners of our worlds before we experience the pervasive absence that death brings. We may miss the presence of the dying in familiar places, especially public places where we have conducted everyday business, shopped together, shared meals, enjoyed entertainments, attended worship services, strolled together, and taken vacations or day trips or the like. If they have become confined to hospitals or extended care facilities, we may miss them in the homes where we shared our lives or where we frequently visited them. We may miss them in any of the rooms where we began and ended the day together, blended our daily routines, shared responsibilities, supported one another, nurtured or were nurtured by them, spent time with family or friends, celebrated special occasions, played together, worked together, found respite from the challenges of the wider world, worried about and planned for the future, knew companionship and intimacy, laughed, cried, argued, or shared silences. We may miss them in the doorways, the yards or the gardens, the garages or the cars, or in the surrounding neighborhoods. Even if they are living out their dying days at home with us, we may miss their participation in many of the old, familiar ways, participation rendered impossible by debilitation, loss of mobility, or other changes related to illness. All of these experiences provide a basis for our saying (as we frequently do) such things as "I feel like I miss her already" or "I know he's still with us, but it's as if he's partially left us."

Still, even in circumstances where our interactions with the dying and their lives are severely compromised, they remain with us. Their simple presence means so much to us. We may resent institutional settings; intrusions of health care staff on our shared time, the imposition of routines, regulations, and treatments; changes in the home necessary for the provision of home care; or the limitations imposed by debilitation and illness themselves. Nevertheless, we are grateful for the time we can have together. There can be much to be grateful for, whether in extended conversation and richly varied exchange or only brief illuminated moments. Embracing warmly, touching softly, holding a hand, wiping a tear, looking into each other's eyes, praying together, listening to or singing a favorite melody, sharing silence, and the like can be precious to us. We go to great lengths to spend time with the dying, no matter how much or how little that time may seem to offer. We borrow time from other obligations, stretch our energies and endurance to the limits, and make many sacrifices. We resist letting go of loved ones' presence even when continued living is obviously difficult for them and witnessing their suffering tests us. We dread the time when they will be gone, even when we sense it will bring welcome release for them and for us. We cannot know the full impact of the complete loss of their presence until it comes.

Dealing with Present Pain

This is not to say that we or caregivers can do nothing about the pain of missing the presence of loved ones before they die. We need to recognize our experiences for what they are and find effective ways to express the hurt we feel. It matters less how we do so than that we find ways that work for us and respect others. Our pain and anguish bear witness to the values and meanings of what we have lost. When we express our hurt, we affirm those values and meanings.

Caregivers can minister to our experiences of the partial losses of presence described here, our first encounters with absence, and the attendant pain. When we as family, companions, or friends tell of such experiences, caregivers should welcome and normalize the expressions as healthy recognition of very real challenges that we are facing. We too suffer, and not only those who are dying. However, we and others tend to downplay the legitimacy of our hurt. When we do not tell of such experiences, caregivers can gently probe and ask whether we are having them. Their willing presence with us in the typical chaos of our lives assures us that they value us, that our suffering matters, and that we do not walk alone. Their patience with our expressions of suffering encourages us to move through the suffering.

Caregivers can help us appreciate the many choices we have and support us as we decide what to do with our feelings. They can help us find opportunities and means to express ourselves. Caregivers can offer, without insisting, to hear our stories of loss and our hurt. If we are reticent to share our troubles and sorrows with them, they can encourage us to bring them to intimates or friends in quiet conversation or correspondence; to support groups where those who know suffering listen without judging us or our feelings; or to higher powers through prayer, meditation, or ritual. We should be careful about bringing too much of such sorrow to the dying to avoid adding to their already heavy burdens. If we are reticent to reach out to others, caregivers can encourage us to use other means to bring our hurt to the surface and release it. They can encourage us to weep rather than choke back the tears, find "screaming places," ventilate through vigorous physical activity, record our pain and anguish in journals or diaries, make music, paint, sculpt, or write poetry. When we produce something tangible, they can encourage us to share it with them or others. When we do, we express ourselves to them indirectly.

Caregivers can help us adjust to the changes in our physical and social surroundings where the dying are no longer present as before. They can help us identify where and how we are most acutely affected and where we feel most safe and secure. They can help us see that we have options and support us as we choose when to approach what affects us most, how long to stay, what to do or say while there, and when to retreat to relative safety. They can volunteer to accompany us when and where we hurt most or encourage us to reach out to others if we do not want to be alone. They can help us to identify, or provide us with, places of retreat, reflection, comfort, and respite. They can help us recognize the practical, social, and spiritual challenges that the absence of the dying already poses in our daily lives. They can encourage us to set our own paces and our own priorities in meeting those challenges, help us identify alternative ways to address them, and support us as we take first steps in the directions we choose.

Caregivers can encourage us to recognize and express or demonstrate our gratitude for what the presence of the dying has meant, or continues to mean, to us. Expressions of our feelings of hurt at losing that presence, as discussed earlier, are only part of the story here. We should hesitate to burden the dying with too much of our hurt. However, we should not hesitate to express in our own ways the gratitude that we feel for their having been and continuing to be parts of our lives. Caregivers can help and support us in finding ways to affirm the values and meanings we have found—and still find—in the presence of the dying. Fuller discussion of acknowledging and expressing and showing gratitude for the contributions of a lifetime follows later in the chapter. Suffice it to say here that such acknowledgment and expressions of gratitude balance, and to some extent mitigate, our experiences of the pain of missing our loved ones.

Anticipating the Painful Path Ahead

The first sections of this essay describe what can be expected in mourning after death and emphasize what is involved in relearning the relationship with the deceased. We often dread the path that will lie ahead after those we love die, especially the pain of missing them and "losing everything." Caregivers can address our dread as they educate us about the probable contours of the path and the experience of walking it. They can help us appreciate how, in some ways, our current missing of the dying, even while they are still with us, provides a partial preview of this experience. Also, they can honestly acknowledge and gently caution that this preview cannot shield us from the full impact of the loss to come. At the same time, they can help us anticipate that the pain of missing the deceased will moderate with time as we move beyond the early intensity of our suffering, pass our most painful first encounters with absence, and find ways to carry the pain of missing the deceased as we reshape our daily lives and move in new directions in the unfolding of our life stories. Caregivers can help us to see how, though our loved ones' presence is most precious, we will not lose everything that we cherish in their lives when they die. They can educate us about the challenges of, and the hope and promise in, making the transition from loving in presence to loving in absence. They can help us see that, in making this transition, we can still provide places in our hearts for our loved ones in our memories and our practical lives as well as in the lives of our souls and spirits. They can help us anticipate how different relationships with the deceased can be integral in our daily individual, family, and community lives and continuing life stories. As they do these things, caregivers can help us foresee a time when the pain of missing the deceased will be balanced by our continuing love for them in their absence.

ANTICIPATING THE TRANSITION TO LOVING IN ABSENCE

We cannot love others in absence until they are absent. We can, however, love them well while they are still with us and interact with them in ways that will make it easier to continue loving them when they are gone. Doing so involves both attending to unfinished business between us and striving for the best possible quality in interactions and time shared at the end of life. It also involves taking beginning steps in the transition from loving in presence to loving in absence. In all instances, caregivers can encourage and support us.

Addressing Unfinished Business

We are often challenged by unfinished business in our relationships with the dying. It is vital to do all we can to come to terms with distressing feelings, resolve past conflicts, heal rifts, forgive omissions or offenses, and find ways to do or say what we feel we must while they are alive. It is not impossible to do these things after death occurs, but it can be extremely difficult. If we do not manage to address and approach resolution or completion of unfinished business, we may be troubled by irresolution, regret, remorse, frustration, or anger after death occurs. Such troubling states of affairs and hard feelings can preoccupy us as we mourn. They can interfere with or even undermine our efforts to make the transition to loving in absence.

Caregivers can help us identify these challenges by asking us to imagine a time several months after death has occurred and to visualize what might then seem unresolved, unfinished, or otherwise troubling about our relationships with the deceased. They can motivate us to address those challenges in the time remaining by inviting us to consider how painful the present irresolution is for us (and may be for the dying) and how irresolution can interfere with or undermine our loving them when they are gone. Caregivers can encourage and support us as we seek ways to address the challenges, ways of doing or saying what we feel we must before it is too late. They can help us identify options, rehearse scenarios with us, help us think and feel our way through hesitations, volunteer to be with us when we try our best, debrief with us after difficult sessions with the dying, and the like. All the while, caregivers need to respect differences among individuals, families, and friendships in styles of confronting such issues. They need especially to recognize that some of us, and some who are dying, may honestly prefer to leave some business unfinished rather than violate comfortable and well-established norms of communication, candor, and honesty. When we make that choice, caregivers can help us process feelings around trouble that lingers in the air and find ways to minimize its interference as we try to live out those final times as well as possible.

Striving for Quality in the Final Times

Other contributors to this book discuss the importance of tending to the wide range of needs of the dying and our needs as their survivors-to-be. If these needs are not recognized and addressed, the quality of life in the final times will be compromised. Moreover, we will accumulate painful memories, regrets, remorse, frustration, anger, and the like that can carry over into and diversely affect bereavement.

Let us focus more narrowly here on the relationships and the quality of interactions between close survivors and the dying as the end approaches. When we are intimates of the dying, we typically draw closer to them in their illnesses. Often, we join with health care professionals in providing care and meeting their needs. As we do, we contribute to their quality of life and can come to feel that we are "doing all that we can do" as family members, companions, or friends in difficult circumstances. This helps to minimize our feelings of helplessness, regret, or guilt both before and after death. When we share in caregiving with others in our intimate circles, we come to appreciate how they share our love for the dying. The dying, in turn, can recognize the depth of our care and concern and benefit from our ministering directly to them. At the same time, we need to be careful not to overextend ourselves, deplete our energies to the point of exhaustion, court resentment of the dying or our fellow intimates, or render ourselves ineffective in giving care.

When caregiving is effective, the dying can know good times in the final times. They can remain themselves within the limits that illness and debilitation dictate. And we can know good times with them. As mentioned earlier, there can be much to be grateful for in the experiences we share as illness progresses and death approaches. It can be burdensome to carry painful memories of the course of illness, debilitation, deterioration, and the hardships of caregiving, sacrifice, and disruption of familiar life rhythms. Still, these memories can be partially balanced with memories of the good that we found together in those difficult times, the moments of joy and laughter, the meaningful things we managed to say and do, the ways in which we touched one another, the closeness we felt.

Leave-taking is a most difficult yet vital aspect of our interactions at the very end of life. Unsaid good-byes can haunt us for years. So, too, can guilt if we cling when the dying are ready to let go or if we do not signal our permission to die, painful though that may be. Effective leave-taking brings closure to the time together, eases our transition to life in separation, and eases the dying toward the transition into death. We can communicate leave-taking in words of acceptance of the inevitable, remembrance, gratitude, or love or in gestures that convey those meanings. It can help to recognize that leave-taking is about separation and ending our presence with one another and not about ending our love. With this in mind, we can imagine a wider range of words and actions to acknowledge the meaning of the diminishing presence and to express how our love will endure. Much of what is discussed in the following section can be understood as part of expressing good-byes and taking leave.

Caregivers can help us to learn ways to participate in caregiving and to balance meeting the needs of the dying with meeting our own needs for rest, respite, and nourishment as well as material, emotional, social, and spiritual support. They can help and encourage us to look for and even create good moments or periods in the final times. They can encourage us to recognize the importance of leave-taking for all concerned. They can talk with us about things we might say or do, tell us what others have done, or even model ways of saying good-bye or signaling permission to die. They can support us in coming to terms with the often intense emotions that leave-taking can arouse.

Anticipating Cherishing the Legacy

We can take beginning steps in the transition from loving in presence to loving in absence as we move toward effectively cherishing the legacies of the dying. We can look to the past and review the life now ending and our life together. And we can anticipate the future. We can do these things privately, with fellow survivors, or, perhaps most powerfully, with the dying themselves.

As we review the past, we remember cherished experiences. Stories of good times shared bring delight, joy, and laughter. When we share memories and stories with others, including the dying, we enrich memory, deepen our knowledge of the life now ending, and multiply delight in it and all we have shared.

We also remember lessons in living that we have learned from those with whom we have shared our lives. Their advice and counsel have often been invaluable for us as individuals and in our families and communities. We have learned about many things that matter to us because we have known them, including caring for and about one another in our intimate circles. They have shaped and influenced our characters and our family and friendship patterns in so many ways.

We remember ways in which the dying have inspired us. They have shown us how, and encouraged us, to be all we can be. They have shown us ways to face and deal with challenges in living, strive to transcend limitations, and cope with adversity.

Remembering all of these things deepens our appreciation of the extent and value of what we will still keep of the dying when they are gone. Remembering with the dying provides opportunities to express our love for them, praise them, and convey gratitude for all that they have given us and all that their presence has meant. It gives them powerful affirmation of the values and meanings of their lives and lets them learn of and be warmed by our gratitude. It also allows them to tell us, in effect, that they too are grateful for their time with us and for the chance to share their lives with us. These expressions can console and comfort us deeply.

Caregivers can listen to our memories or explore with us the possibilities of remembering in private, with fellow survivors, or with the dying. They can help us appreciate the value and potential of such remembering. They can help us see the possibilities of remembering not only cherished experiences but also the influences, life lessons, and inspirations that we find in them. They can encourage and support us in remembering in any or all of these ways and support us in dealing with the feelings such remembering may arouse.

As we look to the future we anticipate separation, a time when pain of missing the deceased can be balanced by continued loving in absence. Life review, as just described, enables us to recognize the legacies of the dying that we will still hold. Privately, or with family members or friends, we can look toward times when we will have memories to cherish and when we, individually and with others, can benefit from our loved ones' legacies. We can make initial plans for those times together and take small, beginning steps toward actualizing those plans. We can anticipate interweaving these legacies more fully into our daily lives after death occurs and in our continuing journeys into the future.

When we join with the dying in anticipating the future, we can hear from them how they would like their desires and interests to be furthered after they die. They may express concerns about such matters as their aging parents, children, or pets; projects they would like to see completed; the quality of our living together in our families, with friends, or in our communities; or the fate of things and places that have special meaning for them. We can learn of their concerns about our well-being and their wishes for us as we mourn. Typically, they do not want us to be overwhelmed by grief or to dwell in the pain of missing them. We can learn of their hopes that we will thrive, find purpose and meaning in life, succeed, know joy, and love. Typically, they want us to hold dear the good in their lives, to use and cherish what they have given.

Anticipating the future with the dying allows us to discuss with them ways in which we can further their desires and interests after they die. We can make promises and assure them that we will abide by long-standing covenants. We can tell them how we will cherish them in memory. We can let them know how we feel ourselves to be, and how we will remain, different for having known them. We can tell them how we will use and cherish the legacies of their influence, their life lessons, and their inspiration. We can pledge to strive to realize their hopes for us as individuals, families, and communities. We can assure them that we will do our best to balance the pain of missing them with loving them in their absence in all of these ways.

Caregivers can listen to our concerns about life in separation and explore with us ways of anticipating that time in private, with fellow survivors, or with the dying. They can help us to appreciate the value and potential of such anticipation. They can help us see the possibilities of cherishing memories and of giving significant places in our individual, family, and community lives to the legacies of lives now ending. They can encourage and support us in anticipating loving in absence in any or all of these ways. They can remind us how such continuing loving can balance the pain of missing those who die.

REFERENCES

Attig, T. (1987). Grief, love and separation. In C. A. Corr & R. Pacholski (Eds.), *Death: Completion and discovery.* Lakewood, OH: Association for Death Education and Counseling.

Attig, T. (1996). *How we grieve: Relearning the world.* New York: Oxford University Press.

Attig, T. (in press). *The heart in grief: The desire for lasting love.* New York: Oxford University Press.

Klass, D. (1988). *Parental grief: Solace and resolution.* New York: Springer.

Klass, D., Silverman, P., & Nickman, S. (1996). *Continuing bonds: New understandings of grief.* Washington, DC: Taylor & Francis.

Lindemann, E. (1944). Symptomatology and management of acute grief. *American Journal of Psychiatry, 101,* 141–148.

CHAPTER 5
Anticipatory Mourning and the Transition of Fading Away

Betty Davies

Families who face the diagnosis of progressive, life-threatening illness face many losses—the loss of health, the loss of hope for a long life, the loss of dreams fulfilled, to name only a few. Rando (1986) has defined anticipatory grief as

> the phenomenon encompassing the processes of mourning, coping, interaction, planning and psychosocial reorganization that are stimulated and begun in part in response to the awareness of the impending death of a loved one and the recognition of associated losses in the past, present and future. It demands a delicate balance among the mutually conflicting demands of simultaneously holding on, letting go of, and drawing closer to the loved one. (p. 24)

The definition of anticipatory grief, in this book now called *anticipatory mourning,* has evolved over many years and reflects the ever-expanding breadth of what the term signifies, while rarely articulating what specific processes might occur for those who confront impending death of themselves or of loved ones.

The Families in Supportive Care research program, upon which this chapter is based, was not conducted within the framework of anticipatory mourning. In fact, because no theoretical framework could be found that provided adequate direction for the study, we selected qualitative methods. (For a discussion of the rationale for choosing qualitative methods and of the challenges faced in conducting qualitative research in palliative care, refer to Davies, Chekryn Reimer, Brown, & Martens [1995], pp. 97–108.) Yet, though not shaped per se by an anticipatory mourning framework, the findings of this project have relevance for a fuller understanding of the phenomenon of anticipatory mourning. Whether what we term *fading away* is in fact anticipatory mourning, or whether it even fits within that phenomenon, is irrelevant; it is important simply to know more about families' experiences. This chapter describes the transition of fading away, a process that a family experiences when one of its members faces terminal illness (Davies et al., 1995). It makes clear that the experience is similar for all members, including the dying person, the spouse, and their adult children, but that there are distinct differences among family members as well. It illustrates how this transition is influenced by contextual variables—in particular, family functioning. Finally, it suggests interventions for practitioners that are specifically geared to the experiences of families facing terminal illness.

BACKGROUND OF THE RESEARCH PROGRAM

The Families in Supportive Care research program arose from the expressed needs of nurses caring for families with members receiving palliative care for advanced cancer. How were they, as nurses, best to support both the patient and family members as they faced the imminent death of the ill person? The literature, though comprising many articles with titles including the word *family*, offered little guidance concerning the actual experiences of families in palliative care. Many of the articles were based solely on the perspective of a single family member, usually the bereaved spouse. Moreover, the studies, conducted after the patients had died, did not reflect the patient's perspective. The purpose of our project, therefore, was to explore the experiences of such families by interviewing patients, spouses, and adult children. Of course, this approach excludes the perspectives of younger children and other family members, such as the parents or siblings of the dying person. Most families in palliative care programs are "older"—that is, the average age of patients is 65. Therefore, for the study to have optimal relevance for these programs, a family included the patient, the spouse, and one child over 18. We recognize that the study is limited by this selection; however, by offering a view on the experiences of families dealing with terminal illness, its findings provide details that help fill in the picture painted by Rando's (1986) definition of anticipatory mourning.

Interviews were held with each family group and with each member individually. A total of 23 families (71 family members) participated in the project. Families were selected from a variety of palliative care settings, including home care, general hospital palliative care units, and a supportive care program in a cancer center. The patients, all in the final stages of advanced cancer, were receiving supportive or palliative care—that is, care given when cure and prolongation of life were no longer paramount and emphasis was on symptom control and quality of life. The first and second phases of the project, conducted with a total of 18 families, resulted in a theoretical schema describing the experiences of families with advanced cancer in one member. The third phase tested the conceptualization with 5 additional families, who reported that the description of the phenomenon made sense to them. (A complete description of the sample, research procedures, and findings is presented in Davies et al., 1995.)

The conceptual analysis of study findings resulted in a description of the transition of fading away. Families were in transition from a time when they could carry on largely as usual (despite the diagnosis of cancer in one family member) to a time when they could no longer carry on as usual. They were in the transition between a time when the patient was "living with" cancer and a time when he or she was "dying from" cancer.

FADING AWAY: THE EXPERIENCE OF TRANSITION IN FAMILIES FACING TERMINAL ILLNESS

The transition the families experienced began with the realization that the patient was, in fact, going to die from the disease. The realization was triggered by the patient's declining physical condition and the resultant perception that the patient was "fading away" rather than, at minimum, maintaining a plateau. The patient's condition had deteriorated to the point where the inevitable could no longer be denied. Insuperable weakness, loss of mobility, loss of independence in personal care, and loss of mental clarity were visible signs of the patient's forthcoming demise. Patients and family members had been told the prognoses months, sometimes years, before: They had been intellectually aware of the possibility that the patients might die, but a time came when that knowledge hit home, suddenly and forcefully. Until that moment, they unconsciously (or, in some cases, consciously) chose to focus on successful treatment outcomes, life-style changes, and "normal" living:

> *I knew, I guess, that cancer could kill, but I didn't ever believe it would kill my dad. We all focused on fighting, on beating this thing. Then, one day, as I was talking to my dad, he just fell asleep in his chair. I saw for the first time how exhausted he was, how thin he had gotten, and it hit me like a truck. . . . Dad isn't going to make it!*

The full realization that death would be the inevitable outcome of the disease initiated the transition of fading away. The transition of fading away comprises seven interrelated and intertwined components: redefining, burdening, struggling with paradox, contending with change, searching for meaning, living day to day, and preparing for death. A natural tendency is to perceive these components as occurring in a linear fashion and sequentially. In reality, however, each recurs and overlaps with the others; together, they constitute the whole of the transition experience.

Redefining

Redefining is central to the transition experience. Redefining entails reconciling what used to be and what is now. It leads to an adjustment in how individuals view themselves and one another as well as how they define the family unit. The patient's redefinition of self, in response to shifts in abilities and capabilities resulting from limitations imposed by the illness, is critical in this process. For patients, redefining means they let go of their view of who they used to be and develop new views of themselves, their capabilities, and others. They alter their identities over time. One woman, an influential politician, took great pride in her work and in her family of three young adult children. Realizing that her condition was worsening and that she could no longer work full-time and still maintain her active family life, she cut back to part-time work. Within a couple of months, she was down to working just one day a week, and then to fulfilling some work responsibilities via telephone from her home. *I am still representing my constituents,* she said, *but not the way I used to. I do it differently now.* As her condition deteriorated, this same woman found new ways of expressing her political views by writing and then by dictating the "lessons she had learned" for the benefit of other female politicians who would come after her. As time passed, she was able to adapt her working life, redefining herself, her abilities, and her contributions. As many other patients did, she reinforced the fact that she was still the same person inside, though her body was no longer recognizable in its previous form. One patient expressed it this way: *The physical me is no longer here as I was. . . . It seems I'm trapped in this sort of helpless little carcass. But my mind and my soul, I think, are the same.*

It is not easy for patients to accept the limitations imposed by disease. They speak about their new selves with sadness and a sense of loss. In the politician's words, *It's not that I like what has happened to me. I am sick and funny looking. . . . I had never been sick a day in my life. Always full of energy and fun. But what can I do?* She, like some patients, was able to make the adjustments that the declining state demands: *It seems as this is the lot that fate has given me—the most I can do is to make the best of what I have left for as long as I have it.* She differentiated between those aspects that remained intact and those that had changed: *I am still here to talk with my kids—and I have so much to tell them—but I have less time now for my constituents.* Such patients conveyed this understanding to others and continued to receive support.

When patients cannot redefine themselves, they experience anger, feelings of worthlessness, and persistent frustration with their altered situations. They perceive changes in themselves but cope with them by refusing to give in. One man, devoted to his accounting practice, refused to modify his regular pattern. Each day, even though barely able to stand alone, he would insist that his wife drive him to the office, where he proceeded to criticize his associates for various decisions made in his absence. He exclaimed, *I am not going to let this get me down. I have worked at getting this business up and running all my life, and I am not going to let it go now!* Such reactions only served to frustrate the man's spouse, friends, and colleagues and diminished the support they wanted—and were allowed—to offer him.

For the spouse, redefining focuses on his or her relationship with the patient. Most often, the spouse perceives changes in the patient resulting from the disease or treatment, rather than a conscious effort on the patient's part to behave in a certain way: *You have to understand that the drugs do strange things to people. He doesn't mean to be forgetful or say such stupid things . . . it's just the drugs.* Spouses' ease in redefining the patients, their relationships, and themselves is directly related to the patients' ability to redefine. The politician's husband, for example, indicated that this time together was . . . *the best time of our lives. We have grown even closer than we were before. I don't know how she manages to keep her spirits up. But she does—and that helps all of us.* When patients redefine themselves, spouses are able to help in constructive ways:

> *We had to get a couple of new phone lines in here so that there was a phone in every room—that way, she could take calls without having to waste energy walking to the phone. The kids and I surprised her one day by hiding the new phones and then waiting for the first call. She was so surprised when we produced the new phones—we all had a good laugh over that. She was thrilled!*

Spouses try to maintain life as normally as possible: *We don't go out like we used to, but we manage to have one or two friends over for just coffee. None of the fancy baking she used to do . . . but we get to visit anyway.*

Spouses have much more difficulty when the patients do not redefine. The accountant's wife, for example, confided,

> *If only he would see that he can't keep going like he used to. I hate driving him downtown—I don't get anything else done. And I am so tired from being awake at night to give him his drugs.*

The driving really gets on my nerves, and it shows. I want to help him—but it's impossible for me to do what he wants me to!

When patients do not redefine themselves, spouses avoid situations that tend to upset the patients:

I tried talking to him once about how tired I was and how it wasn't safe to be driving downtown every day. He got really mad at me and said that if I didn't want to do it, then he would just take a taxi. Right! We live 40 miles from his office. Do you know how much that would cost?

The accountant's wife continued to drive her husband to his office, resenting every mile and finding the relationship increasingly troublesome.

Adult children are profoundly affected by the alterations in their ill parent's physical condition. In response, adult children are forced to undergo a perceptual shift: Instead of seeing the parent as someone in control, they see someone who is now the opposite. The politician's 19-year-old daughter explained:

Seeing my mom so thin and fragile—it's really a shock. She was always full of energy and fun and made us laugh over all the funny things that happened to her each day. It's so hard to get used to her this way.

Adult children deal with these feelings by focusing on the illness or treatment rather than on intentional behavior: *She can't help how she looks now—it's not her fault. So why would we make a big deal of it? Inside, she's still my mom.*

Adult children are the family members who talk most about facing the future without the ill person. Their comments frequently center on their parent's never being a grandparent: *When I have my own children, they won't ever know my mom. That makes me so sad.* They begin to see that death is part of life in ways they had not realized previously. Adult children see that they too will someday die, and in response, they often resolve to take better care of themselves and spend their time in worthwhile ways. Some adult children have difficulty redefining. They continue as if nothing had changed and try, often desperately, to create what they perceive to be a "normal" family. The accountant's son said, *Well, my dad is sick, of course, but not much has changed, really. I visit when I can—probably less than I used to, but no more, no less than other sons probably visit their dads.*

As mentioned earlier, redefining is the central component in fading away. It strongly influences each of the other components. The more the patient and the other family members can redefine themselves, one another, and the situation, the better able they are to manage the other aspects of the transition. Burdening, for example, is strongly affected by redefining.

Burdening

Burdening has many facets. Patients believe themselves to be burdens to the degree to which they have not constructively redefined themselves and their altered situations. When patients do redefine, they use their limited energy for emotional support and encouragement as a way of easing the burden for family members. These patients try to alleviate burden by avoiding complaint: *I try not to complain. My husband has enough to deal with without having to listen to that kind of whining.* They sometimes share their concerns selectively: *I have a wonderful minister—he's my listening post. After I have talked with him, then I feel less need to talk about some of my woes with the kids.* Patients try to be as useful as they can: *I still can manage to get most of me dressed. That helps them a little bit.* And some patients accept and prepare for death as a strategy to relieve the burden on their families: *I know that the grim reaper is waiting for me by the door. I would rather die sooner than later so that my family doesn't have to put up with all of this for too long.* When patients do not redefine themselves or when they perceive themselves as burdens, they use their energy to maintain their former views of themselves, often at the expense of their spouse-caregivers. The accountant, for example, had no perception of the burden his insistence on going to work was placing on his wife.

Although spouses acknowledge their extra responsibilities, many hesitate to describe them as burdens. Rather, they perceive them as "the things you do for those you love." When spouses believe their ill partners appreciate their efforts, they feel even less burdened and express satisfaction with their abilities to provide care. However, spouses who do not feel their efforts are appreciated or even acknowledged experience heavy burden. Their focus is on waiting for the patient to die; they perceive that death is the only avenue for relief. Instead of satisfaction and pride, they feel exhaustion and resentment.

For adult children, burdening takes on an added dimension. Like spouses, they also assume extra work and responsibilities. However, these are superimposed on the demands of their own careers, children, and homes. They often feel both satisfied and exhausted. The degree to which adult children feel burdened is influenced by the health of the well parent. When he or she is healthy and can manage fairly well, adult children feel less burdened than when that parent cannot adequately care for him- or herself or for the patient. When both parents are able to redefine, then adult children are better able to redefine.

Struggling with Paradox

A central aspect of the transition of fading away concerns the paradox of living and dying at the same time. The dilemma for the patient is captured in the words of this man: *I like to think that I will be here for a while yet, but I know it's not to be. I know I am not going to make it, but I have so much yet that I would like to do with my life.*

Patients often refer to the struggle between wanting to fight and wanting to give up—both at the same time, depending on how they feel at any particular moment. Spouses, on the other hand, talk about the paradox, but they do not experience the same dilemma. They find that struggle more relevant to the patients. The dilemma the spouses experience has more to do with how to spend their time. They want to care for and spend time with their dying partners, but at the same time, they also need to continue meeting the requirements of day-to-day life.

Adult children struggle with three major paradoxes. The most common is the struggle between hanging on and letting go. They want the ill parent to live but do not want the parent to suffer:

> There's been a real tug-of-war. . . . On one hand, I want someone to
> do something, find a cure. . . . On the other hand, there's the very
> frustrating knowledge that there is no cure. It would be so much
> better if he just died and released his own pain, his own agony.

Children want to spend as much time as possible with their dying parent but at the same time want to get on with their own lives, and this is the second dilemma. This dilemma is particularly troubling for younger adult children who are just establishing intimate relationships and careers. The third paradox emerges when adult children with families of their own are pulled between the desire to spend time with the parent and the desire to spend time with their own growing children. In coping with this paradox of dual loyalties and demands, adult children devote much energy to weighing the pros and cons of each alternative.

Contending with Change

The ill person and the other family members face major changes in relationships, roles, responsibilities, and social life. When patients are able to redefine, they are better able to alter their responsibilities, to reflect on patterns in their lives, and to change those patterns according to altered needs and abilities: *What it has given me is an opportunity to mend some fences. I realized that in the past 11 years, I had made my son feel like a second-class citizen. . . . Our relationship has improved tremendously.* As patients become more housebound and bedbound, many of them focus their attention on their immediate environments, particularly nature, and find much satisfaction in the little things: *I have lived here for so long, and never before have I noticed that old weather vane up there. Now, I love to just watch it and see how the wind changes its direction.*

Some spouses report that their relationships with their partners grow as a result of the current situation; others describe their relationships as strained. Forced togetherness often results in disharmony and tension, particularly when redefining is limited. Most spouses cope with changes by keeping things as normal as possible within the limitations imposed by the illness. However, in contending with change, very few spouses pay attention to the need for self-care. When patients encourage spouses to take time for themselves, the spouses feel less confined and less tired. When patients disregard spouses' needs, the spouses are greatly fatigued.

Adult children contend with numerous changes, which seem to have more widespread and all-encompassing effects. The changes have to do with taking on additional responsibilities: They often assume financial and legal responsibility for their parents in addition to providing emotional and physical care. Such activities siphon time from their own families, careers, and social lives, and they often entail changes in interactions with adult siblings as well. One daughter-in-law, for example, after experiencing a difficult time pulling together all the siblings, explained:

> *They weren't ready to hear about how serious [the illness] was. Everybody was trying to avoid it. He's dying of cancer, and he's going to go very soon. And it was important for them to know, so I called a family meeting to discuss it—I didn't want to take over, but I felt it was so important for them to know.*

Faced with so many changes, adult children become chronically fatigued.

Searching for Meaning

While experiencing the transition of fading away, family members examine their situations and seek answers that help them understand and come to terms with those situations. The focus of the search for meaning varies among patients, spouses, and children, and not all individuals search for meaning to the same degree.

Patients journey into themselves, reflecting on the spiritual aspects of life. They try to put their experiences in context and endure the turmoil. They try to make sense of their situations by connecting with others or with nature. Connecting with self involves reexamining and affirming values and possibly changing priorities. As one woman said:

> You cannot help but stop and think about what all this means to you. I have never been much of a spiritual person, I guess . . . but this has made me stop and think about it. I feel so much better now—inside myself, I mean. Death doesn't scare me, really—not any more. It feels as if I have found some inner gift, some kind of inner peace from all this.

Patients seek meaning in a variety of ways—with others, with nature, with new forms of contribution. Doing so engenders satisfaction and a feeling of usefulness instead of despair and hopelessness.

Spouses concentrate on the meaning of their relationship with their partners and the ways illness has contributed to their own personal growth. They appreciate and enjoy family life more; in cases where there had been disharmony, they find more mutual tolerance. They see some benefit from their situations, dreadful as the situations are. They often realize that the positive aspects might not have manifested themselves without the cancer experience: *We all realize now that life is more than we thought. . . . Some of the material things we valued are now almost insignificant. We have come to be so much closer, so much more real, in so many ways.* Spouses often reflect on their new spiritual growth as well, often struggling painfully with challenges to previous belief systems. When spouses dogmatically hang on to their belief systems, they do not allow questions or doubts to be expressed, and little search for meaning occurs. Also, if spouses focus mostly on "why" questions—why the cancer occurred in the first place, or why they must be burdened with the current situation—then issues pertaining to the search for meaning are not addressed. They focus more on enduring the experience than on growing through it.

Adult children reflect on the impact of the experience on all aspects of their lives. They come face-to-face with mortality, with their own vulnerability, and with the implications for the future. For them, the search for meaning evolves from this impact. They reevaluate their attitudes, beliefs, and values in relation to themselves, their families of origin and procreation, and their life-styles. Some resolve to make significant changes. One young woman vowed to take better care of herself by starting an exercise program and working fewer hours so she could spend more time with her family and friends. Others, however, focus primarily on the past in the search for meaning and become preoccupied with trying to undo what cannot be undone. They put every other aspect of life on hold and try to restore what they perceive was neglected. Bob S., for example, regretted that he did not share what he considered a close relationship with his mother. During her youth, economic depression had forced her to quit school in the eighth grade. Bob, who was now pursuing doctoral studies, perceived that his uneducated mother had never understood his academic world. During the last months of his mother's life, Bob traveled 600 miles every 2 weeks to visit her in an attempt to capture the closeness he had always yearned for. Though she appreciated her son's visits, Mrs. S. found them exhausting. Her son talked constantly, and Bob made little progress toward his goal of making his mother understand him. Moreover, he neglected his own family in the process and felt lost, frustrated, and resentful. He found little meaning in the experience.

The search for meaning appears to form a bridge between the struggle thus far and a new perspective. When patients and family members find some meaning and are able to put the situation into perspective, they experience less turmoil. This does not mean that they are completely at peace all the time, but they enjoy a sense of having come to terms with what is happening. They see more clearly the need to live day to day and make the most of the time they have remaining. Because not all affected individuals are successful in their search for meaning, not all of them reach the point of living day to day.

Living Day to Day

When patients live day to day, they "make the most of it" and focus on the present. They plan only for the short term and accept events as they are rather than worrying about the future: *There's not much point in going over things in the past—not much point in projecting yourself into the future, either. It's the current time that counts.* However, not all patients manifest this attitude. Those who do not focus on living day to day tend to minimize the experience and focus on "getting through it." In the words of the accountant described earlier, *I'll get through this somehow. . . . I am not going to let it get me down. If things get worse, they get worse, but in the meantime, I have lots to do. This is not going to change anything.*

Many spouses, realizing that the time with their partners is limited, focus on spending as much quality time together as possible. On the other hand, spouses who have not redefined, who have not found meaning, and whose marital relationships are tense simply endure the time that is left. They know little enjoyment of any sort.

Living day to day presents challenges for adult children. They cannot, as spouses more often can, defer their obligations. Living day to day involves taking one day at a time, focusing less on the future, and slowing down to spend quality time. Adult children talk about doing this and about trying to "live one day to the next and worry about tomorrow, tomorrow." However, the reality of their own families' needs and of their jobs and other responsibilities makes living day to day most often an unattainable goal.

Preparing for Death

In preparing for death, patients, spouses, and adult children come to terms with the practical aspects of the patients' dying. For patients, this means taking care of legal matters and ensuring that family members are well informed and equipped to deal with the future. One man, for example, encouraged his wife to learn to drive so she could get around more easily after his death. Patients also attend to such mundane details as house repairs. For some, preparing for death involves reminiscing about the past and leaving legacies for the future. One woman spent her last weeks knitting afghans for her loved ones; another made a tremendous effort to attend church with her family on Father's Day, knowing that this would be the last time they would be in church together and wanting to leave a precious memory.

Spouses complete their preparations in partnership with the patients. They focus on fulfilling the patients' wishes, though this may be difficult: *I am worried sick about having him die at home, but this is what he wants. I am not about to say no. . . . It's his last wish, and I will manage somehow. The home care nurse said she would be here and to call at any time.* Some spouses allude to future times without their partners, but this is not a central aspect of their preparation. They focus on preparing for the death, indicating that they will focus on their own futures when the time comes. Believing that they will at some point be spiritually reunited with their spouses often makes their anticipation of the future easier.

Adult children's preparations for death involve a wider range of activities. They take pains to reassure the dying parent that they will ensure adequate care of the surviving parent. They also must consider how best to prepare their own children and involve them in the grandparent's death. Some spend considerable effort helping their own siblings prepare for the death. When they can remember good things about the past and feel as if they have done their best in preparing for their future without their parent, they feel satisfaction in what they are doing.

FADING AWAY AND FAMILY FUNCTIONING

Families experience the transition of fading away with greater or lesser difficulty, depending on the level of functioning within the family. The way a family interacts on the following eight dimensions contributes to its success or difficulty: integrating the past, dealing with feelings, solving problems, utilizing resources, considering others, portraying family identity, fulfilling roles, and tolerating differences. For each of these dimensions, there is a continuum of functionality; family interactions vary along each continuum. To offer appropriate support, the caregiver needs to note where a family is in level or degree of functioning. There is no value in judging that functioning as good or bad, positive or negative.

Previous experience with illness, loss, and adversity helps some families cope with the current situation. They acknowledge the pain of the past and incorporate what they have learned into subsequent experiences, including the present transition of fading away. One family had previously endured several crises, including escape from religious persecution. They looked back on that experience as a time of learning and talked about it matter-of-factly. In contrast, another family had experienced a similar situation but hung onto that past experience with anger and resentment, dwelling on the painful feelings associated with that event.

Some families express a full range of feelings, from happiness, through uncertainty and dread, to sorrow and sadness. When they express anger, it tends to spring from a specific event related to the patient's care. Anger is a part of the story, not a central theme. Family members acknowledge their vulnerabilities and their ambivalence about what is happening:

> We have good days and bad days. It's not always easy, but we
> have some wonderful times, especially remembering some of the
> silly things we have done along the way. Those moments are
> precious. . . . Though we know they won't last, we focus on them
> while we can.

Other families focus on a narrow range of feelings, with anger, hurt, and fear claiming the most intensity. They tend to avoid the feelings of turmoil associated with impending death: *Our life has always been a struggle . . . [doesn't] seem we can ever get much ahead. Work, work, work—and what do you get? This! We don't even want to think about it!*

Families with higher levels of functioning identify problems as they occur and exchange information openly. Members agree on possible solutions. They participate in problem solving and implement strategies creatively:

We couldn't figure out how to get Mom into that thing that helps put her into the bathtub. You should have seen us—all trying to put one arm in, and then the other, and then realizing we were doing it all wrong. We finally stopped, had a good laugh and a few tears as well, and then decided we needed to call the nurse to come and show us one more time.

In other families, members tend to agree on issues in the group setting but individually disagree with, or blame, others. They focus more on examining why problems occur and placing blame than on finding solutions: *We could never get any help from any of them at the hospital. They were "too busy" to call us back when we left a message. Never did get a call. . . . We can manage on our own, thank-you very much!*

Some families use a wide range of resources and are able to request help from friends and community agencies. Other families use few resources and appear reluctant to seek or accept help, preferring to "do it on their own." Within some families, members show concern for one another; in other families, members focus primarily on their own needs with little regard for others. In some families, members willingly share roles and responsibilities and tolerate differences among themselves:

It's not a lot of fun, you know . . . but Dad does the laundry, and I do the yard now. Grandma makes "meals on wheels" for us, and every once in a while, I call up Aunt Jane and ask her to make us a chocolate cake.

In other families, members do not adapt easily to new roles and tend not to tolerate discrepant views among themselves, or among friends and health care professionals:

Mom did all the cooking until she went to the hospital last week. Now we just eat there, or we get pizza or something on our way home. Becky [neighbor] offered to come in to clean up, but she doesn't know where anything goes, and Dad doesn't want her snooping around.

The family as a whole dies along with one of its members—the family will never be the same again. Every aspect of the family's life and functioning is undergoing change, a change imposed against its will. Inevitably, these changes create stress within the family. The way a family has functioned in the past profoundly influences the way it deals with the dying of one of its members. For some families, the stress of palliative care coupled with the decreased level of family functioning makes the situation almost overwhelming. To manage the transition of fading away, they require assistance, tempered with healthy doses of patience, tolerance, and encouragement—rather than criticism of their existing coping strategies. They need help with the immediate situation more than with planning for a future without the patient.

INTERVENTIONS DERIVED FROM THE STUDY: GUIDELINES FOR CAREGIVERS

By providing insight into the nature of the transition of fading away, study findings suggested approaches for helping patients and families through the experience. Guidelines for care derived from the direct accounts of patients, spouses, and children concerning the strategies they used to cope (Chekryn Reimer, Davies, & Martens, 1991; Davies et al., 1995).

Perhaps most important for professional caregivers to realize is that the transition is an unwelcome, resisted change to which families adapt over time. Disengagement from formerly held views, redefinition of the situation, and adoption of new orientations all occur over time, even though the time elapsed between realization of the inevitability of death and the advent of death may be relatively short. The challenge for practitioners centers on anticipating and preparing family members for each coming step without violating their need to relinquish old orientations and hopes at a pace they can handle. This challenge is complicated by the fact that redefinition may lag behind the receipt of information about the escalation of the illness.

While the patient redefines him- or herself, family members also redefine the patient, their relationships with one another, and interactions within the family; redefinitions may not always be congruent. Practitioners must therefore tailor interventions to the various family members' abilities to assimilate the changes. At the same time, however, the practitioner must support the family as a unit. One way to do so is to normalize the situation, reassuring family members that a range of responses and coping strategies is to be expected. By encouraging dialogue within the family about the changes they are experiencing, the caregiver can foster family members' redefinition of their situation. Because the process requires time, the caregiver must be prepared to listen repeatedly and to discuss often.

Study findings indicated that patients, spouses, and adult children share similar experiences. However, because their experiences also differ in significant ways, the caregiver needs to guard against treating each family member the same: Each requires individualized attention. Because each dimension of the experience is manifested differently for patients, spouses, and adult children, caregiver guidelines for these groups must also differ—not in major ways, but in subtle ways that reflect on the major concerns of each group. For example, to help a patient with redefining, the practitioner might provide opportunities to talk about the losses incurred because of illness, the enforced changes, the adaptations the patient has made, and the feelings associated with these. The practitioner might also focus on what the patient can still do and review alternatives when he or she can no longer function in habitual ways. The practitioner might reinforce those aspects of self that remain intact and acknowledge that roles and responsibilities may be expressed differently. When assisting a spouse with redefining, the practitioner might provide opportunities to talk about the marital relationship and to discuss ways for the spouse to reorganize priorities so as to be with and care for the patient to the degree he or she desires. To help adult children, the practitioner might discuss how they can face their own vulnerability by channeling concerns into positive steps for self-care.

Although each component of the fading away transition yields direction for practitioners, underlying all guidelines is the practitioner's own level of comfort with talking about issues related to death and dying. Practitioners must not force, pull, or push, but they must also not turn away because of their own insecurities. Moreover, practitioners must guard against the tendency to offer solutions, to "fix" families. What families need are practitioners who will listen and walk alongside them, not direct and try to change what they may not want changed.

Guidelines for helping families also must take into account levels of family functioning. For example, when a family is cohesive, offering an array of options is a good approach to assistance with problem solving. However, with some families, problem solving takes considerably more effort on the part of the family and the practitioner alike. The practitioner may have to seek information from more than one family member, as family members may perceive the situation differently and may not feel comfortable sharing their disparate views in a meeting with the family group. The practitioner cannot assume that information given to one member will be shared with the others, and he or she may have to repeat answers to the same questions from various family members. The challenge for practitioners is to use their knowledge, skills, patience, and compassion to help families manage the transition in a manner that supports family integrity.

CONCLUSION

The families' own descriptions of the transition of fading away tell us that our understanding of anticipatory mourning can be developed further through in-depth exploration with those who themselves are living with impending death. Some of the earliest studies in anticipatory mourning were either interviews with, or observations of, parents of terminally ill children (e.g., Bozeman, Orbach, & Sutherland, 1955). Using more quantitative measures than did these earlier studies, later studies attempted to link anticipatory mourning with bereavement outcome. In these studies, anticipatory mourning received various operational definitions, including the presence of a certain cluster of depressive symptoms on the part of the spouse during the patient's terminal illness (Clayton, Halikas, Maurice, & Robbins, 1973); the length of the terminal illness (Bornstein, Clayton, Halikas, Maurice, & Robbins, 1973; Clayton, Halikas, & Maurice, 1972); and advance warning of death, determined by whether the cause of death was from chronic illness or from acute illness (Ball, 1977; Gerber, Rusalem, Hannon, Battin, & Arkin, 1975). In some studies, advance warning of death is positively associated with good subsequent bereavement outcome (Ball, 1977; Lundin, 1984; Parkes & Weiss, 1983). Other studies report no association between advance warning and outcome following the loved one's death (Clayton et al., 1973; Gerber et al., 1975; Jacobs et al., 1986; Sanders, 1980). Attempting to be more specific about the experience of anticipatory mourning and not just to rely on the assumption of its existence on the sole basis of the length of terminal illness, Rando (1983) was the first to identify behaviors indicative of anticipatory mourning. She found that the more anticipatory mourning behaviors parents demonstrated before the death of a child, the less abnormal grief they had following the child's death.

Clinical and personal experience tell us that anticipatory mourning is a relevant phenomenon. The aforementioned studies, and others like them, tell us that the experience of family members prior to a loved one's death in some way influences their subsequent bereavement experience. But to understand this relationship better, we need a more comprehensive understanding of what it is like for a family to face terminal illness in a loved one. Though challenging to the researchers, the qualitative methods used in this project permitted a closer look at the core experiences of patients facing impending death and of their immediate family members. The knowledge thus gained enabled us to articulate more clearly the processes in which patients and families engage during the last phase of illness.

The findings of this project also emphasize the importance of going directly to those at the center of the phenomenon—the patients. To focus only on family members and exclude patients from discussions of anticipatory mourning denies the role of these central players and limits our understanding of the phenomenon.

Including patients along with spouses and adult children not only showed similarities in their ways of experiencing the transition but also revealed subtle differences among the three groups.

Moreover, descriptions of the transition of fading away show that individual experience cannot be separated from the experience of the family as a whole. A family is a complex, dynamic network of interdependent and interacting relationships; this complexity must be considered in discussions about anticipatory mourning. Writings on the subject suggest that the phenomenon is influenced by social and cultural variables, but the findings of this study begin to delineate exactly how that influence is manifested.

By appreciating the complexities involved in the transition of fading away and by following the approaches suggested by our study findings, practitioners can be better prepared to support families in more individualized ways. The findings provide specific guidelines for those wishing to help families who are anticipating the deaths of loved ones. Drawing on this understanding and on their own expertise, practitioners can help families cope with the sadness of the many losses associated with dying and find the satisfaction that comes from creating a new way of living until death occurs.

REFERENCES

Ball, J. F. (1977). Widows' grief: The impact of age and mode of death. *Omega,* *7*, 307–333.

Bornstein, P. E., Clayton, P., Halikas, J. A., Maurice, W. L., & Robbins, E. (1973). The depression of widowhood after thirteen months. *British Journal of Psychiatry, 122*, 561–566.

Bozeman, M. F., Orbach, C. E., & Sutherland, A. M. (1955). Psychological impact of cancer and its treatment: Part I. Adaptation of mothers to threatened loss of their children through leukemia. *Cancer, 8*(1), 1–19.

Chekryn Reimer, J., Davies, B., & Martens, N. (1991). The nurse's role in helping families through the transition of "fading away." *Cancer Nursing, 14*(60), 321–327.

Clayton, P. J., Halikas, J. A., & Maurice, W. L. (1972). The depression of widowhood. *British Journal of Psychiatry, 120*, 71–78.

Clayton, P. J., Halikas, J. A., Maurice, W. L., & Robbins, E. (1973). Anticipatory grief and widowhood. *British Journal of Psychiatry, 122*, 47–62.

Davies, B., Chekryn Reimer, J., Brown, P., & Martens, N. (1995). *Fading away: The experience of transition in families with terminal illness.* Amityville, NY: Baywood.

Gerber, I., Rusalem, R., Hannon, N., Battin, D., & Arkin, A. (1975). Anticipatory grief and aged widows and widowers. *Journal of Gerontology, 30*(2), 225–229.

Jacobs, S., Kasl, S., Ostfeld, A., Berkman, L., Kosten, T., & Charpentier, P. (1986). The measurement of grief: Bereaved versus non-bereaved. *The Hospice Journal, 2*(4), 21–36.

Lundin, T. (1984). Long-term outcome of bereavement. *British Journal of Psychiatry, 145*, 424–428.

Parkes, C. M., & Weiss, R. S. (1983). *Recovery from bereavement.* New York: Basic.

Rando, T. A. (1983). An investigation of grief and adaptation in parents whose children have died from cancer. *Journal of Pediatric Psychology, 8*(1), 3–20.

Rando, T. A. (1986). *Loss and anticipatory grief.* Lexington, MA: Lexington Books.

Sanders, C. M. (1980). A comparison of adult bereavement in the death of a spouse, child and parent. *Omega, 10*, 303–322.

CHAPTER 6

On the Experience of Traumatic Stress in Anticipatory and Postdeath Mourning

Therese A. Rando

I remember thinking how she looked shell-shocked, this woman who had been referred to me in the hope that I could help her contend with the dying of her sister from a rare type of cancer. With emotionless voice and expressionless eyes, she described how her life was centered around trying to meet the varied needs of her sister and her sister's family, while paying some attention, at least in passing, to those of her own husband and three children. While she certainly experienced a deep sense of sadness, she had been unable to cry; in fact, she had been unable to express any emotion for the last 5 months except for a muted combination of anxiety and depression that was manifested through restless sleeping, bouts of irritability, preoccupation with her sister's situation, a considerable blunting of all feelings and interests, a sense of being constantly "revved up" internally despite perpetual physical exhaustion, and an awareness of total powerlessness as she witnessed her sister's life slipping away. At this point, she was like an automaton strung out on amphetamines.

It's almost as though she is traumatized, I remember thinking. She really could benefit from some medication, but, after all, one is not supposed to offer medication to persons dealing with a loved one's dying. Unless very special circumstances exist, the prevailing thought is to avoid medication as much as possible in mourning. Anyway, she needed to feel all of her feelings about her sister's dying, didn't she? Still, it was unfortunate. In any other situation where a person exhibited the same symptomatology, I would make a referral for a medication evaluation and intervene to focus on

---
❋

To all the persons—dying, bereaved, and traumatized—who have informed my thoughts in this chapter

> *traumatic symptoms. I really wished this woman weren't here for*
> *anticipatory mourning. She truly needed potent intervention.*
>
> *It was then I asked myself, What's the difference? Why can't I*
> *treat her as I would anyone else with these symptoms? Why*
> *should she be penalized by not having access to interventions*
> *known to be helpful for her symptoms merely because of what*
> *brought them on? Why should grief and mourning prevent her*
> *from receiving what she needs? Why not enable her to be in the*
> *best possible shape to deal with this traumatic stress? Yes, that's*
> *what it is, I said, traumatic stress. If that's what it is, then I'll*
> *treat her for that.*

For too long, many caregivers of the dying, the bereaved, and their families have, relatively speaking, excluded the integration of general psychiatric and mental health principles and practices in their treatment of anticipatory and postdeath grief and mourning. In depathologizing and normalizing responses to loss, as caregivers we appear to have isolated ourselves somewhat. For example, many of us have not sufficiently incorporated appropriate clinical information about the "normal" psychiatric manifestations of even relatively uncomplicated bereavement (e.g., anxiety and depressive symptoms) or about issues of recovery, resolution, or timing. And we have often failed to appreciate the diverse treatment implications in cases of complicated mourning (e.g., the need for some mourners to be evaluated for antianxiety medication relatively soon after a traumatic death).

Recently, commentary has centered on how failure to respond appropriately to some of these issues (a) has been harmful to the mourners affected (e.g., the need is raised for biologically informed psychotherapy of depression [BIPD] for major depression associated with spousal bereavement; Zisook & Shuchter, 1996); (b) potentially could delay mourning indefinitely or retraumatize the mourner (e.g., when posttraumatic stress is insufficiently treated before the caregiver attempts to intervene in the acute grief of a traumatized mourner; Rando, 1993); (c) perpetuates clinical myths in thanatology (e.g., the strong but unsubstantiated view taken by many clinical thanatologists that antidepressant medication is inappropriate and ineffective in managing bereavement; Simpson, 1997); (d) contributes to myriad pitfalls in the field of thanatology today associated with complicated mourning (see Rando, 1992–1993); and (e) results in many bereaved individuals' coming to feel misunderstood by others and/or experiencing doubts about their own sanity (e.g., Exline, Dorrity, & Wortman, 1996).

The argument is constructed in this chapter that anticipatory mourning, as defined in chapter 2 of this volume, inherently constitutes an experience of significant traumatic stress for those who observe and attend to the dying of someone with whom they sustain a meaningful attachment. After introductory comments about the nature of trauma, traumatic stress, and the historical separation between the fields of thanatology and traumatology, the chapter provides discussion of the conceptual and empirical associations of acute grief with all forms of traumatic stress. This discussion includes, among other topics, investigations into the generic issues provoking anxiety in bereavement, the dynamics of separation anxiety, the role of anxiety in both uncomplicated and complicated mourning, and the phenomenon of traumatic bereavement. Next is a delineation of evidence supporting the notion of acute grief as a traumatic stress response, with particular attention being paid to nine areas of similarity between the two phenomena. An examination of traumatic stress in medical illness is next, leading finally into a discussion of how anticipatory mourning encompasses traumatic stress symptoms, correlates, and processes, and therefore constitutes a legitimate form of traumatic stress.

The reader will note that a great deal of material is presented on postdeath grief and mourning in this chapter. This information is given to capitalize on the greater familiarity most caregivers have with this experience in order to build a case for what happens during the period of anticipatory mourning. The examination of postdeath bereavement is employed as a vehicle to help the reader better discern the issues in anticipatory mourning, to ground the relevant concepts, and to utilize the larger clinical and empirical knowledge base relating to postdeath mourning.

As used here, *traumatic stress* (also termed *posttraumatic stress* if the stressor has ended) is a generic term incorporating the specific and nonspecific symptoms and disorders either associated with or consequent to the human experience of trauma. It may denote currently ongoing or past stress and specifically refers to (a) acute stress disorder (ASD), posttraumatic stress disorder (PTSD), generalized anxiety disorder, or any other anxiety disorder as delineated in the fourth edition of the American Psychiatric Association's *Diagnostic and Statistical Manual of Mental Disorders* (DSM-IV; American Psychiatric Association, 1994); (b) traumatic stress reactions that do not meet the criteria for full-blown PTSD/ASD or other anxiety disorders; and/or (c) posttraumatic personality change (see Krystal, 1984; Ochberg, 1988; Spitzer, 1990; Titchener, 1986). It must be noted that psychological trauma and traumatic stress in general are also directly associated with dissociative disorders, brief psychotic disorders, and borderline personality disorder (Herman & van der Kolk, 1987) and appear related, in varying degrees, to alcohol and other forms of substance abuse, various mood disorders, family dysfunctions, diverse patterns of compulsivity, some eating disorders, and numerous stress-related physical complaints and disorders (Everly, 1995).

The extreme complexity and subtlety of posttraumatic responses has been noted since Kardiner's (1941) postulation of a two-stage response to trauma (Brett, 1996). In this description, the first stage is the core traumatic neurosis (what is now termed PTSD); the second stage can have any diagnostic manifestation and is the personality's adaptation to and reorganization in the face of its compromised functioning caused by the traumatic neurosis. This is why long-term effects of trauma can be witnessed among a whole range of fundamental intrapsychic, relational, social, behavioral, and neurobiological functions (van der Kolk, 1996). Longstanding chronic victimization tends to bring, in addition to quintessential PTSD symptomatology, "complex PTSD," or symptoms indicative of "disorders of extreme stress not otherwise specified" (DESNOS). Incorporated only under the "Associated Features and Disorders" section of PTSD in the DSM-IV, although included within a diagnostic category of enduring personality changes after catastrophic experience that was created in the tenth revision of the *International Statistical Classification of Diseases and Related Health Problems* (ICD-10; World Health Organization, 1992), according to van der Kolk (1996), the five main categories of proposed symptom criteria include (a) alterations in regulating affective arousal (e.g., chronic affect dysregulation, difficulty modulating anger, self-destructive and suicidal behavior, difficulty modulating sexual involvement, and impulsive and risk-taking behaviors); (b) alterations in attention and consciousness (e.g., amnesia and dissociation); (c) somatization; (d) chronic characterological changes, including alterations in self-perception (e.g., chronic guilt and shame; feelings of self-blame, of ineffectiveness, and of being permanently damaged), alterations in perception of perpetrator (e.g., adopting distorted beliefs and idealizing the perpetrator), and alterations in relations with others (e.g., an inability to trust or maintain relationships with others, a tendency to be revictimized, and a tendency to victimize others); and (e) alterations in systems of meaning (e.g., despair and hopelessness, and loss of previously sustaining beliefs).

Suffice it to say, trauma is a central phenomenon that can precipitate a number of traumatic stress symptoms and disorders that may be viewed as "epiphenomena." In fact, the myriad symptoms associated with traumatic stress appear to be one of the reasons for the ongoing debate regarding whether to classify the formal PTSD disorder under the nosological categories of the currently existing anxiety or dissociative disorders, or whether to include it with others to create a new stress response category (see Brett, 1996).

TRAUMA, TRAUMATIC STRESS, THANATOLOGY, AND TRAUMATOLOGY

Stemming from the Greek word for wound, *trauma* is commonly defined as a disordered psychic or behavioral state resulting from mental or emotional stress or physical injury. It is also defined as an agent, force, or mechanism that causes trauma. Thus, in popular usage, the term refers to both *wounding cause* (or agent) and *wounded effect*.

A clinical definition for trauma is offered by Moore and Fine (1990) in *Psychoanalytic Terms and Concepts*. It is not necessary to espouse psychoanalytic theory or treatment to use the framework offered by their definition:

> The disruption or breakdown that occurs when the psychic apparatus is suddenly presented with stimuli, either from within or from without, that are too powerful to be dealt with or assimilated in the usual way. A postulated stimulus barrier or protective shield is breached, and the ego is overwhelmed and loses its mediating capacity. A state of helplessness results, ranging from total apathy and withdrawal to an emotional storm accompanied by disorganized behavior bordering on panic. Signs of autonomic dysfunction are frequently present. (p. 199)

Despite my personal preference for this particular perspective, alternative ways to conceptualize trauma exist, stemming from and relatively independent of the psychoanalytically based one just described. Alternatives are delineated among psychoanalytic contributions to a theory of traumatic stress discussed by Brett (1993). These include the traditional psychoanalytic model of symptom formation (Fenichel, 1945), Freud's stimulus-barrier definition of trauma (Freud, 1920/1955), and Freud's repetition and defense model of trauma based on the operation of the repetition compulsion (Freud, 1939/1953). Alternative post-Freudian psychoanalytic definitions of trauma have been proposed as well. As noted by Brett, these include definitions articulated by, among others, Krystal (1985) and Parson (1984). Another way to view trauma is to identify the specific models that partially explain the phenomenon of one major form of traumatic response—PTSD (Brown, 1996). These include dissociation (e.g., Janet, 1889); information processing (e.g., Horowitz, 1986); attribution (e.g., Janoff-Bulman, 1992); psychobiology (e.g., van der Kolk, 1987); structure/development (e.g., Parson, 1984); and context (e.g., Mollica, 1988).

Although they are conceptually, clinically, and often empirically associated, the fields of thanatology and traumatology traditionally have remained relatively independent. This is quite surprising given that in all trauma there is loss (at the very least, a loss of control) and in the majority of losses there are dimensions of trauma. Yet only fairly recently has a concerted effort been made to bridge these two areas formally and systematically. In 1996, *The Series in Trauma and Loss* was initiated by Charles Figley and Therese A. Rando to describe and promote the research, analysis, explication, and treatment of experiences spanning both trauma and loss. The initial book in this series, *Death and Trauma: The Traumatology of Grieving* (Figley, Bride, & Mazza, 1997) constituted the first examination devoted entirely to a conceptual and phenomenological exploration of traumatic bereavement and death-related PTSD.

Until now and still to a large extent, each field tends to address the issues it has customarily identified and treated. Consequently, after a death under traumatic circumstances, traumatologists generally focus on trauma mastery and thanatologists usually focus on accommodation of loss. Unfortunately, the traumatically bereaved individual requires assistance with both (Rando, 1997a). A few authors in each field have recognized this important reality—for example, Lindy, Green, Grace, and Titchener (1983), Eth and Pynoos (1985), and Nader (1997a) in traumatology and Raphael (1983), Redmond (1989), and Rando (1993) in thanatology. All too frequently, however, either there is clinical work on loss-related aspects but no trauma mastery, or traumatic effects are mastered but the loss is not accommodated in a healthy way. For proof that this "either-or" mentality has predominated, one need only peruse the literature of each field. In reviewing the literature in both grief counseling and trauma counseling, Figley (1997) concludes that "neither literature references the other in spite of the fact that bereavement so closely parallels traumatic stress reactions, and various forms of dysfunctional/abnormal bereavement parallel PTSD" (p. xxii). In examining the similarities, differences, and overlap of thanatology and traumatology, Green (1997) comes to identical conclusions. She observes that mental health researchers and clinicians have studied and treated both survivors of traumatic events such as war, disaster, and assault, and those experiencing bereavement through the death of a loved one, but that for a number of years their study has proceeded mostly in parallel despite the similarity in the features of these events.

ASSOCIATIONS OF ACUTE GRIEF WITH TRAUMATIC STRESS

A variety of associations exist between acute grief and mourning and traumatic stress. My position is that acute grief is located in the beginning parts of the six "R" processes of mourning but that mourning inherently involves a number of processes beyond acute grief in both time and scope (see Table 2.2 in this book; Rando, 1993). By definition, mourning includes acute grief. However, the focus in this chapter primarily is on acute grief *per se* in relation to traumatic stress, given that it is during this period of acute grief that the most dramatic traumatization is witnessed and where relatively more data have been collected. Aspects of trauma are also encountered in later mourning processes after acute grief subsides. Indeed, numerous traumatizing experiences and secondary losses occur in the latter "R" processes. Extrapolations of the information provided in this chapter should be made as appropriate to experiences later in mourning.

While certainly there are other manifestations of traumatic response, the following discussion is limited to anxiety and the anxiety disorders and their association with bereavement. The highlighting of anxiety is legitimized both by the prominence of anxiety symptoms in response to trauma and, notwithstanding cogent arguments for their inclusion in dissociative or stress response categories (see Brett, 1996), the DSM-IV's current grouping of formal traumatic stress disorders such as PTSD/ASD under the domain of anxiety disorders.

Traumatic Stress in Postdeath Acute Grief

The following discussion investigates traumatic stress in postdeath acute grief to capitalize on the greater familiarity most caregivers have with it, to ground the relevant concepts, and to serve as a source for extrapolation of clinical and empirical knowledge. The section first describes the roles anxiety has in uncomplicated acute grief, then focuses on the presence of anxiety in complicated mourning.

There are several reasons anxiety disorders are so frequent in bereavement. Two cardinal features of the anxiety disorders—symptoms of anxiety and avoidance behavior—are major symptoms of complicated mourning. As well, they represent an exacerbation of what often are typical responses to the separation brought about by death or loss. Finally, given Bowlby's (1980) discussion of why anxiety appears before depression after loss, anxiety disorders would reflect earlier, rather than later, problems in mourning. Because many mourners never get past the juncture where anxiety disorders would be found to predominate, one would expect to find more persons having complications associated with anxiety.

Anxiety in Uncomplicated Acute Grief

Along with the relative overfocus on affect over cognition in bereavement, the underappreciation of anxiety in acute grief—in terms of its importance, influence, prevalence, functions, and differing sources—has the dubious distinction of being one of the more potentially serious errors thanatologists and clinicians can make. In the education of and treatment focus undertaken by bereavement caregivers, far greater emphasis is placed on depression, a logical consequence of the loss of a loved one. What caregivers fail to comprehend is that anxiety is just as logical a consequence and is, in fact, more common in bereavement than depression, actually paving the way for it.

Anxiety has been defined as "the apprehension cued off by a threat to some value that the individual holds essential to his existence as a personality" (May, 1977, p. 205). That threat may be to physical existence, as in the threat of death or loss of a body part, or it may be a threat to psychological existence, as in meaninglessness, violations of one's sense of control, or loss of one's identity. The danger stimulating the threat can be either external (e.g., a tornado, a rapist) or internal (e.g., a disease process, overwhelming emotions). The affect of anxiety has both a psychological side (including a sense of imminent danger and apprehensive anticipation, along with a particularly unpleasant feeling state) and a somatic and behavioral side (operationalized by motor tension, autonomic hyperactivity, and vigilance and scanning). In contrast to fear, in which apprehension is directed toward a real, identified threat, anxiety is apprehension occurring in the absence of a specific danger.

As noted earlier, an intimate relationship exists between anxiety and trauma. Whenever an external or internal event presents a person with stimuli too powerful to be dealt with or assimilated in the usual way, psychic trauma occurs. Sudden, intense anxiety increases to the point that it exceeds the person's ability to manage and defend against, causing him or her to be overwhelmed and unable to cope and bringing a loss of control, helplessness, and other flooding affects (e.g., shock, horror, vulnerability) that debilitate the person's adaptive capacities, violate the assumptive world, and exacerbate already present anxiety.

Generic issues provoking anxiety in mourning

Anxiety concretizes itself around a number of generic issues in mourning. Building upon Rando (1991), these generic issues and other concerns on the part of the mourner that explain the frequent presence of anxiety in bereavement fall into four main categories: (a) unknown or inaccurate information, (b) one's reactions to the experience, (c) one's concerns about being changed and different from before, and (d) certain sequelae of bereavement.

Anxiety arising from unknown or inaccurate information is stimulated by the following:

- Facing the unknown, unfamiliar, and uncertain (i.e., the new world without the loved one and one's own difficulty dealing with this new world)

- Struggling with the absence of role models, social guidelines, and realistic information about how to act, think, and feel as a mourner

- Suffering imposed by unrealistic standards or expectations that may be maintained for oneself as a mourner or because of inaccurate information about grief and mourning

Anxiety arising from one's reactions to the experience involves these experiences:

- Responding to the unsettling experiences of acute grief and one's perceptions of oneself and one's actions in it, especially if one perceives these as being significantly different from before

- Being concerned about losing one's mind and control, being unable to adapt, and violating the expectations one has had for grief and mourning

- Coping with concerns about being able to survive—psychologically, behaviorally, socially, physically, financially—without the loved one and fear of what his or her absence will mean in one's life

- Being frightened by the sense of vulnerability caused by the loss

- Experiencing the reactions to the shattering of basic assumptions about life and one's invulnerability in it, particularly the world's being benevolent and meaningful, and the self's being worthy (Janoff-Bulman, 1992)

- Reacting to the utilization of defenses to cope with the loss and its ensuing grief and mourning, which may be foreign or more distressing or numerous than usual

Concerns about one's being changed and different from before include the following:

- Recognizing that one's usual coping patterns and problem-solving strategies cannot eliminate the problem

- Encountering the altered sense of self arising from the loss of the loved one and the changes necessary adapt to it

- Coping with identity confusion, and its ensuing anxiety and insecurity, after the loss of a beloved who had assisted one to know and experience oneself as the person one has come to know oneself to be

Finally, the following sequelae of bereavement can contribute to anxiety:

- Coping with separation from a beloved individual to whom one was integrally connected and experiencing panic about being able to deal with separation pain or its anxiety
- Contending with the insecurity inherent in psychosocial transitions
- Facing the panic of each new day when the reality of the loss reasserts itself and poses questions about the mourner's ability to respond to psychosocial and physical survival needs
- Managing labile emotions that sustain a terrifying degree of intensity and uncontrollability while simultaneously withstanding feelings of unreality, confusion, and incomprehensibility
- Attempting to meet the extraordinarily painful requirements of the six "R" processes of mourning (see Table 2.2 in this volume; Rando, 1993), which one often initially resists
- Coping with the feelings of helplessness, vulnerability, insecurity, victimization, and shattered assumptive world that result from major loss
- Experiencing intrusive thoughts, images, emotional and physical feelings, impulses, and behaviors
- Confronting and managing unacceptable, unexpressed, uncomfortable, or conflictual affects, thoughts, behaviors, impulses, wishes, needs, or images associated with the deceased; the self; the mutual relationship; the illness, dying, and/or death; or other foci of mourning
- Experiencing the "fight or flight" biological response (Cannon, 1927) elicited in the situation without acting on either alternative
- Reacting to the overwhelming of the ego brought about by a major loss's inherent threat to one's stability; dealing with the anxiety relating to the flooding of the psyche with stimuli that disorganize ego functions and create intrapsychic and external disorganization
- Being unable to make sense of the loss, given its basic incomprehensibility, unreality, and the violations of the assumptive world that it stimulates

- Bearing the stress of the cognitive dissonance caused by the loss of the loved one and the ensuing violations of the assumptive world inherent in that death
- Worrying about how other loved ones are coping now and will cope in the future with the death and its sequelae
- Feeling terror at the thought of losing other close loved ones
- Experiencing distress associated with memories of earlier losses, separations, and traumas
- Recognizing existential and personal limitations to power and control over one's life and that of one's loved ones
- Sustaining numerous physical and psychosocial secondary losses consequent to the death
- Repeatedly and painfully learning in countless ways the reality of the death and its implications through the frustration of one's desires to be reunited with the deceased loved one
- Being anxious that the attempts early in mourning to find and recover the lost loved one will not be successful (Bowlby, 1980)
- Experiencing death or annihilation anxiety
- Experiencing heightened emotional and physiological arousal
- Feeling survivor guilt
- Contemplating thoughts of one's own death that have been prompted by the death of the loved one

In addition, numerous aspects of the dying or death may pose certain idiosyncratic threats that generate anxiety in the mourner. For instance, the loved one may have died from cancer, and the mourner has always had a terrifying fear of this type of death.

Separation anxiety

Separation anxiety assumes a prominent position in the works of two individuals often cited in thanatology: John Bowlby and Colin Murray Parkes. The ethological grounding of their theories gives added significance to the critical functions and survival value of separation anxiety, upon which much more of the rest of the mourning experience depends (see, for example, Bowlby, 1973, 1980; Parkes, 1987).

Briefly, Bowlby (1980) advances Freud's (1926/1959) view about anxiety: When a loved one is believed to be temporarily absent, the response is one of anxiety. When the loved one appears to be permanently absent, the response is one of pain and mourning. Therefore, before a loss is truly recognized as final, the mourner is anxious and initiates a series of attempts to find and recover the lost person (e.g., crying, searching, pining). After repeatedly frustrated attempts to reunite with the deceased have convinced the mourner that the person is not recoverable, hope is abandoned. Bowlby paraphrases Shand (1920) when he notes how fear presupposes hope; it is only when one is striving and hoping for better things that one is anxious about failing to obtain them. With no hope, there is nothing to fear. Because there is nothing to hope for, anxiety dissipates and the depression and despair of mourning ensue. Other sources of anxiety exist in the mourning experience (e.g., the threat of the new world or the confrontation with freedom and responsibility), but these are secondary to the mourning experience and are not the same as separation anxiety, which must be relinquished before mourning can progress. The continuation of searching attempts revealed in the restlessness and agitation typical of complicated mourning indicates that a mourner has not truly acknowledged and internalized the reality of the loss.

It only is when acknowledgment leads to the depression, despair, and disorganization of mourning that old patterns break down. This is a prerequisite for the revision of the out-of-date patterns and for the development of new ones. In this regard, then, anxiety has a pivotal role in catalyzing searching for the deceased. The failure of this search brings about depression, despair, and disorganization, which ultimately propel the mourner into the relinquishment and change necessary to accommodate the loss in a healthy fashion. This is one reason psychosocial reorganization (the one of the seven generic operations in anticipatory mourning that incorporates the cognitive processing necessary to learn the reality of loss and to prompt adaptive readjustment to it) is such a pivotal aspect of healthy anticipatory mourning. (See chapter 2 under the heading "Generic Operations" for more on this.)

For his part, Parkes (1987) elucidates the problem of misunderstanding the role of anxiety in bereavement and clarifies its reality:

> When asked how to classify a bereavement reaction, most psychiatrists say "reactive depression," and certainly depression is a prominent feature. Yet more prominent is a special kind of anxiety, separation anxiety. . . . In fact, I think it fair to say that the pining or yearning that constitutes separation anxiety is the characteristic feature of the pang of grief. If grief is to be forced into the Procrustean bed of traditional psychiatric diagnosis, therefore, it should probably become a subgroup of the anxiety states. (p. 26)

Parkes also observes that, in terms of increased use of the health care system, the bereaved seek treatment more frequently for anxiety than for organic physical disease.

Further confirmation of the crucial aspect of separation anxiety is provided by Jacobs (1993). He identifies the cardinal experience of what he terms "normal grief" to be separation distress (a synonym for separation anxiety), which is the anxiety, emotional pain, and suffering experienced when one's ongoing attachment to a loved one is ruptured by death. While he posits that in normal grief three other dimensions are also present (the mourning-depressive, traumatic, and recovery dimensions), Jacobs identifies separation anxiety as the most specific emotional reaction to loss, found in both child and adult bereavement. Pangs, searching, protest, and anxious mood are its hallmarks, and they are evidenced in particular by yearning, preoccupation with the deceased, sighing, crying, a perceptual set for the deceased (including illusions, dreams, and hallucinations), searching, anger, protest, anxiety/arousal, and panic.

It is important to note here the unequivocal association that separation anxiety, as a particular type of anxiety, sustains with complicated mourning:

> These two features, intense separation anxiety and strong but only partially successful attempts to avoid grieving, were evident in all the forms of atypical grief I have come across. The degree of disbelief and avoidance varied considerably, but whatever its degree *there was always an impression that the underlying separation anxiety was severe.* (Parkes, 1987, p. 129, emphasis added)

Therefore, while separation anxiety is a normal component in uncomplicated acute grief, it is often a catalyst for the evolution to complicated mourning.

Empirical findings about anxiety

The role of anxiety in uncomplicated acute grief, as well as in more complicated outcomes, has been supported not only by clinical observation but also by empirical findings. There are perhaps little more interesting and challenging data for those relatively overfocused on the role of depression in loss than those provided by Shuchter, Zisook, Kirkorowicz, and Risch (1986). Their investigation found that biological indices of depression (as measured by dexamethasone suppression tests) were related more to levels of anxiety than to levels of depression, suggesting that

> the pathophysiology of at least some grief-related "depressions" may be more related to separation anxiety than . . . to primary affective disorder. . . . It may be that separation anxiety is a driving force which leads to both

anxiety and depressive symptoms and, in some cases, a
full-blown depressive disorder following bereavement.
(pp. 880–881)

Thus, physiological data confirm the importance of anxiety in acute
grief and support clinical data long supplied by Bowlby and Parkes,
among others. It appears that anxiety in reaction to the separation
initiates the specific processes that eventually culminate in the
depressive symptomatology of uncomplicated bereavement.

More recent research continues to document the relevance of
anxiety during bereavement. A number of studies of mid- to late-life
widowed individuals, conducted by Holly Prigerson and her colleagues, have yielded important information about the role of anxiety in both uncomplicated and complicated mourning (Prigerson et
al., 1995; Prigerson, Bierhals et al., 1996; Prigerson, Shear et al.,
1996; Prigerson et al., 1997). Specifically, Prigerson and her associates found that anxiety is distinct from symptoms of depression and
of grief. Additionally, they found that each factor of anxiety, depression, and grief was differentially affected by treatment, with anxiety
and depression declining more dramatically than grief among subjects treated with a tricyclic antidepressant as opposed to those
untreated. Each of the three factors also differentially predicted subsequent symptomatology. In the case of anxiety, Prigerson and colleagues discovered that baseline anxiety predicted subsequent
depression and anxiety later on in the bereavement.

Prigerson and her research group caution against overlooking
the importance of anxiety or assuming that it merely constitutes a
different aspect of depression:

If the symptoms of anxiety are believed to be normal
manifestations of grief or are not considered to be elements
of a disorder in their own right (e.g., considered aspects of
depression), then they may not receive the professional
attention from which they have been shown to benefit.
(Prigerson, Shear et al., 1996, p. 11)

Other research reveals that the anxiety of mourning can eventuate into a full-blown anxiety disorder. When this occurs, by definition the situation is no longer uncomplicated. Such outcomes are
more prevalent than most caregivers, with their overfocus upon
depression, realize. Jacobs, Hansen, Kasl, Ostfeld, Berkman, and
Kim (1990) reported the first systematic study of anxiety disorders
during bereavement. A total of 44% of their sample reported an
episode of anxiety disorder at some time during the first year—a
percentage that was significantly higher than the normal prevalence

rate for the community from which the sample was drawn. Also in this study, Jacobs et al. demonstrated empirically what had been well known clinically: considerable overlap of and interrelationship between the anxiety disorders and depressive syndromes in bereavement exists. Of those who had an anxiety disorder, 55.6% reported a concomitant major depression. This figure is significantly higher than the rate of depression among those without anxiety. All of those with a generalized anxiety disorder met the criteria for a major depression; 60% of those with panic disorder met those criteria. The 55.6% figure contrasts with a figure of 82.5% for those with a major depression who also reported an anxiety disorder. In these individuals, there was most often a generalized anxiety disorder and less frequently another anxiety disorder.

Jacobs and Kim (1990), in reviewing the literature, concluded that in the first year of bereavement the estimated rate for complications from generalized anxiety disorder is 39% and that for panic disorder it is 14%. This contrasts with estimated rates of 4 to 34% for what they construe as "pathologic grief" and 17 to 27% for unremitting depression. These figures document the relatively greater frequency of anxiety over depression, despite the latter's greater isomorphy with complicated mourning and the popular notion of depression's greater prevalence in bereavement.

Complicated Mourning and Anxiety

Anxiety and avoidance behavior are symptomatic of anxiety disorders and complicated mourning as well as of uncomplicated acute grief. As conceptualized by Rando (1993), complicated mourning is present whenever, given the amount of time since the death, there is some compromise, failure, or distortion of one or more of the six "R" processes of mourning (see Table 2.2 in this volume). Complicated mourning can be manifested in any one or combination of four forms: (a) complicated mourning symptoms; (b) one or more of seven complicated mourning syndromes, which include three syndromes with problems in expression (absent mourning, delayed mourning, and inhibited mourning), three syndromes with skewed aspects (distorted mourning of the extremely angry or guilty types, conflicted mourning, and unanticipated mourning), and one syndrome with a problem of closure (chronic mourning); (c) a diagnosable mental or physical disorder; and (d) death.

There are seven high-risk factors that can predispose anyone to complicated mourning. Four factors are associated with the specific death. They include (a) a sudden and unanticipated death, especially when it is traumatic, violent, mutilating, or random; (b) death from an overly lengthy illness; (c) death of a child; and (d) death associated with the mourner's perception of preventability. Three high-risk factors are associated with antecedent and subsequent variables. They are (a) a premorbid relationship with the deceased that is markedly angry or ambivalent, or markedly dependent; (b) the mourner's prior or concurrent unaccommodated losses or stresses, or prior or concurrent mental health problems; and (c) the mourner's perception of lack of support.

Anxiety is known to be associated with complicated mourning both as a personality trait and as a determinant in the predispositions to make anxious and ambivalent attachments, engage in compulsive caregiving, or assert independence of affectional ties, all of which predispose one to complicated mourning (Bowlby, 1980). As a generic ingredient in the fear and reluctance to confront the implications of the loss or pain of mourning, ambivalence or dependence in the premorbid relationship, or change in the relationship with the deceased, anxiety contributes to all of the symptoms and syndromes of complicated mourning. In addition, it interferes with the successful completion of the six "R" processes of mourning.

Although anxiety contributes in part to all types of complications in mourning, it plays the most prominent role in three specific complicated mourning syndromes. Specifically, anxiety is perceived as a chief cause of chronic mourning via its promotion of a disorder of attachment, hypothesized by Parkes and Weiss (1983) as fostering an emotional dependency that leaves the mourner ill-equipped to function without the deceased and contributes to the mourner's refusal to move forward. In distorted mourning of the extremely angry type (Raphael, 1983), anxiety is a chief and fueling feature of the response. Often such anxiety is manifested after the loss of an extremely dependent relationship through the mourner's perception of threatened survival and inordinate resurrection of the insecurity of earlier losses. Finally, in the unanticipated mourning syndrome (Parkes & Weiss, 1983), anxiety is not the chief cause, but rather the chief result. The lack of preparation for the loss stuns the mourner and illustrates powerlessness to protect oneself and one's loved ones. Thus, profound insecurity is a major consequence, underscoring impaired functioning following the loss.

Recently, two well-respected groups have proposed empirically generated diagnostic criteria for complicated mourning; these criteria prominently feature symptoms of anxiety. One group presented criteria for Complicated Grief Disorder (Horowitz, Siegel, Holen, Bonanno, Milbraith, & Stinson, 1997), the other for Traumatic Grief (Prigerson et al., 1998). While differing in some respects, these two sets of criteria have considerable consistency, suggesting independent validation of each other (Jacobs, 1999). Each of the sets needs additional study and refinement. Nevertheless, they represent important actions taken to fill in serious gaps in psychiatric nosology regarding grief and mourning. In these efforts, anxiety and correlates of traumatic stress are clinically conceptualized and empirically validated as major and pivotal elements of complicated response to the death of a loved one.

Formal anxiety disorders have not been discussed much in the thanatological literature as an outcome of loss; most emphasis has been given to depression. Anxiety states in general, and phobias specifically, are mentioned in passing by Raphael (1983) in a listing of psychiatric conditions described as being outcomes following bereavement. Similarly, Raphael mentions panic, anxiety states, and agoraphobia as being some of the neurotic conditions identified by Jennings and France (1979) for which bereavement therapy has been used. Both Anderson (1949) and Lehrman (1956) mention anxiety states as a form in which complicated mourning presents itself, with Anderson finding that, in his patients with morbid grief, 59% had clinical patterns assuming anxiety states and 7% had obsessional tension states.

Despite this relative lack of recognition in the literature, virtually all forms of anxiety disorder appear to have some association with complicated mourning. The reader is referred to Rando (1993; chapter 5) for an analysis of the specific anxiety disorders as they are related to complicated mourning.

Traumatic bereavement: The intersection of loss and trauma

One variation of complicated mourning is evidenced in cases of traumatic bereavement. The purpose here is to introduce concepts pertinent to the unique intersection of loss and trauma in traumatic bereavement and to address how their combination creates a situation distinctly different from what would be seen by merely adding them together. In this section, there is an examination of the various interrelationships between loss and trauma, and between the ensuing processes of grief and traumatic stress after a traumatic event.

There are six high-risk factors that have the potential to make any death circumstance traumatic for the mourner. Alone or in combination, each of these factors generates posttraumatic stress above and beyond that found in uncomplicated acute grief. Adapted from Rando (1994), these six factors are (a) suddenness and lack of anticipation; (b) violence, mutilation, and destruction; (c) preventability and/or randomness; (d) loss of a child; (e) multiple death; and (f) the mourner's personal encounter with death secondary to either a significant threat to survival or a massive and/or shocking confrontation with the death and mutilation of others.

The work of two clinicians—Robert Pynoos and Kathleen Nader—is germane to the discussion of loss and trauma. Their research and clinically oriented publications have been among the most informative regarding the intersection of grief and trauma (e.g., Eth & Pynoos, 1985; Nader, 1997a, 1997b; Nader, Pynoos, Fairbanks, & Frederick, 1990; Pynoos, Frederick et al., 1987; Pynoos & Nader, 1990, 1993; Pynoos, Nader, Frederick, Gonda, & Stuber, 1987). These observers have repeatedly asserted that an individual's efforts at relieving traumatic anxiety typically take psychological priority over mourning because posttraumatic stress reactions focus the mind on the circumstances of the death and interfere with ego resources and with allotting full adaptational attention to the loss and subsequent life changes. Pynoos and Nader's studies involving children's responses to exposure to violence and traumatic death provide continued evidence of the following interrelationships between loss/grief and trauma/traumatic stress for both children and adults:

1. Two distinct processes (or two separate dimensions of emotional distress) operate after violent or traumatic loss experiences, with the amount of grief being related to the closeness of the survivor's relationship to the deceased and the severity of posttraumatic stress being related to the extent of the survivor's exposure to life threat or witnessing injury or death.

2. There are differential effects of grief and of the encounter with death (i.e., trauma), and posttrauma intervention must include screening and specialized interventions for each of the two reactions and their interplay.

3. When there is a traumatic death, the individual must contend with symptoms of grief, of trauma, and of an amalgam of the two; thus, there is both an independence of and an interaction between grief and trauma reactions.

4. Treatment for grief alone following a traumatic death, without attention to trauma, can be ineffective and even harmful.

5. The interaction of grief and trauma may intensify and complicate reactions in each realm and/or create problems associated with the combination of the two.

Nader (1997a) provides a very useful schematic to illustrate the interaction of grief and trauma as just identified (see Figure 6.1). Particularly valuable is her identification of the overlapping symptoms. These include anxiety, agitation, helplessness, emotional pain, loss of energy, depression, and guilt. Also, Nader articulates four ways in which the combination of grief and trauma may affect the bereavement process: (a) The interplay of grief and trauma may intensify the symptoms common to both; (b) Thoughts of the deceased may lead to traumatic recollections; (c) Traumatic aspects of the death may hinder or complicate issues of bereavement, such as grief dream work, relationship with the deceased, issues of identification, and processing of anger and rage; and (d) A sense of post-traumatic estrangement or aloneness may interfere with healing social interactions.

When loss and trauma collide, they create an experience—traumatic bereavement—that is more than merely the sum of its parts. Thus, ideally the caregiver brings not only experience in treating grief and in treating trauma to the traumatized mourner. He or she also brings familiarity with the interaction or overlapping of the two processes.

A newly proposed diagnostic category: Traumatic grief

As noted previously, a new diagnostic entity has recently been proposed: traumatic grief (Jacobs, 1999; Prigerson et al., 1998). In this disorder the use of "traumatic" in the name refers not to etiology but describes the phenomenological experience of the mourner. The nidus of the disorder for an individual is a "personally devastating" traumatic separation, one which can originate from (a) developmental issues (i.e., the quality of the relationship with the deceased or other personal predispositions of the mourner); (b) environmental circumstances (i.e., the objectively traumatic circumstances of the death—sudden, violent, horrific, etc.); and/or (c) a combination of both developmental issues and environmental circumstances (Jacobs, 1999). The dual underlying dimensions of the disorder involve two distinct domains of distress: separation anxiety and traumatic stress symptomatology.

Rationale for Acute Grief as a Traumatic Stress Reaction

Elsewhere I have asserted that acute grief—whether uncomplicated or complicated—is a form of posttraumatic stress reaction (Rando, 1993, 1997a, 1997b). Here that argument is bolstered by other thanatologists and traumatologists, as well as by a clinical examination of the various levels of association.

Interestingly, in writings since the institution of the DSM-IV, in which the diagnosis was first introduced, ASD has not been cited frequently in the literature despite its pertinence. The traumatic stress diagnostic category most considered has been PTSD. The ASD diagnosis appears to be quite useful, not only in cases where the diagnosis of PTSD has been excluded because symptoms have not persisted beyond a 1-month minimum (ASD requires only a 2-day minimum), but also in situations where the traumatic stress has yet

FIGURE 6.1

Interaction of Grief and Trauma

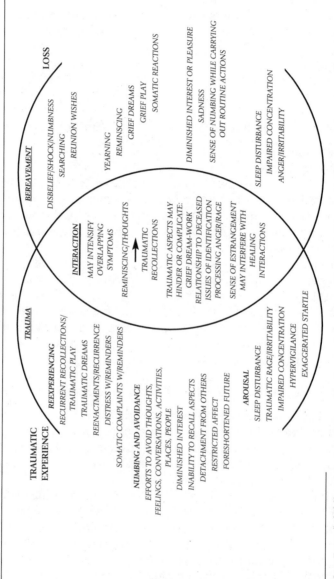

Note. From "Childhood Traumatic Loss: The Interaction of Trauma and Grief" by K. Nader. In *Death and Trauma: The Traumatology of Grieving* (p. 19), edited by C. Figley, B. Bride, and N. Mazza, 1997a, Washington, DC: Taylor & Francis. Reprinted by permission.

to abate (e.g., during a terminal illness). In addressing some of the gaps left by PTSD, the diagnosis of ASD may be particularly informative for those working with anticipatory mourners.

Although full-blown PTSD certainly is the most dramatic and well-known example of traumatic stress symptomatology, even in cases of ASD or where DSM-IV diagnostic criteria for either disorder are not fully met, a mourner can experience traumatization, heightened distress, complication of mourning, the need for interventions designed to address traumatic stress, and numerous other trauma-related sequelae and demands. Consequently, it is not solely when symptoms meet criteria for these disorders that considerations relevant to trauma must be raised. The issue is less the number of traumatic stress symptoms per se than it is the impact of traumatic stress upon the affected person's mourning and subsequent treatment needs. As Everly (1995) observes, the study of psychological trauma is far more than just the study of PTSD (and to this must be added ASD).

There are nine arguments for acute grief and traumatic stress's being variations on a theme or, to put it another way, for acute grief being a form of traumatic stress reaction. Grief and traumatic stress are similar in the following ways:

1. Inherent involvement with both loss and trauma

2. Elemental association with anxiety

3. Qualification as a personal disaster (Raphael, 1981)

4. Suitability of classification under a proposed stress response category

5. Common fundamental issues

6. Manifest symptomatology and associated features

7. Alternating modes of regulation of exposure to distressing material

8. Presentation of two tasks to affected individuals

9. Ultimate treatment requirements for working through of the experience via cognitive completion with affective release

Inherent involvement with both loss and trauma

As noted earlier, there is always loss in trauma. In any definition of trauma, there is a loss of the status quo, an impingement of negative stimuli that robs at least some of the individual's well-being. In the lay definition, the "disordered" state implies the loss of some preexisting order. And certainly "stress" or "injury" suggests a relative loss of comfort or integrity. Much loss is implicit in Moore and

Fine's (1990) psychoanalytic definition in the stimuli that exceed the person's ability to deal with or assimilate as usual (i.e., losses of homeostasis, control, and typical problem-solving efficacy) and breach the stimulus barrier and cause the ego to be overwhelmed (i.e., loss of integrity and the ego's ability to mediate), resulting in helplessness (i.e., loss of power to determine what happens) and frequent autonomic dysfunction (i.e., loss of usual internal autonomic functioning).

Conversely, some dimensions of trauma are evident in most major losses. The following discussion bolsters this claim. At the outset, however, two points must be made. First, it makes sense clinically that if death robs an individual of a loved one whose continued existence is an integral part of that person's phenomenological, psychosocial, behavioral, physical, and assumptive worlds, some elements of traumatization are to be expected secondary to the severing of such a meaningful attachment and consequent to the number and extent of assumptive world violations and other secondary losses. Second, if a loss is considered major from the mourner's idiosyncratic or phenomenological perspective, then the odds are great that elements of traumatic stress will be present and experienced within the myriad responses to that loss. Circumstances of death can exist in which few or no objective situational characteristics of trauma are found, but if the loss has enough significance to the person, it can be expected to generate some traumatic stress reactions. For instance, this is why, no matter how peaceful or anticipated the actual death, the loss of a child is typically considered a traumatic death for the surviving bereaved parents. The clinical and empirical evidence document that the death of a child is the most difficult and problematic loss with which one may contend, and a loss that precipitates particularly severe, complicated, and long-lasting mourning, with unparalleled symptom fluctuations over time (Rando, 1986).

Another confirmation of the existence of trauma in loss is Jacobs' (1993) identification of traumatic distress as one of the four dimensions of what he terms "normal grief." He asserts that this dimension adds avoidant and intrusive components to the experience as manifested in such symptoms and phenomena as numbness, disbelief, horrific images, and nightmares.

In a study significant because it involved a systematic search for traumatic symptoms in a sample of bereaved individuals who were not selected because of a presumed traumatic loss, Schut, de Keijser, van den Bout, and Dijhuis (1991) found impressive levels of traumatic stress symptomatology. Studying 128 bereaved spouses whose family members had died from multiple causes, the authors found evidence of intrusive and avoidant traumatic symptoms in 60 to

80% of the sample (the rate depending upon when the participants were observed at four points in time over the first 25 months of bereavement). PTSD was observed in 20 to 31%, with 9% meeting the criteria for PTSD on all four assessments.

In the Leiden Bereavement Study (Cleiren, 1993), a controlled longitudinal study of 309 family members of individuals who had died from suicide or traffic accident (classified as "unnatural" deaths) or long-term illness, posttraumatic stress was one of the indicators of functioning investigated. As measured on a translated version of the Impact of Event Scale (IES; Horowitz, Wilner, & Alvarez, 1979), both intrusion and avoidance were found to be common among the bereaved. They seemed to be closely related, with one at times following as a reaction to the other. Regardless of mode of death, bereaved individuals showed virtually the same level of intrusions, with the impact of the shock appearing to be equal for mourners after a long-term illness and for an unnatural death by suicide or traffic accident. At 4 months, the avoidance component of the stress response initially was significantly higher for those bereaved from an unnatural death, but the difference disappeared 14 months after the loss.

Other important findings from the Leiden study about the experience of those whose loved ones died from a long-term illness, as contrasted with bereavement after suicide and traffic accident, include the following:

- Preoccupation with the search for a picture of what has happened is only somewhat less important in this group than among the bereaved after an unnatural death.

- The subject of rumination has more to do with the cause of the illness than with the cause of death itself. This suggests a search for meaning in the death virtually as strong as among the unnatural death groups.

- Intensity of reactions to the loss in general do not differ to a great extent from that seen after unnatural modes of death.

- There is as much trouble with detachment from the deceased as with the suicide-bereaved.

- Although slightly less avoidance (which is part of traumatic stress measures) is evidenced at 4 months, the posttraumatic stress reactions at 14 months are at the same level as those for the unnatural death groups. At both points after the loss, the posttraumatic stress response seems to occur as frequently as in the unnatural modes of death.

- Psychological and physical health is generally not systematically different from that connected with other modes of death. Initially, depression is somewhat lower, but at 14 months there appears to be an increase in the proportion of depressed spouses and parents in contrast to the other modes of death.

• The mean level of need for emotional support is moderate and slightly lower than for the unnatural modes of death. Social integration and social activities are at roughly the same level, however.

• Many of those in the long-term illness group felt very relieved after the loss. The reasons seem unambiguous—the death means an end to worry and fear about what is going to happen. The deceased is perceived as finally freed from his or her suffering, and mourners are released from burdensome, even sometimes 24-hour-a-day care.

In brief, these findings suggest that anticipatory mourning encompasses significant traumatic stress. Specifically, those bereaved from a loved one's terminal illness experience just as much traumatic stress as those bereaved from deaths traditionally perceived to impact more traumatically upon the survivors (e.g., unexpected and/or violent deaths). Cleiren (1993) concludes:

> Maybe the intense contact that often developed during the illness makes the contrast with the subsequent absence of the deceased even sharper, thus constituting a relatively great shock. . . . Results indicate that a natural, and to some extent expected, loss such as *death after a long-term illness must not be underestimated in its traumatic impact.* (pp. 200–202, emphasis added)

Elemental association with anxiety

Very simply, both acute grief and traumatic stress inherently assume strong, essential, and basic association with anxiety. Earlier sections of this chapter document the generic issues that promote anxiety in mourning, the separation anxiety that underpins acute grief, and the empirically validated presence of anxiety in acute grief. Plainly, anxiety is a core element of acute grief. In terms of traumatic stress, the current DSM-IV classifies formal disorders of traumatic stress under the anxiety disorders. Although there has been debate in the field of traumatology over precisely where to place PTSD/ASD in the DSM classification (under the anxiety disorders, dissociative disorders, or a new stress response category; see Brett 1996), little if any disagreement exists that anxiety is a cardinal element. As noted previously, reactions indicative of traumatic stress may include symptoms and disorders not exclusively within the domain of anxiety. However, these reactions are still in response to the anxiety occurring at the time of the traumatic event.

Qualification as a personal disaster

A useful concept that unifies acute grief and trauma is that of *personal disaster,* a term introduced by Raphael (1981). In her discussion, Raphael uses the term to describe an "intensely distressing, possibly catastrophic personal experience" (p. 183) that involves "highly distressing, extremely stressful life circumstances" (p. 187).

While the disaster literature is replete with discussions and data about major catastrophes (e.g., the bombing of Hiroshima, concentration camp internment, mass transportation crashes, floods, fires), one also finds similar themes occurring in more ordinary events of lesser scale: The incidents are shocking, beyond the individual's control, and involve the threat of death. In fact, Raphael (1981) has identified five key similarities between a personal disaster (which she exemplifies by such events as the death of a loved one, the personal experience of major disaster, or a serious, especially life-threatening illness or injury/accident) and a more widespread mass catastrophe: shock and denial, distress, helplessness, death and destruction, and images of the trauma. Issues and treatment implications can be extrapolated across categories. In each case, the person's reactions, defenses, behaviors, and coping mechanisms are contingent upon personal history and the idiosyncratic factors involved in the experience in and after the event. As well, Raphael notes that both types of trauma involve psychological defense processes, the need for cognitive completion with affective release, and mitigating behaviors. Raphael writes that situations of personal disaster experience may be encompassed by both acute crisis aspects of the event and by ongoing chronic stresses that, she notes, "may emerge, becoming in themselves of disastrous severity" (p. 187). This finding is particularly relevant to contending with a loved one's life-threatening or terminal illness.

The concept of personal disaster integrates traumatic stress data and information into the grief, loss, and adjustment matrix from which clinical conceptualizations of personally aggrieved and adversely impacted individuals spring. In addition, the concept knits together grief and traumatic stress, and supports the contention that these two are variations on a theme.

Suitability of classification under a proposed stress response category

Among the earliest to argue for the removal of PTSD (as a major form of traumatic stress) from the diagnostic category of anxiety disorders, Horowitz, Weiss, and Marmar (1987) suggested that a set of disorders called stress response syndromes be created and that PTSD could be better served by being located under this new category. They proposed that this category also include the adjustment disorders, the bereavements (normal and pathological grief), brief reactive psychoses, and posttraumatic character disorder (Horowitz, 1986; Horowitz et al., 1987). Thus, these authors explicitly recognized the relative similarity in etiology and consequent response processes between acute grief and traumatic stress reactions. This viewpoint is shared by others who advocate for the creation of this new diagnostic category. (See Brett, 1996, for more on proposal of this category.)

Common fundamental issues

Other common issues are fundamental in the responses to both loss and trauma. Green (1997) has delineated the similarities between bereavement through death and trauma secondary to life threat. Both loss that stimulates acute grief and trauma that occasions traumatic stress contain elements associated with disorganization or disruption, helplessness and loss of control, severing of an important attachment and the protection it provides, and concerns with annihilation.

I submit that the experience of victimization—an experience that in itself typically precipitates traumatic stress reactions—is another fundamental issue in both acute grief and traumatic stress. Victimization is the experience of being acted on and adversely affected by a force or agent. In acute grief, the dynamic of victimization is illuminated by the linguistic origins of the word *bereavement*. Bereavement, or the state of having suffered a loss, comes from *bereave*, a word that shares the same root as the word *rob*. Both experiences involve an unwilling deprivation by force, having something withheld unjustly and injuriously, a stealing away of something valuable—all of which leave the individual victimized. As previously mentioned, Moore and Fine (1990) noted the adverse effects—in other words, victimization—that occur when a traumatic stressor breaches the protective shield of the ego. Recall also that the lay definition of trauma is of an agent, force, or mechanism that causes trauma, itself a disordered psychic or behavioral state resulting from mental or emotional stress or physical injury. Thus, trauma, by several definitions, gives rise to victimization. So also does the loss of a loved one stimulate acute grief and cause an experience of victimization.

The concept of victimization is instructive on many accounts, not the least of which is its identification and explanation of the presence of a number of common phenomena in both loss-generated acute grief and trauma-generated traumatic stress. For instance, in both one may find anger, anxiety, questions as to why one has had to undergo this type of experience, wonder as to how to prevent its recurrence, violation of the assumptive world, elements of reexperiencing and avoidance, and therapeutic demands for processing the experience in a fashion that will enable future empowerment and ultimate integration of the experience into one's ongoing life, among many other sequelae.

Regardless of whether stimulated by loss or trauma, victimization entails a loss of control and a relative helplessness that can, under the appropriate conditions (prior to any potential working through and ultimate transcendence or derivation of positive effects) engender their own traumatic responses in addition to the strong displeasure and negative sequelae typically brought about by having been cast into the role of victim.

Manifest symptomatology and associated features

Expressing his concern that the *Diagnostic and Statistical Manual of Mental Disorders* (American Psychiatric Association, 1987, 1994) "resolutely insists on treating bereavement, alone of all stressors known to mankind, as excluded from significant diagnoses," Simpson (1997, p. 7) brilliantly argues for the integration of grief and bereavement within the traditional classification system. He provides numerous examples of the clinical and research inconsistencies associated with the conceptualization of grief and bereavement in the DSM-III-R and the DSM-IV. Noting that the similarities between typical features of normal grief and PTSD (as a major form of traumatic stress) are striking, Simpson painstakingly compares the DSM-IV symptomatic criteria for PTSD with descriptions of normal grief from major authorities. His analysis is a compelling argument for significant overlap.

Eth and Pynoos (1985) take the position that grief and trauma are different human experiences, although they may be precipitated by a single event. After identifying five factors typically present in traumatic grief (visual horror, guilt, ego constriction, stigma, and reunion fantasies) and discussing how these factors can disrupt bereavement, the authors then address the similarities between grief and trauma. These are impressive in their overlap:

> These two processes share certain salient features in
> common. Traumatized and grief-stricken patients are
> plagued by intrusive thoughts, painful affects, and fears of
> being overwhelmed. There are consequent efforts to avoid
> reminders of the trauma of the deceased, feelings of

hopelessness over the irreversibility of the event, and a sense of personal guilt for having failed to do more. Both processes place enormous demands on psychic energy, which would otherwise be channeled into new relationships or challenges. The courses of trauma and grief are comparable as well. The natural histories are characterized by an abrupt onset after the psychosocial stressor, followed by an acute phase, and then a slow recovery with periodic reactivations, such as anniversary responses. For both syndromes there are a variety of mediating factors, including the presence of supportive objects, which can affect outcome. And importantly traumatized and grief-stricken patients are responsive to focal, brief psychotherapy. In fact, these similarities may have contributed to disguising the elements of trauma in certain cases of grief. (pp. 181–182)

Further discussion of the similarities of loss (generating separa-tion distress) and trauma (creating traumatic distress) is provided by Jacobs (1993):

In emphasizing the distinction between traumatic distress and separation distress, the similarities that exist between these types of distress should not be ignored. Notably, both emotional processes are characterized by episodes of intrusion of thoughts, images, and feelings into consciousness, on the one hand, and avoidance of event-specific cognition and emotion when distress is excessive, on the other hand. Also both processes may be associated with secondary somatic, depressive, or anxious symptoms that add to the appearance, if not the reality, of their being similar rather than different. (p. 84)

Nader (1997a) has identified several associated features that can be common in both grief and trauma. These include (a) guilt or increased sense of responsibility; (b) suicidal ideation; (c) impact from previous loss; (d) issues of identification; and (e) multiple losses (including physical or emotional loss of loved ones and friends, as well as of preexisting relationships; losses due to changed circumstances; loss of one's own expected life course; and loss of previous aspects of the self and of specific competencies).

Despite the observed similarities between acute grief and trau-matic stress, other individuals have carefully analyzed grief and trau-matic stress reactions and found differences. The authors of three works important both conceptually and clinically have been particu-larly proficient in articulating the differences, as well as the similarities, between uncomplicated acute grief and traumatic stress responses: Raphael and Martinek (1997), Nader (1997a), and Jacobs (1993). These writers do pinpoint differences; however, I contend that the differences are primarily in content and degree and not necessarily in process.

Raphael and Martinek (1997) compare and contrast what they call *bereavement reactions* (i.e., grief) and posttraumatic reactions (as manifested in PTSD), specifically addressing, among other phenomena, cognitive and repetitive processes and affects, avoidance phenomena, and arousal phenomena. Nader (1997a) addresses the same three areas as Raphael and Martinek in her comparison of grief with reactions to trauma, although the language is slightly different: traumatic versus grief reexperiencing, issues of numbing and avoidance, and arousal phenomena. Jacobs (1993) also clearly struggles to balance the similarities and differences between loss and trauma, and the reactions they precipitate. He attempts to reconcile them under the umbrella of stress-related disorders:

> There is a fascinating relationship between trauma and loss, two stressful experiences. Although most traumatic experiences involve loss of some sort, and the experiences of trauma and loss are inseparable, the element of loss is minimal in some traumatic situations. Conversely, although it might be argued that losses that lead to pathologic grief are traumatic by definition, certainly there are many losses that are not traumatic. Therefore, it is possible to conceptualize trauma and loss as separate experiences and distinct processes. For example, except in times of war, great social upheaval, or disasters, trauma is not universal and inevitable like bereavement. Dissociation is conspicuous in trauma but rare in bereavement, although less severe attenuating processes such as transient numbness and disbelief and the use of psychological ego defenses are common after a loss. The content of the intrusions after trauma is horrifying and frightening rather than desolate and empty, as is typical of bereavement. The essential affective experience in a traumatic situation is fear. In bereavement, it is separation distress characterized by yearning and pining. Therefore, each experience is distinctive and potentially leads to a unique type of clinical complication.
>
> However, in some ways loss and trauma resemble each other and the study of one clarifies the other. For example, loss and trauma are similar in the intrusive quality of the

distress and the mitigating processes employed by the afflicted individual to cope. Also both loss and trauma are associated with major depressions and anxiety disorders if they do not, in fact, increase the risk of their occurrence. These similarities establish common ground for both loss and trauma that argues for their inclusion together as stress-related disorders. (p. 356)

It is inarguable that the differences between acute grief and traumatic stress are vitally important phenomenologically, to the affected individual, as well as clinically, to the caregiver who is called to intervene. Nevertheless, the case that acute grief after major loss constitutes a form of traumatic stress reaction is reinforced by the similarities between their underlying dynamic processes.

On an everyday basis, those who treat acutely bereaved individuals must contend with differences in content. Certainly, no two mourners will have the exact same bereavement experiences; rather, idiosyncratic constellations of factors combine to give every bereavement its own unique cast. If caregivers must consider different content in their treatment of different mourners because of their individual differences, yet address generic processes that are informed by these differences (i.e., mourners experience the same processes in their own unique ways), why should the case be any different when traumatic and loss-related content are of concern? The specific content may make these experiences appear different, but the underlying dynamics are the same. Thus, just the "window dressing" is different.

It is true that differences in content may bring different levels and qualities of reaction to the affected person. For instance, as part of acute grief a mourner may experience an intrusive image of the deceased loved one as he looked when well. However, an intrusive image of a traumatized person's loved one being crushed to death in an automobile accident would likely prompt a quite different reaction. In both cases, an intrusive image comes unbidden to the person. In the first case, the image generates sadness and separation distress. It may or may not stimulate avoidance reactions on the part of the person experiencing it, and it may or may not constitute further trauma to that person (the image may evoke distress but not be currently experienced as traumatizing). In contrast, in the second case, the person is probably currently traumatized by the image and probably seeks to distance it. (It is worth noting here that such images are not always unbidden; sometimes the mourner may consciously contemplate them.)

Although special issues are attendant to either acute grief or trauma, these two phenomena are variations on a theme, that theme being the processing of impact upon the person, which fundamentally involves elements of loss and trauma. Therefore, in major and meaningful loss we can expect to see traumatic stress reactions because a loss that is "major" and "meaningful" alters the person and his or her world in such ways and to such an extent that the person experiences a traumatic "wound." This is one reason we typically see at least some dimensions of trauma associated with such loss.

Even so, major losses can occur without traumatic circumstances: Surely, a loved one may have a peaceful death that is construed by the mourner to be appropriate in manner and timing. Surely, as well, as Eth and Pynoos (1985) assert, a death can be distressing but not automatically qualify as a traumatic loss. However, one must differentiate between acute grief as a form of traumatic stress and traumatic bereavement, as discussed previously. Even in the absence of a traumatic death leading to traumatic bereavement as a form of complicated mourning—perhaps in the case of relatively "benign" bereavement—acute grief embodies a number of generic elements of traumatic stress and shares, in kind if not in degree, many features with PTSD/ASD.

Alternating modes of regulation of exposure to distressing material

Another area in which acute grief is similar to PTSD as a major form of traumatic stress reaction is in the affected individual's attempts to regulate his or her exposure to distressing material or information associated with the loss or trauma. This regulation is necessary in order ultimately to be able to accommodate the event via cognitive completion with affective release.

In acute grief, most of the phenomena—traditional psychological defenses, processes of cognitive completion with affective release, coping behaviors, and specific attempts at mitigating the pain of loss (i.e., disbelief, sense of the deceased's presence, hallucinations and illusions, linking objects and messages, dreams, avoidance of reminders, and selective forgetting; Parkes, 1987)—serve an important function. According to Parkes, they help to regulate the quantity of novel, unorganized, or in other respects disabling information the person handles at a given time. Parkes notes that the mourner oscillates between twin opposing tendencies. One is an inhibitory tendency, which by repression, avoidance, postponement, and so forth holds back or limits the mourner's perception of disturbing stimuli. The other is a facilitative or reality-testing tendency, which enhances the mourner's perception and thought about disturbing stimuli.

The process described by Parkes is identical to that described as
the denial and numbing–intrusion cycle of the stress response syndrome (Horowitz, 1986). The stress response syndrome, which
develops after traumatic events and is based on an information-
processing model, is a predictable series of responses precipitated
by a stressful event involving news that is severely out of accord
with the way an individual believes him- or herself to be articulated
with the surrounding world. This causes a sudden and powerful
breach in the person's security and violates his or her assumptive
world. The individual is confronted with fear, as well as with implications for short- and long-range personal meaning. The latter
implications extend both into the past, joining with that person's
life story, and into the future, prompting revisions in plans of both
a practical and imaginative nature. Horowitz asserts that, following
a serious life event—which can include medical illness, dying, and
bereavement—and immediate efforts at coping, the individual typically undergoes the following responses in the stress response syndrome: outcry, denial and numbing, intrusion, working through,
and completion. Horowitz's work informs us about the importance
of trauma in creating cycles of avoidance and intrusion as the person struggles to work through the stress response to ultimate completion.

Processes similar to those in Horowitz's denial and
numbing–intrusion cycle are witnessed in Parkes' twin opposing
tendencies of inhibition/facilitation. Both regulate the individual's
exposure to distressing material. Thus, the denial and numbing
symptomatology of Horowitz's stress response syndrome is equivalent to Parkes' acute grief inhibitory tendency, and Horowitz's intrusive symptomatology is the same as Parkes' facilitative tendency. In
both schemas, the individual tries to maintain psychological equilibrium by alternately avoiding and approaching the material in the
attempt to process it and work it through. The similarity between
these two schemas supports the notion of acute grief as a form of
traumatic stress reaction and as an application of the stress response
syndrome (although in its entirety, the syndrome would continue
past the acute grief phase into the latter mourning processes).

An examination of the intricacies of Parkes' and Horowitz's different responses and their phasic interplay reveals remarkable similarity to the six "R" processes of mourning, which I assert in
themselves qualify as a stress response syndrome (see Table 2.2 in
this volume; Rando, 1993). Each of the three models focuses on the
person's coming to cognitive completion with affective release in
order to achieve healthy accommodation of some adverse event and
to integrate it appropriately in the person's life, ultimately leaving

that individual the freedom to go forward in a healthy way and reinvest in the new world without the loved one.

Presentation of two tasks to affected individuals

Acute grief and traumatic stress both present the affected individual with the mandate to achieve the goals of trauma mastery and loss accommodation or, as the latter is otherwise known, healthy mourning (which by definition includes grief resolution).

Depending upon prevailing circumstances, there can be significant differences in the amount of trauma mastery required, as well as in the amount of healthy mourning necessary. While these two tasks are most clearly evident in cases of traumatic bereavement that have eventuated in a clear-cut diagnosis of PTSD that overlays the mourning, they still are present in the relatively more "benign" bereavements in which there are only minimal posttraumatic symptoms interspersed among loss-related reactions. The point is that in both acute grief and PTSD (used here as an example of intense traumatic stress), whatever trauma is present requires mastery—or at least some management. This type of mastery is a clinical issue separate from the loss-related tasks of grief resolution/loss accommodation (i.e., mourning), notwithstanding their concurrence. For this reason, interventions enabling trauma necessarily must be integrated with those promoting healthy mourning. As next discussed, at times they must also take precedence.

Levels of association between acute grief and traumatic stress. Three levels of association can exist between acute grief and traumatic stress. Based on how much traumatic stress symptomatology is present within the acute grief, and depending upon the configuration of symptoms in relation to grief, treatment implications follow. Each of the three levels of association next discussed is illustrated by the situation of a widow's dealing with the death of her spouse.

In the first case, there is insufficient symptomatology to warrant a formal diagnosis of PTSD/ASD. This first level of association may be described as either "acute grief with minimal traumatic stress symptomatology" or "acute grief as a minor form of PTSD/ASD." At this level of association, the woman's husband has died from expected causes subsequent to a well-managed, pain-free terminal illness that has permitted her an optimum amount of time and appropriate circumstances to achieve closure, enable a "good" dying experience for all concerned, and prepare, but not so much time or such circumstances as to deplete and subject her to negative sequelae that outweigh the therapeutic benefits. While there are elements of traumatic stress within the acute grief, they are equal or subordinate to the strictly loss-related issues with which the widow contends. For instance, although she has had the opportunity to address in advance the husband's actual loss, this woman's acute grief is peppered with attempts to block out certain images of her husband on his deathbed, her frequent awakening in the morning with a sense of dread about having to struggle all day with the pain of his absence, her waves of anxiety and pangs of distress, her increased irritability, and her lack of interest in or feeling about anything else currently going on in the world. Nevertheless, her focus is on the loss of her spouse, trying to make sense of his death, and learning to be in the world without him. She is not preoccupied with the need for trauma mastery per se. Rather, she deals with the expectable types of issues just described, which one would find in relatively uncomplicated cases. Although such a bereavement is painful and has the potential for traumatization, it is type of bereavement in which the amount of traumatization is relatively minimal, despite the presence of stress response syndrome processes (Horowitz, 1986).

A second level of association is found between acute grief and traumatic stress when that grief is complicated by one or more of the six high-risk factors for making a death circumstance traumatic. The complication results in more than the "usual" amount of traumatic symptomatology that would be found in a more benign bereavement. This may or may not result in a formal diagnosis of PTSD/ASD, but the traumatic elements the mourner must deal with impinge upon, exacerbate, or at least temporarily interfere with the working through of the loss-related ones. The configuration is of traumatic stress elements being interspersed with loss-related ones. At this second level of association between acute grief and traumatic stress, the woman in our example has been enjoying a quiet Saturday evening dinner with her husband when suddenly he puts his hand to his chest, exclaims that he feels strange, and then slumps over in the chair, dying at once from a massive heart attack. The suddenness of his death, her witnessing of it and being powerless to assist him, and her watching the emergency rescue personnel unsuccessfully attempt to resuscitate him all contribute to additional trauma that impacts adversely upon this woman's bereavement and will leave her relatively more traumatized within it than in the first example. Probably, although not certainly, there will be sufficient traumatic stress symptomatology to meet the criteria for PTSD/ASD, at least for a brief period of time. Phenomenologically, depending upon the factors present to influence her grief, we would expect this mourner to struggle with an exacerbated need for trauma mastery secondary to the circumstances of the death and what they have brought to her. This struggle will be above and beyond that required by loss-related issues that stem from sudden death, such as not getting the opportunity to say good-bye, disbelieving what has happened and being unable to grasp it cognitively, or obsessing about the events that led up to her husband's demise. As compared with the widow's reactions at the first level of association between acute grief and traumatic stress, we may find this woman to have additional trauma-related issues—for example, increased anxiety, irritability, and hyperarousal; flashbacks about the paramedics putting the cardiac paddles upon her husband's chest and causing his body to jump; some increased distress at dinner time every Saturday; inability to remember the precise sequence of events that took place when she called 911; a persistent sense of numbness; and the perception that she is floating above herself watching herself go through the motions of life. The configuration is of traumatic stress elements significantly coinciding with acute grief elements.

The third level of association between acute grief and posttraumatic stress occurs when full-blown PTSD/ASD exists along with acute grief. The factors associated with the death are sufficiently traumatizing that the mourner meets the diagnostic criteria for one of these formal stress disorders. The configuration here is of PTSD/ASD that overlays the acute grief; the grief processes essentially are blanketed by the traumatic stress symptomatology. This third level of association might be expected to develop after the woman in our example loses her husband in the following manner: The two are taking a leisurely stroll around their neighborhood after dinner when suddenly a car pulls over beside them and a clearly drug-crazed youth jumps out of the passenger side, pointing a gun at them and demanding all their money. Terrified, the couple give him their wallets and beg him not to hurt them. The gunman bends down to reenter the car and then looks back, laughs, and shoots the husband in the face before the car speeds away. The widow is covered in her dead husband's blood and fragments of his skin and bone, cradling him in her arms, and screaming for assistance. While in the second case the widow had to contend with a sudden and unanticipated death, unlike this one it was not violent, may not have been preventable, was not random, and did not expose her to a significant threat to her own personal survival or to a shocking confrontation with her husband's mutilation. That these high-risk factors are present in the third scenario, in addition to suddenness and lack of anticipation, causes this survivor to suffer relatively more trauma than the widow in the second example. The traumatization is sufficient to create full-blown PTSD/ASD.

It must be realized that the amount of traumatization experienced can only be determined from the person's phenomenological perspective. One cannot determine the amount merely by objective circumstances. Responses will be based upon perceptions, appraisals, and other factors associated with that affected individual. As caregivers we have the right to make a statement about traumatization only in one direction (e.g., "I'm surprised that she wasn't more traumatized"); we cannot make it in the other (e.g., "She shouldn't feel that traumatized.") Always, an evaluation of the factors influencing the person's bereavement experience and responses must be undertaken if we wish to assess that person's responses accurately.

Configurations and treatment implications of associated acute grief and traumatic stress. Acute grief and traumatic stress intersect in two possible ways, each with its own treatment implications. It is clear that when significant amounts of traumatic stress (either full-blown PTSD/ASD or symptoms very close to reaching diagnostic criteria) overlay mourning, trauma-related issues must be addressed prior to the loss-related aspects of mourning. In other words, interventions to facilitate trauma mastery must take precedence over those to promote loss accommodation (Eth & Pynoos, 1985; Lindy et al., 1983; Nader, 1997a, 1977b; Pynoos & Nader, 1990; Rando, 1993, 1994; Raphael, 1983, 1986; Raphael & Martinek, 1997; Raphael & Wilson, 1993). If the traumatic stress symptomatology does not override the grief but is merely interspersed with it, then the caregiver has the luxury of intermingling work on trauma-related concerns with loss-related ones or of incorporating techniques for addressing traumatic stress symptomatology into overall interventions for grief and addressing the two areas simultaneously.

Briefly, reasons for giving priority to work on the trauma—in terms of its effects and the defenses erected to protect against them—all stem from the fact that the traumatized person's preoccupation with the trauma and its sequelae impedes healthy grief and mourning. The mourner simply is unable to progress with all the aspects of loss accommodation because of the residual traumatic symptomatology. To varying degrees and depending upon the impact of the specific trauma, it is possible to witness an individual who may remain anxious, fearful, and overwhelmed, possibly locked into the dimensions of the helplessness and horror of the traumatic event; at times victimized by repetitive trauma-related intrusions; with some measures of emotional blunting and diminished responsiveness to the external world; exercising as needed various attempts to avoid trauma-related stimuli; often being fragmented and dissociated regarding some elements of the trauma but possibly fixated upon others and upon trauma-related concerns; hyperaroused; and without full and conscious access to the ego functions.

That treatment should focus first on trauma mastery makes sense if one recalls Maslow's (1962) hierarchy of needs. It is only when basic survival needs and needs for safety and security are fulfilled that higher level needs—related to such abstractions as love and belonging, self-esteem, and self-actualization—can emerge. Very simply, a traumatized person does not have the ability to indulge the higher order needs found in grief and mourning. He or she is focused on surviving and achieving stability, safety, and security, all of which have been disrupted by the traumatic encounter, its sequelae, and the defenses erected to contend with them.

It is important to note that the aforementioned feelings of safety and security may pertain not only to physical safety and security, but also to psychosocial or emotional safety and security. According to most definitions, a person can be traumatized by events that arise internally as well as externally. This means that memories, thoughts, images, emotional and physical feelings, impulses, and behaviors associated with the traumatic event, its sequelae, and the defenses aroused by them can re-traumatize the person. Consequently, it is important to address such trauma arising within the individual—to free that person first from preoccupation with it—in order then to be able to turn therapeutic attention toward grief and loss-related matters.

Lindy et al. (1983), studying the impact of psychotherapy with survivors of a devastating supper club fire, observed the process of work on trauma as prerequisite for work on grief:

> In cases where both intrapsychic trauma and loss were present. . . . The psychotherapy seemed to proceed spontaneously in a sequential manner, namely, working through with regard to trauma including the overwhelming anxiety of death, feelings of helplessness, shame as well as defenses protecting against these strong affects came first. When they were sufficiently dealt with within the safety of the treatment setting and cohesion of the self was reestablished, a spontaneous progression seemed to ensue in which the patient was able to take on the as yet not worked-through aspects of grief relating to losses in his experience. (p. 608)

Additional support for assigning trauma work primacy over grief and mourning work comes from a variety of individuals working with diverse populations. Eth and Pynoos (1985) observed that "traumatic anxiety is a priority concern for the ego, compromising its ability to attend to the fantasies of the lost object that are integral to the grief process" (p. 175). Writing about her long-term and in-depth observations of children coping with a parent's death, Furman (1974) noted that no instance was observed in which mourning could appropriately proceed and be completed unless a person had first dealt adequately with immediate concerns and anxieties, such as a child's coping with anxieties about the circumstances surrounding the death, which the child's mind could not master and whose environment failed to allay.

A similar conclusion was drawn by Burgess (1975) when she addressed family reaction to homicide and reported that victim-oriented thought (the horror over the manner of death) interferes with ego-oriented thought (the loss of the family member). As well, even prior to the development of the diagnosis of PTSD/ASD as we know it today, Raphael and Maddison (1976) suggested that bereavement problems were likely to arise in association with traumatic circumstances of the death, which might lead to a "traumatic neurosis" that blocked or interfered with the bereaved's capacity to grieve. Raphael (1983) articulates some of these dynamics when she writes about death that brings an extra effect of shock over and above the normal, in which the bereaved is confronted by the power of death to kill and deprive, and human helplessness in the face of it. She comments that the circumstances of the death may be so stressful as to overwhelm the ego, with ego resources then being taken up with trying to master the helplessness and other flooding affects. This situation prompts the need to help the bereaved face the affects of helplessness and anxiety generated at that time and to gain a new mastery so that the preoccupation with memories of the death scene or situation can be relinquished and the bereaved can carry on the work of mourning (Raphael, 1983).

Pynoos and Nader (1990) arrive at the same conclusions with regard to children who have been exposed to violence and traumatic death. They clarify that posttraumatic stress reactions keep children's minds focused on the circumstances of death and that these reactions interfere with ego resources and the allotting of full adaptational attention to the loss and its subsequent life changes. They note specifically that "thoughts of the deceased themselves become traumatic reminders because the child is unable to think of the deceased without recalling the mutilation. Consequently, it is difficult to reminisce about the deceased, a necessary component of grief resolution. Further, like other traumatic reminders, thoughts of the deceased may trigger traumatic reenactments or other symptoms" (p. 341).

All of the aforementioned notwithstanding, if the traumatized mourner does insist on presenting loss-related issues first (unlikely but not totally impossible), the caregiver will need to make a therapeutic decision about whether to follow the person's stated needs or attempt to persuade the mourner of the importance of addressing the traumatic material first.

Ultimate treatment requirement for working through of the experience via cognitive completion with affective release

A striking similarity between acute grief and traumatic stress— and one that lends further credence to the notion that they constitute variations on a theme or both are, as Jacobs (1993) terms them, stress-related disorders—is their ultimate treatment requirement for working through of the event via cognitive completion with affective release. This is required in order to achieve healthy accommodation of the event and to integrate the event appropriately into the person's life, leaving him or her the freedom to reinvest in the new life. Since *ultimate* treatment requirements are the focus of this discussion, attention is given to the entire array of mourning processes, not just those pertinent to the acute grief phases.

For both loss and trauma, specific processes must be undertaken in order to accommodate the event in a healthy way in the individual's life. Although the language differs slightly, treatment requirements for acute grief and for traumatic stress reveal considerable overlap and similarity.

As outlined in Rando (1993), the six "R" processes that must be successfully accomplished for a loss to be accommodated in a healthy way involve (a) recognizing the loss, (b) reacting to the separation, (c) recollecting and reexperiencing the deceased/lost object and the relationship, (d) relinquishing the old attachments to the deceased/lost object and the old assumptive world, (e) readjusting to move adaptively into the new world without forgetting the old, and (f) reinvesting. (Table 2.2 in this volume lists the subprocesses involved in these main processes.)

In comparison, as delineated in Rando (1994), the courses of action next specified are necessary for successfully working through a traumatic event. These actions appear to differ from those for accommodating loss in that they are reduced to smaller therapeutic steps, more specifically related to trauma (e.g., guilt, helplessness), and more detailed (e.g., images, behaviors). These differences are superficial, however: The loss-related processes can subsume the trauma-related ones, and the trauma-related processes are simply a more explicitly detailed version of the loss-related ones. The requirements for processing trauma, then, are as follows:

- Bringing into consciousness the traumatic experience; repeatedly reviewing, reconstructing, reexperiencing, and abreacting the experience until it is robbed of its potency

- Identifying, dosing, expressing, working through, and mastering the affects of the traumatic encounter (e.g., helplessness, shock, horror, terror, anxiety, anger, guilt)

- Integrating conscious and dissociated memories, affects, thoughts, images, behaviors, and somatic sensations

- Mourning relevant physical and psychosocial losses

- Avoiding maladaptive processes and therapeutically address-ing the defenses and behaviors used to cope both with the trauma itself and the mechanisms employed to deal with it

- Acquiring and developing new skills and behaviors and/or retrieving overwhelmed ones to promote healthy living in the world after the trauma

- Countering the helplessness and powerlessness with experiences supporting mastery; a sense of personal worth and value; con-nectedness to others; coping ability; release of feelings in small doses; undertaking of action to give testimony, help others, or minimize the effects of similar traumatic experiences; and the avoidance of further victimization

- Developing a perspective on what happened, by whom, to whom, why, and what one was and was not able to do and con-trol within the traumatic experience; recognizing and coming to terms with the helplessness of the trauma

- Accepting full responsibility for one's behaviors as is appropri-ate and ultimately relinquishing inappropriate assumption of responsibility and guilt after therapeutically addressing survivor guilt

- Creating meaning out of the traumatic experience

- Integrating the aspects of the trauma and its meaning into the assumptive world; placing the event in continuity within the totality of one's past, present, and future

- Forming a new identity reflecting one's survival of the traumatic experience and the integration of the extraordinary into one's life

- Reinvesting in love, work, and play, reconnecting with others, and reassuring the continued flow of life and development halted by the traumatic experience

In brief, the responses to both acute grief and traumatic stress are ways of coping with events that are inconsistent with the way the person assumes the world is or should be. This inconsistency creates a disarticulation of the individual in his or her world, typically caus-ing pressing demands to reduce stress-related impacts, cognitive dis-sonance, and the distress these effects engender.

TRAUMATIC STRESS IN MEDICAL ILLNESS

Given that anticipatory mourning inherently involves medical ill-ness, the literature on that topic can inform us about the prevalence and clinical realities of traumatic stress in this specific context. Early studies may not have used specific measures of traumatic stress or PTSD/ASD in the investigation of medical illness, given that PTSD and ASD are fairly recent diagnostic categories. However, anxiety per se has been one of the emotions addressed most frequently, clinically and empirically, as a psychosocial reaction to or element of psychological distress stemming from illness of all types. It is typically identified as concomitant with medical illness, its treatment, and its sequelae, such as life-style alterations, dependency on health professionals, fear of recurrence, challenges posed by rehabilitation, and alterations in work, leisure activities, and relations with others (see Taylor & Aspinwall, 1990).

When the illness is life-threatening or terminal, even more sources of anxiety and additional losses are to be expected (see Rando, 1984). For discussions of the experience of anxiety and other trauma-associated reactions of the dying person, one can go directly to the literature on the dying patient. Among others, particularly good discussions on these topics are provided in the writings of Alsop (1973), Barton (1977), Doka (1993), Garfield (1978), Glaser and Strauss (1965), Kalish (1970), Kübler-Ross (1969), Pattison (1969, 1977, 1978), Rando (1984), and Weisman (1972a, 1972b, 1975, 1977, 1979).

Other evidence suggests that the experience of medical illness has been relatively late in being identified as an arena for traumatic stress. In 1993, Kelly and Raphael contributed the sole chapter, among 84 in Wilson and Raphael's encyclopedic *International Handbook of Traumatic Stress Syndromes*, devoted to traumatic stress in medical illness. That among so many chapters such a comprehensive resource only includes one focusing on this topic attests to the insufficient appreciation of the experience of traumatic stress within the complex phenomenological experience of coping with medical illness. The chapter concerns coping with acquired immune deficiency syndrome (AIDS), a life-threatening and terminal illness. Plainly, large gaps remain to be filled pertaining to traumatic stress in injuries or illnesses that are not necessarily life-threatening or terminal. Investigations on the subject do appear to be on the increase, however. In her excellent review identifying survivors at risk and delineating trauma and stressors across events, Green (1993) documents how, in the investigation of trauma, the trend is toward broader definition of potentially traumatic events, including technological and health-related events. While this shift poses some problems, it is important because an expanded definition encompasses more survivors who can be understood within the traumatic stress framework and who are potentially in need of clinical services.

Not surprisingly, recent studies are now documenting the presence of traumatic stress in medical illness. The first feature of Criterion A for PTSD/ASD (as forms of traumatic stress) in the DSM-IV is that a person contends with an event or events that involve actual or threatened death or serious injury, or threat to the physical integrity of self or others. Certainly, this situation exists when one confronts a serious illness. This automatically puts experience with medical illness in the legitimate domain of potential PTSD/ASD–associated events. Additionally, responses involving intense fear, helplessness, or horror (Criterion A2) would not be unexpected or atypical within that domain.

Among the first to explicitly identify an illness-related posttraumatic stress disorder, Hartman and Burgess (1985) described the extension of the concept of PTSD to victims of severe illness—in their case example, those who had experienced a heart attack. They presented a model for structuring intervention efforts with PTSD emerging from serious illness.

Another early work, definitive in the explication of posttraumatic stress associated with medical illness, is Nir's (1985) analysis of PTSD in children with cancer. Nir observed that the diagnosis of cancer plunges children into a medical reality of aggressive treatments, daily painful procedures, and grave treatment sequelae that create a series of overwhelming physical and emotional problems for young patients and their families. This situation explains the conclusion of Nir and colleagues that the primary psychopathology encountered in the majority of child and adolescent patients with cancer falls within the diagnostic criteria for PTSD.

As a major architect of theory and practice in a variety of areas related to traumatic stress, Mardi Horowitz's comments carry particular weight. In his widely referenced book, *Stress Response Syndromes* (1986), he asserts that medical illnesses and disabilities are life events that can lead to stress response syndromes. Horowitz cites the Kaltreider, Wallace, and Horowitz (1979) study involving a group of women of childbearing age who underwent nonelective hysterectomy. A year after surgery, a symptomatic pattern characterizing a stress response syndrome was found at a mild level in 43% of the subjects and at a severe level in 18%. Also at this time, more than a third of the subjects continued to note experiences of denial, with awareness of avoiding thoughts about the hysterectomy (38%) or of having a momentary sense of unreality that it had happened (35%).

Horowitz identifies other precipitants of posttraumatic stress in the medical illness realm, observing, for instance, that life-threatening illnesses such as myocardial infarctions are often associated with early denial and later intrusive thinking, two of the cardinal elements of the stress response syndrome. Horowitz also points out that even the news of being at risk for premature death may set in motion a stress response syndrome. This was reflected in the findings of a large study of men informed that they were at risk for premature heart disease (Horowitz et al., 1983). Elevated levels of intrusive thinking were found at yearly intervals. The study revealed that 18% of the men were substantially upset for a period of 3 or more years after receiving the news. The clinical implication is that caregivers should ask about psychological consequences for a considerable time after a person has had an illness or has been told that he or she is at risk of illness. (Other studies of PTSD and myocardial infarction are summarized in Green, Epstein, Krupnick, & Rowland.)

Kelly and Raphael (1993) have reported preliminary data from a prospective study of the correlates of psychiatric disorder in persons with human immunodeficiency virus (HIV) infection. They were particularly interested in assessing the applicability of conventional notions of posttraumatic stress symptoms (e.g., intrusive and avoidant images, thoughts, and affects) in the processes of adaptation to the chronic adversity of a life-threatening or terminal illness. High levels of both intrusive and avoidant symptoms of PTSD were found. A high correlation existed between the intrusive phenomena concerning HIV infection and those concerning death, indicating the salience of death-related anxiety in the population. Intrusive items were endorsed more frequently than avoidance items and were significantly correlated with overall psychiatric morbidity. The investigators interpreted high preoccupation with having been told of the disease (unrelated to time frame of diagnosis) and with the possibility of death as quite likely reflecting not only posttraumatic symptomatology, but PTSD in the subjects. The authors concluded that although it is not conventional practice to apply models of posttraumatic phenomena to the understanding of adaptation to the chronic and changing stress of a life-threatening illness, the model may help define the cognitive and emotional processes that occur.

What must be one of the most comprehensive works to date to comment on the association of traumatic stress in medical illness is the chapter "Trauma and Medical Illness: Assessing Trauma-Related Disorders in Medical Settings," by Green et al. (1997). Two major aspects of the association are explored: medical illnesses that might serve as stressors for the development of PTSD and trauma as a precipitant of medical problems. The former are briefly reported next.

In terms of cancer, Cella, Mahon, and Donovan (1990) administered the Impact of Event Scale (IES) to patients within 30 days of a recurrence of cancer. They found marked elevations on both intrusion and avoidance subscales, with 43% of the sample exceeding the clinical cutoff score for intrusive symptomatology and 80% exceeding the cutoff for avoidant symptoms. These levels of stress-related symptomatology are comparable to those for individuals presenting with more traditional trauma-induced disorders. Other findings indicated that women who had experienced a prior recurrence tended to exhibit fewer avoidance symptoms than those for whom this was the first recurrence and that 78% of the patients felt that their initial diagnosis of cancer was less distressing than news of a recurrence, with only 8% feeling that the first diagnosis was more distressing.

At the only site examining medical illness as a stressor event for the multicenter DSM-IV field trial for PTSD, Alter et al. (1992) examined the incidence of PTSD in three patient groups who were, on average, at about 5 years posttreatment: adolescent survivors of cancer, their mothers, and adult breast cancer survivors. Adolescent survivors had lifetime and current PTSD rates of 54% and 33%, respectively. Interestingly, no differences were found related to time since treatment or stage of illness. For adult survivors, the lifetime prevalence rate of cancer-related PTSD was 22%, and the current rate was 4% (Alter et al., 1996). Mothers of adolescent survivors of cancer were found to have lifetime rates of 54% and current rates of 25% (Pelcovitz et al., 1996).

Green et al. (1997) also report on the Stuber, Christakis, Houskamp, and Kazak (1996) data on pediatric cancer survivors who had been off treatment for at least 2 years and their parents. The results indicated that 13% of the patients, 40% of the mothers, and 33% of the fathers scored in the "severe" range of the PTSD Reaction Index. The self-report data revealed that for many children the memories lingering after treatment were of the medical procedures themselves (e.g., bone-marrow biopsies, spinal taps, etc.) rather than their life-threatening condition. Consistent with the results of the Alter et al. (1992) study, no difference in PTSD Reaction Index scores were noted as a result of time since treatment ended. This suggests that the problem may be a chronic one. Green et al. point out that while the data provide evidence of PTSD, a diagnosis was not established by diagnostic interview.

Finally, in a recent study by Green et al. (1996), women 4 to 12 months posttreatment for early-stage breast cancer were examined for incidence of PTSD. At some time after their diagnosis of breast cancer, 36% of the women had experienced recurrent, intrusive recollections or ruminations, 8% met full DSM-III-R PTSD diagnostic criteria for numbing/avoidance, and 27% met hyperarousal criteria. At the time of the interview, 20% reported current intrusive recollections or ruminations, 4% met numbing/avoidance criteria, and 11% met criteria for hyperarousal. Only 5% of the women met full criteria for lifetime (postdiagnosis) cancer-related PTSD, whereas 2.5% met current criteria. The authors interpreted the incidence of cancer-related

PTSD to be very low in their population. Another 4% might be conceptualized as meeting criteria for "subsyndromal PTSD" (i.e., meeting intrusive and arousal criteria but having only two rather than three avoidance symptoms). Therefore, about 9% of the sample was highly symptomatic, and up to 20% had intrusion, two avoidance symptoms, or two arousal symptoms. The authors observe that these findings are very similar to those reported by Cordova, Andrykowski, Kenady, McGrath, Sloan, and Redd (1995), who, utilizing the IES and a screen for PTSD symptoms, estimated that 5 to 10% of breast cancer survivors likely would meet DSM-IV criteria for PTSD.

In addition to giving a review of the literature, Green et al. (1997) flesh out two important differences between a life-threatening illness as a DSM-IV Criterion A stressor for PTSD and more traditional stressors (e.g., disasters, rape, combat, or automobile accidents). First, in contrast to these other stressors, where the source of the threat is externally based, in the environment, in life-threatening illness the threat arises internally. This means the threat and the individual cannot be separated. In turn, this may make the experience qualitatively different from one in which the threat arises externally. Second, once a person has been treated for the illness and survived, the ongoing stressor may not be the memory of the past event per se, but rather the threat that in the future the illness may recur or intensify, with death resulting. Thus, the threat is not primarily in the past, but in the future.

Green et al. also note similarities between life-threatening illness and more traditional PTSD stressors:

> For example, the news about having a potentially deadly
> illness can be sudden and unexpected, the treatment may be
> traumatic, and many of the mental/emotional processes for
> avoiding and integrating the experiences are likely similar.
> The anxiety and arousal associated with the information,
> and certainly with some of the associated procedures, may
> be quite similar as well, along with the disruption in
> relationships brought on by the knowledge that one has
> had an experience that others may not be able to
> understand or find equally frightening. (p. 167)

Green et al. describe several concerns to keep in mind when attempting to determine dimensions of traumatic stress. First, it is critically important to differentiate between symptoms characteristic of the stress response and those typically produced by the illness or treatment. For instance, pain can produce sleeplessness or irritability, chemotherapy can cause fatigue and/or depression, and medication can result in concentration problems. Since these symptoms are all associated with PTSD as well, they will require proper identification so effective treatment may follow.

The second concern relates to potential differences in intrusive thinking. As noted previously, for individuals with life-threatening illnesses the content of images and thoughts may be ruminative and future-oriented rather than recollection of past events. Some ill persons do report actual recollections. The same distinction applies to dreaming; for example, some individuals dream about life-threatening illnesses in the future and some dream about the details of their surgery.

A third concern is that, with regard to the denial/numbing symptoms in PTSD Criterion C, the symptom of a "foreshortened future" can pose problems. Obviously, this is appropriate and reality-based when one has a life-threatening illness.

Finally, Green et al. observe that the Criterion D arousal symptom of hypervigilance can take a form in cancer survivors (and, by extension, in others with life-threatening or terminal diagnoses) different from that in survivors of other types of traumas. Rather than being hyperalert to their surroundings, cancer survivors became hyperalert to their physical health and any bodily changes that might signal recurrence (or, by extension, progression) of the disease.

TRAUMATIC STRESS IN ANTICIPATORY MOURNING

After examining traumatic stress first in postdeath grief and mourning, and then in medical illness, it is now time to bring these two areas to the point of their natural intersection—that is, to the anticipatory mourning experience. A comprehensive argument for anticipatory mourning as a form of traumatic stress could have been constructed in no other fashion: One must analyze both issues of loss and issues of trauma (derived from life threat, mutilation, and pain secondary to illness), given that anticipatory mourning inherently incorporates the two.

As a context, the reader needs to recall at this point the definition of trauma and its various manifestations; the pivotal association of anxiety as a central dynamic in and manifestation of acute grief; the diagnostic criteria of PTSD/ASD (as major forms of traumatic stress); and the nine arguments for acute grief's constituting a traumatic stress reaction. In particular, traumatic stress in anticipatory mourning is discussed here as the result of (a) separation anxiety associated with a loved one's dying, (b) the characteristics of the anticipatory mourning situation, and (c) the exposure of and demands placed upon the anticipatory mourner.

Separation Anxiety Associated with a Loved One's Dying

Very simply, the dying of the loved one is the process of separating that loved one from this life and from those who love that person. As a result, significant separation anxiety tends to be stimulated in the dying person, intimates, and concerned others.

In separation anxiety experienced after a death, the mourner must deal with a fait accompli. In contrast, in a situation of anticipatory mourning, the dying person must contend with the gradual slipping away of the self and of others. Intimates, concerned others, and caregivers undergo a similar process. This experience of losing the loved one (whether self or other) and dealing with one's inability to stop the inexorable process of separating and attachment-rupturing deprivation, engenders the traumatizing affect of helplessness, in and of itself victimizing the individual.

The poignancy of watching a loved one slip away, and the anxiety of enduring it until what is often a sadly painful process ceases, is what makes some caregivers prefer to cope with postdeath grief—no matter how traumatic the circumstances—over anticipatory mourning. At least, in the former, the physical separation already has been enacted. In the latter, the separation is currently happening, creating an experience that is both excruciatingly painful and anxiety provoking. A number of factors contribute to the difficulty: the sadness of witnessing the process, the often vain hope the situation could be altered, the press to do and not do things while the ill person is still alive, the awareness that the death has yet to be undergone and still must be faced, the continued experience of loss, the balancing of conflicting demands and emotions, being in the middle of the intense feelings and anxieties accompanying the process of being bereaved of that loved one and having him or her extracted from one's life, and being poised between life and death. One family member of a dying person described the position as being like standing under a huge, cresting tidal wave, waiting for it to descend upon and engulf her. She could see it looming and knew there was no escape: She was forced to wait helplessly until it crashed over her.

None of the foregoing is to suggest that positive, growth-producing dying experiences are not possible. These can and do occur. However, when they do, they are usually set within the context of some separation anxiety; this fact that must be appreciated, particularly if the potential for growth is to be realized.

Characteristics of the Anticipatory Mourning Situation

The majority of factors, characteristics, or elements associated with a traumatic event are present in anticipatory mourning. To recapitu-

late, the following are among those that best illuminate the anticipatory mourning experience:

- Raphael's (1981) five key elements in personal disaster: shock and
  denial, distress, helplessness, death and destruction, and images
- Green's (1997) four fundamental similarities between loss and
  trauma: disorganization or disruption, helplessness and loss of
  control, severing of an important attachment and the protection
  it provides, and concerns about annihilation
- The experience of victimization of the person contending with
  loss or trauma
- The six generic factors that predispose a specific death circumstance to be traumatic: suddenness and lack of anticipation; violence, mutilation, and destruction; preventability and/or
  randomness; loss of a child, multiple death; and the mourner's
  personal encounter with death secondary to either a significant
  threat to survival or a massive and/or shocking confrontation with
  the death and mutilation of others (adapted from Rando, 1994)
- The manifest symptomatology and associated features that
  acute grief and traumatic stress have in common (i.e., the nine
  arguments for acute grief's being a form of traumatic stress)

Clearly, these all combine to place anticipatory mourning squarely
and unequivocally within the domain of trauma.

Exposure of and Demands Placed upon the Anticipatory Mourner

The events to which the anticipatory mourner is exposed and the
demands of the anticipatory mourning experience have the potential
to render that experience traumatic. These events and demands
include (a) exposure to horrific stimuli, (b) multiplicity and chronicity of illness-induced losses and traumas, (c) creation of secondary
traumatic stress, (d) inherent generation of helplessness, and (e) confrontation with overwhelming emotions and conflicting demands
during times of strained resources. The placement of discussion
about these five issues is somewhat arbitrary, in fact reflecting the
interrelationships among them as well as with separation anxiety
associated with the loved one's dying and the characteristics of the
anticipatory mourning situation.

Exposure to Horrific Stimuli

As noted by many traumatologists, the degree of exposure to a specific trauma is a primary determinant of the severity of traumatic

stress experienced by the individual involved, both during and subsequent to the event (see Nader, 1997b; Pynoos & Nader, 1990; Raphael, 1986). Exposure may be to life threat and/or to shocking stimuli, violence, death, destruction, mutilation, and grotesque imagery. Thus, internal (perception of threat) and external (environmental) factors can be involved in creating the person's exposure and determining its influence.

In the period of anticipatory mourning, interaction with life-threatening and terminal illness often provides considerable exposure to trauma-producing elements. As in other disasters, these elements may pertain to the degree of life threat that is stimulated. The degree of life threat may derive from concerns about one's own mortality that are stimulated by the specific event (such as in the HIV-positive person who witnesses a loved one dying of AIDS or the person who is terrified that she will contract the breast cancer that killed her mother and is taking the life of her sister). It may be determined by the degree, proximity, and duration of exposure to horrific stimuli and/or stimulated by the dying process in general (such as the heightened personal death anxiety one may have in response to the dying of a loved one). Finally, it may be influenced by the degree of helplessness and powerlessness experienced by the individual in the face of the trauma or may be occasioned in part by the person's preexisting vulnerability from earlier trauma.

A major cause of traumatization of the anticipatory mourner is the psychic and physical assault that can be experienced secondary to the horrific stimuli encountered. The anticipatory mourner may be forced to contend with the sensory perception of the ravages of the illness—its mutilation, disfigurement, hemorrhages, foul smells, purulent discharges, expressions of pain, diminished capacities, and so forth—as well as with exposure to the reactions of the dying person thereto. These possibly terrifying confrontations with the impacts of dying can cause horror, helplessness, anxiety, hyperarousal, vulnerability, threat, shock, and a perception of absurdity in the situation. Jacobs (1993) observes that trauma in life-threatening and terminal illnesses can be expected, and points out its damaging impact:

> In this sense, lessons learned from traumatic losses offer a perspective on the emotional consequences of deaths that are not conspicuously traumatic in nature. These include not only deaths from acute illness, for which there is a lack of preparation, but also *deaths from chronic, disfiguring, painful diseases that horrify the survivors and break down their usual denial or other defenses used to cope with death.* (p. 87, emphasis added)

In commenting upon disasters, Raphael (1986) notes that the individual's distressing encounter with the deaths of others—the sights, smells, sounds, tastes, and touches of it—produce reactive traumatic phenomena that require integration. There will be intrusive memories, images, and nightmares. Situations and stimulus cues may trigger memories and produce the emotional intensity of the original experience, even when the event is thought to be forgotten.

We may extrapolate Raphael's views on massive disaster to the personal disaster situation of helplessly watching a loved one be impacted, if not ravaged, by illness and pain. This creates anxiety and hyperarousal, and can magnify the sense of trauma and distress. One adult survivor of the death of a brother from head and neck cancer commented: "It wasn't that he died that was so bad; it was how he died. To end up looking so grotesque and hideous, and to have this happen in this day and age of medical miracles, is just totally unacceptable. I just can't get over it. I knew I would be impacted by his death, but I didn't expect this!"

Even in those circumstances where the damage to the loved one is not as visible as it can be with head and neck cancer, similar dynamics can bring trauma to the mourner. The point is that physical wasting away and the destruction of the loved one's body—the stimulus that, for most of us, is the image of the person we love—embody the two Criterion A elements of PTSD/ASD and expose the mourner to circumstances known to be traumatizing.

Rosenblatt's (1983) research is germane to this point about exposure to traumatic stimuli in life-threatening and terminal illness. He found that anticipation of a loved one's death appeared to be associated with less grief in the first 2 years after a loss but only if the person had some disconnection from the dying individual by virtue of not living with that person. He provides evidence that co-residence with the dying person has several possible effects upon an intimate's anticipatory and postdeath mourning. In cases where the anticipatory mourner lives with the dying individual, home care for that dying loved one may (a) interfere with the occurrence of anticipatory mourning; (b) offset its postdeath benefits by providing additional memories, ideas, and behavior links that will need to be worked on after the death; and/or (c) lead to experiences, and conclusions derived from them, that actually augment postdeath grief. While Rosenblatt does not specifically mention exposure to horrific stimuli as a precipitant of problems, it is a reasonable extension of his findings: The potential exists for additional distress as a result of exposure to traumatic stimuli associated with the loved one's dying.

In a kind of "domino effect," in which the specifics of illness-related experiences influence anticipatory mourning and both of these influence postdeath grief and mourning, experiences of traumatization secondary to exposure to horrific stimuli during the illness can be expected to have a significant impact upon current and future grief, mourning, and adaptation. Healthy anticipatory mourning may expose the mourner to perceptual, behavioral, and emotional experiences that are not without significant expense, even if over the long term they can be of positive benefit.

Multiplicity and Chronicity of Illness-Induced Losses and Traumas

The nature of the multiciplicity and chronicity of the losses and traumas associated with a life-threatening or terminal illness also contributes to the creation of traumatic stress in anticipatory mourning. In other words, additional trauma is caused by undergoing processes of illness-induced loss and trauma repeatedly and for an extended time. This trauma is over and above that related to the actual specific content of those losses (e.g., loss of a body part or bladder control) and traumas (e.g., traumatization from exposure to oozing lesions or the coughing up of pieces of lung). Thus, process, as well as content, can traumatize.

Multiplicity

In regard to multiple loss experiences, the notion of *bereavement overload* is particularly relevant. Introduced by Kastenbaum in 1969 to refer to the serial loss of social contacts experienced by the elderly, the term has been used since then to apply to the individual who sustains many bereavements either concurrently (e.g., the loss of multiple family members in the common disaster of a house fire) or serially. In either case, the person's past and/or current experiences of loss leave him or her depleted emotionally and unable to address the loss and other related demands of the current situation.

There are some conceptual and clinical differences between these two types of multiple death (Rando, 1993). Primarily, in simultaneous multiple loss the mourner faces relatively more difficult choices than when one loss precedes the other, no matter how brief the interval between the losses. In the first case, the individual involved must prioritize the losses, differentiate them, contend with conflicts that arise because of the differing issues generated by them, work through the overwhelming nature of the situation, decide whether to address the losses sequentially versus simultaneously, manage the compromise of the six "R" processes of mourning (Rando, 1993; Table 2.2 in this volume) that tends to be created, and, in some cases, struggle with guilt and/or loss of support.

Such multiple losses are traumatic because they confront the mourner with the complicated mourning high-risk factor of unaccommodated concurrent losses and/or stresses when it comes to mourning each individual loss. Mourning for one loss is compromised by the concurrent crisis of the ongoing, stalled, or delayed mourning for the other losses. A vicious cycle often exists: The loss of A cannot be worked on in the fashion desired because of the emotional press and unfinished business of losses B and C; each of these losses, in turn, cannot be worked through because of incomplete mourning and stress associated with A.

In either situation of multiple loss and traumatization, whether concurrent or serial, one's ego struggles to maintain homeostasis. The situation is worsened by the overwhelming nature of so many losses. Frequently, the overload can leave the person psychically numb in defense and often lacking effective self-direction. Sometimes the person is totally immobilized or, in contrast, overly reactive to all stimuli and conflicts. Conflicts causing complicated mourning for one of the losses can generalize to others. This means that for any given loss, an increased chance of complicated mourning exists not only because of the difficulties of mourning multiple losses, but also because of the contiguity of mourning. Individual losses will need to be identified, differentiated, and labeled, and caution observed that resulting defenses and resistances in the mourning of one loss do not become inappropriately generalized to others.

As in cases where the multiple losses are of deaths of loved ones, in cases of multiple losses inherent in anticipatory mourning it will be important for the anticipatory mourner and caregiver to adjust expectations about the intensity of reactions, pacing, and time required for effective processing. Greater intensity, a slower pace, and longer time intervals (if it is even possible for mourning processes for a particular loss to be accomplished prior to the death) will be the norm. The feeling of not knowing where to begin in situations involving multiple losses is typical and must be responded to with great empathy. The person can be educated about the ongoing nature of loss and enabled to recognize the importance of paying attention to those losses that require it. Some losses will not require as much attention as others, but relative importance must be determined from an assessment of time or other needs and not from countertherapeutic avoidance that will cause problems later on. If the mourner can turn attention to relevant issues as they occur, they will not accumulate and create an unhealthy situation. Sometimes a disease-related event occurs and presents multiple losses and traumas, all at once, and a more leisurely approach to confronting the losses at hand is impossible (e.g., when an emergency surgery is required that leaves the person with significant and unanticipated deficits).

With regard to the repeated exposure to traumatic stimuli and/or trauma associated with life-threatening or terminal illness, four areas of information may be particularly helpful. While it is outside of the purview of this chapter to review the literature in all of these areas, several clinical concepts have direct relevance to anticipatory mourning. These concepts, enumerated in Table 6.1, fall into four main conceptual categories: stress management, countertransference, impact of loss and trauma on the family, and vicarious bereavement of others not directly affected. Some of these concepts legitimately could fit into more than one category; each brings information germane to the anticipatory mourner's experience of illness-induced trauma.

The bottom line is that trauma has the potential to develop in a person after exposure to the losses and traumatization of another. During the anticipatory mourning experience, this may take place as a result of witnessing or experiencing sufficient conditions to generate trauma. Specifically, this includes the following:

- Personally witnessing the physical and psychosocial traumatization and suffering of another

- Vicariously experiencing bereavement and/or traumatization secondary to identification with the person actually experiencing the loss or trauma (Type I vicarious bereavement) or experiencing personal losses consequent to Type I vicarious bereavement, resulting in subsequent intense reactions and/or assumptive world violations (Type II vicarious bereavement)

- Personally sustaining losses and/or trauma and/or victimization as a result of one's own experience in the anticipatory mourning situation (e.g., helplessness, loss of assumptive world elements, experiencing the slipping away of the dying person)

- Perceiving traumatic stimuli (e.g., stimuli that are death-related, grotesque, horrific, terrifying)

- Experiencing trauma due to the type, number, nature/characteristics, and conflicts of the demands imposed upon one in the situation (i.e., task-, duty-, or role-related demands)

- Having one's own personal fears, concerns, issues, or sensitivities resurrected and/or touched

Chronicity

It is not solely the number of losses and traumas during anticipatory mourning that account for the mourner's traumatization, but also their chronicity. Given the vicissitudes of today's life-threatening and terminal illnesses, a number of problems develop that may contribute to the traumatizing nature of the experience. These can include the following, among others: numerous remissions and relapses, with myriad psychological reactions to each; lengthened periods of anticipatory mourning; increased emotional, social, physical, time, and financial pressures; long-term family disruption; progressive decline of the ill person and emotional responses of loved ones to this decline; longer periods of uncertainty; intensive treatment regimens and their side effects; dilemmas about decision making and treatment choices; confusion about how to relate to a person who, although dying, is also still living; the extended and uncertain up-and-down course of many illnesses; distress magnified by excessive and lengthy periods, breeding inconsistency, resentment, and ambivalence; longer illness duration, providing increased potential for experiences and emotions that complicate pre- and postdeath grief and mourning (e.g., prolonged time and intensified circumstances leading to psychological conflicts, emotional exhaustion, and physical debilitation); depletion secondary to the stress of demands for major readaptations and investments of self, time, and finances; extended social isolation; more circumstances for family discord; lack of norms and clearly specified expectations and responsibilities; and the adverse impacts on the optimal carrying out of other functional roles outside of caregiver.

In addition to these problems, even relatively innocuous symptoms can serve as signs of additional loss and may come to constitute traumatic stimuli: Every event or nonevent can be interpreted as a possible harbinger of the loved one's death. When anxiety is present at high levels and for extended periods of time, an individual's ability to adapt and cope becomes impaired. Very simply, the person gets worn out, experiencing a depletion in coping capacity and a consequent increase in distress associated with these diminished capabilities.

While many writers focus on the dramatic and acute sequelae of all sorts of traumatic experiences, Raphael (1981) goes a step further and explicates the long-term chronic impacts. Her words have direct application to the anticipatory mourning experiences occasioned by today's chronic illnesses:

> Adults as well as children may experience a period or even a
> lifetime where they are dogged by the chronicity of debilitating
> illness and its associated changes, or by other stresses cumulatively.
> Each of these stresses may in itself seem minor, a small
> score on the life events schedule, but nevertheless, together
> and continuously they constitute ruinous misfortune or
> mishap. . . . Similarly for the bereaved there are the stresses
> of longer term adaptation to the altered roles, changed

TABLE 6.1

Areas of Information Pertinent to Illness-Induced Trauma

STRESS MANAGEMENT

1. Loss-related
   - Generic stress management adapted to those working with the seriously medically ill, dying, or bereaved (e.g., Harper, 1977; Vachon, 1987)
   - Specific "care for the caregiver" strategies (e.g., Larson, 1993; Rando, 1984)
2. Trauma-related
   - Interventions for stress in emergency services personnel (e.g., Mitchell & Bray, 1990; Raphael & Wilson, 1994)
   - Critical incident stress debriefing and management (e.g., Mitchell & Everly, 1996)
   - Death overload (e.g., Pine, 1984)

COUNTERTRANSFERENCE

1. Generic and applied analyses of countertransference reactions (e.g., Wilson & Lindy, 1994a, 1994b; Wilson, Lindy, & Raphael, 1994)
2. Secondary traumatic stress and stress disorder (e.g., Figley, 1993, 1995a, 1995b, 1995c)
3. Vicarious traumatization (e.g., McCann & Pearlman, 1990)
4. Compassion fatigue (e.g., Figley, 1995a, 1995b, 1995c)
5. Stress in dealing with complicated mourning (e.g., Rando, 1993)

IMPACT OF LOSS AND TRAUMA ON FAMILY

1. Secondary catastrophic stress reactions (e.g., Figley, 1982)
2. Co-victimization (e.g., Spungen, 1998)
3. Secondary victimization (e.g., Remer & Elliot, 1988a, 1988b)

**IMPACT OF VICARIOUS BEREAVEMENT
ON OTHERS NOT DIRECTLY AFFECTED**

Vicarious bereavement—Type I and Type II (e.g., Rando, 1997c) patterns of interaction and gratification of this new "deprived" state. These components of chronicity then appear to bring their own stress or effect and their own pattern of psychiatric morbidity. . . . *Chronic "disastrous" effects of long-term or terminal illness for patient and family members have been identified in a number of investigations.* (pp. 186–187, emphasis added)

In a life-threatening or terminal illness, the anticipatory mourner embodies Raphael's notions of being bereaved for past losses as well as contending with current and future losses, all the while coping with the stresses of chronicity and the disastrous effects of the illness. Raphael's work confirms Rando's assertion that in anticipatory mourning, one contends with past, present, and future losses that transpire over an often extended period of time.

In 1991, Terr proposed a categorization of childhood traumas. This classification has been adopted by many as useful for adult traumas as well. It has particular applicability to contending with life-threatening or terminal illness in anticipatory mourning in terms of understanding the traumatic impact of chronic losses and trauma.

Terr identified a *Type I trauma* as being a single, discrete, unanticipated, overwhelming event of limited duration (e.g., murder, natural disaster, accident). Vividly remembered, the event produces questions such as "Why?" and "Why me?" The affected individual attempts to gain retrospective mastery and invests considerable mental energy in developing reasons and purposes for the event and ways the disaster could have been averted. This type of trauma produces classic PTSD symptoms of repetition, avoidance, and hyperarousal and is prognostic of quicker recovery and fewer long-term problems than Type II events.

In contrast, a *Type II trauma* stems from multiple, repeated, or long-standing exposure to extreme events, often of intentional human design (e.g., sexual abuse, torture, witnessing chronic aggression between parents). While the first such event in the series creates surprise and a Type I trauma, subsequent unfolding of events creates a sense of anticipated trauma from which the person attempts to protect and preserve the self by defenses such as massive denial, repression, dissociation, self-anesthesia, self-hypnosis, identification with the aggressor, and aggression turned against the self. Psychic numbing, rage, and unremitting sadness commonly exist, along with fear. These reactions and defenses often lead to profound character changes and result in long-standing interpersonal and characterological problems, frequently exhibited in the symptoms of "disorders of extreme stress not otherwise specified" (DESNOS), delineated earlier in this chapter.

Crossover conditions is the term employed by Terr to refer to the coincidence of features of both Type I and Type II conditions. Typically, a single shock (Type I) occurs, and the ongoing stresses subsequent to it tend to push the changes in the survivor to those characteristic of Type II traumas.

With a little extrapolation, the experience of anticipatory mourning can be seen to embody both Type I and Type II trauma, thus serving as a type of crossover condition. In this regard, the Type I element in the situation is the dying of the loved one. However, the dying occurs over time and with many associated traumatic experiences, including the anticipation of future and continued traumatization and the effects of chronic living with and defending against the Type II trauma.

Finally, with regard to chronicity, convincing clinical and empirical data reveal that illnesses that are overly lengthy predispose survivors to poorer postdeath adjustment. (See chapter 1 in this volume under "A Combination of Positive and Negative Findings," as well as Rando, 1983, and Sanders, 1982–1983, for more in-depth discussion of this issue.) What these findings suggest is that there can be "too much of a good thing." While illness of a certain length can provide opportunities to engage in therapeutic processes of anticipatory mourning, over a longer time the benefits appear to be washed out or offset. Problems are generated by excessive amounts of time, during which secondary conflicts and other issues arise, and resources become progressively depleted.

Creation of Secondary Traumatic Stress

Several of the concepts discussed in relationship to traumatic stress in anticipatory mourning can be subsumed under a discussion of secondary traumatic stress and stress disorder (see Figley, 1993, 1995a, 1995b, 1995c). Briefly, *secondary traumatic stress* refers to "the natural consequent behaviors and emotions resulting from knowing about a traumatizing event experienced by a significant other—the stress resulting from helping or wanting to help a traumatized or suffering person" (Figley, 1995b, p. 7). Secondary traumatic stress disorder (STSD) is a syndrome of symptoms nearly identical to PTSD, except that exposure to knowledge about a traumatizing event experienced by a significant other is what triggers and is associated with the symptoms. In contrast, in PTSD symptoms are directly connected to the sufferer, who is the person actually experiencing primary traumatic stress.

Certainly, observing the physical and psychosocial losses, suffering, and pain of the dying individual will impact upon an empathetic, concerned anticipatory mourner. Witnessing what the dying person is facing—and particularly how he or she is reacting to what is being faced—affects the anticipatory mourner in addition to seeing that dying loved one's personal control be robbed, assumptive world be violated, terror at the unknown, anxiety at annihilation and its ensuing separation from loved ones, and ongoing contention with loss. In many cases, knowing that the person is being reluctantly taken away and faces possible physical, spiritual, and/or psychosocial suffering—coupled with needing to say good-bye and tolerating the awareness that one will continue to exist while the loved one will die—increases one's own personal primary traumatization at the same time it creates and escalates secondary traumatic stress.

Inherent Generation of Helplessness

One cannot find a more formidable adversary than death: No one escapes it. Consequently, there is no situation in which human beings are in a more vulnerable position than in relation to their demise. This means that the confrontation with death played out in life-threatening or terminal illness will generate some amount of helplessness. It inevitably produces encounters with limit, finitude, existential anxiety, loss, and awareness of relative impotence. Not infrequently, fear is significant, at least for many persons at certain points in the illness. Since these encounters exist around the other set of events known to be traumatic precipitants—injury to and actual death of a loved one that meet Criterion A for PTSD/ASD— we can expect some measure of traumatic stress to result.

Much of the material in this chapter converges on the relative helplessness and fear experienced by many anticipatory mourners. The issues of separation anxiety, the characteristics of the anticipatory mourning situation, and the various exposure of and demands placed upon anticipatory mourners are often attended by feelings that contribute to trauma. Caregivers must be aware of the potentially horrific nature of the loved one's dying and deeply appreciate the sense of helplessness, fear, frustration, and eventual anger that may accompany witnessing a dearly loved person being permanently, irretrievably, and in some cases, unwillingly pulled away. This is not to indicate that positive experiences and growth cannot occur, only that helplessness is part of the experience. Indeed, for many the decision to grow within or transcend the experience is a direct response to the perception of helplessness with regard to death.

Confrontation with Overwhelming Emotions and Conflicting Demands During Times of Strained Resources

Part of what can make anticipatory mourning traumatic is the encountering of overwhelming emotions. Such emotions may be directly stirred up by the illness and overpowering in number, intensity, or type, or they may result because the ego and its coping abilities are so compromised by the anxiety and distress associated with the illness and its implications that affect cannot be appropriately modulated or mediated. Whatever the reason, the result often is that the individual is overwhelmed and overcome, feeling out of control and helpless. A primary task for all anticipatory mourners is maintaining a balance between experiencing feelings and being overwhelmed by them. Precisely because emotions are often quite intense, possibly unfamiliar, and usually painful, the anticipatory mourner struggles to keep his or her emotions in check, to avoid being too inundated by or distanced from them.

Depending upon the point in the illness trajectory, the person's current coping capacities, his or her preexisting vulnerabilities, and any of the other factors known to influence anticipatory mourning (see chapter 2 in this volume), the anticipatory mourner's abilities to contend with the psychosocial and physical vicissitudes of the illness experience will be impacted. For instance, Pattison (1977, 1978) notes how during the acute crisis of diagnosis, the ill person temporarily manifests regressive, immature, or primitive ego-coping mechanisms and defenses. More age-appropriate ones come into play during the chronic living-dying phase. We can extrapolate this finding to the reactions of other parties in the anticipatory mourning situation as well.

If resources are strained because of the chronicity of the illness, obviously this will affect the anticipatory mourner's ability to cope and his or her experience of traumatization. It only makes sense that it is easier to traumatize an exhausted, depleted, and strained individual than it is to traumatize one who is in better psychological and physical shape.

One of the seven generic operations in anticipatory mourning, balancing conflicting demands, is a primary source of strain and a major task (see chapter 2 in this volume). The anticipatory mourner is often called upon to struggle with a number of such demands, to say nothing of the obligation to reconcile what is associated with them: opposing needs, clashing responsibilities, discordant roles, antagonistic tasks, incompatible obligations, and irreconcilable expectations.

As I have noted in chapter 2, conflict can erupt on each of three contextual levels in anticipatory mourning. Intrapsychic conflict involves competing demands inherent in the anticipatory mourning itself (e.g., holding on versus letting go of the dying person or acknowledging the terrible reality and its implications versus trying to maintain hope). Interpersonal conflict may occur among any combination of parties concerning demands for tending to the needs of one party (often but not always the ill person) and reconciling such demands with the needs of another (or others). For example, conflict can transpire between and among individual mourners and various others in the family/intimate network (e.g., struggling to give the dying person sufficient attention while continuing to take care of others in the family), concerned others, or caregivers. Systemic conflict takes place among persons within the different systems involved, such as between certain members of the family/intimate network and members of other participating systems, such as caregivers (e.g., when the family orders the caregivers not to inform the children), other social and organizational groups, or the health care system. Conflicts can arise between other parties and systems as well—for instance, between caregivers and the health care system.

Although relatively unacknowledged in the professional literature, a primary source of stress involves efforts to balance oneself and what one expects oneself to do. In addition to trying to bring some order to the chaos created by conflicting demands, the anticipatory mourner struggles to withstand and respond to them. Great tension arises as a consequence of being pulled from different directions and from the anxiety of having to identify, prioritize, and choose from divergent existing demands. It can be traumatic for some to be aware that incorrect choices can impact significantly and adversely upon those they love as well as on themselves. The actual stress of trying to decide how to proceed in any one or combination of the unlimited dilemmas that present themselves in anticipatory mourning only heightens the normal emotional responses that accompany that experience.

REFERENCES

Alsop, S. (1973). *Stay of execution: A sort of memoir.* Philadelphia: J. B. Lippencott.

Alter, C., Pelcovitz, D., Axelrod, A., Goldenberg, B., Harris, H., Meyers, B., Grobois, B., Mandel, F., Septimus, A., & Kaplan, S. (1996). The identification of PTSD in cancer survivors. *Psychosomatics, 37*(2), 137–143.

Alter, C., Pelcovitz, D., Axelrod, A., Goldenberg, B., Septimus, A., Harris, H., Meyers, B., Grobois, B., & Kaplan, S. (1992, October). *The identification of PTSD in cancer survivors.* Paper presented at the 39th meeting of the Academy of Psychosomatic Medicine, San Diego.

American Psychiatric Association. (1987). *Diagnostic and statistical manual of mental disorders* (DSM-III-R). Washington, DC: Author.

American Psychiatric Association. (1994). *Diagnostic and statistical manual of mental disorders* (DSM-IV). Washington, DC: Author.

Anderson, C. (1949). Aspects of pathological grief and mourning. *The International Journal of Psycho-Analysis, 30,* 48–55.

Barton, D. (1997). The family of the dying person. In D. Barton (Ed.), *Dying and death: A clinical guide for caregivers.* Baltimore: Williams & Wilkins.

Bowlby, J. (1973). *Attachment and loss: Vol. 2. Separation: Anxiety and anger.* New York: Basic.

Bowlby, J. (1980). *Attachment and loss: Vol. 3. Loss: Sadness and depression.* New York: Basic.

Brett, E. (1993). Psychoanalytic contributions to a theory of traumatic stress. In J. Wilson & B. Raphael (Eds.), *International handbook of traumatic stress syndromes.* New York: Plenum.

Brett, E. (1996). The classification of posttraumatic stress disorder. In B. van der Kolk, A. McFarlane, & L. Weisaeth (Eds.), *Traumatic stress: The effects of overwhelming experience on mind, body, and society.* New York: Guilford.

Brown, D. (1996). *Phase-oriented treatment and hypnotherapy of trauma patients* (Parts 1/2). Workshops presented at the second annual conference on "Trauma, Loss and Dissociation: The Foundations of 21st Century Traumatology," Alexandria, VA. Presented by Georgetown University Medical Center and Kairos Ventures II, Ltd., February 29–March 4.

Burgess, A. (1975). Family reaction to homicide. *American Journal of Orthopsychiatry, 45,* 391–398.

Cannon, W. (1927). *Bodily changes in pain, hunger, fear and rage* (2nd ed.). New York: Appleton-Century-Crofts.

Cella, D., Mahon, S., & Donovan, M. (1990). Cancer recurrence as a traumatic event. *Behavioral Medicine, 16,* 15–22.

Cleiren, M. (1993). *Bereavement and adaptation: A comparative study of the aftermath of death.* Washington, DC: Hemisphere.

Cordova, M., Andrykowski, M., Kenady, D., McGrath, P., Sloan, D., & Redd, W. (1995). Frequency and correlates of postttraumatic-stress-disorder-like symptoms after treatment for breast cancer. *Journal of Consulting and Clinical Psychology, 63*(6), 981–986.

Doka, K. J. (1993). *Living with life-threatening illness: A guide for patients, their families, and caregivers.* Lexington, MA: Lexington Books.

Eth, S., & Pynoos, R. (1985). Interaction of trauma and grief in childhood. In S. Eth & R. Pynoos (Eds.), *Post-traumatic stress disorder in children.* Washington, DC: American Psychiatric Press.

Everly, G. (1995). Psychotraumatology. In G. Everly & J. Lating (Eds.), *Psychotraumatology: Key papers and core concepts in post-traumatic stress.* New York: Plenum.

Exline, J., Dorrity, K., & Wortman, C. (1996). Coping with bereavement: A research review for clinicians. *In Session: Psychotherapy in Practice, 2*(4), 3–19.

Fenichel, O. (1945). *The psychoanalytic theory of neurosis.* New York: W. W. Norton.

Figley, C. R. (1982, February). *Traumatization and comfort: Close relationships may be hazardous to your health.* Paper presented at the conference "Families and Close Relationships: Individuals in Social Interaction," Texas Tech University, Lubbock.

Figley, C. R. (1993). Foreword. In J. Wilson & B. Raphael (Eds.), *International handbook of traumatic stress syndromes.* New York: Plenum.

Figley, C. R. (Ed.). (1995a). *Compassion fatigue: Coping with secondary traumatic stress disorder in those who treat the traumatized.* New York: Brunner/Mazel.

Figley, C. R. (1995b). Compassion fatigue as secondary traumatic stress disorder: An overview. In C. R. Figley (Ed.), *Compassion fatigue: Coping with secondary traumatic stress disorder in those who treat the traumatized.* New York: Brunner/Mazel.

Figley, C. R. (1995c). Epilogue: The transmission of trauma. In C. R. Figley (Ed.), *Compassion fatigue: Coping with secondary traumatic stress disorder in those who treat the traumatized.* New York: Brunner/Mazel.

Figley, C. R. (1997). Preface. In C. R. Figley, B. Bride, & N. Mazza (Eds.), *Death and trauma: The traumatology of grieving.* Washington, DC: Taylor & Francis.

Figley, C. R., Bride, B., & Mazza, N. (Eds.). (1997). *Death and trauma: The traumatology of grieving.* Washington, DC: Taylor & Francis.

Freud, S. (1953). Moses and monotheism. In J. Strachey (Ed. & Trans.), *The standard edition of the complete psychological works of Sigmund Freud* (Vol. 23). London: Hogarth Press. (Original work published 1939)

Freud, S. (1955). Beyond the pleasure principle. In J. Strachey (Ed. & Trans.), *The standard edition of the complete psychological works of Sigmund Freud* (Vol. 18). London: Hogarth Press. (Original work published 1920)

Freud, S. (1959). Inhibitions, symptoms, and anxiety. In J. Strachey (Ed. & Trans.), *The standard edition of the complete psychological works of Sigmund Freud* (Vol. 20). London: Hogarth Press. (Original work published 1926)

Furman, E. (1974). *A child's parent dies: Studies in childhood bereavement.* New Haven, CT: Yale University Press.

Garfield, C. (Ed.). (1978). *Psychosocial care of the dying patient.* New York: McGraw-Hill.

Glaser, B. G., & Strauss, A. (1965). *Awareness of dying.* Chicago: Aldine.

Green, B. (1993). Identifying survivors at risk: Trauma and stressors across events. In J. Wilson & B. Raphael (Eds.), *International handbook of traumatic stress syndromes.* New York: Plenum.

Green, B. (1997, June). *Traumatic loss: Conceptual issues and new research findings.* Keynote address presented at the 5th International Conference on Grief and Bereavement in Contemporary Society and the 19th Annual Conference of the Association for Death Education and Counseling, Washington, DC.

Green, B., Epstein, S., Krupnick, J., & Rowland, J. (1997). Trauma and medical illness: Assessing trauma-related disorders in medical settings. In J. Wilson & T. Keane (Eds.), *Assessing psychological trauma and PTSD.* New York: Guilford.

Green, B., Rowland, J., Krupnick, J., Epstein, S., Stockton, P., Stern, N., Spertus, I., & Steakley, C. (1996). *Posttraumatic stress disorder in women with breast cancer: Prevalence and phenomenology.* Manuscript submitted for publication.

Harper, B. (1977). *Death: The coping mechanism of the health professional.* Greenville, SC: Southeastern University Press.

Hartman, C., & Burgess, A. (1985). Illness-related post-traumatic stress disorder: A cognitive-behavioral model of intervention with heart attack victims. In C. Figley (Ed.), *Trauma and its wake: The study and treatment of post-traumatic stress disorder.* New York: Brunner/Mazel.

Herman, J., & van der Kolk, B. (1987). Traumatic antecedents of borderline personality disorder. In B. van der Kolk (Ed.), *Psychological trauma.* Washington, DC: American Psychiatric Press.

Horowitz, M. J. (1986). *Stress response syndromes* (2nd ed.). Northvale, NJ: Jason Aronson.

Horowitz, M. J., Siegel, B., Holen, A., Bonnano, G., Milbraith, C., & Stinson, C. (1997). Diagnostic criteria for complicated grief disorder. *American Journal of Psychiatry, 154,* 904–910.

Horowitz, M. J., Simon, N., Holden, M., Connett, J., Borhani, N., Benfari, R., & Billings, J. (1983). The stressful impact of news of premature heart disease. *Psychosomatic Medicine, 45*, 31–40.

Horowitz, M. J., Weiss, D., & Marmar, C. (1987). Diagnosis of posttraumatic stress disorder. *The Journal of Nervous and Mental Disease, 175*(5), 267–268

Horowitz, M. J., Wilner, N., & Alvarez, W. (1979). Impact of Event Scale: A measure of subjective stress. *Psychosomatic Medicine, 41*, 209–218.

Jacobs, S. (1993). *Pathologic grief: Maladaptation to loss.* Washington, DC: American Psychiatric Press.

Jacobs, S. (1999). *Traumatic grief: Diagnosis, treatment, and prevention.* Philadelphia: Brunner/Mazel.

Jacobs, S., Hansen, F., Kasl, S., Ostfeld, A., Berkman, L., & Kim, K. (1990). Anxiety disorders during acute bereavement: Risk and risk factors. *Journal of Clinical Psychiatry, 51*, 269–274.

Jacobs, S., & Kim, K. (1990). Psychiatric complications of bereavement. *Psychiatric Annals, 20*, 314–317.

Janet, P. (1889). *L'automatisme psychologique.* Paris: Balliere.

Janoff-Bulman, R. (1992). *Shattered assumptions: Towards a new psychology of trauma.* New York: The Free Press.

Jennings, L., & France, R. (1979). Management of grief in the hypochondriac. *Journal of Family Practice, 8*, 957–960.

Kalish, R. A. (1970). The onset of the dying process. *Omega, 1*, 57–69.

Kaltreider, N., Wallace, A., & Horowitz, M. J. (1979). A field study of the stress response syndrome: Young women after hysterectomies. *Journal of the American Medical Association, 242*, 1499–1503.

Kardiner, A. (1941). *The traumatic neuroses of war.* New York: Hoeber.

Kastenbaum, R. (1969). Death and bereavement in later life. In A. H. Kutscher (Ed.), *Death and bereavement.* Springfield, IL: Charles C. Thomas.

Kelly, B., & Raphael, B. (1993). AIDS: Coping with ongoing terminal illness. In J. Wilson & B. Raphael (Eds.), *International handbook of traumatic stress syndromes.* New York: Plenum.

Krystal, H. (1984). Psychoanalytic views on human emotional damages. In B. van der Kolk (Ed.), *Post-traumatic stress disorder: Psychological and biological sequelae.* Washington, DC: American Psychiatric Press.

Krystal, H. (1985). Trauma and the stimulus barrier. *Psychoanalytic Inquiry, 5*, 131–161.

Kübler-Ross, E. (1969). *On death and dying.* New York: Macmillan.

Larson, D. (1993). *The helper's journey: Working with people facing grief, loss, and life-threatening illness.* Champaign, IL: Research Press.

Lehrman, S. (1956). Reactions to untimely death. *Psychiatric Quarterly, 30*, 564–578.

Lindy, J. P., Green, B., Grace, M., & Titchener, J. (1983). Psychotherapy with survivors of the Beverly Hills Supper Club fire. *American Journal of Psychotherapy, 37*, 593–610.

Maslow, A. (1962). *Toward a psychology of being.* Princeton, NJ: Van Nostrand Reinhold.

May, R. (1977). *The meaning of anxiety* (rev. ed.). New York: Norton.

McCann, I., & Pearlman, L. (1990). Vicarious traumatization: A framework for understanding the psychological effects of working with victims. *Journal of Traumatic Stress, 3*(1), 131–149.

Mitchell, J., & Bray, G. (1990). *Emergency services stress: Guidelines for preserving the health and careers of emergency services personnel.* Englewood Cliffs, NJ: Prentice Hall.

Mitchell, J., & Everly, G. (1996). *Critical incident stress debriefing: CISD: An operations manual for the prevention of traumatic stress among emergency service and disaster workers* (2nd ed.). Ellicott City, MD: Chevron Publishing.

Mollica, R. (1988). The trauma story: The psychiatric care of refugee survivors of violence and torture. In F. Ochberg (Ed.), *Post-traumatic therapy and victims of violence.* New York: Brunner/Mazel.

Moore, B., & Fine, B. (Eds.). (1990). *Psychoanalytic terms and concepts.* New Haven, CT: American Psychoanalytic Association and Yale University Press.

Nader, K. (1997a). Childhood traumatic loss: The interaction of trauma and grief. In C. R. Figley, B. Bride, & N. Mazza (Eds.), *Death and trauma: The traumatology of grieving.* Washington, DC: Taylor & Francis.

Nader, K. (1997b). Treating traumatic grief in systems. In C. R. Figley, B. Bride, & N. Mazza (Eds.), *Death and trauma: The traumatology of grieving.* Washington, DC: Taylor & Francis.

Nader, K., Pynoos, R., Fairbanks, L., & Frederick, C. (1990). Children's PTSD reactions one year after a sniper attack at their school. *American Journal of Psychiatry, 147,* 1526–1530.

Nir, Y. (1985). Post-traumatic stress disorder in children with cancer. In S. Eth & R. Pynoos (Eds.), *Post-traumatic stress disorder in children.* Washington, DC: American Psychiatric Press.

Ochberg, F. (1988). Post-traumatic therapy and victims of violence. In F. Ochberg (Ed.), *Post-traumatic therapy and victims of violence.* New York: Brunner/Mazel.

Parkes, C. M. (1987). *Bereavement: Studies of grief in adult life* (2nd ed.). Madison, CT: International Universities Press.

Parkes, C. M., & Weiss, R. S. (1983). *Recovery from bereavement.* New York: Basic.

Parson, E. (1984). The reparation of the self: Clinical and theoretical dimensions in the treatment of Vietnam combat veterans. *Journal of Contemporary Psychotherapy, 4,* 4–56.

Pattison, E. M. (1969). Help in the dying process. *Voices: The Art and Science of Psychotherapy, 5,* 6–14.

Pattison, E. M. (Ed.). (1977). *The experience of dying.* Englewood Cliffs, NJ: Prentice Hall.

Pattison, E. M. (1978). The living-dying process. In C. A. Garfield (Ed.), *Psychosocial care of the dying patient.* New York: McGraw-Hill.

Pelcovitz, D., Goldenberg, B., Kaplan, S., Weinblatt, M., Mandel, F., Meyers, B., & Vinciguerra, V. (1996). Posttraumatic stress disorder in mothers of children with cancer. *Psychosomatics, 37,* 116–126.

Pine, V. (1984, December). The disaster worker and death. Paper included in *The proposed F.E.M.A. manual (Early 1985),* manual for Mass Casualty Disaster seminar, sponsored by the Federal Emergency Management Agency, New York State Emergency Management Agency, and others, Syracuse, NY.

Prigerson, H., Bierhals, A., Kasl, S., Reynolds, C., Shear, M., Newsom, J., & Jacobs, S. (1996). Complicated grief as a distinct disorder from bereavement-related depression and anxiety: A replication study. *American Journal of Psychiatry, 153,* 1484–1486.

Prigerson, H., Frank, E., Kasl, S., Reynolds, C., Anderson, B., Zubenko, G., Houck, P., George, C., & Kupfer, D. (1995). Complicated grief and bereavement-related depression as distinct disorders: Preliminary empirical validation in elderly bereaved spouses. *American Journal of Psychiatry, 152*, 22–30.

Prigerson, H., Shear, M., Bierhals, A., Pilkonis, P., Wolfson, L., Hall, M., Zonarich, D., & Reynolds, C. (1997). Case histories of traumatic grief. *Omega, 35*, 9–24.

Prigerson, H., Shear, M., Jacobs, S., Reynolds, C., Maciejewski, P., Davidson, J., Rosenheck, R., Pilkonis, P., Wortman, C., Williams, J., Widiger, T., Frank, E., Kupfer, D., & Zisook, S. (1998). Consensus criteria for traumatic grief: A preliminary empirical test. *British Journal of Psychiatry, 174*, 247–253.

Prigerson, H., Shear, M., Newsom, J., Frank, E., Reynolds, C., Maciejewski, P., Houck, P., Bierhals, A., & Kupfer, D. (1996). Anxiety among widowed elders: Is it distinct from depression and grief? *Anxiety, 2*, 1–12.

Pynoos, R., Frederick, C., Nader, K., Arroyo, W., Steinberg, A., Eth, S., Nunez, F., & Fairbanks, L. (1987). Life threat and posttraumatic stress in school-age children. *Archives of General Psychiatry, 44*, 1057–1063.

Pynoos, R., & Nader, K. (1990). Children's exposure to violence and traumatic death. *Psychiatric Annals, 20*(6), 334–344.

Pynoos, R., & Nader, K. (1993). Issues in the treatment of posttraumatic stress in children and adolescents. In J. Wilson & B. Raphael (Eds.), *International handbook of traumatic stress syndromes*. New York: Plenum.

Pynoos, R., Nader, K., Frederick, C., Gonda, L., & Stuber, M. (1987). Grief reactions in school-age children following a sniper attack at school. *Israeli Journal of Psychiatry and Related Sciences, 24*(12), 53–63.

Rando, T. A. (1983). An investigation of grief and adaptation in parents whose children have died from cancer. *Journal of Pediatric Psychology, 8*, 3–20.

Rando, T. A. (1984). *Grief, dying, and death: Clinical interventions for caregivers.* Champaign, IL: Research Press.

Rando, T. A. (Ed.). (1986). *Parental loss of a child.* Champaign, IL: Research Press.

Rando, T. A. (1991). *How to go on living when someone you love dies.* New York: Bantam.

Rando, T. A. (1992–1993). The increasing prevalence of complicated mourning: The onslaught is just beginning. *Omega, 26*, 43–59.

Rando, T. A. (1993). *Treatment of complicated mourning.* Champaign, IL: Research Press.

Rando, T. A. (1994). Complications in mourning traumatic death. In I. Corless, B. Germino, & M. Pittman (Eds.), *Dying, death, and bereavement: Theoretical perspectives and other ways of knowing.* Boston: Jones and Bartlett.

Rando, T. A. (1997a). Foreword. In C. R. Figley, B. Bride, & N. Mazza (Eds.), *Death and trauma: The traumatology of grieving.* Washington, DC: Taylor & Francis.

Rando, T. A. (1997b). Living and learning the reality of a loved one's dying: Traumatic stress and cognitive processing in anticipatory grief. In K. J. Doka (Ed.), with J. Davidson, *Living with grief: When illness is prolonged.* Washington, DC: Taylor & Francis.

Rando, T. A. (1997c). Vicarious bereavement. In S. Strack (Ed.), *Death and the quest for meaning.* Northvale, NJ: Jason Aronson.

Raphael, B. (1981). Personal disaster. *Australian and New Zealand Journal of Psychiatry, 15*, 183–198.

Raphael, B. (1983). *The anatomy of bereavement*. New York: Basic.

Raphael, B. (1986). *When disaster strikes: How individuals and communities cope with catastrophe*. New York: Basic.

Raphael, B., & Maddison, D. (1976). The care of bereaved adults. In O. Hill (Ed.), *Modern trends in psychosomatic medicine*. London: Butterworth.

Raphael, B., & Martinek, N. (1997). Assessing traumatic bereavement and post-traumatic stress disorder. In J. Wilson & T. Keane (Eds.), *Assessing psychological trauma and PTSD*. New York: Guilford.

Raphael, B., & Wilson, J. (1993). Theoretical and intervention considerations in working with victims of disaster. In J. Wilson & B. Raphael (Eds.), *International handbook of traumatic stress syndromes*. New York: Plenum.

Raphael, B., & Wilson, J. (1994). When disaster strikes: Managing emotional reactions in rescue workers. In J. Wilson & J. Lindy (Eds.), *Countertransference in the treatment of PTSD*. New York: Guilford.

Redmond, L. (1989). *Surviving: When someone you love was murdered*. Clearwater, FL: Psychological Consultation and Education Services.

Remer, R., & Elliot, J. (1988a). Characteristics of secondary victims of sexual assault. *International Journal of Family Psychiatry, 9*(4), 373–387.

Remer, R., & Elliot, J. (1988b). Management of secondary victims of sexual assault. *International Journal of Family Psychiatry, 9*(4), 389–401.

Rosenblatt, P. (1983). *Bitter, bitter tears: Nineteenth-century diarists and twentieth-century grief theories*. Minneapolis: University of Minnesota Press.

Sanders, C. M. (1982–1983). Effects of sudden versus chronic illness death on bereavement outcome. *Omega, 13*, 227–241.

Schut, H., de Keijser, J., van den Bout, J., & Dijhuis, J. (1991). Post-traumatic symptoms in the first year of conjugal bereavement. *Anxiety Research, 4*, 225–234.

Shand, A. (1920). *The foundations of character* (2nd ed.). London: Macmillan.

Shuchter, S., Zisook, S., Kirkorowicz, C., & Risch, C. (1986). The dexamethasone suppression test in acute grief. *American Journal of Psychiatry, 143*, 879–881.

Simpson, M. (1997). Traumatic bereavements and death-related PTSD. In C. R. Figley, B. Bride, & N. Mazza (Eds.), *Death and trauma: The traumatology of grieving*. Washington, DC: Taylor & Francis.

Spitzer, R. (1990, May–June). *Problems and promises in the classification of post-traumatic psychopathology*. Paper presented at a course on psychological trauma cosponsored by the Harvard Medical School and the Massachusetts Mental Health Center, Cambridge.

Spungen, D. (1998). *Homicide—The hidden victims: A guide for professionals*. Thousand Oaks, CA: Sage.

Stuber, M., Christakis, D., Houskamp, B., & Kazak, A. (1996). Posttraumatic symptoms in childhood leukemia survivors and their parents. *Psychosomatics, 37*, 254–261.

Taylor, S., & Aspinwall, L. (1990). Psychosocial aspects of chronic illness. In P. Costa & G. VandenBos (Eds.), *Psychological aspects of serious illness: Chronic conditions, fatal diseases, and clinical care*. Washington, DC: American Psychological Association.

Terr, L. (1991). Childhood traumas: An outline and overview. *American Journal of Psychiatry, 148*, 10–20.

Titchener, J. (1986). Post-traumatic decline: A consequence of unresolved destructive drives. In C. Figley (Ed.), *Trauma and its wake: Vol. 2. Traumatic stress theory, research, and intervention.* New York: Brunner/Mazel.

Vachon, M. (1987). *Occupational stress in the care of the critically ill, the dying, and the bereaved.* Washington, DC: Hemisphere.

van der Kolk, B. (1987). The psychobiology of the trauma response: Hyper-arousal, constriction, and addition to traumatic reexposure. In B. van der Kolk (Ed.), *Psychological trauma.* Washington, DC: American Psychiatric Press.

van der Kolk, B. (1996). The complexity of adaptation to trauma self-regulation, stimulus discrimination, and characterological development. In B. van der Kolk, A. McFarlane, & L. Weisaeth (Eds.), *Traumatic stress: The effects of over-whelming experience in mind, body, and society.* New York: Guilford.

Weisman, A. D. (1972a). *On dying and denying: A psychiatric study of terminality.* New York: Behavioral Publications.

Weisman, A. D. (1972b). Psychosocial considerations in terminal care. In B. Schoenberg, A. Carr, D. Peretz, & A. H. Kutscher (Eds.), *Psychosocial aspects of terminal care.* New York: Columbia University Press.

Weisman, A. D. (1975). Thanatology. In A. M. Freedman, H. I. Kaplan, & B. J. Sadock (Eds.), *Comprehensive textbook of psychiatry* (Vol. 2, 2nd ed.). Balti-more: Williams & Wilkins.

Weisman, A. D. (1977). The psychiatrist and the inexorable. In H. Feifel (Ed.), *New meanings of death.* New York: McGraw-Hill.

Weisman, A. D. (1979). *Coping with cancer.* New York: McGraw-Hill.

World Health Organization. (1992). *ICD–10: International classification of dis-eases and related health problems* (10th ed.). Geneva, Switzerland: Author.

Wilson, J. P., & Lindy, J. D. (Eds.). (1994a). *Countertransference in the treatment of PTSD.* New York: Guilford.

Wilson, J. P., & Lindy, J. D. (1994b). Empathic strain and countertransference. In J. P. Wilson & J. D. Lindy (Eds.), *Countertransference in the treatment of PTSD.* New York: Guilford.

Wilson, J. P., & Lindy, J. D., & Raphael, B. (1994). Empathic strain and therapist defense: Type I and II CTRs. In J. P. Wilson & J. D. Lindy (Eds.), *Counter-transference in the treatment of PTSD.* New York: Guilford.

Wilson, J. P., & Raphael, B. (Eds.). (1993). *International handbook of traumatic stress syndromes.* New York: Plenum.

Zisook, S., & Shuchter, S. (1996). Psychotherapy of the depressions in spousal bereavement. *In Session: Psychotherapy in Practice, 2*(4), 31–45.

CHAPTER 7

Anticipatory Mourning and Coping with Dying: Similarities, Differences, and Suggested Guidelines for Helpers

Charles A. Corr
Donna M. Corr

This chapter examines similarities and differences between *anticipatory mourning* and *coping with dying*. At first glance, this investigation would appear to be a rather straightforward undertaking. After all, anticipatory mourning and coping with dying both concern events that can or do take place shortly before death. These events occur during the period of the "dying process" or the "living-dying interval" (Pattison, 1977), as it has been called.

To put this another way, anticipatory mourning and coping with dying are different perspectives from which to try to appreciate what takes place between the time when dying begins (itself not an easy moment to define) and the moment when death occurs. Many who work with dying persons and their family members recognize the experiences that are part of anticipatory mourning and coping with dying. The dying and their loved ones are often aware of these experiences, as well. Granted this phenomenological foundation, researchers and scholars strive to clarify and explain these experiences through the conceptual prisms of anticipatory mourning and coping with dying, in part by describing each of the concepts in its own right and in part by drawing out their similarities and differences.

In fact, however, our proposed investigation is more complicated and less easily undertaken than it might first appear. So far as we know, there is no existing body of literature that attempts to compare and contrast anticipatory mourning—previously often termed *anticipatory grief*—and coping with dying. Moreover, there are disagreements about and gaps in the explication of both concepts. Therefore, this chapter should be regarded as a tentative exploration of this complex subject, an effort to stake out some central landmarks in this area and to advance certain suggestions concerning the issues.

We begin with a brief excerpt from a letter written early in 1848 by the celebrated American writer Edgar Allan Poe. Reflection on Poe's reactions to and struggles with events preceding his wife's death helps to lay the groundwork for our analysis. Next, we offer a brief review of what has been written about the concept of anticipatory grief, followed by an account of some relevant concepts and language taken from postdeath experiences of bereavement, grief, and mourning. We proceed to an interim summary of some important points concerning anticipatory mourning and postdeath bereavement. The subsequent sections of the chapter examine the central concept of coping, some issues that may arise in coping during the dying process, and lessons to be drawn from three theoretical approaches to explication of the dying process. This chapter concludes with comparisons between anticipatory mourning and coping with dying and practical guidelines for those who work with dying persons and their family members.

EDGAR ALLAN POE: ONE MAN'S EXPERIENCES

On January 4, 1848, Edgar Allan Poe sent the following response to a question put to him in a letter of July 26, 1847, by George W. Eveleth.*

> You say—"Can you hint to me what was the terrible evil which caused the irregularities so profoundly lamented?" Yes; I can do more than hint. This "evil" was the greatest which can befall a man. Six years ago, a wife, whom I loved as no man ever loved before, ruptured a blood-vessel in singing. Her life was despaired of. I took leave of her forever & underwent all the agonies of her death. She recovered partially and I again hoped. At the end of a year the vessel broke again—I went through precisely the same scene. Again in about a year afterward. Then again—again—again & even once again at varying intervals. Each time I felt all the agonies of her death— and at each accession of the disorder I loved her more dearly & clung to her life with more desperate pertinacity. But I am

---

*We thank our colleague, Dr. Clyde Nabe, for drawing our attention to this extract from Poe's letters, and we express our continuing gratitude to him for helping us strive for conceptual clarity in matters such as those explored in this chapter.

constitutionally sensitive—nervous in a very unusual degree. I became insane, with long intervals of horrible sanity. During these fits of absolute unconsciousness I drank, God only knows how often or how much. As a matter of course, my enemies referred the insanity to the drink rather than the drink to the insanity. I had indeed, nearly abandoned all hope of a permanent cure when I found one in the death of my wife. This I can & do endure as becomes a man—it was the horrible never-ending oscillation between hope & despair which I could not longer have endured without the total loss of reason. In the death of what was my life, then, I receive a new but—oh God! how melancholy an existence. (Poe, 1966, p. 356)

One can see in this account the tortured story of Poe's 6-year struggle with a series of threats to the life of his wife, Virginia; his tormented responses to those events; his turning to drink as a way to cope with his anguish and his wife's health problems; and his experience when she eventually died in January of 1847 at age 25. Because Poe recounts the story in reply to an inquiry about his recent behavior, his comments on these events do not say much about—and perhaps even obscure—his wife's experiences during this period. And because Poe is describing his own reactions to the threatened and eventually the actual loss of his wife's life, he frames much of his message in the anguished language of grief.

The concept of anticipatory mourning provides a useful perspective from which to try to understand and empathize with the experiences of Poe and his wife. They initially confronted the consequences of a ruptured blood vessel in her lungs, apparently associated with tuberculosis, or "pulmonary consumption," as it was then called (Shulman, 1996; Silverman, 1991). In the expectation that this disorder would lead to Virginia's imminent death, Poe "took leave of her forever & underwent all the agonies of her death"—a classic portrait of grief distinguished mainly by the intensity of Poe's reactions and by the fact that these reactions occurred before rather than after his wife's actual death.

However, Virginia Poe did not die immediately as a consequence of this first threat to her health and life. She recovered partially, only to undergo repeated similar experiences over the next several years. On each of these occasions, Poe reports that he "felt all the agonies of her death" all over again. Evidently, Poe's life became dominated by escalating grief, oscillations between despair and hope, desperate eruptions of love and clinging, and bouts of what appear to be mania and aberrant behavior—including both alcohol abuse and what he terms "long intervals of horrible sanity."

Although Poe reports repeated experiences of leave-taking and anguished feelings that would have been expected had his wife actually died, on each occasion he also declares that he "loved her more dearly & clung to her life with more desperate pertinacity." In short, Poe lived through a roller coaster–like sequence of events. It was a period filled with powerful feelings of pain and love, of being pushed apart and drawn together, ending only in what Poe ironically terms "a permanent cure" upon Virginia's death. No doubt, Poe's experiences after her death were also difficult—he describes the time after the death as a melancholy existence that he must endure. But his focus in the extract from the letter is mainly on experiences prior to the death, experiences that he reports he could not much longer have borne without going completely insane.

In connection with the concept of anticipatory mourning, one might ask: Can a husband experience grief and mourning prior to, and as a result of, the expectation of the death of his wife? The answer to be drawn from Poe's letter is obviously affirmative. More broadly, is this merely a portrait of one man's experiences of anticipatory mourning? Or is it characteristic in its general features of what anyone might experience? To consider these broader questions, we must consider how anticipatory mourning is described in the professional literature.

ANTICIPATORY GRIEF: A BRIEF REVIEW OF THE LITERATURE

The concept of "anticipatory grief" was apparently first put forward by Lindemann (1944) in his landmark article describing bereavement and grief associated both with mass death from a fire at the Coconut Grove nightclub in suburban Boston and with other losses. Drawing especially on studies of relatives of members of the armed forces, Lindemann referred to anticipatory grief as a syndrome of "genuine grief reactions in patients who had not experienced a bereavement but who had experienced separation . . . [a separation that] is not due to death but is under the threat of death" (p. 147).

Since the mid-1940s, anticipatory grief has been the subject of intermittent attention from a variety scholars (e.g., Aldrich, 1963; Fulton & Fulton, 1971; Fulton & Gottesman, 1980; Schoenberg, Carr, Kutscher, Peretz, & Goldberg, 1974). Perhaps the concept received the most sustained attention in a landmark book, *Loss and Anticipatory Grief*, edited by Rando (1986b). In her introductory chapter in that book, Rando (1986a) outlined the history of the concept, noted some reasons why it had been misunderstood and (in some quarters) rejected or found controversial, and undertook to define its key elements with new rigor and precision.

Rando (1986a) defined anticipatory grief as

the phenomenon encompassing the processes of mourning, coping, interaction, planning, and psychosocial reorganization that are stimulated and begun in part in response to the awareness of the impending loss of a loved one and the recognition of associated losses in the past, present, and future. (p. 24)

That is a complicated and wide-ranging definition. Indeed, it may be too broad a definition to sustain what is meant by either the adjective *anticipatory* or the noun *grief*. We can test this concern and clarify some of the complexities associated with the concept of anticipatory grief by locating anticipatory grief in the more familiar landscape of what is known about postdeath bereavement, loss, grief, and mourning, as we do subsequently. First, however, we must note the use of the term *anticipatory mourning* to encompass more than mere grief. As we will discuss later, there are reasons to prefer this term over the one historically used. Henceforth, anticipatory mourning will incorporate what had been denoted by the older term. *Anticipatory grief* will be used either to conform to a particular writer's usage or to denote situations in which grief—but not necessarily mourning—transpires. The full rationale for this will be explained later.

POSTDEATH EXPERIENCES: LANGUAGE AND CONCEPTS

Bereavement, Loss, and Grief

If anticipatory grief and mourning as they are experienced prior to or independently of a death are truly a type of grief and mourning, then they must be similar in some ways to postdeath experiences of bereavement, loss, grief, and mourning. We can evaluate the truth of this supposition by examining these various postdeath experiences, with special attention to the key concepts of grief and mourning.

To begin, the term *bereavement* is widely understood to designate the objective situation of an individual who has experienced the loss of a significant person or other attachment figure (Osterweis, Solomon, & Green, 1984; Parkes, 1996; Rando, 1984; Raphael, 1983; Stroebe, Stroebe, & Hansson, 1993). Clearly, if there were no loss of such an attachment object, there would be no bereavement. However, it is also true that if there had been no such significant object in the first place, there would be no bereavement. For example, in a loveless relationship or one involving purely nominal affiliation to a distant relative or acquaintance, there may be no significant bonds of attachment. In such circumstances, termination of the relationship may not result in any experience of bereavement for the remaining member. And it is probably correct to say that if there were no awareness of a significant loss, even though that loss had actually occurred, there would also be no bereavement. This latter alternative might apply during the period between the death of a loved one in a far-off land and the communication of that fact to the survivor.

The noun *bereavement* and the adjective *bereaved* apply to one who has been deprived of something that is important to him or her. Both words derive from a verb not often used today in colloquial English. That word is *reave;* according to the *Oxford English Dictionary,* it means "to despoil, rob, or forcibly deprive" (Simpson & Weiner, 1989, Vol. 13, p. 295). In short, a bereaved person is one who has been deprived, robbed, plundered, or stripped of something that he or she valued. That which is taken away in this manner may be a person or an object, a physical being or a valued symbol. The important point is that the taking away of the valued person or object has done violence to the bereaved survivor.

As a result of having been "reaved" or having experienced one or more significant losses, an affected individual typically reacts to what has happened and is happening to him or her. It would be surprising if this were not the case. Failure to react would seem to indicate that the loss the individual is confronting does not involve a person or thing that was truly prized, that the individual is somehow unaware of the loss, or that other factors intervene.

In its most fundamental sense, *grief* is the term used to designate the reaction to loss. The term arises from the grave or heavy weight that presses upon those who are bereaved and burdens them (Simpson & Weiner, 1989, Vol. 6, pp. 834–835). Quite often in the literature, however, one finds grief described or defined as "the emotional reaction to loss." At first glance, this definition may appear obvious, but on closer examination it is also inadequate in important ways. Most individuals who have experienced significant losses *do* respond emotionally to their experiences; however, their reactions are not confined to *emotions* alone or, at least, may not always be well described by that term.

In reflecting on the term *emotions,* Elias (1991) observed that "broadly speaking, emotions have three components, a somatic, a behavioral and a feeling component" (p. 177). As a result,

> the term *emotion,* even in professional discussions, is used
> with two different meanings. It is used in a wider and in a

narrower sense at the same time. In the wider sense the term *emotion* is applied to a reaction pattern which involves the whole organism in its somatic, its feeling and its behavioral aspects. . . . In its narrower sense the term *emotion* refers to the feeling component of the syndrome only. (p. 119)

According to this view, the importance of *feelings* in the overall grief reaction to loss is undeniable. But equally undeniable is the importance of other aspects of the grief reaction. These include *somatic or physical sensations* and *behaviors or behavioral disturbances,* as well as matters involving *cognitive, social, and spiritual functioning.* It is not important to set forth here a comprehensive list of all aspects of the grief reaction to loss. The main point is that human beings may, and indeed are likely to, react to important losses in their lives in a broad spectrum of ways and with their whole selves, not just in a limited set of ways or solely with some narrowly defined aspect of their humanity.

In principle, grief is a natural and healthy reaction to loss. Surely there can be unhealthy reactions to loss; one of these would be a failure to react in any way to the loss of a significant person or object in one's life. But insofar as the grief reaction is a natural and healthy phenomenon, it should be described in the language of "signs," "manifestations," or "expressions." Illness language such as that associated with the term *symptoms* should be avoided in relationship to grief unless one consciously intends to use the latter terminology to indicate some form of aberrant or unhealthy reaction to loss.

Mourning

Some use the term *grief* to refer not only to the reaction to loss as previously outlined but also to everything else that follows in bereavement after a death. Others (e.g., Attig, 1991) draw a distinction between *grief* and *grieving.* Still others prefer to differentiate between *grief* and *mourning.* We have found it useful to follow this last option and, therefore, need to add to the foregoing description of postdeath bereavement some additional comments on mourning.

Many aspects of the grief reaction to loss are in character very much like a reflex. They seek to push away the hurt of the loss with denial, or turn back upon it with anger, or respond to its implacability with sadness. Most of this is defensive. But there is more to bereavement than defensive reactions or passive reflexes (Rando, 1993, 1995). The other central element is the effort to find some way to live with the loss. This is *mourning,* the attempt to incorporate one's loss and grief into ongoing living. Mourning is what one does to try to learn to live with one's bereavement.

Note that *mourning* is a participial word indicating action or activities of the sort expressed by verbs. Lindemann (1944) called this "grief work," although he defined that phrase in a specific way. Here, it is enough to think of mourning as an active, effortful attempt to manage what bereavement has brought into one's life. In this context, note that bereavement brings both loss and grief. A bereaved person needs to do something to integrate into his or her life both the loss that has been experienced and the grief reactions that the loss has provoked. For example, when a spouse dies, the survivor must mourn or try to learn to live in healthy ways with both his or her loss ("My spouse has been taken away from me; I am deprived of that ongoing presence") and with his or her grief reaction ("I am angry at what has been done to me" or "I am sad about the barrenness of my new mode of life").

Because humans are both individuals and social creatures, mourning has two complementary forms or aspects. It is both an internal, private, or intrapersonal process—an individual's inward struggles to cope with or manage the loss and the grief reaction to that loss; and an outward, public, or interpersonal process—the overt, visible, and characteristically shared public efforts to cope with or manage the loss and associated grief reaction. Some authors (e.g., Wolfelt, 1996) prefer to emphasize the distinction between these two aspects of bereavement by describing its intrapersonal dimension or internal meaning as *grieving* and reserving the term *mourning* for the interpersonal or outward and public expression of grief. There is justification for some linguistic distinction between intrapersonal and interpersonal coping with loss and grief. However, that usage is not adopted here. The central point for purposes of this chapter is the distinction between grief as reaction and mourning as coping.

INTERIM SUMMARY: ANTICIPATORY MOURNING AND POSTDEATH BEREAVEMENT

From this analysis of postdeath experiences of bereavement, grief, and mourning, there is no reason to deny that a dying person and his or her family members may experience many losses during the dying process or before death itself. For example, losses associated with illness and dying are likely to intrude into the lives of the individual and the family. These intruders may take away many things, such as health, energy, a sense of the self as invulnerable, the ability to work at a job or around the home, time to effect changes in difficult relationships, or long-cherished prospects for the future. We are "reaved" by such losses; they spoil or tear apart our lives.

Especially in cases involving the long-term, chronic, or degenerative diseases (the leading causes of death in our society), losses associated with life-threatening illness and dying are likely to take place in an incremental but often intermittent and unpredictable way over an extended period. At any given point, some losses will already have occurred (they are *past* losses), others may be ongoing or currently taking place (they are *present* losses), and still others will not yet have happened (they are *future* losses). Insofar as they are foreseeable, only these last—the future losses—can properly be said to be awaited or *anticipated*. After all, used properly, *anticipation* involves a kind of precognition or presentiment wherein we represent to ourselves or realize something before it actually occurs (Simpson & Weiner, 1989, Vol. 1, p. 522). That is why talk about predeath grief as merely "anticipatory" misdescribes its proper character. And that is why Rando (1988)—who insists that we are exploring an experience that really does occur—has argued that it is, nevertheless, a misnomer to speak of "anticipatory" grief because the grief response can be prompted not only by losses that are currently only anticipated but by past or present losses as well.

A further sense in which *anticipatory grief* misdescribes or misnames the experience concerns the term *grief*. First, for any of the losses mentioned in the previous paragraph (past, present, or future), an individual's reactions may range from a positive welcoming or looking forward to the occurrence to a negative response or expectation. This range can be seen in the comments of Edgar Allan Poe. He hoped for his wife's recovery or cure and eventually just for any sort of end to the trials that he shared with her. At the same time, his reactions to the threats to his wife's health and life also took the form of despair and a melancholy dread of what he anticipated. Reactions to any of the losses experienced prior to death need not always take the form of grief.

Second, as noted earlier in the analysis of postdeath bereavement, the term *grief* points to a wide spectrum of natural and healthy reactions to any loss. As such, grief is not confined solely to reactions that occur after a death. It applies with equal validity to losses experienced prior to a death and even to losses that are not death related in any way, such as those entailed in getting a divorce, being fired from a job, or having to give up one's home. Only in some cases will these losses that one is grieving be anticipated (that is, not yet having occurred); in all other instances, the losses will already have occurred or be in the process of occurring.

One important point made by scholars who have studied the concept of anticipatory grief is that it is not the same as "forewarning" or merely being warned in advance of the expected occurrence of a loss (Rando, 1986a). Forewarning or some sort of awareness of an actual or expected loss is a necessary condition for anticipation, but it is neither equivalent to nor sufficient for grief. The reason for this is that one may simply not react to the warning—and it is the reaction that is the heart of what has been termed *anticipatory grief*.

This fact draws attention again to our earlier characterization of grief as reaction to loss. Strictly speaking, if the noun in the phrase "anticipatory grief" is understood as described previously, then anticipatory grief is limited to *reactions* to predeath losses (whether those losses have already occurred, are in the process of occurring, or are expected to occur). If it is meant also to include the processes of *coping* with those losses and with the grief reactions that they stimulate (as in the definition of anticipatory grief offered by Rando, 1986a), then it is more appropriate to speak of "anticipatory mourning" or "anticipatory grief and mourning." That is, use of "anticipatory grief" in the larger sense in which that phrase has been most frequently defined appears to be a further instance of the misnaming of this phenomenon. One can concede, however, that discussions of all types of bereavement frequently blur the lines between what is meant by *grief* and what is meant by *mourning*. We concur with Rando's comments in the introduction of this book that these important distinctions mandate a renaming of the general phenomenon as anticipatory mourning, of which anticipatory grief is a part.

COPING DURING THE DYING PROCESS

The concept of mourning as coping with loss and grief suggests another way to learn about similarities and differences between anticipatory mourning and coping with dying. We can take a new approach by turning to the concept of coping with dying and beginning with reflection on the nature of coping. This will involve a definition of *coping*, some comments on the differences between coping and reacting, attention to different types of stressors that may generate both grief reactions and coping (represented here by contrasts between losses and new challenges), and a renewed emphasis on the temporal and social dimensions of all aspects of experiences associated with dying.

Reacting and Coping

Reacting and coping are clearly related. As we have already suggested, *reacting* is often automatic and defensive, as when one throws up a hand to ward off a stone that would otherwise strike one. *Coping*, as Lazarus and Folkman (1984) define it, is "constantly changing cognitive and behavioral efforts to manage specific external and/or internal demands that are appraised as taxing or exceeding the resources of the person" (p. 141; cf. Monat & Lazarus, 1991; White, 1974). From this standpoint, coping is essentially constructive (Weisman, 1984). It seeks—not always successfully and not always in the most effective ways—to *manage* a perceived source of stress. Efforts to cope may not always master the situation, but ineffective coping is still an attempt to manage that which is perceived as stressful. Consequently, ineffective coping should not be confused with not coping, or a failure to try to cope.

Often, defensive or primitive reactions to loss may be replaced by or develop into more sophisticated and constructive coping mechanisms. In this sense, they can be closely related. This is what people mean when they say that their bereavement has taught them both about their vulnerability to loss (and to their grief reactions) and about their resilience. They now realize that they are vulnerable because they see that loss can touch them and provoke strong reactions; they recognize that they are resilient because they have found ways to go on living productive and meaningful lives in the wake of significant losses. The nature of the grief reaction has highlighted how important the attachments were in their lives; the work of mourning has indicated the marvelous capacities they have developed to cope with loss and grief, and eventually to find comfort and solace by reorganizing their lives and restructuring their relationships to the lost persons or objects.

Losses and New Challenges

In the context of bereavement, discussions of reactions and coping are understandably framed in terms of loss, grief, and mourning. But it is worth keeping in mind that stress is not limited to that which originates in loss. Stress can arise in many aspects of life and in many ways; in particular, it can come into an individual's life not only through losses but also through new challenges. We can illustrate this fact by briefly describing two women with advanced, metastatic breast cancer whom we met many years ago during our initial visits to a British hospice.

The first of these women, whom we will call Jane, was admitted to the inpatient hospice unit in an advanced state of distress. When the sources of her distress were ameliorated and after receiving good nourishment and care, Jane rebounded to a condition in which she no longer needed to remain in the hospice facility. It was evident that her condition would continue to decline over a relatively short period of weeks or months, even with the support of the hospice home care team. But at the moment, Jane felt good and wanted to go home. However, discharging Jane to home did not seem feasible because she had lived alone for many years after being divorced and was not fully able to care for herself in her present condition.

Nevertheless, the discharge was arranged after the hospice staff informed Jane's ex-husband of the situation and initiated contacts between them. The ex-husband agreed to move back into the couple's former home to provide the presence and support that Jane would need during the time between her discharge and what everyone expected would be her eventual readmission to the hospice unit. Hospice staff were extremely pleased with this arrangement. They commented that, in their experience, ex-wives had frequently stepped in to help dying ex-husbands, but a similar act by an ex-husband had no precedent.

On the morning of her discharge, one of us happened to ask Jane if she was looking forward to going home and living once again in the same house with her ex-husband. Both her words and her physical presentation (for example, new blouse, hair carefully arranged, and makeup in place) clearly conveyed her excitement about returning home. For the rest, she commented that she intended to give her ex-husband a try and "put him through his paces."

The second woman, whom we will call Mary, was a long-term hospice inpatient. In an ideal world, perhaps she should have received most of the care she needed at home. However, during the course of her illness, Mary's husband had essentially abandoned her and taken up a relationship with another woman. And Mary's adult daughter, who only rarely visited her in the hospice, turned out to be an extremely fragile personality, incapable of coping effectively with the stresses presented by her mother's illness or of providing much support to her beleaguered mother.

That there were multiple and ongoing losses in Mary's life at this point is obvious. But it is also worth recognizing that the hospice staff had taken Mary in and had become for her a kind of substitute family. Her eccentricities were tolerated, the difficulties associated with her advancing illness and some peculiar habits were addressed with patience and love, and she had no fear of being abandoned by her new hospice community. In a 25-bed institution that experienced the death of approximately one patient per day, Mary became over many months a figure of constancy for members of staff and a mentor in some ways for other dying patients (and their family members) who were admitted to her 5-bedded ward. In coping with the challenges of her new situation, Mary came to see that when her death eventually came, it would be peaceful and she would be safe in her new hospice home/community.

Both of these women were dying from long-term and widespread cancer. Both were confronted with many past, present, and future (expected) losses, including the prospect of looming death in the not-too-distant future. In their behavior and in our conversations with them, it was evident that both were reacting to their losses with grief. But that was not the whole story. New challenges arose for these two women every day in their lives, many of the challenges—though not all—directly associated with their disease. Each woman was coping with her losses and with the new challenges she faced. And each was the beneficiary of skilled intervention by a caring team of professionals and volunteers and by new sources of social support to assist in the work of coping. Unrelieved loss and grief is not a fair or adequate description of this period in the life of either Jane or Mary.

Temporal and Social Aspects of Dying

Temporal and social aspects of the experiences associated with dying can be seen both in terms of losses and in terms of new challenges. We will consider each of these dimensions in turn.

Losses

At any given point in the dying process, there may be past, present, and future losses involved in the overall experience. A husband who is diagnosed with a terminal illness may already have lost his job, he may currently be confined to bed, and it may be clear that he will soon lack sufficient energy to wrap his wife in the great bear hugs that had marked their relationship ever since they first fell in love, kept them close in later years, and been so comforting throughout their shared life together.

As unique individuals, these spouses may act separately and/or as a couple to react to and cope with the vocational loss of status (and income) that is now in their past, the loss of the husband's mobility that is ongoing in their present, and the loss of a special and treasured kind of intimacy that they expect will soon come upon them. As members of a social unit, they face their losses together, share their reactions to some degree, and perhaps cope in more or less similar ways. As distinct individuals, this husband and this wife inevitably differ to some degree in what they perceive as significant in those losses, how they react to the losses, and how they cope with both the perceived losses and their grief reactions. In all of this, they experience both anticipatory mourning and coping with dying.

There is another aspect to the temporality and the social character of anticipatory mourning and coping with dying. Past, present, and future losses as described thus far have all been identified in terms of a fixed moment, the present. But what is present today will be past tomorrow. As time passes, the future becomes first the present and later the past. As it does, the loss of the husband's ability to hug his wife, which both expected, may already have occurred, and they may now have shifted their focus to center on anxieties concerning the time when he will decline further and slip into a coma as his disease progresses. The changing losses associated with dying are likely to initiate changing grief reactions and changing patterns of coping with dying.

New Challenges

Thus far, our discussions have been framed in terms of actual or symbolic losses that occur or are perceived prior to death. However, loss is only one part of the story of that predeath period. Along with the losses come *new challenges*. With a husband's past loss of his job may come challenges to social status, to job-related identities, and to establishing ways of meeting ongoing household expenses. With the husband's present confinement to bed and loss of mobility come challenges to reorganize the everyday workload of household duties, to bring food to his room, and to find ways of managing the many demands of a bedfast person. And with the prognosis of further declines in the husband's energy, the couple can soon expect to be challenged to find new ways to express and communicate their love for each other.

Issues encountered during dying are not limited solely to reacting to and coping with a changing set of losses. Encounters with dying also include a need to cope with new and often heretofore unexperienced sorts of challenges that are likely to arise. In part, new challenges such as those described in the preceding paragraph may be consequences of various types of losses. But they can also be related to other aspects of the dying process. For example, a hospice patient who is invited to talk to an audience about his or her experiences might find that prospect stressful if he or she lacks prior experience in public speaking. Similarly, family members might find it difficult to cope with a dying relative who reacts to a life-threatening illness by unilaterally liberating him- or herself from former social roles and responsibilities.

Even events unrelated to the cycle of disease and loss can pose new and daunting challenges during the living-dying interval. For example, in the case of the couple described earlier, someone might steal their car from the driveway, a new grandchild might be born, an old friend might die, or they might win the lottery. These and many other events present new challenges in everyday life. Here they represent an additional overlay or potential source of stress beyond what is already being experienced as a function of death-related losses. To understand these new challenges correctly, we must address the concept of coping with dying more directly and more fully.

COPING WITH DYING: THREE THEORETICAL APPROACHES

As Kastenbaum and Thuell (1995) note, "Strictly speaking, there are no scientific theories of dying, if by 'theory' we mean a coherent set of explicit propositions that have predictive power and are subject to empirical verification" (p. 176). Nevertheless, Kastenbaum and Thuell also note that there do exist at least three distinctive theoretical approaches to understanding and interpreting the dying process, each of which draws attention to specific dimensions of the overall experience. Brief descriptions of these theoretical approaches will help draw out some of the complexities involved in the dying process and in coping with dying.

Glaser and Strauss: Awareness Contexts and Dying Trajectories

Working as medical sociologists in hospitals in California during the 1960s, Barney Glaser and Anselm Strauss published two important books that are relevant to an understanding of processes involved in dying. The first of these books, *Awareness of Dying* (Glaser & Strauss, 1966), described four types of *awareness contexts*, or patterns of interaction and interpersonal communication between a dying person, his or her family members, and his or her professional care providers. In brief, a context of "closed awareness" is structured around a situation in which a person who is dying does not realize that fact while the caregiving staff, and perhaps family members, do have that information. In this context, Glaser and Strauss observed, actions of staff and family members are guided by two principles: (a) an assumption that patients do not want to know their illnesses are terminal and (b) an unwillingness to share such information. As a result, the information is withheld, and (in this respect, at least) communication (and presumably awareness also) is closed.

In a context of "suspected awareness," there may be suspicion on the patient's part that important diagnostic and/or prognostic information is not being shared. Thus, the ill person may begin to suspect that more is going on than is being said. Nevertheless, the implicit rule of communication for staff and family members remains that the information is not to be shared.

In a context of "mutual pretense," all parties to the interaction know the anxiety-provoking truth; however, each party acts as if it were not the case. Once again, the critical information is not shared among all parties to the interaction, this time because of a kind of shared drama in which all involved act out roles intended to say that things are not as they know them to be. Glaser and Strauss added that mutual pretense may even go so far as to involve individuals' covering up missteps in which they or others reveal in some way either the information itself or the fact that they possess it. Thus, mutual pretense requires constant vigilance and a great deal of effort to maintain or correct failings in the basic strategy of dissembling.

Finally, in a context of "open awareness," all involved are willing to share information or concerns that each may possess, and such sharing is actually implemented. In fact, the parties involved may not actually spend much time discussing the fact that the ill person is dying; the central point is the willingness to discuss the realities of the situation when any party to the interaction wishes to do so.

Note that Glaser and Strauss did not present these awareness contexts as steps in a linear progression from inhibitedness to openness, nor were they recommending one or another context. As sociologists, they were simply describing four different patterns of group interaction that they had observed in connection with terminal illness. The point is that social interactions are likely to be affected by the awareness context of coping with dying. And any awareness context is likely to entail some potential costs and some potential benefits.

In a second book, *Time for Dying*, Glaser and Strauss (1968) described what they called *dying trajectories*. Such a trajectory is defined in part by "duration," or the time involved between the onset of dying and the arrival of death. In addition, the authors singled out as important a second variable: "shape," or the characteristic course of the dying process. The meaning of *shape* can be understood by analogy with the differences between the relatively flat trajectory of a cannon shell and the more exaggerated curve (and consequently shorter range) of a howitzer or mortar shell. A disease that has a relatively short dying trajectory tends to move more or less directly to death, whereas one with a longer dying trajectory may involve either a fairly consistent decline or one that is more variable and ambiguous.

Dying trajectories, as originally described by Glaser and Strauss, have both objective and subjective dimensions. For example, as a matter of objective fact, many communicable diseases display a relatively brief dying trajectory, moving fairly rapidly from the first signs of disease (e.g., elevated temperature, flushed skin) either to death or to a point at which it will become clear whether or not the body's own internal defenses and any external interventions that may have been mobilized will overcome the threat to life (e.g., the fever will "break" and recovery will begin). By contrast, a chronic or degenerative disease typically displays a much longer and perhaps more ambiguous dying trajectory.

But Glaser and Strauss also saw a subjective element in the concept of dying trajectories as they incorporate a before-the-fact estimation or an element of prediction on the part of professional care providers. That is, Glaser and Strauss noted that a professional, when confronted by an ill person, often makes a fairly rapid estimation or assessment about whether or not that individual will die and how. On the basis of such estimates, professionals organize their work, and ill persons are treated in differential ways. For example, the predicted inevitability and duration of the dying trajectory might lead to assignment to one or another ward in the hospital, and treatment might or might not include implementation of more or less aggressive interventions. For Glaser and Strauss, dying trajectories do not merely involve internal processes within ill persons; much more to the point, they describe important elements of communication and interaction between dying persons and their care providers.

Kübler-Ross: Stages of Dying

By far, the best-known theoretical approach to dying is the one set forth by Elisabeth Kübler-Ross (1969) in a book entitled *On Death and Dying*. She postulated a sequence of five stages or psychosocial reactions to awareness of impending death: denial, anger, bargaining, depression, and acceptance. Kübler-Ross also noted that "the one thing that usually persists through all these stages is *hope*" (p. 138). However, popular attention focused mainly on the so-called "stages" and far less on hope or its implications. Kübler-Ross described the stages themselves in various ways: as "reactions" or "responses," as "defense" mechanisms, and as "coping" strategies.

Although all stage theories are inherently sequential and directional (one moves forward or backward in a progression or regression, toward or away from some boundary marker), Kübler-Ross often suggested that dying persons and others who were coping with dying could jump from one stage or psychosocial reaction to another and that various stages could sometimes exist side by side. That notion tends to undercut the intrinsic connectedness and linearity inherent in the concept of stages.

In fact, few professionals who work with dying persons would now accept many of the claims associated with this theoretical approach. There is no preordained or universally desirable goal—no "perfect" way to die—that will or must be sought by all who are coping with dying. There are no essential or inevitable stages involved in a common process of seeking that goal. Nor are there only five ways of reacting or responding to impending death. Neither the early research literature (e.g., Metzger, 1979; Schulz & Aderman, 1974) nor observations from knowledgeable clinicians and scholars (Feigenberg, 1980; Kastenbaum, 1995; Pattison, 1977; Shneidman, 1980/1995; Weisman, 1977) have supported the claims Kübler-Ross made on behalf of this theoretical approach, and she has not brought forth further evidence on its behalf since its initial presentation in 1969.

Nevertheless, there are positive aspects of Kübler-Ross's theoretical approach that should not go unnoticed. Perhaps its most salutary feature is the emphasis on the individual's responses to what is happening in the dying process. If individuals can respond to dying in these (and other?) ways, then dying persons must be alive and not already dead or as good as dead. If individuals can respond to dying in these (and other?) ways, then such responses need not be limited to dying persons alone; similar reactions may be experienced by family members and care providers. If individuals can respond to dying in these (and other?) ways, then such responses are likely to be expressed and shared in both verbal and nonverbal communications as well as in other behaviors.

Drawing in particular on the preface to Kübler-Ross's book, C. M. Corr (1993) proposed three lessons that can be learned from her work on coping with dying: First, dying persons (and others who are coping with dying) are *still alive* and may have important things they need or want to do; second, others cannot expect to provide effective care for dying persons and all who are coping with dying unless they *listen actively* to those people and determine with them the priorities that should govern such care; and third, there is much that all humans can *learn from* dying persons and all who are coping with dying about our common mortality and ways of responding to imminent death.

Corr: A Task-Based Approach to Coping with Dying

A third theoretical approach to understanding and interpreting dying has been proposed by C. A. Corr (1992). This approach emphasizes efforts that are involved in coping with dying on the part of anyone caught up in such coping. Those efforts are interpreted as *tasks* or *task work*. Corr noted four areas or dimensions of task work—physical, psychological, social, and spiritual—in a holistic account of coping with dying. In a general way, physical tasks center on the satisfaction of bodily needs and the minimization of physical distress; psychological tasks typically emphasize security, autonomy, and richness in living; social tasks involve interpersonal attachments to particular individuals and social groups; and spiritual tasks center on the identification, development, or reaffirmation of sources of spiritual energy and the fostering of hope.

Corr chose to speak of *tasks* rather than *needs* because of his concern that use of the latter term leads too quickly to a shift in many minds to the roles of care providers in helping to meet needs. By contrast, the emphasis in a task-based model is on the goals, objectives, and efforts of the individual who is striving to cope with dying, whether that be the dying person, one of his or her family members, or a care provider. The point is to begin with the efforts of the coping person and only then to consider how the tasks of others in the environment might facilitate, impede, or have nothing to do with that individual's coping.

Central Themes in the Three Theoretical Approaches

When these three theoretical approaches to the dying process are juxtaposed, each can be seen to emphasize some aspects of the process. Each approach thus contributes to our overall understanding of the subject. For instance, the concept of dying trajectories reminds us that the disease process itself is an important determinant of both the quantity and the quality of the dying experience. Similarly, both dying trajectories and awareness contexts reveal the importance of human interactions and communication patterns in the overall experiences of dying and coping with dying.

Moreover, as noted earlier, if we set aside the framework of stages in the approach proposed by Kübler-Ross, there is much to be learned from her work about the vitality of dying persons, about some (if not all) of their psychosocial responses to awareness of impending death, about the fact that similar responses may be identified in all parties who find themselves coping with dying (ill persons, their family members, and their care providers), and about the possibility and the importance of hope as an aspect that can pervade the entire experience.

Corr's approach perhaps focused most deliberately on the concept of coping with dying. Glaser and Strauss did not articulate that concept, and Kübler-Ross spoke of coping with dying only on some occasions in setting forth her theory of stages. By contrast, Corr made issues involved in coping with dying central to his concerns. He did this by emphasizing "task work" in such coping and by arguing for the need to attend to this coping in a holistic way. Corr's approach (along with others in the field of bereavement; cf. Attig, 1991; Corr & Doka, 1994) responds to what are perceived as overly passive qualities in stage- and phase-based models. Against that, Corr argued that, at least in principle, individuals can select which tasks they wish to pursue, as well as how and when they wish to do so.

The concept of dying trajectories can accommodate a broad variety of identifiable trajectories, including such highly complex and variable trajectories as those associated with HIV disease and AIDS—phenomena identified only after Glaser and Strauss had published their work. In a similar way, Glaser and Strauss had simply described four different types of awareness contexts, without claiming either that they were intrinsically linked in some way or that they were exhaustive of all possible awareness contexts.

In her stage-based theory, Kübler-Ross seemed, at least at times, to be suggesting that there were only five ways (her identified "stages") of responding to awareness of impending death and that they were somehow connected in a stage-like sequence. Corr was concerned that this approach, with its laudable grounding in clinical attention to the experiences and concerns of individuals who were coping with dying, risked converting legitimate generalizations associated with a particular population into universal claims about and even stereotypical depictions of all such persons. Perhaps this danger has been more evident in others' applications of Kübler-Ross's approach than in the theoretical framework itself. Nevertheless, when one person who was coping with dying in the early 1970s commented, "Being invisible I invite only generalizations" (Rosenthal, 1973, p. 39), it became evident that one should at least be cautious about the seduction of overgeneralization in some theoretical approaches.

By contrast, the "task-based" approach proposed by Corr (along with some other similar models; see, for example, Corr & Doka, 1994; Doka, 1993) avoids such generalizations by claiming universal validity for the task-work schema and for its four principal dimensions (physical, psychological, social, and spiritual) and by calling for careful, active listening to identify the specific tasks that are of functional concern for any individual who is coping with dying.

COMPARISONS BETWEEN ANTICIPATORY MOURNING AND COPING WITH DYING

Although we have yet to develop a comprehensive or fully adequate theory of coping with dying, and though our understanding of anticipatory mourning has elements of imprecision or incompleteness, the present state of our knowledge does permit some instructive comparisons between anticipatory mourning and coping with dying. First, as a mode of grief, anticipatory grief that is the beginning of anticipatory mourning understandably emphasizes reactions to loss. In this context, such losses are associated with awareness of impending death. Some of these losses have already been realized or are currently being realized in the lived experience and conscious awareness of the mourner. Other losses known to the griever's mind have yet to occur in objective reality, although he or she expects them. Properly speaking, only these last are "anticipated losses."

If anticipatory grief is only grief and not more, then it is confined to reactions to loss (i.e., anticipatory grief). If it also involves mourning processes, then it encompasses both reacting to and coping with loss (i.e., anticipatory mourning). In any case, it remains associated with some realized or anticipated experience of loss in which the realization occurs prior to death.

By contrast, coping with dying is explicitly concerned with coping and is not restricted to associations with loss. Loss may be part of what one copes with during dying, but the stressors that generate such coping may also include a variety of new challenges. As a result, anticipatory grief may be a part of, but cannot be coextensive with or equivalent to, coping with dying. By itself, anticipatory grief is just one distinct, identifiable part of the full range of events that occur or may occur as part of the process of coping with dying. Together, anticipatory grief and coping with dying are central features in the dying process.

Anticipatory mourning and coping with dying have many similar features. Both originate in the responses of individual mourners and copers to events arising in their lives. Both take place within social networks that center on, but are not confined to, a dying person. Both are heavily influenced by interpersonal communications and interaction patterns that arise at the intersections of individuals who are experiencing grief and striving to cope. Both have strong temporal components in that sources of stress and responses to that stress can be expected to change as dying progresses and other issues intervene.

In our view, it is not too elementary to note that both anticipatory mourning and coping with dying are experiences of living persons. Life is the fundamental condition for both phenomena. Dying persons are living human beings, as are all other individuals who are drawn into and engage in anticipatory mourning and coping with dying. From this perspective, it is the ways in which dying persons and involved others live out their lives that are most relevant to anticipatory mourning and coping with dying. As the American humorist Josh Billings (1818–1885) is reported to have observed, "Life consists not in holding good cards but in playing those you do hold well."

How we play our cards when we are dying, or when a significant other is dying, is what this is all about. In other words, the central concept in this human drama is clearly the concept of *coping*. As a set of reactions to perceived losses, anticipatory grief is a part of or the beginning of a coping process. As a set of processes that attempt to manage stressors encountered in connection with dying, coping with dying is clearly a coping process.

Recall the key elements in the definition of coping quoted earlier. Coping is (a) "constantly changing" (b) "efforts to manage" (c) perceived stressors (Lazarus & Folkman, 1984). This interpretation of coping is fully consistent with our analyses of anticipatory mourning and coping with dying. It emphasizes the coping processes and the attempt to manage perceived stressors. It does not confuse coping with outcome because it acknowledges that coping may or may not ultimately be successful. More specifically, this understanding of coping does not confuse efforts to "manage" stress with efforts to "master" stress. Quite often, one can manage a situation without mastering it—for example, by accepting, enduring, minimizing, tolerating, or avoiding its demands.

In their well-known analysis of coping, Moos and Schaefer (1986) identified three broad focal domains or types of coping: appraisal-focused coping, problem-focused coping, and emotion-focused coping. If we fit Moos and Schaefer's work into the analyses outlined in this chapter, we might say that they have drawn attention in the first place to the way the person who is coping appraises or understands his or her situation as an individual who is dying or as someone attached to such an individual. In the examples of the two British hospice patients presented earlier, both Jane and her ex-husband and Mary and her husband clearly have different and perhaps changing appraisals of their respective situations. One way to cope with the losses and challenges experienced during the dying process is to rework one's appraisal of the situation. In the popular comic strip, when Dr. Zook told Hagar the Horrible that he would soon be unable to get through the door of the house if he persisted in his current life-style, Hagar interpreted this to Helga, his wife, as medical advice to remodel the entryway to their home.

A second way to cope with losses and challenges experienced during the dying process is to do something about them. This is not simply a matter of appraisal. It may involve taking actions to change the sources of stress. More typically, problem-focused coping is expressed in interventions of the sort that are central to the hospice philosophy of palliative care. These are interventions designed not to eradicate the cause of the stress but to minimize sources of distress and to maximize present quality of life. When possible, coping in this way can achieve much during the dying process.

According to Moos and Schaefer, a third way of coping with the losses and challenges of the dying process involves emotion-focused coping. In light of our earlier comments on the terms *emotion* or *emotional* as involving a potentially misleading narrowing of grief from a holistic reaction to loss to one of feelings alone, we might prefer to describe this as "reaction-focused" coping. Here, what is central is not the experienced loss, but one's reactions to that loss, not the new challenge in itself but one's responses to that challenge. In this regard, Edgar Allan Poe found himself led to excessive drinking by the intensity of his reactions to his wife's afflictions, and he took pains to note that it was not the excessive drinking that led to his intense grief reactions.

Dylan Thomas (1971) recommended a distinctive type of reaction-focused coping in his famous poem "Do Not Go Gentle into That Good Night." Thomas urged his reader to "rage, rage against the dying of the light" (p. 128). That may be good advice for some, although it will not be helpful for persons who seek to come to terms with death in their own minds. These latter individuals often best cope by reorganizing their reactions or making peace with sources of stress. This point of view is captured in an anonymous saying noting that "although we cannot direct the wind, we can adjust our sails." In other words, even when it does not help to reappraise the wind or to try to change its force or direction, adjusting sails and tacking with the wind may be good advice for many sailors on the troubled seas of life.

In short, individuals may experience anticipatory mourning and strive to cope with dying in many and varied ways. Grief, mourning, and coping may be influenced directly by a particular set of losses and challenges or indirectly by lifelong patterns of personality and behavior. Helpers should not expect that people will experience anticipatory mourning or coping with dying only in ways that might gain their approval. Insofar as their grief, mourning, and coping are not intrinsically harmful to themselves or to others, who are we to engage in "killing them softly with our song"?

PRACTICAL CONCLUSIONS: TEN GUIDELINES FOR HELPERS

An improved understanding of the similarities and differences between anticipatory mourning and coping with dying can be of value in a variety of ways to those seeking to help the dying and their family members during the dying process. On the basis of the preliminary investigation in this chapter, we suggest the following 10 guidelines for such helpers.

Guideline 1: Dying individuals and (of course) others who are experiencing anticipatory mourning and/or who are coping with dying are living human beings. This is a lesson stressed by Kübler-Ross, who often insisted that such people need to address what she called "unfinished business." But others who have studied experiences of anticipatory mourning and/or coping with dying have more or less explicitly advanced similar lessons. What this means for helpers is affirming the value in the lives of people who are experiencing anticipatory mourning or coping with dying, as well as our shared humanity, by reaching out to assist them in their struggles. Enabling people to mourn as they should and to cope as they must is the noble work of helping in a context of dying.

Guideline 2: At any given point in the dying process, the sources of stress that confront an individual experiencing anticipatory mourning and/or coping with dying are likely to be multiple, complex, and overlapping. This is true whether the stresses arise from the various losses being experienced or expected in anticipatory mourning or from any of the other challenges associated with dying. Helpers need to look for and be sensitive to the multidimensional aspects of these experiences.

Guideline 3: When seeking to help individuals who are experiencing anticipatory mourning and/or coping with dying, it is always essential to approach them from a holistic perspective. Both anticipatory mourning and coping with dying are experiences of whole human beings. As a result, they may have physical, psychological, social, and spiritual dimensions. Effective help for people experiencing anticipatory mourning, as well as for those coping with dying, must attend to them as whole human beings. Do not limit or fail to appreciate all of their grief reactions, mourning processes, or coping tasks because of preconceptions that arise from misunderstandings of anticipatory mourning or coping with dying.

Guideline 4: When seeking to help individuals who are experiencing anticipatory mourning and/or coping with dying, it is always essential to appreciate that the losses and new challenges to which they are reacting or with which they are coping will change over time during the dying process. Helpers must be alert to this inevitable and characteristic temporal element of all that is taking place during the living-dying interval. Ask what the individual is responding to in anticipatory mourning or coping with in dying at the present moment. Do not be surprised if the person's focus of concern has changed; expect that it may change again in the near future. Life is not static; neither are anticipatory mourning and coping with dying. Assess, reassess, and reassess again each time you come to offer help.

Guideline 5: When seeking to help individuals who are experiencing anticipatory mourning and/or coping with dying, it is almost always essential to take account of the social networks within which those experiences take place and the interactions among different mourners and different copers caught up in shared involvement in a dying process. This social quality is especially evident in Rando's (1986a) account of anticipatory grief and in the work of Glaser and Strauss (1966, 1968) on both awareness contexts and dying trajectories. Because of the social aspects of both anticipatory mourning and coping with dying, it is not a waste of resources to address care to all who are involved in a dying process and to call upon or mobilize all of those same people to share in providing care to one another. Pay attention to friends and co-workers, aged parents, grandparents, and children; ask the mourner or coper who are the really significant people at this point in his or her life.

Guideline 6: We can expect to provide effective help to those experiencing anticipatory mourning and/or coping with dying only when we listen actively to them and determine with them the priorities that should govern our assistance. Once again, this lesson is prominent in the work of Kübler-Ross, but it is really implicit in all good care. Ask questions or make observations that encourage individuals to share their concerns. Listen to what they say, as well as to what they do not say and what is behind such communications. Pay attention to verbal and nonverbal communications, to literal and symbolic disclosures.

Guideline 7: In efforts to help those who are experiencing anticipatory mourning and/or coping with dying, the grief reactions and coping processes should attract primary attention. The work of any helper is or should be principally guided by an assessment of how individuals react to stressors during the dying process and how their reactions extend into or are superseded by efforts at coping. This is evident in earlier comments concerning grief and mourning in postdeath bereavement, as well as in Corr's emphasis on task work in coping with dying. Notice which losses are being grieved and how the grief is being expressed, as well as which tasks are being undertaken and how they are or are not being carried out in an individual's coping. Alertness to grief reactions and coping processes can assist helpers in identifying sources of stress as they are perceived by individuals involved in the dying process; ways in which those individuals respond to perceived stressors; the coping tasks that they pursue; physical, psychological, social, and spiritual resources at their disposal; and the ways in which interventions of various types can be implemented most effectively.

Guideline 8: Much can be done to minimize distress and to improve quality in living for individuals who are experiencing anticipatory mourning and/or coping with dying. Helpers can offer much to such individuals if they are confident that they have something useful to offer. Typically, this confidence is founded on a realistic assessment of the helper's own strengths and limitations. Know yourself and what you bring to the mourner/coper. Also, the helper should realize that experiences associated with the dying process (losses and challenges, stressors, reactions, and coping) are often complex, both in themselves and in their temporal and social aspects. Not surprisingly, in such circumstances optimal care is usually best provided by an interdisciplinary team of helpers who respect and draw upon one another's strengths and limitations in appropriate ways. Learn to work with and rely upon others in your team. Learn also to call upon your team when you are preparing for this work and when you need support in carrying it out.

Guideline 9: In assisting persons who are experiencing anticipatory mourning and/or coping with dying, helpers have much to learn about their own humanity as people who will likely one day have similar experiences and much satisfaction to gain from this work. Once again, this lesson is particularly evident in the work of Kübler-Ross, but appreciation of the rewards inherent in helping is a commonplace among those who work with others during the living-dying interval. People are grateful not to be abandoned at this juncture when they face so many losses and challenges, often for the first time. We all need one another—especially in these moments that are both pressured and precious. Imagine what the situation would be like if you were not there to help. Imagine what you would want in a similar situation in your own life.

Guideline 10: The more that we can learn about and appreciate in experiences of anticipatory mourning and coping with dying, the better off we will be as helpers and as students of the human condition. In an effort to contribute to a better understanding of experiences of anticipatory mourning and coping with dying, this chapter seeks to improve both our appreciation of these phenomena and our ability to respond to them in caring ways. In the long term, better understanding and appreciation are a constant goal; in the short term, sensitivity to fellow human beings and genuine caring are most highly prized. As Carl Jung (1954) once remarked about theories in psychology, "We need certain points of view for their orienting and heuristic value; but they should always be regarded as mere auxiliary concepts that can be set aside at any time" (p. 7).

REFERENCES

Aldrich, C. K. (1963). The dying patient's grief. *Journal of the American Medical Association, 184,* 329–331.

Attig, T. (1991). The importance of conceiving of grief as an active process. *Death Studies, 15,* 385–393.

Corr, C. A. (1992). A task-based approach to coping with dying. *Omega, 24,* 81–94.

Corr, C. A. (1993). Coping with dying: Lessons that we should and should not learn from the work of Elisabeth Kübler-Ross. *Death Studies, 17,* 69–83.

Corr, C. A., & Doka, K. J. (1994). Current models of death, dying, and bereavement. *Critical Care Nursing Clinics of North America, 6,* 545–552.

Doka, K. J. (1993). *Living with life-threatening illness.* Lexington, MA: Lexington Books.

Elias, N. (1991). On human beings and their emotions: A process-sociological essay. In M. Featherstone, M. Hepworth, & B. S. Turner (Eds.), *The body: Social process and cultural theory.* London: Sage.

Feigenberg, L. (1980). *Terminal care: Friendship contracts with dying cancer patients* (P. Hort, Trans.). New York: Brunner/Mazel.

Fulton, R., & Fulton, J. (1971). A psychosocial aspect of terminal care: Anticipatory grief. *Omega, 2,* 91–100.

Fulton, R., & Gottesman, D. J. (1980). Anticipatory grief: A psychosocial concept reconsidered. *British Journal of Psychiatry, 137,* 45–54.

Glaser, B. G., & Strauss, A. (1966). *Awareness of dying.* Chicago: Aldine.

Glaser, B. G., & Strauss, A. (1968). *Time for dying.* Chicago: Aldine.

Jung, C. G. (1954). The development of personality (Vol. 17). In H. Read, M. Fordham, & G. Adler (Eds.), *The collected works of C. G. Jung* (20 vols.). New York: Pantheon.

Kastenbaum, R. (1995). *Death, society, and human experience* (5th ed.). Boston: Allyn and Bacon.

Kastenbaum, R., & Thuell, S. (1995). Cookies baking, coffee brewing: Toward a contextual theory of dying. *Omega, 31,* 175–187.

Kübler-Ross, E. (1969). *On death and dying.* New York: Macmillan.

Lazarus, R. S., & Folkman, S. (1984). *Stress, appraisal, and coping.* New York: Springer.

Lindemann, E. (1944). Symptomatology and management of acute grief. *American Journal of Psychiatry, 101,* 141–148.

Metzger, A. M. (1979). A Q-methodological study of the Kübler-Ross stage theory. *Omega, 10,* 291–302.

Monat, A., & Lazarus, R. S. (Eds.). (1991). *Stress and coping: An anthology* (3rd ed.). New York: Columbia University Press.

Moos, R. H., & Schaefer, J. A. (1986). Life transitions and crises: A conceptual overview. In R. H. Moos & J. A. Schaefer (Eds.), *Coping with life crises: An integrated approach*. New York: Plenum.

Osterweis, M., Solomon, F., & Green, M. (Eds.). (1984). *Bereavement: Reactions, consequences, and care*. Washington, DC: National Academy Press.

Parkes, C. M. (1996). *Bereavement: Studies of grief in adult life* (3rd ed.). New York: Routledge.

Pattison, E. M. (1977). *The experience of dying*. Englewood Cliffs, NJ: Prentice Hall.

Poe, E. A. (1966). *The letters of Edgar Allan Poe, with new foreword and supplementary chapter* (Vol. 2; J. W. Ostrom, Ed.). New York: Gordian Press.

Rando, T. A. (1984). *Grief, dying, and death: Clinical interventions for caregivers*. Champaign, IL: Research Press.

Rando, T. A. (1986a). A comprehensive analysis of anticipatory grief: Perspectives, processes, promises, and problems. In T. A. Rando (Ed.), *Loss and anticipatory grief*. Lexington, MA: Lexington Books.

Rando, T. A. (Ed.). (1986b). *Loss and anticipatory grief*. Lexington, MA: Lexington Books.

Rando, T. A. (1988). Anticipatory grief: The term is a misnomer but the phenomenon exists. *Journal of Palliative Care, 4*(1/2), 70–73.

Rando, T. A. (1993). *Treatment of complicated mourning*. Champaign, IL: Research Press.

Rando, T. A. (1995). Grief and mourning: Accommodating to loss. In H. Wass & R. A. Neimeyer (Eds.), *Dying: Facing the facts* (3rd ed.). Washington, DC: Taylor & Francis.

Raphael, B. (1983). *The anatomy of bereavement*. New York: Basic.

Rosenthal, T. (1973). *How could I not be among you?* New York: George Braziller.

Schoenberg, B., Carr, A., Kutscher, A. H., Peretz, D., & Goldberg, I. (Eds.). (1974). *Anticipatory grief*. New York: Columbia University Press.

Schulz, R., & Aderman, D. (1974). Clinical research and the stages of dying. *Omega, 5*, 137–144.

Shneidman, E. S. (1980/1995). *Voices of death*. New York: Harper and Row/ Kodansha International.

Shulman, E. (1996). Edgar Allan Poe: Drawing the line between self-destructive life style and actual suicide. *Omega, 34*, 29–69.

Silverman, K. (1991). *Edgar A. Poe: Mournful and never-ending remembrance*. New York: HarperCollins.

Simpson, J. A., & Weiner, E. S. C. (Eds.). (1989). *The Oxford English dictionary* (2nd ed., 20 vols.) Oxford, England: Clarendon.

Stroebe, M. S., Stroebe, W., & Hansson, R. O. (Eds.). (1993). *Handbook of bereavement: Theory, research, and intervention*. New York: Cambridge University Press.

Thomas, D. (1971). *The collected poems of Dylan Thomas: 1934–1952*. New York: New Directions.

Weisman, A. D. (1977). The psychiatrist and the inexorable. In H. Feifel (Ed.), *New meanings of death*. New York: McGraw-Hill.

Weisman, A. D. (1984). *The coping capacity: On the nature of being mortal.* New York: Human Sciences Press.

White, R. H. (1974). Strategies of adaptation: An attempt at systematic description. In G. V. Coelho, D. A. Hamburg, & J. E. Adams (Eds.), *Coping and adaptation.* New York: Basic.

Wolfelt, A. D. (1996). *Healing the bereaved child: Grief gardening, growth through grief and other touchstones for caregivers.* Fort Collins, CO: Companion Press.

CHAPTER 8
Denial and the Limits of Anticipatory Mourning

Stephen R. Connor

INTRODUCTION

Controversy continues over the understanding and use of the term *anticipatory mourning*. It has been the belief that anticipatory mourning is like postdeath mourning except that it occurs prior to the loss of the loved one. Mourning expressed before the loss has been thought to mitigate against abnormal mourning reactions after death and enhance adjustment to loss. Research on the links between anticipatory mourning and postbereavement adjustment is, however, inconclusive (Evans, 1994).

Initial criticism of what formerly was referred to as anticipatory grief was based on the belief that "real" grief could occur only following the death event (Parkes & Weiss, 1983; Silverman, 1974). Predeath responses were thought to be emotional or coping reactions but not grief. Grieving could occur only following an actual loss.

Rando (1986) pointed out that anticipatory grief—referred to hereafter in this chapter as *anticipatory mourning,* a phenomenon that inherently incorporates anticipatory grief at its inception—can be seen as separate from postdeath grief and mourning. She argued that the phenomenon is not composed exclusively of anticipated losses but includes as well mourning for losses that have already happened or are currently being experienced. These predeath losses can affect either the dying person or the family; can relate to past, present, or future losses; and can encompass psychological, social, or physiological factors.

It has also been noted that anticipatory mourning cannot be assumed to occur simply on the basis of the length of illness or because a patient has been informed of a life-threatening diagnosis. The purpose of this chapter is to explore the limits of anticipatory mourning, to ask how it is that anticipatory mourning can occur in some individuals and not at all in others. It is proposed that denial plays a crucial role in people's responses to the knowledge of impending death. I will examine the clinical implications of this proposition.

RELEVANT CONCEPTUALIZATIONS AND DISTINCTIONS

Much of the conflict over the relevance of anticipatory mourning comes from a lack of clarity about its definition. *Anticipatory* implies that the phenomenon is mourning over something that has not yet happened. However, rather than concerning what is anticipated (i.e., the forthcoming death), the term is often directed toward losses that have happened or are currently happening (e.g., loss of work, altered perception of health, limitations in use of body parts, loss of sexual functioning, changed body image, etc.). To the extent that these changes are cognitively acknowledged, responses will occur.

There is still debate over the nature of these responses. Thanatologists tend to view them as mourning reactions. Researchers in the field of stress and coping tend to see them as cognitive, behavioral, and emotional reactions to external stresses or threats. An individual response will be based on the patient's or family member's perceptions of how significant the threat is to his or her well-being (Lazarus & Golden, 1981). If the threat is minimized or denied, it will not result in a significant cognitive or emotional reaction. If the threat is perceived as great, it will elicit a coping reaction. Lazarus and Golden categorize such reactions as either problem-focused or emotion-focused coping tendencies. The usual reaction to threat is problem focused. One tries to solve the problem through curative treatment attempts. When (and if) it becomes apparent that no cure is possible, the person shifts to emotion-focused coping. This is the avenue available in terminal illness: If one cannot change the situation, one can at least change one's reaction to it.

Rather than taking only one position (i.e., that predeath emotional reactions are all mourning responses or that they are all coping reactions), it makes more conceptual sense to posit that both phenomena are occurring. The individual has experienced significant losses and thus is mourning at the same time as he or she is attempting to cope with new threats. It may be helpful for clinicians to assist individuals in sorting out these differing dynamics so that losses can be identified and mourned while new coping reactions are strengthened.

One proposed explanation for the presence of anticipatory mourning is that it functions as a kind of rehearsal or prior imagination of the loss (Arkin, 1974; Ramshorn, 1974). The individual rehearses the loss better to prepare emotionally for the real event. Some individuals do seem to try to master the situation by working it over and trying to incorporate the future loss into their schemes of the world. Doing so is not always adaptive, however. It is similar to Lindemann's (1944) description of a spouse who had so thoroughly prepared for the death of her husband who was away during World War II that, when he returned, she no longer loved him and wanted a divorce.

Another difficulty is the distinction between death-related loss and other types of loss. Some believe that postdeath grief and mourning are unique and different from those generated by other losses. Weiss (1988, 1994) suggests that grief is possible only when one is separated from a relationship of attachment with another human being. But what about the loss of a limb or the loss of a healthy future? Although complete separation from a loved one is a profound loss, it also seems likely that other personally significant losses can elicit real grief responses and catalyze mourning processes.

There are many different kinds of death. Sweeting and Gilhooly (1992) describe three different forms of death: clinical, biological, and social. Clinical death can occur before biological death; social death can occur even earlier. Social death precedes the other forms and can lead to anticipatory mourning. However, these mourning and coping reactions can occur only if there is cognitive awareness that a loss has occurred or that a real threat to integrity or well-being exists. To the extent that these are not acknowledged, there is no opportunity to mourn or to muster adaptive coping.

RELEVANT RESEARCH

The general literature on anticipatory mourning is summarized earlier in chapter 1 of the present book. This section will review important findings related to denial in terminal illness and its impact on anticipatory mourning.

A number of important texts have examined the use of denial in terminal illness. Avery Weisman's (1972) classic book, *On Dying and Denying,* provided a number of important contributions to further the understanding of denial. Weisman introduced the concept of "appropriate death," which he describes as purposeful death, pain free, with emotional and social impoverishments kept to a minimum and conflicts resolved. If denial is used, however, this is difficult to accomplish. Weisman went on to posit three degrees of denial. First-order denial is the patient's obvious denial of the main facts of the illness. Second-order denial, which may appear after the diagnosis is accepted, is denial of the significance or implications of the illness. Third-order denial is the inability to believe the illness will result in death; the patient believes he or she will remain in the incapacitated state indefinitely.

Elisabeth Kübler-Ross (1969) included denial in her stage theory of response to impending death. She identified denial as a first-stage response, a kind of shock absorber that allowed one time to develop more adaptive coping responses. Other authors have contributed to an understanding of denial. Breznitz (1983) expanded on Weisman's concepts to propose seven different kinds of denial, each related to a different stage in the processing of threatening information. Thomas Hackett (Hackett & Weisman, 1964; Weisman & Hackett, 1966) emphasized denial as arising from the social sphere and saw the importance of denial in preserving significant relationships. He proposed a scale (Hackett & Cassem, 1974) that classified denying patients as either mild, moderate, or major, though the criteria were never precise. In his 1973 book *The Denial of Death*, Ernest Becker proposed that inability to deal with death was a cultural failure. He had been influenced by Otto Rank, who questioned society's inability to inculcate the values of the hero, who faces death without denial.

Though early researchers viewed denial as a negative reaction (Freud, 1924/1964; Freud, 1940/1964; Sjoback, 1973), many others perceived it as a more adaptive coping process (Beilin, 1981; Beisser, 1979; Dansak & Cordes, 1978–1979; Haan, 1965; Hackett & Cassem, 1970) or as a useful strategy in the early stages of cancer. More recent authors have focused on both the negative and the positive functions of denial in the seriously ill. Lazarus and Golden (1981) observe that "denial like processes have both beneficial and harmful consequences depending on the timing, circumstances, and pervasiveness" (p. 30). Taylor (1989) sees denial as unhealthy when it is reality distorting; she also sees the use of positive illusions as helpful in getting people through difficult crises. Repression and denial alter perceptions of reality, whereas illusions simply interpret it in the best possible light.

Rando (1986) notes that there is probably a balance between denial (which presumably would forestall anticipatory mourning work) and acceptance (which presumably would facilitate it). This may explain why anticipatory mourning does not necessarily increase as the loss grows nearer. There are a number of reasons not to assume the presence of anticipatory mourning in situations where the likelihood of death is high. Fulton and Gottesman (1980) warn against assuming that forewarning of loss is the same as anticipatory mourning. Forewarning is the perception that a death may occur; it does not tell us how the person will respond to the information. The response will be greatly affected by psychological, interpersonal, and sociocultural factors. For instance, Vachon et al. (1977) reported that, although 66% of widows of cancer patients acknowledged having been told that their husbands were dying, 40% refused to accept the warnings, even from the physicians. Of 162 widows, 61% had not discussed impending death with their spouses. For those who had discussed it, 81% said that having talked made the bereavement experience easier. Those who refused to accept the forewarnings of death saw the illness as lingering, and death came as a complete shock.

When I studied the effects of psychosocial intervention on denial in terminally ill patients (Connor, 1992), I found that most denial was in the service of preserving important interpersonal relationships. Interventions had positive effects by decreasing the need for use of defenses and presumably facilitated the expression of anticipatory mourning. A later study (Connor, 1996b) revealed that widows and widowers who were more involved in the care of their spouses and had more psychosocial interventions to facilitate anticipatory mourning utilized hospitals and outpatient medical services significantly less than those without this support.

It seems clear that denial can have significant impact on the presence of anticipatory mourning. The more denial is used, the less likely it is that a loss will be perceived or that a threat will be identified. One cannot assume that anticipatory mourning will occur on the basis of length of an illness or the delivery of a fatal prognosis. The following research example further strengthens this argument.

RESEARCH EXAMPLE

A large research project conducted in 1987 and 1988 examined the effects of bereavement follow-up on widowed persons' use of health care services (Connor, 1996b). The study, conducted in the Northern California Kaiser Permanente health care system, tracked the widowed persons' utilization of inpatient and outpatient services in the year before and the year after the death of a spouse.

As part of the study, 143 widows and widowers were extensively interviewed one year after their spouses' deaths. The group consisted of 41 males (29%) and 102 females (71%), with a mean age of 67 years. Their spouses died of a variety of conditions, as Table 8.1 shows.

One question asked of the surviving spouses was "Was the death sudden or expected?" This question was followed by a detailed discussion of the circumstances of death. Questionnaire

TABLE 8.1

Causes of Spousal Death

Malignancy	60	42%
Heart disease	22	15%
Cardiovascular accident (CVA)	13	9%
Chronic obstructive pulmonary disease (COPD)	8	6%
Alzheimer's disease	4	3%
Other causes	36	25%

results were then analyzed. Because of an apparent incongruity between subjects' expected responses to the sudden-versus-expected-death question and their descriptions of the circumstances, the results were further analyzed. Each description of circumstances of death was rated as either "sudden" or "expected" on the basis of the details provided.

Criteria for sudden death were fairly obvious. Patients who had died of nonterminal illness or injury, where the circumstances allowed no forewarning, were considered in the sudden death group. Examples included victims of accidents, sudden CVAs, and arrhythmic heart attacks. Also included were some patients who had been diagnosed with advanced terminal illness and then died within days or weeks.

Criteria for expected death were more difficult to assign. Included were cases of terminal illness where the patient had been diagnosed for more than a month. In a number of cases, the presence of forewarning was difficult to assess. Chronically ill patients with multiple problems don't always have definitive prognoses. In cases where there was doubt, death was classified as sudden.

To address possible rater bias, two clinicians with many years experience in health care reviewed each case to make independent ratings of all subjects, using the foregoing criteria. Both raters' assessments of the actual events of death as sudden or expected agreed in 141 out of 143 cases, or 98.6% of the time. Concerning all deaths described by subjects as expected, both raters agreed 100% of the time. However, 31 of the deaths described as sudden by subjects were rated by both independent raters as expected.

The 31 subjects who perceived death as sudden when events offered much opportunity for forewarning had spouses with the causes of death shown in Table 8.2.

Of these 31 subjects, 8 (26%) were male. The patients with malignancies had all had extensive treatment histories. Two had been diagnosed with pancreatic cancer for over 6 months. Those with CVAs were very elderly and had had multiple strokes and other major illnesses. Patients who had died from other causes included one with a 7-year history of Alzheimer's disease; one with a 10-year history of asthma and congestive heart failure; and one with a long history of Parkinson's disease, who had been admitted to the hospital in a coma.

Table 8.3 summarizes a chi-square analysis of the differences between the widowed person's responses and independent assessment of the circumstances leading up to the death.

Why was it that those 31 individuals refused or were unable to perceive that their loved ones were dying? A number of possibilities can be put forward. First, it appeared that most responded to the sudden-versus-expected question as relating to the actual experience of death. It is possible that they knew how seriously ill their spouses were but that they were experiencing Weisman's (1972) third-order denial and didn't believe that the illness would actually result in death.

When someone is ill for a long time, the caregiver can grow accustomed to seeing the person in a debilitated state. There may have been prognoses issued that were not realized. It is not unusual for someone to be given a 6-month prognosis and live well beyond it. When this happens, the person loses confidence in medicine's ability to predict. Because death tends to be hidden away in our culture, few people have much direct experience with people who are actually dying; most people do not know what to look for. It may also be that there is no substitute for the actual experience of death. You can imagine losing someone you love, but until it actually happens, it is difficult to believe it will occur.

CLINICAL INTERVENTION

If we adopt the premise that a significant number of people who have forewarning or knowledge of impending death will not benefit from or accept the reality of that information, we must ask ourselves, "What next?" Do we attempt to intervene psychologically so that people will be better able to face reality or to experi-

TABLE 8.2

Causes of Death Perceived As Sudden

Malignancy	22	71%
CVA	3	10%
Other causes	6	19%

TABLE 8.3

Widower Responses versus Independent Assessment

	Sudden	Expected	Total
Subject responses	67	76	143
Actual events[a]	36	107	143
Totals	103	183	286

df = 1, cv = 6.64, X2obs = 14.6, p = <.01
[a] As rated by independent assessment

ence anticipatory mourning? These questions are explored in two case examples.

Prior to any good psychological intervention, there must be an accurate assessment of the client's circumstances and internal state. A professional dealing with a person who appears to be experiencing anticipatory mourning must have detailed knowledge of the client's losses and coping ability. The psychosocial assessment needs to include questions about present or past losses, as well as open questions about how the client perceives the currently anticipated loss.

Case Example 1

A woman is caring for her husband, who is dying of lung cancer. She does not appear to be very upset about his deteriorating condition, and hospice staff are concerned about her. The hospice social worker visits and talks with the woman about how she and her husband are doing. The wife expresses confidence in her ability to care for her husband and makes no mention of his diminishing strength. The social worker asks her what she understands of his condition. She replies that she knows he is very ill but is hopeful that he will improve. The social worker acknowledges her desire for him to improve and asks if she has any worries about his not getting better. The wife says that she cannot think about his dying and that she is sure he will hang on. The social worker asks the woman about people she has known who have died. She recounts many experiences with loss, including the deaths of her parents, a cousin, a co-worker, and several close friends. When asked about her responses to these losses, she reports that she has always been uncomfortable dealing with loss and just couldn't face up to it. The social worker asks about changes that have happened since the husband's illness and how they have affected the couple's relationship. The wife describes a growing isolation from family and friends and from her husband, who is unable to work, show intimacy, or relate to her.

In this case example, the social worker has gathered a great deal of critical information about how and why the client is reacting the way she is. She has learned that the wife has a long history of avoidant coping and has tended to avoid dealing with any losses. She knows that the wife is experiencing many current stresses and losses and that she is isolated and lacking a good support system.

At this point, the social worker has three options: (a) support the client's avoidant coping style and join her in hoping for a very unlikely improvement, (b) attempt to confront the client with the reality of the seriousness of her husband's condition, or (c) support the client's need for hope while gradually helping her face the reality of her current losses and her husband's impending death.

The conventional thinking in psychology has been not to challenge defenses. However, to collude with the wife's unrealistic hopes may not be therapeutic. Her comments lead us to believe that she has never learned how to deal with loss. To confront her in an effort to make her face reality is obviously countertherapeutic. The third choice appears best: It meets her where she is emotionally in seeking hope, which may have many meanings for her. At the same time, it offers an opportunity to help her explore how she might face the possibility of her husband's death. As the social worker learns more about the client's other losses, she may find clues that suggest why the woman has never learned how to face loss. Perhaps an early, devastating loss was too much for her to tolerate.

With some people who have few internal resources for coping with stress and trauma, it may be best not to try to intervene psychosocially. If all attempts to help a person face the reality of loss are rebuffed, it is best to leave things be. However, most people avoid discussing impending death out of a misguided belief that open talk will cause harm to the individual or the relationship. Actually, the opposite is usually true. It is *not* talking about the obvious reality that causes people to withdraw or to miss important opportunities for healing. Therefore, presuming that the client can benefit from more open communication, our social worker could continue to pace her interventions (Connor, 1992) to promote the idea that it is possible for the wife to face reality even as she continues to hope for improvement.

A second case example illustrates work with anticipatory mourning on the part of the patient.

Case Example 2

Ben was a 38-year-old engineer diagnosed with metastatic melanoma. He lived with his wife and two young daughters. He belonged to a wellness group and was receiving chemotherapy. A positive thinker, he refused to believe that the disease would kill him. Ben had spent a year off with his family sailing around the Caribbean, and apparently the excessive sun exposure had triggered his disease. He was on the verge of a breakthrough in his field and wanted to continue working. When I saw him, he was too weak to get out of bed, yet he was adamant that he would live and beat the disease. He just needed to regain his strength. His wife knew how seriously ill he was and was very concerned that he have an opportunity to say good-bye to his daughters before he died.

We agreed that the best approach was to continue to support Ben's hope but gradually to work on his ability to face the current reality. He was focused on the wellness philosophy and feared that if he doubted his ability to get well, it would make him sicker. His wife and I enlisted the help of the wellness group facilitator. The man visited Ben and let him know that Ben had done all he could to help in his healing but that the end was near. We all continued to support his need for hope, but after this visit Ben was able to begin allowing for the possibility that he could die. A gradual change began to occur as Ben was able to face the reality of his situation. He was able to let his family, including his daughters, help with his care. We appealed to his paternal side and encouraged him to talk with his daughters about his life and the possibility that he might not always be there.

Ben never regained his strength, nor was he able to deal with his guilt over having triggered his disease during the boat trip. He did decide against being resuscitated and managed to express some anger at not being able to complete his work. He was able to be more comfortable until his death, and his daughters were able to say good-bye before he died.

Having refused to accept the possibility of death in spite of the seriousness of his condition, Ben was unable to express any anticipatory mourning. Perhaps the enormity of his impending losses and his rational, nonemotional engineer style also got in the way. Once Ben began to face the possibility of his death, there was some opportunity to reach closure, but he avoided dealing with any unpleasant emotions. His wife needed for him to face his situation so she could go on with her life. She did benefit from our interventions and, after Ben's death, felt that her grief was made more bearable by the knowledge that he had been able to say good-bye.

DISCUSSION

Anticipatory mourning is a complex and multidimensional phenomenon that represents the variety of reactions of individuals facing impending death and the experiences of significant people in their lives. It is multidimensional in that it affects and is affected by an individual's social, psychological, physical, and spiritual experience. It is complex in that its presence, quality, duration, and intensity vary greatly from one individual to another.

People facing similar dire circumstances can vary in their reactions from no discernible anticipatory mourning response to profound mourning processes that affect all spheres of experience. This chapter has explored the variability in this phenomenon. Although anticipatory mourning is affected by many factors, a key issue is the individual's coping style and ability to face the reality of impending death. The more denial-like coping is used, the less opportunity there will be to acknowledge ongoing losses.

The issue of whether or not to intervene with clients who appear to be using denial-like coping in order to promote the experience of anticipatory mourning is an important one. In previous publications (Connor, 1992, 1994, 1996a), I have argued that intervention can be therapeutic. The most important distinction is whether the use of denial is in the service of preserving interpersonal relationships. If it is, then intervention is usually helpful and can result in growth.

There is nothing inherently wrong with avoiding opportunities for anticipatory mourning. Some individuals lack the inner resources to face such tragic situations, whereas others may benefit from opportunities to work through their losses and to say good-bye. For some, the experience of facing death straight on also affords an opportunity to grow. The period before dying can see the emergence of new experiences that may accelerate the process of human development. Some of these growth experiences, described by Byock (1997), are acceptance of the finality of life and of one's existence as an individual, development of a new self beyond personal loss, a sense of meaning concerning life in general and a sense that life goes on with or without one, and the possibility of surrender to the transcendent or the unknown.

The important point regarding anticipatory mourning is not whether one can experience it or whether one needs to experience it.

What is important is for us to understand why someone does or does not experience it and to accept that position as a reflection of the individual's life history.

REFERENCES

Arkin, A. M. (1974). Notes on anticipatory grief. In B. Schoenberg, A. Carr, A. H. Kutscher, D. Peretz, & K. Goldberg (Eds.), *Anticipatory grief*. London: Columbia University Press.

Becker, E. (1973). *The denial of death*. New York: Free Press.

Beilin, R. (1981). Social functions of denial and death. *Omega, 12*, 25–35.

Beisser, A. R. (1979). Denial and affirmation in illness and health. *American Journal of Psychiatry, 136*, 1026–1030.

Breznitz, S. (1983). The seven kinds of denial. In S. Breznitz (Ed.), *The denial of stress*. New York: International Universities Press.

Byock, I. R. (1997). *Dying well: The prospect for growth at the end of life*. New York: Putnam.

Connor, S. R. (1992). Denial in terminal illness: To intervene or not to intervene. *Hospice Journal, 8*(4), 1–15.

Connor, S. R. (1994). Denial, acceptance and other myths. In I. Corless, B. Germino, & M. Pittman (Eds.), *Dying, death, and bereavement: Theoretical perspectives and other ways of knowing*. Boston: Jones & Bartlett.

Connor, S. R. (1996a). The ethics of hope and denial. In J. Morgan (Ed.), *Ethical issues in the care of the dying and bereaved aged* (Death, Value, and Meaning Series). New York: Baywood.

Connor, S. R. (1996b). Hospice, bereavement intervention and use of health care services by surviving spouses. *HMO Practice, 10*(1), 20–23.

Dansak, D. A., & Cordes, R. S. (1978–1979). Cancer: Denial or suppression. *International Journal of Psychiatry in Medicine, 9*(3–4), 257–262.

Evans, A. J. (1994). Anticipatory grief: A theoretical challenge. *Palliative Medicine 8*, 159–165.

Freud, S. (1964). The loss of reality in psychosis and neurosis. In J. Strachey (Ed. & Trans.), *The standard edition of the complete psychological works of Sigmund Freud* (Vol. 22). London: Hogarth Press. (Original work published 1924)

Freud, S. (1964). An outline of psychoanalysis. In J. Strachey (Ed. & Trans.), *The standard edition of the complete psychological works of Sigmund Freud* (Vol. 23). London: Hogarth Press. (Original work published 1940)

Fulton, R., & Gottesman, D. J. (1980). Anticipatory grief: A psychosocial concept reconsidered. *British Journal of Psychiatry 137*, 45–54.

Haan, N. (1965). Coping and defense mechanisms related to personality inventories. *Journal of Consulting and Clinical Psychology, 29*(4), 373–378.

Hackett, T. P., & Cassem, N. H. (1970). Psychological reactions to life threatening stress: A study of acute myocardial infarction patients. In H. S. Abram (Ed.), *Psychological aspects of stress*. Springfield, IL: Charles C Thomas.

Hackett, T. P., & Cassem, N. H. (1974). Development of a quantitative rating scale to assess denial. *Journal of Psychosomatic Research, 18*(2), 93–110.

Hackett, T. P., & Weisman, A. D. (1964). Reactions to the imminence of death. In G. H. Grosser, H. Wechsler, & M. Greenblatt (Eds.), *The threat of impending disaster: Contributions to the psychology of stress*. Cambridge, MA: MIT Press.

Kübler-Ross, E. (1969). *On death and dying*. New York: Macmillan.

Lazarus, R. S., & Golden, G. (1981). The function of denial in stress, coping, and aging. In E. McGarraugh & S. Keissler (Eds.), *Biology, behavior, and aging*. New York: Academic.

Lindemann, E. (1944). Symptomatology and management of acute grief. *American Journal of Psychiatry, 101*, 141–148.

Parkes, C. M., & Weiss, R. S. (1983). *Recovery from bereavement*. New York: Basic.

Ramshorn, M. (1974). Selected tasks for the dying patient and family members. In B. Schoenberg, A. Carr, A. H. Kutscher, D. Peretz, & K. Goldberg (Eds.), *Anticipatory grief*. New York: Columbia University Press.

Rando, T. A. (1986). A comprehensive analysis of anticipatory grief: Perspectives, processes, promises, and problems. In T. A. Rando (Ed.), *Loss and anticipatory grief*. Lexington, MA: Lexington Books.

Silverman, P. (1974). Anticipatory grief from the perspective of widowhood. In B. Schoenberg, A. Carr, A. H. Kutscher, D. Peretz, & K. Goldberg (Eds.), *Anticipatory grief*. New York: Columbia University Press.

Sjoback, H. (1973). *The psychoanalytic theory of defensive processes*. New York: Wiley and Sons.

Sweeting, H. N., & Gilhooly, M. (1992). Doctor, am I dead? A review of social death in modern society. *Omega, 24*, 251–269.

Taylor, S. (1989). *Positive illusions: Creative self deceptions and the healthy mind*. New York: Wiley and Sons.

Vachon, M., Freedman, K., Formo, A., Rogers, J., Lyall, W., & Freeman, S. (1977). The final illness in cancer: The widow's perspective. *Canadian Medical Association Journal, 117*, 1151–1154.

Weisman, A. D. (1972). *On dying and denying: A psychiatric study of terminality*. New York: Behavioral Publications.

Weisman, A. D., & Hackett, T. P. (1966). Denial as a social act. In S. Levin & R. Kahara (Eds.), *Geriatric psychiatry: Creativity, reminiscing, and dying*. New York: International Universities Press.

Weiss, R. S. (1988). Is it possible to prepare for trauma? *Journal of Palliative Care, 4*(1 & 2), 74–76.

Weiss, R. S. (1994). Loss and recovery. In M. Stroebe, W. Stroebe, & R. Hansson (Eds.), *Handbook of bereavement: Theory, research, and intervention*. New York: Cambridge University Press.

CHAPTER 9
Towards an Appropriate Death

J. William Worden

It is always a challenge in medicine when the aim of treatment changes from curative to palliative. It is a challenge to the patient not to give up and become depressed; it is a challenge to physicians and caregivers not to lose interest and move on to other cases where there is the possibility of cure. This challenge is particularly evident in a large teaching hospital. Implicit in this scenario is the issue of failure, the failure to cure the patient. It is the thesis of this chapter that when the aim of treatment is palliative and not curative, one must change the criterion of success. One way to do this is to understand the concept of appropriate death. One of the generic operations of anticipatory mourning (see chapter 2 in this volume), the facilitation of the most appropriate death possible is a crucial target goal for professional caregivers and loved ones of the patient.

We coined the term *appropriate death* in the Omega Project at the Massachusetts General Hospital (MGH). This project involved a series of NIH-funded studies on terminal illness, cancer care, suicide, and bereavement codirected by Avery D. Weisman, M.D., and myself. An appropriate death is defined as "a death that one might choose for oneself" or "a death one could live with." All individuals whom we treat in the hospital represent varying life goals, values, and life-styles. An appropriate death is one in which the person can experience a dying that reflects personal goals, values, and style of life. For example, if a physician or nurse who has devoted a career to good medical care dies with less than adequate medical care, his or her death would be less appropriate. I recently spoke to a longtime colleague who is close to death. This colleague was one of the pioneers in palliative care and was an early associate of Dr. Kübler-Ross. Among his contributions to the field was creative pain management. When I spoke to him, I discovered that his current pain was uncontrollable despite various medical interventions. Continuing to experience this intractable pain until his death would make his death less than appropriate. For a person whose life has been highly organized, with great attention to detail, dying with his or her affairs in disarray would make death less than appropriate.

The concept of appropriate death is useful in medical care in the following way. When the aim of treatment changes from curative to palliative, we, the staff, change our criterion of success. We see success no longer in terms of cure but rather in terms of how much we can help the patient have a death consonant with his or her goals, values, and life-style. After the person dies, we evaluate the extent to which this happened and judge our effectiveness—success, if you will—on the degree to which the patient had an appropriate death. This shifting of criterion not only helps keep the staff creatively connected with the dying patient but also keeps them focused on who the patient is and what is important to him or her. It helps the staff to see the patient as a person and not the colon cancer case in Room 323.

I first saw the effectiveness of this approach when asked to work in a liaison capacity with the gynecological unit at the MGH, a very fine and well-run unit. Patients who were dying were often allowed to remain as inpatients until death. However, because of the high level of care offered in this unit, its staff members frequently became demoralized when they experienced a number of deaths during a brief period. When we changed the criterion of success from one of cure to one of appropriate death and conducted staff debriefings after a death, morale improved and the end-stage interventions of the staff became more creative. Caregivers paid more careful attention to what had been important in the patients' lives and tried to help them experience aspects of these things in their terminal care, if at all possible. Staff members were often pleased that they were able to make certain things happen for the patients before death came.

Even though *appropriate death* refers to the individual and what has been important to him or her, there are certain psychosocial parameters that define appropriate death for all patients. Let me say at the outset that adequate palliation of symptoms is part of this concept. However, what I want to focus on are five psychosocial parameters that define appropriate death and that we evaluated after a patient's death. The five parameters are provision of continuing support, sensitive communication, reduction of fears, encouragement of patient and family to finish business, and identification of "mini-hopes." These concepts are useful in hospice care as well as in treatment in a general hospital facility. In fact, I use them when training hospice volunteers for the Hospice of Pasadena in California.

PROVISION OF CONTINUING SUPPORT

"Continuing support" may sound like a bit of a cliché, but let me define what I mean. About the time we began the Omega Project in

1968, an anthropologist conducted a study of staff behavior in a general hospital. The anthropologist found that the sicker the patient was, and the closer to death the patient was, the longer it took staff to answer the call light over the door. In other words, it is not easy to work with very sick and dying patients.

Elisabeth Kübler-Ross and I once did a study of 6,000 health professionals from all over the country (Worden & Kübler-Ross, 1978). They included physicians, nurses, psychologists, social workers, and clergy. One question we asked was "Is there a kind of dying person that you have difficulty working with?" The responses revealed that 92% found some dying persons difficult to work with; only 8% said they could work with all dying persons. This finding only confirmed my personal experience that some patients are not easy to work with and that at some times I would rather be in my office processing data than at the bedside of a dying person. Certain dying patients touch our own issues and make it difficult to work with them in any kind of intimate way.

When we analyzed the 6,000 responses by professional groups, we found that physicians, as a group, often had difficulty working with dying patients who were experiencing considerable anxiety. Nurses often had difficulty working with dying patients who were younger or who were their peers in age and gender. Social workers and psychologists had difficulty working with dying patients in pain. Clergy, most of whom were chaplains, had difficulty working with nonreligious dying patients or patients they did not know but were required to see. The point is that some dying patients and their plights give us personal difficulty, and we tend to want to avoid them or not work with them in any intimate way. One aspect of ensuring appropriate death is recognizing this tendency and making sure that other staff members who are less personally affected by those particular patients can be there for continuing support until death—support that supplements adequate palliation of symptoms.

I believe not only that continuing support affects a patient's quality of life but that it can also affect the quantity of life. In the Omega Project, we looked at a large group of cancer patients, of whom some had lived longer than medically expected and some had lived for briefer times. Most variations in survival time are accounted for by tumor site, dissemination of the disease, tumor histology, and treatments. We statistically accounted for all of these medical and treatment variables and then looked to see what psychosocial characteristics differentiated the long from the short survivors (Weisman & Worden, 1975). Here is what we found.

Patients who survived longer than medically expected were those who were cooperative and compliant with hospital staff, who had histories of good social relationships, and who had a lot of emotional support while they were dying. These were patients who did not want to die, who were frightened by the prospects of dying, who would not let themselves believe that death was inevitable, and who showed some denial of the facts and implications of their illnesses. Late in their illnesses they could express some anger over their plight, but it was not the kind of anger that alienated others around them.

On the other hand, those considered short survivors, those who succumbed to early death, were less cooperative and compliant with hospital staff and hence had less emotional support from the staff and from others. These patients often had histories of poor social relationships. They showed less denial of all types, believed that the situation was hopeless, and expressed more desire to die, something that caused them less fear and anxiety than the long survivors experienced. For the short survivors, depression was the affect most present in the terminal phase; if they were angry, the anger was of the destructive and alienating kind.

These findings imply that length of survival not only involves interpersonal aspects of patients' lives at the time of illness but also suggests differences in life histories and psychological characters. According to LeShan (1969), there is a good deal of evidence that deep psychological isolation, the loss of ability to relate and to love, lessens the ability to fight for health. LeShan reminds us of Freud's observation that in the last analysis, we must love in order not to fall ill and must fall ill when, in the consequences of frustration, we cannot love.

SENSITIVE COMMUNICATION

A second psychosocial dimension related to appropriate death is sensitive communication. After the publication of Kübler-Ross's *On Death and Dying* in 1969, the media conveyed a popular notion that there were all these dying people out there wanting to talk to someone about their dying but that the conversations were not taking place because of the reticence of caregivers and families. At that time, we even had some young nurses who would go into dying patients' rooms and say, "I know you want to talk and I am here to talk," using a can opener approach in attempts to initiate such conversations. They may have been well meaning but they were ill informed.

In the Omega Project, we studied communication patterns and discovered that wanting to talk about one's death was an intermittent phenomenon (Worden, 1987). Some patients wanted to talk about it now but not later, others later but not now. Patients were selective regarding interlocutors for such conversations, choosing some staff members and rejecting others. Because such conversations were intermittent, we wanted to be sure that they were encouraged if and when patients wanted them. This is what I mean by sensitive communication: being sensitive to *when* a patient wants to speak about his or her dying and *with whom*.

Weisman (1972, 1974) has written about the denial found in the terminal patients whom we studied. Denial in such patients is an intermittent phenomenon and not merely a stage in the dying process. When Kübler-Ross writes about the stage of denial, she is referring to what we call "impact denial." A person receiving bad news relating to diagnosis and prognosis tends to say, "Not me," "They must have the wrong X rays," "I couldn't be sick," and so on. This type of denial is quite common close to the time of diagnosis. However, denial of facts of the illness and its implications appears intermittently throughout the course of the illness. What triggers denial is usually some threat to an interpersonal relationship or some intrapsychic conflict. When the threat abates, so does the denial. A good clinical intervention sees denial as a fever and searches for the underlying cause rather than attacking the denial directly. The patient needs the denial for some purpose; identifying this purpose and helping the patient resolve underlying conflicts will cause the denial to abate.

REDUCTION OF FEARS

Our research with terminally ill patients shows that they tend to be more afraid of dying than of death (Worden, 1989). One could speculate that the fear of dying is nothing more than a displacement of the fear of death. However, it is easier for the clinician to deal with the former than with the latter. Most patients have some type of fear regarding dying. A fourth dimension of appropriate death is the reduction of such fears. Clinicians need to assess carefully their patients' fears with regard to the dying process and try to reduce these fears through creative intervention.

Not all patients have the same fears. Some fear that in dying they will lose control over personal decision making and lose the esteem that goes with that. Even though the process of dying is regressive and many decisions are made for the patient by others, the patient can still be given choices. Limitation in physical functioning does not mean limitation in mental functioning. "Do you want to take this now or later?" or "Do you want to lie on this side or that side?" may seem like small choices, but they can be important to the person who is afraid of losing control over decisions.

Offering a patient these seemingly small choices may take the care-giver's time when it would be easier to give directives, but it can be so important to this type of patient.

Not every patient wants control over personal decisions. Some patients have been waiting all their lives to regress and are happy to say, "Here I am; take care of me." For these patients, losing control of decisions is not what underlies the fear of dying. Something else may be.

Another fear that affects some patients is the fear of loneliness. It is true that dying can be a lonely business. No one can do it for you. Earlier in this chapter, we looked at the difficulty caregivers have in working closely with some patients, a difficulty that can lead to isolation. Such isolation was the experience of a dying student nurse, who some years ago wrote the following to her friends and colleagues:

> I sense your fright and your fear enhances mine. Why are you afraid? I am the one who is dying. I know you feel insecure, don't know what to say, don't know what to do. But please believe me, if you care, you can't go wrong. Just admit that you care. That is really for what we search. We may ask for whys and wherefores, but we don't really expect answers. Don't run away . . . wait . . . all I want to know is that there will be someone to hold my hand when I need it. I am afraid. Death may get to be routine for you, but it is new to me. You may not see me as unique, but I have never died before. To me, once is pretty unique!

> You whisper about my youth, but when one is dying, is he really so young anymore? I have lots I wish we could talk about. It really would not take much more of your time because you are in here quite a bit anyway.

> If only we could be honest, both admit our fears, touch one another. If you really care, would you lose so much of your valuable professionalism if you even cried with me? Just person to person? Then, it might not be so hard to die . . . in a hospital . . . with friends close by.

For the patient who is afraid of dying alone, the remedy is fairly easy. The caregiver can give reassurance that he or she will not abandon the patient but will be there until the end. Of course, one must not make such a promise unless it can be honored. Such reassurance can go a long way in alleviating this particular fear of dying.

For some patients, another element of the fear of dying is the fear of pain. Thirty years ago we treated pain cautiously because we didn't want the terminal patient to become addicted to pain medications. We now do a much better and more creative job in treating the pain some terminal patients experience. Not only is the philosophy of pain management more advanced—thanks to the work of Robert Twycross, Balfour Mount, and others—but also we are more alert to the potentiating effects of anxiety and depression on the experience of pain. If a patient is afraid of pain in the dying process, caregivers can offer pain management that includes the careful titration of doses, along with a subjective record of the person's pain experience recorded over time.

Another fear in dying is the fear that one's quality of life will be severely compromised as a by-product of treatment. It is true that treatments can compromise the patient's energy levels as well as locomotion, elimination, and other abilities. Patients with this fear can be included in treatment decision making all along the way.

Some dying patients are troubled by the fear that they will not know what is happening to them. For most patients, the wish to know is the rule rather than the exception. However, some patients experience this need more strongly than others, and the fear of not knowing is a major focus in their dying. I once interviewed a dying patient in front of the medical staff of a Pennsylvania hospital. The patient was a schoolteacher with a very strong need to know what was happening. He would read up on his medical condition and bring stacks of reprints into his oncologist's office with the query "Have you read these?" To his pleasure, his oncologist was very capable and had read them. The day of the interview, the oncologist was in the front row of the auditorium. The patient told his oncologist that he knew the doctor was a busy person but that he also knew that he himself had a strong need to know. He thanked the doctor for taking extra time with him (Worden, 1976). Physicians sometimes feel that if they spend extra time informing one patient, all patients will want extra time and extensive information. However, not every patient has that same need. For those who do, taking the extra time will do much to alleviate this fear.

The foregoing are just a few of the fears of dying that I have seen. Helping a patient to have an appropriate death means carefully assessing the patient's fears of dying and trying to address them through creative intervention. On the occasion of a community lecture in Colorado, a woman asked me to speak to her 92-year-old mother, who was in the audience. The mother told me that she was not afraid of death but was afraid of being put in a coffin before she was dead. Because she lowered her voice when telling me, I suspected that she had not shared this fear with others; my suspicion turned out to be true. I suggested there were two things she might do: tell her daughter of this fear and tell her physician, who would probably attend her death in that small town. A month after I returned home, I received a note from this 92-year-old thanking me for helping her address her one fear of dying. My intervention probably took all of 15 minutes, but the attenuation of her anxiety was obvious.

ENCOURAGEMENT OF PATIENTS AND FAMILY TO FINISH BUSINESS

A fourth dimension of appropriate death that we assess concerns the patient's ability to complete unfinished business before dying. I am not referring to the completion of wills or the making of funeral arrangements, although these considerations are important. I am referring to the patient's and the family's saying what needs to be said, expressing appreciations and resentments so as to not leave important things unsaid. Many patients do this task naturally, but others need encouragement. The same is true for family members, who often want to say something to the dying person but are hesitant and look to the caregiver for permission.

This need for permission came to my attention shortly after I began my work in terminal illness care 30 years ago. A woman asked me whether or not her husband, who was in a coma, could hear her if she spoke to him. I started to respond with a physiological answer and then stopped myself, realizing that she was not asking a physiological question but rather was saying, "There are some things I want to say to my husband before he dies. Is that all right?" I told her that I wasn't sure if he could hear or not but encouraged her to sit beside his bed and tell him what she wanted him to hear before he died. She took my suggestion and later manifested considerable relief that she had done so. My sense is that she would not have talked to her husband if I had not given her permission to do so. This experience opened my eyes to the number of patients and family members who want to speak but need encouragement or permission to do so.

Permissions are not only granted verbally. At times, our very behavior as caregivers encourages this communication. A patient with very invasive stomach cancer signaled that he wanted to speak to me, though he was weak and close to death. I put my ear close to his mouth, and he took considerable time to get out the words. Essentially, what he wanted me to know was of his long estrangement from his youngest son. He told me that my talking openly with him about his death had given him permission to talk to his son about it and to effect a reconciliation. In this case, permission was given nonverbally.

After a patient dies and we are assessing the dimensions of appropriate death for him or her, we try to judge to what degree the patient and family members were able to say what needed to be said before the death. As a grief counselor, I have seen the value of communicating those important feelings to a dying loved one rather than waiting until after the death and expressing them to an empty chair in my office. This communication is an important dimension of anticipatory mourning that can ease the course of the survivors' bereavement after the loved one dies.

IDENTIFICATION OF MINI-HOPES

When hope for recovery is exhausted and the aim of treatment changes from curative to palliative, patients often give up hope, show signs of depression, and turn their faces to the wall. A possible counter to this response is what I call "mini-hopes"—hopes this side of recovery. The caregiver can encourage the patient at this point: "You are not dead yet. What do you still want to do while you are alive?" Some patients will reply with ideas like "I hope to live until Christmas"; "I hope to live until my daughter marries"; "I hope to live until so-and-so comes to visit me." It is important to have hope. Our research at Harvard confirms what Schmale and Engel (Engel, 1968) found at Rochester: that when patients give up hope, they soon die, sometimes in spite of prognoses that are not too grim. Encouraging the patient to identify mini-hopes can help attenuate this depression.

Not all patients have mini-hopes within their grasp; some need extra encouragement to find them. I was in the room of a 52-year-old single woman with no family when her oncologist said they were stopping active treatment. The woman was devastated and turned her face to the wall in a serious depression. "What do you still want to do while you are alive?" I asked. I received no response, though I prodded her for a number of days to think along these lines. (One can do this if one has a good relationship with the patient and the patient knows one cares.) After a week of prodding, the woman told me that she wanted to return once more to Cape Cod and see the bridge that crossed the canal onto the cape. When I went to the cape, I would take a look at the bridge for her and describe it to her on my return. I brought her pictures of the bridge for her room, which had no windows. She never did make it to see the bridge, but the hope of one day doing so helped her extend her future for some time. Eventually, the disease took her, but her last days were filled less with depression and more with hope.

When we assess the dimensions of appropriate death, we look to see if the patient was able to maintain some hope until the end—not hope for recovery but the mini-hopes that can enhance quality of life and perhaps extend life to some degree.

Dr. Kübler-Ross wrote about the final stage of dying as the stage of acceptance. Many of the patients we worked with in the Omega Project never reached such a stage of acceptance. Many resented right to the end that they were dying, and this was true regardless of their age. Even if a patient never reaches this stage of acceptance, we can still help him or her have an appropriate death, help the patient to have things in the final weeks of life that are consonant with his or her goals, values, and life-style.

One patient who never approximated the stage of acceptance was a well-known 82-year-old writer. Although she had come from a prominent family and had had an illustrious career in writing, she resented until the very end that she was dying. Despite this resentment, we were able to help her experience in her final months of life things that were important to her. Because music was one of them, we were able to have someone come in once a day and play the piano for her. Because of her interest in literature, we were able to have someone read to her twice a day. Because she did not want to die in Massachusetts, we helped arrange an ambulance to take her the hundreds of miles to her home so she could spend her last days there. For some time, she had been estranged from one family member in a well-known family feud. A reconciliation took place, and the family member was able to assist in her care until the end. All these things helped make the woman's death more appropriate, even though she resented dying until the very end. Death can be appropriate if not acceptable.

The concept of appropriate death can help both patients and caregivers. It enables the dying to be seen as people and not just as patients or the carriers of certain diseases. It helps caregivers evaluate their care of dying patients by applying a new criterion of success when the aim of treatment changes from curative to palliative.

REFERENCES

Engel, G. (1968). A life setting conducive to illness: The giving-up, given up complex. *Annals of Internal Medicine, 69,* 293–300.

Kübler-Ross, E. (1969). *On death and dying.* New York: Macmillan.

LeShan, L. (1969). Psychotherapy and the dying patient. In L. Pearson (Ed.), *Death and dying.* Cleveland: Case Western Reserve.

Weisman, A. D. (1972). *On dying and denying.* New York: Aronson.

Weisman, A. D. (1974). *The realization of death.* New York: Behavioral Publications.

Weisman, A. D., & Worden, J. W. (1975). Psychosocial analysis of cancer deaths. *Omega, 6,* 61–75.

Worden, J. W. (1976). *Personal death awareness.* New York: Prentice Hall.

Worden, J. W. (1987). Communication: A critical factor in survival. In *Proceedings of the fifth national conference on human values and cancer.* San Francisco: American Cancer Society.

Worden, J. W. (1989). The experience of recurrent cancer. *CA—A Cancer Journal for Clinicians, 39,* 305–310.

Worden, J. W., & Kübler-Ross, E. (1978). Attitudes and experiences of death workshop attendees. *Omega, 8,* 91–106.

PART II

Anticipatory Mourning from Different Perspectives

CHAPTER 10
Grief in Dying Persons

William M. Lamers, Jr.

INTRODUCTION

Dying is a major universal human condition, yet it has received little attention in the medical literature. Early in this century, Sir William Osler (1904) wrote of his observations on the dying process in over 400 persons at Johns Hopkins Hospital. Just after midcentury, Kübler-Ross (1969) offered a simplified schema of the grieving process in dying persons. Physicians as a rule have little or no training, experience, or interest in working with dying persons and their families. When I was in medical school, we were urged to have the next of kin sign permission for an autopsy. To graduate we had to attend 40 live births but not one single death. I recall hearing a physician, looking back over 55 years of practice, state, "I have never actually seen a patient die." In this chapter I will focus on personal observations during 25 years of work as a hospice physician. During that time I worked closely with hundreds of dying persons and their families. My work included numerous home visits during the final stages of illness and at the time of death.

Current health care reimbursement focuses on the physical needs of dying persons, whereas psychological, spiritual, and social needs usually receive scant attention. Communication between family members and the attending physician is frequently less than satisfactory, even when the dying patient is a physician (Calland, 1972) or the relative of a physician (Netske, 1976). The latest major study of dying in the United States suggests that we know little about the experience of dying, that pain and other symptoms are commonplace and troubling to patients, and that family members believe that patients prefer comfort (palliation) but that life-sustaining treatments are often used instead (Lynn, Teno, Phillips et al., 1997). In the absence of services such as hospice, patients usually continue to receive aggressive and life-prolonging therapies past an optimal point, and patients are rarely identified as "dying" until too little quality time remains during which constructive psychological, social, and spiritual change can occur.

Modern medicine has the technology to prolong many types of chronic illness. The side effects of life prolongation include denial of the inevitability of death and avoidance of the necessity to consider one's finitude. In general, hospital personnel are preoccupied with treatments, charting, administration, and other routines to the neglect of patient concerns with the implications of diagnoses and prognoses. Not only are they slower to respond to calls to the bedside of a dying person, they spend less time once in the room (Glaser & Strauss, 1965). By default, hospital personnel work to maintain mechanisms that deny the proximity and inevitability of death. They focus on providing routine physical care, transporting patients to treatments, and bringing trays of food that may never be touched.

Because of a general disinclination on the part of hospital staff to deal with the reality of impending death, patients and families are denied opportunities openly to discuss shared hopes, fears, needs, spiritual concerns, and unfinished business. Death becomes the elephant in the room—recognized by all, yet unacknowledged and dreaded because of misplaced fears of what would happen if the taboo against discussing it were violated.

In the United States today, dying is usually a grim experience for a number of reasons. Many patients die in needless pain. Many are not identified as dying until their last few days or hours, a circumstance that leads patients and families to have false hopes regarding survival. Most elderly patients and those with chronic diseases die in hospitals where little care is given to the multidimensional needs of the dying and their families. To paraphrase Byock (1996), one of the leading advocates of palliative care, dying without medical care can be horrible, but when the human dimension of dying is nurtured, the transition from life can become as profound and intimate as the miracle of birth. One patient, nearing death from pancreatic cancer, said, "This last few months has been the best time of our 30 years of marriage." He had been cared for at home during his last illness by hospice with the assistance of his wife and children.

The professional literature on grief and mourning has largely focused on the emotional reactions of survivors to the deaths of loved ones. Current popular notions of how people react to their own impending deaths derive largely from the pioneering work of Elisabeth Kübler-Ross (1969), who postulated that learning of one's impending death sets in motion a train of psychological phenomena starting with denial and progressing through anger to bargaining, depression, and, ultimately, acceptance. Although this conceptualization has been helpful in alerting the public to the needs of dying persons, we know today that the psychological processes associated with experiencing one's dying usually do not follow such a circumscribed course but depend upon a host of variables. Whereas some patients facing death work through difficult transitions and come to accept their fate, others show a wide range of adjustments from passive acceptance to angry resistance or even sublime transcendence. There is no standard way to die, no single set of guidelines to use in helping dying persons, and no way to predict readily the outcome of the work of dealing with one's own dying.

Today we are less likely to stress the importance of acceptance and are reluctant to include depression as a requisite element in the process of dying. Acceptance to some extent represents a cultural adaptation to a fatal diagnosis: Meaningful life is over; get your affairs in order and prepare to meet your maker. In our society, dying persons undergo a process called "disidentification." They resign from work, withdraw from meaningful activities, try not to make scenes or become burdensome to friends or family, turn toward religion, and generally keep low profiles. At one time, many dying persons were seen as harboring pathogenic organisms, transmissible diseases. That is generally not the case today, yet our attitude toward the dying—which they sense and adapt to—is not far removed from the days of polio epidemics and tuberculosis sanitaria.

Kübler-Ross (1969, 1975) and others (Freud, 1917/1957) have suggested that depression is an inherent part of the dying process. Freud and Kübler-Ross saw grief and depression as inextricably bound in the process of acceptance of loss. Common sense would suggest that dying persons should be depressed, if only because of the losses incurred during an incurable illness. But not all dying persons are depressed. Melvin, Ozbek, and Eberle (1992) performed psychological studies on a group of patients with advanced illness and found that only 44% showed signs of serious depression. They stated that this "lack of a statistically significant relationship between depression and other known physical indicators can be interpreted as further support for the conceptualization of depression as an unnecessary element in the process of death" (p. 45).

We know from work with dying persons that depression is a major side effect of inadequately managed chronic pain. When pain is adequately controlled, depression—together with associated anxiety, insomnia, anorexia, anger, and a host of other distressing psychological symptoms—vanishes. When we see depression in a dying patient whose pain and other physical symptoms are adequately managed, we look elsewhere for the basis of the depression. A careful interview will usually reveal its source. Common sources of depression are shame and guilt associated with the development of disease; the multiple losses (family, friends, health, mobility, future, identity, etc.) associated with the dying process; disidentification secondary to change in social status; loss of productivity; social isolation and miscommunication; and mistaken assumptions and misinformation regarding the illness, prognosis, and treatment alternatives.

Pattison (1978) has observed that the psychological resources of dying persons may not be equal to the tasks posed by dying. Although this may be true for some, many of the older persons I have been with as they were dying had been present at the deaths of parents or of close friends or relatives. They recognized dying as a challenging time of high emotion that afforded an opportunity to exchange farewells, to profess and receive love, and to bring relationships to meaningful conclusions. However, those who have not witnessed traditional deathbed experiences may not know what to do. On several occasions, dying persons have looked up at me and asked, "Am I doing this right?" I also recall an elderly Christian Scientist who was dying of bowel cancer. He denied pain and even had a slight smile on his face. At one point I remarked that he seemed to have things in pretty good control. He glanced at me, pointed toward the heavens, and said calmly, "No . . . He does." I once visited a 7-year-old boy who was dying of cancer. When I asked if there was anything I might do to help him, he replied, "I know I'm dying, and I'm all right with that. Would you please help my mother? She's having a tough time."

As a result of these and other experiences and observations in work with dying persons, I feel that the psychological resources of the dying are usually equal to the tasks of dying. When that appears not to be the case, we must first address any physical symptoms, especially inadequately managed pain, and then address the psychological, social, and spiritual realms to find out what is complicating the dying process. Sometimes dying persons know what is bothering them. Others are unaware or feel guilt or shame over their illnesses. Some feel their deaths will unfairly burden their survivors. Whatever the source of the conflict, it can usually be identified, and quite often measures can be taken to improve the situation.

Over the last 25 years, a number of patients have asked me to kill them or to get something they could use to kill themselves. In each instance, it was possible to help the patient identify the underlying cause for the request. The most common cause, especially among dying physicians, is the fear of endless, untreatable ("intractable") pain. Other reasons expressed include economics (not wanting to exhaust funds that survivors will need), feelings of inadequacy ("I don't deserve the care I am receiving"), compassion ("I don't want to put my wife through any more of this"), and need for control ("I can't stand the waiting"). The first man who asked me to hasten his death was immobilized by severe, chronic pain secondary to metasta-tic cancer. He had recently visited two major pain clinics where he was told that his pain was intractable. I prescribed a different narcotic in a dose adequate to relieve his pain around the clock. Two days later he drove to his office and began to put his affairs in order. Before he died 2 months later, he made peace with a son from whom he had been estranged, entertained friends and relatives, enjoyed the company of his wife, and completed plans for his memorial service.

Learning of impending dying may stimulate a crisis period dur-ing which either integrative or disintegrative mechanisms come into play. Although some may react initially with disorganized panic, most people are able to gather strength from friends and family and go on to develop a more balanced outlook than at first seemed pos-sible. They also turn to internal resources, such as faith and benevo-lent expectancy. Denial may be an effective temporary protection. It takes time to patch things together when one has received a termi-nal diagnosis. During the most difficult transitions, the dying person may appear depressed. The apparent depression may not be due solely to the approach of one's death. Pattison (1978) says that the dying process reactivates unresolved problems from both the near and distant past, including dependency, passivity, aggression, narcis-sism, and identity issues. At the same time, these reactions are nor-mal responses to the massive upheaval caused by serious illness, and with time, education, and appropriate support, they can be turned to the dying person's advantage.

Enforced dependency is intolerable for most active persons, yet it may become a refuge for those who regress in the face of the chal-lenge ahead. The passivity seen in some dying persons is often the result of poorly managed physical symptoms, especially pain. Effec-tive analgesia and attention to physical symptoms may somewhat alleviate passivity. Aggression also may be aggravated by inade-quately managed pain and other physical symptoms, but like many other emotional symptoms, it may be the outward expression of feelings, conflicts, hopes, and fears that need to be discussed—if not with family members, then with an experienced counselor. I have not seen narcissism as a problem in dying persons, but I have often been involved in helping patients address questions of identity related to changed physical appearance.

AWARENESS OF DYING

Persons who develop chronic diseases for which no cures as yet exist (e.g., cancer, HIV disease, or progressive renal failure) learn to monitor their advancing physical symptoms, their changing needs for medication, and their communications with health care workers. Some dying persons ask direct questions of their physicians; others are reluctant to ask the questions to which they already presume to know the fateful answers. Reactions to the development of an awareness that one is dying produce a wide variety of emotional responses that depend on one's psychological makeup, the circumstances, the quality of communication, and the availability of support.

Pattison (1978) analyzed the knowledge of death in terms of crisis and wrote that in the crisis phase persons respond to news of their impending death as a problem insoluble in the immediate future, to which they can only surrender. In my opinion, this is an extreme and uncommon response that represents the absence of hope and the shattering of benevolent expectations for the future. Usually, this phase is a temporary adjustment that responds favorably to focused supportive counseling. At the opposite extreme, some see forthcoming death as a blessing, as a way to be reunited with deceased loved ones or as the necessary passage to a pleasant life hereafter. Some treat the news of impending death as a challenge and never surrender to it; they continue to push their limits to the very end. Some respond with anger to the threat of death and seek any treatments that offer hope of prolongation of life, no matter what the side effects. Some stubbornly persist in whatever abuses contributed to their fatal illnesses. Some sense dying as high adventure and approach it eagerly. I heard a very old Jesuit priest whisper excitedly as he was dying, "Now we'll see!"

Cousins (1974) wrote of the plight of all too many dying persons in our high-technology medical environment, emphasizing that the ultimate tragedy is not death, but dying alone and unable to achieve spiritual comfort from others. All too often persons with advanced, incurable illnesses are institutionalized, and their dying is medicalized. They receive treatments that not only prolong life but also impair the quality of whatever life remains. They are generally separated from their natural environments and absent from normal sources of emotional support. For example, I worked in one health care system in which nursing home occupants, as they approached death, were transferred by ambulance to the nearest intensive care unit, where they were not allowed to die without full technical support, including attempts at resuscitation. The most telling part of this practice was that while the loved one was dying in a nearby intensive care unit, the grieving relatives commonly gathered at the empty bedside in the nursing home. At present in the United States, it is estimated that only one-sixth of dying persons who might benefit from it are referred for hospice care.

Forewarnings

Eliot (1946) introduced the term *forewarning* of death to describe the unanticipated, strong awareness of the proximity and/or the inevitability of dying and death. The first forewarnings of death may be subtle or dramatic, but they alert the person to physical changes, to nuances in communications with physicians, or even to an interest in learning more about the meanings of symptoms and the progression of disease. The implications of forewarnings can be exaggerated, misunderstood, denied, or suppressed. Most of us at some time experience forewarnings of our own finitude, much as we experience anxious moments when considering the fact that someone we love might die. Personal forewarnings usually come as a surprise. Most can be put out of mind shortly, especially if one is in reasonably good health. But certain physical signs or clinical symptoms carry added weight and contribute to an increasingly undeniable realization that, barring a miracle or an unanticipated response to treatment, one's days are numbered. Responses to forewarnings range from unquestioning acceptance to stout resistance. Where one person might have anticipated and almost sought confirmation that death is imminent, another might be intellectually or psychologically disposed not to recognize the message inherent in the forewarning.

The experience of forewarning does not of itself lead to the development of grief over one's impending death and the multiple losses that dying usually entails. Some people look forward to dying; others never accept the fact that they are dying. Those who die young, those who predecease their mates, those who will leave young children, and those in the midst of significant tasks usually have more intense feelings associated with forewarnings of death and more commonly grieve their dying and its associated separations.

In my experience, reaction to forewarnings of death is largely an ongoing, conscious process. Some dying persons have difficulty expressing concern about the forewarnings manifest in their changing physical conditions. They may have difficulty expressing their fears about what is happening to them. Yet, if they can develop trust in their caregivers, inevitably they will reveal concerns, fears, hopes, and objectives that may not have been shared with their own families or with their physicians. Therefore, health care personnel who work with dying persons must have training that alerts them to the special needs and fears of persons with advanced illness. It takes time for patients to develop trust and rapport with care providers. Optimal support and symptom management likewise take time. Communication cannot be forced. Often, dying persons will ask those who clean their rooms or deliver their meals the sorts of questions that only their physicians can answer.

The most obvious forewarning I know of involved a call to me in the middle of the night from an oncologist who knew my work as a hospice physician. When I picked up the phone, I heard a voice shouting, "I'm dying! I'm dying!" After the physician calmed down, he told me that he had just discovered a hard lump in his groin that, as a cancer specialist, he knew to be a metastatic lesion from an unknown primary cancer. He was right. I spent considerable time with him during his last months and was at his bedside as he died as well as in attendance at his funeral. From the time he discovered his fatal cancer, he was unable to deny the implications of his disease. For several weeks, he made every effort to find the primary lesion. Then he pursued every avenue that offered any hope of cure or remission. No treatment modality was overlooked. Several hours before his death, he begged me to try to save him because, as he pleaded, "I've only now begun to live." The first late-night forewarning resonated through diagnosis; through repeated, unsuccessful attempts at treatment; and into the last moments of the physician's life. This man did not want to die. He did not go through customary phases of adjustment to his fatal diagnosis. The closer he came to death, the more he was determined to live. From prior contact with him, I knew that he had felt his life was always in jeopardy. He had suffered serious injuries during World War II. It seemed to me that his work as a physician and radiation oncologist represented a counterphobic stance toward the death he had narrowly escaped in combat. Discussions with him as he lay dying affirmed his extraordinary fear of death, a fear that was not allayed by his strong religious heritage and training.

Encounters with death during terminal illness produced a different effect in Carl Sagan (1997), who apparently experienced forewarnings of impending death:

> Six times now I have looked Death in the face. And six times Death has averted his gaze and let me pass. Eventually, of course, Death will claim me . . . as he does each of us, it's only a question of when. And how. I've learned much from our confrontations . . . especially about the beauty and poignancy of life, about the preciousness of friends and family, and about the transforming power of love. In fact, almost dying is such a positive, character-building experience that I'd recommend it to everybody . . . except, of course, for the irreducible and essential element of risk. (p. 214)

I have heard similar statements from patients facing death. They have come to terms with their living and with their dying. They have gained a new perspective. A number of persons have told me something like "I did not really begin to live until I knew that I was dying." Patients approaching death are able to make such statements, providing they are aware of their situations and are utilizing whatever time remains to complete unfinished business. To face death with equanimity, they must be able to put their lives in perspective with what they perceive as the implications of their dying. For one who has lived a "full life" (whatever that means to the individual) and who has a sense of accomplishment and task completion, that may be a reasonable demand, but it can be most daunting for one who leaves unfinished business, especially for a young mother who senses she will not be able to raise her offspring.

What may be an innocuous forewarning to one patient may have ominous portent for another. Multiple variables determine how forewarnings will be interpreted. A young woman was referred to me by a counselor because he said the co-workers in his building could no longer tolerate her screams during therapy sessions. The patient was in her thirties, pregnant, and suffering from a highly malignant brain tumor. Her oncologist had advised her to have an abortion, as the fetus would be damaged by the medications required to suppress grand mal seizures; the patient wanted to deliver the baby as a last gift to her husband. Each seizure was a stern forewarning of her impending death, as was each chemotherapy and radiation treatment. She called one morning and asked me to come to her home. Earlier that morning she had asked her husband to drop the cat at the veterinarian's for a checkup. The veterinarian called to say that he had "put the cat down," as it was riddled with cancer. Her new fear was that she had transmitted her cancer to the cat and would do the same to her unborn child and to her husband and their two sons. Cancer in the cat, though unrelated to her own cancer, served as a forewarning that was understandably blown out of proportion by a frightened and most vulnerable patient. When the woman could discuss the fears engendered by the veterinarian's call, she was able to let go of a lot of previously unexpressed anxieties, fears, and mistaken assumptions. As her disease progressed, she appeared to make an increasingly successful adaptation to her fate, based, it appears, on mastery of some very frightening confrontations or forewarnings. She grieved the many losses that accompanied her dying. Later, the fact that she gave birth to a healthy infant helped offset the many losses attendant to her dying.

Patients who attend to repeated forewarnings of dying begin to accept and adapt to their situations in graduated phases. They ask the meanings of symptoms; they ask caregivers for confirmation. A woman recently referred for hospice care after the sudden onset of ominous physical symptoms looked up at me as I was examining her and asked quite directly, "Am I dying now?" She asked not out of fear of impending death but rather out of concern for a daughter overseas who would have to make travel plans if her mother was imminently dying. Because of her directness, it was very easy to communicate with her about a broad range of subjects, including death. She rapidly developed new priorities and seemed to have new energy to deal with life. An anonymous person once said, "For it is only in daring to accept death that we may be said to truly accept life." I have heard similar comments from numerous dying persons.

Adjusting to a Terminal Diagnosis

In general, once the prospect of death is openly discussed with patients they begin to deal with their dying in a rational manner. They may develop lists of those whom they want informed of their condition; they also begin to decide what they want to do. They balance their available energy against the tasks at hand and develop priorities. They inquire how and where they will receive care during their final days. They ask how their survivors will be cared for. They consider their financial and social responsibilities. Many deal with spiritual and religious issues and seek the support and advice of experts in these areas.

On learning of impending death, some people find new meaning, purpose, and freedom. As quoted by Beresford in 1997, William Bartholme, a pediatrician and medical ethicist with esophogeal cancer, said, "I never understood the intensity of life before. Now I know a sunset can knock you down. I never had a sense that I could be or say whatever the hell I felt like being or saying or that I could invest my time on a minute-by-minute basis" (p. 13).

When dying persons receive accurate information about their diagnoses, prognoses, and treatment alternatives; when they have the 24-hour, 7-day availability of coordinated teams of specially trained and supervised health care professionals and volunteers; and when they know that they and their families will be supported throughout the final illnesses at little or no out-of-pocket cost, they begin to experience relief that gradually increases as they learn to trust, to share their hopes and fears, and finally to learn that pain and other symptoms can be successfully managed so that they and their loved ones can concentrate on their goals and priorities during the time remaining.

Some dying persons experience more profound loss than others. Some grieve the untimeliness of their dying. As noted earlier, young mothers, especially, bemoan the fact that they will not be able to care for their children. Young fathers protest that they will not be able to provide for their families. Some people express grief over not being able to fulfill their hopes, dreams, and plans. Others may grieve the loss of relationships with friends, family, and loved ones. For older persons, especially widows and widowers, dying inevitably brings a recapitulation of the death of the spouse as well as renewal of other prior losses. For some dying persons, however, progression toward death brings an end to suffering and makes possible a hoped-for reunion with deceased loved ones.

FACTORS INFLUENCING THE DYING PERSON'S PSYCHOLOGICAL STATE

Many variables affect the ways in which dying persons begin to deal with the losses that accompany their own dying. I will discuss cognitive, affective, social, and spiritual dimensions of the dying process from the standpoint of the dying person's anticipatory grief. It is significant that the grief of survivors receives a disproportionate share of attention and that, by default, the grief of dying persons is rarely discussed—much less attended to—in current health care practice in the United States.

Numerous variables may confound the clinical picture, but in my experience several central factors influence the psychological state of the dying person:

The management of pain and other physical symptoms. In the absence of effective pain and symptom management, there is little chance the dying person will be able to address or successfully meet the social, psychological, and spiritual challenges inherent in the last phases of life.

The identification of the patient as "dying." Patients need to know they are dying and to understand the alternatives available to them before they can begin to adjust to their fate and make optimal use of their time and energy.

The timely use of support services, especially hospice care. Late referral (for example, in the last 2 weeks of life) does not allow for the development of trust and openness among the dying person, the family, and hospice staff. Late referral is often complicated by attempts to identify patient/family needs, to organize resources, to manage physical symptoms, and to assist the patient and family in adjusting to rapidly changing physical symptoms. Optimal benefit from hospice services often requires 4 to 6 weeks' involvement in care. All too often, we have heard families say, "If only we had known of hospice earlier."

The type of dying: medicalized versus nonmedicalized. Do the patient and the family desire aggressive therapies until death is imminent? Do they want everything possible done to extend life? Or are they interested in palliative care, in the relief of pain and other symptoms without attempts to seek a cure or unduly extend life through artificial means? We cared for a young physician who had many medical devices delivered to his home, where he was under the care of a hospice team. Despite his intellectual understanding that he was dying of cancer, he asked that we resuscitate him when he died.

The duration of dying. As is generally the case with survivors' grief, dying persons need time to make successful adjustment to their fate. In the absence of forewarnings, beneficial adaptive processes are not set in motion; there is little time for the dying person or family members to attend to all that must be done. At the other extreme, persons identified as dying who experience prolonged remissions may encounter what has been termed the "Lazarus phenomenon." They may wonder why they are still alive, may wait for recurrent forewarnings, and may provoke unease in family members who had resigned themselves to earlier death.

The site of dying. Research shows that the percentage of people who die in hospitals is highest in areas with the highest concentrations of hospital beds (Wennberg, 1997). We also know from recent research that survivors express considerable dissatisfaction with the terminal care provided to their loved ones in major medical institutions (Robert Wood Johnson Foundation, 1995). Most physicians prefer to treat patients in a hospital setting, where resources are immediately available and they can visit several patients in close proximity. Dying at home, in favor early in this century, has given way to dying in a hospital. Some patients do not know that there is an alternative to hospitalization until the time of death. Others take control of their lives and determine to be cared for at home, if not by their regular physicians, then by physicians who will make home calls. In the past two decades, rapid growth in home care for dying persons has opened the possibility of excellent palliative terminal care at home for most dying persons.

Time

It takes time to react thoroughly to a fatal diagnosis/prognosis. Time may loom out of proportion in the early phases of adjustment to one's coming death. Later, time may be less important, especially as the dying person has had a chance to prioritize new objectives; to share thoughts and feelings with friends and loved ones; to deal with fears, misunderstandings, and mistaken assumptions; and to gain confidence in the availability of excellent pain and symptom management during the weeks and months ahead. Someone once remarked that work tends to be accomplished within the time available. Some dying persons do not attend to the tasks at hand no matter how much time they have. Others whom I have known put their affairs in order in a few days and then began to deal with a whole new set of priorities: enjoying whatever time remains in the company of loved ones while at the same time saying good-byes to their own lives and to their loved ones.

As noted, if the time between diagnosis and death is too long, the dying person may rightly feel that he or she has beaten the odds. Family and friends may feel awkward in the presence of a person who has outlived his or her prognosis. They may feel guilty about their wish to have the person get on with the business of dying. Similarly, the dying person may sense a lack of completion, a failure to fulfill the role of the dying patient. Persons who have adjusted successfully to their own dying and yet found themselves alive have told of their feelings of unreality, as though they had dodged the bullets that were supposed to kill them.

Physical Symptoms

It is obvious that the physical state plays a significant role in determining how the impact of the overall situation is processed, both intellectually and emotionally. Persistent or recurrent severe pain can profoundly affect a person's perception of his or her condition. Pain, especially poorly managed pain, can have ominous significance for a seriously ill patient. Unrelieved chronic pain brings with it a host of psychological sequelae including (but not limited to) anxiety, depression, insomnia, anorexia, frustration, anger, and eventually thoughts of suicide. Unrelieved pain is augmented by memories of past pain combined with premonitions of pain yet to come. The pain threshold is lowered during chronic pain so that what would otherwise be a minor irritation may become a major source of distress.

The presence of other distressing physical symptoms (weakness, nausea, vomiting, constipation, diarrhea, skin breakdown, muscle cramps, etc.) compounds the problem of pain and impairs the dying person's ability to process in an orderly fashion the significance of the fact that he or she is dying. Advancing physical symptoms make it harder to deny the reality of progressive illness. The patient's thinking may rush forward to a belief that death is imminent. Neurological symptoms such as dementia, paralysis, and pain may make it more difficult for the dying person to understand or communicate with caregivers. The patient may express a wish to die or, out of fear, ask to have life ended as a way to bring an end to the suffering.

Clinical conditions are not a factor in most bereavement studies because it is usually assumed that the bereaved person is alive and functioning and will, after a certain period of time, be better. For a dying person, his or her level of functioning and clinical condition are all-important. Clinicians now speak of the quality of life (QOL) of dying persons. Instruments exist to measure various aspects of the QOL. Needless to say, the higher the quality of life, the more likely it is that a dying person can make use of opportunities to adjust satisfactorily to impending death.

Medicalized Dying

When dying is seen as a purely medical condition by the patient, the physician, the family, or some combination thereof, the dying person is likely to remain in some sort of medical institution until death supervenes. On the other hand, when dying is seen as a normal part of the human condition and the limits of aggressive and life-prolonging therapies are apparent, the patient can be referred to a hospice program for palliative care. I first learned the distinction between medicalized and nonmedicalized dying from a friend who called me as soon as he learned that he had cancer of the pancreas and that his surgeon (who proclaimed that he did not make home visits) said my friend had to remain in the hospital. My friend pleaded with me to have him released to home. He said, "Get me out of here! I'm not sick; I'm only dying!" He recognized the finality of his diagnosis and limited prognosis. He was clear headed. He saw that he had a lot to do before he died, and he wanted to get about the business of living with his family, not in a hospital where he would be forced into the "patient" role. He fully recognized that he was dying, yet the implications of what it meant to die unfolded only gradually with one forewarning after another. He withdrew from the outer, business world to focus attention on his wife, his children, and the task of putting his temporal affairs in order. During my conversations with him, it was apparent that he was also dealing with broader spiritual issues, with values and priorities that had been relegated to secondary importance as he worked his way to success in the business world. He developed new objectives, new priorities. The scope of his interests narrowed. His bed was in the living room of the home. Visitors were restricted to a short list of family and friends; he had no time for idle chatter. In the background at all times was the music of Puccini's La Bohème, his favorite opera. It served as a constant reminder of the beauty of love and the tragedy of death. Listening to La Bohème many hours a day served my friend as a reminder, a forewarning of the inevitability of death.

Serola (1975) provides the interesting account of her father, a professor of medicine. When he suspected that his increasing anemia was probably due to prostate cancer that had metastasized to his bones, he asked his daughter to buy him three pairs of blue silk pajamas. He withdrew from an active medical practice and lived comfortably until his death a few months later. His daughter, also a physician, suggested that her father's nonmedical approach to his advancing disease should be considered as an alternative to extended diagnostic testing and futile aggressive therapies.

Family Dynamics

Family dynamics exert a strong influence on the patient's attitude toward dying. A woman who was well aware that she was dying of metastatic breast cancer asked me to come to her home to help convince her husband and sons that she was dying. During the discussion, it was obvious that they knew she had advanced cancer, yet they could not openly consider that she was going to die. The patient wanted them to acknowledge her impending death so she could deal realistically with the tasks she wanted to accomplish, including saying her good-byes to her husband and sons and having these good-byes acknowledged as such. The husband and the sons had been led to believe that a positive attitude would improve her chances of survival; they hoped that their united benevolent optimism would alter the course of disease. They did not want to lose their mother and wife to cancer. Yet the strength of their defenses prevented the patient from dealing with the obvious fact that she was dying. Once the issues were identified and clarified, the family began to deal with the difficult facts in a timely manner. The sons and the father began to express their grief, and the mother was able to express her feelings about the losses she was experiencing.

The Physician

The physician generally sets the tone for discussion about diagnosis, prognosis, and treatment alternatives. The reactions of the physician and other health care workers to the changing clinical picture have tremendous power to affect the emotional state of the patient and the patient's loved ones. The physician's personal feelings about death and dying are also important determinants of care and attitudes toward the dying person. Aring (1971) asserts that "a physician unaware of his personal feelings about death and dying by the same token permits them to interfere with his effective treatment of patients. On one hand, indifference has resulted in undertreatment and neglect and, on the other, in overtreatment and an officious striving to keep alive" (p. 160). The extreme positions occur all too often and have negative impact on the dying person as well as the family. The middle road is more difficult for physicians, who often find it hard to blend clinical objectivity with sensitive, empathic identification with dying persons. Part of the problem lies in the education of physicians. It was not until long after medical school that I saw how the death of a loved one often had a profound, enduring impact on survivors, especially if the death was sudden and unanticipated or if the impending death was not openly discussed with the patient and family.

Byock (1996) has addressed the areas of responsibility for physicians and the teams who attend to the needs of dying persons. First of all, the physician must be present to the patient; he or she must go to where the patient is, examine the patient, speak with (not to) the patient:

> We may not have answers for the existential questions of life and death anymore than the person dying. We may not be able to assuage all feelings of regret or fears of the unknown. But it is not our solutions that matter. The role of the clinical team is to stand by the patient, steadfastly providing meticulous physical care and psychosocial support, while people strive to discover their own answers. (p. 251)

Dying persons sometimes develop close relationships with caregivers with whom they can communicate and in whom they trust. The availability of reliable, knowledgeable caregivers experienced in working with dying patients and comfortable with their own feelings about dying can be of inestimable value in helping the dying person make a positive adjustment to approaching death.

ANTICIPATORY GRIEF AND MOURNING

Horowitz (1980), writing of postdeath bereavement, defined *mourning* as "the processes in which states of grief are eventually attenuated as the person recognizes and adapts to loss" (p. 1157). Anthropologists describe mourning as the complex series of postdeath rituals and ceremonies that bereaved persons use to adapt to the loss of a loved one or to the death of an important member of their social group. I have not seen dying persons mourning their own deaths or the losses associated with their impending deaths in this strictly anthropologic sense of the term. But, from time to time, we hear of someone "mourning his or her own death." This usage applies more to psychoanalytic than to anthropologic terminology. Some dying persons grieve their dying and associated losses. Some make successful adjustments to their dying regardless of age or the circumstances of dying.

Anticipatory mourning in dying persons and intimates has been defined in this volume as including responses to a number of losses (see Rando, chapter 2). The dying person grieves not only the loss of life but all attendant losses as well: the loss of the prior level of functioning; loss of abilities; loss of body parts and functions; loss of anticipated future with loved ones; loss of hopes, dreams, and expectations invested in relationships with loved ones; loss of security, predictability, and control; and loss of the notion of personal invulnerability. Further, Rando (1986) observes that

> whereas in conventional mourning secondary losses will accrue, they will at some point diminish in number in contrast to the dying patient, for whom they will only increase. These realities plus those intrinsic to pain, facing the unknown, and the ultimate experience of permanent separation and death, combine to intensify the emotions of anxiety, depression, sorrow, anguish, sadness, anger, hostility, frustration, guilt, and shame that most mourners must confront. (p. 28)

In my experience as a hospice physician, dying persons usually do not emotionally emancipate themselves from their loved ones as death approaches. Many dying persons tell of increased closeness to their spouses and loved ones as life comes to an end. On the other hand, dying persons clearly do let go of mundane realities when they can no longer perform as they once did. They adapt, commensurate with experiences of forewarning, to the reality that life is coming to an end. They let go of the routines of life, accept limitations on their activities, experience and repeatedly assess physical changes consistent with dying, focus on their finitude, consider themselves in the role of "sick" and "dying," interact with others who are responding to their dying, confront spiritual issues, redefine self-image in terms of the progression of disease, adjust to lower levels of energy, and accommodate to new physical symptoms. In this sense, their anticipatory grief differs from that in the case described by Lindemann (1944), in which a wife unconsciously became emancipated from the relationship with her soldier husband. Such situations do present themselves, however: I once worked with a patient who made an unexpected, spontaneous recovery from malignant melanoma. Her husband, repeatedly told by the oncologist that his wife would not recover, had emancipated himself from his wife, but the wife had never freed herself from the bonds to her husband. She sought my help to try to persuade her husband that she was not going to die and that he should return to her.

There is no single, common path or time interval between diagnosis of a fatal illness and death. Even when the circumstances are similar, the manner of facing death varies greatly from person to person. Each one reacts to the imminence of dying in his or her own way. Some fear dying, others welcome death; some accept their fate regardless of age, others seek any means to prolong life. Yet others change their position midway through the process of dying. The variables are so numerous, and some of them are so central to the course of the dying process, that it is problematic to say that any single factor predominates. Experience, however, suggests that dying persons who make knowledge-based decisions affecting their care, obtain optimal pain and symptom relief, and remain mentally alert can prioritize their goals and use whatever time remains to complete unfinished business; say their good-byes; and attend to any remaining personal, family, and spiritual issues. Attention to these tasks reduces the severity of grief in dying persons.

Dying persons grieve the losses that accompany advancing illness; the loss of strength, mobility, employment, and independence; the loss of an anticipated future; and the premature severance of relationships. Each new loss is a further reminder of the inevitable loss of self, of identity, and of continuity. Some people grieve each new loss openly, whereas others appear able to transcend multiple losses with equanimity. The process of adjusting to these sequential losses is multidimensional; it involves processing information from observation of one's own physical changes, processing the observations of caregivers and loved ones, and integrating them with perceptions of one's changing role and one's fears, hopes, expectations, and spirituality. The dying person's adjustment to all these changes is rarely smooth. Anxiety, insomnia, and transient depression are not uncommon as death approaches. A minor crisis can occur when a change in physical condition or a reminder of the prognosis heightens awareness of approaching, inevitable death. These intimations of finitude, these forewarnings, are commonly disconcerting, yet they focus the dying person on the tasks at hand. Each forewarning provides further opportunity to clarify the situation, to refocus on reality, and to identify and reprioritize objectives. Successful adaptation to forewarnings is not an automatic process but usually requires sharing with a trusted person, allowing feelings to be discussed and expressed, determining the meaning of the forewarning, and ultimately integrating and internalizing the experience.

Denial versus the Need to Know

The need to know what is happening is universal, but for certain reasons knowledge can be suppressed by the occasional patient who does not want to face the facts. At times, the mechanism of denial persists and dominates past a point that seems reasonable to observers. If we operate on the assumption that all behavior has meaning, we can usually gain some understanding of the reason for the persistence and hypertrophy of a normal mental defense mechanism. I worked with a man who had a history of exposure to asbestos, many years of smoking, exposure to fallout from nuclear explosions, and metastatic lung cancer. He was receiving nasal oxygen and gasping for breath. A short while before he died he gasped, "I'm gonna beat this thing, Doc!" Outwardly, he never gave in to the diseases that killed him, nor did he outwardly grieve his dying or the many personal losses it entailed. His wife had difficulty accepting a death to which he vowed he would never succumb. From a psychological point of view, we may speculate that the man could not accept the fact that he was dying for a variety of reasons: He had lived through some perilous wartime experiences. He had just begun to experience success in business but had accumulated debts that his wife could not handle. And, because he could not begin to deal with the fact that he was dying, his wife felt that she could not undercut his massive denial so that together they could develop an alternative plan should he not experience the hoped-for cure or prolonged remission of symptoms. This example supports the contention that the dynamics of dying must be considered in a broader family or social context. Also, the example suggests that preexisting attitudes toward life tend to carry over into the period of dying. In this case, denial was a predominant psychological process in the lifestyle of the dying person, with physical invulnerability as a counterpart to repeated serious toxic exposures.

Denial is a mechanism, not a phase. It is the cornerstone of all our psychological defenses and must be respected as such because some people, for whatever reasons, cannot face the discomfort of total awareness of impending death. On the other hand, it is unreasonable to participate knowingly in denial if to do so deprives the patient or family members of the opportunity to understand their situation; to begin to develop new objectives and priorities; and to participate in decisions affecting treatment, care, and the timely resolution of all manner of social and economic necessities.

Nuland (1995) advises us that "it is by knowing the truth and being prepared for it that we rid ourselves of that fear of the terra incognita of death that leads us to self-deception and disillusions"

(p. xvii). The presence and persistence of denial reduce the possibility that a dying person can benefit from the repeated forewarnings that commonly occur during the dying process. The forewarnings fulfill a function: They help the patient maintain focus and perspective. They can, as Fulton (1978) observed, ease the process of dying itself.

Styles of Dying

Some people approach their dying with clarity of mind and remain in open communication until the last moments of life; others, because of the impact of illness, the side effects of treatment, or declining mental abilities, appear unaware of their circumstances. In general, people tend to approach dying and death as they have approached life. Some face their dying directly and matter-of-factly; others use a variety of denial defenses to give the appearance that they will never die. Some people accept dying as a series of tasks to be taken seriously. Others, for various reasons, regress in the face of incurable illness and relinquish control to family, friends, or caregivers. More commonly, dying includes a sequence of forewarnings interspersed with more or less successful attempts at denial.

The daughter of an 84-year-old woman diagnosed with fatal cancer was advised to place her in a nursing home. With the assistance of hospice, two daughters and two grandchildren, the woman received excellent care in a daughter's home. She remained alert and involved throughout her final illness. Pain and other physical symptoms were well controlled. During the last few days of life, she reflected on many of the events of the past. On the day before she died, she declared to me, "Dying, you know, is the experience of a lifetime." As death approached, she was happy and at peace. She had apparently completed whatever unfinished business remained at the time of diagnosis, and now she looked forward to dying. Just before dying, she closed her eyes, dramatically blew a kiss to those in the room, folded her arms across her chest, and calmly waited for death.

A young boy we worked with who died of osteogenic sarcoma was asked by his mother what he wanted for breakfast on what turned out to be the last day of his life. He replied simply, "A kiss." The boy and his mother had had a close and difficult relationship aggravated by other family stresses during the son's final illness. His response on that last morning typifies the optimal result of a great deal of work on the part of patient, family, and caregivers. The boy knew he was dying and knew that his mother was distraught. He, too, had a great deal of difficulty adjusting to his dying. The struggles and strong feelings of loss of both mother and son were smoothed and defused by his ultimate response to her caring question.

For some, however, the glass will always be half empty, never half full. I recall a young woman who asked shortly before her death, "Is this all there is?" Despite the best of care, not everyone feels good about his or her dying. I have been with persons who, as they died, expressed anger at the unfairness of their illnesses. Others have expressed regret over wrongs never righted, unfinished personal business, or unrelieved guilt from prior transgressions. People in this general category do not actively accept their dying; they become resigned to it and do not depart gently. But those who learn to accept their dying as part of their living see it as natural and inevitable. They are less likely to feel cheated by death no matter when it comes.

NEEDS OF DYING PERSONS

Dying persons need good communication with their physicians. They need to know that their wishes will be respected. They need honest answers to their questions. They need to know that they will be neither abandoned nor encouraged to receive unneeded or inappropriate treatments. They need to know that they will receive prompt attention to their symptoms.

Dying persons need time to discuss the impact of their diagnoses and all the ramifications. They need to be able to express their hopes, fears, and concerns. They need time to consider options and alternatives for treatment and care. They need to know that when it is appropriate, they will be considered as dying. They need to be able to discuss impending death in a realistic manner without euphemisms, dysphemisms, or symbolic expressions to cover the facts. Dying persons need time to reflect on whatever unfinished business remains in their lives. They need to know what is happening and what is going to happen to their cognitive abilities as illness progresses. They need to be involved in treatment decisions. They need to know what care will be needed as symptoms progress.

In practical terms, dying persons need others experienced with "the system" to advise, guide, assist, review, and help them develop plans that include options, alternatives, and analyses of available resources. They will need assistance in dealing with the complications of disease and the side effects of treatments. They will require answers to questions about health insurance, life insurance, and other economic considerations. If the patient and the family opt for end-of-life care in the home, family members will require instruction and supervision in management of the patient's changing physical condition and in the administration and recording of medications. They may also require assistance with transportation, medical appointments,

communication with health care workers, child care, shopping, cleaning, cooking, and keeping track of those who volunteer their help.
Family caregivers will require emotional support and perhaps respite
from the continuous responsibility of patient care.

Dying persons need to be able to communicate, to share their
fears and feelings with people they trust—people who are experienced, nonjudgmental, trustworthy, and objective. They may want
to explore what is happening to them. They may want to tell parts
or all of their life stories, to reflect on their lives, their losses, their
work, their regrets, their loves. They need opportunities to express
and share feelings with loved ones, to thank those who have helped
them. They need opportunities to explore the spiritual dimensions
of their lives, to help plan for what will happen later to their loved
ones. They may feel the need to speak out of the anxiety of the
unknown. They may need the reassurance that can come only from
one who possesses knowledge and experience about dying and
death.

As dying persons identify and deal with their needs and are reassured that they will continue to be cared for, they can begin to
adjust positively to their fate, to their awareness of impending death.
They gradually begin to disengage from some of their worldly concerns, some of which are mourned, others of which are no loss. I see
distinct changes in the attitudes of dying persons as they make peace
with their fate. They become more outgoing, they begin to show
concern for the well-being of others, they sleep better, and they
become more involved in living than in dying. This happens only
when they have excellent relief of pain and other major physical
symptoms and have begun to resolve the challenges presented by
their dying.

Dying persons also need reasonable hope. At first they may
hope that their diagnoses are in error or that the prognoses are
incorrect. They may hope for the timely discovery of a cure. Gradually, hopes are transformed to meet the changing clinical picture. In
time, some persons hope to die without pain and suffering, to sum
up their life experiences, to be able to express gratitude and say
good-bye to loved ones, to share their thoughts and reminiscences,
and to die with comfort. Some look forward to an afterlife in which
they will be reunited with loved ones.

GROWTH AT THE END OF LIFE

Can dying persons experience growth despite all that is happening
to them? I have found that when excellent physical care and proper
emotional support are provided to patients and family members,

they can make productive use of what might otherwise have been a devastating experience. Erikson (1950) pointed out that successfully handled grief can serve as the focus for social and psychological growth. I believe that Erikson's dictum applies to the grief of dying persons as well as to that of survivors. The operative phrase is "successfully handled." That includes somehow integrating a variety of primary and secondary losses into a meaningful resolution, usually on a spiritual level, that allows the dying person and the survivor to focus on the positive aspects of the relationship rather than to dwell on the negative aspects of the situation.

Byock (1996) finds that those who can be said to have grown in their dying express satisfaction in the direction of the personal change taking place in response to the progressive stresses of disabling illness and that they experience an enhanced subjective sense of self during the process. He points out that those who die progressively rather than suddenly have opportunities to acknowledge achievements and enjoy their accomplishments. As noted previously, if the trajectory of dying is too brief or if referral to a supportive, palliative program like hospice is not made in a timely fashion, patient and family may not be able to make optimal use of available services.

I have seen many individuals rise above the fact of their dying to a new level of comfort with the situation. The essence of this attitude becomes manifest when the patient experiences less concern about his or her own situation and takes more interest in the well-being of family, friends, and caregivers. This "transcendent" response is qualitatively different from the responses characterized as acceptance or resignation. I have observed this dramatic change in patients dying of a variety of illnesses. In my experience, this transcendent sensation comes only if the patient is fully aware of all that is happening; is involved in decisions affecting care; has received optimal relief of pain and other physical symptoms; has completed remaining unfinished business; and feels secure in the affection of family, friends, and caregivers.

I had never witnessed this transcendent experience until I began working as part of an interdisciplinary team with dying persons receiving hospice care in their own homes. Had I not witnessed this experience time and again, I would not have imagined it could happen, save as the result of a delirious process caused by chemical derangement of the dying person's mind. Having seen it repeatedly in dying persons aware of what is happening to them supports the belief that conscious dying can be accompanied by a feeling of exaltation. This phenomenon does not occur every time, yet it is a reasonable objective that can be attained through identification of and attention to the complex, changing needs of dying persons. Although it would be a mistake to glorify the situation, experience in hospice validates historic and literary observations that at times the suffering of the sick and dying can give way to a heightened sense of well-being and quality of life.

SUMMARY AND CONCLUSIONS

Dying persons grieve impending death and its attendant losses: the loss of relationships, identity, and future. Recapitulation of prior losses is also commonly observed in older dying persons. With excellent care and symptom management, together with sufficient time and support, the normal psychological symptoms associated with loss and dying can yield to a recognition of the finitude of life and the importance of the spiritual dimension.

The positive impact of observing and participating in the excellent care of a dying person cannot be overemphasized. It assures family and friends that their efforts have been worthwhile, that they have truly assisted the dying person in a meaningful way, and that the act of dying has been transformed into a positive experience for all involved. Survivor grief is attenuated because of an awareness that all was done that could or should have been done. Further, involvement in such an experience provides a model for approaching other deaths in the future, including one's own.

REFERENCES

Aring, C. (1971). *The understanding physician.* Detroit: Wayne State University Press.

Beresford, L. (1997, Fall). Living in the light of death. *The Hospice Magazine,* pp. 12–16.

Byock, I. R. (1996). The nature of suffering and the nature of opportunity at the end of life. *Clinics in Geriatric Medicine, 12*(2), 237–252.

Calland, C. (1972). Iatrogenic problems in end-stage renal failure. *New England Journal of Medicine, 287,* 334–336.

Cousins, N. (1974). *A celebration of life.* New York: Harper & Row.

Eliot, T. (1946). War bereavements and their recovery. *Marriage and Family Living, 8,* 1–6.

Erikson, E. (1950). *Childhood and society.* New York: Norton.

Freud, S. (1957). Mourning and melancholia. In J. Strachey (Ed. & Trans.), *The standard edition of the complete psychological works of Sigmund Freud* (Vol. 14). London: Hogarth Press. (Original work published in 1917)

Fulton, R. (1978). *Death and dying: Challenge and change.* Reading, MA: Addison-Wesley.

Glaser, B. G., & Strauss, A. (1965). *Awareness of dying.* Chicago: Aldine.

Horowitz, M. J. (1980). Pathological grief and the activation of latent self-images. *American Journal of Psychiatry, 137,* 1157–1162.

Kübler-Ross, E. (1969). *On death and dying.* New York: Macmillan.

Kübler-Ross, E. (1975). *Death, the final stage of growth.* New York: Prentice Hall.

Lindemann, E. (1944). Symptomatology and management of acute grief. *American Journal of Psychiatry, 101,* 141–148.

Lynn, J., Teno, J., Phillips, R. et al. (1997). Perceptions by family members of the dying experience of older and seriously ill patients. *Annals of Internal Medicine, 126,* 97–106.

Melvin, T., Ozbek, I., & Eberle, D. (1992). Recognition of depression in hospice patients. *International Hospice Institute.* (On-line publication)

Netske, M. (1976). Dying in a system of good care. *Pharos of AOA, 39*(2), 57–61.

Nuland, S. B. (1995). *How we die: Reflections on life's final chapter.* New York: Vintage Books.

Osler, W. (1904). *Science and immortality.* Boston: Houghton Mifflin.

Pattison, E. M. (1978). The living-dying process. In C. A. Garfield (Ed.), *Psychosocial care of the dying patient.* New York: McGraw-Hill.

Rando, T. A. (1986). A comprehensive analysis of anticipatory grief: Perspectives, processes, promises, and problems. In T. A. Rando (Ed.), *Loss and anticipatory grief.* Lexington, MA: Lexington Books.

Robert Wood Johnson Foundation. (1995). *On dying in America* (Annual Report). Princeton, NJ: Schmitz Press.

Sagan, C. (1997). *Billions and billions.* New York: Random House.

Serola, I. K. (1975). The death of an old professor. *Journal of the American Medical Association, 232,* 728–729.

Wennberg, J. (1997). *Dartmouth Atlas of Health Care,* quoted in Reuters, 97–10–17.

CHAPTER 11

Promoting Healthy Anticipatory Mourning in Intimates of the Life-Threatened or Dying Person

Therese A. Rando

It is a role for which there is no formal preparation and often minimal recognition. It is ill-defined and ambiguous at a time when definition and clarity tend to be valued. Support for it may wax and wane, if indeed there is much at all. Implicit assumptions may be held about how one should behave in it, yet it lacks explicit instruction and direction. There are no norms for appropriate behavior in it, yet those who deviate from the expectations of others typically are criticized. It frequently involves experiences that traumatize, yet the person affected, as well as those around him or her, often do not appreciate the ensuing traumatic stress. The individual operating in it usually struggles with monumental stressors and conflicting tasks but may find him- or herself unsupported and possibly disenfranchised. In its domain, the individual attempts to control what is essentially an uncontrollable situation. While it ostensibly focuses upon a person who is physically dying, it involves the psychosocial dying of parts of the mourner's self and the intimate network.

It is the experience of the anticipatory mourner contending with the life-threatening or terminal illness of a loved one. *Intimate anticipatory mourning* is a wide ranging and often profound set of experiences and demands associated with the role of an intimate whose loved one is life-threatened or dying. The purpose of this chapter is to examine a variety of those specific experiences and to identify therapeutic strategies that can promote healthy anticipatory mourning.

In this chapter, the term *intimate* often refers to family members. However, an ill person may feel strongly and reciprocally connected to nonfamily members. Therefore, restricting the term to biological

---
❋

To the children of my siblings—Laura, Alex, Carla, and Marielle—for all they are and will be

307

family or those with kinship ties is inappropriate. Doka (1993) makes the point that one of the first tasks for the caregiver should be to determine precisely who constitutes the person's circle, "family," or intimate network. The intimate network may be composed of family, nonfamily, or a combination of the two; hereafter, unless otherwise specified, the term *family* will refer to the intimate network in a broader sense, and the term *intimate* may denote a family member, but not necessarily.

It is important to identify the significant others in an ill individual's life both in order to access them as needed for the care of the person and to pinpoint those who also may require assistance. It is also necessary for caregivers to appreciate family systems concepts when working with the intimates of the ill person because dynamics similar to those found in traditional family systems often operate as well within the intimate network, regardless of whether or not some or all of its members have kinship ties. Increasingly, the majority of a person's intimates are nonfamilial, and very close friends and compassionate caregivers or volunteers may take the place of biological family during that person's illness and dying.

The chapter commences with a brief outline of clinical concepts related to anticipatory mourning. Subsequently, there is an overview of family systems dynamics associated with illness and disability and particularly pertinent in anticipatory mourning. Following a brief sketch of how stress, crisis, and secondary traumatization affect intimates, discussion turns to factors that complicate intimate anticipatory mourning. The chapter concludes with discussion of therapeutic strategies and interventions, presented within the context of the Four-Plus Phase Model for Intervention in Intimate Anticipatory Mourning.

INTIMATE ANTICIPATORY MOURNING

As delineated in chapter 2 of this volume, anticipatory mourning is

> the phenomenon encompassing seven generic operations
> (grief and mourning, coping, interaction, psychosocial
> reorganization, planning, balancing conflicting demands,
> and facilitating an appropriate death) that, within a context
> of adaptational demands caused by experiences of loss and
> trauma, is stimulated in response to the awareness of life-
> threatening or terminal illness in oneself or a significant
> other and the recognition of associated losses in the past,
> present, and future.

Anticipatory mourning may be viewed, experienced, and understood from four distinct perspectives: patient, intimate, concerned other, and caregiver. The anticipatory mourning of any of these four parties may occur on three contextual levels: (a) the intrapsychic level (including processes grouped into the categories of awareness of and gradual accommodation to the threat, affective processes, cognitive processes, and planning for the future); (b) the interpersonal level (including processes grouped into the categories of directing attention, energy, and behavior toward the life-threatened or dying person; resolution of personal relationship with the life-threatened or dying person; and helping the life-threatened or dying person; and (c) systemic level processes. Like all anticipatory mourning, that of an intimate will be shaped by classes of psychological, social, and physiological influencing factors, also identified in chapter 2. The seven generic operations can be expected to occur at varying points and intensities throughout the period of mourning, with experiences of loss and trauma serving as major sources of adaptational demands throughout.

FAMILY SYSTEMS CONCEPTS RELATING TO ILLNESS AND DISABILITY

In order to help both patients and intimate anticipatory mourners, the caregiver must be aware of the particular characteristics of the system (i.e., intimate network) within which both operate. While a complete discussion of family systems theory as it relates to the dying and/or death of a family member is beyond the scope of this chapter, a few pivotal concepts must be explained here. (For in-depth discussion and clinical information regarding dying, death, and families, see Bowen, 1976; Doka, 1993; Figley, 1989; Grebstein, 1986; Krieger & Bascue, 1975; Nadeau, 1998; Pincus, 1974; Prichard, Collard, Orcutt, Kutscher, Seeland, & Lefkowitz, 1977; Rando, 1984; Rolland, 1994; Rosen, 1990; Shapiro, 1994; and Walsh & McGoldrick, 1991.) There also must be an appreciation of how these concepts are affected by chronic illness and disability.

Family Constellation

In any family system—including the entire intimate network—the whole is more than the sum of the parts. In this regard, the family is composed not only of individuals, but also of relationships among individuals that define the family unit. As a system, the family operates under the same conditions as does any system. Causality is circular rather than linear—that is, anything that affects the system as a whole will affect the individual members, while anything that affects the individual members will affect all other members, as well as the system as a whole. In the case of chronic disorders, professionals involved in the patient's care become part of the "health-related family unit," or treatment system. In the case of protracted, disabling conditions, it is not uncommon for professionals in home health care to become central to family life. Such persons must be considered in any evaluation of the system. In stigmatizing disorders or those that affect groups subject to discrimination—such as AIDS in the gay community—caregiving networks emerge that function as family units and should be viewed as such (Rolland, 1994).

Homeostasis

Like all systems, the family operates to maintain its own balance and equilibrium. To do so, families develop stabilizing mechanisms to preserve continuity. These include uniquely distinct roles, rules, norms, boundaries, expectations, communication patterns, and patterns of behavior that reflect the family's beliefs, values, assumptions, experiences, coping strategies, system alliances, and coalitions. These function to keep the family system consistent and stable. When the family loses its homeostatic balance because a significant change affects its members, the system will move to compensate and adapt to that change in order to reestablish its homeostasis.

Cohesion and Boundaries

One of the central dimensions of family organization, *cohesion* refers to the degree of closeness, emotional bonding, and connectedness among family members. Ideally, families balance needs for closeness and connectedness with a respect for separateness and individual differences, a balance that shifts as families move through the life cycle. *Boundaries* define and separate individual members and promote their differentiation and autonomous functioning, and they exist on the interpersonal, generational, and family-community levels (Rolland, 1994). Among families, there is a continuum of differentiation of the family member's self from the family. This range runs from extreme overinvolvement or "enmeshment" (where there are few to no boundaries among family members and no tolerance of individuality, autonomy, privacy, or separation) to extreme isolation or "disengagement," where individual autonomy and separateness, differences, uninvolvement, and low bonding are promoted at the expense of family relatedness.

Rolland (1994) observes that cohesion—a central dimension of family organization that has been shown to be a major predictor of family coping with illness (Olson et al., 1989)—changes as families move through the life cycle. A relatively greater need for teamwork or cohesion exists when the family has small children than when the children are in adolescence, at which point the family organization typically becomes less cohesive and places greater emphasis on differentiation and autonomy of adolescent members. In the case of a disabling chronic condition, these normal transitions may be intensified and prolonged. In some illnesses, such as cerebral palsy or the developmental disability of mental retardation, the need for high cohesion may be permanent and can derail family members from normative developmental shifts. Degree of cohesion is also cultural. A highly cohesive family style is normal in many ethnic groups and may not signal the dysfunction it does in families where it is not part of the culture.

Interpersonal boundary patterns of enmeshment and disengagement are risk factors for successful family coping and adaptation. Rolland (1994) asserts that, for any disorder, caregivers must assess the fit between the psychosocial demands for cohesion and family patterns of closeness. He notes that at a pragmatic level, conditions requiring teamwork, such as home-based dialysis for end-stage renal disease, will be especially difficult for the disengaged family, which avoids closeness and cooperative efforts. Alternatively, the self-contained tasks of taking medication and going for regular check-ups involved in a disorder such as a stomach ulcer may not create such problems for this family because of the minimal demands for teamwork. At the other end of the continuum, enmeshment in families can contribute to problems when families overprotect the patient and inhibit the development of autonomy with regard to self-care and pursuit of realistic life goals. This frequently happens with chronically ill children and adolescents as they strive for normal independence. The transition from the crisis to the chronic phase of the illness can be difficult for these families. Enmeshment, helpful in the initial crisis, interferes with the shift to autonomy that the latter phase requires. Enmeshed families also tend to be wary of outsiders and to maintain rigid boundaries around the family unit, both of which create problems if conditions necessitate professional help, especially within the home.

Flexibility and Adaptability

While it is important for the family to have a sense of cohesiveness and stability to maintain continuity, it is also imperative that the family be able to integrate new information and adapt suitably to change. Adaptability in families has been defined as "the ability of a relationship system to change its power structure, role relationships, and relationship rules in response to a situational or developmental stressor" (Russell & Olson, 1983, p. 26). Transformational mechanisms are therefore necessary to ensure optimal morphogenesis (Keeney & Thomas, 1986). Recent writings in family therapy emphasize the balance of change and continuity—that is, that families need to be able to adapt to changing circumstances while maintaining a sense of cohesiveness and stability (Shapiro, 1994). In other words, the system must adapt to changing circumstances or life cycle developmental tasks while meeting the family's needs for enduring values, traditions, and predictable, consistent rules for behavior (Rolland, 1994).

Citing family adaptability as one of the chief requisites for well-functioning family systems (Olson, Russell, & Sprenkle, 1989), Rolland (1994) observes that family adaptability is essential, particularly when patients have progressive, relapsing disorders or acute medical crises. Rolland notes that flexibility is required for a family to adapt to the internal and external changes serious illness may require and that, internally, the family must reorganize in response to (a) new developmental imperatives brought on by progressive illness and (b) the disorder's continual interaction with the family's and individual members' life cycle development. Families at the extremes of adaptability will have more problems with certain types of conditions. Because rigid families have difficulty with change, their style of functioning will be ill suited to the rapid shifting of roles required by relapsing disorders. According to Rolland, such families will function better with constant-course conditions, such as permanent injuries. Families that are chaotic and disorganized have problems with illnesses in which strict adherence to regimens is required, such as diabetes. Major illnesses, such as stroke or Alzheimer's disease, cause the family sufficient stress to require major adaptational shifts in family rules in order to ensure continuity of family life. Rolland cites the example of a disabled husband who may have to alter traditional gender-based rules to assume the role of homemaker while his wife takes a job outside the home.

Communication

All verbal and nonverbal behaviors communicate. There is no way to avoid communicating; whatever is done or not done delivers a message. Communication may be about pragmatic or factual information or issues, or about emotional or affective information or issues. Characteristics of communication—style, clarity, openness, directness, patterns, topics, constraints and avoidances, sender and recipient roles, and so forth—reveal critically important information about the system. From a family systems viewpoint, individual symptoms are understood in terms of both the communication that occurs and the function of the symptoms in relation to the current state of the family system.

Rolland (1994) contends that effective communication is vital to family mastery of illness and disability, and that in families facing major, long-term health problems, communication cannot regularly be left unclear or unresolved without pathological consequences or possible dissolution of family relationships. He believes communication about emotional issues is generally more difficult than communication about pragmatic or instrumental issues and that communication about feelings may be particularly compromised in disorders that involve threatened loss and, by inference, many situations of anticipatory mourning.

CLINICAL CONCEPTS RELEVANT TO INTIMATES OF THE LIFE-THREATENED OR TERMINALLY ILL PERSON

Several clinical concepts must be apprehended for successful work with the intimate anticipatory mourner. Specifically, the caregiver must adequately appreciate the issues of stress, crisis, and secondary traumatization that typically apply when an individual contends with the possibility or inevitability of a loved one's death. This information can help the caregiver understand and, as necessary, interpret the reactions of affected parties, as well as to design therapeutic strategies and identify specific interventions to enable appropriate and healthy anticipatory mourning. Although for the purpose of discussion the concepts are differentiated here, in reality great interrelatedness and overlap exists.*

Stress

In essence, stress is a demand placed upon the human being for an adaptational change. Therefore, the occurrence of stress is an inherent part of life-threatening or terminal illness. The experience of a loved one's life-threatening or terminal illness and ensuing anticipa-

---

*Topics that cannot be addressed in this chapter are discussed at greater length in the following resources: For issues of coping with the crises of physical illness, see Moos (1977, 1984); for issues concerning families, illness, and disability, see Rolland (1994). For information about generic, individual, and family issues in life-threatening and terminal illness, see Doka (1993) and Rando (1984). For issues of families contending specifically with terminal illness, see Rosen (1990). For treatment of traumatized families, see Figley (1989). For information about family systems, death, and bereavement, see Shapiro (1994) and Walsh and McGoldrick (1991).

tory mourning, whether from the perspective of ill person or intimate, places a number of major demands upon the individual for
adaptation. Disequilibrium occurs in the balance within the person,
and strain or tension is felt to some degree as one perceives the
demand and attempts to restore the previous balance.

Sources of stress in families with a chronically ill child have
been delineated by Patterson and McCubbin (1983). These can be
extrapolated to families and intimate networks contending with
the chronic illness of a member of any age. Regardless of whether
an illness is life-threatening or terminal, chronicity alone often
brings with it the following stresses: (a) strained relationships,
(b) modifications in activities and goals, (c) increased tasks and
time commitments, (d) increased financial burden, (e) need for
housing adaptations, (f) social isolation, (g) medical concerns,
(h) differences in school and work experiences, and (i) grieving.
An additional source of stress is that the normal developmental
tasks of the family and its members must be played out in an atypical context, where the ill member's special needs or changing
medical condition interacts with the tasks, often exacerbating
demands and hardships.

Another precipitant of stress identified by Patterson and
McCubbin is "pile-up." This is what happens when multiple stressors (i.e., changes and demands) and their ensuing strains occur
simultaneously, all demanding attention at once. Among the components of pile-up are (a) normative changes; (b) strains and hardships associated with the illness; (c) persistent hard-to-resolve or
irresolvable specific difficulties that serve as a source of chronic
strain; (d) specific efforts at coping attempted to remedy the situation (which can cause their own stresses and strains); and (e) ambiguity about such matters as decisions, the ill person's prognosis, and
how to plan for the future. Patterson and McCubbin assert that multiple impacts on the family and its members can derive from the
size of the pile-up alone, including effects on the health and well-
being of the chronically ill person and, if unresolved, contribution
toward undesirable characteristics in the family environment.

Crisis

Very simply, a crisis occurs "when a person faces an obstacle to
important life goals that is, for a time, insurmountable through the
utilization of customary methods of problem solving. A period of
disorganization ensues, a period of upset, during which many
abortive attempts at solution are made" (Caplan, 1961, p. 18). Thus,
crisis involves stress that has become excessive. The person experiences a threat that he or she cannot resolve, thereby creating a state

of psychological disequilibrium and causing an increase of inner tension, anxiety, and disorganization of function that results in a period of emotional upset. This is almost identical to what happens in trauma (see chapter 6 in this volume). In this regard, it is probably fair to say that in many cases a crisis is traumatic, and that in all cases a trauma prompts a crisis.

The new balance achieved after a crisis may represent a healthy adaptation that promotes personal growth and maturation or a maladaptive response that foreshadows psychological deterioration and decline. Thus, a crisis is a transition or turning point that can have lasting implications for an individual's adaptation and ability to meet future crises (Moos & Schaefer, 1984).

In life-threatening or terminal illness, the issue of crisis arises in two general ways: (a) as a particular phase in the illness, such as Pattison's (1977) acute crisis phase of diagnosis, and (b) as an ongoing or periodic experience that punctuates the course of the illness. In this latter vein, a crisis may be physically related—caused by the vicissitudes of the illness, its treatment, or sequelae—or it may result from reactions to the psychological, behavioral, or social concommitants of the illness at a particular point in time (e.g., an individual's reaction to the ill person's increased dependency). An incongruence between demands and resources can occasion a crisis, as when the sick loved one needs 24-hour-a-day assistance but the intimate cannot respond to the need and finances are insufficient to hire professionals.

Similarly, lack of fit between the needs of the family at its point in the life cycle and the demands of the illness can prompt a crisis. For instance, a crisis can erupt when the family that has been granting an adolescent increased independence must monitor that teenager more closely and insist that he or she relinquish some autonomy because of illness.

Fears about the likelihood and severity of disease-related crises are often a major source of a family's underlying anxiety (Rolland, 1994). It is important for families to consider such crises (Strauss, 1975) and to plan for them in a noncrisis context early in the chronic phase of the illness (Doka, 1993). Ways to prevent crises, to manage them when they occur, and to enhance coping are all important considerations. Contingency planning with caregivers and family to identify possible sources of formal and informal support, medical assistance, and various response options can forestall panic that can immobilize people. Planning regarding future illness-related crises is helpful as long as the parties are not so inundated with potential future adversities that they become threatened or lose hope. In such cases, merely listing resources to be contacted should the need arise may be the best way to proceed (Doka, 1993).

A crisis always must be understood in terms of the phenomenological perspective of the person experiencing it. Related to this, Rolland (1994) observes that, in terms of family adaptation to serious illness as a developmental process over time, the central reference point must be the "goodness of fit" between the family's functioning style (i.e., the family system dynamics, multigenerational patterns, family and individual life cycles, and family belief systems) with its own particular strengths and vulnerabilities and the psychosocial demands of different disorders over time. Thus, from the perspective of his Family Systems–Illness Model, Rolland notes that no single family pattern is inherently healthy or unhealthy. Additionally, families need to be educated to appreciate the fact that there is a changing fit between the demands of a chronic disorder and new developmental issues for the family unit and its individual members. For Rolland, interaction is at the heart of all systems-oriented biopsychosocial inquiry, and in physical illness, particularly chronic and life-threatening disorders, the primary focus is the system created by the interaction of a condition with an individual, family, and other biopsychosocial systems.

Secondary Traumatization

In 1985, Figley wrote about *chiasmal effects,* in which support system members are themselves indirectly affected emotionally by the victimization of a member of the family or intimate network. In their attending to this person, and through their efforts to help, they are exposed to the reactions of the victimized member. In turn, they become personally and adversely impacted by the member's reactions. This has been called "secondary catastrophic stress response" (Figley, 1983), a label that was a forerunner of what is now termed "secondary traumatic stress." These are "the natural consequent behaviors and emotions resulting from knowing about a traumatizing event experienced by a significant other—the stress resulting from helping or wanting to help a traumatized or suffering person" (Figley, 1995, p. 7). Secondary stressors can give rise to secondary traumatic stress disorder (STSD), a syndrome of symptoms nearly identical to those of posttraumatic stress disorder (PTSD) except that exposure to knowledge about a traumatizing event experienced by a significant other is what is associated with onset and not, as in PTSD, the individual's primary exposure to traumatic stressors.

The experience of anticipatory mourning is replete with instances in which one member of the family system or intimate network is impacted by another. Sometimes this is the ill or dying person; at other times, it is another member of the system. In brief, observing the physical and psychosocial losses and suffering of another—witnessing that person's traumatization—is conducive to promoting a personal experience of loss and traumatization in individuals empathically and emotionally connected to that person.

FACTORS COMPLICATING INTIMATE ANTICIPATORY MOURNING

The anticipatory mourner today may experience difficulties that stem, either singly or in combination, from (a) unique problems of bereavement for the contemporary American family, (b) particular characteristics of today's life-threatening or terminal illnesses, (c) inherent systemic pitfalls in intimate anticipatory mourning, and/or (d) situational problems within the intimate's anticipatory mourning experience. Treatment must be designed to address and/or compensate for these types of difficulties.

Unique Problems of Bereavement for the American Family

A series of social changes occurring within this century have contributed to the evolution of the American family as an institution. These social changes, occurring at an increasingly rapid rate, include the following processes, among others:

- Greater industrialization, urbanization, technicalization, social mobility, secularization, and deritualization
- Increasing unemployment, poverty, and economic problems
- Rising societal, interpersonal, and institutional violence
- Declines in family integration, primary group interaction, and extended families
- Escalating divorce rates
- Significant social reorganization (specifically, a diminution—or, some would say, a breakdown—of the nuclear family, increases in single parent and blended families, multiple caretakers for children, and the relative exclusion of the aged and dying)
- The engendering of undesirable personal and social consequences (e.g., severance or weakening of the links between adults and children; attachment deficiencies; impaired psychosocial development; personal disenfranchisement and social alienation; senses of personal helplessness and hopelessness;

parental absence and neglect of children; larger societal discrepancies between the "haves" and the "have nots"; and epidemic drug, alcohol, physical, psychological, and sexual abuse)

All of these changes bear directly on contemporary anticipatory mourners by influencing their experience within families and intimate networks.

Today's more isolated nuclear family has fewer resources for interpersonal support as a result of geographical and social distance from family, intimate networks, and other primary groups; strains and depletions of resources secondary to the aforementioned social changes; and the limited ability of the family/intimate network to meet the needs of its members. Increasingly, tasks formerly met in the family have had to be delegated to society. Lengthier chronic illnesses, increased age spans, altered mortality rates, and intensified bioethical dilemmas place additional stresses on the American family contending with the dying or death of one of its members.

The psychological impact of the death of a family member is relatively greater in American culture than in other cultures (Volkart, 1957). This stems from the fact that the limited range of interaction possible in the American family fosters unusually intense emotional involvement. In societies where the extended family or intimate collective group is larger and permits more than just the biological parents to be actively involved with child rearing, psychological involvement is more dispersed. Death of a family member in these societies does not generate such an overwhelming impact as it does in this country, where relationships are more exclusive.

Another psychological problem arising in contemporary American society is the greater potential for ambivalence and hostility as a consequence of death (Volkart, 1957). This occurs because, in the American family, self-identification and personal dependency are rooted in the limited scope of family members and because the social tendency exists for American families to breed overidentification and overdependence, factors known to complicate mourning (Rando, 1993). These problems are often exacerbated by today's extended developmental period of adolescence and the recent trend for adult children to return with their own children to their parents' homes after divorce or economic downturn, making overidentification and overdependence even more common and, at the very least, more protracted. Another important issue is that, although family members are major sources of love and gratification, they are at the same time sources of punishment, frustration, anger, and ambivalence. This necessarily leaves individuals in this country with more negative and ambivalent feelings with which to contend after a death, with these feelings serving as factors that complicate mourning (Rando, 1993). The fact that it is the norm in contemporary American families to have emotional attachments to particular people, as opposed to roles, further increases the risk for complicated bereavement responses. All of these factors contribute to high vulnerability after the death of a family member, as well as to the life-threatening and terminal illness experience leading to that death.

Characteristics of Contemporary Life-Threatening or Terminal Illnesses

In contrast to decades past, today's life-threatening and terminal illnesses have a number of characteristics that, while affording more time prior to death, also present the affected parties with more dilemmas and stressors than ever before. Thus, recent medical advances are truly mixed blessings for ill persons and families. Some of these characteristics are common to chronic illness in general; others are exclusive to the dimension of life threat or terminality. Most are a blend of the two and demonstrate the impact of the singular phenomenon identified by Pattison (1977, 1978) as the *living-dying interval*. While not every life-threatening or terminal illness circumstance involves all of the issues delineated in this section—and those noted are not exhaustive by any measure—the issues next discussed are among the most common.

Elsewhere I have described numerous problems resulting from the chronic nature of illnesses today (Rando, 1986, 1993). Among those having the most impact are the following:

- A more prolonged illness experience, exposing the mourner to the possibility of an "overly lengthy illness," a high-risk factor for complicated mourning (Rando, 1993), and depletion of psychological, social, physical, financial, and pragmatic resources, plus various sequelae therefrom

- Numerous remissions and relapses, along with myriad illness-generated losses, disabilities, and dysfunctions, as well as exposure to sights, sounds, smells, tastes, touches, and demands of debilitating illness, all of which generate their own psychological reactions

- Lengthened periods of anticipatory grief and mourning, often including intense and frequent and/or long-lasting times of uncertainty, anxiety, and traumatization

- Increased financial, social, physical, time, and emotional pressures

- Long-term individual and/or family disruption, disorganization, and physical and emotional exhaustion

- Progressive decline of the ill person over time and the emotional response of loved ones to this decline and their helplessness to stem it

- Longer periods of uncertainty

- The need to balance for an extended period of time conflicting demands, opposing needs, antagonistic tasks, clashing responsibilities, and discordant roles, and to contend with a loved one who while still living is also slowly dying

Problems regarding chronicity—due both to duration of the illness and to not having a genuine reprieve within the situation—are only one type of adversity that comes with contemporary illnesses. Other present-day issues that can exacerbate the stress and increase the number of problems for anticipatory mourners include the following:

- Intensive treatment regimens and their side effects

- Pressures that place uncommon stress and demands on the ill person and concerned others, such as the uncertainty of some situations, the certainty of others; the inconsistency of the illness in its various aspects, or its relentless and persistent consistency in progressing towards death; the steady debilitation, or the up-and-down nature of the loss of control; the wish that the end would come and the fear that it will

- The increased involvement of a more limited group of people secondary to a decline in extended families and greater social mobility that takes some family members away from the extended family. This means fewer respites, more responsibility, and a greater intensity of involvement for those caring for the ill person.

- Decision dilemmas centering on ethics, morality, and legality, which result from an expanded range of options regarding treatments, end-of-life care, and assisted suicide, increasing the potential for negative reactions if one retrospectively perceives oneself to have made the wrong choices or is perceived by others as having done so. Previously, restricted options meant fewer things over which one might ultimately feel guilty.

- Losses of possible sources of structure, comfort, and guidance during this tumultuous time, given the secularization and deritualization of contemporary Western society

- Potential failures to identify important anticipatory mourners, given today's reconfigured family and intimate networks, and greater chance of someone's disenfranchisement (Doka, 1989)

- Assumptive world elements (i.e., the mourner's assumptions, expectations, and beliefs; see discussion in chapter 2 in this volume) associated with the notion that in this day and age one can "beat death" and that there is always something that can be done, with consequent experiences of loss and traumatization when this is not the case for the loved one

- Adverse reactions to the increased medical technicalization that may be a part of a loved one's pre-palliative care (e.g., feeling useless, remote, or believing that others who are more skilled or technologically proficient are better caregivers)

All of these problems occur in a situation where existing confusion is magnified by situations in the illness that breed inconsistency, resentment, and ambivalence. The lack of norms and clearly specified expectations and responsibilities—along with the depletion that results from the stress of demands for major readaptations and investments of self, time, and finances—have the potential to further an intimate's psychological conflict, emotional exhaustion, physical debilitation, social isolation, and family discord. Difficulties are compounded by the typical emotional reactions of anxiety, sorrow, depression, anger, and guilt, so routinely reported by intimates whose loved one is life-threatened or dying.

Adding to stress caused by specific characteristics of today's life-threatening and terminal illnesses are demands placed upon the intimate network caring for a seriously ill member. This network must develop strategies for meeting the needs of the ill person. Depending on the nature of the illness, the system and its individual members may be required to adapt to a loved one who, though slowly dying, will go on living for an extended period of time because of advancements in health care. Frequently, this results in intervals where the individual sometimes appears completely normal, allowing life to be resumed as previously. At other times, the person may become severely ill, creating demands for major readaptation in the system.

This up-and-down nature of illness does not preclude the fact that the affected individual—although perhaps somewhat changed by confrontation with mortality, pain, loss, disease, disability, or psychological reactions thereto—is in many cases still much the same person as before. (In cases where the individual's personality does change significantly, there is even more pressure on the intimates to apprehend and respond to those alterations.) In a great percentage of cases, until a point relatively close to death the ill person has many of the same needs, preferences, hopes, and desires as previously and still requires intimacy, enjoyment, productive work, and social and intellectual stimulation. That person often expects to be treated in many of the same fashions he or she always has been. This is not to suggest that people cannot change, that priorities may not be reordered, or that terminality does not have the potential to impact positively on and transform individuals. The main point is that the diagnosis of a life-threatening or terminal illness does not take away the human needs of the seriously ill or dying person—if anything, it heightens them. And it is to these needs that the intimate anticipatory mourner must respond, within the context of a family system or intimate network additionally stressed by troublesome aspects of today's serious illnesses.

Inherent Systemic Pitfalls in Intimate Anticipatory Mourning

As an anticipatory mourner, the intimate is in a "good news–bad news" situation. The good news is that, in many cases, the system (i.e., the family and/or intimate network) surrounding the intimate can be uniquely supportive because of the dynamics of families and intimate networks. The bad news is that precisely because there is such a system surrounding the intimate, he or she is subject to problems stemming from those same dynamics.

A number of complicating issues associated with intimate anticipatory mourning arise specifically from system dynamics. These include the following:

- The struggle with balancing the conflicting demands inherent in anticipatory mourning (see chapter 2 for a discussion of these). These can arise on the intrapsychic, interpersonal, or systemic levels.

- The systemic dilemma of being immersed in the context of illness or death and caring for the ill loved one while simultaneously continuing to respond to the needs of the individual members in the family, assist the family system to continue to function as a social unit in society, and provide a structure for the growth and development of its members (Barton, 1977), while also performing those ongoing functions the family is charged with providing to its members in terms of nurturance, relationship, communication, emancipation, and recuperation (Fleck, 1975).

- Being susceptible to absorbing or "catching" others' traumatic stress in addition to one's own, also known as the chiasmal effect (Figley, 1985)

- System issues resulting in the inability to have respites or to take them without guilt

- The loss of some of the most important sources of support, given that other members of the system are also losing the same loved one and contending with their own anticipatory mourning

- Inadequate appreciation of the uniqueness of a person's anticipatory mourning experience—how each person sustains a different relationship with the dying person and has different experiences and losses based upon the idiosyncratic factors applicable to him or her in this situation and how this makes for dissimilarities in such areas as phenomenologies, perceptions, needs, reactions, and attempts at coping, among others

- The proximity that can make other members in the system vulnerable to displacement of the anticipatory mourner's anger, frustration, guilt, and so forth, causing difficulties with the people he or she is closest to and who are typically most relied upon for support

- Communication and/or sexual problems that can develop between the anticipatory mourner and those closest to him or her when their discrepant ways of responding to anticipatory mourning cause conflicts or impairments in these areas

- Additional pain and distress that can be caused by witnessing the pain and distress anticipatory mourning is bringing to other loved ones in the system who are also contending with the illness and dying of the one they love

- Problems that can erupt when one intimate anticipatory mourner tries to "rescue" other intimates from their own anticipatory mourning

- Frustration, guilt, further loss of control, poor self-evaluation, a sense of incompetence, and other negative attributions and emotions that may be experienced when one perceives deficiencies associated with anticipatory mourning to be adversely affecting others in the system

- Resentment if others in the system are not feeling, thinking, or behaving as the anticipatory mourner believes they should, with this exacerbating the distress of that mourner over and above that directly associated with the ill loved one

- Concerns that relationships with other loved ones are receiving less-than-desired attention secondary to the fact that focus and resources are being devoted to the ill person and/or that the anticipatory mourner is preoccupied with loss, trauma, and their sequelae

- Overprotection of other loved ones (often, although not exclusively, children) out of the anticipatory mourner's desire to shield them from what the ill individual is undergoing, with such overprotection having the potential to compromise the relationship and interfere with normal developmental and life-cycle tasks and resulting in many negative consequences on the parts of those being "protected" (e.g., hostility, estrangement, resentment)

- Problems, confusions, and stresses associated with the lack of norms and defined behaviors and expectations for the role of intimate anticipatory mourner

- Anxiety and distress associated with concerns that any genetic similarity (secondary to being a blood relative) or experiential similarity (e.g., having worked in the same environmentally toxic environment or shared the same habit of cigarette smoking) with the seriously ill or dying person means that the same illness and dying experience is potentially in store for oneself and/or for other loved ones

Basically, intimates of the life-threatened or terminally ill person must deal with three areas of loss. First, they mourn the potential loss of the loved one. Second, there is also grief and mourning for the death of the family unit or intimate network as it has existed in the past. Finally, mourning takes place for the loss of the part of the self that had existed within that family unit, given that, from a symbolic interactionist and phenomenological viewpoint, the self experiences not only the loss of the dying person, but also of the part constituted by the relations that were anchored in that other person. For example, as Weigert and Hastings (1973) note, the death of a father forever destroys that part of the interactional self that was son and that is sedimented in the memories and role enactments mutually constituted by father and son. Consequently, in the losing of the loved one and the family one has formerly known—the context for the relationship with that loved one—a mourner can experience a number of losses of self.

Thus, family members are left in a position of coping simultaneously with multiple loss experiences. Such a situation usually constitutes bereavement overload (Kastenbaum, 1969) and leaves affected individuals with profound feelings of loss and a predisposition for complicated mourning (Rando, 1993). However, multiple losses are an inherent part of the experience and cannot be avoided.

One final note about family systems or intimate networks and death: Unlike other institutions (e.g., political, educational, religious, economic), the family is vulnerable to *time death*—that is, it will gradually die with the death of its members (Weigert & Hastings, 1973). Time eventually will end that specific institution, whereas others will endure long beyond the lifetimes of specific individuals.

Situational Problems in Intimate Anticipatory Mourning

Situational factors within the context of anticipatory mourning can cause complications. Although specific situational factors must be ascertained from assessment of the individual in the particular situation, common problems that negatively impact the intimate's anticipatory mourning include the following:

- There is a lack of a relatively invariant, step-by-step, specifically delineated process, given that anticipatory mourning is such a nonlinear process, involves the participant in multileveled and contradictory courses of actions (e.g., holding on to the dying person in the here-and-now relationship and, at the same time, starting to let go of that person in the assumptive world).

- The traumatization of the anticipatory mourner can severely interfere with anticipatory mourning processes, as it can with postdeath processes (see chapter 6 in this volume).

- Exhaustion and depletion of the anticipatory mourner on all levels complicates the person's mourning. Such exhaustion and depletion may occur psychologically (including emotions, cognitions, philosophy/spirituality, conations, perceptions, defenses, and attempts to cope), behaviorally, socially, and physically.

- Bereavement overload (Kastenbaum, 1969) can overwhelm the anticipatory mourner, leaving the person unable to benefit from direction, and may interfere with his or her own anticipatory mourning processes.

- Conflicting demands occurring during times of strained resources, exhaustion, and depletion add to the stress experienced and complicate anticipatory mourning. This is not unlike the high-risk factor of prior or current unaccommodated losses and/or stresses, which has been identified as interfering with mourning in general (Rando, 1993).

- To the extent that the intimate anticipatory mourner is disenfranchised (Doka, 1989) in his or her role, anticipatory mourning may be negatively affected and require intervention that enfranchises that mourner and accesses appropriate support and avenues for processing mourning that may have been needed but were unavailable (see Doka, 1989; Rando, 1993).

FACILITATING FACTORS AND THERAPEUTIC PERSPECTIVE IN INTIMATE ANTICIPATORY MOURNING

In terms of factors that facilitate the individual's ability to experience healthy anticipatory mourning, it is instructive to examine Figley's (1983) list of characteristics that appear to differentiate the functional family's ways of coping with catastrophe from that of the dysfunctional family. These characteristics must be added to the ones known to promote healthy mourning in general. As noted earlier in this chapter, while Figley speaks of "family," in most cases this legitimately can be replaced by the term *intimate network*. The characteristics are as follows:

1. Ability to identify the stressor

2. Viewing the situation as a family problem, rather than merely a problem of one or two of its members

3. Adopting a solution-oriented approach to the problem, rather than simply blaming

4. Showing tolerance for other family members

5. Clear expression of commitment to and affection for other family members

6. Open and clear communication among members

7. Evidence of high family cohesion

8. Evidence of considerable role flexibility

9. Appropriate utilization of resources inside and outside the family

10. Lack of overt or covert physical violence

11. Lack of substance abuse (p. 18)

Rando (1984) reviewed the literature and summarized findings regarding variables associated with positive adjustment for families contending with the terminal illness of one of their members. These overlap with some of Figley's and include the following:

• Appropriate and adaptive role reassignment

• Direct communication in an open awareness context (Glaser & Strauss, 1965)

• Open emotional expression

• Appropriate family participation in the care of the dying member

- Flexibility in family rule patterns
- Awareness and empathy in relationships
- Appropriate and flexible boundaries
- Flexibility in relationships
- "Energized family" (Pratt, 1976), encompassing (a) varied contacts with community groups in an active attempt to cope and master their lives; (b) fluid internal organization, including flexible role relationships; (c) shared power, with each member participating in decisions affecting him or her; and (d) high degree of autonomy within the family, with relationships among members that support personal growth

To the degree that the caregiver can enable a healthier approximation of these characteristics within a given family or intimate network, the probability of therapeutic anticipatory mourning is increased. Of course, the caregiver must be mindful of the premorbid history of a given system and its members and must be realistic in terms of expectations and goals. While positive growth certainly can and does occur in families during the severe illness of a loved one, this is not the time for extensive attempts to remake the family totally. Rather, the caregiver needs to be aware of the characteristics of the system beforehand and, within these constraints, work to promote as much healthy movement as possible in the system and in its individual members. For some systems and in some intimates, movement will be minimal or nonexistent, but for others this time can promote significant therapeutic changes. Positive changes may be beneficial for all concerned, but the caregiver must be mindful not to further destabilize either the family system or its individual members. The caregiver must support existing healthy processes and offer alternatives to supplant, minimize, and try to avoid unhealthy ones. It is a delicate task to maintain awareness of the synergy between the system and individual members and coalitions thereof, and to intervene appropriately and effectively for all parties. At times, the caregiver must give priority to either the system or the individual, although often compromise is possible.

PROTOCOL FOR THE FOUR-PLUS PHASE MODEL FOR INTERVENTION IN INTIMATE ANTICIPATORY MOURNING

Healthy experiences in anticipatory mourning have a potentially profound and positive influence on postdeath bereavement (Rando, 1986), and anticipatory mourning provides an area of primary prevention opportunities for the caregiver. This section presents a protocol for intervention in anticipatory mourning. As depicted in Figure 11.1, the four phases of this protocol are assessment, triage, treatment, and follow up. The "plus" refers to the fact that, throughout the phases, a general set of processes is sustained: support, education, and advocacy (SEA). The protocol can be modified for use by any type of caregiver (i.e., it is not exclusively for mental health professionals) and for any party in the anticipatory mourning experience (i.e., patient, intimate, concerned other, or caregiver). Inasmuch as this chapter's focus is on anticipatory mourning in intimates, the following discussion primarily concerns the application of the model to that group. If the anticipatory mourner him- or herself is the life-threatened or dying person, other considerations would obviously apply, and the interventions suggested would need to be extrapolated accordingly. Similar adaptations would be required for interventions with concerned others and caregivers.

Even among the intimates group, members are quite heterogeneous. Idiosyncratic factors—psychological, social, and physiological—profoundly affect any given intimate's anticipatory mourning. Of particular concern are the following factors: (a) the point at which the ill person, intimate, and family or intimate network are in the illness trajectory; (b) the amount of time since the diagnosis; (c) the circumstances that have transpired since the diagnosis, including the nature of the illness experience and its sequelae, along with the ill person's attitude, disposition, and approach to life after diagnosis, and his or her quality of life; and (d) the meaning of the disease to the mourner and his or her perceptions of the suffering of the ill person. It would be inappropriate, for instance, to compare the anticipatory mourning of an intimate whose loved one has been newly diagnosed with AIDS to that of a person whose loved one has been in a remission for 2 years and is able to resume the majority of previous functioning, or to that of a person whose loved one is very close to death. It would be equally incorrect to assume that all interventions appropriate for the terminal phase of an illness would be as suitable for one contending with life threat but not imminent death.

Plainly, anticipatory mourning occurs on a number of different levels, involves many simultaneously conflicting demands, is influenced by actors and events that are out of the mourner's control, and is not necessarily a sequential or linear process. Therefore, caregivers must consider the protocol described here as a set of guidelines, not a rulebook, for enabling healthy anticipatory mourning.

All of the information about this protocol and its specific treatment suggestions presupposes that the caregiver is well-versed and clinically adept in the skills required in mental health intervention

FIGURE 11.1

Protocol for the Four-Plus Phase Model for Intervention in Intimate Anticipatory Mourning

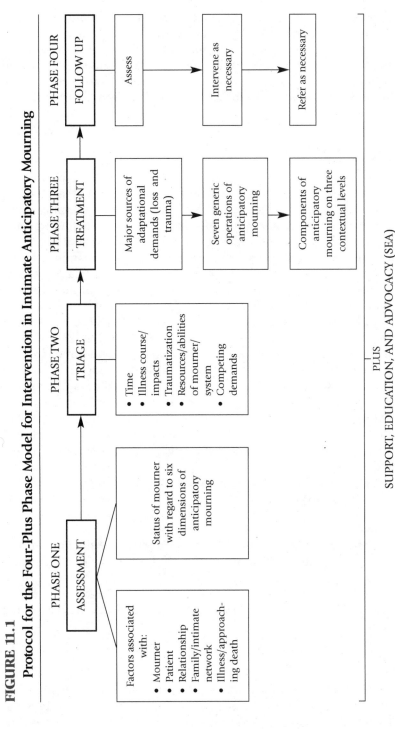

PLUS
SUPPORT, EDUCATION, AND ADVOCACY (SEA)

in general, as well as in techniques for facilitation of uncomplicated mourning. (Knowledge of and skill in the treatment of complicated mourning are desirable but not mandatory.) These generic skills are the foundation upon which the following treatment suggestions are built. An underlying presumption is that all caregivers operate according to the specific ethical and legal guidelines for their respective professions.

Phase One: Assessment

In *Treatment of Complicated Mourning* (Rando, 1993), I expressed my concern about the adequacy of assessment in the area of thanatology and presented a specific clinical tool, the Grief and Mourning Status Interview and Inventory (GAMSII), which I believe useful in gathering general data on an individual's mental and physical health, as well as specific loss-related information. Such information is essential in formulating treatment goals and in making treatment decisions: It is inadvisable to attempt to intervene in anticipatory mourning prior to conducting an assessment, even if it must be brief.

Although the GAMSII is written specifically with the postdeath mourning experience in mind, its components are the same as those necessary to evaluate the status of the anticipatory mourner. In both postdeath and anticipatory mourning, it is important to obtain demographic and loss history information and to undertake an evaluation of the individual's history, mental status, and premorbid personality. With respect to anticipatory mourning, the assessment must elicit at least basic information about the mourner, the ill person, the relationship between the two, the family or intimate network, and the illness and approaching death. It must be remembered that because of fluctuations in the illness experience, the anticipatory mourning context can be expected to change. The caregiver will need to remain mindful to update assessments continually to ensure effective treatment intervention.

The caregiver also should attempt to evaluate the anticipatory mourner's status with regard to the six dimensions of anticipatory mourning, detailed in chapter 2 of this volume. Three of these dimensions have particular implications for treatment and are discussed at length in the section devoted to the treatment phase of the protocol.

Phase Two: Triage

In contrast to the situation of postdeath bereavement, where in theory the caregiver can take as much time as required to address the mourner's issues, anticipatory mourning operates under time constraints. The ill person will live for just so long, and the conditions of this life (e.g., the vicissitudes of the illness, its impact upon the person) affect whether and how anticipatory mourning is experienced by all parties during that time. Consequently, problems must be triaged in light of the realities of the disease: expected trajectory, loss of function, pain, diminishing consciousness, and so forth. However, estimations of the amount of time left to a dying individual often turn out to be less than accurate, and triage decisions must be made with this fact in mind.

In addition to time, the main issues affecting triage decisions are the course of the illness and its effects on the ill person, the amount of traumatization being experienced by the anticipatory mourner, the resources available to and abilities of the intimate and the system, and the presence and relative importance of other competing demands.

Based on their assessments, caregivers will place different emphases on the various issues to be addressed and will prioritize them accordingly. For example, one caregiver may spend considerable time working with an anticipatory mourner around issues concerning unfinished business with the dying person, given the short trajectory of that person's illness. In another situation, the initial therapeutic focus may be more on understanding family dynamics, given the knowledge that in this case the illness is not yet terminal and that, until the intimate comprehends past difficulties in communicating with the ill loved one, unfinished business can be only partially addressed.

Phase Three: Treatment

It is possible to conceptualize specific treatments as occurring across three of the six dimensions of anticipatory mourning: (a) the major sources of adaptational demands (the experiences of loss and trauma, and the emotional sequelae to which they give rise), (b) the seven generic operations of anticipatory mourning, and (c) the components of anticipatory mourning as found on its three contextual levels (intrapsychic, interpersonal, and systemic).

The order in which these dimensions are discussed does not imply that any sequential or invariant stages, phases, or processes exist when it comes to coping with the life-threatening or terminal illness of a loved one. While some activities are necessary for the unfolding of others in the development of the person's mourning (e.g., if the mourner does not recognize the seriousness of the illness, then he or she cannot deal with its ramifications), it is also true that people's abilities to contend with these experiences wax and wane, and that what is witnessed today, or at this hour, or at this minute may be quite different from what is seen at another time. For instance, it is well known that dying persons can drift in and out of the conscious awareness of death, at times acknowledging and at other times denying its imminence—sometimes even doing both simultaneously. Quite often, a similar process can be seen in intimates. For this reason, assessments must be continually updated to reflect current realities, and treatment strategies must follow from them and not be permanently fixed.

An important point must be kept in mind: Caregivers always must act with the awareness that "opening up," confronting, and/or in other ways treating an anticipatory mourner is often quite different from, and riskier than, doing the same with a post-death mourner. In the former, death has not yet occurred, and the potential that omissions or commissions could adversely affect the ill person, the self, or others in the experience can restrict the options the mourner will permit him- or herself in terms of dealing with aspects of anticipatory mourning. In postdeath mourning, nothing that can occur will alter the dying and death experience—it is a fait accompli. Essentially, the postdeath mourner has more freedom to explore issues without fear, notwithstanding the fact that the opportunity for dealing with them with the loved one present is gone.

Major Sources of Adaptational Demands: Loss and Trauma

Caregivers must be aware that intimate anticipatory mourning encompasses a combination of loss and trauma; therefore, grief and mourning along with traumatic stress play pivotal roles in the intimate's anticipatory mourning experience. This awareness demands a shift in focus from the traditional thanatological emphasis on exclusively loss-related concerns and mandates that trauma-targeted interventions be included as well in any intervention plan.

The adaptational demands of loss and trauma—and their combination—have the potential to provoke significant emotional responses. Because of the intensity, conflict, and problematic clinical issues associated with these emotions, they have a special relevance for the treatment of the anticipatory mourner. (For discussion of loss and trauma as they fit within the six dimensions of anticipatory mourning, see chapter 2; for the relationship of these adaptational demands with traumatic stress, see chapter 6.)

Figure 11.2 illustrates the anticipatory mourning experience in terms of its loss and trauma aspects and their respective major psychological sequelae. The association of certain psychological responses with loss, trauma, or a combination of loss and trauma is

FIGURE 11.2

Loss and Trauma Components and Their Major Emotional Sequelae

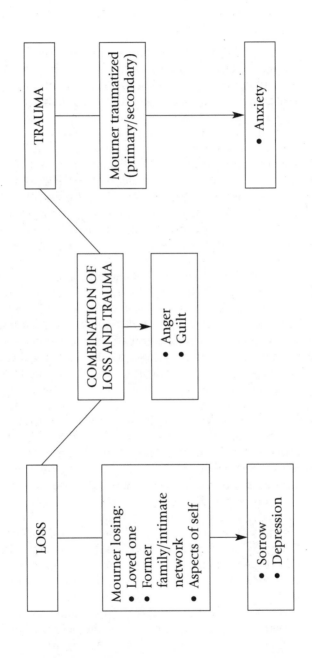

meant to suggest the predominant origins of these sequelae; in reality, each of these reactions can stem from any of the three origins.

Loss

Loss is, of course, the central theme running throughout life-threatening or terminal illness. Very simply, during a loved one's life-threatening illness and dying process, the intimate anticipatory mourner is losing that loved one, the previously existing intimate network that included them both, and aspects of the self (i.e., the interactional self constituted within the relationship with the ill person and with the former intimate network, as well as associated assumptive world violations). While this does not mean that the intimate's focus constantly is on deprivation, it does mean that he or she will encounter myriad experiences of physical and psychosocial loss. These experiences will stimulate grief and mourning, even if not acted upon, for any number of reasons (e.g., pressure of simultaneously competing demands, resistance, failure to acknowledge the loss).

The six "R" processes of mourning (see Table 2.2 in this volume) is a useful model to help the anticipatory mourner understand and contend with his or her losses in attending to the illness, dying, and death of a loved one. *Treatment of Complicated Mourning* (Rando, 1993) presents detailed discussion of how to assist the mourner in undertaking the "R" processes successfully and describes many specific treatment guidelines and protocols. These can and should be employed in the treatment of the anticipatory mourner. Additionally, the emotions and associated interventions discussed, along with those generated by the combination of loss and trauma, require appropriate integration of treatment strategies and techniques for facilitation of the six "R" processes of mourning. Maintenance of the clinical perspectives identified as necessary for treatment of both uncomplicated and complicated mourning is also important, as is the incorporation of the generic guidelines for treatment of complicated mourning. These issues are likewise discussed in Rando (1993).

Because sorrow and depression have been associated with loss historically, Figure 11.2 shows these emotions as stemming from the loss-related components of anticipatory mourning. It is important to note, however, that sorrow and depression are not unrelated to trauma.

Sorrow. Sorrow is the sadness, pain, and anguish that intimates feel in their grief and mourning over losing a loved one and in recognizing associated secondary losses. Many individuals fear that they will be overwhelmed by this mental suffering. Because of this, they may distance themselves emotionally or physically from the seriously ill or dying loved one, only contributing further to that person's own sorrow. Some may overcompensate for this fear with aggressive or demanding actions to hide their true vulnerability, whereas others may adopt an attitude of indifference to camouflage their feelings. Caregivers need to recognize that sorrow, and the depression that frequently accompanies it, are difficult to cope with, especially when the individual involved is concerned about remaining in emotional control.

Caregivers must keep a number of points in mind when intervening in the sorrow of intimates. First, they need to identify, label, normalize, and legitimize feelings of sorrow. They then need to assist the mourner in differentiating and tracing these feelings, to reduce the intimate's fear of them and to help him or her respond and process them appropriately—giving the feelings some form of expression and working them through as much as possible. All of this must be done in ways that do not interfere with the intimate's remaining time with the ill loved one. Caregivers may need to redefine ideas such as "lose control" or "break down," acknowledging these fears but reframing them more positively, using such language as "emotional release" or "intense feelings." The intimate should be informed that these are normal reactions, often requiring strong expression, and that in this case they follow norms that are different than usual and do not denote loss of control. Caregivers will do well to assist intimates in understanding that it is precisely those unexpressed emotions that prompt "loss of control" responses and that there is great value in expressing a little emotion at a time in order to avoid an accumulation that eventually may explode.

It often helps intimates to understand that they hurt so much expressly because they love the ill or dying person so much. Placing their sorrow in a context of personal meaning—philosophical, spiritual, or religious—can help them avoid being overwhelmed by it. Intimates can be given a sense of control of their feelings if they are helped to understand that the processing of emotions must take place but that they can choose how and when. The caregiver can encourage expression of feelings in places that are comfortable and relatively safe—hospital corridors and waiting rooms do not offer the privacy intimates may require. Caregivers must legitimize pain while holding out the expectation that, although the situation is difficult and the emotions hurtful, they can be contended with and at some future point there will be less pain.

Caregivers need to be mindful of the limits and capabilities of intimates. They must recognize when one or more of the intimates may need assistance, such as to be given information in smaller bits and pieces or at a slower pace, or to receive gentle closure in a situation in order to avoid being overwhelmed. This does not mean patronizing members of the intimate network nor helping them avoid reality. Rather, it means modifying the experience to maximize their ability to cope and continue without becoming so inundated that they give up. Most importantly, caregivers must focus on enabling intimates to experience the joys and pleasures that are still available, so as not to detach prematurely from the life-threatened or dying person or to relinquish satisfactions that continue to be possible in the relationship.

Depression. Feelings of depression can be expected to arise in those who are losing a loved one through a life-threatening or terminal illness. This emotion is both a natural aspect of grief over the past, present, and future losses in anticipatory mourning and an expected consequence of the multileveled depletion that occurs during the course of caring for a seriously ill or dying individual.

Depression is concomitantly an indication of, and tool for, preparation for the loss of the patient. Bowlby (1961) has written that depression is adaptive in the postdeath mourning process. His theory can be extended to anticipatory mourning. Bowlby views depression as the subjective aspect of the state of disorganization ensuing when one's behavior is no longer organized and self-sustaining. Such a state typically arises when the functioning interaction ceases between oneself and important aspects of one's world. In anticipatory mourning, this disorganization results from loss of the relationship with the ill loved one as it had existed prior to the illness, when all of the assumptions, expectations, and beliefs attendant to that relationship and their contingent hopes, wishes, fantasies, and dreams (i.e., assumptive world elements pertinent to the loved one) were still intact. It also refers to the other past, present, and future losses inherent in the loved one's illness and dying. In anticipatory mourning, the former patterns of behavior that had existed in interaction with the loved one are gradually ceasing to be appropriate, as loss follows loss and the ill person relinquishes roles, capacities, and abilities. These losses signal the ending of the relationship as it used to be. Consequent feelings and violated assumptive world elements lead to disorganization of the mourner's usual behavior patterns, which in turn evoke feelings of depression.

Although painful, disorganization and depression are necessary and adaptive because they facilitate the breakdown of old patterns of behavior and assumptive world elements (based on the old relationship and former realities) and make way for new ones in the future. Failure to relinquish patterns of behavior or assumptive world elements that have grown up in interaction with the loved one and that are no longer appropriate in the situation of the loved one's illness or dying result in maladaptive behavior if they persist. Only if such patterns are broken down and assumptive world elements relinquished or appropriately modified will it be possible for new patterns and assumptive world elements, adapted to new objects and experiences (or, in the case of the seriously ill or dying person, to the new realities of his or her current situation), to be assumed.

Therapeutic intervention in the depression that accompanies anticipatory mourning should focus on encouraging the expression of feelings associated with the illness or impending death of the loved one while continuing to facilitate whatever ongoing involvement and relationship remains possible. As appropriate, emotions, thoughts, wishes, fears, symptoms, and so forth can be normalized and legitimized. Past, present, and future losses can be identified and mourned. These entail not only tangible or easily recognized losses, but also the symbolic or psychosocial ones, such as losses of assumptive world elements, meaning, status, roles, and relationships. It is helpful to assist intimates in identifying, labeling, differentiating, and tracing the specific emotions and thoughts they are experiencing. If this is not done, such emotions and thoughts accumulate and act as one undifferentiated mass of painful stimuli. In such instances, people lose the ability to understand the experience clearly, cannot problem solve or deal with its specific components, and tend to feel overwhelmed by its sheer mass.

Intimates should be helped to express and work through the emotions they experience in whatever therapeutic fashions meet their idiosyncratic needs. As well, it is therapeutic to enable them in identifying any unfinished business that remains with the ill or dying person and in discovering appropriate ways to facilitate closure without premature detachment. Physical activities and social support can provide intimates with outlets that facilitate expression of emotion and reduce the intensity of affect. Self-help or mutual support groups can also serve these purposes and have the added benefit of providing information, validation, and socialization into the intimate anticipatory mourner role. Finally, psychotropic medications are often helpful when symptoms warrant.

Trauma

In all trauma there is loss, and in most major losses there are aspects of trauma. A strong association of acute grief with traumatic stress exists, given the following similarities: (a) inherent involvement with both loss and trauma, (b) elemental association with anxiety, (c) qualification as a personal disaster (Raphael, 1981), (d) suitability of classification under proposed stress response category, (e) common fundamental issues, (f) manifest symptomatology and associated features, (g) alternating modes of regulation of exposure to distressing material, (h) presentation of two tasks to affected individuals, and (i) ultimate treatment requirements for working through of the experience via cognitive completion with affective release.

As argued in chapter 6, significant traumatic stress is also present in anticipatory mourning. This stress stems primarily from the separation anxiety associated with a loved one's dying, the particular characteristics of the anticipatory mourning situation, and the exposure of and demands placed upon the anticipatory mourner. These last include (a) the exposure to horrific stimuli, (b) the multiplicity and chronicity of illness-induced losses and trauma, (c) the creation of secondary traumatic stress, (d) the inherent generation of helplessness, and (e) the confrontation with overwhelming emotions and conflicting demands during times of strained resources. These situational issues may or may not be present in conjunction with the mourner's idiosyncratic developmental or characterological ones (e.g., overly dependent premorbid relationship, preexisting mental health problems). Both sets of issues, and their combination, can make a loss traumatic. I will focus on the objective situational demands, although the caregiver must be aware of and responsive to the characterological demands as well.

The traumatization of the intimate anticipatory mourner may come from primary or secondary exposure to trauma. Traumatic stressors are of two types: Either they are individual, internally originated stressors that stem from and accrue to persons undergoing difficult experiences, or they are system-originated stressors that are transmitted to an individual by virtue of an individual's membership in a system that is strained or that includes a traumatized member. Some stressors involve a combination of both.

It is important to note that experiences of trauma vary widely within anticipatory mourning. Some illness and dying experiences will stimulate little trauma in most, if not all, intimates; others will engender huge differences in diverse intimates' appraisal and experience. Finally, there are those illness and dying experiences that will be severely traumatic to almost every intimate. Personal predispositions of the mourner, along with other influencing factors, also contribute to the variety of reactions that can be witnessed.

Anxiety. The predominant emotion connected to trauma is anxiety. Elements of anxiety and traumatic stress arise in response to the current or impending separation from and loss of a loved one. In addition, the experiences during a loved one's life-threatening or terminal illness in themselves often are anxiety provoking and may be traumatizing. Recent data reflect substantial anxiety and trauma in those mourning after the death of a loved one from a long-term illness (Cleiren, 1993).

The emotion of anxiety is brought to the fore in anticipatory mourning from the loss side as well as the trauma side. However, because of anxiety's relatively stronger clinical association with trauma, it is shown in Figure 11.2 as accruing from the traumatic aspects of anticipatory mourning.

Anxiety has been defined as "the apprehension cued off by a threat to some value that the individual holds essential to his existence as a personality" (May, 1977, p. 205). The threat may be to physical life, as in the threat of death, or it may be a threat to psychological existence, such as meaninglessness or the loss of one's sense of identity. Anxiety can be expected in anticipatory mourning, given the experience confronting the anticipatory mourner. It is a central dynamic in, generic response to, and cardinal manifestation of traumatization and loss during life-threatening and terminal illness. However, anxiety on the part of intimates is probably the emotion least appreciated by caregivers and others dealing with the family or intimate network of a life-threatened or dying person. Whereas allowances may be made for individuals to experience other, more expected emotions—such as sorrow, depression, anger, and even guilt—awareness of the manifestations of anxiety and the need for interventions to address them is limited.

Knowledge of the different types of anxiety is important for the caregiver. Certain types will never diminish completely (e.g., existential anxiety, separation anxiety), while others are much more amenable to reduction and/or eradication (e.g., anxiety arising from internal conflicts about unexpressed or unacceptable feelings, anxiety caused by heightened physiological arousal). It is inappropriate to expect to eradicate all anxiety; rather, the therapeutic goal is to reduce anxiety to the extent possible and then to manage what remains as well as possible.

Certain points in time within the illness experience are known to generate particularly intense amounts of anxiety. This is especially true in the acute crisis phase at the time of diagnosis, which tends to elicit the most extreme and primitive defenses from those involved (Pattison, 1977, 1978). Times of relapse are exceptionally anxiety provoking as well.

It is important for caregivers to differentiate among the various sources of and design interventions for the forms of anxiety present in anticipatory mourning. The primary sources of anxiety are the losing of the loved one and the experiences of illness bringing that loss. Anxiety is present because it confronts the individual with the unknown and the unfamiliar. Violations of the assumptive world—numerous in this experience and conducive to, as well as resulting from, trauma and loss—engender significant anxiety and insecurity. These factors, plus concerns about separation from and life without the loved one, fear arising from the sense of vulnerability caused by the process of loss, distress associated with memories of earlier losses and separations resurrected by this loss, and heightened emotional and physical arousal all contribute to intimates' panic and anxiety, occurring either intermittently or chronically during anticipatory mourning.

Anxiety is also a normal accompaniment to the uncertain, sometimes mutually exclusive demands of the life-threatening or terminal illness. This anxiety can be exacerbated as changes and losses occur, either unpredictably or as part of a continual process that the intimate perceives as bearing down on the intimate network and feels relatively powerless to deter. Other reasons for anxiety include the sense of helplessness aroused when a loved one is endangered and the outcome cannot be altered; the flood of acute emotions experienced during the illness and the reactions to them; the defenses used to cope with the illness and gradual loss of the dying loved one; the intense separation anxiety experienced in anticipation of parting from the loved one; and the contemplation of one's own death, stimulated by the experience of watching another die (McCollum & Schwartz, 1972).

Additional sources of anxiety in anticipatory mourning are unexpressed emotions and thoughts—for example, when an intimate struggles to hide his or her sadness or anger from the seriously ill loved one or wants to talk with the person about the illness but has been forbidden by the family to do so. Psychological conflicts in one's feelings, thoughts, wishes, fantasies, or impulses concerning the life-threatened or dying individual also can stimulate feelings of anxiety. Such conflict is exemplified in the intimate who becomes anxious at the recognition of a wish for some relief through the death of the ill person.

One of the greatest stimulators of anxiety is the disorganization that occurs both intrapsychically, within the individual, and intrasystemically, within the intimate network. Intrapsychic disorganization occurs as the assumptive world is violated and there are mandates for revision. As well, it is an expected by-product as the mourner attempts to replace old patterns of behavior with new and more adaptive ones that reflect the current reality (Bowlby, 1961). Intrasystemically, it takes place within the intimate network as members cope with altered life-styles and reassignment of roles and responsibilities. Coinciding with these anxiety-provoking issues is uncertainty regarding the ill loved one's deterioration; concern about depletion of emotional, physical, financial, and time resources; and the stress of decision making and balancing conflicting demands.

At times, the distressing anxiety and ambiguity of the situation breeds ambivalence. An increase in negative feelings or a reactivation of longstanding unresolved issues can develop within and between intimates and everyone else with whom they come into contact, including the ill person. Caregivers can become the targets for displacement of these feelings.

Treatment of anxiety in intimates involves paying as much attention as possible to trauma mastery, as well as loss accommodation, within an ongoing illness experience. Since anxiety can be generated by trauma and/or loss, both present in anticipatory mourning, the caregiver must assess the origins of the anxiety and intervene appropriately. If anxiety (or other traumatic sequelae) is of sufficient severity, it must be given priority. Trauma reduction is often crucial for anticipatory mourners, notwithstanding the fact that trauma tends to be overlooked in favor of loss-related aspects. The presence of trauma raises issues about the use of psychotropic medication in anticipatory mourning and implies that caregivers must consider incorporating formal techniques and protocols for treating traumatic stress into their interventions.

Another approach to intervention in anxiety with intimates is much the same as that for the dying person (Rando, 1984). Since anxiety is apprehension in the absence of a specific danger and differs from fear in that it is nondirected, a major way to assist an individual is to help him or her break down the anxiety into its component parts. In this fashion, specific fears, concerns, or underlying emotions or issues are identified, labeled, differentiated, traced, and problem-solved or worked through individually (e.g., anger at the illness, sadness at the deprivation, jealousy of others not affected, guilt at relief that "It isn't me"). It is always easier to cope with well-defined, explicit fears than to attempt to grapple with global, undifferentiated, and thus more terrifying anxiety.

Each individual has his or her own unique combination of fears about dying and death in general—and the dying and death of a certain loved one specifically. What is of utmost concern to one person may be of negligible importance to another. It should be the caregiver's goal to work with the intimate to ascertain which specific fears and issues are of most concern and then, to reduce the overall level of anxiety, to assist that person in isolating each one and confronting each one individually. Examples of such concerns include fears centered around the unknown, loneliness, loss of identity, not knowing how to accept the sympathy of others, being overwhelmed by sorrow, missing the loved one at happy occasions in the future, economic problems, disintegration of the family after the death, guilt for previous omissions or commissions, unceasing sadness and grief, loss of social status, inability to cope with practical matters in the absence of the loved one's guidance, and so forth. To the extent that the individual's anticipatory mourning includes some contemplation of his or her own death, some normal annihilation fear or existential anxiety also would be expected.

It is clear that a remedy for much of the anxiety associated with anticipatory mourning entails the provision of information. Offering information minimizes the uncertainty and fear of the unknown with which the intimate must contend. It legitimizes and normalizes feelings, thoughts, and impulses that heretofore may have been unacceptable—and therefore conducive to anxiety and the assorted mechanisms mobilized to handle it. In brief, the caregiver offers information that allows the intimate's experiences to be less of a threat. Where threat is diminished, anxiety is lowered.

As an adaptive coping behavior on the part of the anticipatory mourner, information seeking is helpful on several accounts and in appropriate amounts should be facilitated by caregivers. Information seeking gives intimates the ability to take some control—a critical issue since they have so little power to challenge the ultimate threat of the loved one's illness. If the information seeking generates treatment options, this also renders control and works against passivity and victimization. It may serve as a vehicle for the intimate's participation in the care of the life-threatened or dying person. Such participation, in appropriate amounts, has been identified as a positive factor in postdeath mourning and adjustment (Rando, 1983).

Some cognitive techniques have been identified as being particularly helpful in the amelioration of anxiety in general. These, adaptable for anxiety in anticipatory mourning, include problem solving and a number of the specific techniques of cognitive restructuring, such as thought stopping, cognitive reprocessing, reattribution, logical analysis, decatastrophizing, evaluation of belief, reframing, hypnosis, metaphor, and guided imagery.

Still other forms of anxiety intervention can be therapeutic in anticipatory mourning. Numerous behavioral and cognitive-behavioral interventions can be adapted for use. Specifically, relaxation techniques (e.g., breathing exercises, progressive relaxation, safe-place imagery, yoga) have been shown to be quite positive for all who must cope with chronic stress. In addition, encouraging and providing permission for appropriate respites from the ill loved one offer anticipatory mourners with much-needed replenishment, and suggesting physical activities to release tension can go far in helping intimates cope with the anxiety inherent in anticipatory mourning. In one study investigating group treatment of cancer patients and their spouses, education and information about the illness, its treatment, its stresses, and methods of coping with its changes—especially relaxation techniques—were reported to be the most helpful aspects of the intervention (Heinrich & Schag, 1985). The therapy of eye movement desensitization and reprocessing known as EMDR has offered significant assistance to anticipatory mourners in therapeutically addressing a number of issues, anxiety among them (Shapiro, 1997). Other types of intervention in anxiety shown to be important include assertiveness training, role-playing, and social networking and support. Mutual support groups have proven quite beneficial for many anticipatory mourners contending with a wide variety of emotions, including anxiety. It must be remembered, however, that some anxiety is appropriate given the current and potential separation the anticipatory mourner faces and that not all anxiety can (or even should) be eliminated. Nevertheless, the interventions described can ameliorate much anxiety.

Combination of loss and trauma

The unique experience formed by the combination of loss and trauma creates the often difficult emotions of anger and guilt. While certainly each of these emotions could be generated either by loss or trauma alone, in my clinical experience it is the joining together of loss and trauma in the fashion that they are in the anticipatory mourning experience that gives anger and guilt the particular character they assume in that phenomenon.

Anger. Overall, people in Western society have significant problems contending with anger. Not surprisingly, the loss of a relationship accompanied by excessive amounts of anger or ambivalence has been demonstrated to be a high-risk factor for complicated postdeath mourning and adaptation (Rando, 1993). Similarly, excessive experiences of anger during a loved one's illness, dying, or death (or problems in dealing with the emotion in general) can be expected to complicate an intimate's anticipatory mourning, as well as to affect his or her postdeath mourning and adaptation adversely.

As used here, *anger* refers to any amount of hostile or aggressive emotion, whether minor (e.g., annoyance) or major (e.g., rage). Anger in intimates may exist as one or a combination of the following: (a) a normal reaction to the illness and its losses; (b) a reaction to loss of a relationship characterized by the mourner's excessive dependency; (c) a reaction after particular losses with specific characteristics (including instances involving a great sense of desertion on the mourner's part, loss of a special and irreplaceable relationship, great suffering or a sense of preventability, or in which the loss is violent or sudden, unexpected, and one for which someone is blamed); and (d) a major characteristic of the premorbid relationship.

Anger is a component of an innate biological predisposition to attempt to find and recover what has been (or is being) lost and to ensure that no future separations occur (Bowlby, 1961). Both these goals can be expected of intimates whose loved one is dying. The emotion is also witnessed because whenever a person is being deprived of something or someone valued, anger is a natural response and an expectable emotional consequence.

In anticipatory mourning as in other areas of life, anger, and associated hostility and frustration, may be expressed in myriad ways—for example, negative verbalizations, aggressive behavior, sarcasm, intolerance, negativity, irritability, tension, anxiety, obstinacy, belligerence, criticality, passive aggressiveness, withholding, withdrawal, jealousy of others, self-reproach, and stinginess, among others. During a loved one's illness, anger can be directed at the self, the ill or dying loved one, or third parties, such as other intimates, caregivers, or anyone else with whom the intimate comes into contact. Frequently, anger is vented without the intimate's conscious knowledge or intent. Although anger at the life-threatened or dying person for abandoning the intimate network is quite common, it is most difficult to admit and is not generally deemed socially appropriate. It can be evidenced in the frustration, impatience, resentment, and withdrawal of intimates vis-à-vis the ill or dying loved one. In lieu of dealing directly with anger at the loved one, intimates can retroflect it inward and may become depressed, experiencing such feelings as worthlessness, self-reproach, and guilt. These feelings also can emanate from the guilt, loss of control, or frustration that normally accompany experience with life-threatening or terminal illness of a loved one. Not infrequently, anger is displaced onto other persons who may or may not be directly involved in the illness. Sometimes a certain intimate is targeted as a scapegoat, and this can be destructive.

Anger may result from violation of one's assumptive world, particularly because of shattered assumptions (Janoff-Bulman, 1992) regarding safety, invulnerability, meaning, and self-worth. In dealing with the illness and dying of a loved one, some of these violations result in loss of faith in God or one's spiritual or existential philosophy. The situation may precipitate a quest for meaning to make sense out of the illness, the impending death, and their impacts on and consequences for the survivors-to-be. "Why my loved one?" and "Why me?" are common questions that may fail to elicit acceptable answers. Many mourners experience—at least temporarily—a profound sense of injustice and disillusionment, feeling that they have played life by the rules but have lost the game. Values and beliefs that formerly were comforting may now be useless. Some can become embittered and alienate others when their value systems fail them in their attempts to understand and control what is happening to their ill or dying loved one and to themselves.

The experience of the illness itself, and what it does to all involved, tends to stimulate anger. Few things generate more feeling than watching deprivation continue—particularly if one witnesses a loved one suffering or in pain. The vicissitudes of the disease, its ravages, the continuing process of loss it involves, the traumatization it causes, the sense of impotency it generates, the pain, the confusion, the unfairness, the frustration, and the ultimate separation of the impending death all can give rise to angry feelings. In addition, intimates often must struggle with anger over consequent emotional, physical, economic, and social drains, along with ensuing impacts on life-style. The situation becomes increasingly problematic as resource demands escalate and, despite sacrifices, the loved one continues to decline.

Other possible sources of anger in anticipatory mourning concern the failure of the ill loved one to fulfill the dependency needs of intimates and/or to finish unfinished business with them. Both of these problems result from the ill person's decreased ability to function, as well as from the shifting of roles and responsibilities to other members of the intimate network to cope with this reduced functioning. (Sometimes this shifting causes its own anger over the changes brought.) Disappointment over unfulfilled ambitions, lack of closure, and expectations that will never be realized also may serve to catalyze the anger and frustration of intimates. Frustration is an emotion that often fuels the flames of anger throughout the entire illness experience.

The ill person himself or herself can contribute to the aggression and aggravation intimates feel through illness-induced personality changes, his or her own previous personality traits, or perceptions on the part of intimates that the illness has been self-inflicted or caused by the person's own neglect. When intimates or others involved with the ill or dying person act out their anger by withdrawing or avoiding the individual, serious problems can follow. Such behavior is typically recognized by the ill person, who may escalate his or her own aggressive behavior and/or experience increased feelings of loss of control, anxiety, grief, and anger at being in the situation. For this reason, it is important that intimates receive assistance in coping with angry feelings and channeling them in the most appropriate and therapeutic ways available.

There are a number of prerequisites for treating anger in mourners. As adapted from Rando (1993), these include the caregiver's ability to do as follows:

- Understand the purposes of the anger
- Be able to promote healthy psychological, behavioral, social, and physiological processing and management of anger
- Determine when the anger reveals a lack of acceptance of the illness or dying of the loved one and when the anger is a response to that which is accepted
- Recognize anger's myriad forms and varying intensities
- Inquire specifically about—and not merely assume—which aspects of the experience are generating the anger
- Relabel emotions, if necessary, in order to increase the mourner's tolerance of them
- Expect that certain types of illnesses, particular loved ones, and specific experiences will engender more intense anger than others
- Recognize that some repetition in processing and expressing anger may be required in order for the mourner to work through the emotion

A number of therapeutic interventions can assist intimates in coping with the anger and its derivatives generated in anticipatory mourning. Foremost, caregivers must convey their recognition of the normalcy of these emotional responses under the conditions of life threat or terminality. Psychoeducational and normative information about anger must be communicated implicitly, and sometimes explicitly, to all concerned. Likewise, caregivers will usually need to give intimates specific permission to ventilate and channel these feelings, as long as this is done in an appropriate way. For example, although verbalization of anger under most conditions can be tolerated, the physical attack of another cannot, and appropriate limits must be established.

For some anticipatory mourners, the debilitating effects of the loved one's chronic illness and/or the number of loss and traumatization experiences sustained, in combination with multileveled depletion, leaves them with insufficient energy to express their anger. Unfortunately, holding in anger that requires expression can create additional anger, anxiety, guilt, and depression. For this reason, caregivers ought to encourage physical, as well as psychosocial, ways to discharge aggression. As in other instances involving loss, traumatization, or its combination, physical release of emotion during anticipatory mourning is most therapeutic. Too often caregivers fail to capitalize on this important dimension. Physical outlets such as pounding a pillow, playing a sport, chopping wood, smashing old dishes or glasses in a safe area, punching a punching bag, kicking an empty and open paper bag, and so forth can siphon off emotions that, lacking other means of release, may prompt emotional and/or physical acting out in inappropriately aggressive ways. Similar interventions can offer a means of therapeutic catharsis for all types of emotions in anticipatory mourning: anxiety, sorrow, depression, guilt, and so forth. The caregiver also can encourage anticipatory mourners to take breaks or respites from the ill or dying loved one to ensure that these emotions do not build up to unhealthy levels.

Obviously, it is important for the caregiver to understand and help the person involved to understand the true sources and causes of anger. Often this means ascertaining which of many emotions, thoughts, fears, concerns, strivings, wishes, and so forth may be camouflaged by the anger. Feelings of grief, fear, anxiety, frustration, dependency, impotence, sadness, and depression frequently underlie aggressive feelings and behaviors. Effective and therapeutic interventions will help the individual address these feelings as well as superficial anger. Processing underlying feelings involves identifying, labeling, differentiating, and tracing the affective experience, and then working with the person to feel, accept, examine, give some form of expression to, and work through all its associated emotions. In this fashion, the anticipatory mourner can cope with the feelings more effectively than if presented with them en masse. Only when the underlying concerns prompting the anger are known will the individual be able to respond most productively.

As with all other emotions in the anticipatory mourning experience, intimates manifest feelings of anger, hostility, frustration, and so forth according to idiosyncratic psychological, social, and physical determinants. These determinants interact with factors associated with the ill loved one, the relationship, the illness, and the intimate network. Intimates must be allowed to express their feelings in ways consistent with these individual influences and should not be forced into predetermined or culture-bound manifestations. Caregivers will do well not to take a patronizing attitude toward intimates' aggressive feelings, nor to push intimates to experience these feelings as the caregivers believe they should.

In helping intimates identify their specific, idiosyncratic concerns, the caregiver must refrain from assuming that an intimate's actions legitimately may be interpreted according to the caregiver's previous learning, either personal or professional. For example, the statement "I know that he [the anticipatory mourner] is really angry that my loved ones are healthy while one of his is dying, and that is why he is saying that I don't understand him" may be more about the speaker's guilt than about the anticipatory mourner's true feelings. In fact, the speaker may not sufficiently understand the mourner. This can be determined only if and when the caregiver assesses the situation without overreliance upon preconceived notions.

If anger exists because of unfinished business between the intimate and the ill or dying loved one, it will be important for the caregiver to work to provide vehicles for resolving the unfinished business with the loved one. If the condition of the loved one prevents resolution, the intimate should be enabled to do what can be done within the constraints operating. Often, therapeutic bereavement rituals, which may or may not involve the ill loved one, can be helpful in this regard (see Rando, 1993).

A lack of information about what is happening to the loved one and what they can do to help often prompts intimates to feel resentment, frustration, and infantilization, as well as a sense of being out of control and unprepared. As already mentioned, healthy individuals frequently use information seeking as an adaptive coping response to stress. It is important to provide intimates with appropriate information not only to allow them to prepare for what is going to occur and to participate maximally in the care of their loved one, but also to avoid the negative sequelae that result when they are prohibited from receiving such information. Appropriate information can be quite empowering—can even begin to somewhat dissemble some of the victimization that may occur in anticipatory mourning. Although in some cases caregivers may feel that intimates want to know too much, the importance of their need to be included, not to feel that the care of their loved one has been taken away from them by strangers, and to feel some amount of control in the situation cannot be overstated. Each request for information should be evaluated with these normal psychological needs in mind. For caregivers who routinely hold conferences with the intimate network and who treat the ill person and intimate network as a unit, this will not be a new notion.

It is helpful for caregivers to keep in mind that intimates may have difficulty admitting to being angry at their ill or dying loved one. In such cases, it may be more prudent to use less emotionally charged words that convey sentiments to which the anticipatory mourner can more readily admit. For example, instead of admitting to anger, it may be more acceptable for some people to admit to being "irritated" or "annoyed" (Lazare, 1979). When it would be therapeutically productive, the caregiver can address the intimate's idiosyncratic resistances to dealing with anger.

Because intimates are often confined under one roof, the potential for volatility is high. Each person, struggling to cope with the aggression that is part of his or her experience, may have the normal tendency to displace it onto those closest. When several people in a household are feeling this same way (or intensely feeling different emotions), they can potentiate one another's anger. This "multiplier effect" (Rando, 1984) is another reason it is imperative for caregivers to be aware of aggressive feelings, as well as of those emotions, thoughts, fears, behaviors, and various other stimuli that prompt them. Without intervention, aggression can build up in an intimate network and initiate a chain reaction among its members, with the end result being more anger. While this can happen with other emotions, it tends to occur more frequently with anger and its variations.

In situations where anger is inappropriately displaced onto others or one or more intimates are being scapegoated, the process will need to be identified and intervention undertaken to confront the displacement and provide healthier channeling of the emotion. Frontline caregivers are frequent targets for such aggression. Theirs is a most delicate position. They are cognizant of the fact that excessive amounts of aggression and hostility must be channeled to others besides the dying person, yet they are also aware that they must appropriately limit what they tolerate from that person's intimates.

Guilt. Intimates almost always experience some guilt for the feelings, thoughts, wishes, impulses, and behaviors that are a natural outgrowth of living, or having intimate association, with a dying person. Numerous precipitants of this very painful and anxiety-provoking emotion exist. Guilt may accompany the recognition of anger and other hostile feelings toward the life-threatened or terminally ill person. These may have preexisted the illness or derived from it. Guilt frequently develops from the interpersonal conflicts that often arise during a serious illness, when frustration, anxiety, and irritation can be so much a part of the experience. Guilt is not uncommon when intimates feel responsible for the illness in any way: through heredity, omissions, or commissions; because they failed to protect the loved one from the illness; or because they will survive the loved one. It also can be stimulated by the repugnance intimates feel when they confront the ravages of the illness (e.g., scars, smells, medication side effects). Intimates frequently experience guilt when they wish the end would come.

The normal reactions to the arduous task of contending with the illness usually are major factors prompting an anticipatory mourner's guilt. These reactions include ambivalence about being in the situation; negative feelings about the demands of the sick loved one and the illness; resentment about resources spent on the ill person; distress when other intimates violate the mourner's own particular expectations and/or standards about devoting time, energy, and focus to the ill person; stress in making choices about incompatible responsibilities, roles, and tasks; and relief because the intimate is not the one dying.

Guilt feelings can serve a number of latent functions. For instance, a person may use guilt psychologically to protect the self from other even less acceptable emotions (e.g., sadness, anger). In other words, it is more tolerable for him or her to deal with the feelings of guilt—uncomfortable though they may be—than to deal with whatever these feelings are camouflaging. Guilt may also serve as (a) a defense against helplessness, (b) a self-punishment or tool for retribution, (c) a vehicle for maintaining a sense of social enfranchisement, (d) a way to keep the individual from forgetting a particular event and continuing its sense of meaning, (e) a form of connection to the loved one, and (f) a form of specific resistance to the requirements of mourning in the situation (Rando, 1993).

Guilt (where one perceives one's *behavior* as bad and fears punishment) is closely related to but different from shame (where one perceives *oneself* to be bad and fears abandonment). Both are known to be stimulated by loss and trauma, individually or in combination. Many anticipatory mourners struggle with shame secondary to the type of illness the loved one has (e.g., a socially stigmatized illness like AIDS). A variety of behaviors or experiences in contending with the illness also may provoke shame. These include one's perceiving oneself as needy or incompetent; one's reactions to outbursts of anger, fear, or other emotions, which can suggest to the person a lack of control; or one's discomfort about one's own wellness and survival). If shame appears, caregivers must consider appropriate treatments for its amelioration.

The therapeutic goals in treating guilt are to help the anticipatory mourner to (a) adopt the proper perspective about ambivalence, human error and imperfection, and normalcy of some amount of guilt when dealing with a loved one's illness or dying; (b) identify, label, differentiate, trace, feel, accept, and give some form of expression to the guilty feelings; (c) identify precipitants of these feelings (i.e., the behaviors, omissions, emotions, thoughts, attitudes, needs, wishes, fantasies, or impulses); (d) understand the impacts of these precipitants, how and why they occurred, and reduce their number via cognitive and emotional processing and psychoeducation; and (e) work through remaining guilt, transform it to regret, or learn to live constructively with that which remains (see Rando, 1993, for specific treatment interventions in guilt that can be adapted here). With respect to the second goal, it is important for the caregiver to help the mourner recognize "illegitimate guilt," or guilt that comes from inappropriate self-condemnation or violation of an irrational or unrealistic standard. Because illegitimate guilt feels the same as legitimate guilt, for which there is cause, the mourner may not be able to distinguish between the two.

To help the anticipatory mourner cope with guilt, the caregiver needs to identify its sources, its type, and the functions, if any, that it serves. The caregiver must be aware of opportunities to intervene sensitively in the intimate's struggles with guilt. During the illness, the caregiver needs to observe the intimate's reactions and encourage the appropriate expression of negative feelings whenever suitable, looking for constructive ways to expiate subsequent guilt if necessary. The caregiver can assure the person of the normalcy of some negative thoughts toward sick persons and note that these human reactions to stressful situations are acceptable providing they do not prompt hostile, destructive, or abandoning actions. Negative actions must be identified and alternative ways of responding discovered to avoid hurting the loved one or the self (this last by acting in a way that would precipitate further guilt now or later, after the death). If not dealt with, guilt can compromise the intimate's current relationship with, and involvement in the care of, the dying loved one. Compromise of this sort can lead to numerous and serious problems after the death. However, where the demands of the situation do not permit processing of guilt, the caregiver should remain watchful for potential opportunities to intervene but focus on the healthy anticipatory mourning that can occur.

The caregiver often will have to educate intimates that angry feelings can coexist with loving ones, that one does not preclude the other. It may be necessary to point out the positive feelings that have been observed in the relationship with the seriously ill patient. Education about the normalcy of ambivalence can be especially therapeutic. It is useful also to convey to intimates that in times of stress people sometimes dwell on the negative aspects of a relationship, forgetting the positive ones. While a caregiver should not prematurely reassure or overemphasize positives—the mourner must be permitted to express his or her feelings and not be closed down by caregiver response—it is important to identify genuine positives in the relationship and work to minimize overemphasis of negatives. Emphasizing the positives helps diminish illegitimate guilt. It also helps the intimate tolerate negative or ambivalent thoughts that might give rise to guilt, thereby permitting such thoughts to coincide with positive and constructive ones.

In their association with an ill or dying loved one, it is not uncommon for intimates to have inappropriate ideas about what they can and should do. Unrealistic and irrational expectations of self and situation must be identified and more appropriate ones offered. If intimates are able to care for the loved one with realistic self-expectations, they will sustain less guilt and self-reproach—common human responses to the failure to meet standards. Basically, to reduce potential or actual guilt, caregivers must help anticipatory mourners reality test the self-image and/or standards, expectations, and elements of conscience against which they judge themselves deficient. Doing so will enable mourners to determine whether the sources of their guilt actually are inappropriate and unrealistic standards, as opposed to wrongdoing, and whether more appropriate and realistic standards are required. Reality testing also helps educate mourners about the current experience (e.g., recognizing that it is not "bad" to wish one were not burdened with so many demands during the illness and that it is normal for human beings to want to eliminate distress in their lives).

Further prevention or relief of guilt can be provided by enlisting intimates' appropriate participation in the ill or dying person's overall care. This gives them the opportunity to make restitution for any acts of omission or commission in the past and provides them with experiences that illustrate to themselves and others their concern for the patient. However, this process must be monitored to assure that the participation allows intimates enough time to attend to critical personal needs, or it can become destructive to both the ill person and his or her intimates. A study by Rando (1983) found that too much participation with a terminally ill loved one, like too little, was associated with poorer postdeath adjustment.

Although intimates may respond to their guilt by putting all their time, energy, and resources into the care of the ill or dying person, overextension can stimulate further resentment and, consequently, more guilt for feeling this way. When such behaviors are recognized, caregivers should speak to the intimate about the need to rest and replenish energy. They can explain that continual neglect of one's own needs ultimately leads to resentment. As appropriate, caregivers can bring up guilt as a precipitant of the worrisome behaviors and enable more therapeutic ways to contend with the situation. Caregivers are often in an excellent position to time interventions sensitively, promoting a break or time-out between intimate and loved one when both parties can benefit from it. For example, it is at times helpful to encourage intimates to go home and rest, shower, change clothes, and then return more refreshed to spend time with the ill person. Those caring for the loved one at home can be encouraged to arrange for respite care to allow themselves the freedom to leave the house, tend to their own personal needs, and get a different perspective. The loved one can benefit from this as well, if the separation is timed correctly and care is taken that it does not signal abandonment.

Although intimates frequently recognize that they require respites, they may be reluctant to initiate them without the caregiver's implicit or explicit permission. Receiving such permission is therapeutic, especially near the end of an illness when intimates may be keeping a vigil with the patient. Being present for the dying person is very important for intimates, but even in the best of circumstances people need time away from one another and from the contemplation of threatening situations if they are going to continue to cope in healthy ways. Mourning, whether before or after a death, requires energy. The emotionally and/or physically exhausted, depleted person is simply unable to attend optimally to the requisite tasks of this important work. Nevertheless, there will be some intimates, especially near the end of the loved one's illness, for whom it is simply unacceptable not to spend all their time with the ill person. While the caregiver can point out consequences of this, the decision ultimately must be respected and interventions geared to help such individuals undergo the experience as best as possible and to cope with the sequelae of their lack of respite.

When guilt serves the functional purpose of protecting the anticipatory mourner from other feelings, thoughts, impulses, or issues (e.g., anger at the ill person), or of meeting latent needs (e.g., distancing the helplessness), the caregiver must work gently to enable the mourner to discern and directly address the underlying concerns. The caregiver may use therapeutic interventions to help the mourner identify the sources of the guilt, its type, and the functions, if any, that it serves, and then to problem solve and work it through to the extent possible. Therapeutic rituals can be quite effective. Often sharing guilt with a nonjudgmental other, or others, in a supportive relationship can be very useful in assisting the anticipatory mourner in diffusing and reducing the guilt, normalizing it, and learning to live with it. Mutual support groups for patients and intimates have been quite helpful in this regard. Such groups can also help anticipatory mourners deal with current traumatization and cope with guilt about survival after the loved one's death.

Interventions must not attempt to take away, absolve, or rescue the anticipatory mourner from guilt. He or she will not be aided by efforts to explain guilt away, only by being enabled to relinquish it or reevaluate it as regret. Regret can be lived with in a much more healthy way than can guilt. If the mourner truly has done (or not done) things warranting guilt, the caregiver must intervene with strategies designed for coping with legitimate guilt that promote reducing it to the extent possible, taking responsibility for it, engaging in symbolic experiences and discovering constructive ways to make restitution and expiate it, and, ultimately, forgiving the self (see Rando, 1993).

Finally, it may be helpful for caregivers to remember that, although some claim the contrary, few people get through the illness and death of a loved one without experiencing at least some guilt. Even though guilt is a natural and expectable part of the antici-patory mourning process, in my experience it is frequently the most difficult emotion for human beings to handle. I often approach guilt more slowly than other emotions, unless the mourner is bring-ing the issue to me in a fashion suggesting the need for quicker intervention or the guilt is preventing the mourner from doing things that must be done prior to the death.

Seven Generic Operations

The task of treatment in the seven generic operations is to facilitate healthy engagement in each one: (a) grief and mourning, (b) cop-ing, (c) interaction, (d) psychosocial reorganization, (e) planning, (f) balancing conflicting demands, and (g) facilitating an appro-priate death. How this will be accomplished will be different depending upon both the caregiver and the anticipatory mourner, given that variables affecting both will lend a distinct complexion to each case.

Chapter 2 offers an in-depth description of these seven generic operations, so these details will not be repeated here. With regard to intimate anticipatory mourners, caregivers may find a great deal of variation in ability to engage in these processes. Some individuals may be fairly successful in all of them except, for example, facilitating an appropriate death. For idiosyncratic personal or systemic reasons, this operation may be more difficult to accomplish. Consequently, the caregiver must not assume that merely because an individual engages effectively in one operation, all others are being appropri-ately addressed as well. This is why the anticipatory mourner's status with regard to each generic operation must be evaluated in the assessment phase of the treatment protocol. It is important for the caregiver to monitor continually for changes.

With the exception of the last, facilitating an appropriate death, these generic operations are not exclusive to anticipatory mourning, and the caregiver is free to choose interventions he or she feels most effective from a wide range of treatment choices established to pro-mote appropriate undertaking of these operations.

Finally, treatment in this arena often requires the caregiver to bring together diverse approaches, dissimilar modalities, and differ-ent styles. What works to help someone who needs to grieve may be quite different from what is required to assist that person in balanc-ing conflicting demands. The diversity of operations mandates the integration of a wide range of strategies and techniques. For instance, a caregiver may be more directive and behavioral when working with an anticipatory mourner to facilitate an appropriate death for the loved one but more nondirective and insight oriented when addressing the mourner's grief and mourning. He or she may adopt a more cognitive-behavioral focus when working to enable optimum coping. Assuredly, no single way of intervening will be suitable for all operations, to say nothing of a single approach for all anticipatory mourners. Part of the skill of the effective caregiver is in knowing when and how to use diverse interventions and in what fashion to combine and coordinate them to create a helpful treatment package.

Component Processes of the Three Contextual Levels of Anticipatory Mourning

The anticipatory mourning of the intimates of a life-threatened or dying person is a complex phenomenon. It encompasses a number of emotional responses and a host of psychosocial processes in response to demands to adapt to experiences of loss and trauma engendered in the experience. These demands often occur during a time of intense confusion, chaos, and competing responsibilities, and within a system (i.e., the intimate network) that has its own processes and needs to be met, as do each of its individual members.

This section examines specific interventions that promote and enable the components of the interrelated processes of anticipatory mourning. These components are found across the three contextual levels of anticipatory mourning: the intrapsychic level, the interpersonal level, and the systemic level. Chapter 2 of this volume identifies the components; their facilitation is discussed here.

Intrapsychic-level processes

On the intrapsychic level, the intimate becomes increasingly aware of the threat of the loved one's life-threatening condition and/or impending death and copes with the reactions generated by this awareness. These responses involve affective processes (dealing with the emotional responses stimulated) and cognitive processes (pertaining to revising one's assumptive world, changing one's sense of self, attempting to crystallize memories for the future, bargaining for a reprieve, and contemplating one's own death). These processes also interface with those involved in planning for a future that is an uncomfortable but natural outgrowth of the increasing recognition that future losses will occur and that the intimate must be prepared to deal with them.

Awareness of and gradual accommodation to the threat. For intimates to come to an awareness of and gradual accommodation to the threat of the loved one's status, they must have received and understood appropriate warnings. Frequently, diagnoses are given in medical jargon, with insufficient time allowed for processing of implications. It is not unusual for intimates to know the name of the loved one's disease but to have minimal understanding of its implications. If the illness or the impending death are not made real for intimates, they cannot deal with the present situation in an appropriate way or prepare for future losses. This does not mean the caregiver takes away all hope or establishes a self-fulfilling prophecy. Rather, it means the caregiver provides information intimates need to recognize and deal with reality. Like the postdeath mourner who cannot begin to mourn the death of a loved one if that person's status is unknown (as in the case of individuals missing in action or whose bodies cannot be found), an intimate will have difficulty commencing anticipatory mourning if the impending loss is not clear. This reality must be presented very gently. For example, the crass statement "The cancer will kill your husband in a straight, downhill course very quickly" is better phrased "Your husband has a cancer that will soon make it increasingly difficult for him to function. It is not clear exactly how long his body will be able to tolerate the illness. However, you should know that based on current knowledge we would expect that in the near future he will start to experience a series of debilitations and that, in most cases, death eventuates very rapidly once the process has begun."

In order to prepare intimates adequately, caregivers must be supportive yet at the same time as specific as possible when giving information. Caregivers should ask intimates what they have understood in order to check their comprehension and should be prepared to deliver information more than once. The emotional defenses of intimates—especially at the time of diagnosis or commencement of the terminal phase—may have prevented them from taking everything in all at once. Recognizing the confusion intimates often feel, caregivers should encourage them to ask questions and then give adequate time for them to integrate the answers. Intimates should be informed that it is acceptable to ask questions in the future, as they occur.

Notwithstanding the typical need for sensitivity and gentleness, at some times the caregiver may have to be rather blunt. Frankness is necessary when the illness is progressing and it is clear that the intimate is denying that process and/or its implications and that the denial interferes with actions the intimate must undertake. At this point, the caregiver may have to be very specific: "Mr. Smith, it is important that you understand that your wife is not going to recover from this illness. As far as medical knowledge can predict, she will not be able to make it to the holidays to see your children. I suggest that you contact them and have them come home to see their mother now." In the same manner, some intimates may have to be

confronted if time is limited and unfinished business will complicate their postdeath mourning. There are times when caregivers
actually may have to prompt intimates to talk with the dying person: "You only have a limited amount of time left. Make sure that
you say or do the things that you need to so you will not feel guilty
later on." At these times, it is permissible to be more direct than normal with intimates. Although intimates' desires ultimately must be
respected, caregivers should point out the deleterious consequences
of leaving certain business unfinished.

A goal of the caregiver is to assist the mourner in reality testing
and appropriate planning. Sometimes, this entails helping intimates
understand the implications of medical information; at other times,
it means helping them make practical plans for pre- and postdeath
activities. In many situations, the caregiver also must encourage
repeated recollection of events leading up to the illness and the
loved one's current condition in order to help intimates gradually
adapt to the shock of the losses they are encountering. Normally,
the experiences of the illness itself prompt intimates gradually to
realize that the loved one is life-threatened or dying. As the loved
one deteriorates, as hopes must be relinquished, and as medical
interventions are of little use, family members are confronted with,
and ultimately taught about, the reality to which they must eventually accommodate. Caregivers can be helpful in assisting the
mourner to accommodate gradually to the loved one's illness
and/or dying by identifying assumptive world violations and
addressing reactions to them, along with processing the nature and
extent of the revisions currently required. There should be identification of constructive coping techniques and the development of
strategies to minimize ineffective or harmful responses as the
mourner contends with the changes in the ill person that now mandate this psychosocial reorganization. At this point, self-help or
mutual support groups can be helpful.

Affective processes. The life-threatening or terminal illness of a
loved one engenders a host of affective processes in those close to
that person. The major ones—sorrow, depression, anxiety, anger,
and guilt—have already been discussed in this chapter as they
impact the intimate's anticipatory mourning consequent to experiences of loss and trauma. Knowledge of the threat of death and
potential loss and assumptive world violations that mandate psychosocial reorganization escalate the levels of emotion present and
in themselves are often causes of traumatization. The remissions
and relapses of the illness may bring about shifts in the type and
intensity of emotions intimates experience. In the presence of the
seriously ill or dying loved one, attempts may be made to modulate
or suppress negative feelings in order to eliminate potential stress.

These negative feelings later can erupt in less appropriate ways, increasing resentment and eventually undermining the cooperation of intimates.

Caregivers can be helpful if they anticipate and communicate to intimates the emotional reactions and traumatic sequelae they may experience; normalize them, as appropriate, when they are encountered; and suggest and enable appropriate ways for intimates to express, cope with, process, and work through these responses. This entails the caregiver's (a) legitimizing appropriate affects, cognitions, wishes, fears, behaviors, experiences, and symptoms; (b) assisting the intimate in identifying, labeling, differentiating, and tracing affective experiences and their component parts; and (c) enabling the mourner to feel, accept, examine, give some form of expression to, and work through all of the feelings aroused. The caregiver engages strategies to assist the intimate to deal with any bereavement overload (Kastenbaum, 1969). Rando (1993) delineates a wide variety of therapeutic guidelines, strategies, interventions, and formal protocols to facilitate and treat affective responses and processes in postdeath bereavement, including bereavement overload; these may be adapted for anticipatory mourning. All interventions must provide support for the intimate to cope with the anticipatory mourning process.

Additionally, caregivers must identify intimates' idiosyncratic fears, concerns, and needs in the specific situation, as well as in general, if they are to understand the intimates' emotional reactions, the ways in which each member of the intimate network chooses to cope with them, and what specific interventions are required. Clearly, the need for assessment is ongoing.

Cognitive processes. Cognitive processes are stimulated by the loved one's terminal illness. Two major sets of cognitive processes occur during psychosocial reorganization in anticipatory mourning. The first pertains to the mourner's learning about the reality of the loved one's illness and its implications; the second—contingent upon the success of the first—pertains to adjusting cognitively to the reality of the loved one's deterioration and dying. This then ideally leads into necessary adaptive readjustment.

As with any stressful event, the threatened loss of a loved one causes an individual to be hyperalert, scanning the environment for potential cues related to the stress, often searching for personally effective ways of coping with the situation. The illness and threatened loss strike at an intimate's security, sense of self, assumptive world, and so forth. Many intimates become increasingly preoccupied with the illness and its meanings. In some, this may be a sign that necessary psychosocial reorganization is transpiring. In addition, as losses and changes accumulate over time and experiences with the illness teach about the reality of the loved one's illness and/or dying, intimates begin to recognize that the world is now different and that they must change in order to adapt to that new reality. Cognitively, this means revisions of the assumptive world and changes in identity as intimates start to incorporate their various intrapsychic and behavioral changes and begin the gradual transformation from being a "we" to an "I" in terms of their interactive relationship with the loved one. Although this transformation is relative to the former relationship, which is now precluded by the current reality, there still can be—indeed, should be—interaction with the loved one in the present, even if it is different from before.

Because it is very important for intimates to construct a composite mental image of the patient that can endure after the death, it may be helpful for caregivers to encourage reviewing the past in order to crystallize memories that will continue on after the death. The "life review" (Butler, 1963) is often beneficial to the ill or dying person, as well as to intimates, because it puts the loved one's life in perspective and may help him or her to integrate it. Life review can help intimates develop a view of the loved one that perhaps is more balanced than before and that has a more longitudinal dimension. Many times, review affords insight into the loved one that heretofore had been lacking.

Although life review has great potential therapeutic value, Weisman (1988) cautions against a concerted effort to initiate a formal, all-inclusive review. He feels that the technique does not necessarily confer much benefit, given that it may recall unresolved conflicts that are beyond repair or may turn out to be a romanticized denial of difficulty. Nevertheless, Weisman believes that a sense of continuity is a prerequisite for an appropriate death, and he looks for ways to bring the best of the past into functional relation with the present in order to strengthen positive support. This can be accomplished via reminders of past struggles successfully completed or of outstanding accomplishments still recollected with a sense of pride. In this regard, tokens of earlier activity from the preterminal life can be encouraged, such as visits from associates, letters from friends, greeting cards, photographs, and so forth—anything that establishes a positive link between then and now. Given that the main purpose of continuity is to protect authentic self-identity during the last stages of life, intimates can help themselves, and their loved ones, by making sure life review is productive in a therapeutic sense, not merely exhaustive.

Other cognitive processes may occur, such as thinking about one's own death and bargaining for a reprieve. In the former, thoughts of one's own demise often are stimulated by watching the dying of another. This can give rise to death anxiety and certainly contributes to some of the traumatization the anticipatory mourner may experience. In such instances, caregivers can intervene to reduce traumatic stress, allow ventilation, and encourage planning for one's own death. When intimates bargain for the life of their loved one, it is best for caregivers not to interfere unless the situation is either distinctly unhealthy for the intimate or interferes with the ill person's receiving appropriate treatment or having medical needs met. Taking away the hope that one's bargaining will work is not in the caregiver's purview, although this does not mean that the caregiver should support unrealistic hopes.

Throughout anticipatory mourning, but especially in the terminal phase, many intimates, implicitly and at times without conscious knowledge, develop a philosophy of coping during the loved one's remaining time. Some will try to do as much as possible to create memories of the ill or dying person, from which they can later derive sustenance. Others prefer not to feel pressured and take a more passive, laissez-faire approach, not letting themselves get caught up in a whirlwind. The caregiver can help by asking the ill person and intimates how they are most comfortable in spending the time left. Problems can arise when the ill loved one's attitude differs from that of the intimates. In this case, the caregiver must mediate to help them come to a mutually agreeable arrangement or, at the very least, to understand one another on this issue. My own belief is that the dying person must be given as much consideration as possible—after all, it is his or her remaining life that is being debated.

Related to a philosophy of coping is the need many intimates have to find personal meaning and put their loved one's suffering and death into some philosophical, spiritual, or religious context. For some this occurs after the death, but for many others it occurs during the illness. The best posture for the caregiver to assume is a nonjudgmental and empathic one, supporting the family member's quest for meaning if it is not detrimental to that person or the ill loved one. For many, addressing spiritual or existential issues created or resurrected by the illness or dying is a prerequisite to trauma reduction and healthy coping. This may be considered part of the process of assumptive world revision. It is also a way for mourners to explain or give meaning to the situation and to integrate it into their unique life stories.

Intimates also may contemplate old issues (previous losses, griefs, vulnerabilities, traumas, experiences, etc.) revived by the current situation. In this regard, the caregiver is best guided by the principle of promoting whatever appropriate ventilation, processing, and achievement of closure the intimate deems or can be convinced is necessary; that is possible under the circumstances; and that would not be detrimental to the life-threatened or dying loved one. This latter point is important because what may be helpful to the intimate (e.g., admission of an extramarital affair years ago) may be harmful to the ill or dying person. In such instances, caregivers are well advised to weigh the costs and benefits of pursuing the particular matter, consider who should engage in it with the intimate if it is undertaken (e.g., perhaps a referral is necessary), and clarify what the ground rules would be. Most importantly, the caregiver must be clear on the person to whom he or she owes primary therapeutic allegiance and how conflicts of needs would be handled. Supervision and/or collegial support is desirable here as at times when ethical, moral, and/or clinical dilemmas present themselves.

Planning for the future. When the threat has been recognized and while the feelings and thoughts associated with it are being processed, planning for the future, one of the seven generic operations in anticipatory mourning, becomes a natural outgrowth. As a matter of course, effective planning implies having some realistic understanding of future losses and changes. Caregivers should support intimates' attempts to incorporate the ill or dying loved one in planning discussions. However, it also must be recognized that some planning is for the intimates alone and, despite their inclusion of the ill person in most things, some intimates may want or feel the need to consider certain issues privately. This especially can be the case if such planning is combined with unresolved survival guilt.

Caregivers can facilitate appropriate planning for the future by asking what specific plans have been made for certain events. For instance, the soon-to-be widow can be asked how she will manage child care once she returns to work. Inquiries must be made in a way that will help stimulate planning; the mourner should not be bombarded, overwhelmed, or frightened. It is often uncomfortable for intimates to recognize that they are considering a future without their loved one, so it is imperative that caregivers normalize this discomfort and convey that it is a natural part of accommodating to the undesirable, but inevitable, loss. In addition to rendering him or her some control, involving the ill or dying person also may decrease intimates' guilt over contemplating the future without the loved one and increases opportunities to benefit from that person's input, guidance, and preferences. A caveat: It is important that such planning and discussion occur at the appropriate time in the illness. When broached prematurely, these issues can isolate the ill loved one and/or provoke premature detachment.

Interpersonal-level processes
with the life-threatened or dying person

In these processes, depending on the person's status in the illness, the anticipatory mourner actively continues to be involved with the ill or dying loved one. Such involvement is necessary not only to continue to support the person and ensure that there is no premature detachment, but also to provide the time and opportunities for the intimate to care for the loved one and to resolve their mutual relationship—actions that can be particularly therapeutic for postdeath mourning and adjustment.

Directing attention, energy, and behavior toward the life-threatened or dying person. In a loved one's life-threatening or terminal illness, it is normal for intimates to find themselves directing attention, energy, and behavior toward the life-threatened or dying loved one. The main therapeutic focus here is on promoting whatever communication, interaction, control, living, and meaning remains available to the ill or dying person. Intimates may need to be assisted in adopting a commitment to this and to remaining as involved as possible with the patient. Clearly, the former relationship will have to change somewhat to accommodate the current realities of the illness and its sequelae, but despite these alterations, connections to the loved one still can be maintained until such time as it is appropriate to change them or let go. It must be remembered that withdrawal will not accentuate just the ill person's losses. It will deprive intimates of the therapeutic benefits of appropriate participation in the loved one's care, a factor identified as an important influence on one's postdeath mourning and adjustment (Rando, 1983).

At appropriate times, caregivers can explain to intimates the inevitability of having to struggle with mutually conflicting demands. In terms of orientation vis-à-vis the ill or dying person, anticipatory mourning necessitates that the intimate simultaneously move toward the person (e.g., directing attention, energy, and behavior toward him or her), stay the same with the person, (e.g., attempting to maintain some of the premorbid status quo, remaining involved with him or her), and move away from the person (e.g., revising the assumptive world by letting go of the expectation of that person's being as before or of being alive in the future). The caregiver must help the intimate balance these conflicting demands and cope with the stress their incongruence creates. The intimate will need guidance in identifying how to simultaneously, yet differentially, respond to these demands. For example, one can move toward the ill person behaviorally and socially (increasing time spent interacting with that person) while moving away intrapsychically (starting to detach from former images of the individual as alive in the future and revising relevant aspects of the assumptive world).

As can be seen, the competing demands may be met in different realms of the personality. The possibility of such differential responses means that the loved one does not have to be prematurely abandoned in the here-and-now despite the commencement of a decathexis process regarding the future. It will be critical for the caregiver to assist the mourner with this important but complex realization. The caregiver must continually emphasize the importance of ongoing involvement, for as long as is appropriate and in whatever ways are appropriate, modeling this for intimates by interacting with the ill or dying person and incorporating that individual into as many family activities as possible and appropriate.

Balancing conflicting demands is one of the seven generic operations of anticipatory mourning. Intimates often require the caregiver's assistance in learning how to meet the challenges they are subject to in this area. The caregiver must educate and assist intimates in taking appropriate respites in order that, when they are with the ill or dying person, they are able to focus their energy on caring for that loved one. Normal resentment, ambivalence, frustration, and the like are frequently part of the process of living with a seriously ill or dying individual. When caregivers explain this, intimates often can be liberated from guilt and other negative responses that could interfere with their relating to the loved one. There are cases where intimates refuse to take proper respites or to engage in anything that will occupy what time they do have remaining with the person. Frequently, although not exclusively, this attitude is found in parents whose children are dying. Many relinquish jobs, peer relationships, hobbies, and so forth, saying, "There'll be time for all of that later. Right now my responsibility is to be with my loved one." While caregivers can express their concern about this and identify potential consequences, the decision is ultimately the intimate's and must be respected.

It often takes a great deal out of intimates to participate in activities that are uncomfortable for their loved one (e.g., taking him or her for painful medical procedures) or that prevent their loved one from having access to things that he or she enjoys (e.g., refusing to buy cigarettes). Caregivers can encourage intimates to discuss such matters and, in situations where the practice does not appear to make sense (e.g., "So what if he smokes now? He's dying anyway"), help them decide whether or not they want to continue with them. In situations where the "cure mentality" is minimal and palliative care is the norm, intimates are not usually put in such situations.

Resolving the personal relationship with the life-threatened or dying person. One of the most important aspects of anticipatory mourning is that it allows time for resolution of the personal relationship with the life-threatened or dying person, the most critical aspect of which is finishing unfinished business. Addressing psychosocial issues that have never been addressed or that have lacked successful closure can involve many behaviors. Such behaviors include not only expressing feelings and resolving past conflicts, but also such actions as saying good-bye, asking for or giving forgiveness, explaining past omissions or commissions, articulating important messages, informing the person of the meaningfulness of the relationship, or providing other pieces of necessary feedback. Again, before recommending that intimates be candid, caregivers must consider the premorbid characteristics of the intimate and the ill or dying loved one, as well as their mutual relationship and the ability of the intimate network to withstand open and honest communication. As noted previously, it may be necessary to urge intimates to do or say those things that need to be done or said to prevent them from feeling guilty later on. Often it is helpful for caregivers to ask intimates to identify what they think they will feel uncomfortable, incomplete, or guilty about 6 months down the road, then to suggest that they attend to these issues now in order to finish unfinished business and come to closure with the loved one.

Many times the caregiver will have to work with the mourner to decide what needs to be communicated, how to do so, and what concerns or resistances have to be addressed in the process. Communication may be nonverbal as well as verbal; symbolic acts, little rituals, touch, and presence can be powerful vehicles for communicating with an ill or dying loved one. As noted under the discussion of cognitive processes, issues can arise if what the intimate desires to communicate or to do to finish unfinished business could adversely affect the ill person. My own position is that the life-threatened or dying individual has the right to be free of the unnecessary and unhealthy burdens that can be imposed, although often unwittingly, by an intimate in this regard. Caregivers will have to differentiate between those situations in which the ill person can actually be harmed and those in which there is concern about "distressing" the loved one by conveying love or caring in ways that are different than usual. The caregiver may or may not intervene in the latter; there is an obligation to intervene, if warranted by assessment, in the former.

It is critically important, although frequently quite painful, for intimates to say good-bye to the loved one and to give him or her permission to die. At the appropriate time, caregivers may need to model saying good-bye to the dying person. This can be accomplished, for example, by letting the person know how he or she will be remembered: "I will miss you when you are gone. Whenever I watch *Casablanca* I'll remember you and how much you loved that movie." Saying good-bye involves acknowledging that the leave taking is occurring and can be demonstrated through concrete or symbolic actions as well as through verbal communication. Again, the caregiver should be aware that different words or actions will be meaningful for different people in saying good-bye. Personality, cultural, and ethnic factors play influential roles.

Permission to die is essentially what intimates convey to the dying person that makes it acceptable for him or her to let go. Intimates refrain from attempting to keep the loved one alive through guilt, responsibility, or unfinished business. Giving permission does not mean that the intimates are unmoved. Rather, it signifies that, despite their wishes to the contrary, they love the dying individual enough to recognize that death is natural, inevitable, and at hand. Therefore, they do not act in ways that will meet their own needs at the expense of the dying person's need to let go. At the appropriate time, they can permit the peaceful transition. Sometimes just making a verbal or nonverbal statement to the effect that "It is OK to let go" or recognizing that the loved one is dying sends the message that the intimates understand and accept what is happening, although reluctantly. Often, to assuage concerns about leaving the anticipatory mourner behind—concerns that may bind the dying individual or interfere with his or her letting go—it can be helpful for the anticipatory mourner to mention that he or she will be "sad, but OK" in the loved one's absence.

Helping the life-threatened or dying person. Throughout the period of anticipatory mourning, intimates ideally work on helping the life-threatened or dying person maximize and optimize life as much as possible, cope as effectively as possible with their own anticipatory mourning, deal with specific fears and concerns, and achieve a sense of closure that contributes to the feeling of peace and the ultimate ability to let go at the appropriate time. This entails facilitating an appropriate death (Weisman, 1972), one of the seven generic operations of anticipatory mourning (see chapter 2). This facilitation ideally involves the concepts of safe conduct, significant survival, and dignified dying. Interventions could include such things as helping the person be relatively pain and symptom free, determining and meeting physical and psychosocial needs, assuming necessary body and ego functions, reducing suffering, maximizing the control of personal comfort, keeping losses (particularly social and emotional impoverishments) to a minimum, enabling as high a level of functioning as possible, helping to resolve residual conflicts and find meaning, and tending to the last wishes of the loved one. Most important, it means providing specific emotional and psychosocial support and acceptance necessary for the person to communicate about and cope with all aspects of his or her illness, its related losses, and the impending death, as well as with all of the feelings, thoughts, fears, concerns, and needs generated by it. (For complete discussion of therapeutic concerns with dying persons, see Doka, 1993; Pattison, 1977, 1978; Rando, 1984; and Weisman, 1979, 1988.) Finally, instrumental and logistical support, assistance with treatment regimens and relations with caregivers, and the enabling of appropriate decision making and action around end-of-life issues are additional ways to assist the ill person.

Obviously, in order to meet the needs of seriously ill or dying loved ones, intimates must be aware of what these needs are. Therefore, a major responsibility of the intimate network is to create an atmosphere in which the dying person feels free to make needs and wants known without fear of incurring resentment or disapproval. In this regard, caregivers can work to facilitate an open awareness context (Glaser & Strauss, 1965) or at least one that is as open as the system can tolerate. Intimates can be directed not to assume what the loved one's needs are, but instead to ask the person directly. Caregivers may need to advise intimates to balance support for the ill individual's increased dependency with the continued need for autonomy; too much of either can be countertherapeutic. Because the person's status shifts, there will be fluctuations in what is necessary for an appropriate balance. Consistent reevaluations are mandatory.

Intimates often require assistance in coping with processes that mark the decline toward death. Some may need help to refrain from abandoning the loved one in order to avoid witnessing the decline. It can be particularly painful for intimates to watch the loved one deteriorate and be forced to relinquish the roles and responsibilities that once were sustained. Intimates cope with and defend against feelings of helplessness and lack of control—frequent precipitants of, as well as reactions to, traumatization—through a variety of coping mechanisms. Certain coping mechanisms can be functional for an intimate in a given situation. These are mechanisms that are expected and appropriate at the time, safeguard the individual against incapacitating anxiety or depression, enable the individual to maintain need-fulfilling relationships, and do not interfere with the medical care of the ill person (McCollum & Schwartz, 1972). The caregiver can work to support those mechanisms that are healthy, functional, and adaptive, and gently supplant those that are not.

Along with helping the dying person in the aforementioned ways, intimates can provide the loved one continued control and self-determination by asking how he or she wishes to be remembered and then attempting to bring this to pass. Suggestions include writing letters or making videotapes for young children who will be left behind, establishing an endowment in the ill or dying person's name, bequeathing precious possessions to certain loved ones, choosing a headstone, and so forth. If the loved one desires, intimates can help preplan the funerary rituals. In facilitating ongoing communication between intimates and the seriously ill or dying person, the caregiver serves as a reality tester, a source of comfort, and a resource for helping to discharge negative feelings that could impinge on these important relationships.

Systemic-level processes

Like all other systems, the intimate network struggles to regain functional equilibrium and achieve homeostatic balance after change. The illness and dying of the loved one, and the person's consequent inability to function as previously in the intimate network, will necessitate the redistribution and reassignment of roles and responsibilities to other intimates. Caregivers can help by explaining and enabling this process, working to minimize the distress of those undergoing and/or observing it (including the ill or dying person, whose roles and responsibilities are being reassigned), advocating the most appropriate assignment of roles, and pointing out where assignments may be inappropriate or incongruent with a member's present responsibilities (e.g., the 8-year-old boy who is expected now to be the "man" of the house). As well, caregivers can help intimates anticipate future permanent changes and direct them toward restructuring their roles in mutually adaptive ways. However, caregivers must resist the impulse to take over for the intimate network while restructuring occurs, either with the dying patient or among the intimates themselves.

Children occupy unique roles as anticipatory mourners and as members of the intimate network. Their uniqueness and disadvantage in these roles must be understood, responded to, and incorporated into the overall intervention with the intimate network. (See Rando, 1995, for more on this important topic.) Caregivers may need to provide psychoeducation and actively intervene to enable the intimate network to overcome—or at least minimize—the resistance, in the name of protecting the children, to appropriately including them in the anticipatory mourning processes.

Another systemic issue during anticipatory mourning concerns the fact that intimates typically are called upon to negotiate relationships outside the network. Many of these are with medical personnel and other caregivers. Intimates often benefit from being encouraged to be assertive and taught to express anger and discontent in ways that will not jeopardize either their future relationship with caregivers or the care of the ill loved one.

Other social relationships are frequently put under stress when a loved one is dying, as a result of the disruption that occurs during the illness. Lack of energy, losses, and traumatic sequelae consequent to the illness can interfere with intimates' ability to maintain and nurture outside relationships. These relationships often are assigned lower priority, with many intimates choosing to reserve energies for matters associated with the seriously ill or dying loved one.

Caregivers can help by explaining the social avoidance of friends. Because of their own anxiety about the life-threatening or terminal illness or their lack of knowledge about how to be supportive, friends may become distant. Intimates may need guidance to take the lead in dealing with friends who are interested in helping but do not know what to do. Caregivers also may need to normalize the resentment intimates feel over the relative good fortune of friends or over their feelings that others cannot understand their plight. Mutual support groups for intimates of seriously ill persons can be exceptionally helpful, and caregivers should be aware of these resources.

Finally, not only must intimates learn how to communicate with the dying loved one and with health caregivers and friends outside the intimate network, they also must learn to work with one another. Communication will be especially important when the intimate network is in flux due to the reassignment of roles; when the members need to make plans for the future; or when mutually contradictory needs, desires, and expectations arise among the members. Caregivers must work to facilitate and reinforce intrasystem communication among the intimate network, demonstrating its importance by including all intimates in relevant meetings whenever appropriate, respecting the feelings and opinions of all, and modeling healthy skills for communication and compromise. Caregivers also need to be cognizant of the premorbid issues and communication patterns in the network that may preclude healthy communication and interaction at this time. While it is not impossible for differences to be overcome, long-standing problems typically do not completely vanish as a loved one is dying. Caregivers must have appropriate expectations for the intimates, their system, and what realistically can be accomplished at this point under the prevailing conditions.

Phase Four: Follow Up

As demonstrated unequivocally in the classic Institute of Medicine study (Osterweis, Solomon, & Green, 1984), if the factors are conducive, bereavement is a state of appreciable distress, dysfunction, and potential risk for the mourner. As well, the literature suggests that the death of a loved one from an overly lengthy illness predisposes the bereaved individual to complications in mourning (Rando, 1993) and that, as noted throughout this chapter, certain experiences that commonly occur within such illnesses can create additional problems for the mourner. Finally, as concluded in the Institute of Medicine study *Approaching Death: Improving Care at the End of Life* (Field & Cassel, 1997), today in the United States too many ill persons suffer needlessly at the end of life, as do those close to them. We know this can predispose survivors' postdeath bereavement to complications.

Given what we know about the potential sequelae of the loss of a loved one, particularly if there has been a prolonged life-threatening illness, some type of follow up should be provided to the intimate, if at all possible. In the Four-Plus Phase Model of Intervention in Intimate Anticipatory Mourning, it is part of the treatment plan.

The type and depth of follow up that can be offered depends on the role the caregiver has occupied vis-à-vis the intimate. For instance, a cleric may be able to make an unsolicited postdeath visit to the intimate's home, sit down and share a cup of coffee with him or her, and have an informal discussion that not only provides the intimate with support but enables the caregiver to garner information about the status of that mourner. A mental health professional may be more limited in his or her ability to reach out without solicitation. This dilemma can be anticipated, and the caregiver can schedule a visit for a specified time after the death or at least suggest such a visit. If counseling or therapy will continue with the caregiver after the loved one's death, access is a moot issue. Sometimes, hospice bereavement visits are an expected mode of follow up. Although they must follow certain guidelines and restrictions, hospice workers may not have the same constraints as the mental health counselor. Clearly, substantial variation exists in the ways caregivers will engage in this phase of intervention.

Follow up can take the form of a one-time meeting or consist of many contacts over time and at different intervals. Contacts can be personal and face-to-face or by telephone, computer, videotape, teleconference, e-mail, facsimile, audiotape, standard mail, or any other form of communication. Content and/or process may range widely in depth and form. At minimum, follow up should provide relevant assessment and, if appropriate, brief intervention.

Regardless of how the follow up is conducted, the caregiver must keep in mind and account for a number of issues in any assessment of the mourner. The major issues, among others, are as follows:

- Timing of the follow up
- The artificial deflation that occurs after death of a loved one from prolonged illness
- The need to attend to traumatic stress responses, not exclusively loss-related ones
- The current effects of any type of depletion (emotional, cognitive, spiritual, conative, behavioral, social, physical, financial) on the individual and on the intimate network
- The status of the intimate network as a bereaved, and possibly traumatized, system and what impact this status is having on the mourner
- The number, type, and consequences of secondary losses experienced by the mourner

A primary purpose of follow up is to permit the caregiver to determine whether the mourner requires additional treatment and/or referral. The caregiver can employ a variety of types of assessment instruments, along with a number of clinical tools and interviews, to determine these needs. Briefly, anything that facilitates an accurate assessment at follow up is therapeutically valuable. The caregiver must be familiar with effective community resources. To determine that a person requires assistance but be unable to refer him or her does little good.

Follow up also provides the opportunity for brief intervention that may obviate the need for deeper intervention down the road. In other words, if the caregiver ascertains that issues or concerns are present and require minimal intervention, this often can be provided at that point. Follow up furnishes the opportunity to address any issues that lack closure. For example, a mourner may have worked diligently to achieve a desired type of death for his or her loved one and then, at the end, this did not occur—for instance, the death was traumatic and not peaceful, with the person dying at the hospital instead of at home because the family panicked and called 911. Leaving such matters unfinished can result in subsequent problems; it is in the best interests of most parties to address these issues directly, and the follow up can provide the opportunity to do just that. During this time the caregiver also is able, as appropriate and warranted, to normalize and depathologize many of the aspects of postdeath mourning that often are inaccurately perceived as pathological.

Another purpose of follow up, especially if there has been significant contact during the illness, is to illustrate to the mourner that he or she has not been forgotten, is not unimportant now that the loved one has died, continues to require attention and support, and is experiencing something (i.e., postdeath mourning) that is of concern to the caregiver. In cases where involvement between caregiver and intimate anticipatory mourner has been extremely intense and close, follow up can confirm and validate the importance of the earlier work, communicate that the mourner is more than merely a "case" to the caregiver, and permit termination or gradual transitioning into a new relationship. As pertains to this last point, it is often important to enable a good ending with the anticipatory mourner if for no other reason that this is what the caregiver had been working with the mourner to achieve. A good ending with a caregiver can be therapeutic to the mourner and underscore the importance of such work at times of future loss. Not everyone will require the same types of intervention, but the ending ideally should be therapeutic for the parties involved.

Unfortunately, many mourners have reported to me experiencing a profound blow when, at the precise time they were struggling to deal with the death of their loved one, they also unexpectedly had to contend with the loss of others who had become like family to them (i.e., caregivers). This "double whammy" can combine with the normal disorientation that occurs after the death of a person around whom one's life had revolved. Such a death can leave intimates unsure of their roles and without structure, given that they have relinquished so many other interests, investments, and relationships in order to concentrate upon the dying person. Sharing a loved one's dying with another individual is very intimate. Losing that intimacy, and loss of the "life" one had for so long during the illness, can be a powerful event. Therefore, appropriate termination is necessary. From a personal standpoint, the caregiver should follow up with persons with whom he or she has worked intensely to facilitate his or her own sense of closure. It is well-documented that caregivers adept at assisting others in dealing with losses can lack the same skills to deal with the losses they encounter professionally.

Where the mourner has characterological issues around dependency or where the circumstances have promoted an intense dependency, concerns about the loss of the caregiver are even more relevant. Follow up that addresses these issues definitely classifies as "treatment," even if it occurs after the formal treatment time has terminated. It is important to remember, however, that if follow-up time is limited, it is inappropriate to open up certain issues—even in the name of closing down others—unless the mourner has access to help in processing the issues that have been addressed and/or stimulated.

Plus: Support, Education, and Advocacy (SEA)

Plus refers to a sustained set of processes that occur throughout all of the phases in this model. In other words, the caregiver provides support, education, and advocacy throughout the duration of his or her relationship with the intimate anticipatory mourner.

Support

In all types of research and clinical investigations, as well as in a variety of therapeutic situations, support has been found to be a key element in any person's coping and adaptation. Technically, the provision of information (i.e., education) is a form of support, but for the purpose of this discussion it is examined separately. If the mourner perceives the external world as providing support for mourning, that perception is an extremely positive factor. The perception that support is unavailable, available and not forthcoming, or available but insufficiently provided can have a profoundly negative impact on coping, as can the perception that the loss is not socially acknowledged. In fact, any of these perceptions constitutes a high-risk factor for complicated mourning (Rando, 1993).

According to Rando (1993), types of support include emotional support, instrumental support, validational support, informational support, support of presence, relational support, and support for social activities. Depending upon the role of the caregiver, avenues of support may or may not be open. Some specific ways in which caregivers can support the mourner in anticipatory mourning are as follows:

1. Instructing the mourner in how to "dose" himself (i.e., direct attention toward and then away from disturbing stimuli before they become intolerable) and control the pace of mourning by structuring respites

2. Helping the mourner discover ways to replenish himself following the severe emotional, social, physical, intellectual, and spiritual depletion resulting from the loss (e.g., rest, nutrition, social support, physical activity/sports, religion, philosophy, literature, media)

3. Encouraging physical activity or exercise to release pent-up emotion

4. Acknowledging pragmatic concerns and referring the mourner to the proper resources for assistance in these areas

5. Promoting appropriate support from others

6. Working with the mourner to maintain the proper balance between experiencing pain and other

unpleasant affects and maintaining sufficient defenses to avoid being overwhelmed

7. Assisting the mourner to maintain good physical health and avoid or keep to a minimum use of drugs, sedatives, alcohol, caffeine, nicotine, and other self-medication

8. Helping the mourner develop the proper perspective on what accommodating the loss will mean (Rando, 1993, pp. 375–376)

Education

Education, the provision of psychoeducational and normative information, is one of the most effective ways to help mourners cope with the vicissitudes of a loved one's illness or dying and the traumatization and mourning that ensue. As in any other human situation, understanding makes the circumstances more tolerable. Along with advocacy, clinical education interventions provide practical information to help intimates cope.

Caregivers too often fail to appreciate the therapeutic value and significance of providing psychoeducational material. This cognitive information is critically important in a number of ways (Rando, 1993): (a) it corrects misinformation and debunks myths establishing unrealistic expectations that eventuate in feelings of guilt and failure; (b) it provides a framework to help the mourner feel less overwhelmed, out of control, and helpless; (c) it offers specific data that promote healthy mourning; and (d) it normalizes and legitimizes aspects of mourning that the intimate erroneously may have interpreted as indicating negative things about him- or herself. To these I would add a fifth point: that information can prevent any existing difficulties from becoming more problematic by minimizing potentially exacerbating issues.

Members of the intimate network need to be assisted in understanding many things when a member is seriously ill or dying. At some point, and perhaps more than one, the caregiver may have to interpret the dying person's responses for the intimate network and educate them about the person's feelings. Intimates often need help to understand the dying experience from the ill loved one's perspective, the intense anticipatory mourning that individual may feel at losing everything known and familiar, that person's specific fears, his or her emotional reactions and coping mechanisms stimulated by thinking about the oncoming death, and his or her struggles with dependency and independence, among other topics. Frequently, the intimate network needs to be helped to appreciate, if applicable, the person's fears of dying in pain and dying alone, along with any other idiosyncratic fears the loved one may have and how these can be assuaged. Caregivers can explain the concept of social death and work with the intimate network to avoid it. Intimates can be shown how to support the dying individual's self-esteem and sense of control and will benefit from recurring guidance on how to help him or her achieve an appropriate death.

In addition to specifics about the dying person, intimates usually need information about the illness, its sequelae, and medical treatment, as well as facts pertinent to the institutions with which they must deal. They also may require assistance in identifying existing or potential resources. For instance, they may need specific guidance in identifying, locating, and utilizing material, financial, and social assistance. They often are aided by concrete information to help them contend with other practical realities of the illness and death, such as how to meet future medical needs, plan needed respites, and arrange postdeath rituals. Intimates can benefit from discussion with the caregiver regarding how to explain the illness and its implications to others. Intimates should be instructed as to what can be expected at the time of death and afterward.

Very important, intimates usually are greatly helped by explanations about the experiences of anticipatory and postdeath loss, mourning, and traumatization for individuals, families (including children), and intimate networks. Intimates can benefit from knowledge about the systemic functioning of these families and intimate networks and how these systems need to reorganize themselves. Good psychoeducational information that promotes sound principles of mental health will never hurt. Enlightenment can help intimates avoid potentially destructive behaviors (e.g., cessation of communication with other intimates, reliance on drugs/alcohol, or running away by commencing an extramarital affair). The goal of all education and advocacy is to support strengths and offer alternative ways to deal with weaknesses.

Advocacy

Like support and education, advocacy is a process that depends on the role the caregiver has with the intimate. In common usage an *advocate* is one who pleads the cause of another. Sometimes the vicissitudes of the illness and demands on the intimate overwhelm that person or the system, or problems are insufficiently addressed by the resources at hand. In such situations, the caregiver can direct, if not take actual steps to ameliorate, the situation for the intimate. For example, the caregiver might advocate for extended health benefits, speak with a supervisor about the stress an employee is under due to the illness of a family member, and so forth.

Again, the specific role of the caregiver will be instrumental in determining to what extent that caregiver can or will advocate for the intimate. The important point to bear in mind is that, throughout the process of anticipatory mourning, the caregiver can undertake constructive instrumental/informational activities to provide support both for the intimate anticipatory mourner and for the system as a whole.

A FINAL PERSPECTIVE

Although this chapter has outlined the many difficult issues, demands, and situations encountered in the life-threatening or terminal illness of a loved one, it would be incorrect to assume that all sequelae are invariably negative. As illustrated so well by Byock's (1997) work, the end of life can be a time that offers unique prospects for growth, reconciliation, meaning, and spiritual peace. Many survivors can attest to the "gifts" received as a result of their involvement with the illness, dying, and death of a loved one. Reordered priorities, increased communication, enhanced appreciation for life, closer relationships, heightened sensitivity to others, improved self-esteem, and more acute awareness of life's preciousness, brevity, and fragility are among the many positive effects of healthy anticipatory mourning. Caregivers are remiss when they focus exclusively on the demands and overlook the potential in this experience. This is not to dismiss the distress, pain, trauma, and conflict inherent in these circumstances, but rather to assure that they need not dictate ultimate outcome.

REFERENCES

Barton, D. (1977). The family of the dying person. In D. Barton (Ed.), *Dying and death: A clinical guide for caregivers.* Baltimore: Williams & Wilkins.

Bowen, M. (1976). Family reaction to death. In P. Guerin (Ed.), *Family therapy: Theory and practice.* New York: Gardner.

Bowlby, J. (1961). Childhood mourning and its implications for psychiatry. *American Journal of Psychiatry, 118,* 481–498.

Butler, R. (1963). The life review: An interpretation of reminiscence in the aged. *Psychiatry, 26,* 65–76.

Byock, I. R. (1997). *Dying well: The prospect for growth at the end of life.* New York: Riverhead Books.

Caplan, G. (1961). *An approach to community mental health.* New York: Grune & Stratton.

Cleiren, M. (1993). *Bereavement and adaptation: A comparative study of the aftermath of death.* Washington, DC: Hemisphere.

Doka, K. J. (Ed.). (1989). *Disenfranchised grief: Recognizing hidden sorrow.* Lexington, MA: Lexington Books.

Doka, K. J. (1993). *Living with life-threatening illness: A guide for patients, their families, and caregivers.* Lexington, MA: Lexington Books.

Field, M., & Cassel, C. (Eds.). (1997). *Approaching death: Improving care at the end of life.* Washington, DC: National Academy Press.

Figley, C. R. (1983). Catastrophes: An overview of family reactions. In C. R. Figley & H. McCubbin (Eds.), *Stress and the family: Vol. 2. Coping with catastrophe.* New York: Brunner/Mazel.

Figley, C. R. (1985). From victim to survivor: Social responsibility in the wake of catastrophe. In C. R. Figley (Ed.), *Trauma and its wake: The study and treatment of post-traumatic stress disorder.* New York: Brunner/Mazel.

Figley, C. R. (1989). *Helping traumatized families.* San Francisco: Jossey-Bass.

Figley, C. R. (1995). Compassion fatigue as secondary traumatic stress disorder: An overview. In C. R. Figley (Ed.), *Compassion fatigue: Coping with secondary traumatic stress disorder in those who treat the traumatized.* New York: Brunner/Mazel.

Fleck, S. (1975). The family and psychiatry. In A. Freedman, H. Kaplan, & B. Sadock (Eds.), *The comprehensive textbook of psychiatry* (Vol. 1, 2nd ed.). Baltimore: Williams & Wilkins.

Glaser, B. G., & Strauss, A. (1965). *Awareness of dying.* Chicago: Aldine.

Grebstein, L. (1986). Family therapy after a child's death. In T. A. Rando (Ed.), *Parental loss of a child.* Champaign, IL: Research Press.

Heinrich, R., & Schag, C. (1985). Stress and activity management: Group treatment for cancer patients and spouses. *Journal of Consulting and Clinical Psychology, 53,* 439–446.

Janoff-Bulman, R. (1992). *Shattered assumptions: Towards a new psychology of trauma.* New York: Free Press.

Kastenbaum, R. (1969). Death and bereavement in later life. In A. H. Kutscher (Ed.), *Death and bereavement.* Springfield, IL: Charles C. Thomas.

Keeney, B., & Thomas, F. (1986). Cybernetic foundations of family therapy. In F. Piercy, D. Sprenkle, & Associates (Eds.), *Family therapy sourcebook.* New York: Guilford.

Krieger, G., & Bascue, L. (1975, July). Terminal illness: Counseling with a family perspective. *The Family Coordinator,* pp. 351–355.

Lazare, A. (1979). Unresolved grief. In A. Lazare (Ed.), *Outpatient psychiatry: Diagnosis and treatment.* Baltimore: Williams & Wilkins.

May, R. (1977). *The meaning of anxiety* (rev. ed.). New York: Norton.

McCollum, A., & Schwartz, A. (1972). Social work and the mourning parent. *Social Work, 17,* 25–36.

Moos, R. H. (Ed.). (1977). *Coping with physical illness.* New York: Plenum.

Moos, R. H. (Ed.). (1984). *Coping with physical illness: Vol. 2. New perspectives.* New York: Plenum.

Moos, R. H., & Schaefer, J. (1984). The crisis of physical illness. In R. H. Moos (Ed.), *Coping with physical illness: Vol. 2. New perspectives.* New York: Plenum.

Nadeau, J. (1998). *Families making sense of death.* Thousand Oaks, CA: Sage.

Olson, D., Russell, C., & Sprenkle, D. (Eds.). (1989). *Circumplex model: Systemic assessment and treatment of families.* New York: Haworth.

Osterweis, M., Solomon, F., & Green, M. (Eds.). (1984). *Bereavement: Reactions, consequences, and care.* Washington, DC: National Academy Press.

Patterson, J., & McCubbin, H. (1983). Chronic illness: Family stress and coping. In C. R. Figley & H. McCubbin (Eds.), *Stress and the family: Vol. 2. Coping with catastrophe.* New York: Brunner/Mazel.

Pattison, E. M. (Ed.). (1977). *The experience of dying.* Englewood Cliffs, NJ: Prentice Hall.

Pattison, E. M. (1978). The living-dying process. In C. Garfield (Ed.), *Psychosocial care of the dying patient.* New York: McGraw-Hill.

Pincus, L. (1974). *Death and the family: The importance of mourning.* New York: Random House.

Pratt, L. (1976). *Family structure and effective health behavior: The energized family.* Boston: Houghton Mifflin.

Prichard, E., Collard, J., Orcutt, B., Kutscher, A. H., Seeland, I., & Lefkowitz, N. (Eds.). (1977). *Social work with the dying patient and the family.* New York: Columbia University Press.

Rando, T. A. (1983). An investigation of grief and adaptation in parents whose children have died from cancer. *Journal of Pediatric Psychology, 8,* 3–20.

Rando, T. A. (1984). *Grief, dying, and death: Clinical interventions for caregivers.* Champaign, IL: Research Press.

Rando, T. A. (1986). Understanding and facilitating anticipatory grief in the loved ones of the dying. In T. A. Rando (Ed.), *Loss and anticipatory grief.* Lexington, MA: Lexington Books.

Rando, T. A. (1993). *Treatment of complicated mourning.* Champaign, IL: Research Press.

Rando, T. A. (1995). Anticipatory grief and the child mourner. In D. Adams & E. Deveau (Eds.), *Beyond the innocence of childhood: Vol. 3. Helping children and adolescents cope with death and bereavement.* Amityville, NY: Baywood.

Raphael, B. (1981). Personal disaster. *Australian and New Zealand Journal of Psychiatry, 15,* 183–198.

Rolland, J. (1994). *Families, illness, and disability: An integrative treatment model.* New York: Basic.

Rosen, E. (1990). *Families facing death: Family dynamics of terminal illness.* Lexington, MA: Lexington Books.

Russell, C., & Olson, D. (1983). Circumplex model of marital and family systems: Review of empirical support and elaboration of therapeutic process. In D. Bagarozzi, A. Jurich, & R. Jackson (Eds.), *Marital and family therapy: New perspectives in theory, research and practice.* New York: Human Services Press.

Shapiro, E. (1994). *Grief as a family process: A developmental approach to clinical practice.* New York: Guilford.

Shapiro, F. (with M. Forrest). (1997). *EMDR: The breakthrough therapy for overcoming anxiety, stress, and trauma.* New York: Basic.

Strauss, A. (1975). *Chronic illness and the quality of life.* St. Louis: Mosby.

Volkart, E. (with S. Michael). (1957). Bereavement and mental health. In A. Leighton, J. Clausen, & R. Wilson (Eds.), *Explorations in social psychiatry.* New York: Basic.

Walsh, F., & McGoldrick, M. (Eds.). (1991). *Living beyond loss: Death in the family.* New York: W. W. Norton.

Weigert, A., & Hastings, R. (1973, October). *The family as a matrix of tragedy.* Paper presented at the Child Development and Family Relations Meetings, Toronto.

Weisman, A. D. (1972). *On dying and denying: A psychiatric study of terminality.* New York: Behavioral Publications.

Weisman, A. D. (1979). *Coping with cancer.* New York: McGraw-Hill.

Weisman, A. D. (1988). Appropriate death and the hospice program. *The Hospice Journal, 4*(1), 65–77.

CHAPTER 12

Anticipatory Mourning: Challenges for Professional and Volunteer Caregivers

Dale G. Larson

Professional and volunteer caregivers who work with people facing grief, loss, and life-threatening illness have extensive encounters with anticipatory mourning, both in themselves and in the people they care for.* This chapter will examine how these helpers (a) cope with anticipated losses, (b) experience empathic anticipatory mourning, and (c) facilitate anticipatory mourning in patients and their loved ones. After a look at the adaptive and helping challenges these encounters pose, some guidelines for meeting the challenges are offered.

HELPER ANTICIPATORY MOURNING: COPING WITH LOSS

What is anticipatory mourning? A review of the literature on anticipatory mourning in family members, partners, and significant others of hospice patients, people with AIDS, children with terminal cancer, and people with Alzheimer's disease reveals that the concept and its measurement are in an early stage of development (Rando, 1986; Reynolds, Miller, Jelalian, & Spirito, 1995; Rolland, 1990; Rosen, 1990; Walker, Pomeroy, McNeil, & Franklin, 1994, 1996). Basically, the term has been used to refer to almost all the predeath coping behaviors exhibited in these situations. There have been few

---

*The terms *caregiver* and *helper* are used interchangeably to refer to human service workers (e.g., nurses, physicians, social workers, clergy, mental health workers, and hospice staff and volunteers) who provide care to people facing life-threatening or terminal illness. The term *caregiver* is also commonly used for family members, partners, or friends who care for the ill or disabled, and although many of the ideas presented here apply equally well to these laypersons, my use of the term *caregiver* is not meant to include them.

attempts to measure or operationalize *anticipatory grief* (Levy, 1991; Rando, 1983), which is the term previously used to describe what in this chapter and book is termed *anticipatory mourning*. *Anticipatory grief* is reserved for the initial parts of mourning—that is, the reactions to the perceptions of loss. *Anticipatory mourning* will be used to encompass not only these reactions, but also the efforts to cope with and readjust to the loss(es) that gave rise to them. As such, anticipatory mourning inherently assumes anticipatory grief.

Despite its expansive conceptual boundaries, anticipatory mourning has a fundamental meaning that most bereavement experts agree on—namely, that it is a normal mourning reaction to an expected death that allows emotional preparation for the loss (Middleton, Moylan, Raphael, Burnett, & Martinek, 1993, p. 460). Rando further delineates the construct by specifying that anticipatory mourning includes processes of mourning, coping, interaction, planning, and psychological reorganization that are stimulated and begun in part in response to the awareness of the impending loss of a loved one and the recognition of associated losses in the past, present, and future (1986, p. 24). Although a more precise definition of anticipatory mourning is somewhat elusive, it is fairly easy to recognize when it occurs: Openly discussing death, planning for a funeral, saying good-bye, and expressing strong anger or sadness about losing one's life or loved one are some examples of coping behaviors that we intuitively consider expressions of anticipatory mourning.

Although helping relationships are not ongoing *relationships of attachment* (Sperling & Berman, 1994; Weiss & Richards, 1997) like the romantic or family relationships we typically associate with normal mourning reactions, we must not underestimate the significance of the helping relationship—and its loss(es)—for both caregiver and patient. The fact that so little has been written about mourning in the professional and volunteer caregiver, let alone about helper anticipatory mourning, reflects a long-standing bias of researchers against attributing much significance to such experiences. The reasoning beneath this bias must go something like this: For there to be mourning, there must be attachment, and trained helpers are not supposed to become attached to their patients. The helper is the caregiver; the patient is the care-seeker. The flow of caregiving is predominantly unidirectional, and it is the care-seeking patient—if anyone—who experiences attachment and loss in this context. But this formulation fails to recognize that caring, empathic involvement with people in distress naturally leads to the development of relationships with significant personal meaning and investments for the caregiver and that when these relationships end through death, the caregiver suffers real, incontrovertible loss.

At least three conditions can deepen the personal meanings and commitments that such a relationship holds for the caregiver. First, the relationship can span a long period. For example, staff in nursing homes can spend countless hours with elderly patients; pediatric oncology staff often care for a child for many years, living through remissions, recurrences, and often death with the child and the child's family. Second, the anticipation of loss can often increase a sense of attachment (Rando, 1986). Therefore, as death approaches, the caregiver-patient bond can become more significant to both participants. Finally, caregivers often become more deeply emotionally involved with certain patients. For any number of reasons, a particular patient and helping relationship may take on special significance. As Lederberg (1990) notes, this kind of greater involvement (sometimes overinvolvement) with "special patients" is common, and it can lead to more intense, and sometimes unexpected, mourning reactions in caregivers. It can also lead to other internal conflicts, such as feeling guilty about the absence of a special relationship with other patients.

When these three variables coincide—long duration, closeness enhanced by the approach of death, and a special connection—the caregiver's mourning, both before and after the loss, will be correspondingly intense. Intensity can vary widely, but all caregivers who care for terminally or chronically ill patients must learn to cope with the adaptive challenges that these losses present.

The patient's actual death, though often a significant stressor for the caregiver, can sometimes pose fewer adaptive demands than other kinds of losses or stressors that occur in the process of helping. These other losses are rooted in the caregiver's helping goals or commitments (Lazarus, 1991). Caregivers have commitments or stakes in many helping outcomes—for example, achieving good pain control, enhancing quality of life, or facilitating anticipatory mourning. As they assess how well they are achieving these goals, they ask themselves, "Is the family addressing its unfinished business? Am I doing all I can to enhance this person's quality of life?" The outcomes of these appraisals determine to a large extent the amount of stress caregivers experience in their work. If they perceive that they are not moving toward their helping goals and do not see any way to do so, a stress response is initiated. The greater a caregiver's commitment in any of these areas, the more vulnerable he or she is to psychological stress in the area of that commitment (Lazarus & Folkman, 1984, p. 58). Thus, the death of a patient might be less distressing than the way the patient dies because the caregiver is so powerfully invested in making a positive difference in the dying process. The process of helper anticipatory mourning goes beyond mourning the loss of the patient; it can also include confronting a loss of self-esteem, a loss of one's sense of making a difference, or a loss of a principle one believes in.

In the following sections, I examine how professional and volunteer caregivers experience three of the anticipatory mourning processes identified in family caregivers: (a) moving closer while preparing to let go, (b) assisting the dying person, and (c) saying good-bye (Rando, 1986).

Moving Closer while Preparing to Let Go

A key element of the anticipatory mourning process is a dynamic of simultaneously moving closer and preparing to let go (Rando, 1986; Rosen, 1990). This paradoxical process of withdrawing emotional investments and at the same time intensifying them requires, says Rando (1986), "a delicate balance among the mutually conflicting demands of simultaneously holding onto, letting go of, and drawing closer to the dying patient" (p. 24). "Letting go" can mean many things for the caregiver: It can mean letting go of hopes for a medical cure or hopes for an "appropriate death" as well as letting go of a dying patient.

In the context of the helping relationship, this paradoxical process becomes even more complex. The notion of becoming intensely emotionally involved with a patient and being able to let go at the same time can lead to many difficult experiences. For example, consider a hospice worker who is forming a relationship with a patient with a prognosis of 1 or 2 weeks. Each step toward greater intimacy, each discovery of a new quality in the patient, of a way the relationship enriches both participants, becomes more poignant with the awareness of the impending death, and each must ultimately be assimilated as a loss the caregiver must endure.

In a long-term helping relationship, the caregiver's struggles with holding on versus letting go may more closely parallel those of patients' significant others. In this situation, the helping relationship has a history, and a deeper attachment has developed. The caregiver anticipates the loss of the relationship and must cope with the personal losses this death signifies while at the same time moving closer to assist the dying person.

For professional and volunteer caregivers as well as for family caregivers, this dimension of anticipatory mourning can lead to maladaptive, as well as adaptive, outcomes. A family member may disconnect from the dying patient before the death, and this can interfere with that person's expressions of caring and support. Among professional and volunteer caregivers, this same kind of negative outcome can occur when "letting go" becomes instead avoidance. This avoidance can take many forms. The caregiver might avoid developing a deep, caring connection or might shy away from contact with the patient in a variety of ways. Later I will take a closer look at these and other caregiver avoidance behaviors when I discuss the notion of empathic anticipatory mourning.

Helper anticipatory mourning can also be hindered by the responses of the caregiver's peers, friends, and family. Mourning for the impending loss of a patient is an important aspect of anticipatory mourning. Yet there are many ways in which public display of this process is discouraged. In this sense, the caregiver's mourning is disenfranchised grief (Doka, 1989), and strong grief reactions can be met with criticism from peers who interpret these emotions as signs of being overly involved with patients and of not maintaining an appropriate professional stance.

In the face of these responses, every caregiver must nevertheless find a way to mourn the anticipated losses that most affect him or her. If the caregiver can reflect on the significance of a relationship, explore the personal feelings that are present, and discuss them with a supportive colleague, friend, or family member, coping with these losses can be greatly facilitated.

A problem can arise when caregivers conceal their anticipatory mourning. Because few of these hidden mourners share how much the anticipated losses of certain patients are affecting them, each individual caregiver must struggle with the fallacy of uniqueness— that is, the belief that he or she alone has these kinds of reactions (Larson, 1993b). A deleterious chain of events can ensue: Social comparison data are not received, difficulties are not normalized, the stakes involved in confiding are increased, additional help is not sought, and the caregiver becomes further isolated. If, however, the caregiver does talk about anticipatory mourning with supportive colleagues and learns to see it as an inevitable part of the work, constructive action can take place. For example, the caregiver can arrive at a better understanding of the personal significance of the particular helping relationship and, in the time that is left, use this understanding to assist the patient more effectively.

Assisting the Dying Person

For the family member or loved one, assisting the dying person is one way to mourn in anticipation of the impending loss. Such lay caregivers can attend to the dying person's needs, respond to last wishes, listen to feelings, and be a haven of safety and security in this time of crisis. Offering these kinds of assistance requires directly approaching the reality of the loved one's condition—and the loss implicit in this reality—in a constructive manner.

For the professional or volunteer caregiver, assisting the dying person takes many of the same forms and has some of the same significance. By assisting the patient with his or her moment-to-moment needs, the caregiver is directly confronting the patient's declining condition and simultaneously confronting the impending loss as well.

These various ways of helping the dying person also strengthen the helper-patient connection. They are an integral part of the healing relationship because they contribute to the patient's experience of the caregiver as reliable, caring, and responsive. Not just chores or professional responsibilities, they are something more: something rooted in the connection between us all, in the human response to suffering and loss.

Saying Good-bye

As for significant others in the patient's life, saying good-bye is another way caregivers can confront their anticipatory mourning. Although this is generally viewed as a positive coping behavior and as part of an uncomplicated process of anticipatory mourning, it can actually create a conflict for many caregivers. When avoidance wins out in the inner struggle over whether or not to say good-bye to a dying patient, the following kind of experience can result:

> I sometimes have patients who become very close, yet when
> they are getting close to the end, I avoid them. Yes, I want to
> go and talk with them and tell them how special they are to
> me and hold their hands, but I just can't. I had one very
> dear lady that I distanced myself from. After she died, I went
> back to the hospital room where she died, many times, over
> almost a year. I talked with her and told her how much I
> missed her. Why couldn't I do that while she was still alive?
> (Larson, 1993a, pp. 74–75)

This caregiver is struggling with the aftereffects of what might be considered complications in helper anticipatory mourning. The caregiver's responses to her distress are also not adaptive. Her negative ruminative thinking (i.e., regrets over things not said or done, intrusive thoughts, and a tendency to focus on negative feelings) is the type of thinking associated with unfavorable bereavement outcomes (Nolen-Hoeksema, McBride, & Larson, 1997).

Professional and volunteer caregivers, like family members and other loved ones of the dying, can be pulled in contrary directions as they encounter the challenges of anticipatory mourning. We are just beginning to unravel how the outcomes of this process relate to the caregiver's long-term adjustment and health.

The most important guideline for coping with one's own antici-patory mourning as a caregiver is to acknowledge its presence, accept it as part of the work one does, and find supportive col-leagues with whom to share one's experiences safely. Because helper anticipatory mourning is not often discussed, and is even to some degree stigmatized in the professional helping world, normalization of these feelings and acceptance from self and peers are essential. A coping style in which self-doubts and other experiences of personal distress are not confided can increase personal distress, decrease empathy, and possibly compromise the health of the caregiver (Lar-son, 1985, 1987, 1993b; Larson & Chastain, 1990).

EMPATHIC ANTICIPATORY MOURNING

The personal loss when patients die and the losses when helping goals are not met may still not be the most stressful encounters with loss that caregivers face. Perhaps their most challenging encounters with loss occur as they empathically experience all the traumas and mourning of the people they care for. Their empathy, which is at the heart of effective helping, can be a double-edged sword: It is the caregiver's greatest asset as well as a point of true vulnerability.

The Helper's Pit

Empathic anticipatory mourning is empathy for the anticipated, cur-rent, and past losses of patients and loved ones. The helper imagines walking in the other person's shoes and then has a vicarious emo-tional response based on this sensing of the other person's state or condition. Rogers (1957) describes empathy this way: "To sense the client's private world as if it were your own, but without ever losing the *as if* quality—this is empathy" (p. 99). Empathy requires remaining separate while at the same time drawing closer to the other person (a paradox resembling the "holding on while prepar-ing to let go" experienced in anticipatory mourning). If the helper's empathy loses the "as if" quality, he or she risks being dragged into what I call the Helper's Pit.

Emotional involvement as a helper varies not only in intensity but also in the quality and kinds of emotions the caregiver has. The varieties of possible emotional experience are illustrated in the metaphor of the Helper's Pit. Imagine that the patient is in a pit and the caregiver is on its edge. If the caregiver identifies with the patient's problems, what happens? The caregiver falls into the pit! If the caregiver sympathizes, he or she is concerned and compassionate but remains safely on the edge of the pit—sympathy is *feeling for* the person in distress. If the caregiver empathizes, he or she *feels with* the person in the pit and gets inside his or her experiential world (Larson, 1993a, p. 38).

How does one know whether one has fallen into the Helper's Pit or is just intensely emotionally involved with the person in distress? Strong emotions are a natural part of helping people cope with grief, loss, and chronic illness. Almost every veteran caregiver has been visibly moved and cried with someone in great pain and distress. This display of deep feeling almost always strengthens the helping relationship because it shows the patient that the caregiver truly cares. The caregiver can be balanced even while shedding tears, as long as he or she remains focused on the other person and his or her own feelings do not shift from caring to distress. The latter distinction is clarified if we think about the difference between crying and sobbing: When we sob, our attention has shifted to our own distress.

Burnout, Personal Distress, and Vicarious Traumatization

A crucial question concerning emotional balance in caregivers is a long-term one: How can they keep the flame of caring burning brightly within as they continue to make powerful, caring connections with their patients? The hazards of empathic involvement with distressed people are extensively documented in the literature on burnout in the helping professions. The hallmarks of burnout are emotional exhaustion, diminished caring, and a profound sense of demoralization. Frustrated idealism, failing to move successfully toward important personal helping goals, guilt, and self-reproach combine to create a downward spiral, deepening the caregiver's distress and exhaustion. The idealistic, highly motivated, empathic helper is often the first to burn out; after all, a bright flame is, by virtue of its intensity, more likely to burn out (Larson, 1993a).

The burned-out caregiver is personally distressed much of the time. Personal distress is different from empathy and sympathy: In personal distress, one loses one's balance and falls into the pit. Personally distressed caregivers can feel drained, troubled, angry, worried, or grieved. They may "go to pieces," feel helpless in highly emotional situations, or lose control during emergencies (Batson, Fultz, & Schoenrade, 1987). Their caring connections with their patients become weak or even nonexistent as they focus their attention on their own pain, feelings of failure, and other emotional reactions (Thompson, Cowan, & Rosenhan, 1980).

Frustration in the pursuit of helping goals is not the only factor contributing to personal distress and burnout in caregivers working with the dying and chronically ill. Another major contributor is exposure to the high levels of trauma and grief in their patients. How does such exposure affect caregivers? For example, what are the cumulative effects of repeatedly empathizing with mothers of dying children, giving people bad medical news, and listening to the anger and pain of family members who are coming to terms with the impending losses of those they love most?

Recent research and theory on vicarious traumatization or compassion fatigue in trauma workers (e.g., rescue workers and therapists who treat victims of trauma and disaster) shed light on the dynamics and cumulative effects of such exposure. Pearlman and Mac Ian (1995) describe vicarious traumatization as a "transformation that occurs within the therapist (or other trauma worker) as a result of empathic engagement with clients' trauma experiences and their sequelae" (p. 558). According to Pearlman and Mac Ian, repeated exposure to graphic depictions and processing of traumatic events while one is empathically engaged with patients can lead to psychological distress and disrupted cognitive schemata in the areas of safety, trust, intimacy, self-esteem, and power. Like the trauma victim (Janoff-Bulman, 1992), the trauma worker must struggle to develop new mental schemata to replace those shattered by the traumatic event.

Figley (1995) uses the terms *compassion fatigue* and *secondary traumatic stress disorder* to describe these same phenomena. He agrees that "the process of empathizing with a traumatized person helps us to understand the person's experience of being traumatized, but, in the process, we may be traumatized as well" (p. 15).

Wilson and Lindy (1994) point out that "sustained empathic inquiry," which they consider the sine qua non of psychotherapy with traumatized persons, is not easy to maintain as aspects of the trauma are introduced into the therapeutic encounter. Left unmanaged, "empathic strain" can lead to a rupture of empathy and a loss of therapeutic role for the helper. Wilson and Lindy argue further that helpers are often subject to strong countertransferential processes in these situations and must be alert for them (p. 7). Countertransference reactions in the therapist can lead either to avoidance, distancing, and detachment reactions or to tendencies to overidentify and become overinvolved with the client (p. 16). Similarly, Massie, Holland, and Straker (1990) note that in response to the complex psychological stressors of oncology, staff can become caught in the dynamics of either rescue (emotional overinvolvement) or withdrawal (emotional distancing).

Extremes of closeness and distance are the endpoints of a continuum of emotional involvement on which all caregivers constantly move back and forth. Personal distress occurs at both poles of the continuum. The two poles are vividly described by a nurse who said, "I feel either like I am encased in steel [the distant, uninvolved position] or like my skin has been ripped off [the overly involved position]." Most veteran caregivers have experienced both ends of the continuum. When caregivers cannot maintain their emotional balance, when their empathy loses the "as if" quality or becomes hollow and detached, and when personal distress derails a sustained empathic focus on the patient, they fall into the Helper's Pit, and their helping is severely compromised.

The derailment of empathy, and with it of the helping relationship, is often expressed in psychological and physical distancing by caregivers. In a study of helper secrets (i.e., self-doubts, strong emotions, and other experiences of personal distress related to the caregiver's work that are kept inside and not confided) reported by 495 nurses, I found that the most common secret concerned wanting to distance oneself emotionally or physically, or actually having done so, from patients, patients' families, staff, or one's own family members (Larson, 1987). This distancing took many forms: Becoming emotionally distant, ignoring patients' needs, not visiting difficult patients, and feeling cold and unsympathetic are just a few examples. However, these efforts to decrease stress had the reverse effect because they led to feelings of self-doubt, guilt, and personal and professional inadequacy. These outcomes make this style of coping an untenable long-term stance. The stress-avoidance-guilt sequence is reflected in the following disclosure from that study: "I feel guilty that my care-giving has become more emotionally distant. It seems I am protecting myself. I don't want to give so much of my energy to others' lives or my work" (p. 24).

Coping with Personal and Universal Loss

Our capacity for empathy is rooted in the emotional knowledge of loss. As Szalita (1976) observed, "Empathy becomes more accessible as we come to grips with fears of death. Confrontations with sorrow, grief, and bereavement are always painful, but often engender a more compassionate attitude toward others and a commitment to life" (p. 151). However, in empathic anticipatory mourning, the double-edged nature of empathy again stands out: Losses deepen empathy, yet as one struggles to look openly and courageously at some of the most frightening of human experiences, reminders of personal pain can push one either toward avoidance or into the Helper's Pit.

Extant research can tell us something about the interaction between a helper's personal history and vulnerability as a caregiver.

Pearlman and Mac Ian (1995) found that trauma therapists with personal histories of trauma showed more negative effects from their work than those without such histories. However, we do not know whether their helping and empathic engagement were also adversely affected. It is possible that these more distressed helpers were the best helpers, despite having suffered themselves.

In another study, hospice volunteers with lower scores on a measure of death anxiety continued working in the hospice program longer than volunteers with high scores. This finding suggests that those with high death anxiety had greater difficulty keeping their emotional balance (Amenta, 1984).

It has also been found that people can work through their own losses and fears of loss by participating as caregivers. Palliative care nurses working with the terminally ill have more positive attitudes toward death and less death anxiety than nurses who do not work regularly with the dying (Brockopp, King, & Hamilton, 1991).

Raphael and Wilson (1994) note that rescue workers experience "*identificatory empathy*, grieving for the human condition for other human beings devastated by this event, and for themselves within this context" (p. 339) even when the victims involved are not personally connected to them. Working with dying and chronically ill patients in high-mortality settings, where the presence and awareness of suffering and pain are pervasive and bereavement overload (Kastenbaum, 1977) is common, requires a balanced, empathic engagement with both immediate and more universal dimensions of loss. No satisfactory prescription for this kind of balanced expanded empathy exists. It must surely be something like what Lief and Fox (1963) describe as "detached concern"—a state of being emotionally involved and yet at the same time maintaining a certain emotional distance, of being united but also separate. It must also begin with an acceptance of one's own vulnerability and losses, and then it can grow to include compassion for the pain of all human beings.

Thus, the adaptational process of the caregiver exposed to such mortality and morbidity includes a kind of personal grief work— mourning not just the losses that have already occurred in one's life but those that inevitably lie ahead as well. As is often said, when we cry at funerals, we are also crying about our own deaths. This personal grief work, though fraught with pain and difficulties, can also be a source of growth for the caregiver. Lederberg (1990) observed that if oncology workers make it through an initial, difficult phase of adaptation, which includes adjusting to working in settings where loss is commonplace, they are likely to have satisfying careers.

The likelihood of positive adaptation is increased if caregivers (a) have exceptional stress management skills that will help them maintain emotional balance (Larson, 1993a), (b) know their limitations and the "emotional buttons" they possess that can lead to idiosyncratic (i.e., countertransferential) responses to trauma and loss, (c) have excellent interpersonal helping skills, and (d) have and use strong social support systems.

FACILITATING ANTICIPATORY MOURNING

In addition to personal and empathic anticipatory mourning, there is another way professional and volunteer caregivers encounter anticipatory mourning. This encounter occurs as the caregiver facilitates anticipatory mourning in the patient and the patient's loved ones. The facilitation might take the form of coaching anticipatory mourning in the family (Rosen, 1990), doing a life review with a dying patient, helping a spouse plan for life after widowhood, or any number of similar interventions.

Empathy is essential to all these interventions, and most of the dynamics and challenges of empathic anticipatory mourning discussed earlier in this chapter apply here. However, successfully facilitating anticipatory mourning poses an additional challenge: The caregiver must decide which specific coping processes to encourage and which to discourage. This is necessary because coping processes differ widely in their therapeutic potential, from highly adaptive to highly maladaptive.

Fortunately, some preliminary guidelines for making these decisions are emerging from research in the stress, coping, and bereavement areas. At the broadest level, an emerging theme in stress and coping research is the overall adaptive advantage of approach over avoidance in coping with stressful events. Approach coping includes such behaviors as cognitive reappraisal, seeking of guidance and support, and active problem solving. Avoidance coping includes behaviors like distancing, engaging in fantasy and wishful thinking, and emotional discharge (Moos & Schaefer, 1993). In general, when difficult and threatening experiences are actively faced, new dimensions of personal growth and improved health result, although illusory optimism and distraction can sometimes, in small doses, be adaptive (Larson, 1993a; Roth & Cohen, 1986; Taylor & Aspinwall, 1993).

Thus, the general principle of supporting approach coping versus avoidance coping can be a touchstone for interventions meant to facilitate anticipatory mourning processes. Patients and family members must be supported as they struggle actively to approach the frightening and difficult experiences of anticipatory mourning.

We saw earlier how this principle also applies to the caregiver's coping processes. The caregiver must be able to approach the often intense emotions of anticipatory mourning, and there is no anxiety-free, easy way to accomplish this task. The seduction of short-term relief (e.g., through avoidance) must be resisted if one is to achieve long-term helping goals.

Research has also begun to pinpoint some of the coping processes that determine bereavement outcomes. In a recent study, four teams of investigators separately examined the bereavement narratives of 30 gay men whose partners had died of AIDS within the past month (Folkman, 1997). Numerous coping processes were examined and related to measures of bereavement outcome. Among the findings were that self-analysis and negative rumination were associated with poorer adjustment (Nolen-Hoeksema et al., 1997), whereas positive appraisals or interpretations by the survivors about what had happened, what they had done, and how they felt about what had happened predicted less depression and more positive well-being at bereavement and better recovery 12 months later (Stein, Folkman, Trabasso, & Christopher-Richards, 1997). Studies like this can aid in the development of models for adaptive coping throughout the grief trajectory, from anticipatory mourning processes to postdeath coping responses.

Although research findings like those just presented offer some general guidelines for facilitating anticipatory mourning, the caregiver still faces the daunting challenge of distinguishing the therapeutic processing of feelings from emotional discharge, healthy life review from negative rumination, acceptance of loss from emotional withdrawal, and, in general, approach from avoidance coping.

The much larger ongoing debate about whether anticipatory mourning is good for one's health, or for the quality of the life that remains for the patient, will not be answered until systematic outcome studies are conducted. Only a handful of preliminary studies exist (Levy, 1991; Rando, 1983), and more are sorely needed. Future empirical work must include measures that permit a more fine-grained analysis of the individual's emotional, cognitive, and behavioral coping responses and that can be related to current models of stress and coping processes.

The following vignettes (Larson, 1999), which show caregivers facilitating anticipatory mourning, convey some of the poignancy and adaptive potential of this process. In the vignettes, the caregivers sensitively encourage patients and family members to say good-bye, finish unfinished business, confront and work through loss, and prepare family members for a future that does not include the mate or child:

I was called when an elderly patient was dying. At the bedside were six granddaughters. They had decided not to call their mother to come for her sake, but would all stand together during those last hours. They were weeping. I suggested to them that since their grandmother could still hear and knew they were present that they should share some of the fun times they had with their grandmother through the years. For almost two hours they shared stories, laughing and crying together.

A rather young patient of ours had a real problem accepting his deteriorating condition and terminal diagnosis. He carried on with us and with his family as if everything would be OK, and he was going to get better. Shortly before he lapsed into semiconsciousness, he told me how much he liked me and what a wonderful nurse I was. He then proceeded to cry out in anguish, "Make me better . . . do something . . . help me . . . I don't want to die." He sobbed afterwards, almost uncontrollably. I held him in my arms. I had to tell him that I couldn't make him well. At that moment I learned what touching one's very soul really meant.

A family was having great difficulty accepting their father's death. One by one they would talk to me, trying to convince me to say he was getting better. However, I tried to point out his progressive disease and encouraged them to spend time with him and allow him to express his feelings to them. After a period of time they started to open up with their dad and on the Sunday before he died—Father's Day—he had each of his children in to tell them why he was proud of them. Later, the children told me how special that day was to them.

A final vignette beautifully captures the work of facilitating anticipatory mourning:

I was involved with a young family. He was dying and she had been a protected wife with two small children. I was able to support and assist this wife and husband to grow and change throughout the dying process. By the time her husband died, all their work was done, and she was able to become independent. She told me, "I think I can do it now."

CONCLUSION

For the patient and family members, anticipatory mourning often begins at the moment of diagnosis. For the professional or volunteer caregiver who cares for these people, the encounter with anticipatory mourning usually begins with the initial helping encounter. Anticipatory mourning challenges professional and volunteer caregivers on many fronts. The caregiver must (a) deal with personal losses encountered in the care of people with terminal or chronic illnesses, (b) find a way to remain empathically engaged with the anticipatory mourning of patients and their loved ones without succumbing to burnout, and (c) facilitate adaptive anticipatory mourning processes in the people he or she is caring for. Although the challenges are great, learning how to cope with them can make the caregiver a more effective and balanced helper. Haan (1993) suggests that confrontations with stress can make one more "tender, humble, and hardy" (p. 259). This most surely is true of the caregivers who maintain their sense of compassion while courageously assisting others to live with hope in a world in which loss is inescapable.

REFERENCES

Amenta, M. M. (1984). Death anxiety, purpose in life and duration of service in hospice volunteers. *Psychological Reports, 54,* 979–984.

Batson, C. D., Fultz, J., & Schoenrade, P. A. (1987). Distress and empathy: Two qualitatively distinct vicarious emotions with different motivational consequences. *Journal of Personality, 55,* 19–39.

Brockopp, D. Y., King, D. B., & Hamilton, J. E. (1991). The dying patient: A comparative study of nurse caregiver characteristics. *Death Studies, 15,* 245–258.

Doka, K. J. (1989). Disenfranchised grief. In K. J. Doka (Ed.), *Disenfranchised grief: Recognizing hidden sorrow.* Lexington, MA: Lexington Books.

Figley, C. R. (1995). Compassion fatigue as secondary traumatic stress disorder: An overview. In C. R. Figley (Ed.), *Compassion fatigue: Coping with secondary traumatic stress disorder in those who treat the traumatized.* New York: Brunner/Mazel.

Folkman, S. (1997). Introduction to the special section: Use of bereavement narratives to predict well-being in gay men whose partners died of AIDS—Four theoretical perspectives. *Journal of Personality and Social Psychology, 72,* 851–854.

Haan, N. (1993). The assessment of coping, defense, and stress. In L. Goldberger & S. Breznitz (Eds.), *Handbook of stress: Theoretical and clinical aspects* (2nd ed.). New York: Free Press.

Janoff-Bulman, R. (1992). *Shattered assumptions: Toward a new psychology of trauma.* New York: Free Press.

Kastenbaum, R. J. (1977). Death and development through the life span. In H. Feigel (Ed.), *New meanings of life.* New York: McGraw-Hill.

Larson, D. G. (1985). Helper secrets: Invisible stressors in hospice work. *American Journal of Hospice Care, 2*(6), 35–40.

Larson, D. G. (1987). Helper secrets: Internal stressors in nursing. *Journal of Psychosocial Nursing and Mental Health Services, 25*(4), 20–27.

Larson, D. G. (1993a). *The helper's journey: Working with people facing grief, loss, and life-threatening illness.* Champaign, IL: Research Press.

Larson, D. G. (1993b). Self-concealment: Implications for stress and empathy in oncology care. *Journal of Psychosocial Oncology, 11*(4), 1–16.

Larson, D. G. (1999). *Great moments in caregiving.* Unpublished manuscript.

Larson, D. G., & Chastain, R. L. (1990). Self-concealment: Conceptualization, measurement, and health implications. *Journal of Social and Clinical Psychology, 9,* 439–455.

Lazarus, R. S. (1991). *Emotion and adaptation.* New York: Oxford University Press.

Lazarus, R. S., & Folkman, S. (1984). *Stress, appraisal, and coping.* New York: Springer.

Lederberg, M. (1990). Psychological problems of staff and their management. In J. C. Holland & J. H. Rowland (Eds.), *Handbook of psycho-oncology: Psychological care of the patient with cancer.* New York: Oxford University Press.

Levy, L. H. (1991). Anticipatory grief: Its measurement and proposed reconceptualization. *The Hospice Journal, 7*(4), 1–28.

Lief, H. I., & Fox, R. C. (1963). Training for "detached concern" in medical students. In H. I. Lief, V. F. Lief, & N. R. Lief (Eds.), *The psychological basis of medical practice.* New York: Harper & Row.

Massie, M. J., Holland, J. C., & Straker, N. (1990). Psychotherapeutic interventions. In J. C. Holland & J. H. Rowland (Eds.), *Handbook of psycho-oncology: Psychological care of the patient with cancer.* New York: Oxford University Press.

Middleton, W., Moylan, A., Raphael, B., Burnett, P., & Martinek, N. (1993). An international perspective on bereavement related concepts. *Australian and New Zealand Journal of Psychiatry, 27,* 457–463.

Moos, R. H., & Schaefer, J. A. (1993). Coping resources and processes: Current concepts and measures. In L. Goldberger & S. Breznitz (Eds.), *Handbook of stress: Theoretical and clinical aspects* (2nd ed.). New York: Free Press.

Nolen-Hoeksema, S., McBride, A., & Larson, J. (1997). Rumination and psychological distress among bereaved partners. *Journal of Personality and Social Psychology, 72,* 855–862.

Pearlman, L. A., & Mac Ian, P. S. (1995). Vicarious traumatization: An empirical study of the effects of trauma work on trauma therapists. *Professional Psychology: Research and Practice, 26,* 558–565.

Rando, T. A. (1983). An investigation of grief and adaptation in parents whose children have died from cancer. *Journal of Pediatric Psychology, 8,* 3–20.

Rando, T. A. (1986). A comprehensive analysis of anticipatory grief: Perspectives, processes, promises, and problems. In T. A. Rando (Ed.), *Loss and anticipatory grief.* Lexington, MA: Lexington Books.

Raphael, B., & Wilson, J. P. (1994). When disaster strikes: Managing emotional reactions in rescue workers. In J. P. Wilson & J. D. Lindy (Eds.), *Countertransference in the treatment of PTSD.* New York: Guilford.

Reynolds, L. A., Miller, D. L., Jelalian, E., & Spirito, A. (1995). Anticipatory grief and bereavement. In M. C. Roberts (Ed.), *Handbook of pediatric psychology* (2nd ed.). New York: Guilford.

Rogers, C. R. (1957). The necessary and sufficient conditions of therapeutic personality change. *Journal of Consulting Psychology, 21,* 95–103.

Rolland, J. S. (1990). Anticipatory loss: A family systems developmental framework. *Family Process, 29,* 229–244.

Rosen, E. J. (1990). *Families facing death: Family dynamics of terminal illness.* New York: Lexington Books.

Roth, S., & Cohen, L. J. (1986). Approach, avoidance, and coping with stress. *American Psychologist, 41,* 813–819.

Sperling, M. B., & Berman, W. H. (Eds.). (1994). *Attachment in adults: Clinical and developmental perspectives.* New York: Guilford.

Stein, N. L., Folkman, S., Trabasso, T., & Christopher-Richards, A. (1997). Appraisal and goal processes as predictors of well-being in bereaved caregivers. *Journal of Personality and Social Psychology, 72,* 872–884.

Szalita, A. B. (1976). Some thoughts on empathy. *Psychiatry, 39,* 142–151.

Taylor, S. E., & Aspinwall, L. G. (1993). Coping with chronic illness. In L. Goldberger & S. Breznitz (Eds.), *Handbook of stress: Theoretical and clinical aspects* (2nd ed.). New York: Free Press.

Thompson, W., Cowan, C., & Rosenhan, D. (1980). Focus of attention mediates the impact of negative affect on altruism. *Journal of Personality and Social Psychology, 38,* 291–300.

Walker, R. J., Pomeroy, E. C., McNeil, J. S., & Franklin, C. (1994). Anticipatory grief and Alzheimer's disease: Strategies for intervention. *Journal of Gerontological Social Work, 22,* 21–39.

Walker, R. J., Pomeroy, E. C., McNeil, J. S., & Franklin, C. (1996). Anticipatory grief and AIDS: Strategies for intervening with caregivers. *Health and Social Work, 22*(3/4), 21–39.

Weiss, R. S., & Richards, T. A. (1997). A scale for predicting quality of recovery following the death of a partner. *Journal of Personality and Social Psychology, 72,* 885–891.

Wilson, J. P., & Lindy, J. D. (1994). Empathic strain and countertransference. In J. P. Wilson & J. D. Lindy (Eds.), *Countertransference in the treatment of PTSD.* New York: Guilford.

PART III
Applied Cases

CHAPTER 13
Anticipatory Mourning and Prenatal Diagnosis

Donna Jeane Hitchcock Pappas

"Are you having a boy or a girl?" This innocent question posed to expectant parents marks a fundamental way in which pregnancy has changed. Prior to the advent of prenatal diagnosis, there was news of a pregnancy, and in 9 months a baby was born. The identification of a birth defect took place after the birth. With today's technology, it is possible to identify birth defects prenatally. There are sometimes decisions to be made with the information available to expectant parents. The detection of a potential problem in utero may give them an opportunity to prepare emotionally for the anticipated outcome. On the other hand, it may instead spiral them into a course of emotional upheaval (Zuskar, 1987). When prenatal diagnosis results in the identification of a potential problem, a structural defect, or a chromosomal abnormality, how can practitioners bring into context the experiences of expectant parents who receive this news? This chapter uses the theory and research on anticipatory mourning as a matrix to provide clinical perspectives and strategies for therapists who work with clients experiencing this significant life event.

CURRENT OPTIONS AND DILEMMAS

For many, prenatal diagnosis is a double-edged sword. The state of technology can pressure expectant parents into choosing prenatal diagnosis without providing many options for treatment, particularly in utero (Gregg, 1993). However, there are times when the information derived can influence treatment options or the management of the pregnancy (Zuskar, 1987). Whether pregnant women feel a covert pressure to access prenatal diagnosis is open to question. However, the experience of pregnancy has changed. A decision against prenatal diagnosis has consequences. If a birth

---
✳

To all my Pappas boys, especially Jim, who has always been there for me, and J. P., who was with us for such a short time but has impacted our lives so enormously

defect that could have been identified prenatally is found at birth, then the mother must come to terms with the fact that she could have known. A decision about prenatal testing entails balancing the risk of the procedure and the need to know (Kolker & Burker, 1993).

Clearly, technology has changed the landscape surrounding pregnancy. At present, the following are options available prenatally.

Alpha-fetoprotein (multimarker) screening. At between 16 and 18 weeks' gestation, a pregnant woman may choose to have her blood drawn for a multiscreen test (American College of Obstetrics and Gynecology [ACOG], 1991). The results of this test indicate the pregnant woman's risk of having a baby with a neural tube defect, Down syndrome, or Trisomy 18 (American College of Medical Genetics, 1994). This test is not diagnostic; it can yield false positive results: A pregnant woman may receive results that show her to be at risk, yet further prenatal testing (i.e., ultrasound and/or amniocentesis) may not find the potential problem.

Ultrasound. Today, ultrasound is an expected part of obstetric care (Chescheir, 1996). Ultrasound is the standard way of detecting structural birth defects in utero. The technological advances in equipment, coupled with the advanced skills of ultrasonographers, have improved the ultrasound as a diagnostic tool. Performing an ultrasound at 15 to 18 weeks can ensure reasonably adequate views of the fetal anatomy. It is at this time that structural defects may be detected. These include defects of the central nervous system (i.e., anencephaly and spina bifida), congenital heart defects, urinary defects, and skeletal abnormalities (Sabbagha, 1993).

Chorionic villus sampling (CVS). Chorionic villus sampling (CVS) is a prenatal test available in the first trimester. It is performed at 10 to 12 weeks' gestation. When test results indicate abnormal findings, the family has the option of terminating the pregnancy before physical signs of pregnancy become overt (Kuller, 1996).

Amniocentesis. Amniocentesis is the primary technique used to diagnose genetic disorders (Elias & Simpson, 1993). The growing fetus sheds cells into the amniotic fluid surrounding it in the uterus (Eisenberg, Murkoff, & Hathaway, 1988). A needle is inserted into the amniotic space and fluid is removed. The cells from the fetus are then tested for genetic defects. Common defects found are Trisomy 21 (Down syndrome), Trisomy 18, and Trisomy 13. The standard period during which amniocentesis is performed is 15 to 18 weeks' gestation (Cabiness, 1996). Early amniocentesis can be performed at 12 to 14 weeks.

For most people choosing it, prenatal diagnosis is a means to gain reassurance about the baby. If the multiscreen test shows an abnormal result, ultrasound and amniocentesis can let them know that everything is normal.

Parents have told me that they expect it will always be the other person whose baby has a problem. Therefore, even when on one level parents are concerned, on another level they do not believe it can happen to them. For this reason, when expectant parents are told of a problem, they experience shock and trauma. It is a moment when everything changes. They talk about life before the news and life afterward.

When parents receive news of a disturbing prenatal diagnosis, they often become overwhelmed by the information. Intervention begins at the moment the diagnosis is given. Frequently, the information will be delivered by the patient's obstetrician or by a perinatologist, a physician who specializes in prenatal diagnosis. Because this is a moment that will change the couple's lives forever, attention must be given to small details, such as having the parents sit down rather than stand. Because the parents' filter systems will quickly become overwhelmed, it is important to pace the delivery of information and to repeat information several times. Often, parents are told the diagnosis and then return home immediately afterward. Over the next few days, as they are ready, more information can be given. For many, the adjustment involves learning a whole new language—"medicalese."

After the shock of the diagnosis, the couple begin to absorb the information. This process can take weeks. In some cases there may be external time pressure from a medical standpoint to assimilate complex information and make decisions (Fonda, Allen, & Mulhauser, 1995). Ideally, there should be a partnership between the clinician and the family, and this partnership should determine the pace at which information is provided.

During the time from diagnosis forward, a couple has the opportunity to prepare emotionally and medically for the birth of their baby (Palmer, Spencer, Kushnick, Wiley, & Bowyer, 1993). This preparation includes making decisions about the pregnancy, the delivery, and—for some parents—even the way they want their child to die. A mother who was expecting twins and knew that one had a lethal renal abnormality had two requests. She wanted to be sure she would be able to see and hold her twins together, and she asked to be placed in a room with a window. She said that she wanted her son to see the sky before he died.

IMPLICATIONS OF KNOWLEDGE OF A PRENATAL DIAGNOSIS

When parents are told there is a problem with their baby, one of their first questions is "What does this mean for the baby?" There are a number of possible scenarios. In some cases, the identified problem indicates the necessity of surgery after birth, with the strong likelihood of total recovery. In other situations, parents may learn that the anomaly found is a lethal defect, which means that the baby will die at birth; an example of this is anencephaly. Still another possibility is learning that problems are evident on the ultrasound but that it is unclear exactly what the problem is or what it may mean for the baby. Sometimes a diagnosis is known, but the outcome is still uncertain; this is the case with Trisomy 21 (Down syndrome). Although a diagnosis can be given, the parents cannot be told what precisely it will mean for their baby because there is a range of possible functioning. Finally, when rare chromosomal abnormalities are detected, the parents are informed but, because of the rarity of the condition, may not be able to receive information about the impact of the chromosomal change on their baby. Thus, given the current status of genetic research, parents may receive disturbing data without knowing exactly what to do with it.

Many parents learn more than they ever wanted to know about medical conditions. On-line access has given people great freedom in accessing information. However, there is no quality control filter for on-line information. One role of the health care professional is to help parents sift through the information. This must be done carefully because there is danger of an adversarial relationship if parents perceive the health care professional as being an "information watchdog."

When bad news is delivered, the parents expect that the next step is to talk about what will be done about the problem. In some cases, indeed, the problem can be "fixed." However, in even more cases, a problem exists and there is nothing to do about it. Some parents wrestle with the decision whether to continue or interrupt the pregnancy. Even if the problem is not lethal, parents face a deadline by which they must make a decision if they are to have the option of termination. Some couples want to wait and see how things progress in the pregnancy before they make a final decision. For others, the decision is easy: There is no question about continuing the pregnancy regardless of the possible outcome. One woman whose baby was identified with a lethal skeletal problem said that she and her husband never discussed the choices. They both moved forward to address how they were going to manage the rest of the pregnancy.

Parents who do entertain options think about the baby's quality of life (such quality of life, of course, being personally defined), the impact on the children they already have, the impact on the couple's relationship, the financial aspects of the situation, and the medical care aspects. With the nature of medical insurance changing at a rapid pace, parents want to know about the coverage that will be available for their child, both in the short term and in the long term. Unfortunately, nobody can give them the answer. This in itself is anxiety provoking.

Whatever decision a couple makes about their baby after a prenatal diagnosis, it is an intensely personal decision with consequences that they must live with forever. For parents choosing to end the pregnancy, the diagnosis, decision making, and termination happen at a quick pace. Frequently, the events take place within a couple of weeks. Such parents report that only afterward do they mourn the loss of their baby. For those who choose to continue the pregnancy because the diagnosis came too late for termination to be an option, there is a period of adjustment until the baby's birth. This time of preparation, reflection, and anticipation revolves around the realization that this birth will not be what was imagined.

ANTICIPATORY MOURNING AND ITS LOSSES

Rando asserts that in *anticipatory mourning* (previously termed *anticipatory grief*) the past, the present, and the future are mourned (see Rando, chapter 2 in this volume). As parents come to terms with the news of a problem while their baby is still in utero, all three aspects of mourning take place.

Losses in the Past

A woman may mourn the loss of her identity as the mother of a healthy baby. Many women say they just assumed they would have healthy children. Motherhood is so integral to their identities that they fear they will never fulfill this important part of who they are. Couples who have delayed conception frequently reflect with sadness that things might have been different if they had just not waited so long. Any ambivalence about the pregnancy, even that experienced in the early stages of an unplanned pregnancy, can result in a flood of emotion, blame, and regret. Parents may worry that their ambivalence caused their baby's problem. They mourn the loss of innocence. One woman said, "I want to go back to the time that I believed everything would be OK."

Losses in the Present

When parents learn of a problem in utero, their attention naturally becomes focused on the diagnosis and what it means for the baby. Consequently, they become active parents at a much earlier stage than most expectant parents. As the acuteness of the initial diagnosis diminishes, the couple must deal with the ongoing pregnancy, but the knowledge of the diagnosis has changed the present. Often, in view of the baby's significant health problems, it seems shallow to the parents to permit themselves to be sad about the loss of their pregnancy as they had imagined it would be. Parents can fully explore this part of anticipatory mourning only when they know that it is a natural part of the process.

Parents are in love not only with the idea of having a baby but typically with being pregnant and all the things surrounding pregnancy. As committed as a couple may be to continuing a pregnancy, they must alter the way they are doing things and the way they are thinking about the pregnancy.

Frequently, parents struggle with how much to tell family, friends, and co-workers about the problem with the pregnancy. The positive side of sharing the news is receiving additional support through a difficult period. On the other hand, couples talk about the difficulty of managing the flow of information to family members and friends. Imparting information can take enormous energy. Every time there is a doctor visit to check the status of the baby, there are multiple phone calls to make that require repetition of the same information. For some, telling people adds an additional burden. One woman said that at such times she would need to comfort her family and that she just did not have the energy. Another couple wanted to wait until after the birth, when they would have a more definitive diagnosis, before telling anyone. For couples whose family members are geographically distant, friends often become the family-like support systems to which they turn.

Practical matters must be considered as well. One expectant mother said that she did not know what to do about her work. She was uncertain how she would manage to go to her job each day and function. Yet, from a financial standpoint, she could not afford not to work.

Another difficult issue that a couple may face is how much to prepare for the baby. Should they begin to buy things for this baby? Should they set up the nursery? Should they have a baby shower? Obviously, there are no correct answers to these difficult dilemmas. One couple just wanted to wait and see what happened. One woman, even though her baby was at great risk of dying at birth, proceeded with attending to all the usual preparations. She believed that this was her way of letting her baby know that she expected everything to turn out fine.

As we can see, all the little things associated with being pregnant are what a couple mourns. The essence of the pregnancy has now changed. All of these things are parts of the process of anticipatory mourning.

Losses in the Future

As pregnancy progresses, a couple's attention shifts from managing the details of the present to imagining life in the future. The diagnosis of a birth defect can create a great black hole where a wonderful planned future once existed. In a first pregnancy, the man and woman are beginning to cope with the transition in their lives and roles (Duval, 1977). As part of anticipatory mourning, they may begin to deal with the ways their roles as parents may be different from what they had imagined. If the baby is expected to die at birth, the couple's parenting takes place during the pregnancy. If the baby may be hospitalized for a time after birth, there is the issue of the mother's preparing to leave the hospital without the baby in her arms. When the diagnosis indicates developmental disabilities, there is often a shifting of the parents' expectations for the child and the way they had believed they would live their lives. Some parents use this time to contact appropriate organizations and parents with children in similar circumstances. For them, dealing with grief and mourning involves preparation and education. Another response may be to stay in the present without looking too far in the future. Whether awareness is actively addressed or suppressed, the fact exists that the future is altered. Part of the couple's anticipatory mourning focuses on the dreams of the future that are now forever changed.

UNIQUE ASPECTS OF PRENATAL ANTICIPATORY MOURNING

A unique feature of anticipatory mourning around prenatal diagnosis is that it encompasses a family's major developmental stage (Duval, 1977). This is particularly true with a first pregnancy. However, even the entry of a subsequent child represents a milestone and a change in the family's existence. If nothing else, the couple may see that entry into parenthood is not as simple as once was thought. Parents often say that they never imagined anything would be wrong with their baby. They talk about their loss of innocence. They are amazed that others they know coast along without concern or worry about a pregnancy. And they know they can never return to that place again.

Anticipatory mourning means that a person whom you care about is dying or has a devastating disease that will change him or her so that the person you knew and loved no longer exists. When parents receive a discouraging prenatal diagnosis, they mourn the person they imagine would have been. Unlike the situation when a family member or friend is dying, the parents do not have a history of memories to reflect on. Instead, they mourn hopes and dreams. Also, the person to be mourned is not in a room somewhere for the family to visit and be with. This tiny being is yet within the mother, the ultimate caretaker.

The Pregnant Mother

Four general tasks have been identified for a pregnant woman: (a) seeking safe passage for herself and her child through pregnancy, labor, and delivery; (b) ensuring acceptance by significant persons in her family of the child she bears; (c) bonding with her unborn child; and (d) learning to give of herself (Rubin, 1975). In the situation precipitating anticipatory mourning, the first task is unattainable. The next two tasks are often difficult. The woman is forced into the fourth task without the preparation time a normal pregnancy provides. This mother must actively advocate for her baby in a way that normally is not necessary until after the baby is born.

The mother's process of attaching to the baby is related to the degree to which the pregnancy was planned (Hughes, 1987). This process begins earlier for a woman who had little ambivalence about pregnancy than for one who experienced great ambivalence. A woman who is still coming to terms with her ambivalence may receive news of the prenatal diagnosis just as she is beginning to attach to her pregnancy. Parents' ability to visualize their baby physically (often via ultrasound), along with their perception of activity in utero, marks a point of parental awareness of this baby as a separate and unique being, and elicits a sense of closeness. Notwithstanding this fact, from a clinical standpoint, experience has shown that it is difficult to make absolute statements about the nature of parents' attachment to and bonding with their baby. For some, that relationship begins prior to conception. For others, it requires the physical feeling of the presence of the baby.

Some men have difficulty identifying with their babies until the time of birth. The reality for the mother is that the baby is constantly with her. This reality is often a source of comfort for the mother, yet it also can add to her stress. One woman observed that her husband could go to work and essentially escape for a while the reality that their baby was so sick; she could not put her uterus on the shelf in the morning and go to work.

Although carrying a baby and caring for an ill person are different, the sense of having to be "on" is similar. However, a caregiver to an ill family member or friend usually can get some type of respite, perhaps from other loved ones or from a formal system like hospice. The pregnant woman has fewer options to turn "off." Sometimes, a woman struggles to take responsibility for the life inside her and come to terms with the diagnosis. One woman, knowing her baby was going to die at birth, decided to have a glass of wine in the evening—something that she would never have done with a healthy baby. She said she still loved her baby; it was her way of coming to terms with the diagnosis and beginning to let go.

Personal and Gender Differences

Because the physical experience of pregnancy is quite different for a woman and a man, the mother and the father often have different levels of attachment to the baby. When a couple receives the news of a poor diagnosis, the parents' qualitative experiences of anticipatory mourning will differ, along with the intensity of their anticipatory mourning. As mentioned, the man typically has the safety valve of work for an escape. He may be quite frustrated at witnessing his wife's roller-coaster emotions and at being powerless to make things right for her or for their baby. One man, at the end of a meeting with a physician about the possible diagnosis and probable outcomes for his unborn child, angrily said that he had not come to the medical center for an opinion. He had come for an answer. Suddenly, the neat package with "the" answer does not exist.

Couples talk about the rhythm of their mourning during this time of anticipation. Some have commented that they took turns being down. One woman, noting that she was always the more optimistic one whereas her husband was the pessimist, said that she had to keep herself balanced so she could help him actively during his low times.

The need for information varies for each member of the couple. One person may want to know everything that can be known. In fact, this desire is often less about finding information per se and more about occupying time and feeling that one is doing something. As with any life crisis, the style of the couple's relationship and the patterns of communication will most probably be reflected throughout this life experience.

Other Children

When the family includes other children, the mother and father not only must confront all the emotional upheaval of their own anticipatory loss, they must face as well the emotional ramifications of this life crisis for their already born children. Parents often mention being very guarded, often secretive, about what is happening as the diagnosis is unfolding. They need time to digest the news before they can inform their children. For a very young child, who can barely grasp the concept of a new baby, it probably will be quite difficult to comprehend the problems. However, children do know intuitively when there is something wrong in the family. Withholding the information too long leaves children wondering and anxious about what is transpiring. For most children, such uncertainty and anxiety are far worse than distressing news.

One couple's strategy was to use the time they had during the pregnancy to disclose the information gradually. Their children were preschool and early elementary ages. Although the parents knew that the potential outcome of the pregnancy could be the death of the sibling, they chose not to begin with this information. They first told their children that the doctor was worried the baby was not growing big enough inside the mother. They said that this meant the parents would be needing to return and have the doctor check on the baby, just as they did when one of the other children was sick. As the weeks progressed, the parents continued to unveil more information: "The baby's heart is not working. The doctor may not be able to fix it. You know when a toy breaks and we cannot fix it?" This couple did a marvelous job of providing a framework of anticipatory mourning from a child's perspective.

For another family, knowing that a birth defect meant the baby would not look physically normal at birth led them to communicate to their other children that there was a problem but that everything was going to be OK. While preparing their children, they also wanted to normalize the experience and the baby. Tragically, the baby—a boy—died at birth of an undetected lethal heart defect. A subsequent pregnancy about 2 years later was extremely stressful for the parents and their 8-year-old daughter. Their stress multiplied when this baby, too, was diagnosed with a heart defect. Although this heart defect could be surgically repaired, the reality for the little girl was that babies with heart problems died. As the parents struggled with their own demons around those very same issues, it was difficult to ask their daughter to take in much more information. They tried to reassure her quietly, but they felt hesitant about how far to go. They themselves were not sure how much they could trust. They were sad that their daughter not only had been robbed of one brother already but also had missed out on the joy of anticipating a new sibling.

Extended Family and Friends

As a couple awaits the outcome of a prenatal diagnosis, the sense of loss and the experience with anticipatory mourning ripple out to extended family and friends. Grandparents-to-be juggle the overwhelming emotions elicited by watching the transformation of what should be the happiest time in their children's lives and their need to cope with their feelings vis-à-vis their expected grandchild. For some grandparents, there may be mistrust of the technology and disbelief in the diagnosis. This attitude can compromise their ability to prepare for and mourn the loss. Other extended family (e.g., siblings, aunts, uncles) and friends may have invested in the pregnancy. Although their mourning does not approach the level of the parents', it still is very real. If these individuals have children of their own, they often can appreciate the magnitude of the loss as they extrapolate from their parental feelings to what it must be like for the expectant parents. For people who have not begun families, the loss is a reminder of what everyone knew potentially could happen but thought happened only to strangers.

As they come with their own sad feelings, family and friends wonder how they can support the expectant family. In the best-case scenario, they ask how they can help; they state that they are not sure what to say or do but that they want the family to indicate how to be of assistance. In the worst-case scenario, they impose their own opinions, wishes, and desires upon the anticipatory mourners. Quite hurtful are family members and friends who just disappear and never make any contact during this difficult time or its aftermath.

ISSUES COMPLICATING ANTICIPATORY MOURNING

At times there are roadblocks to the anticipatory mourning processes. Absence of choice is one of them. In many situations, parents actively choose to access information prenatally. For some, a diagnosis is found during the management of the pregnancy. Couples who have no choice but to continue pregnancy because of a late diagnosis express regret (Sandelowski & Jones, 1996). For them, mourning becomes difficult. Their focus is on what could have been rather than what is happening now.

Ambivalence is another issue complicating anticipatory mourning. If the mother had mixed feelings about the pregnancy, her energy may focus on her ambivalence. Coinciding with this phenomenon may be feelings of guilt. The mother thinks, "If I had only wanted my baby, this would not have happened." The belief that thoughts and feelings caused the problem can be deeply rooted. When there is a family history of a problem, family members struggle with guilt. One father with a congenital heart problem was devastated when he and his wife learned through prenatal ultrasound that their baby had a heart problem. It was not totally clear that there was a link between the fetal problem and the father's heart problem. Nevertheless, in the father's mind, such a link existed.

No one can predict what it will feel like to hear the diagnosis of a problem and what the reaction will be. A deeply religious couple received the news that their baby had Down syndrome and significant heart problems. Although termination was against their religious beliefs, they considered it. In the end, they chose to continue the pregnancy, and the mother became clinically depressed. She had difficulty bonding with the baby she was carrying. Six weeks prior to delivery, at a friend's urging, she began to bond with the baby and let it into her heart. In retrospect, this mother is very disappointed in herself. She hates the way she felt early in her pregnancy. She has difficulty seeing the journey she made and understanding that what matters is where she ended, not where she began.

THE IMPORTANCE OF HOPE

What keeps a couple going as they try to manage all the pieces of this horrendous life crisis? Hope. Hope is ever present as long as there is some life left. For some, it may be hope for a miracle. One mother, when Down syndrome was diagnosed in her fetus, did not want any more information. She said she would pray for her baby to be cured. The genetic counselor working with her worried what would happen when the baby was born and there was no miracle. Would she think that she had not prayed enough or had not done it right? Concerned, the genetic counselor called the mother after the birth. She discovered that this woman saw the fact that her baby did not have a heart defect as the answer to her prayers.

Sometimes the health care community confuses hope with denial. In the case of one couple, no fluid was detected early in the pregnancy (at 14 weeks). Problems with the kidneys were detected by ultrasound. A dismal prognosis was pictured. Nevertheless, the couple decided to continue the pregnancy. Throughout the pregnancy, the physicians and nurses would continually revisit the diagnosis and prognosis with the couple. The counselor on staff was called to see them out of concern that the couple "just was not getting it." When asked, the couple could relate the medical details and the prognosis, yet they were committed to this baby and to giving the baby every chance possible. The mother said that to continue to carry this baby, she had to reserve some hope that maybe the experts were wrong. This hope did not preclude the couple's speaking to the neonatologist and having a frank discussion about the care of the baby postdelivery. When the baby was born, and after the evaluation of the baby took place, the couple declined intrusive medical care that ultimately would not have changed the outcome.

For a family dealing with a diagnosis that requires monitoring throughout the pregnancy, there is constant challenge to maintaining hope. A day or so before each scheduled appointment, the stress and anxiety begin to build. One woman recalled that every visit had meant hearing worse news. It was a relief to the couple when they went to one appointment and learned that everything looked the same. To them, this was good news. For another mother, hope was shaken by a change in the diagnosis. The doctors had outlined the worst-case scenario and told the couple that at least they did not have to contend with that situation. However, later in the pregnancy, that worst-case scenario became the diagnosis. The mother said that she had never expected to be dealing with the worst case; that understanding had been the one thing she had held on to. For her, there was still some hope, but it was not the same.

Hope can be intertwined with reality. One couple, told that their baby would most likely die because of a chromosomal abnormality, began during the pregnancy to make plans for the funeral. They researched funeral home costs, and they discussed how they would like to handle the service. Meanwhile, they also researched and found cases of survival. They searched out and talked to the parents of these children. This couple was able to visit both places. When the baby died at birth, they felt both prepared and at peace.

TREATMENT IMPLICATIONS

For the medical community and society at large, there is no turning back to the time when parents had no information prenatally. In fact, with the human genome project, there is an increase in the volume of available information. Even today, at some for-profit labs, expectant parents are offered a menu of possible genetic tests, including testing for cystic fibrosis and other hereditary diseases. And these procedures are offered to people without any family histories of those disorders! The burden of deciding whether to know or not to know may accelerate anticipatory mourning to a point we just cannot imagine.

Even though a disturbing prenatal diagnosis constitutes an intense life crisis, parents usually do find ways to return to their lives. Pursuing normal life is a way of taking a vacation from the diagnosis. As a family navigates through this time, the support of surrounding people is not only helpful but therapeutic. Clearly, health care personnel are in a unique position to facilitate anticipatory mourning (Rando, 1983). The advance knowledge permitted in this situation allows for a measure of control, and with this control, long-term coping can be optimized (Fonda et al., 1995). As clinicians, we can help families by acknowledging the changes in the way pregnancy is experienced. When there is bad news, we can provide information and support. We can guide couples through the choices and decisions they must face.

The challenge of the health care team involved in the mother's care during the pregnancy after a problem has been identified is to ensure that communication is consistent and information complete. This communication should occur across the various disciplines and specialties with which the family has contact.

How can the family access the system and to whom should they speak if they have concerns or questions about what they are being told? The ideal situation for communication includes a case manager who can help the family negotiate the system. Early on, parents will need to know how information will be provided and that throughout the course of the pregnancy different health care professionals may have different interpretations of the problem and the best ways to manage it. Whoever is in a position to communicate with the family must recognize that new information may disrupt a delicate equilibrium the family has established within this crisis. Although they may seem fine, it may be days after they receive a new piece of information before the family can reestablish this balance.

The reactions, responses, and needs of each family are unique. They will decide how they will fold this news into the fabric of their lives. As clinicians, we give families information and guidance; in return, families tell us how to provide appropriate support at any given moment. The most important tool we have is not some high-tech medical device. Instead, it is simply listening. As we listen, we should ask ourselves, "What will the memory of this experience be for the family?" and "What role during this most difficult time can I play in creating a memory that will be positive upon reflection years from now?"

Although receiving a negative prenatal diagnosis is an incredibly emotionally draining experience, when asked in retrospect if they are glad they knew, parents typically say that knowing was helpful. The process of anticipatory mourning brought many of these people to a place where they would not have been otherwise. Although the process involved pain and sadness, it also allowed them to parent in ways they would have missed if they had not known. In this way, their healing also began.

REFERENCES

American College of Medical Genetics. (1994). *CMG position statement on multiple marker screening in women 35 and older.* Bethesda, MD: Author

American College of Obstetrics and Gynecology. (ACOG). (1991). *Alphafetoprotein* (ACOG Technical Bulletin No. 154). Washington, DC: Author.

Cabiness, M. (1996). Amniocentesis. In J. Kuller, N. Chescheir, & R. Cefalo (Eds.), *Prenatal diagnosis and reproductive genetics.* St. Louis: Mosby.

Chescheir, N. (1996). Overview of obstetric sonography. In J. Kuller, N. Chescheir, & R. Cefalo (Eds.), *Prenatal diagnosis and reproductive genetics.* St. Louis: Mosby.

Duval, E. N. (1977). *Marriage and family development* (5th ed.). Philadelphia: Lippincott.

Eisenberg, A., Murkoff, H., & Hathaway, S. (1988). *What to expect when you're expecting.* New York: Workman.

Elias, S., & Simpson, J. (1993). Amniocentesis. In J. Simpson & S. Elias (Eds.), *Essentials of prenatal diagnosis.* New York: Churchill Livingston.

Fonda, J., Allen, J., & Mulhauser, L. (1995). Genetic counseling after abnormal prenatal diagnosis: Facilitating coping in families who continue their pregnancy. *Journal of Genetic Counseling, 4,* 251–265.

Gregg, R. (1993). Choice as a double-edged sword: Information, guilt, and mother-blaming in a high-tech age. *Women and Health, 20,* 53–71

Hughes, C. B. (1987). Assessing the pregnant family. In L. N. Sherwin (Ed.), *Psychosocial dimensions of the pregnant family.* New York: Springer.

Kolker, A., & Burker, M. (1993). Grieving the wanted child: Ramifications of abortion after prenatal diagnosis of abnormality. *Healthcare for Women International, 14,* 513–526.

Kuller, J. (1996). Chorionic villus sampling. In J. Kuller, N. Chescheir, & R. Cefalo (Eds.), *Prenatal diagnosis and reproductive genetics.* St. Louis: Mosby.

Palmer, S., Spencer, J., Kushnick, T., Wiley, J., & Bowyer, S. (1993). Follow-up survey of pregnancies with diagnoses of chromosomal abnormality. *Journal of Genetic Counseling, 2,* 139–151.

Rando, T. A. (1983). An investigation of grief and adaptation in parents of children who have died from cancer. *Journal of Pediatric Psychology, 8,* 3–20.

Rubin, R. (1975). Maternal tasks in pregnancy. *The Journal of Maternal Child Nursing, 4,* 143–153.

Sabbagha, R. (1993). Ultrasound diagnosis of fetal structural anomalies. In J. Simpson & S. Elias (Eds.), *Essentials of prenatal diagnosis.* New York: Churchill Livingston.

Sandelowski, M., & Jones, L. (1996). Healing fiction: Stories in the aftermath of the detection of fetal anomalies. *Social Science Medicine, 42,* 353–361.

Zuskar, D. M. (1987). The psychological impact of prenatal diagnosis of fetal abnormality: Strategies for investigation and intervention. *Women and Health, 12,* 91–103.

CHAPTER 14
Dealing with the Chronic/Terminal Illness or Disability of a Child: Anticipatory Mourning

Joyce Ashton
Dennis Ashton

With today's technology, an increasing number of children are being discharged from hospitals with complex medical plans, involving sophisticated equipment and treatment regimens in which families are expected to participate. More than 20 million children are living with a chronic and/or terminal illness or disability (Heaman, 1995). Most children with chronic illnesses or disabilities will live into adulthood (Angst & Deatrick, 1996).

Anticipatory mourning, previously termed *preparatory* or *anticipatory grief*, is the process of preparing for an upcoming death. Parents of a child with a chronic illness or disability may fear that they will walk into their child's room one morning and find the child no longer breathing. Families of a terminally ill child work toward accepting death as inevitable.

To understand the intense grief felt at the time a diagnosis or prognosis is given, it is helpful to understand the developmental processes parents and children experience: claiming, entitlement, bonding, and attachment.

PARENTAL CLAIMING, ENTITLEMENT, BONDING, AND ATTACHMENT

The moment one fantasizes about becoming a parent, certain expectations, hopes, and dreams begin to form. These dreams may begin in childhood. A child plays with a doll or stuffed animal, pretending to love, protect, and nurture it as his or her own. Rarely do these fantasies include bearing or parenting a child with disabilities or serious illnesses.

At conception, hopes and dreams become a reality, as parents begin the process of *claiming:* "Will we have a boy or girl? Should we move to a bigger apartment? Will the baby be here by the holidays? When should we take off work?"

Often parents celebrate the pregnancy by buying baby clothes or decorating the nursery. Every time they see someone with a baby or a child, they envision themselves as parents, holding, rocking, strolling, swinging, or throwing a ball to their own child. Names may be chosen, or money put aside, as they feel a strengthening sense of *entitlement.* As the baby starts to grow and develop, parents begin to envision their future. They may hear the heartbeat and feel the baby move and kick. Although mothers feel the movement and most often experience *bonding* before fathers, fathers too are forming *attachments* and making plans. Finally, with the ultrasound appointment, parents see their baby! When the long-awaited day of birth comes, they watch the little body emerge. At last, they can hold, kiss, and smell their *own* baby! They are flooded with overwhelming feelings of love, protection, concern, and joy.

Let's now consider the 25% of parents who do not carry their child to term or whose baby is born ill, disabled, or dead.

CONTENDING WITH A CHILD'S ILLNESS OR DISABILITY

The Diagnosis

Receiving the diagnosis of a disability, terminal illness, or chronic illness is an overwhelming experience for anyone. Many parents' initial reactions are similar to the reactions of parents who are informed that their child has died suddenly. They find themselves experiencing acute grief. This traumatic experience, for many, will also satisfy the DSM-IV diagnostic criteria for acute stress disorder (American Psychiatric Association, 1994).

> *I couldn't believe it! Not me, not us! I closed the drapes, took the phone off the hook, and cried and cried. My child, my child, what do I do now? How can I care for him? Why us? I was so afraid, how can I do this? What IS ahead? What is going to happen, to me, to my child?*

> *When I was given the initial diagnosis of leukemia by our pediatrician, I felt like I was in a huge hole, trying to keep my composure so I could call my husband. When the diagnosis was*

*confirmed by specialists, I was overcome with hopelessness and
dread.*

Perinatal Diagnosis and Demise

More than 250,000 babies are born each year with one or more birth
defects—about one in every 13 births. One in four pregnancies is lost.
With advances in medical technology, many serious diagnoses are
made before a child is even born. Armed with this advance knowledge, parents and professionals today face many difficult choices.

> *We were told our baby was incompatible with life and would die
> before, during, or shortly after delivery. I was still a few months
> from term. The doctor asked us, Did we want to continue
> carrying the child or interrupt the pregnancy to aid my own
> health? How can I choose when to end my child's life? How can I
> cope with such a decision? I wish I didn't even have a choice. I
> just want my baby!*

A parent's mourning after a serious perinatal diagnosis or
demise may become "complicated" or "chronic" due to the following factors:

1. A high degree of personal investment in the pregnancy, emo-
    tionally or financially

    *I had two in vitro fertilization pregnancies. Both failed. I was so
    hopeful the second time because we had seen a healthy fetus and
    heartbeat on ultrasound! Each procedure cost about 10,000
    dollars. It was devastating!*

2. Prolonged infertility

    *I had three tubal pregnancies. The first one took my right tube,
    and the third one my left. The hardest part for me is knowing I
    cannot conceive again.*

3. The age of the mother

    *I am 40 years old and had been trying for years to conceive.
    When I finally got pregnant, we were thrilled! Although I only
    was pregnant a few weeks, I had planned my whole life around
    this baby. I was heartbroken when I miscarried. My time is
    running out, and I wonder if I will ever be a mother.*

4. No medical explanation for the demise

    It is confusing for many parents who have lost a child not to
    receive an explanation for the death. We assume medical tech-
    nology and doctors have the knowledge to prevent, or at least to

explain, why a child has died. Cognitively, individuals cannot process their loss as successfully when there is no known cause or reason for why their child is no longer a part of their lives.

We had tried for 2 years to have a child. Now, I was 2 weeks over my due date, and I knew any minute I would be holding a baby! During the night I had several contractions off and on; however, by morning the baby had stopped moving. Fear gripped us as we anticipated something might be wrong with our baby. When we arrived at the hospital, no heartbeat could be found. A few hours later, after much pain and pushing, I delivered a beautiful baby girl, almost 7 pounds. She looked perfect. However, she was dead. A reason was never found. I was in shock for days! Sadness and despair set in. It was a sorrow I had never felt before.

5. Delayed diagnosis

   Often physicians delay sharing an unfavorable diagnosis. They, too, have insecurities. They want to make sure that they are correct first, or they may fear how parents will react to and cope with the news. In some instances, parents may have sensed before the doctor that something was wrong. They may wonder why the doctor took so long to give them a diagnosis. Like parents, health professionals experience a type of anticipatory mourning. They may need to assimilate what the diagnosis means to them, as well as to their patients. Some bury their emotions as a way of coping with and avoiding professional burnout. This tendency causes some professionals to appear cold, uncaring, and distant. These reactions may be masking their own uncomfortable emotions and anticipatory mourning.

Additional factors that may complicate the mourning process include the family's coping skills, as well as members' personality styles, psychological health, beliefs, values, history of losses, and belief that the current loss was preventable.

Testing and Procedures

Putting together all the facts for a diagnosis can take time. It may require extensive testing, poking, X rays, CAT scans, or other procedures as parents sit in specialists' waiting rooms. All this usually represents additional money and pain for both parents and child.

Our daughter was too compromised to undergo the sedation for an EMG and muscle biopsy, so she just had an MRI and blood test. This was done right after our first unsuspecting visit to the pedi-neurologist. He sent us immediately to the pedi-ICU with a very

*probable terminal diagnosis. . . . The MRI was so loud, and us
alone with that big machine, it felt so surreal, as though we were
the only two people in the world—that nobody cared about us.*

Hearing the Diagnosis

Hearing the diagnosis and/or prognosis can bring some relief by
eliminating confusion and uncertainty.

*Strangely, I was relieved in a sense knowing she wouldn't have to
live for years and years not being able to even sit up or move a
muscle. I would rather [she had] died at the time of diagnosis
than live longer and be in pain.*

For others, the painful truth and reality can be overwhelming.

*I'm sick, I'm scared, I'm bitter. Why couldn't the test be normal?
My soul is in an awful state. . . . NO ONE KNOWS MY PAIN.
Help me, Lord. Help me, Christ. Help my daughter, give me
peace. Let me know, let this baby be normal, please, please, please!*

Withdrawal

The process of anticipating a diagnosis, hearing it, and accepting it is
draining. Some are left alone to cope with the details. Others choose
solitude, trying to sort out what the diagnosis means. Some may
want to talk about the diagnosis over and over again, obsessively trying to reconstruct and alter the reality of their lives, while others lack
the ability or energy to even explain the details accurately to family
and friends. Social withdrawal is common. Parents may become
completely consumed with testing, doctors, and treatments.

*I was so tired and overwhelmed most of the time. It became more
and more difficult to get out. My son became harder and harder
to load in the car and take places.*

Denial and Disbelief

Other parents may not be able to accept or believe, for a time, what
the diagnosis or prognosis means for them or their child.

*I received the diagnosis of cerebral palsy for my child when he
was about 1 year old. He looked so healthy and happy, and
continued to grow and develop. He tried so hard to sit, move, roll,
drag himself, and to stand holding on, I knew he would learn to
walk someday! He was determined, too! I wasn't ready, for many
years, to accept that he would spend most of his life in a*

*wheelchair. I wasted time searching for the right treatment and
cure. When he died, I wished I had spent more time with him,
not trying to make things different.*

Parents' present reactions to the diagnosis or prognosis will be
directly correlated to their level of understanding and current phase
of grief recovery. In the beginning, most children and parents fight
for life. They seek a cure or at least hope for a lengthy remission.
During this phase of the illness, it is perfectly normal for them to
deny that death is coming.

> I am still in denial of my child's cystic fibrosis. I tell the
> doctors that one day they'll do his sweat test and it will be
> negative. There are times when I feel that I would sell my
> soul to cure him. Money is not the issue. I ignore the
> diagnosis in a way, in order to get through a day without
> depression and tears. (Ashton, 1996, p. 19)

It may take exposure to additional opinions, information, or time in
order for families finally to realize the magnitude of the diagnosis or
prognosis.

Some parents wonder, "Aren't the medical professionals sometimes wrong?" They spend their lives in search of a miracle cure that
usually doesn't exist. Specialists can help parents find a balance
between services that will help the child and those that will not. A second opinion can help individuals through their disbelief and denial.

Other parents wear "masks," pretending to feel different, and
are unable or unwilling to share their true emotions. This denial
may delay or complicate their mourning.

When the child dies, parents who have remained in disbelief or
denial may be no more prepared for the loss than those parents
who lose a child to sudden, unexpected death. Although painful,
anticipatory mourning can help parents prepare. It can soften
extreme shock and reduce acute grief reactions. Anticipatory mourning provides opportunity for special good-byes, rituals, and celebra-
tions of life. The letting go or detachment (decathexis) can begin.

Some professionals fear, however, that this process may occur
too soon. The concern is that premature detachment may result in
emotional abandonment and withdrawal, leaving a child fearful
and confused.

Accepting the Diagnosis

Anticipatory mourning is most beneficial when one understands
and accepts the diagnosis or prognosis. If a prognosis is not given,
this may delay or complicate the process. Accepting a diagnosis and

giving up hope are not necessarily the same thing. Hopes may be altered and expectations changed along the way. As Pearl Buck wrote in *The Child Who Never Grew:*

> Only to endure is not enough. Endurance can be a harsh and bitter root in one's life, bearing poisonous and gloomy fruit, destroying other lives. Endurance is only the beginning. There must be acceptance and the knowledge that sorrow fully accepted brings its own gifts. (1950, p. 25)

It is very difficult for parents to accept a terminal diagnosis and begin their grief work when they are given any possibility of the child's survival. Any remote chance is a light at the end of a dark tunnel: "We just assumed we would beat this. We never dreamed in the beginning he could really die."

An attitude of beating the odds is common. How very difficult it is when a child relapses or does not survive:

> *He relapsed after the bone marrow transplant. We were told all that could be done had been done. I felt such guilt for what I had put him through all these months. There were blood tests, bone marrow aspirations, spinal taps, radiation, and chemotherapy that made him so sick. I was with him through them all. They were difficult to watch. Now, after all he's been through, it didn't work. I'm angry, nervous, uneasy, and totally devastated.*

Those who lose a child to sudden death often envy parents who have additional time with their child to prepare for death and experience anticipatory mourning. Those who watch their child suffer a long and painful illness may disagree: "There is nothing worse than watching a child you love with all your heart and soul SUFFER."

The loss of a child is a difficult task in any circumstance, and the choice of how or when is not usually ours to make.

THE MOURNING PROCESSES

The mourning processes are an individual experience. With advanced technology and early diagnosis, many begin mourning long before death. Anticipatory mourning can begin as soon as someone suspects something is wrong. Parents' minds may race through all the frightening possibilities as they consider the future and how best to care for their child. In most instances, anticipatory mourning cannot truly begin until disbelief and denial leave. For some, this acceptance occurs with the diagnosis; for others, it develops somewhere farther along the journey toward death.

As Rando asserts in chapter 2 of this volume and elsewhere, anticipatory mourning includes contending with issues from the past, present, and future. Mourning may bring up regrets and feelings of guilt with regard to former life events: "Have I been a good parent? Did we do all we could for our child? Were the testing and diagnostic procedures the best available? Did we wait too long to seek medical care?"

Parents may mourn the present mounting losses as the illness causes additional changes in daily life. They may watch helplessly as each new day brings pain, wasting away, and additional challenges for their child. They mourn a future once filled with hopes and dreams, now lost without their child.

Once a parent or child comprehends the reality of the terminal illness, it is possible to move forward through anticipatory mourning. The mourning experienced with a terminal illness differs from that experienced with a sudden loss. It entails losing someone slowly, "bit by bit" over time (Davies, 1997). Parents are continually assaulted cognitively and emotionally as they try to accept that this child will not be in their future. With sudden death, the child is gone immediately, and parents must assimilate their "new normal" (Limbo & Wheeler, 1986) all at once, without the child at their side. Each circumstance creates a uniquely different set of challenges.

A multitude of factors influence how individuals mourn. Some are as follows:

- The type of illness and how it is viewed ("appropriate death"; Rando, 1984)
- The duration and intensity of pain and suffering
- The age and maturity of the child and other family members
- The nature and quality of the relationship
- The interplay of faith, beliefs, and expectations
- The quality and quantity of support
- The number of past losses and current stressors
- Personality styles and past coping abilities

In addition to these eight factors, the phase of illness the child is currently experiencing influences specific mourning reactions. Acute grief is followed by a chronic phase (Doka, 1997), where family and professionals may be searching for a cure or remission. The chronic phase may last for months or years. If a remission is obtained, the family may return to their former life, hoping the illness is behind them. Unfortunately, for many a relapse follows, and more hopes and dreams are dashed.

The ups and downs of remissions and relapses are extremely draining. However, they do often have a preparatory effect. At some point, the family and child realize the situation is not going to get better. This is the terminal phase. Mourning may be different now, with this new acceptance of impending death.

Most adults and children will experience symptoms of mourning across all five dimensions of the human system (see Figure 14.1). *Intellectually,* individuals attempt to comprehend and understand what is happening. *Emotionally,* reactions appear as intense feelings. *Physically,* anticipatory mourners may become depleted, experiencing physical aches and pains throughout their bodies. *Spiritually,* mourners can become angry at God or begin to search for meaning to make sense out of the event. *Socially,* mourners often withdraw as they lose old identities and eventually reclaim new ones.

Intellectual Aspects of Mourning

A traumatic experience can cause the mind to shut down and be unable to assimilate painful information. One may become confused, disorganized, or disoriented. These intense reactions often result in the inability to concentrate or absentmindedness.

In the beginning, parents may repeatedly go over and over the details of the hurtful event. They ruminate on each bit of information. Intellectually, they are attempting to assimilate, grasp, and understand what has occurred. They may engage in repetitious thoughts in a vain attempt to come up with a different or better diagnosis or prognosis. They hope on a conscious or unconscious level to prevent or alter what has happened. If the child or parents recognize that these reconstructed thoughts are symptoms of the intellectual mourning process, they are less likely to feel they are "out of control," "losing their minds," or "going crazy."

Emotional Aspects of Mourning

Some anticipatory mourners, typically more men than women, try to intellectualize the details of their loss, not permitting themselves to emote. However, emoting can be healing, and some individuals may need help transmitting knowledge from their heads to their hearts.

As the disbelief, shock, and numbness of acute grief leave, parents may become painfully aware of what is happening. Their safe assumptive world has been shattered. Now other emotions follow—depression, guilt, anxiety, and anger. These emotions and the yearn-

FIGURE 14.1

Five Dimensions of the Human System:
Common Grief Reactions

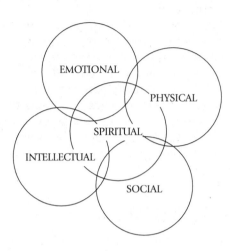

INTELLECTUAL	PHYSICAL	SPIRITUAL
INTELLECTUAL	sadness	**SPIRITUAL**
confusion	denial	impressions
disorganization	anxiety	dreams
lack of	confusion	loss of faith
concentration	fear	increase of faith
intellectualizing		anger at God
disorientation	**PHYSICAL**	spiritual injury
absent mindedness	changes in appetite	questioning values
denial	blurred vision	feeling betrayed by God
	sleep changes	disappointment in
EMOTIONAL	muscle twitches	religious clergy and
shock	restlessness	members
numbness	breathlessness	
anger	heart palpitations	**SOCIAL**
guilt	loss of sexual desire	loss of identity
relief	changes in weight	isolation
depression	headaches	withdrawal
irritability	bowel changes	lack of interaction
loneliness	crying	energy
yearning	exhaustion	loss of ability to
disbelief	dry mouth	function

Note. Adapted with the permission of M. A. Ryan, R.N., M.S., from materials presented at a seminar held by the American Academy of Bereavement, Tuscon, January 1993.

ing for something different can remain with parents for many years and in some instances indefinitely (i.e., as chronic or "shadow grief").

Depression

Sadness, deep sorrow, and depression are normal emotional responses to loss for both children and adults. Depression can influence thoughts, moods, and behaviors. As one parent remarked, "I've lost my song."

Over time, prolonged depression resulting from loss can develop into clinical depression, which can complicate or thwart the mourning process. Parents may be unable to function at home, school, or work. They may not be able to interact with others appropriately or care for themselves or for their ill child.

Guilt

Guilt often emerges with loss. Its exhausting flames can consume any parent. As Bush (1991) notes, "Guilt feelings are often a combination of many different feelings rather than one simple feeling. . . . It's a messy mixture of insecurity, self-doubt, self-condemnation, self-judgement, anxiety, and fear" (p. 2). Many parents have described guilt as their most painful emotion: "If I had just noticed something was wrong and caught it sooner, I know I could have prevented this whole thing, protected my son, and he would be alive today!"

Children experience guilt, too: "If I hadn't said, 'I wished my sister was dead,' she wouldn't be dying now"; "If I had been a better boy, I wouldn't have gotten sick."

Much of what children and adults experience during these early stages of loss is *false guilt*. False guilt occurs when an individual unrealistically feels responsible for another's (or even one's own) misfortune or death: Because of the complexity and potential harm to self and others, professional therapy may be helpful to sort through these feelings.

Anxiety

Anxiety is an intense reaction to loss and fear. Many symptoms can accompany this emotion. The loss of control over one's future is overwhelming and frightening. Sometimes parents may respond by trying to overcontrol. Some parents and children become overactive—unable to sit still, constantly planning or doing something. These activities keep them from thinking about the frightening reality of their lives.

My pulse raced, I couldn't breathe, sit still, or concentrate. I went into overactivity, trying to do a hundred things at once. I got a lot of things done, but my anxiety wouldn't leave me.

Anger

Anger can be a healthy emotion if directed productively. Anger that is repressed, ignored, shelved, or turned toward oneself can lead to depression, confusion, or guilt. Anger can hide other emotions: "When I act mean and angry, it just means I'm sad inside."

Angry parents may strike out at their spouses or health care providers. This is usually a sign of unmet needs or expectations. The loss of a safe, protective world often leads to increased vulnerability and fear concerning future losses.

Physical Aspects of Mourning

The physical symptoms of anticipatory or postdeath grief and mourning are extensive. The acute symptoms may include numbness, heart palpitations, breathlessness, or tightness in the chest or stomach. In addition, changes in bodily functions can occur. Weight and bowel changes are not uncommon. Eating and sleeping patterns can be altered.

With any major loss, the immune system can become depleted or shut down. One study that monitored the immune systems of bereaved parents discovered that three biochemicals were abnormal 3 weeks after the death of their child; levels remained abnormal 8 months later (Spratt & Denney, 1991). Another study showed an increase in illness and death among mourners for up to 2 or more years following their loss (Jackson, 1946).

Spiritual Aspects of Mourning

Spirituality is an integral part of most individuals' lives. It may be expressed personally or through collective religious practices. It may or may not include formal religious worship. Often it is associated with one's relationship to God and the universe. Spirituality provides meaning and purpose to this world and one's place in it. Many individuals successfully nourish their spirituality through formal religious practices and beliefs.

When someone is diagnosed with a terminal illness, that person may turn to spirituality, faith, or religion for strength and comfort. Some who previously did not believe report that their trial turned them to God. Unfortunately, others become spiritually injured. Spiritual injury results when life's realities contradict and/or conflict with previously held spiritual assumptions. Such injury occurs to faithful, good people in all religions.

> *Why did God allow this to happen? I've been a good person all my life. Why does he allow an innocent child to suffer? Why didn't he protect us? I feel judged at church, too. Do they think I caused or deserved this?*

A child may promise or bargain with God: "I will be good, never do anything wrong, pray, go to church, if I can get better."

Parents and children may plead and pray for a miracle or other divine intervention. They may fast and perform healing rituals that are unsuccessful in preserving the life of the child. They may see or hear of others who were healed and question why they did not receive their own miracle. Some blame themselves or question their faith when their child is not cured.

> *I just knew if I prayed hard and believed, God would make my son whole. It's been so hard to understand why He didn't heal him. Doesn't he love us? Are we being punished?*

Such self-talk is one way spiritual injury occurs. In families like these, their world has crumbled, and fear or anger that God is not with them or has failed to protect them complicates the mourning process.

Many parents feel confused, judged, or unaccepted. Others fear that if they don't heal quickly they may be considered weak, unworthy, or unfaithful. If they attend religious services, they often isolate themselves from other church members. Their mourning is further complicated as they turn from family and friends, their faith, and their God.

As quoted in Ashton (1996), the minister Marilyn Dickson says:

> Because having faith is a sense of belonging to God, and is often felt through God's family and servants, mourners may feel great spiritual rejection during grief. The isolation compounded by these negative emotions are usually of no benefit to the bereaved, or their church. (p. 133)

It has been said that we bury more people outside the church doors than in the ground following a funeral.

Many parents and children are confused because they felt their faith would protect or shield them from painful experiences, or at least would help them heal quickly. It is helpful for them to understand that their responses to grief are normal and do not indicate a lack of faith. Parents can miss a child intensely, even when they have faith that they will see their child again in an afterlife. Faith and belief alone are seldom sufficient to eliminate the need to mourn: "It's like you're on a desert and you are dying of thirst, and someone says, 'Yes, you can have a drink, but not for thirty years!'" (Edwards, 1989, p. 151).

Social Aspects of Mourning

Clearly, loss affects mourners' behaviors and how they function and interact socially. A child and parents' social lives can be forever altered by the child's disability or by a chronic or terminal illness. Identities and self-esteem can be changed or lost for each family member. Social interactions outside the family are affected, as well as those within. In some instances, everything and everyone have to be put on hold. Some parents will have to relinquish former responsibilities or their careers to care for a child full-time. One mother quit her job to care for her daughter, as her daughter's health declined: "I thanked God every day for giving me the strength to give her my time unconditionally. I felt very fortunate to be part of her life."

Other parents rush to help their child live the fullest life possible in the relatively short time the child has remaining to function or live: "After a serious incident, I thought my disabled child was going to die. He recovered, and I promised myself we were going to make the most of the time we had left together!"

Socially, children go through many changes with an illness. These social changes are secondary losses. Some cannot attend school or church with their peers. Others lose their identities as cheerleader, computer whiz, football star, and so forth. They may not be able to go bowling, skating, or to the movies with their friends.

At home, assumptions and expectations about these children may change. They may no longer have chores and responsibilities around the house. They may see a brother or sister doing the things they used to do. These interactions can cause confusion, stress, fear, guilt, anger, and irritability within the family.

Interpersonal and psychosocial changes can become overwhelming; finding an appropriate balance is not an easy task for families.

> I'm pretty miserable. I'm sad, I'm frustrated, I'm angry, and I'm trying to figure out what I have done so wrong in my life to deserve so many bad things. Now my son's behaviors are going from bad to worse.

HELPING THE FAMILY COPE: CLINICAL INTERVENTIONS

Health care providers can offer families a variety of self-help tools and clinical interventions. Many families are searching for help and readily accept offers of support. Others will not be as amenable to interventions. Health care providers can serve as guides, offering ideas. However, making use of these tools and responding to the interventions is ultimately the responsibility of each family member.

Before discussing specific interventions, we must first consider a more general question: how and when to include the child in the diagnosis and prognosis. A child may be aware of his or her diagnosis from the onset. The degree of knowledge and timing of disclosure will depend on the child's age, developmental maturity, and emotional stability. Disclosure also will be influenced by the parents' experiences, expectations, beliefs, and past styles of coping. The child initially may have reported signs and symptoms of the illness, or the absence of feeling well. Children often watch their parents' reactions and coping styles to determine their own.

Professionals generally encourage parents to inform the child of the diagnosis within 24 hours (Rando, 1984). To the extent that a family's communication style has been open in the past, this disclosure will be easier. Families who don't share feelings and tend to deal with problems individually probably will have difficulty acknowledging the illness and its impact (Wolfelt, 1996). Such families may need additional intervention to break the traditions of silence and secrecy.

The advantages of an open communication style are that individuals may respond more fully to the realities of their diagnosis and that doctors can treat the illness more appropriately. An open style also allows those involved the opportunity to plan medical treatments jointly and to make other timely arrangements. If a closed communication style exists, it may complicate the postdeath grief and mourning.

Much progress has been made in our understanding and treatment of the complete human system (see Figure 14.1). Because individuals experience anticipatory mourning and stress intellectually, emotionally, physically, spiritually, and socially, we need to offer self-help tools and clinical interventions in all these areas. Since each dimension affects the others, we need to keep each individual area as strong and healthy as possible. Many individuals will focus on only one or two dimensions and then wonder why they become "stuck," unable to resolve important issues in their mourning.

The following self-help tools and clinical interventions may prove valuable to family members, as well as to friends, relatives, and caregivers.

Intellectual Interventions

It is common for parents to question, analyze, and search for information. The caregiver should offer all the medical information possible. Families should then be encouraged to take time to think and sort through all of the information they have received.

Stress Reduction

Losing a child is likely the most stressful event parents could ever experience. Typically, parents will need to find ways to reduce other stressors in their lives. There will be times when those mourning must stop thinking about their loss and rest their minds, through thought control, meditation, visualization, hypnosis, yoga, or other relaxation exercises. Even the dying child can be taught to use some of these tools:

> I started Lyndsay doing active relaxation with me. We would prop up some pillows and get comfortable—sometimes after a session of giggling and wrestling around. . . . To show her what "relaxed" meant . . . I used her Raggedy Ann. . . . "Breathe in the magic from the air and send it . . . through the body." (Kübler-Ross, 1983, p. 116)

Experiment to find what works best for parents and their child. Most individuals need guidance to find ways to reduce stress during anticipatory and postdeath mourning. Some will try to maintain or resume a full life and will become frustrated or feel failure when the "grief attacks" continue to knock them down. They will need to limit stress and temporarily decrease some of their personal expectations in order to mourn in a healthy way.

> *I found I was unable to concentrate and remember all the things I needed to do. I had to eliminate several of my outside commitments. I just couldn't function like I used to. I required a lot more down time. I wasn't able to perform at my job as well either. This took a long time to accept. It was a secondary loss, in addition to losing my child.*

Journaling/Writing

Journaling is a self-help tool that allows individuals to process their thoughts and thus facilitate mourning. Journaling provides a record of both cognitive insights and changes in emotions. It also provides the evidence some need to recognize subtle improvements and to track their progress. This helps parents and their children recognize even small improvements. Those who write about their traumatic experiences have been found to have fewer illnesses, less time off from work, fewer doctor visits, and a more positive outlook (Sobel, 1997).

Reading and Talk Therapy

Many parents have found it valuable to read. Becoming educated about their child's illness or the mourning process itself can help both parents and children. Reading what others in similar circumstances have felt and experienced may also be useful.

Others need a lot of talk time to process all that is going on emotionally and cognitively. Caregivers, family, or friends may help by lending a listening ear on a regular basis. Some may prefer professional counselors to help them sort through it all.

Control Issues

When parents discover their child is chronically ill, disabled, or dying, the loss of control leaves them feeling vulnerable. As a result, parents, caregivers, or children may begin to overcontrol people and situations in their environment. This may be an attempt to compensate for not being able to control the real circumstances of the illness.

> *I know I am driving my husband and children crazy! They claim I expect perfection from them! I become so frustrated when they don't do what I think they "should." The need to control is an overpowering force since my son died.*

There may be conflicts among parents, relatives, or caregivers as they struggle over the question "Which of us really knows what is best for the child?" Fighting for control can add significant stress to families.

> *I felt the nurses and doctors were keeping things from me. They disagreed with my decision regarding duration of life support and resuscitation measures. I often felt their judgment and unacceptance. I knew they were talking about me. This added so much unnecessary stress in addition to watching my child die. I am still angry and hurt. I am having to work through these issues in addition to the grief of losing my child. I really needed the nurses' and doctors' compassion and support, not their judgment.*

Another said:

> When I finally figured out what I did and didn't have control
> over, I was able to let go of a lot of things. My anxiety left and to
> my surprise those around me quit fighting, too. It seemed I had
> broken the power struggle between us. I actually got what I
> wanted by letting go.

Thought Control

There are times when mourners must put a limit on their worry.
This means that although they need to spend time mourning and
doing grief work, they also need time away from grief. One cannot
spend every waking hour thinking about problems without becoming totally exhausted.

Positive Attitude

It is not the situation that causes our stress but how we view it.
Reframing how one chooses to look at a significant event is not an
easy task. This perception change is referred to as a *paradigm shift*
(Covey, 1991). When one gets stuck in a victim role, depression and
other serious problems can develop. If one can view challenges as
growth opportunities, coping abilities may be enhanced. In this
regard, it is useful to remember Nietzsche's observation that "what
doesn't kill me, strengthens me."

Families can come to understand that even though they have
lost control over some aspects of their lives, they still can be in
charge of their thoughts and feelings. No one can *make* us angry—
we *choose* to feel that way. This is not to suggest that we should stuff
our anger and pretend that it is not there. It does mean redefining
and changing how we look at life's circumstances and tragedies.
When we change our perceptions, we begin to change how we feel.

> I spent a lot of time mourning, doing my grief work, and trying to
> accept the disability and death of my son. I heard a presentation
> on Gratitude Therapy . . . developing an "Attitude of Gratitude." I
> tried to focus more on the positive things in my life; slowly joy
> began to come back into my soul.

In 1950, Pearl Buck wrote of her disabled daughter:

> Why must this happen to me? . . . To this there could be no
> answer and there was none. . . . My own resolve shaped into
> the determination to make meaning out of the meaningless,
> and so provide the answer, though it was of my own
> making . . . her life must count. (p. 26)

Vicklor Frankl survived a Nazi concentration camp. His father, mother, brother, and wife died with millions of other Jews in the gas chamber. In addition to all of these losses, Frankl also endured physical torture. With time, he discovered that although his captors could torment his body, he had control over his mind. He wrote, "Everything can be taken from a man but one thing: the last of the human freedoms—to choose one's attitude in any given set of circumstances" (Frankl, 1946, p. 75).

The way we feel is often a direct result of what we have been thinking. When someone becomes depressed, we may ask that person, "What have you been telling yourself?" It is hard work to talk positively to yourself when traumatic events are going on. It is not easy to alter negative thinking. It may require a professional psychotherapist to help us identify why we choose to think the way we do and to alter erroneous or unhealthy thinking patterns.

Why? What? Where?

Parents are continually trying to find meaning and sort through the "whys" of their tragedy. When both parents and children have processed the "whys" long enough, professionals can help them redirect their focus. Parents may never understand why their child is ill, disabled, or dying. However, they can work on "*What* has happened?" "*What* do we do now?" and "*Where* do we go from here?"

Emotional Interventions

Emotional health affects physical health. When parents discover that their child is chronically ill or dying, many emotions emerge. How these emotions are expressed may decrease or eliminate other emotional, mental, and physical symptoms.

Feeling Is Healing

Health care providers can encourage families to express their emotions. A primary objective of caregivers is to validate feelings. Acknowledging and accepting feelings provides a safe environment and encourages additional emoting.

As quoted in Rosof (1994), nearly three centuries ago Dr. Samuel Johnson wrote, "Sorrow that hath no vent in tears maketh the organs of the body weep" (p. 246). Crying is not the only way mourners grieve; however, it seems to be beneficial physically as well as emotionally. Tears shed during grief in fact have more toxins than do regular tears. Thus, tears actually can be healing (Limbo & Wheeler, 1986).

Processing emotions is an important task in mourning. The following *As* can help individuals deal more successfully with anger or other emotions (Dickson, 1991).

1. ADMIT and validate the feeling. Do not stuff, repress, or bury it deep inside.

2. ANALYZE and cognitively process the feeling and identify where it is coming from.

3. ACT on the feeling through talking, crying, writing/journaling, or following up on issues.

4. ABANDON or accept the feeling.

Grief work takes time. It is the hardest work most will ever do. Families must be encouraged to find the time to think, feel, cry, and talk to one another. Some parents are afraid of the intense emotions they feel. They fear "going crazy" or losing control. Try offering parents a safe place to release their emotions, and then teach them some thought control, which may help them in public places. Encourage them to *think* first, *act* second, then *feel*.

Depression

Situational depression is a normal response to loss; clinical depression is not. Professional therapy and/or medication should be sought when the following symptoms (American Psychiatric Association, 1994) persist for an extended period of time without improvement:

*   A preoccupation with worthlessness or guilt
*   Diminished interest or pleasure in activities
*   Prolonged functional impairment
*   Psychomotor retardation
*   Sadness or irritability most of the day
*   Five percent or more change in weight
*   Fatigue or change in sleeping patterns
*   Inability to think or concentrate
*   Suicidal thoughts

Clinical depression often abates if treated with psychotherapy and medication. Self-help strategies (e.g., exercise, sunlight, journaling, proper rest, and diet) and some natural remedies have been useful to some individuals whose depression is not too severe.

Physical Interventions

If someone is physically fit and healthy, he or she is more successful in enduring emotional and mental stress. It is very difficult to focus on other issues if one is physically ill or in physical pain. Exercise increases endorphins and the re-uptake of serotonin, giving one a feeling of well-being.

While many families will drop everything to care for their ill child, it is important for them to understand the importance of caring for themselves physically as well. Whether in anticipatory or postdeath mourning, it is a good idea for family members to have a routine medical exam. Grief and stress can alter chemicals and hormones, which in turn regulate metabolism, heart rate, digestion, and immune responses. Clearly, our hormonal balance is crucial to our state of mind, and any changes in that balance, whether caused by endocrine diseases or self-imposed by conditions like stress, can radically alter our mood, behavior, and personality (Morgan & Morgan, 1989).

As part of a physical exam, the physician might discuss the following preventive health and life-style practices.

Exercise

Individuals who exercise regularly have more energy, need less sleep, have less depression, and get ill less frequently. Many have found mood boosts from a brisk walk outside. Sunlight and some artificial lights to the iris of the eye also can decrease seasonal depression (Lewy, 1987).

Diet

Health care providers can help mourners understand the importance of eating properly. Keeping a balance in blood sugar levels also affects mood and energy levels. Certain dietary carbohydrates (fruits, vegetables, and whole grains) are thought to increase the quantity of serotonin present within the brain synapses (Ornstein & Swenciconis, 1990). Going several hours without nourishment often leaves one irritable and sluggish.

Sleep

The quality and quantity of sleep affect human brain chemistry. When people are grieving or stressed, they may have insomnia or extreme fatigue. It is important to help individuals return to their normal sleep cycles. Most people sleep 7 to 9 hours each night. Professionals can offer over-the-counter or prescription sleep aids for

short durations if the following self-help tools do not restore normal sleep cycles.

- Unwind before going to bed. This may include a warm bath or
  warm milk, which contains tryptophan, a natural chemical that
  usually causes individuals to feel relaxed and sleepy (Ornstein &
  Swenciconis, 1990).
- Avoid exciting television programs or novels before bedtime.
- Resist napping during the day.
- For parents who find it relieves tension, have sexual intercourse.
- Practice meditation or listen to relaxing music.

Spiritual Interventions

It is critical for caregivers and counselors to understand the importance of focusing clinical interventions where the client is phenomenologically. Assessing this requires listening and time. It would be
unethical to impose one's own belief system and values on a patient
or family. It could also contribute to their spiritual injury and complicate their grief recovery. The caregiver can, however, support and
guide the family in finding their own spiritual meaning. This search
for meaning is a common phenomenon in families as they reconstruct their new life and imagine a future without their child.

If unhealthy magical thinking has become part of this spiritual
redefinition, professionals or clergy may intervene to guide family
members to healthier assumptions. This may entail helping them
come to terms with the reality that life just isn't fair. As expressed in
the Book of Matthew (5:45), they may need to come to recognize
that it rains on both the just and the unjust and that bad things happen to good people (Kushner, 1981).

Many terminally ill children and their parents have spiritual
experiences. These can include impressions, thoughts, feelings, fore-
bodings, dreams, visions, or visitations. These spiritual experiences
can act as *death preparations* and play an important role as individuals deal with anticipatory mourning. Through these spiritual experiences, many find meaning and final reconciliation.

One father in a bereavement support group was dealing with
the loss of his son, who had died 2 weeks earlier. We were surprised
at how few of the expectable acute grief symptoms he seemed to
experience. His wife also mentioned to me how much beyond her
he appeared to be in his grief recovery and acceptance. We assumed
that he was in shock or denial and would later experience symptoms of posttraumatic stress. Along with his wife, we had questions
about his grief and mourning. However, after listening to him and

following him for several years, we realized a spiritual death preparation that occurred during his anticipatory mourning had profoundly and positively impacted his recovery after his son's death. While he had been lying on the hospital bed next to his son, he was thinking about how he was going to cope if his son died. He subsequently reported that he felt his son's spirit leave his son's body. He then saw his son's spirit walking down the hospital corridor with that of his deceased great-grandfather. This spiritual experience was a death preparation that made a significant difference in this father's postdeath experience.

Dreams

Death preparations in the form of dreams also may play a significant part in anticipatory mourning.

> *About a week before my son was to have surgery, I dreamed his surgery was over and the doctors told me he had to be on life support. They wanted my permission to remove the life support. I entered his room and watched his heart monitor. I ran out of his room crying—I could not decide to remove life support. I wanted him alive at all costs! When I woke up from the dream, I felt as if it had happened. I cried for a long time. I shared the dream with my mother and husband and wondered if we should cancel his surgery. We decided it was just a dream and went ahead with the surgery. Our son died unexpected[ly], 36 hours after a successful surgery. They think he might have aspirated in his sleep.*

Another parent said:

> *One night I dreamed my deceased grandmother was holding and rocking my baby (I was still pregnant). The dream didn't make sense to me until my baby died. In my sadness I have found some comfort picturing my grandmother holding my baby.*

Impressions

Impressions that have come to chronically or terminally ill children and their parents seem to prepare them for the upcoming death. They also can help parents resolve the death afterward. One disabled child wrote the following, 6 weeks before his sudden death:

> I really feel that I can walk in the next life, and that I can talk better. And that I live forever in the next life after this, and that I will see God again. And I get to see my grandma and grandpa who died a couple years ago, again. And you can too someday. I guess I don't have to say any more . . . signing off. (Ashton, 1996, p. 149)

Some children have been prepared for their upcoming deaths by seeing deceased relatives during their illnesses or at the time of their deaths (Morse, 1990). Others have called out a deceased relative's name or reached for someone just prior to death. Some have heard angels singing. One young boy, dying of leukemia, sat up in bed and started talking to someone. When his father asked to whom he was talking, he said, "Can't you see him? Jesus is here. He's come to get me!" He lay back down in his bed and closed his eyes for the last time. This experience seemed to help the parents in their postdeath grief.

While many have reassuring spiritual experiences, others have become spiritually injured hoping for a vision or visitation that did not come.

> *I felt something could go wrong with the surgery, so I asked my son if by chance he didn't make it, would he try to "appear" to me after and tell me he was OK. He hesitantly agreed. I then said, "If you can't, I'll understand and try to have faith you're OK." After his death, I watched for him for months! I was really hurt he wasn't allowed to return for just a brief moment. My faith was shaken for several years.*

Spiritual tools exist and can offer healing. In the beginning, many do not feel like using them, especially if they have been spiritually injured. Caregivers can suggest that families attempt to nourish themselves as they have in the past. They might increase or reestablish their faith and healing through prayer, scripture study, blessings, church attendance, charitable service, imagery, or meditation. The choice of spiritual tools will be different for each individual. With time, most can return to their religion and gain increased or re-identified spirituality.

Studies show that most bereaved parents believe in life after death, and that they hope for a reunion with their child (Doka & Morgan, 1993; Knapp, 1986). This seems to aid in their grief work and recovery. The thought of never seeing their child again is extremely difficult for most parents to accept.

Memorials, Rituals, and Funerals

Creating memorials, participating in rituals, and planning the funeral can be a healthy part of the anticipatory mourning process. Caregivers can assist during the illness by encouraging parents to create memories with their child. Buying a special statue, gift, or something that reminds the parents of their child is one way to memorialize the child. Planting a tree or flowers can be another. Parents can tell the child that every time they see these items they will think of and remember the child. Special songs, rainbows, sunsets, birds, and so forth all can become symbolic or ritualistic reminders that offer comfort. Children want to be remembered, and parents never want to forget them. Memorials can be helpful in meeting these needs.

Some families will not want to think about a funeral until after the child dies. At that point, decisions frequently are hurriedly made, following the advice of others, even strangers. Many parents have later regretted some of their hastily made choices. Rituals help people adjust to major changes in life: birth, graduations, marriage, and death. Funerals give validation to a life that has ended and offer support, comfort, and closure to those left behind.

Generally, it is valuable for families to participate in postdeath rituals. Some have written poems or letters to be read aloud. Others have planned special music. Some have selected the speakers, casket, flowers, clothing, or headstone.

> *I spoke at my both my mother's and my son's funeral services. It was very difficult. However, I wanted them to be honored by one who knew and loved them. I also offered the dedicatory prayer at my infant daughter's graveside service. It was the only thing I could really "DO" physically for her in this life.*

Social Interventions

Socially, parents and ill or disabled children often withdraw from others. They isolate themselves because they may not feel comfortable sharing the details of their circumstances or their emotions. They fear that others will not understand their pain. They are also extremely vulnerable and fearful of additional things going wrong in their lives. The fear of additional loss brings on feelings of helplessness and being out of control. Many parents describe social changes as being damaging to their self-esteem. Health care workers can provide a safe environment and a listening ear as parents share their vulnerabilities, fears, and loss of self-esteem.

It is helpful to explain to a child and his or her parents that a disability or serious illness will likely limit many of the activities that have become part of his or her identity. One's identity may include personal characteristics, body image, talents, abilities, and disabilities. Most of these self-perceptions are learned through interacting with the environment and others.

> It's safe to say that the self image is the core personality
> ingredient which directs every aspect of our being. The way
> we communicate, the way we handle our emotions, the way
> we behave publicly as well as privately is all a commentary

on our image of ourselves. (Carter, personal communication, June 15, 1994)

Children must be helped to realize that when the physical body or environment changes, they must also make emotional, behavioral, and mental adjustments. The caregiver may help parents and children prepare for and normalize the following challenges: (a) physical and mental discomfort and suffering; (b) difficulties with social acceptance and rejection; (c) limitation of experience, which can lead to emotional suffering and feelings of inferiority; and (d) negative, degrading, and devaluating experiences with interpersonal relationships (Buscaglia, 1975).

Parents as well as children struggle with these losses. Their own identities may be strongly linked to their child's. Children, as well as adults, sense others may be viewing and valuing them differently. As a result, some may experience a loss of self-esteem. If children can be helped to identify positive self-concepts, this can help them though their illnesses.

Finding Self-Worth When Self-Esteem Is Not Enough

It can be valuable for both parent and child to understand that focusing on self-worth may combat feelings of worthlessness or loss of self-esteem. As quoted in Ashton (1996), Fred Riley shares, "*Self-worth* is defined as 'who I am'; *self-esteem* as 'what I do.' Self-worth focuses on BEING rather than DOING" (p. 49). An ill or disabled child can feel his or her value without having to DO or perform in any way. That child can feel confidence and peace based on his or her unique, purposeful existence and by understanding that he or she is loved and approved by God. Self-worth is not solely dependent on the opinions or evaluations of others; it comes from inside one's being or soul. It has to do with finding personal meaning or purpose for one's existence and circumstances. Children and parents may find it beneficial to switch their external or physical goals and aspirations to inner, character-based achievements, attitudes, and aspirations. Internal security simply does not come via external striving (Covey, 1991). In brief, parents need to help their children realize they are valued for who they are (self-worth), not what they do (self-esteem).

One child, who had a very limiting disability, had an impressively strong sense of inner strength and self-worth, as illustrated in the following dialogue:

What would you never change about yourself?
My name.

What is the most important thing you own?
My wheelchair.

What is your most important achievement?
To learn to read.

How do you feel on the inside?
Happy.

If your life ended today, what would you like people to say about you?
Hey, that was a neat kid! He also had a cool wheelchair.

Who do you love and admire most?
God, and my mom and dad.

Six weeks before his death, he said the following in an interview, which we have annotated:

> *It not easy being handicapped.* [Realistic and open.] *It looks easy, but not really. It like hard, I guess. Like for example, I can't do a lot.* [Honest about abilities.]*, but I can play with my computer. . . .* [Looks for the positive things he can do.] *I hope you can understand me OK, and learn what it like to be me.* [Shows internal concern for others, while acknowledging his lack of external ability to speak clearly.] *It fun to ride my bike* [feet and waist straps on it] *and wheelchair* [electric]. *I can swim with a little help from this* [a flotation device]. [Focuses positively on the simple things he can do that bring personal joy and achievement.]

Clearly, this boy's inner strength came in spite of his external limitations.

If parents and caregivers are continually open and honest, the ill or disabled child can become aware of false guilt, unrealistic fears, magical thinking, or other faulty perceptions. We cannot change the personality of a child. However, parents and caregivers can significantly influence positive thoughts and behaviors through unconditional love, appropriate expectations, and compassionate service.

> *My friend's child recently was diagnosed with leukemia. When I told my 5-year-old his buddy would be losing his hair from the chemotherapy, he agreed to shave his head, too. I bought matching baseball caps for both of them.*

Negative Labels

Understanding the power of positive and negative labels can help parents and children develop healthy self-talk habits. If children engage in negative self-talk or receive negative feedback from adults long enough, these ideas can become instilled in their minds as truth: "I'm ugly," "I'm stupid," "No one loves me," "I can't do this."

The chronically or terminally ill child or the child with a disability may be even more vulnerable and self-critical. Parents and caregivers can help dispel some of the negative labels children attach to themselves through open, honest communication; unconditional love; and frequent fun and humor.

> Faulty perceptions are kept alive and hidden within the individual when either good communication or sufficient love are missing. . . . In stressful moments people tend to say or do damaging things to children and let the damaging impressions stand unchallenged and unchanged in the child's mind. (Chamberlain, 1978, p. 62)

Negative concepts can be talked out and corrected before deep fears or negative habits develop. Listening to children exhibits love, concern, and respect for them. This usually helps them feel valued and esteemed. When children repress negative emotions and feelings for fear of judgment or reprisal, these emotions often become expressed in other ways. Children who are unable to share their feelings may exhibit nightmares, physical ailments, negative behaviors, regression, or poor mental health. Emotions usually occur for a reason, and denial seldom resolves those issues (feeling is healing). Adults need to allow and accept children's feelings and tears. Telling children that they shouldn't feel a certain way does not enhance understanding or positive self-esteem.

Caregivers can remind parents that overindulgence is an easy trap to get into when a child is ill, and it seldom builds lasting character. Children thrive and heal best when parents establish positive relationships with their children through clear rules and consistent discipline. Children with low self-esteem often come from homes where there are overly permissive or overly harsh forms of discipline.

CARING FOR THE CHILD

Helping a child live fully until the end is no simple endeavor. There will be numerous struggles and ambiguous feelings and experiences during the anticipatory mourning period. For instance, how do parents hold on to the child, knowing they must eventually let go (decathexis)? How do parents protect their child while at the same time allow their child independence? How do parents balance their child's and his or her siblings' needs with their own?

The first priority in caring for anyone who is ill is helping the person to be as physically comfortable as feasible. A child must be kept warm, dry, and as pain free as possible. It is impossible for a child to work on emotional or spiritual issues if basic physical requirements are unmet or if the child is in severe pain.

Understanding the illness and grief from a child's perspective is critical. One may need to watch for nonverbal clues, which are more common in times of stress. Children also communicate through their behaviors and play. It is important to avoid giving children double messages: Because they can read nonverbal cues easily, it is better to be open and honest with them.

During anticipatory mourning, parents frequently overdo, over-give, or over-buy. As parents try to calm fear, guilt, and pain for their child, they may find it difficult to reprimand or discipline in the same ways they did before the illness. They will still need to set realistic expectations and limits. Rules and discipline offer children security in an insecure world. Parents should be informed that realistic limits will aid siblings also. When siblings see a brother or sister receiving everything he or she wants and breaking family rules, they may become resentful, wish they were ill, or start breaking rules themselves.

Home Care

Many families are private and want to do everything themselves. Other families feel guilty seeking outside help for their personal problems. Some try to go it alone, fail, or burn out, thereby adding additional feelings of guilt, stress, and frustration to their grief. Caregivers can help parents balance time away from their child for other commitments. Frequently, after time away parents will return with renewed patience, energy, and inner peace. They are then better able to give to their child, as well as to other family members.

Most communities have resources to help families and children with special needs. Families can make contact with hospice programs, home nursing associations, respite care, parent support groups, local schools, and church groups. It can also be beneficial to encourage families to ask for and accept help from their friends and relatives.

Social and Recreational Needs

Parents should be encouraged to take their child on outings whenever possible. Little pleasures make the day-to-day hardships a little lighter. If a child must stay inside, caregivers can work with parents to bring activities and recreation into the home. Parents will recall the shared joy and laughter expressed during these activities as sweet memories later. A play therapist may have additional ideas for games, music, or other creative activities. In addition, occupational therapists are trained to provide ideas, exercises, and activities for ill, frail, or disabled children. When siblings are involved in these activities, special bonds often form, never to be forgotten.

Parents will find that others' reactions to their child's illness vary. Some people may not want to associate with the family anymore. Such reactions from others can feel like rejection (another loss). Being around dying children can be depressing and reminds us of our own mortality and vulnerability. Caregivers can explain to parents and children that outsiders don't always know better and that their reactions can result from their own insecurity, fear, pity, or denial. If someone has not experienced illness, loss, or the death of a loved one, it is difficult for that person to know what to say or do. As caregivers, we can help educate and sensitize friends and relatives so they can become the more compassionate support system the family desire. We can also encourage friends and relatives to avoid abandoning the child or parents at a time when love, acceptance, and support are most critical.

> I knew people were staring at us. I didn't like their pity. I knew
> every time we went out in public, people could tell something was
> wrong with my child. I hated feeling their disdain as we helped
> him eat. Yet in spite of it all, I felt very proud to be his mother, as
> did my husband. We were happy we could offer the love and care
> to him in a way that no one else could.

Education

The education of a disabled, chronically ill, or terminally ill child is influenced by many factors. How ill is the child? How long is he or she expected to live? What are the desires of the child and the family? Priorities must be established. It is important to recognize that school is a large part of a child's social life and that any changes in this area can become a loss for a child. In planning educational interventions, health care providers must keep in mind that these children are already mourning numerous losses.

Children may choose to attend school and associate with peers in their regular classrooms, especially during remissions. During relapses or treatment, they can be schooled at home or in the hospital. A disabled child may spend part or all of the day in a self-contained classroom.

Care in the Hospital

Hospital stays are often necessary. It can help to educate both parents and child as to what they might expect during their visits. Most hospitals provide a reclining chair-bed for a parent to stay day and night. Children usually feel more secure if a parent is by their side. Often young children have separation anxiety when they are removed from their homes or parents.

Both parents and children must realize that hospitals run on schedules. This means that inevitably they will be disrupted and wakened for medications, meals, vital signs, X rays, doctor visits, and other tests. Parents may be asked to leave for some of these procedures. Afterward, a child may exhibit anger or withdraw from a parent, thinking the parent did not protect him or her from the unpleasant experience. Saying that you are sorry the child has to endure the pain or that you wish you could take his or her place often provides the comfort required. Especially during a hospital stay, families need times to play games, read, and share fun activities. Siblings can visit often and be a part of hospital life whenever possible. Caregivers will also need to encourage parents to take occasional breaks from the hospital environment. Families still maintain a life outside the hospital setting and can benefit from inviting friends, relatives, and fellow church members to help wherever possible. They may need the caregiver's encouragement and permission to do so.

Medical Costs

The costs of a disability or long-term illness have soared in recent years. Seriously ill children are living longer. As a result, we are seeing more relapses and remissions, which means additional treatments and the use of additional specialized equipment. All these medical improvements significantly increase the financial expense for families. In one study, parents listed financial responsibility as a significant stress in caring for their child (Heaman, 1995). The feeling that they could not afford the best treatment can seriously complicate a family's postdeath grief and mourning.

HELPING THE MARRIAGE

The basic needs of most individuals in a marriage relationship, in no particular order, are (a) affection and touch; (b) acceptance and belonging; (c) communication; (d) friendship, freedom, and fun; (e) security and trust; and (f) the complementary expression of sexuality. Relationships often become strained with the added pressure and responsibility of caring for a child with a disability or a chronic or terminal illness. Some couples, especially those whose child has a chronic illness, report that their challenges brought them closer. Although the finding is debated, Kupfer (1971) reports couples parenting a disabled child divorce at a rate of 70%.

Incongruent Grief

Parents may employ very different management styles during their child's serious illness (Knafl, 1996). It is vitally important to explain to parents that they will likely respond to and mourn their child's illness and death differently. Each has a unique relationship with the child. The particular ways in which they appraise the situation and its meanings, along with numerous other factors, will influence their grief and mourning.

Men and women are biologically different, and these differences affect how they do their grief work. Socially, men and women are raised to view and respond to events quite differently. In our society, stereotypically boys are encouraged to be strong and silent, whereas girls are encouraged to express emotions. Loss causes both men and women to feel helpless and powerless, although they may express these feelings in different ways. Caregivers can reassure couples that these feelings are normal and that it will take mutual understanding and healthy thought processes to work through their mourning issues over considerable time.

> Before we were diagnosed we had a good relationship and got along very well. During the diagnosis process we were both shocked, scared, and ignorant about the facts. We started having a little tension between us. My husband and I have been raised differently. I have a lot of questions, but my husband accepts things and goes on. I had some resentment toward him because there were no tears, no screaming, no emotion! He just accepted it. I couldn't!

It may help the couple to understand that men's and women's brains function differently. The differences influence thoughts, moods, and behaviors. Although exceptions occur, men tend to cope with their grief by using logic, concrete facts, and objective reasoning. On the other hand, many women tend to rely more on their feelings and emotions to grieve. They are more focused on happenings at home, relationships, interpersonal process, and resolution of details. Generally, women are more tender, intuitive, nurturing, and talkative than men.

Both fathers and mothers worry about what illness or disability means for their child's life and future. Mothers often report feeling that there is not enough time to do all that is required of them and are typically exhausted as a result. They may show concern over the unavailability of community and other resources to meet the needs of the child. In addition to financial worries, the father typically is also concerned for the health of the child and not having enough time alone with his spouse (Heaman, 1995).

Encouraging parents to use the following Four Cs can strengthen their relationships during stress. These are commitment, communication, cooperation and tolerance, and conflict resolution.

1. COMMITMENT: Parents can be encouraged to stay committed to each other, as well as to their child. They can be helped to acknowledge that they face a long, hard, yet worthwhile road ahead. Interestingly, those couples who do not consider divorce as an option to every conflict usually find mutual solutions that allow them to keep their marriages intact.

2. COMMUNICATION: Communication challenges remain the number one cause of divorce. Parents who are exhausted and actively mourning often have difficulty finding the time and energy that is vital for healthy marital interactions. Advocating that parents discuss their child's illness and the challenges they face openly, honestly, and frequently will help enhance meaningful communication.

3. COOPERATION AND TOLERANCE: Parents can be assisted to accept each other's individual feelings. Negative feelings often go away more quickly when accepted and expressed. Parents must avoid discounting each other's true feelings by using roadblocks such as "Yes, but . . . ," shoulds, or shouldn'ts. Cooperation and compromise break down barriers and power struggles. Many professional therapists have discovered that "tolerance therapy" saves more marriages than other, conventional therapies.

4. CONFLICT RESOLUTION: Caregivers can work to help parents realize that all marriages have conflict and that not all issues can be resolved. Parents may have to "agree to disagree" on some issues. Encouraging and teaching couples to focus their anger and disappointments on their challenges, not each other, will save marriages.

Parents need to be encouraged to accept help with their child so that they can get away and spend time alone together. A short weekly date is worth the time, money, and effort. When possible, an overnight trip away together can be therapeutic. Communication and conflict resolution cannot occur if effort is not made to be alone together on a regular basis.

Touch Therapy

Touch and massage therapy have been healing arts for centuries. Touch can bring comfort to parents as well as to the ill child.

Touch also works well in the marriage relationship because it keeps the partners connected. It can dissolve anger and frustration, and melt away tension. During time alone together, each partner takes a turn massaging the other, using lotions or oils if desired. Partners may talk about their concerns or just take the time to totally relax in silence. Touch or massage can, but does not have to, involve sexual intimacy.

Many have used a combination of massage and music to comfort the terminally ill. This combination can become a healing ritual as death nears.

The Sexual Relationship

Often during the mourning process there are discrepant feelings toward sexual intimacy. One partner may find comfort in intimacy, feeling that not all is lost. The other may not be able to participate, wondering how anyone could think of pleasure at such a sad time. Parents will need to try to understand their differences around these issues.

HELPING SIBLINGS

Whether sibling relationships are peaceful or conflicted, there is a bond between brothers and sisters. The illness and death of a child affect each sibling's identity, as well as the family dynamics. Some children react to the grave condition of a sibling with confusion, withdrawal, depression, or intense emotions. Others may not feel deep grief. Most children appear to recover from loss more rapidly than do their parents or other adults, although for many, the loss will be a lifelong issue.

Children often sense increased stress and anxiety in the home. They may become confused, frightened, and insecure if they are not told the truth or allowed to share in what is happening within the family. They may lose their level of trust and their personal identity within the family unit. Children look to their parents as examples of how to respond to life events. Seeing and sharing in their parents' grief and mourning can validate their own emotions.

Most siblings report that it is hard to talk to their parents during anticipatory and postdeath mourning. Parents are often unable to respond to their other children because of their own grief and mourning. Consequently, siblings may be mourning the loss of their parents' attention, as well as other losses associated with their ill, disabled, or dying sibling.

At first I was afraid to talk to my parents. Then I decided to go back into the family room. I remember sitting on the couch,

listening to my parents cry. I didn't cry—I just sat there staring at
the balloons that said, "Get Well Soon!" The next day was worse.
I became more angry and depressed.

Some siblings, especially teens, may not want to be involved with the anticipatory mourning process. They are often self-focused, and this self-focus occupies most of their time and energy. They are also consumed with friends and concerned with day-to-day events. As one sibling remarked, "I just wanted to speed my life up about 2 years and forget what was happening." Younger children may not be developmentally ready to process some aspects of their sibling's illness and death. They may process their grief at subsequent developmental stages or after other significant life events.

We cannot force children to grieve or react as we think best, nor should we attempt to lecture, compare, or overcontrol them. However, we can be available to guide them through whatever phase they are currently in and to assist them when they need us: "Available evidence suggests that not to assist the bereaved child in actively dealing with the death is to predispose him to significant pathology and life long problems" (Rando, 1984, p. 155).

Children, like adults, fear illness and loss. Their fears can make them feel vulnerable and anxious. Seeing an ill sibling suffer or receive treatments can arouse fears that they might become ill themselves (Thibodeau, 1988). Some children are embarrassed by a sibling's disability or appearance and fear peers' ridicule (Faux, 1991). This reaction can cause them to feel guilty, especially after the death. Discussing ambivalent feelings and helping them realize that such feelings are normal may help them relinquish their guilt.

Parents and caregivers should encourage siblings to experience as normal a childhood as possible, recognizing that siblings will continue to laugh and fight with each other. With time, reassurance, and love, siblings can regain a sense of security. Parents and caregivers can help siblings build important and meaningful memories by encouraging them to play games with their brother or sister or to listen to or sing favorite songs, as well as by encouraging other opportunities for them to express love and concern. Adults can also help siblings memorialize the dying child by allowing them to keep something that reminds them of their brother or sister, or by encouraging them to help plant a tree or buy a symbolic gift. The memories of these events can bring comfort and reduce guilt in postdeath adaptation.

Most children can attend a sibling's funeral. If they are old enough to love, they are old enough to grieve. It may help them actualize their loss if they see others mourning, saying good-bye, and experiencing closure.

HELPING FRIENDS AND RELATIVES

It is often hard for those who have never experienced a major loss or serious illness to understand all that a family is going through. Friends and family may offer well-meaning cliches that discount the need to mourn: "It is for the best," "You can have another child," "It is God's will," and "She is an angel now." While these are often sincere attempts to comfort, they may in actuality create communication barriers that hurt those who are mourning. More helpful comments include the following: "I'm sorry you're having to go through all of this," "I'm sad for you. It must be very hard," "How are you doing with all of this?" and ""What can I do? I'm here as long as you need me."

Relatives and friends may need encouragement to listen and accept any feelings, including anger, that the parents or child might express. It is generally appropriate and helpful to cry with, touch, and hug the bereaved. It is also helpful to offer meals, house cleaning, and child care. As time progresses and healing begins, family and friends need to remember most parents want to talk about and share memories of their child. Sending cards or gifts on special occasions keeps the communication lines open.

Grandparents are often the forgotten mourners. They lose twice: First, they lose their future legacy as they watch a grandchild suffer or die. Second, they experience another loss as they helplessly watch their own adult offspring mourn.

NEED FOR PROFESSIONAL COUNSELING OR MEDICATION

Knowing when someone needs more than insight and self-help tools is not always easy. If someone has a cut or a broken arm, we can see the injury. We don't hesitate to send that person to the hospital to have the problem treated, perhaps with antibiotics or pain medications. When someone has a broken heart and soul, we may not directly perceive the wound. Because grief wounds are often invisible, individuals may fail to seek help soon enough. Often mourners feel broken, bruised, and shattered by their loss. Psychotherapy and medication may be of benefit. If in doubt, help should be sought.

Professional help should be considered when one's emotions, thoughts, or behaviors become debilitating, distorted, or exaggerated. When sadness turns to clinical depression, anger turns to prolonged bitterness or rage, fear turns to anxiety or panic attacks, and guilt to shame, professional help is in order.

If a person decides to go for professional assistance, he or she would do well to seek a counselor trained in grief therapy. If it is a child who is struggling, someone who has experience treating grieving children should be enlisted. Similarly, if the marriage is in trouble, a professional who understands the dynamics of grief and marriage therapy is preferable to one whose experience is less specific.

WHEN DEATH IS NEAR

The diagnosis, illness, and death of a child are catastrophic for most parents. In our attempt to help parents adjust and cope, we must also continue to remain aware of the dying child's needs. Generally, it is the child who first realizes that he or she is close to death. He or she then attempts to share this awakening awareness with the parents. Frequently, parents resist this sharing because they are not ready for, or cannot comprehend, the child's effort to disclose such information. Consequently, the child may take on the role of caregiver, perhaps asking that information not be shared with the parents in an attempt to protect them. A supportive caregiver can become a valuable listening ear. He or she may also make gentle attempts to open communication between parents and child.

The child should be told that it is acceptable to talk about death, cry, and feel sad or angry. If families cannot communicate verbally, caregivers can help them explore options. For example, parents and children can be helped to plan ways to say good-bye to each other through drawings, poems and other writings, or music.

It is valuable for both parents and children to achieve some acceptance of death's eventuality. This requires openness and communication that are natural in some families but almost impossible in others. Caregivers can help parents understand that they can relieve some of their child's guilt and anxiety by openly sharing their own sorrow. Children sense when parents are trying to hide their true emotions. It can be emotionally draining for parents after the child has died if love has not been expressed, a damaged relationship mended, or special good-byes said.

Many caregivers and parents are surprised at the maturity of dying children. It is as if these children are cramming in a lifetime of growing. Dying children often assume adult roles as they try to comfort those around them. Even little children can hug and comfort tearful parents, and having done so be left with a sense of value, control, and competence. This maturation may give children a sense of purpose, but they are still children, often needing to discuss their childlike fears and emotions. If they are repeatedly told how strong and brave they are, they may bury or repress the feelings. Caregivers and parents can help establish an appropriate balance between sharing, showing emotion, and having courage to face the future. Hearing our fears, seeing our tears, and sharing our feelings validate and encourage the expression of children's own emotions.

Difficult issues will continue for families as death approaches. Initially, parents may have had to decide if they should try another round of chemotherapy, radiation, or a bone marrow transplant. Now they may need to decide when it is time to discontinue life-saving measures. How much pain medication and sedation will make the dying easier? Will the child die at home or go to the hospital? Parents ask, "Have I answered all the questions and fears my child has about death?"; "Have we really done all we could do?"; "How do we hold on and at the same time let go?"

Parents can better deal with their fears if they know ahead of time what the dying process is like. Knowing that some children become confused or delirious, have seizures, or lose consciousness is important. The actual process may occur over several days. Typically, a child's breathing and heartbeat will become irregular, and the heart rate will slow. The skin may turn grayish or a pale white as less oxygen is being circulated. The child's hands and feet become cool to the touch. Although there are stories of anguish and suffering, with today's technology, health care providers usually are able to help children die peacefully. Adults can help children understand that they will not be alone when they die and that they will be kept as pain free as possible.

In the end, many parents are relieved to know their child is no longer in pain.

> I felt relief! I don't think you're ever prepared to lose a child, but we were both done hurting and it was very comforting knowing she was pain free.

As part of their anticipatory mourning, parents may try to imagine what life will be like without their child. How can they picture themselves driving by the school where all of the children are at recess except theirs? How can they imagine going to the grocery store, reaching for a special box of cereal, then remembering that no one at home eats it anymore? How will they feel seeing the bike, swing, computer game, or baseball unused? What will it be like to walk by the empty bedroom every night for the rest of their lives? Unfortunately, the future parents face is often beyond their imagination.

The death of a child is the most traumatic event in a parent's life. Some view it as the worst loss anyone must endure (Rosof, 1994). Professionals have classified the death of a child as "catastrophic," ranked by the American Psychiatric Association (1987) as more stressful than the death of a spouse. A family's future is dramatically altered with the death of a child. The word *bereaved* is derived from the Old English word *berêafian*, which means "to rob." Parents truly feel robbed of their child. The relationship they had with that child is irreplaceable. Inordinate amounts of time and energy invested in caring for an ill or disabled child will, in the end, add to the intensity and duration of grief and mourning. It will require months and years of hard work to adjust to the loss. Grief work and mourning will be the hardest task most parents will ever face. However, the job can be accomplished, the loss acknowledged, a "new normal" (Limbo & Wheeler, 1986) established, and joy once again rediscovered. With time and support, parents can choose to transform their pain and anger into hope, forgiveness, and peace.

REFERENCES

American Psychiatric Association. (1987). *Diagnostic and statistical manual of mental disorders* (DSM-III-R). Washington, DC: Author.

American Psychiatric Association. (1994). *Diagnostic and statistical manual of mental disorders* (DSM-IV). Washington, DC: Author.

Angst, D. B., & Deatrick, J. A. (1996). Involvement in health care decisions: Parents and children with chronic illness. *Journal of Family Nursing, 2*(2), 174–194.

Ashton, J. (with D. Ashton). (1996). *Loss and grief recovery: Caring for children with disabilities, chronic or terminal illness.* Amityville, NY: Baywood.

Buck, P. S. (1950). *The child who never grew.* Bethesda, MD: Woodbine.

Buscaglia, L. (1975). *The disabled and their parents: A counseling challenge.* Thorofare, NJ: Charles B. Slackin.

Bush, B. (1991). *Guilt—A tool for Christian growth.* St. Meinrad, IN: Abbey Press.

Chamberlain, J. M. (1978). *Eliminate your SDB's (Self-Defeating Behaviors).* Provo, UT: Brigham Young University Press.

Covey, S. R. (1991). *Principle-centered leadership.* New York: Summit Books.

Davies, B. (1997, April). *Living with grief/when illness is prolonged.* Paper presented at a teleconference sponsored by the Hospice Foundation of America, Washington, DC.

Dickson, M. (1991). *Grief recovery seminars.* Dallas, TX: Ann's Haven Hospice.

Doka, K. J. (Ed.). (1997). *Living with grief: When illness is prolonged.* Washington, DC: Hospice Foundation of America.

Doka, K. J., & Morgan, J. D. (Eds.). (1993). *Death and spirituality.* Amityville, NY: Baywood.

Edwards, D. (1989). *Grieving: The pain and promise.* Salt Lake City, UT: Covenant.

Faux, S. A. (1991). Sibling relationships in congenitally impaired children. *Journal of Pediatric Nursing, 6*(3), 175–184.

Frankl, V. E. (1946). *Man's search for meaning.* New York: Simon and Schuster.

Heaman, D. J. (1995). Perceived stressors and coping strategies of parents who have children with developmental disabilities: A comparison of mothers and fathers. *Journal of Pediatric Nursing, 10*(5), 311–320.

Jackson, E. N. (1946). *Understanding grief.* Nashville, TN: Abingdon.

Knafl, K. (1996). Family response to childhood chronic illness: Description of management styles. *Journal of Pediatric Nursing, 11*(5), 315–326.

Knapp, R. J. (1986). *Beyond endurance—When a child dies.* New York: Schocken Books.

Kübler-Ross, E. (1983). *On children and death.* New York: Macmillan.

Kupfer, F. (1971). *Before and after Zachariah.* New York: Delacorte.

Kushner, H. S. (1981). *When bad things happen to good people.* New York: Avon.

Lewy, A. J. (1987). Treating chronobiologic sleep and mood disorders with bright light. *Psychiatric Annals, 17,* 664–668.

Limbo, R. K., & Wheeler, S. R. (1986). *When a baby dies: A handbook for healing and helping.* La Crosse, WI: La Crosse Lutheran Hospital/Gundersen Clinic.

Morgan, B. L. G., & Morgan, R. (1989). *Hormones (brainfood).* Los Angeles: The Body Press.

Morse, M. (1990). *Closer to the light.* New York: Villard.

Ornstein, R., & Swenciconis, C. (1990). *The healing brain.* New York: Guilford.

Rando, T. A. (1984). *Grief, dying, and death: Clinical interventions for caregivers.* Champaign, IL: Research Press.

Rosof, B. D. (1994). *The worst loss.* New York: Henry Holt.

Ryan, M. A. (1993, January). [Seminar material]. Tucson, AZ: American Academy of Bereavement.

Sobel, D. S. (1997, Summer). The "write" way to cope with trauma. *Partners in Health Newsletter,* p. 23.

Spratt, M., & Denney, D. (1991). Immune variables, depression, and plasma cortisol over time in suddenly bereaved parents. *Journal of Neuropsychiatry and Clinical Neurosciences, 3*(3), 299–306.

Thibodeau, S. M. (1988). Sibling response to chronic illness: The role of the clinical nurse specialist. *Issues in Comprehensive Nursing, 11,* 17–28.

Wolfelt, A. D. (1996, August). *Lessons in caring for the dying.* Materials presented at a workshop sponsored by funeral homes of Dallas, TX.

CHAPTER 15
Anticipatory Mourning in HIV/AIDS

Sandra Jacoby Klein

Anticipatory mourning refers to grief over an indeterminate period that precedes an inevitable loss, such as the death of a person suffering from an illness that is known to be untreatable and certainly fatal. HIV/AIDS has been such an illness. Once someone is infected by the human immunodeficiency virus (HIV), the virus is present in the person for the remainder of his or her life. There is no cure. For almost two decades, HIV-positive people have been preparing to die. Since 1996, however, treatment with new medications has dramatically altered these preparations and affected the anticipatory mourning. This chapter examines the contemporary realities of anticipatory mourning in HIV/AIDS.

THE FACTS ABOUT HIV/AIDS

AIDS, or acquired immune deficiency syndrome, is a disease caused by the human immunodeficiency virus (HIV) that destroys the body's natural ability to fight illness. Opportunistic diseases such as pneumonia and rare cancers develop as the virus causes a breakdown in the body's immune system. Death is actually caused by one or more of these opportunistic infections. The current life-prolonging treatments, for various reasons, may or may not prevent one or more of the opportunistic infections that lead to AIDS and eventually to death from AIDS-related illness.

Estimates by the Joint United Nations Programme on HIV/AIDS (UNAIDS) and the World Health Organization (WHO) indicate that at the end of 1998 over 33.4 million people were living with HIV, the virus that causes AIDS, and that 13.9 million people around the world had already lost their lives to the disease ("WHO Report," 1998). According to the Centers for Disease Control (CDC; 1998), the cumulative number of AIDS cases in the United States

---

For Julian, whose smiles continue to remind me of the preciousness of life

has reached 688,200. Children account for 8,461 of these cases. Also in the United States, the total deaths from AIDS-related disease have reached 415,784—including 410,800 adults and adolescents, and 4,984 children.

Leveling or decline in AIDS opportunistic infections has occurred in some populations, whereas increases continue in other groups. Drops in AIDS-related deaths, probably due to new medications and prevention efforts, indicate that people are living longer with the disease and that more people will need care over long periods. Even as newer and better treatments are developed, they are proven to not work for everyone. Because of the expense involved, they are not available to everyone. Persons with HIV may be living longer, but, at the same time, they are developing conditions that were practically unheard of during the epidemic's early years. The unpredictability of the disease process creates ongoing opportunities for anticipatory mourning. This pandemic is far from over.

The numbers of those infected with HIV will be larger than the numbers of AIDS cases simply because being infected doesn't mean having AIDS. The time between infection and the development of AIDS can be longer than 10 years. HIV is a contagious disease: An infected person appearing to be in good health can transmit the virus to others. HIV is contagious only when passed from an infected person by way of bodily fluids such as blood, semen, or vaginal secretions. It is not transmitted by casual contact such as shaking hands, kissing, touching the deceased, or using a toilet seat. A person is diagnosed with AIDS after he or she develops one of the opportunistic diseases associated with this virus.

ANTICIPATORY MOURNING IN HIV/AIDS: WHAT MAKES IT DIFFERENT?

What makes anticipatory mourning related to HIV/AIDS different from anticipatory mourning experienced in relation to other illnesses? What if *everyone* is expected to die? What if people are so caught up in worry about those who are sick and dying that there is no time to mourn? People don't know how to respond.

The populations most greatly affected by HIV/AIDS (gay, male bisexual, female, African American, substance addicted, imprisoned) are the ones most discriminated against, most disenfranchised, and least accepted by society. In many of their communities, networks of chosen family units or supportive family-like structures have formed. These units can consist of individuals and couples, adults and children, gay men, lesbians, bisexuals, and heterosexuals who provide support and caregiving to AIDS-affected individuals. AIDS has an impact on people of all races, cultures, and ethnic groups. There is an unavoidable climate of loss in affected communities as illness and expectation of death continue (Schwartzberg, 1992).

Another distinction of anticipatory mourning related to HIV/AIDS is that organizations of professional and nonprofessional caregivers that have sprung up to offer support and resources to people with AIDS are often composed of people who are infected and dealing with their own life-threatening illnesses. Also, the clinicians, friends, and family members who offer care and support to persons living with AIDS (PLWA) are often HIV infected and in need of the same for themselves.

Since the outbreak of AIDS in the early 1980s, the homosexual community has been the one most affected by the disease in the United States. Because of the large number of gay men who are still HIV infected, anticipatory mourning continues within this population even as the levels of death among gay men are declining. The effects of this pandemic are far reaching. As Rofes (1996) observes, "The replacement of pre-epidemic gay life by a death-saturated culture has caused a profound alteration of the social fabric and the reorganization of [gay] communal life" (p. 31).

Anticipatory mourning manifests itself in the gay community in painful ways. Most of those who are ill are from the same generation; this situation differs from that in the IV drug–using communities, where different generations of families are infected and affected. Also, in the gay community, familiarity with death and loss over the long years of living with HIV/AIDS does not seem to make the mourning process easier. Grief and mourning are often more difficult as many withdraw from community and relationships to protect themselves from the anticipated deaths and from the pain they know so well. It is not unusual to see an HIV-infected person abandoned by friends and the friends then filled with guilt if death occurs. People who have been in intimate relationships often distance from each other, and longtime friendships evaporate (Odets, 1995, p. 87). Will this behavior be seen in other HIV/AIDS-affected populations?

TEMPORAL AND CHRONOLOGICAL DIMENSIONS OF ANTICIPATORY MOURNING IN HIV/AIDS

A roller-coaster effect seems to characterize the concept of anticipatory mourning and HIV/AIDS. In the beginning years of the epidemic, the time between diagnosis and death was fairly predictable—often a few weeks. HIV-positive people in support groups would become very emotional with each group member's new opportunistic infection, as if they were previewing their own future course. As new medications and treatments were found, the opportunistic infections were treatable and no longer immediately fatal for those fortunate enough to receive and respond to treatment. Recently, there seems to be much more denial of the seriousness of HIV/AIDS and of death itself. This response may be appropriate because of the success of new treatments that continue to bring the infected person back to life and health (Mark Katz, M.D., personal communication, March 25, 1998). But living longer is opening new emotional, financial, and psychosocial issues.

Anticipatory mourning in HIV/AIDS is complicated. It manifests itself in the HIV-infected and HIV-affected populations in several different ways, depending on whether the mourner is (a) a person who is HIV negative mourning for friends and loved ones; (b) a person who is HIV positive mourning for self as well; or (c) a person who does not know, or care to know, his or her HIV status. Anticipatory mourning is also affected by the relationship of the mourner to the person who is dying. Perhaps he or she is a domestic partner who might be either HIV negative or HIV positive. Maybe the mourner is the dying person's parent and, again, may or may not be HIV infected. Dealing with anticipatory mourning surrounding HIV-infected children presents a totally different perspective as social circumstances often isolate HIV-positive parents and children, placing them at risk for a variety of behavioral, social, educational, financial, and health problems (Wiener, 1994). Professional caregivers working in the HIV/AIDS community have special needs, depending upon their own HIV status. Because of the nature of the disease, HIV infects and affects diverse populations, most members of which may be mourning simultaneously.

Anticipatory mourning in relation to HIV/AIDS begins when test results come back positive and for two reasons: The infected person mourns for the loss of health and, more important, mourns because the disease has always been associated with death. The infected person faces a great challenge because of the deep fear attached to this disease. For the duration of the infection, the person is living not only with the disease but also with the stigma attached to it and the fear that the next infection will be the one that kills. Grief comes and goes during the entire life of the infected person—for him- or herself, for caregivers, and for the HIV-infected community.

As people live longer with HIV, AIDS can become more like a chronic illness offering constant opportunities for anticipatory mourning. A chronic illness is defined by

> numerous remissions and relapses; increased financial, social, physical, and emotional pressures; long-term family disruption; progressive decline and the attendant emotional responses of caregivers; elaborate treatment regimens and their often debilitating side effects; and recurring dilemmas surrounding decision making and treatment choices. (Walker, 1996, p. 49)

Anticipatory mourning is experienced at each of the following stages of HIV/AIDS.

- Upon learning that one is HIV positive

  Allison celebrated her twenty-first birthday at an all-night bash thrown by her friends. She felt rather ill for a couple of days after and attributed that feeling to the partying she had done. After several weeks of not feeling well, she went to the doctor. Because Allison is a recovering intravenous drug user and her symptoms were somewhat severe, the doctor tested her for HIV. The test came back positive. Allison was devastated and cried, "I can't believe this is happening to me! I've been clean for 3 years now, and I've been using condoms. It just isn't fair. Now I'm going to die. I'm young and I want to live and get married and have kids. Who is going to want me now?"

- At the time of the first opportunistic infection

- At the occurrence of each successive opportunistic infection

  Dave was so tired of this disease. He said, "I feel fine, then I get an infection. I get treated, feel fine again but a little more tired. Sometimes I even have enough energy to go back to work. Then, BAM—another infection, another setback. I can't work any more. I can't pay my bills. I just want to die already. I wonder what it will be like."

- When treatment is no longer effective

- During the acknowledged approach of an expected death

  Tod, an HIV-positive patient, said, "Jack is dying now. I cannot accept that he will die soon. And what am I going to do if I become sicker? Who will take care of me? So many of our friends are dead that we have hardly anybody to help us. I can't do so much. I'm afraid my health will suffer, and I am at my wit's end. I have no time or energy to deal with this."

DIFFICULTIES ASSOCIATED WITH ANTICIPATORY MOURNING IN HIV/AIDS

Stigmatization

There are many reasons why anticipatory mourning cannot be acknowledged and discussed freely. Society has not found a way to dispel the myths or get rid of the stigma and judgments attached to the diverse populations infected by HIV. The stigma extends to anyone perceived to be associating with the PLWA. An association implies a certain sexual orientation, certain behaviors, and even possible HIV infection. Because of prevailing attitudes and beliefs, people are afraid to tell the truth about their connections to HIV. They cannot share with family, friends, or employers for fear of discrimination, ridicule, rejection, and physical violence. AIDS has been called "the Great Disenfranchiser" (Doka, 1989).

Infection of Multiple Family Members

Multiple family members infected with HIV create another difficult situation related to this disease. Such occurrences are most frequently due to injection drug use by multiple family members, engagement in unsafe sexual practices after infection, or transmission of HIV to a fetus. The illnesses and deaths extend over a prolonged period, maybe 5 to 10 years, which is often more than anyone can cope with. The drug abuse, the sexual orientation, or other situation may have been hidden before the emergence of HIV/AIDS, but it cannot be kept secret so easily any more. The issues surrounding HIV/AIDS—including homosexuality, substance use, and existence of multiple sex partners—are confusing, and it is helpful to determine how each of these issues affects the anticipatory mourning experience.

Unique Issues

The devastation of HIV/AIDS affects anticipatory mourning for individuals and communities in the following important ways, which affect understanding, support, and validation:

- The disaster of AIDS is ongoing. Infected and affected individuals are in various stages of coping with its never-ending devastation. There is no posttrauma. In contrast, when a disaster affects a community, the change usually happens all at once and has a beginning, a middle, and an end. The whole community experiences a sudden, negative change. There is usually widespread emotional and financial support available.

- Those with AIDS are more likely to face discrimination, homo-phobia, and fear of contagion. They are also more likely to be seen as being individually responsible for their disease. They are then placed at greater risk of being stigmatized and socially isolated.

- Infection and disease are linked to sexuality. People's conflicts and discomfort concerning sex, sexuality, and HIV/AIDS make many less willing to offer support during the illness and in the face of impending death. The belief that HIV infection was acquired during sexual relations only increases the stigmatiza-tion of and discrimination against someone whose sexual orien-tation or sexual behaviors are seen as unacceptable.

- Those with AIDS often become ill in their 20s to 40s. PLWA are often younger than 45. Young people are rarely equipped, psy-chologically or developmentally, to deal with recurring illness, impending death, and multiple losses.

- The possibility of developing an opportunistic infection and being diagnosed with AIDS will continue to be part of the life of anyone infected with HIV.

- Some people dealing with ongoing, multiple losses are so over-whelmed that they withdraw and are perceived as uncaring and unsympathetic. They appear to be unaffected by the illnesses or approaching deaths. They may not be able to recognize or deal with anticipatory mourning in a healthy fashion.

When James was asked how he was coping with all his friends' life-threatening illnesses, he told us, "I know they are all dying, but I just forget about them and move on. There's nothing I can do about it, anyway. What's the point of getting all upset?" His refusal to talk about his friends or to express his sad feelings increased his isolation. He became depressed and withdrew from most of his activities. He found himself unable to function at work. With support, he was finally able to relate the changes in his behavior to the avoidance of the grief surrounding him. He began crying and sharing his intense feelings. He was able to talk about his friends—what they meant to him and how much he regretted the changes in his relationships due to the disease. His performance at work improved, and he became an advocate for learning how to mourn.

Complicating Factors

A number of factors complicate anticipatory mourning in HIV/AIDS. Although many of the following factors may be common in relation to other diseases and among other population groups, their particular constellation is most burdensome in HIV/AIDS. These factors are important to recognize and accept in relation to HIV/AIDS.

- The constant possibility of current and future deaths within one's social network, causing an ongoing fear of forming new relationships
- Difficulty in differentiating between symptoms of grief and depression and symptoms of HIV disease
- Shortage of health care workers willing to treat PLWA, along with unavailability of the health care that is usually available for people with other illnesses and often inferior quality of the care that can be accessed
- Increasing dependency on overused, underfunded community resources with constantly changing demographics
- Homophobia (both internalized and externalized), discrimination, and secrecy
- Suicidal thoughts, often common among PLWA because of the ups and downs of the disease, side effects of treatment, and debilitating and disfiguring aspects

Allen, a member of a support group, was beset by fears for his own health and said he would kill himself before he suffered in the same ways he had seen others suffer. As he expressed these fears, other group members began to share similar thoughts and feelings. They had seen friends with dementia and disorientation, friends who had wasted away to less than 100 pounds, and others with disfiguring skin diseases. They vowed to have plans to kill themselves before the same things happened to them.

Psychosocial Issues

Multiple Losses

When the diagnosis is HIV/AIDS, loved ones mourn for losses already experienced and losses that are ongoing. The following types of multiple losses delineated by S. J. Klein (1994) interact with and affect one another, adding yet another dimension to the traditional understanding of anticipatory mourning:

- Loss of validation from society, often including the loss of family support due to rejection and fear
- Loss of health
- Loss of physical and emotional well-being

- Loss of previous life-style and sense of community
- Loss of sexual freedom
- Loss of employment stability due to the stigma attached to HIV/AIDS
- Loss of (discretionary) income due to illness-related expenses
- Loss of free time due to constraints of caregiving
- Loss of privacy and personal power resulting from the "outing" of sexual orientation when HIV status becomes known
- Loss of caregiver role when the PLWA dies
- Loss of a person still alive due to personality changes caused by the infection and the disease
- Loss of personal history
- Loss of a sense of world order
- Loss of role models and leaders who became activists in the cause
- Loss of dreams of growing old together
- Loss of hope for the future

As these frequent and multiple losses are experienced, people affected by HIV/AIDS may find themselves withdrawing and turning inward, away from possible support systems. The deep and intense emotions they feel can be devastating. It is likely that some individuals reach a threshold of saturation "where their capacity to integrate any more loss is reduced. For one person, one loss conceivably could create as much upheaval as would occur when another individual had experienced many times that number" (Corless, 1997, p. 111). The individual personality would determine the amount of distress each person could tolerate. The changing nature of the long-term illness and the intensity of the caregiving are two issues one must take into account when assessing tolerance for loss.

Long-Term Consequences

People dealing with anticipatory mourning may begin experiencing some or all of the following long-term, and possibly irreparable, consequences:

- They may experience emotional numbing, depression, and inability to express feelings. Feelings of pessimism, cynicism, fatalism, and insecurity are common. As these may be new feelings and behaviors, people believe that something is seriously wrong with them and that they will never get better.

"Every death is a reminder of my own mortality." Before Mac died in 1995, he shared with me that he felt "shell-shocked, angry, scared, numb, like I'm looking in a mirror. I isolate in defense. I dream of escaping it all, moving to a cabin in the mountains where the nightmare would slowly fade. 'Who's next?' is the most frequent question that crosses my mind. 'Where am I in line?' runs closely behind."

- People who anticipate loss after loss in short periods cannot realistically be expected to function well in life. The grief of each anticipated loss can hardly be acknowledged before the next potential death appears.

- Anticipatory mourning can influence the intensity of the feelings associated with death. Anger, resentment, frustration, and concern are evident to a great extent at this time. As a patient begins the living/dying process, the dementia that often accompanies AIDS becomes apparent. Loved ones frequently begin to recognize that the person they knew is changing and disappearing and begin mourning for the one "who used to be." The caregiver may also be isolated if other friends find themselves in similar situations.

- It is hard to concentrate and focus on what will be needed after the death. Financial matters, legal issues, and funeral arrangements may never be discussed.

- The PLWA may deal with the anticipatory mourning of his or her own impending death by being hurt and angry and may pull away from relationships. Some of this behavior may be in response to the real or perceived withdrawal of family, friends, and/or caregiver(s). AIDS itself, and the destruction it brings to mind and body, may be the real culprit. The PLWA may not want to be seen by others.

- When one or more members of a family are HIV infected, there will be anticipatory mourning for the currently expected death as well as for the deaths and losses to come. It becomes increasingly difficult to maintain an acceptable balance between engagement and detachment. There is a need to detach to protect oneself while still mattering and making a difference to others. Maintaining this balance requires ongoing self-monitoring, difficult in the best of circumstances (Carmack, 1992). The goal is to support mourners in the anticipatory mourning process without having them withdraw from their loved one before death occurs.

- Anticipatory mourning may manifest itself in the development of indifference, or what elsewhere I have termed "compassionate detachment," among caregivers and friends who repeatedly watch others die after prolonged illnesses. This detachment often is connected to feelings of numbness and an attitude of "I just don't care anymore." I believe that detaching in this manner allows people to continue involvement with those who need them. The prolonged emotional numbing commonly described by those experiencing multiple losses is a natural result of surviving ongoing losses; it is not a lack of sensitivity or caring (S. J. Klein, 1998).

Issues Related to Living Longer with HIV/AIDS

Unique to HIV/AIDS is the fact that many patients have dealt with anticipatory mourning and made arrangements to die, only to learn that they may continue to live. The time during which they survive may or may not be free of disease. For the HIV infected, it will certainly not be free of treatments and medications. Anticipatory mourning is never far from consciousness as they are never certain how long they will remain healthy.

In a recent article in the *Los Angeles Times* (Rothman, 1996), an AIDS patient is quoted as saying, "I realized this week that I have been prepared to die, but I'm not prepared to live. I know it may sound crazy." The author reflects, "But it doesn't sound crazy. Not to the thousands who have put affairs in order, written wills, bought cemetery plots, said their good-byes, sold life insurance policies, maxed out credit cards, given up jobs, gone on disability—only to find themselves getting better, thanks to these new drugs (p. E1). Many AIDS service organization providers find themselves planning support around wellness, not illness, and there is no time to deal with anticipatory mourning even though it is still an issue.

These patients' hopes are raised with caution but raised, nevertheless; however, they remember other promising treatments that failed. As with any new treatment, some patients will respond and others will not. People who are getting better do not know what to do with their lives and they feel as if they are starting over. They have to think about getting jobs, earning livelihoods, and saving for a still uncertain future. Those who are not responding to the drugs blame themselves, believing that it is their fault that the medications have failed. They feel happy for, and at the same time envious of, their friends who are responding to the drugs while their own hopelessness, frustration, and grief continue. The normal anger of grief turns to rage and depression in those for whom the medication is or was too late.

Coping

How do people cope with anticipatory mourning in HIV/AIDS? How does one mourn for the patient and mourn for oneself? To find the answers, one often needs not to explore the future but rather to examine how coping with life was accomplished in the past. Who was there when support was needed? Who was not? How did a family respond to grief in the past? How is physical, emotional, social, and spiritual support accessed in the present? Answering these questions can bring a greater understanding of the need for a person to deal with anticipatory mourning. Recalling what previously gave one strength to survive stressful events will help one focus on strategies for the present.

ANTICIPATORY MOURNING OF CAREGIVERS

Those who are constantly involved in ongoing caregiving for people with AIDS will find feelings and reactions of anticipatory mourning continually being stimulated. They will experience—and try to cope with—sadness, anger, resentment, fear, denial, despair, helplessness, confusion, and numbness. Professionals and lay people who find themselves giving care and being cared for may better understand their behavior by being aware of these normal responses to anticipatory mourning.

A disease or an illness affects the entire "family," not just the diagnosed patient. Yet caregivers sometimes believe that any needs they have are secondary to those of the people with AIDS. These caregivers often ignore their own sense of predeath bereavement, life stresses, and concerns, stating, "The patient is more important"; "I should be grateful that I'm not sick"; "My problems don't really count. I have to be strong." Many caregivers have told me that they are just fine even though they are obviously exhausted and filled with grief that they do not even recognize.

> Jan denied any feelings of grief. She reminded me that Don was still alive. "Even if Don is very ill, he is still alive, and people don't grieve for someone who is alive. I can't give up on him. He needs me to be strong. I can't show him that I am not able to cope, that I need help. That would be letting him down."

Comments similar to this illustrate that education about the role of anticipatory mourning in AIDS illness is imperative. If a caregiver does not understand this type of grief, he or she will not be able to take care of "self" and will have little to give to another person. Attendance at a support group for caregivers or individual sessions with a counselor can bring understanding of and support for one's needs. Talking with others helps a caregiver learn to accept the normal emotions a loved one feels when caring for a terminally ill person. Activities to refresh and renew can be explored. Most important of all, caregivers can learn not to feel guilty about taking care of themselves.

Anticipatory Mourning for Self When HIV Infected

Being at risk for AIDS, HIV-infected people may be witnessing in others what they see as their own futures, and they go through mourning for themselves. If a newly diagnosed person who is medically stable is surviving a partner who died of AIDS-related illness, the person may see him- or herself as following in the footsteps of the deceased. This perception can be extraordinarily stressful and has great impact on self-esteem. The psychological impact of each individual's HIV status has to be sorted out. The goal is to help HIV-positive persons view themselves in their own light, define their own quality of life, become comfortable with themselves, and be confident in their own ways of negotiating life (Shelby, 1992).

MENTAL HEALTH PROFESSIONALS AND THE ANTICIPATORY MOURNING OF HIV/AIDS

Mental health counselors can best direct their efforts toward PLWA and their significant others by helping them examine possible new ways of relating within the context of the hopeful environment now surrounding HIV. People can explore ways to talk with potential partners about their conditions, about safe sex and intimacy, and about planning for the future. They can explore their anticipatory mourning and their angry feelings. They can learn how to take personal responsibility for their lives and how to develop their potential for a future in which hope figures along with HIV.

A clinician working with HIV/AIDS will experience many deaths. Some of these deaths will be personal losses; others will be the losses experienced by those who come for help.

> *Dr. Z., whose partner was dying of AIDS, was a member of a support group for caregivers and was also a health professional. In the group sessions, he frequently used his training to answer medical questions. He became intensely involved with others in the group who had AIDS. His involvement in this way increased his self-esteem, which had been badly damaged by his inability to use his medical knowledge to save not only his patients but also his partner.*

Some practitioners develop exaggerated expectations of comforting their clients and then feel unable to meet those expectations as the clients become sicker. Clinicians must find ways to deal with these feelings as well as their work-related mourning and any unfinished mourning related to their personal lives. A professional's emotional reactions to the devastation caused by AIDS are no less important than the clients' reactions. Counselors who do not understand their own issues around death and dying will it find difficult to be fully available to those they hope to help.

In addition to the professional's need to deal with the impending deaths of clients with AIDS, anticipatory mourning occurs in other distinct contexts in the therapeutic relationship: The therapist may be dealing with his or her own HIV infection and possible death, and the client must then contend with the possibility of the death of the therapist. The mental health professional who is HIV positive must address, with his or her own special anticipatory mourning, issues that include maintaining the ability to work, confronting one's own death, sharing one's serostatus with colleagues and/or clients, and mourning one's own personal losses, even while helping clients with mourning issues. Paul L. Plate, who is HIV positive, discusses his approach to continuing his practice:

> I have the opportunity to model a personal and
> professional life plan that incorporates my illness,
> continuing to do fulfilling work, being committed to goals,
> being involved, and making a contribution. But desire was
> not the only criterion I considered when facing the question
> of continuing to practice. It was crucial for me to consider
> two other areas of my life: physical and mental health and
> the support of colleagues. It is contingent on ongoing
> physical and mental health and my ability to deliver quality
> service. I had to deal with depression; resolve feelings like
> anger, denial, and shame; and ensure that I was not facing
> organic decline or an illness that signaled incipient
> disability. (1996, p. 5)

At some point in the illness of the therapist, the need for self-disclosure will arise. This is a sensitive issue: Premature self-disclosure can be threatening to the client; it can make the client feel as if he or she doesn't count and that the helper is more important. If the integrity of the therapeutic relationship is to be maintained, boundaries must be maintained. Preparing for the possibly premature death of one's therapist and possible early termination of therapy are concerns to be discussed, not avoided. These are difficult issues to confront. They point up the need for the professional to be open to seeking counseling and support while helping clients. The client must overcome fears of confronting the therapist, discussing feelings, evaluating the therapy, dealing with mourning, and moving on to termination or to another counselor.

Tasks for Mental Health Professionals

A clinician may find some clients experiencing emotional problems as a result of frequent changes in their HIV treatments. Wells (1996) discusses the emotional backlash for those who had resigned themselves to AIDS as a terminal illness and who then realize that this mind-set may no longer work. Feelings of regret from past choices made as the client prepared to die may become a central theme of counseling. A sense of wasted or lost time may emerge as the client reflects on choices such as quitting school, not saving money, selling a life insurance policy, running up debts, or engaging in health-compromising behaviors.

The therapist can place these concerns in context by reminding the client that one part of anticipatory mourning is making similar choices when faced with expected death. There may be regrets, but the individual can be encouraged to find a focus for the future with goals that are possible to attain. Now it is time to explore the specific AIDS-related losses and feelings that the client is experiencing.

The mental health professionals counseling people anticipating death—their own or a loved one's—from AIDS-related illness are urged to undertake the following specific tasks. The unpredictable course of the disease mandates flexibility and offers opportunities for therapeutic support, validation, and advocacy.

- Know the person you are counseling, particularly in regard to HIV status, legal and social status, and mental health status. Knowing the client's history of AIDS-related losses will help in the assessment of coping skills, suicide risk and self-destructive tendencies, and degree of depression (Scheps & Klein, 1998).

- Explore the client's relationship with the person who is dying. Discuss how fears of contagion affect physical intimacy. Besides the obvious consideration of the relationship's duration, explore unfinished business, feelings of resentment, anger, financial responsibilities, family issues, and other relevant topics.

- Assist the patient and the family in gathering information that will educate them about HIV/AIDS and help them negotiate the various systems and bureaucracies with which they must deal. The information needed will change constantly as the illness progresses.

- Increase your own awareness in regard to anticipatory mourning, death issues, and knowledge about how one tends to die from AIDS. Be sensitive to the existential issues of confronting death. Many clients become preoccupied with their own mortality, experiencing a sense of dread, existential anxiety, and other feelings associated with personal death awareness. Helping clients sort out their feelings will be more difficult and confusing if you have not developed and accepted your own understanding of death and spiritual beliefs.

- Understand and examine your attitudes and beliefs about HIV/AIDS-infected and HIV/AIDS-affected people of different cultures, religions, races, and ethnicities, as well as about those who are substance abusers or practice behaviors considered to be out of the norm.

- Recognize whether and to what extent you judge those with different sexual orientations and practices.

- Know how HIV infection occurs, and be aware of your comfort level with this information.

- Be aware that the client often wants to talk about his or her illness and death and finds it difficult because of the nature of AIDS. One patient saw that his friends seemed very lost and sad and did not know what to do or how to talk to him. He agreed to have them come to the hospital to share memories of their time with him. A visit of this kind often takes some preparation by the patient and the counselor. Possible outcomes can be discussed, time limits for the visit can be set, and a post-visit debriefing for the participants can be arranged.

  Nina wanted to talk about her coming death from AIDS. Linda, her caregiver, felt anxious about listening. She was afraid that Nina would become emotional, agitated, or angry. I encouraged her to approach Nina in a gentle, open manner, and she agreed to try to do so. I also suggested that part of Linda's anxiety was related to her own mourning over Nina's impending death. She was surprised at this suggestion because she believed that one mourned only after a person died, not before. Exploring her feelings and thoughts, she saw the reality of the situation. Nina did start to cry but for a different reason than anticipated. Nina said, "I am so grateful that you were willing to discuss this with me. I know I am dying, and since I got AIDS, everyone avoids me."

- Be aware of the power and consequences of the secrets and secret keeping that often accompany this disease. Remember that it is not uncommon for the patient's sexual orientation to be disclosed at the same time as the HIV infection is announced. The support system, under these circumstances, may be overwhelmed by anger, guilt, and shame.

- Support open communication about HIV infection and AIDS to the fullest extent possible. Individual and family styles will define the level of communication during anticipatory mourning.

- Provide a safe environment for people to talk. There are not many places where PLWA feel safe meeting and discussing their concerns. The offices of AIDS service organizations tend to be comfortable, but at the same time, being in this environment may be difficult.

- Acknowledge that there may be no answers to the client's difficult and challenging philosophical questions. The PLWA often says, "Most of my friends and I participated in the same activities. Why are some of us dying and others not even infected?"

- Accept that the task at hand is to do work on anticipatory mourning, not to change the client or challenge the life-style.

Counselors who have accomplished the aforementioned tasks and are comfortable with the constantly changing emotions of anticipatory mourning will find their work rewarding. By increasing self-awareness and by understanding anticipatory mourning in AIDS, they will be able to guide clients by asking explicitly, "What would be most helpful for you at this time?" Counselors can offer hope and help PLWA explore how life can have meaning again.

COPING STRATEGIES FOR THE INFECTED AND AFFECTED

Certain questions arise repeatedly when someone is experiencing anticipatory mourning in AIDS: "Is there a way to bring meaning to the losses in my life that will help me to survive?"; "How can I learn to cope with the impending absence of my loved ones?"; "How can I motivate myself to move on even as I struggle with this disease?" Clients can find answers to these questions by exploring the following activities or coping strategies (S. J. Klein, 1994, 1998):

- Avoid isolation. Identify people who understand you and who will listen as you express your feelings and thoughts openly. Find time to spend with them. Find and use support systems: Becoming actively involved with social and/or therapeutic support systems and networks affords opportunities to discuss problems, concerns, and the normal feelings of anticipatory mourning. Reaching out and connecting with others will help alleviate uncomfortable, lonely, and scary feelings. You will avoid the temptation to withdraw as you find a balance between solitude and socializing.

- Counter the conspiracy of silence. Most people will avoid mentioning the disease AIDS. This only serves to increase the sense of isolation and abandonment. So take the lead, and let others know that speaking openly is comforting and not upsetting.

- Identify stresses. People may say, "You have no reason to be stressed—you are healthy." But if you feel stressed, it is important to trust those feelings. After identifying stresses, you can then choose to make changes that will alter the level of stress. Some hidden stresses to uncover might include unrealistic goals, like the need to visit every friend with AIDS or the need always to be a caregiver; keeping sexual orientation hidden, which can be a source of great stress, often relieved if one chooses to "come out of the closet"; and dealing with the pressures of finances, home, and job.

- Focus on soothing activities. Resting the mind as well as the body is important in order to relieve stresses. Quiet time gives a much-needed mental vacation.

- Take breaks from HIV/AIDS. For anyone living in a community where people are constantly living with and dying of HIV/AIDS, dealing with the impending loss of loved ones reflects the reality that there is no way to avoid this disease. The world is infected, and we all need to be aware of how each of us is affected. AIDS is not going away soon, but taking a time-out will leave you feeling somewhat refreshed and better able to face ongoing activities and responsibilities.

- Explore the arts. As one explores the living/dying process, one can also explore the meaning of life by participating in a creative arts program, playing an instrument, dancing, writing creatively, or joining a choral group. These are all healing ways to express oneself and one's feelings.

- Use anger to empower, not to depress. Anger is one of the most prevalent emotions related to this disease. Holding it in can contribute to physical pain and additional illness. Anger can be focused, acknowledged, validated, and then expressed in healthy modes such as exercise, dance, drawing or painting, writing, public speaking, or political action. Redirecting the anger will provide increased energy to explore the anticipatory mourning of HIV/AIDS.

- Pay attention to self-care, grooming, exercise, relaxation, and nutrition.

In the mid- to late 1980s, George Solomon and his colleagues in San Francisco studied long-term survivors who were living with AIDS and published a list of their attributes that still applies today (Solomon, Temoshok, O'Leary, & Zich, 1989). Acquiring some or all of these attributes can give any person struggling with AIDS and the feelings of anticipatory mourning more control over his or her life, thereby increasing longevity and decreasing illness. The list developed by Solomon et al. includes some of the following traits and orientations:

- Perceiving health care as a collaboration between patient and doctor

- Becoming educated about one's personal health issues in order to participate in treatment decisions

- Having a sense of meaningfulness and purpose in life and finding a new meaning as a result of the disease

- Accepting diagnosis but not seeing it as a "death sentence"

- Being assertive and learning to say no in order to withdraw from taxing involvements and to nurture oneself

- Communicating openly about the illness and one's concerns

- Being sensitive to one's body and to physical and psychological needs

Along with exploring the attributes associated with long-term survival, one must become aware of activities and behaviors that may, in fact, be self-defeating or self-destructive. Some people believe that because they are already HIV infected, they do not need to take precautions with other HIV-positive people. This is not true. Reinfection is possible and may lead to an acquisition of a strain that is already resistant to medication; this can cause faster progression of the underlying HIV infection. There is often a desire to make impulsive changes, to run away from the pain. But one cannot run away from the illness or the grief. People dealing with anticipatory mourning in AIDS should be encouraged to seek professional help to identify behaviors that may be self-defeating. Awareness of these behaviors will enable these individuals to make healthier, less impulsive changes.

Additional coping strategies are as follows:

- Understand that you always have choices. One makes choices using the best alternatives available in any situation with current knowledge and resources. Yet one can get stuck in believing no choices exist when none of the alternatives seems to produce what one wants. Learning to see the options helps one take control by identifying those areas in which one still can be in charge.

- Nurture hope. Hope means different things to different people at different times. The object of hope also can change. At some point, one may wish for recovery of oneself or a loved one or pray that new medication will eliminate the virus. If health worsens, the hope will be for less suffering, then for release and peace. Preserving even a tiny bit of hope is essential for surviving the pressures of an AIDS-related situation.

Andrea told me, "It's about having support and resources so when you feel scared with things in life you can talk to someone. You can look with a positive attitude at the things that scare you and have hope instead of despair."

- Participate in rituals such as the Names Project AIDS Memorial Quilt. The quilt includes over 43,000 panels made in memory of people who have died of AIDS. In recent years, people have made panels for loved ones who are dying of AIDS-related illnesses as a positive way to deal with anticipatory mourning. Others can plan the panel with the one who is dying, incorporating his or her specific needs and wishes. The panel then becomes something to honor the loved one after death.

- Connect or reconnect to a religious/spiritual base. HIV/AIDS can create conflicts between the teachings of some religions and the love and compassion some family members feel toward PLWA. The problem inevitably raises spiritual or religious issues because AIDS is often seen as a punishment from God. A PLWA who is estranged from his or her religion may feel as if the early teachings of his or her family are being betrayed. Exploring spiritual options can often relieve the distress caused by this dilemma: Even if religion is a turnoff, comfort can be found in other aspects of spirituality. Turning to religion can constitute a coping strategy. Religious faith may arise from the possibility of imminent death, with many people finding that faith palliates their concerns (Bivens, Neimeyer, Kirchberg, & Moore, 1994–1995).

- Keep your sense of humor. Humor can be one of the best coping resources for dealing with anticipatory mourning and anger. Holding on to a sense of humor helps one appreciate the lighter side of even the darkest situations. A. Klein (1987), in a commentary on humor and death, acknowledges that most of us believe that death is "serious business" without a place for humor. Humor can, however, provide relief for our anxieties about death by taking some of the mystery away and reminding us that laughter can be beneficial.

CONCLUSION

Anticipatory mourning is a subjective experience with no clear-cut definitions. Understanding of this phenomenon has value if caregivers can assess their observations in order to identify those who might be at risk for psychological or physical complications of postdeath mourning. It is helpful to accept individual reactions on the basis of previous loss experience, relationships with the dying/deceased person(s), and meanings attached to illness and death (Sweeting & Gilhooly, 1990).

AIDS-related disease and impending death challenge the ways people see themselves in the world. They force reexamination of beliefs and values and encourage people to explore what is truly meaningful in their lives. They allow a process of rediscovery; a look at possible attainment of earlier, neglected goals; and the discovery of strengths that can take people out of the "victim" role. The energy of this exploration can be used to move forward into growth opportunities previously unrecognized.

> Mac McCoy, a friend of mine who died of AIDS-related illness, was more than willing to share with me his feelings and thoughts on the subject of living with this disease. He was trying to reach some resolution of personal grief for his imminent death and also for the many friends who had died. "What has all this taught me?" he asked. "That life is to be lived in the now, that death is not to be feared when I truly live my life to the fullest, and that I'll be ready when it comes. That taking action helps even if I can't truly fix anything. Doing something gives me a measure of control over my own life and thoughts and feelings. Most important to me, I have learned better to take care of myself and my needs and really enjoy life and the people in it." (S. J. Klein, 1998, pp. 137–138)

REFERENCES

Bivens, A. J., Neimeyer, R. A., Kirchberg, T. M., & Moore, M. K. (1994–1995). Death concern and religious beliefs among gays and bisexuals of variable proximity to AIDS. *Omega, 30,* 105–120.

Carmack, B. J. (1992, Spring). Balancing engagement/detachment in AIDS-related multiple losses. *IMAGE: Journal of Nursing Scholarship, 24*(1), 9–14.

Centers for Disease Control. (1998). *CDC HIV/AIDS surveillance report* (Vol. 10, No. 2). Atlanta: Author.

Corless, I. B. (1997). Modulated mourning: The grief and mourning of those infected and affected by HIV/AIDS. In K. J. Doka (Ed.), *Living with grief: When illness is prolonged.* Washington, DC: Taylor & Francis.

Doka, K. J. (Ed.). (1989). *Disenfranchised grief: Recognizing hidden sorrow.* Lexington, MA: Lexington Books.

Klein, A. (1987). Commentary—Humor and death . . . You've got to be kidding! *Hospice Team Quarterly,* p. 4.

Klein, S. J. (1994). AIDS-related multiple loss syndrome. *Illness, Crises and Loss, 4,* 13–25.

Klein, S. J. (1998). *Heavenly hurts: Surviving AIDS-related deaths and losses.* Amityville, NY: Baywood.

Odets, W. (1995). *In the shadow of the epidemic: Being HIV negative in the age of AIDS.* Durham, NC: Duke University Press.

Plate, P. L. (1996, July). Through the looking glass: Providers with HIV disease. *FOCUS: A Guide to AIDS Research and Counseling,* pp. 5, 6.

Rofes, E. (1996). *Reviving the tribe: Regenerating gay men's sexuality and culture in the ongoing epidemic.* New York: Harrington Park Press.

Rothman, C. (1996, November 5). A world turned upside-down: With promising new drugs, are HIV patients ready for life? *Los Angeles Times,* Section E, p. 1.

Scheps, R., & Klein, S. J. (1998). Negative consequences: Issues for HIV-negative gay/bisexual men. *Journal of Gay and Lesbian Social Services, 8*(2), 51–68.

Schwartzberg, S. (1992). AIDS-related bereavement among gay men: The inadequacy of current theories of grief. *Psychotherapy, 29*(3), 422–429.

Shelby, D. (1992, November/December). Complicated mourning in the wake of AIDS. *The Forum,* pp. 5–6.

Solomon, G., Temoshok, L., O'Leary, A., & Zich, J. (1989). An intensive psychoimmunological study of long-surviving persons with AIDS. *Annals of the New York Academy of Science, 496,* 651.

Sweeting, M., & Gilhooly, M. (1990). Anticipatory grief: A review. *Social Science Medicine, 30,* 1073–1080.

Walker, R. J. (1996). Anticipatory grief and AIDS: Strategies for intervening with caregivers. *Health & Social Work, 21*(1), 49–57.

Wells, E. (1996, January/February). New prognosis for HIV: A mental health perspective. *HIV Frontline,* p. 4.

WHO report on the global HIV/AIDS epidemic. (1998, December). *http://www.us.unaids.org*

Wiener, L. (1994). The HIV-infected child: Parental responses and psychosocial implications. *American Journal of Orthopsychiatry, 64,* 485–492.

CHAPTER 16
Mourning Psychosocial Loss: Anticipatory Mourning in Alzheimer's, ALS, and Irreversible Coma

Kenneth J. Doka

In the beginning, Margaret had just dismissed it as absentmindedness. But slowly over the next year it had gotten worse. Her husband, Bob, had been brought home by the police just a few weeks ago. Walking to a neighborhood store, he had forgotten where he lived and had panicked. That night Margaret had sought to comfort him by reminding him of the morning some years before when they had gone for an early morning jog on a vacation and could not remember the way back to their hotel. But as she recounted the story, Bob looked at her vacantly. It was clear he no longer remembered the incident.

For the past 2 years, Tyler, now 17 years old, has remained in a coma. His mother visits almost daily, sitting by his side, softly talking and stroking his arm. Tyler's father has not visited for over a year.

It began for Mark as a noticeable slur in his speech. A battery of tests failed to establish a definitive cause, leading to a suspicion of ALS, which was later confirmed. Now on disability, Mark adheres both to a limited medical regimen and to a variety of alternative forms of therapy that he hopes will heal him. Absorbed in this self-healing, he is far less available to his family. Meanwhile, his wife and college-age children struggle with the problems posed by this disease.

In an earlier essay, Rando (1986) reminded us that the concept of "anticipatory grief" is both misunderstood and useful. It is misunderstood if it is perceived only as grief that is generated by the prospect of future loss. It is useful insofar as one remembers that the course of an illness entails many losses that are concurrently experienced and mourned. Hence, *anticipatory mourning*—the term used herein to incoporate what previously was called anticipatory grief, along with the coping it engenders—may be described as the reaction to a perceived impending loss, as well as reactions and responses to losses already experienced within the new reality of the illness. Such a definition reinforces and reminds us of the wide range of losses felt and grieved in the progression of an illness.

This phenomenon is illustrated by the three opening vignettes. In each situation, the patient remains alive. Yet in each it is clear that family, friends, caregivers, and, in some cases, the patient as well experience a wide variety of losses that engender mourning.

In each of these cases there is, among other losses, a psychosocial loss, or a loss in which the psychological essence, individual personality, or self is perceived as dead even though the person physically remains alive (Doka & Aber, 1989).* In other words, the persona of the individual is so changed that others experience the loss of that person as he or she previously existed. Psychosocial loss can arise in a variety of circumstances, including religious conversion, mental illness, substance abuse, and even recovery from the latter two conditions. In other cases, traumatic or exceptional circumstances can so alter an individual that others may find it too difficult to relate to him or her. Although psychosocial loss can occur in many situations, it often is profoundly experienced in cases where there is dramatic and irreversible physical or mental deterioration—the kinds of deterioration that inevitably occur in such diseases as amyotrophic lateral sclerosis (ALS) or Alzheimer's disease (and other causes of dementia), as well as in circumstances that cause irreversible coma.

This chapter explores the ways in which anticipatory mourning may be experienced as individuals cope with psychosocial loss as well as other related losses that accompany such conditions. The chapter begins by exploring the nature of these diseases and conditions in order to outline fully the range of losses that may be experienced in their wake. The nature of these losses and the ways they may complicate mourning are then considered. Finally, the chapter concludes by offering interventive strategies to assist patients, their intimate networks of family and friends, and professional caregivers.

---

*The use of the term *psychosocial death* or *psychosocial loss* to refer to the loss of the persona of a given individual as experienced by others in the relational environment (Doka & Aber, 1989) differs from Weisman's (1972) use of the term to refer to psychological and social factors that interact with physiological ones in determining death.

DISEASES AND CONDITIONS
THAT CAUSE PSYCHOSOCIAL LOSS

Dementia and Alzheimer's Disease

The Diagnostic and Statistical Manual of Mental Disorders (DSM-IV) describes dementia as being characterized by the development of multiple cognitive deficits, including memory impairment (American Psychiatric Association, 1994, p. 133). In addition to memory deficits, other cognitive disturbances can include aphasia (or deterioration of language function), apraxia (impaired motor function), agnosia (failure to recognize or identify objects), and impaired executive functioning (deficiencies in abstract thinking, behavioral planning, monitoring, etc.). Conditions such as poor nutrition, trauma, drug abuse, medication difficulties, or inflammatory illness, among others, also sometimes lead to dementia, but in these cases it can be reversible.

Alzheimer's disease is the leading cause of chronic or irreversible dementia, accounting for approximately half of the cases. A variety of theories exist regarding the etiology of the disease, including genetic factors and those suggesting environmental, viral, and metabolic causes. The incidence of Alzheimer's disease does increase with age. Approximately 10% of persons over 65 have been clinically diagnosed with the disease. This figure rises to over 47% by age 85 (Kaplan, 1996). Very new and tentative data from a longitudinal study of Sisters of Notre Dame recount the case of Sister Mary, who had multiple lesions, suggesting advanced Alzheimer's but little clinical evidence of the disease (Snowdon, 1997). This case suggests that a wide range of subtle to severe manifestations of the disease may exist and that perhaps other coexisting factors may influence the decline of cognitive functioning.

In Alzheimer's there is a progressive deterioration of cognitive processes. Early in the disease, individuals may experience loss of memory and judgment skills, which may cause both anxiety and a tendency to compensate by avoiding new situations (Kaplan, 1996). In the end stages, they may be incontinent and totally dependent on others. Throughout the course of the disease, affected individuals may respond with paranoia, depression, delirium, anxiety, and other psychiatric symptoms. As in many of the diseases and conditions addressed in this chapter, the course of Alzheimer's can be highly unpredictable.

The second most common cause of dementia is vascular (or formerly multi-infarct) dementia. In this condition, blood vessels within the brain are destroyed by strokes of varied intensities, as well as by other conditions such as heart failure that deprive the brain of oxygen. Here, the onset of the disease tends to be more sudden and progresses in a more stepped pattern than is normally seen in Alzheimer's. Early diagnosis can sometimes assist here in preventing or slowing deterioration through treatment of underlying conditions such as high blood pressure or diabetes. Other diseases such as Parkinson's, Pick's disease, Huntington's, Creutzfeldt-Jakob, and AIDS also can cause dementia.

The critical commonality is that each of these dementias creates a chain of loss. The afflicted individual experiences significant losses of cognitive functioning that in turn lead to changes in relationships, mental well-being, and self-esteem. Others experience these changes as a consequent loss of the person who was.

Amyotrophic Lateral Sclerosis (ALS)

ALS is the most serious of a group of motor neuron diseases that affect the larger nerve cells, called motor neurons, which connect the voluntary muscles to the spinal cord and the brain. When motor neuron cells are affected by the disease, they are no longer able to transmit impulses to the muscles. The voluntary muscles themselves then atrophy.

ALS has an insidious course. Initial symptoms are very nonspecific and include such things as twitching and cramping in the extremities, weakness in the arms and legs, impaired speech, and perhaps mood swings and uncontrollable bouts of laughing or crying. There is no diagnostic test for ALS. Thus, once symptoms appear, physicians need some time to rule out other diseases that might cause these effects, such as multiple sclerosis, muscular dystrophy, or tumors. The cause of ALS is not known, although genetic factors may account for a small portion of cases. Environmental toxins and autoimmune factors are suspect as well.

Not only may the initial symptoms of ALS differ among individuals, but the course of the disease also varies. Although the disease is progressive and fatal, approximately half of its victims live more than 3 years after diagnosis. Another 20% survive at least 5 years, while 10% live beyond 10 years. Nevertheless, all gradually lose voluntary muscle functioning. In the end stages, the patient will be quadriplegic, bedridden, and totally dependent, yet with intact sensory and mental functioning. But though ALS does not affect mental functioning, depression and anxiety reactions are not uncommon. In the final phase of illness, the patient will lose the ability to breathe and to swallow, becoming dependent on life support and prone to opportunistic disease. Naturally, the cost of such total care can be devastating to the family.

Irreversible Coma

Irreversible comas, sometimes (unfortunately) called "vegetative states," can occur in a wide variety of circumstances, including, for example, trauma, heart failure, aneurysm, cancer, or drug reaction. In such cases, the brain is deprived of oxygen or otherwise damaged. The result is that the patient can remain—sometimes indefinitely, with hydration and feeding—in a netherland between life and death. Again, as with the other conditions, the course and timing may be unpredictable.

Social, Psychological, and Psychosocial Deaths

The two diseases—Alzheimer's and ALS—and the variety of circumstances that create irreversible comas illustrate different conditions of loss. In Alzheimer's disease, there is a gradual and progressive loss of mental faculties. The losses in ALS are also gradual and progressive, but in this case the losses are of physical function; mental functioning remains intact. In irreversible comas, losses include both physical and mental abilities. These losses can be sudden or gradual.

Three concepts are useful for understanding and exploring both the commonalities and the differences in the aforementioned circumstances. Sudnow (1967), in his classic study of dying, defined social death as "that point at which socially relevant attributes of the patient begin permanently to cease to be operative as conditions for treating him and when he is, essentially, regarded as already dead" (p. 73). For example, a comatose patient's condition may be discussed in front of him or her, because the family or caregivers no longer consider the person alive.

Psychological death can be said to occur whenever there is a loss of individual consciousness. The person ceases to be aware of self: "Not only does he not know who he is—he does not know *that* he is" (Kalish, 1966, p. 249). Naturally, this state can only be inferred by others. Psychosocial death has already been defined as the point at which the individual's persona is lost.

In a sense, all of these concepts represent points on a continuum. As Kalish reminds us, "a given person may be socially dead to one individual, to many individuals, or to virtually everyone" (1966, p. 73). Similarly, psychological and psychosocial death can be perceived as partial or total. For example, in Alzheimer's disease, the patient and others may experience times of normal behavior. Even in ALS there may be many times when patients transcend the physical limitations of the disease and they and those around them experience periods that are reminiscent of times prior to the onset of illness.

These concepts provide a context for understanding the range of losses likely to be experienced. In Alzheimer's, patients and their intimate networks experience a gradual psychological dying of consciousness that can lead to psychosocial loss and death and perhaps, particularly in cases of institutionalization, to social death. Irreversible comas often force families to experience the full range of losses associated with all these forms of death. In ALS, deterioration of physical functioning leads to patients' and their families' mourning ongoing psychosocial loss. These losses are mourned throughout the experience of illness, and they reemphasize the fact that anticipated physical death is not the only object of mourning.

THE NATURE OF LOSS

Rando (1986) emphasizes that anticipatory mourning (which she formerly called anticipatory grieving) means mourning not only an expected death but the variety of losses that accompany an illness experience. This concept acknowledges three critical time foci for loss: past, present, and future. One mourns not only an expected future death but also losses that have been experienced in the past and losses being experienced in the present. One can extend the concept by noting that anticipated losses may comprise not only death but additional losses projected within the illness experience as well.

These concepts are unfortunately yet pristinely displayed in the types of diseases and conditions explored in this chapter. For example, in Alzheimer's disease, the extent of loss is profound. First, there is the very loss of past, to which memory links us. As we cease to remember, those connections to the past are severed. This loss was poignantly expressed by a client in the early stages of Alzheimer's. Struggling to recall an incident in his childhood, he began to sob, "I used to remember." In these early phases of the disease, clients can both acknowledge and grieve the lapses of memory and fear that future decline may sever all links to the past.

Memory also links us to the present. It allows us to recall the histories that bind us in relationships, shared experiences that join us to one another. As memory lapses, these links can become tenuous. This is illustrated by an Alzheimer's patient who, when shown a photograph of her daughter, said, "She is either my sister or the lady that cleans the house."

In addition, memory links us to ourselves. As we lose memory, our sense of who and what we are dims, and these lapses of memory can lead to other losses. As one can no longer function effectively, certain roles, such as work roles, may have to be relinquished. One may also experience a loss of independence, perhaps entailing institutionalization with all its attendant losses. Naturally, the degree to which the disease has progressed will affect the level at which the patient can identify and experience grief and mourning.

Although a patient in advanced stages of Alzheimer's disease or some other form of dementia may not recognize the extent of loss, patients with ALS clearly do. As Leach and Keleman state, ALS "is unique in the combination of possibilities it extends for suffering. It is the classic nightmare in which you want to run and your legs won't move, to speak and you make no sound" (1986, p. 57). Patients experience a continuing array of incremental losses—of independence, self-sufficiency, self-image, self-esteem, and eventually even survival—yet they face these losses with no diminution of intellectual skills.

As the disease progresses, patients experience many present losses. They may have to relinquish work, career, and other roles. When disabilities render them unable to participate in habitual activities, significant relationships may change. In one instance, when a man with ALS experienced slurred speech, he began to see the withdrawal of many friends. This was exacerbated by his own embarrassment and humiliation over his speech, which made him reluctant to pursue relationships.

In ALS, each new symptom or further decline can create a new cycle of losses. And the patient continues to be conscious that future losses are likely to lead to total disability, immobility, and incontinence as he or she faces death.

In a case of irreversible coma, the nature of the condition will determine the extent of the patient's mourning. When coma follows a lengthy illness, many of the aforementioned losses may be experienced. In a traumatic event, it is unclear to what extent the patient may mourn.

Whatever the condition and the patient's experience, the family will certainly mourn. In many ways, their losses will parallel the patient's. The loss of memory in Alzheimer's, for example, severs a link to a past that the family shares. The inability to recall and reminisce together can be a significant loss. A family member's own past may seem less real if there are not opportunities for sharing and validation.

Families and friends deal with the continued realities of psychosocial loss. The person is alive, albeit in a different way. The persona that family and friends know is irrevocably lost, yet they have an ongoing relationship with this very changed person. In Alzheimer's, other forms of dementia, or irreversible coma, the only aspect of the person remaining over time may be the physical self. In conditions such as ALS, the changes may be far beyond the physical. The increasing level of disability may make family and friends surrender shared activities. Communication difficulties such as slurred speech may hinder interaction.

Varied psychological responses to devastating illness can also be a source of loss. For example, the patient can become angry or depressed. Mood swings can be a symptom of the disease or a side effect of varied medications. And self-absorption, described earlier in the case of Mark, is not atypical in life-threatening illness (Doka, 1993). All these responses accentuate the sense of psychosocial loss: The patient is now no longer the same person he or she once was. Yet mourning that loss may itself seem selfish and unsympathetic.

Like the patient, family and friends may mourn anticipated losses in the future as well as the expected death. They can look toward further decline, increased responsibilities, and perhaps agonizing end-of-life decisions. These increased demands mean that they lose freedom as well as key roles that formerly provided meaning, bolstered self-esteem, and offered respite and social support. For example, the husband of one ALS patient continued to work as a teacher but experienced the loss of a coaching position that provided income and enjoyment, as well as leadership roles in his church and union. In fact, in a recent study of families of Alzheimer's patients, the losses associated with the caregiving role loomed as the most significant losses persons experienced. Loos and Bowd (1997) found that caregivers very much grieved the loss of social and recreational interactions and occupations. In addition, extensive caregiving responsibilities had two other implications: Caregivers felt a loss of control over life events, and some, especially the elderly, experienced negative effects on their own health and well-being, which created additional losses.

Family and friends may, moreover, grieve the loss of their assumptive worlds. The concept of the assumptive world is critical for appreciation of the concept of anticipatory mourning. All of us possess sets of beliefs and assumptions about our worlds and our places within them. Some of these are assumptions about future lives—how we expect to grow older, how we perceive the next phase, how we envision retirement. These assumptions are both shattered and mourned throughout the course of illness.

Some of these shattered assumptions may be deeply spiritual ones. Beliefs about the nature of the universe or the benevolence of God may be challenged by the circumstances surrounding the loss. The world may no longer seem fair or orderly, and God may no longer be seen as kind. Such spiritual pain exacerbates mourning, adding spiritual losses to the litany of losses mourned, while inhibiting what previously might have been a strong and effective coping mechanism.

The intensive demands of an illness like those discussed here usually mean that caregivers outside the family will be extensively involved in the patient's care. The condition may necessitate a wide range of involvement by nurses' aides, home attendants, nurses, physicians, physical therapists, and, in a case of institutionalization, hospital or nursing home staff. The long period of decline that often characterizes these diseases and conditions can lead to significant attachment. The attachment can be particularly strong in ALS, where the patient's persisting mental capacities and probable middle age can lead both to intensive interaction and, perhaps, to identification.

It is not unusual for caregivers, too, to have grief. In a case of institutionalization where the family may have long experienced the social death of the patient, staff may be, in fact, the primary mourners. Although it is beyond the scope of this chapter to explore implications and helpful interventions relative to such circumstances, it is critical to acknowledge and validate the mourning. Individual caregivers will need to develop effective strategies of self-care, and organizations should review their own strategies for assisting staff. (See chapter 12 in this book, by Larson, and Vachon, 1987.)

Family, friends, and other caregivers will experience a series of losses that are mourned throughout the course of the patient's condition. A variety of factors complicate this mourning process.

One of the myths concerning anticipatory mourning is that it mitigates reactions following the death (see Rando, 1986). This myth is based on the misperception that anticipatory mourning causes others to withdraw slowly from the patient as they anticipate and mourn the death. The emphasis on the fact that anticipatory mourning entails grief for losses previously or currently experienced reminds us that these people do not mourn the death alone, nor is there necessarily any disengagement.

In fact, in the conditions considered in this chapter, involvement in the life of the dying person is likely to intensify. Caregivers and others are faced, then, with a difficult paradox: to mourn the loss of a person dramatically changed by the illness or condition while increasing their involvement in the person's life. In addition to personal losses associated with an expanded caregiving role (Loos & Bowd, 1997), these new and ever-increasing care demands may lead to stress, perhaps complicating relationships with the patient or other family members and thus possibly exacerbating later mourning.

In one case, for example, a daughter who had assumed major care responsibilities when her mother developed Alzheimer's later felt guilty about the occasions when she had been impatient with her mother. At the same time, she was resentful of other family members who had limited their involvement. Even when conflict is not apparent, the increased demands of care may leave little time for others, disrupting the caregiver's supportive network at a time when, paradoxically, it is needed most. And these demands may not even allow the time and energy to mourn.

Another complicating factor is role confusion due to the now ambiguous status of the relationship. For example, as Alzheimer's progresses, spouses may no longer relate to one another in the same roles. The caregiving spouse has lost a mate, though a formal tie remains. In effect, spouses in this situation exist in a netherland, neither married nor divorced or widowed. They become "pseudowidows" (Grossman & Grossman, 1983) or hidden or "cryptowidows" (Doka & Aber, 1989). This condition may intensify with institutionalization: They are alone but still married. Irreversible comas lead to similar circumstances. In ALS, many aspects of the marital relationship, such as the sexual dimension, may be slowly surrendered even as the person remains mentally alert and conscious.

Finally, this mourning is disenfranchised. It involves loss that is not openly acknowledged, socially supported, or publicly shared (Doka, 1989). In short, the mourner is not perceived as having a right to mourn. There are many reasons for disenfranchised grief and mourning, but a lack of open acknowledgment is often the case when the loss is psychosocial. As long as the patient is alive, family, friends, and even the patient may be encouraged to make the best of these changed circumstances. This stance leaves little room to acknowledge the profound losses already experienced.

INTERVENTIVE STRATEGIES

The previous section emphasized the variety of losses that patients, family, friends, and other caregivers may experience throughout the course of these illnesses or conditions. Because these losses are both extensive and current, they will need to be addressed and mourned. For this reason, interventive strategies always begin with validation. Validation means acknowledging and allowing grief, valuing the reality of loss, and providing opportunities to mourn the various losses.

One interesting concept in the psychology of life-threatening illness, introduced by Weisman (1972), is that of "middle knowledge." Middle knowledge is the phenomenon in which the dying person drifts in and out of the awareness of dying, sometimes acknowledging impending death, at other times ignoring or denying that reality. This concept can be extended to family and friends, and it can be applied to other losses as well. The implication is that one should always follow the patient's lead. Sometimes individuals will need to acknowledge these losses and mourn them, but at other times they may choose not to acknowledge the losses they experience or expect. Anticipatory mourning is one of the multiplicity of responses possible within the illness experience.

Patients may benefit from a variety of other strategies, some specific to their illnesses. For example, one of the most promising new clinical approaches to Alzheimer's and other forms of dementia is "validation therapy." Previously, if a confused client made a nonsensical reference to a person or event—for example, an 80-year-old woman searching for her grandmother—it would be dismissed as disoriented rambling. An attempt would perhaps be made to reorient the patient to reality with a reminder that her grandmother had died long ago and that she herself was now a grandmother. According to validation therapy, such seemingly confused comments may in fact point to some unresolved issues that the patient retains and should therefore be taken seriously and explored. For example, one woman with Alzheimer's, unmarried and without children, began to search for her baby. Her social worker validated her quest, asking where her baby could be. Further exploration led to the woman's long-suppressed confession that as a teenager she had become pregnant, gone to another state on the pretext of going to school, had the child, and given it up for adoption. Once this loss was acknowledged, the searching behavior ceased.

In ALS, complementary therapies such as imaging, meditation, nutritional approaches, and biofeedback, to name just a few, may be valuable adjuncts to the therapeutic process. Beyond this inherent value, these approaches offer a renewed sense of control to patients struggling with a disease that is both relentless and unpredictable.

Counselors can draw on a number of interventive strategies in working with aware patients as well as with families and friends. As mentioned earlier, central to every intervention is the issue of acknowledging and validating mourning over losses already experienced or expected. Beyond that critical step, a number of specific strategies can be helpful.

Help Clients Understand the Underlying Condition

The degree to which family and friends understand the underlying condition may either ameliorate or exacerbate grief and stress. In ALS, for example, common symptoms such as fatigue and mood swings may not be recognized as manifestations of disease but rather be perceived as responses under the patient's control. Such misrepresentations create unnecessary tension between patients and their intimate networks. Some cultural groups may be deeply shamed by conditions such as Alzheimer's, with increased isolation of both the patient and the family resulting (Yeo & Gallagher-Thompson, 1996). In addition, in some of these conditions, suspected genetic components may create unnecessary anxiety.

Exploring beliefs about the disease provides opportunities to educate clients, as well as to review coping strategies and assess expectations about the future. Organizations such as the ALS or Alzheimer's association can provide information and referral to self-help networks, support groups, and counselors. Support groups can be particularly useful as they offer validation of responses, education, suggestions for coping, information about resources, and respite. Education also enhances coping by providing meaningful activity that gives clients a sense of control.

Help Clients Deal with the Affective Issues Aroused by the Loss

Clients often lack opportunities to ventilate the emotions aroused by the situation. Because the patient is alive, family and friends may feel disloyal, unfeeling, or inhibited in expressing emotion. The patient, too, may feel it inappropriate to express his or her emotional reactions. All parties may struggle with a series of emotions— among them anger, guilt, anxiety, and shame. The latter two emotions can be very common when the disease has a suspected genetic component. Education about the condition may alleviate some of the affective issues, but clients may need additional opportunities to explore and ventilate their emotions. Counselors should encourage emotional expression, identify and validate the emotional responses that clients experience, and explore strategies for coping with these emotions. Questions such as "Many times clients in your situation have expressed to me feelings of _____. Have you experienced this?" can provide the freedom to explore previously unacknowledged affect.

In addition to the illness, the caregiving experience may arouse affect as well. Caregivers may feel resentful of the burdens placed on them, perhaps angry that others are not more helpful. These feelings are likely to be exacerbated when the relationship before illness was ambivalent. Caregivers may feel resentful of their new responsibilities, guilty about the times their patience lapses, or even regretful that they cannot do more. Patients, particularly in ALS, may resent their increasing dependence, ambivalent about the help they need. Exploring these reactions can allow them to acknowledge their own limits or to develop alternative strategies for future contingencies that can reinforce a sense of control. It is critical that counselors recognize the broad range of ways in which clients may achieve emotional release. For some, ventilating or crying can be helpful; for others, emotions can be expressed in activity or cognition (Martin & Doka, 1995).

Explore Spiritual Issues Raised by the Patient's Condition

Much of the time, clients experience a shattering of assumptions—most of their beliefs about the nature of the world or the future—which can give rise to a profound spiritual struggle. This struggle can be complicated, particularly as the demands of caregiving can limit opportunities for spiritual support—for example, limiting time for participation in religious services or spiritual practices. Again, counselors can validate this struggle, provide space to explore the spiritual issues raised by the illness, and allow clients to assess the ways in which they can effectively utilize their beliefs, rituals, and faith communities.

Help Clients Recognize and Respond to the Changes in Their Own Lives

An individual who experiences loss is likely to experience a series of secondary losses that spring from the initial loss. In psychosocial loss, these secondary losses can be profound. As mentioned earlier, clients may lose prior companionship, shared activities, and contact with others. They may have less personal time and thus be forced to relinquish significant roles or pleasurable activities. They may even experience spiritual crises, finding little control or meaning. These changes are likely to affect all dimensions of their lives: psychological, social, spiritual, sexual, and economic. And the changes may occur so rapidly that they may not realize how significantly their lives have been altered and how the changes have added to their stress.

Many times helping clients to acknowledge these changes can be beneficial. Simply asking "In what ways has your own life changed since _____?" allows clients to enumerate these losses. Sometimes clients themselves will be surprised at the extent to which their lives have changed. Having identified the losses, clients can then develop strategies for coping with them, perhaps regaining some of what was lost (possibly in modified form) and mourning the loss of what cannot be salvaged.

Explore Methods of Coping

Coping can be defined as the "constantly changing cognitive and behavioral efforts to manage specific external and/or internal demands that are appraised as passing or exceeding the resources of the person" (Lazarus & Folkman, 1984, p. 141). Coping strategies can be diverse: Some may be helpful (such as reframing thoughts or sharing emotions with others) and others unhelpful (such as using alcohol to numb emotions). Because the conditions surrounding loss can create periods of sustained stress, counselors will find it useful to explore individual clients' coping strategies. In this exploration, coping strengths can be identified and encouraged. Unhelpful coping strategies can also be identified, and clients can then assess alternative strategies.

Among the issues that might arise in a discussion of coping strategies are concerns about support and respite. One key coping skill is utilizing one's support system effectively. Asking clients to identify and assess their informal support systems can be useful in many ways. It can reinforce the idea that there are others to whom they may turn. It can lead to discussions about who has or has not been forthcoming, allowing the assessment of "surprises"—that is, individuals who did not come through as expected or those who provided unexpected support. This discussion can identify barriers to support, such as a reluctance to use or seek support.

These considerations can in turn lead to a discussion of respite. For the aware patient, respite in the form of visitors or other activity can provide needed diversion. For family caregivers, respite is essential to effective adaptation. Counselors may find these caregivers reluctant to consider their respite needs for a number of reasons, such as inability to find or trust alternate caregivers, concerns of the patient, feelings of guilt, or perhaps even the gratification experienced when one feels essential and needed. Nonetheless, family caregivers should be encouraged to explore both their respite needs and their respite strategies. The very question of how they meet their own needs for respite validates the legitimacy of deriving strategies to meet their own needs.

Help Clients Plan Realistically for the Future

Both aware patients and their family members and friends need to plan for the future. This concern, too, has many dimensions. One issue involves the question of advance directives. Clients may be resistant to planning for three reasons: First, in many of their situations, future possibilities may seem dismal. Second, many may have learned to adapt by simply taking each day as it comes. Third, given the reality of middle knowledge, clients—whether patients or families—may simply choose not to discuss an uncertain future at the time. For all of these reasons, counselors should respect clients' decisions.

Nonetheless, it is important to allow discussions of advance directives should the subject arise, even to invite clients to address these issues (see chapter 17 in this book, by Meagher and Quinn). First, in addition to the process of anticipatory mourning, there is a concurrent process of anticipatory bereavement (Gerber, 1974). This means that patients may need to take objective actions prior to further decline or death. Second, addressing future possibilities can allow patients to consider options that may be available. Even if certain options are not, for various reasons, viable, discussion of alternatives still reinforces a sense of control.

In addition, as clients experience losses, they may wish to develop small ritual acts that allow validation of those losses. For example, as one client's husband was institutionalized with advanced Alzheimer's, she needed a ritual to mark the fact that now, for the first time, she would live alone in her house. Her ritual was simple yet poignant. She neatly folded "his" towel from their bathroom and placed it in her bedroom near a picture of her once vibrant husband.

CONCLUSION

Each of the conditions discussed in this chapter will lead, eventually, to the patient's death. But long before that event, the patient will experience a series of other small, and sometimes not so small, deaths—of function, of consciousness, of memory. All of these losses will have to be mourned along the way.

REFERENCES

American Psychiatric Association. (1994). *Diagnostic and statistical manual of mental disorders* (DSM-IV). Washington, DC: Author.

Doka, K. J. (Ed.). (1989). *Disenfranchised grief: Recognizing hidden sorrow.* Lexington, MA: Lexington Books.

Doka, K. J. (1993). *Living with life-threatening illness: A guide for patients, their families and caregivers.* Lexington, MA: Lexington Books.

Doka, K. J., & Aber, R. (1989). Psychosocial loss and grief. In K. J. Doka (Ed.), *Disenfranchised grief: Recognizing hidden sorrow.* Lexington, MA: Lexington Books.

Gerber, I. (1974). Anticipatory bereavement. In B. Schoenberg, A. Carr, A. H. Kutscher, D. Peretz, & I. Goldberg (Eds.), *Anticipatory grief.* New York: Columbia University Press.

Grossman, S., & Grossman, C. A. (1983, May). *And then there was one.* Paper presented at the meeting of the Northeastern Gerontological Society, Newport, Rhode Island.

Kalish, R. A. (1966). A continuum of subjectively perceived death. *The Gerontologist, 6,* 73–76.

Kaplan, M. (1996). *Clinical practice with caregivers of dementia patients.* Washington, DC: Taylor & Francis.

Lazarus, R. S., & Folkman, S. (1984). *Stress, appraisal and coping.* New York: Springer.

Leach, C. F., & Keleman, J. (1986). Reflections on suffering prompted by ALS. *Loss, Grief, and Care, 1,* 57–68.

Loos, C., & Bowd, A. (1997). Caregivers of persons with Alzheimer's disease: Some neglected implications of the experience of personal loss and grief. *Death Studies, 21,* 501–514.

Martin, T., & Doka, K. J. (1995). Masculine grief. In K. J. Doka (Ed.), *Living with grief: After sudden loss.* Bristol, PA: Taylor & Francis.

Rando, T. A. (1986). *Loss and anticipatory grief.* Lexington, MA: Lexington Books.

Snowdon, D. (1997). Aging and Alzheimer's disease: Lessons from the nun study. *The Gerontologist, 37,* 150–156.

Sudnow, D. (1967). *Passing on: The social organization of dying.* Englewood Cliffs, NJ: Prentice Hall.

Vachon, M. (1987). *Occupational stress in the care of the critically ill, the dying and the bereaved.* New York: Hemisphere.

Weisman, A. D. (1972). *On dying and denying: A psychiatric study of terminality.* New York: Behavioral Publications.

Yeo, G., & Gallagher-Thompson, D. (Eds.). (1996). *Ethnicity and the dementias.* Washington, DC: Taylor & Francis.

CHAPTER 17
Advance Directives and Anticipatory Mourning

David K. Meagher
Marsha (Max) Quinn

> *If it be a short and violent death, we have no leisure to fear it; if otherwise, I perceive that according as I engage myself in sickness, I do naturally fall into some disdain and contempt of life.*
>
> —Michael de Montaigne

INTRODUCTION

Modern medical technology has significantly improved the survival odds in many diseases that in the past had been perceived as synonymous with death. Even in cases where medical success has not been so complete, as in illnesses for which no cures have been found, the chances are that the moment of death can yet be significantly delayed. However, there is a price attached to this successful medical research, a price that many have come to fear more than death itself. This costly price is the possibility of being forced to live beyond any personal consideration of human dignity and respect. At the same time, a surcharge of severe chronic pain and a loss of the ability to control the decisions rendered around one's care may be added. As suggested in the quotation from Montaigne, fear of dying may replace the fear of death when the illness and/or the treatment may force one to live with the dying process longer than is personally acceptable. One may become even more resolute in a personal desire for a quick death if dying is seen as a long, painful wasting away in a sterile medical environment, surrounded by strangers.

The goal of this chapter is threefold:

1. To examine the influence of patients' perceptions of loss of autonomy and self-determination on their ability to cope with the process of anticipatory mourning

2. To demonstrate how the availability of advance directives may help patients feel that they still possess personal autonomy and are still in control of their own destinies

3. To suggest ways in which professional caregivers can utilize advance directives to protect patients' rights to self-determination

THE PATIENT'S PERSPECTIVE

A great deal has been written about postdeath mourning and bereavement. Since the mid-1980s, the findings of numerous research studies on mourning have been published in the professional literature or presented in public forums. In contrast, however, research on the dying process, the needs of the dying patient (apart from discussions of pain management and the legal debate about a right to die), and the mourning experienced by the dying patient and those surrounding him or her (i.e., anticipatory mourning) has been noticeably scarce. The reported activities of Dr. Jack Kevorkian and the writings of Dr. Timothy Quill (1991, 1994) have forced society to take notice of the total human cost of prolonging the dying process. Two major controls that patients may exercise over their own dying have evolved. One comprises the various forms known collectively as advance directives; the other, a result of Kevorkian's admitted participation, is physician-assisted suicide.

The issues of advance directives and physician-assisted suicide have been debated extensively from the perspectives of ethics and law, less from the perspective of their fit with the needs of patients and their loved ones. Although society seems to have accepted to some degree the inclusion of advance directives within the legal realm of patients' rights, assisted suicide seems to be viewed as an unrealistic request a patient makes while in the throes of acute depression. In the current debate, opponents of physician-assisted suicide often claim that the frequency of requests would dwindle to nearly none if the pain of terminal illnesses were adequately managed. This assertion has not been demonstrated by research. Moreover, Cassell (1991) has eloquently argued that pain is neither a necessary nor a sufficient condition for suffering (which he defines as directly proportional to loss of personhood). Not only can a person in great pain experience no suffering, but great suffering can exist even in the absence of physical pain.

Pain, Suffering, and Patient Autonomy

Although the words *pain* and *suffering* are often used together, in order truly to understand the sense of anticipatory mourning in the terminally ill, the caregiver must be able to distinguish between physical pain and its concomitant suffering and the more profound existential suffering. Traditionally, pain has been considered a physically based sensation, a manifestation of discomfort and distress brought on by injury to or pathology of bodily tissue. The experience of pain is the result of the transmission of impulses between pain receptors and pain sites. Therefore, drugs that block this transmission should reduce the intensity of pain or eliminate it altogether. Pain is usually classified as either acute (resulting from some specific and readily identifiable tissue damage and being time limited) or chronic (beginning as an acute episode but becoming unending; Gatchel & Baum, 1983).

It is LeShan's (1979) position that pain should not be considered as a thing or as an event. Rather, pain should be seen as a situation, the total circumstances of a person's existence. LeShan offers four components of this situation that may, in fact, be better considered criteria for the presence of a person's suffering:

1. Terrible things are being done to the person.

2. The person does not know if the situation will get worse in the future.

3. The person feels impotent and helpless to take any effective action.

4. The person perceives that this situation has no time limit or that death is the only limit.

Whether it be called pain or suffering, what LeShan is describing is a situation that (a) forces a person to withdraw into him- or herself, with the attenuation of relationships a result; (b) makes the person believe that he or she cannot take any action against the pain except to learn to bear it; and (c) causes the person to experience a loss of time perspective that makes it almost impossible to focus on a future. This situation results in a cycle in which the person attempts to defend against the pain by reaching deep inside to gather all energy to create a sensory block. Paradoxically, this shift in energy may increase the focus of attention on the pain. In essence, the more the person tries to block out the pain, the more the person thinks about the pain, thereby increasing the intensity and duration of the distressing feeling.

Suffering, according to Cassell (1991), occurs when an impending destruction of the person is perceived; it continues until the threat of disintegration has passed or until the integrity of the person can be restored in some other manner. It follows, then, that although suffering often occurs in the presence of acute pain, shortness of breath or other bodily symptoms, it extends beyond the physical. Most generally, suffering can be defined as the state of severe distress associated with events that threaten the intactness of the person (p. 33). For the individual, it is a total—physical, emotional, psychological, spiritual, familial, and social—situation. Although suffering may hurt in much the same manner as physical pain, there is a qualitative difference that may allow one to think of suffering as acute agony. Suffering can encompass felt pain, a sense of helplessness and hopelessness, deep depression, sadness, loss of autonomy, loneliness, rage, a feeling of futility, a sense of rejection, and a host of other feelings either singly or in any combination.

Suffering, as Cassell (1991) suggests, may include pain, may be caused by pain, and may bring on an increased sensation of pain. Suffering, though, goes beyond the sensation of pain. Suffering that emanates from a sense of loss or potential loss of aspects of personhood—such as a sense of control over one's destiny and personal integrity—may be perceived as acute agony and, as such, may be a significant factor in prompting requests for assistance in suicide. It would be an oversimplification, however, to blame a patient's demand that the medical system honor an advance directive or a desire for assistance in ending life only on the presence of acute depression or the fear of ongoing, potentially intractable physical pain and suffering. The anticipation of existential suffering in the presence of a low personal threshold for this agony may be an even more significant influencing variable; it needs to figure in any assessment of a patient's emotional state or competency. It may be a reason for the not-so-uncommon request for assisted suicide (physician and/or nonphysician assisted) in nondepressed patients who have received prognoses of terminal illness or who believe (accurately or not) that such prognoses will be given very soon. If the profiles of the individuals who sought Dr. Kevorkian's assistance are accurate and represent a heretofore overlooked set of needs, then we must consider the possibility that a patient's request for physician-assisted suicide may be an attempt both to avoid anticipated existential suffering and loss of control and to avoid being relegated to a quality of life that falls below any acceptable minimal level. The reduction of pain may reduce the frequency of such requests, but adequate pain management may also cause the patient to lose autonomy, the ability actively to take charge of his or her life, and the ability to give or withhold informed consent for ongoing treatment, be it aggressive or palliative. This is especially true if the issue is viewed only from the perspective of physical pain and if suffering and existential suffering are ignored. To be human is to be innately endowed with the ability to govern one's own life. The absence of choice in life removes one from the genus of humans and can itself produce great suffering.

Patient autonomy should be the guiding principle in medical decision making (Pearlman, Cole, Patrick, Starks, & Cain, 1995). The legal and ethical basis of informed consent is an embodiment of this principle. When conflict between patient autonomy and any other medical-ethical principle exists, the principle of patient autonomy and self-determination should almost always take precedence (Angell, 1997). Self-determination may be defined as the capacity to plan, amend, and pursue one's own plans for life. Self-determination is a primary element of personal worth and integrity. The Patient Self-Determination Act (PSDA) of 1971 legally extended this principle of patient autonomy and self-determination to the care received by terminally ill patients. All caregiving institutions receiving government insurance payments are now required (a) to inform all patients (terminal and nonterminal) of their right to decide on life-support measures and formulate advance directives, (b) to educate staff and patients on issues related to advance directives, and (c) to document in a patient's record if an advance directive has been executed (Greer, 1995).

Dying, Self-Determination, and Anticipatory Mourning

Rando (1986), while suggesting that the term is a misnomer, offers a concept of anticipatory mourning (at that time called *anticipatory grief*) that encompasses the total existence and experience of the terminally ill person. The term *anticipatory mourning* is technically a misnomer because it tends to imply that such mourning is caused only by the anticipation of a loss. The concept outlined by Rando not only addresses the mourning one may experience in anticipation of not being, but also includes the mourning of losses already incurred, losses anticipated to occur before death, and anticipated losses that death will cause. The dying process entails a significant loss of control over one's life. The process will often cause a person to become totally dependent on others for even the most simple of needs—taking a drink of water or getting dressed. The manner in which one dies is an issue of great import. In the face of a terminal illness, it is often not death that a patient fears but rather pain, abandonment, and the loss of dignity, control, and social value (Hendrickson & Crase, 1995). When a patient suffers a loss of control, a sense of helplessness ensues. This feeling may result in increased anxiety and depression and a heightened physical reaction to symptoms. When demands for attention do not result in change in caregiver response, the patient may engage in some form of self-sabotage (Gatchel & Baum, 1983), such as seeking assisted suicide.

Loss of Control

Dying represents a loss of the self, and the basic force that drives the dying person's struggles is the sense of imminent loss of self. Each loss along the way signals a progressive encroachment on and ero-

sion of the total self. Life for the dying patient is a constant readjustment of expectations and activities to accommodate an ever-dimin-
ishing healthy person and an ever-expanding patient role. The
patient's perception of control is related to the level of adjustment
achieved. *Control* is defined as the ability to determine what one
does or what others do to one. A sense that one is in control of one's
life is an important motivation and an influential determinant of
mood and behavior. A sense of control is an intrinsically reinforcing
goal that directs much of an individual's behavior toward being able
to predict daily events confidently and to plan future experiences.
Feeling in control of one's life is, in and of itself, very ego rewarding,
regardless of whether one may actually be able to effect significant
change in one's environment. For the patient, dying results in a significant loss of control; no behavior on his or her part will alter the
prognosis.

Recent interest in control has centered on two issues: first, the
effects of believing that one has control and that outcomes are contingent on behavior; and second, the effects of believing that outcomes are not contingent on behavior and are therefore not
controllable. The latter issue relates to learned helplessness and the
debilitating effects of believing that one cannot control what happens (Gatchel & Baum, 1983).

Events that are seen as unchangeable may also be seen as
uncontrollable. The receipt of a terminal prognosis may be such an
event. A patient is told by the physician that medicine can do nothing more to control or eliminate his or her illness. This prognosis
includes a prediction (which the patient may perceive as a guaran-
tee) by the physician that the patient will be dead in the very near
future. All hope for a successful medical outcome has been lost. Any
chance for the patient to receive some possible future treatment has
been lost. The prognosis from the medical point of view includes a
foregone conclusion that there is nothing anyone, including the
patient, can do to alter the outlook. Uncertainty and confusion may
permeate the patient's cognition and affect. The patient's perceived
powerlessness to change his or her life may produce a feeling of a
total loss of control. This may lead to anticipation, uneasiness, and a
perception that the frequency of losses in life is increasing at a pace
that the patient finds almost impossible to accommodate. What the
patient *can* control is how the time until death will be spent, the
quality of life he or she will permit, and his or her destiny—however
limited the choices.

An important aspect of control is choice. The psychological
model of locus of control illustrates what happens when control is
not available, when one cannot, under any conditions, gain some
sense of control over what happens to one. The model predicts that

a sense of loss of control leads to a type of capitulation in which the patient learns that he or she cannot affect the outcome and, therefore, stops trying to do so. Repeated exposure to uncontrollable events condition a person to expect responses and outcomes to be noncontingent and produces a learned helplessness in the person.

The Experience of Dying

Dying is a frightening experience for which one cannot totally prepare. A person enters this experience only once and often alone. It is a process that is both unknown and known to all involved—patient, caregiver, and significant others. Both the unknown and known qualities of dying are potential objects of fear. Patients with advanced cancer suffer numerous physical and psychological symptoms that negatively affect the quality of life experienced. The physical symptoms may include pain, sleep disruption, fatigue, dyspnea, and nausea. Psychologically, the patient may experience intense anxiety and depression, adjustment problems, and delirium. The patient may experience both the fear of what he or she has learned or observed dying to be and the fear of entering into the unknown. Following are some of the fears of the dying person that have been identified:

1. Fear of the loss of self-control

2. Fear of pain and suffering

3. Fear of the loss of identity and the loss of self-control and total consciousness that threaten one's sense of identity (Pattison, 1977)

One of the more frequently expressed fears about dying concerns the possibility of chronic pain that may increase in intensity with each passing day and may prove intractable. Not all pain in dying is physiologically based. If it were, pain would not be perceived as a common experience in the dying process. Pharmaceutical substances are readily available to eliminate physical pain. The pain of dying, however, is based in the patient's psycho-emotional-spiritual-familial reality. It springs from contemplation of the incomprehensible wonderment of not being. It comes from seeing the sadness and fear in the eyes of loved ones as they wait for the patient's death to happen. The fear of pain may be responsible for an increase in anxiety. The result may be an unending cycle where, as the intensity of anxiety increases, so does the sensitivity to pain, which further exacerbates the felt anxiety.

Pain is seen has having no value or purpose in the dying process. It does not give an early warning to the possibility of an iatrogenic outcome to the application of a life-saving technique. In curative medicine, pain has a symptomatic value. The presence of pain may serve as an indicant of a potential iatrogenic outcome. However, in palliative medicine, pain is perceived as the source of needless and senseless suffering. Senseless pain is intolerable pain. Pain in the terminally ill is significantly different from the acute pain of the patient with a curable illness. Acute pain, the sensation generally experienced by patients with non-life-threatening conditions, is usually characterized by a heightening of anxiety as pain increases, followed by a reduction in anxiety once treatment begins. However, for patients with chronic pain, the pain of end-stage diseases, the cycle is very different. For these patients, the initial anxiety associated with the pain persists and may eventually lead to feelings of greater anxiety, despair, and helplessness because of the failure of medical care to alleviate it. These feelings may result in a wearing down that creates a layer of behavioral-psychological problems on top of the original pain and gives rise to a belief that the only relief or escape from the pain will be in death. The very fear of pain may lower the pain threshold. A pain experience in which the only change is escalation with each passing day may bring increased fear in anticipation of that future pain.

Society places a strong emphasis on self-control and self-determination. As discussed earlier, dying entails a risk of losing this value. A result may be an increase in anxiety and a fear about the integrity of the self. One may be placed in a position of dependency and inadequacy so that, in a sense, the ego is no longer perceived as master of its own fate nor captain of the self.

ADVANCE DIRECTIVES

An advance directive is a document that allows an individual to anticipate a time when active participation in decisions about his or her own medical care might not be possible. There are two types of advance directives: instructive directives and proxy directives (President's Commission, 1983). An *instructive directive* is a form that specifies the types of care a person wants or does not want to receive; a *proxy directive* does not specify care but rather identifies an individual who will act as the patient's legal surrogate to make decisions for the patient in the event the patient is not able to do so. The designation of a proxy must be made while a patient is considered competent. It is generally accepted that the documents that constitute acceptable advance directives—living wills, health care proxies, and do-not-resuscitate (DNR) orders—give the patient the opportunity to control the treatment that might be rendered if a time arrived when he or she was judged to be incompetent because of unconsciousness, severe depression, or the effects of treatment. Advance directives evolved in law from the accepted belief that adult persons have a fundamental right to control the decisions concerning the rendering of their own medical care, including the decision to have life-sustaining procedures withheld or withdrawn in the event of a terminal condition (President's Commission, 1983).

The current medical-ethical-legal debate about a right to die or a right to demand assisted suicide is ongoing. It has expanded the principles of autonomy, self-determination, and medical decision making into the possible acceptance of more active forms of patient control over the end of life. For some proponents of physician-assisted suicide, the distinction between what may be considered a passive form of control—a living will or DNR order that specifies a do-nothing wish—and an active form manifested in a request for physician-assisted suicide is insignificant at best. Whether the death is facilitated by the withholding or withdrawing of treatment, is hastened by the use of high doses of very potent pain medication, or is initiated by the patient with the assistance of a physician or others, the only differing factor is time. Living wills and proxies provide for death to be the logical outcome of the prevailing condition, with some time elapsing between the decision to withdraw or withhold and the death. The active controls involve techniques that bring an end to the life at the moment the intervention is applied—thus the use by some of the words *suicide* and *homicide* to describe these forms of intervention.

The Rational Choice Debate

Opposition to active controls is generally based on two arguments. The first questions the emotional state of the patient making the request. It is suggested that the patient is in an acute state of depression brought on by severe chronic pain that may be eliminated by effective palliation. Once pain is removed, the argument continues, the patient will not persist in the request for assisted suicide. However, no reported studies, save one small project involving six patients, have examined the effect of treatment for depression on the patient's desire to hasten death and on requests for assistance in doing so (Foley, 1997). The second argument addresses the issue of best interest. This position suggests that a physician directly assisting in death (the equivalent of causing a patient's death) is not acting in the best interests either of the patient or of the medical profession. Further discussion of the ethics and legalities of assisted suicide is beyond the scope of this chapter and would be better pursued in a forum designed to confront the dilemma. Suffice it to say here that the U.S. Supreme Court, in a 1997 decision, stated that a person does not have a constitutional right to die; therefore, one cannot legally demand that a physician assist in one's death. However, the decision did not rule out the possibility of the states' enacting their own laws concerning assisted suicide.

A number of studies have explored the issue of advance directives. These studies have examined the frequency with which patients elect to complete advance directives (Burg, McCarty, Allen, & Denslow, 1995; Palker & Nettles-Carson, 1995; Terry & Zweig, 1994; Walker, Schonwetter, Kramer, & Robinson, 1995); the characteristics of patients who do choose some form of advance directive (Hanson & Rodgman, 1996; Mark, Bahr, Duthie, & Tresch, 1995); and the impact of the Patient Self-Determination Act (PSDA) on the medical caregiver (Arras, 1993; Bassett, 1993; Fade, 1994; Nieuw, 1993) and on the patient (Danis, Garrett, Harris, & Patrick, 1994; Elpern, Yellen, & Burton, 1993; Jacobson et al., 1994).

Few studies have been reported that examined the influence of completed advance directives on patients' fear or anxiety concerning dying and death. Greer (1995) suggests there is a relationship between a higher degree of life satisfaction and a willingness to forego CPR. She theorizes that if a person senses that his or her cognitive status may be slipping, he or she will have less life satisfaction, and the anticipated loss may influence the person to complete an advance directive. Hanson and Rodgman's (1996) findings seem to support Greer's hypothesis. They report that the more functionally independent a person was, the more unlikely he or she would be to have a living will. In their study, prevalence of completed advance directives increased with the patients' perceptions of increased dependency, suggesting attempts on the part of the patients to maintain autonomy and control over medical treatment decisions in anticipation of even further loss of control. Daly and Sobal (1992) conclude from their interviews of 120 elderly, homebound patients that advance directives are important mechanisms whereby patients can extend their autonomy over the circumstances of dying. The work of Palker and Nettles-Carson (1995) seems to indicate that this perceived extension of autonomy and control does not result in a reduction of the patient's anxiety. In fact, they conclude from their interviews of elderly nursing home patients that completion of advance directives does not seem to be a significant variable influencing a patient's death anxiety.

Notwithstanding the legal and ethical arguments supporting the enactment and enforcement of the PSDA, it appears that many people do not choose to employ one or more advance directive options. Following are the identified reasons why a person will not elect an advance directive:

1. Lack of understanding of the language of the advance directive (Joos, Reuler, Powell, & Hickman, 1993)

2. Procrastination (Elpern et al., 1993)

3. Failure to understand the circumstances under which the advance directive controls medical decisions (Jacobson et al., 1994; Walker et al., 1995)

4. Discomfort in discussing impending death (Elpern et al., 1993; Jacobson et al., 1994; Joos et al., 1993)

5. Unavailability of advance directive forms (Burg et al., 1995)

Supporting the Patient and the Family

Fostering patient autonomy and control in medical treatment decisions not only constitutes ethical medical care, it is also consistent with human dignity and respect. Advance directives may not be ends in themselves; however, their usefulness in pain management programs may be significant. Severe pain and diagnoses of AIDS or neurodegenerative disorders are the most common conditions among patients requesting assistance in dying. The limited data available tend to indicate that the factors most commonly involved in requests for assistance are concerns about future loss of control, being or becoming a burden to others, being unable to care for oneself, and fear of severe pain (Angell, 1997).

Concern with regard to advance directives and the potential for anticipatory mourning should focus not only on the patient but also on the loved ones around the patient. Rando (1986) describes two perspectives on anticipatory grief, now termed *anticipatory mourning.* In current terminology, these would be the patient's anticipatory mourning and that of the others who are somehow emotionally involved with the patient. Like the dying person, family members may also be severely affected by a perception that few or no choices exist and that the patient and the family are excluded from control of what happens in the dying process. Among the survivor grief reactions identified by Shuchter and Zisook (1994), three major forms of survivor guilt seem to be related to the absence of control and self-determination. They are as follows:

1. Guilt experienced because the survivor feels some responsibility for the death and/or suffering of the deceased loved one

2. Guilt caused by a feeling that the survivor has betrayed the deceased in some way

3. Guilt associated with the perception that the survivor may have contributed to the deceased's death or suffering, whether by commission or omission

The potential for assuaging the guilt, reducing the destructive consequences of self-incrimination, reducing the fear, and palliating the pain is more easily realized when the patient and loved ones believe that they still have choices and still maintain significant control over what the rest of their lives is going to be like. Advance directives can serve to maintain a patient's autonomy and self-determination. In the absence of advance directives, or in the absence of confidence that completed advance directives will be honored by the system or the family, the patient may seek physician-assisted suicide, believing that it will alleviate fears, allow for a stronger sense of autonomy, and permit determination of the quality of life he or she is willing to accept. An important value inherent in what Logue (1994) labels "a good death" is the dying person's control of the experience.

Protecting Patient Autonomy

Although physicians are considered the ultimate authorities on medical care needs, they do not know enough about their patients, themselves, or suffering itself to provide assistance with dying as a medical treatment for the relief of suffering. Physicians need to explore their own perspectives on the meaning of suffering before they begin to plan the care they intend to give the dying. Physicians need to understand better how the nature of the doctor-patient relationship influences their own decision making as well as that of their patients. Palliative care for the dying must become a required area of study for the physician-in-training if the medical professional is to take a more active role in developing guidelines for good care of dying patients. Until the time when every hospital, nursing home, and home care program has included palliation as part of its standard operating procedures, society will have to rely on hospice to provide most of the necessary care for the dying and their loved ones.

The hospice movement in this country has long championed individual autonomy, patients' rights, and a commitment to maximizing the quality of life even if doing so means hastening death. The movement has worked to empower patients and their families to make choices about their medical care and has emphasized that these choices include all forms of intervention. The patient and the family are nominally in control of all care decisions. However, although hospice has been extremely successful in meeting its stated goals, patient choices are limited. Active aid in dying, as in assisted suicide, is not on the list of options. Hospice and palliative care programs employing successful pain management programs are often expected to be the answer to the question of medically assisted suicide. But effective palliative care must go beyond pain management programs and incorporate techniques and interventions designed to restore patient autonomy and a sense of self-determination. Although the law has become increasingly clear about the issue of advance directives and patients' rights, it has not been clear about who is responsible for informing patients about advance directives. Most patients believe it is the physician's responsibility to discuss advance directives, whereas most physicians believe it is the patient's responsibility (Pugh & West, 1994–1995). Lack of information prevents informed decisions about rights and options. Schonwetter, Walker, and Robinson (1995) report that major barriers to advance directive completion in hospice populations are a lack of physician-patient discussions as well as a lack of understanding of patients' diseases, their prognoses, and advance directives.

Helping patients work through to accepting death, letting them know they have not been rejected and they are still very important, restores their sense of not being alone. Professional caregivers and the patient's family and close friends have four major roles to play in helping a patient cope with pain and suffering and make decisions about advance directives. The first and possibly most basic task is to help the patient make sense of what is happening to him or her. LeShan (1979) suggests that helping a dying person arrive at the knowledge that he or she is unique and irreplaceable supports the person's ability to cope with the situation. Second, those involved need to help the patient find ways to act and react in the situation, help him or her take some semblance of control. Third, caregivers must understand that their actions, words, and presence help to shape the patient's assessment of the best course of treatment. Fourth, the ability and willingness of those around the patient to carry out various decisions often define the range of options available to the patient.

In addition to giving patients control over treatment options, advance directives give patients permission to die, letting them know that they need not continue the struggle if they do not wish to. The permission to die gained through an advance directive restores a person's self-determination. Simply having the opportunity to complete an advance directive may relieve the patient's fear and anxiety with an awareness that "I could fill out a directive if I wanted to."

In providing care and comfort to the terminally ill, the caregiver cannot direct attention to the dying person alone. The definition of *care recipient* must encompass members of the family and other loved ones as well. A patient does not function within a vacuum, unaffected by the anticipatory mourning manifested by those who constitute the significant relationships in his or her life. Support, both in the search for the right decision and ultimately in the decision itself, is crucial for the person's psychological and emotional dimensions. Although the ideal may be for the patient and significant others to arrive at the same decision, such agreement must not be the result of the patient's completely compromising his or her needs. Families, as well as patients, need to cope, to achieve a resolution that all parties can live with. However, coping does not necessarily mean the same thing as accepting (i.e., totally agreeing with or liking). Coping with an advance directive decision requires loved ones to be sensitive and empathic toward the patient's experiences. The patient needs to feel secure that whatever the choice he or she makes, everyone will respect the decision and protect his or her right to the execution of that decision. The mutual nature of support requires open communication among all who are affected by the prognosis of death. However, loved ones often need help communicating about advance directives with the patient. Often, they experience difficulty due to their own suffering from fear, anxiety, and grief. Family members' ability to respond to the patient's needs is determined by their own capabilities under the circumstances.

CAREGIVER TASKS

Caregivers can help the dying cope with anticipatory mourning by helping them regain control over their lives—over the process of dying. There are three principal tasks involved in helping a patient regain autonomy and self-determination: educating the patient and the family, facilitating fulfillment of the patient's wishes, and honoring the patient's signed orders.

Educating the Clients

The caregiver must make certain that patient and family are aware of their rights to advance directives, know what these orders mean, and understand the implications of signing or not signing an advance directive. The patient needs help understanding that advance directives will restore a measure of autonomy and self-determination. The patient and the family need to be educated about the various advance directive options. They need to learn when and how these directives are executed and when they do not affect the patient's care. Education about advance directives is best accomplished in an environment in which the patient and family members can openly discuss their feelings, wishes, and concerns about the impending death and about the potential consequences, both desired and undesired, of completing an advance directive. The caregiver can help establish this environment.

If advance directives are to be consistent with the requirement of informed consent, the patient will need to communicate with the physician about the prognosis; this communication must include a realistic discussion of the patient's chances for an acceptable quality of life. Discussions between doctor and patient (and family, if the patient permits) about quality-of-life potential should address pain management options; the value of suffering, if any, to the patient; and some estimate of the time the patient may expect to experience rational consciousness that would allow for coping with encountered losses and achieving closure. Closure, in this instance, means resolving differences and healing relationship wounds. Achieving closure is more difficult when the patient is uncertain about the likely time of death or when he or she is physically too weak or mentally incompetent. The patient will also need assistance in coping with losses arising from the necessity of letting go of those goals and relationships that have become unachievable.

Facilitating Fulfillment of Wishes

The caregiver must be certain that completed advance directives are included in the patient's medical records or charts and that everyone who may have occasion to provide care to the patient is aware of the documents. Recent surveys have revealed that many physicians have admitted ignoring completed advance directives and continuing the treatments they believed would be in the best interests of everyone. In addition, if an unconscious or incompetent patient has named a health care proxy, the caregiver must provide any and all support this surrogate may need to meet his or her responsibilities. If the proxy is not a family member, the caregiver needs to work with both the legal proxy and the members of the patient's family to prevent friction and to facilitate fulfillment of the patient's wishes as made known by the proxy.

Honoring Signed Orders

The caregiver must be willing to honor any signed order. This task may be extremely difficult for the medical practitioner: Death is the unrelenting enemy of medical practice, and to permit what may be considered a premature death may be seen as a medical defeat. Nevertheless, the prolongation of life for its own sake cannot be the value controlling the way in which the medical caregiver ministers to the terminally ill. In its place, the caregiver must substitute the quality and desirability of life as perceived by the dying person. The patient's needs should guide every action or plan of care.

SUMMARY AND CONCLUSIONS

In coping with anticipatory mourning, the dying patient needs to find a way to regain and maintain autonomy and self-determination. A prognosis of terminal illness carries with it an unstated consequence of loss of control for the patient. Accompanying and, at times, exacerbating this sense of helplessness and impotency is a realization of losses already experienced and an anticipation that whatever future time the patient may have will be spent confronting even greater losses. If the loss experience is accompanied by pain and suffering, if the patient feels rejected and alone in dying, then there may be an increase in fear and anxiety, an onset of acute depression, and a deep visceral feeling that it may be better to "go gently into that dark night."

Advance directives are important tools for helping to restore and maintain a sense of patient autonomy and self-determination. Among the various choices of advance directives are living wills, health care proxy forms, and do-not-resuscitate (DNR) orders. Many patients and family members, however, are uninformed about these options and about their rights vis-à-vis the directives. This uncertainty exists even among those who have signed or completed some form of advance directive. If the provision of good palliative care is the concern of a caregiver, then education of the patient and family along with the protection of the rights of the patient must be integral to any support plan.

Important questions remain, however. Should assisted suicide become an accepted option for terminally ill patients? Can the society permit a terminally ill patient who is not severely depressed, and who is the recipient of effective pain management, the right to physician-assisted suicide? Do patient autonomy and self-determination include the right of a person to decide when, where, and how he or she will die and who will be present at the moment of death? These are questions that all segments of the society, medical and nonmedical, will have to answer in the very near future.

REFERENCES

Angell, M. (1997). The Supreme Court and physician assisted suicide: The ultimate right. An editorial. *New England Journal of Medicine, 336,* 50–53.

Arras, J. (1993). Ethical issues in emergency care. *Clinics in Geriatric Medicine, 9,* 655-664.

Bassett, C. C. (1993). The living will: Implications for nurses. *British Journal of Nursing, 2,* 688-691.

Burg, M. A., McCarty, C., Allen, W. L., & Denslow, D. (1995). Advance directive: Population prevalence and demand in Florida. *Journal of the Florida Medical Association, 82,* 811-814.

Cassell, E. J. (1991). *The nature of suffering and the goals of medicine.* New York: Oxford University Press.

Daly, M. P., & Sobal, J. (1992). Advance directives among patients in a house call program. *Journal of the American Board of Family Practice, 5*(1), 11-15.

Danis, M., Garrett, J., Harris, R., & Patrick, D. L. (1994). Stability of choices about life-sustaining treatments. *Annals of Internal Medicine, 120,* 567-573.

Elpern, E. H., Yellen, S. B., & Burton, L. A. (1993). A preliminary investigation of opinions and behaviors regarding advance directives for medical care. *American Journal of Critical Care, 2*(2), 161-167.

Fade, A. E. (1994). Advance directive: Keeping up with changing legislation. *Today's OR-Nurse, 16*(4), 23-26.

Foley, K. M. (1997). Competent care for the dying instead of physician-assisted suicide. *New England Journal of Medicine, 336,* 54-58.

Gatchel, R. J., & Baum, A. (1983). *An introduction to health psychology.* New York: Random House.

Greer, M. B. (1995). Factors affecting opinions on life support issues in the elderly. *Issues on Aging, 18*(2), 1-11.

Hanson, L. C., & Rodgman, E. (1996). The use of living wills at the end of life: A national study. *Archives of Internal Medicine, 156,* 1018-1022.

Hendrickson, K., & Crase, D. (1995). Self-determination in end-of-life decisions: The application of advance directive. *Illness, Crises & Loss, 5*(1), 19-29.

Jacobson, J. A., White, B. E., Battin, M. P., Francis, L. P., Green, D. J., & Kasworm, E. S. (1994). Patients' understanding and use of advance directive. *Western Journal of Medicine, 160,* 232-236.

Joos, S. K., Reuler, J. B., Powell, J. L., & Hickman, D. H. (1993). Outpatients' attitudes and understanding regarding living wills. *Journal of General Internal Medicine, 8,* 291-301.

LeShan, L. (1979). The world of the patient in severe pain of long duration. In C. V. Garfield (Ed.), *Stress and survival: The emotional realities of life-threatening illness.* New York: Mosby.

Logue, B. J. (1994). When hospice fail: The limits of palliative care. *Omega, 29,* 291-301.

Mark, D. H., Bahr, J., Duthie, E. H., & Tresch, D. D. (1995). Characteristics of residents with do-not-resuscitate orders in nursing homes. *Archives of Family Medicine, 4,* 463-467.

Nieuw, A. D. (1993). Informed consent. *Medicine & Law, 12*(1-2), 125-130.

Palker, N. B., & Nettles-Carson, B. (1995). The prevalence of advance directives: Lessons from a nursing home. *Nurse Practitioner, 20*(2), 7-18.

Pattison, E. M. (Ed.). (1977). *The experience of dying.* Englewood Cliffs, NJ: Prentice Hall.

Pearlman, R. A., Cole, W. G., Patrick, D. L., Starks, H. E., & Cain, K. C. (1995). Advance care planning: Eliciting patient preferences for life-sustaining treatment. *Patient Education and Counseling, 26,* 353-361.

President's Commission for the Study of Ethical Problems in Medicine and Bio-medical and Behavioral Research. (1983). *Deciding to forego life-sustaining treatment: Ethical, medical, and legal issues in treatment decisions.* Washington, DC: U.S. Government Printing Office.

Pugh, D., & West, D. J. (1994–1995). Advance directives and the Self-Ddetermination Act: A patient's perspective. *Omega, 30,* 249–256.

Quill, T. E. (1991). Death and dignity: A case of individualized decision making. *New England Journal of Medicine, 324,* 691–694.

Quill, T. E. (1994). Physician-assisted death: Progress or peril? *Suicide and Life-Threatening Behavior, 24,* 315–325.

Rando, T. A. (Ed.). (1986). *Loss and anticipatory grief.* Lexington, MA: Lexington Books.

Schonwetter, R. S., Walker, R. M., & Robinson, B. E. (1995). The lack of advance directives among hospice patients. *The Hospice Journal, 10*(3), 1–11.

Shuchter, S. R., & Zisook, S. (1994). The course of normal grief. In M. S. Stroebe, W. Stroebe, & R. O. Hansson (Eds.), *Handbook of bereavement: Theory, research and intervention.* New York: Cambridge University Press.

Supreme Court of the United States. (1997). *Dennis E. Vacco, Attorney General of New York et al., Petitioners v. Timothy E. Quill et al.,* No. 95–1858.

Terry, M., & Zweig, S. (1994). Prevalence of advance directives and do-not-resuscitate orders in community nursing facilities. *Archives of Family Medicine, 3,* 141–145.

Walker, R. M., Schonwetter, R. S., Kramer, D. R., & Robinson, B. E. (1995). Living wills and resuscitation preferences in an elderly population. *Archives of Internal Medicine, 155,* 171–175.

CHAPTER 18
Anticipatory Mourning and Organ Donation

Sue C. Holtkamp

Today Anna Grace would get her driver's license—yet another reminder that his little girl was growing up. At 16 she was beautiful, moving out of that gosling stage right into young womanhood. "Where had the time gone?" he wondered. And even as he wondered, Anna Grace made a very grown-up decision as she checked "yes" in the organ donation box on her new license.

"It makes sense, Dad," she had grinned. "Might as well help someone else if I'm not here."

"Anna Grace, if you were not here," he said soberly, "the world would stop spinning."

Three months, 2 days, and 7 hours later, it did just that. Anna Grace was struck by a drunken driver, and 4 days later the physicians informed her family that she was brain dead.

Anna Grace became the Taylor family's first organ donor.

Organ donors belong to a group of individuals who die in a unique fashion.* Following some type of brain trauma, these potential donors "progress" to a medical status involving total and permanent cessation of brain and brain stem activity. This status is termed *brain death*, and it is a prerequisite for organ donation.

Though the donor's death may be perceived as sudden by the family, it is never instant. There is always some period of time—hours or days—between the trauma and the declaration of death. This chapter will explore that period of forewarning before the donor's death to determine how caregivers' awareness of anticipatory mourning can help them address the family's needs. The story of one family's response to this period of anticipation will be woven throughout the chapter to clarify the use of such intervention.

---

*Special thanks to Lyn Simpson, whose assistance as typist and editor was invaluable.

ORGAN DONATION

Organ donation is a remarkable act of altruism in which an individual or his or her family makes the decision to donate organs to save or enhance the life of another human being. Each year in the United States, more than 5,000 people become organ donors; as a result, approximately 20,000 organs are placed in other human beings ("Transplants in 1996," 1997). This modern medical miracle is possible primarily because of a policy that recognizes the phenomenon of brain death.

Brain death is not a cause of death but rather the outcome of some pathological process that injures the brain or brain function. According to the New York Regional Transplant Program (1990), such processes include trauma, cardiovascular accident, stroke, hemorrhage, tumor, and anoxia. Brain death occurs in a relatively small number of patients who suffer complete and irreversible cessation of brain function, including brain stem function. The criteria for brain death developed progressively during the 1970s within the medical community and through a number of court decisions and numerous state statutes (Fox & Swazey, 1992):

> These developments led to the Uniform Determination of Death Act proposed in 1981 by the President's Commission for the Study of Ethical Problems in Medicine and Biomedical and Behavioral Research. . . . The model act, which defined death as either irreversible cessation of cardiopulmonary function or of the functions of the whole brain, including the brain stem, was endorsed by the American Medical Association, the American Bar Association, and the National Conference of Commissions for Uniform State Laws, and subsequently enacted by most state legislatures. (p. 61)

The patient may experience brain death almost immediately or within hours of the precipitating event, or the patient may progress toward brain death over a period of days. There is almost always some brief time lapse between the actual trauma and the declaration of brain death. During this period, the patient is being supported with a ventilator—initially in an attempt to save the life, eventually to maintain the organs for transplantation. Without this forewarning, there would be no organ donation: Only patients who experience total cessation of brain function, including that of the brain stem, and who are being maintained on ventilators can provide viable organs for transplantation.

This nontraditional way to die creates a new category of people who are closely related. They are the family members or significant others of the uniquely deceased, brain-dead patients. With approximately 5,000 individuals becoming donors each year in the United States and with 8 to 10 others affected by each donor's death (Rando, 1993), there are more than 200,000 people directly affected by the deaths and donations of organ donors over a 5-year period. Obviously, as the rate of donations increases, so will the number of mourners affected by this unique experience. These people experience grief and mourning in an unusual fashion: Although the death of the loved one was sudden and unexpected, there was also a narrow window of time to contemplate the possibility of the death. Though the period between the traumatic event and the declaration of brain death may be only hours or days, it has significant implications for the family and the health care professional because it permits certain anticipatory processes and interventions (Holtkamp, 1997).

ANTICIPATORY MOURNING

Since Erich Lindemann first introduced the concept of anticipatory mourning in 1944 under the term *anticipatory grief,* the theory that people can respond to the threat of death with a bereavement reaction has been challenged (Parkes & Weiss, 1983; Silverman, 1974). The problem appears to rest with the term *anticipatory mourning.* For regardless of semantic hairsplitting among scholars, there is little doubt among thanatologists that there are responses on the part of family members being informed that their loved one's death has changed from an inevitable future abstraction to a very real, time-bound condition (Stephenson, 1985). Campbell (1991) suggests that "scholarly speculation does little to comfort a soul actually experiencing the reality of suffering" (p. 32). Anyone who has experienced being told that a loved one may die from an injury can speak to the existence of suffering prior to actual loss.

In a provocative article "Recognizing Suffering," Eric Cassell (1991) defines suffering as

the distress brought about by the actual or perceived *impending* threat to the integrity or continued existence of the whole person. . . . That the wholeness threatened by suffering is more than the individual as physically defined can be deduced from the observation that suffering requires a sense of the future. (p. 24, emphasis added)

When one of its members is injured and a family is summoned to the hospital, much of the family's anxiety is focused on what the future will bring. The suffering experienced by donor families is based on the actual or perceived threat, which requires a sense of that future.

But rather than merely defining what anticipated mourning is, it may be even more important to understand clearly what it is not. It is not the start of a linear process that begins prior to the death and continues on as postdeath mourning. It is a process all its own.

The donor family's experience mirrors in miniature what happens when a family is informed that their loved one is going to die at some future date. From the time the family learns of the patient's trauma to the declaration of brain death, the family members experience, in varying degrees, what Lebow (1976) declares to be "the total set of cognitive, affective, cultural and social reactions to expected death" (p. 459).

It might be argued that the brief warning that death is approaching may be inadequate to be significantly helpful to the donor family. For instance, Rando (1984) and Sanders (1982–1983) have indicated that those with less than 6 months prior knowledge of impending death may experience comparatively fewer benefits than those with longer forewarning. And according to Parkes and Weiss (1983), individuals with less than 2 weeks notice that a spouse was fatally ill and less than 3 days warning that death was imminent fared considerably worse than those who experienced longer warning. Yet anticipatory interventions may work well to optimize the quality of the time between notification of impending death and the actual advent of death. And support given the donor family during this crucial time can facilitate mourning or at the very least help set the tone for healthy processing of that mourning in the postdeath future. To determine how these interventions might work, a review of the donor family experience is helpful.

THE DONOR FAMILY EXPERIENCE

"Organ donors must be . . . healthy individuals who have suffered sudden and fatal trauma to the central nervous system. In practice [this means that] most donors are young and have been killed in accidents" (Prottas, 1989, p. 43). Not only do all potential donor families contend with the sudden death of previously healthy relatives, but nearly three-quarters of all donations involve the parental loss of a child (Kirste, Muthny, & Wilms, 1988). The disbelief that accompanies sudden loss is combined with the unique and unspeakable pain associated with the loss of a child. The devastation experienced by parents whose child dies must never be underestimated. Other responses—shock, denial, and intense expressive reactions—are also present. Paradoxically, though donor families experience all the sequelae that follow sudden death, they also share with other forewarned families a sense of helplessness and vulnerability associated with the threat of loss. The donor family mourns in reaction to a loss that has already occurred plus the threat of impending loss. Yet, in spite of these similarities with mourning related to sudden loss and to forewarned loss, several other factors render the donor family experience distinctly unique.

Brief Forewarning

There is, for the donor family, a period of anticipation that is extraordinarily brief—perhaps a matter of hours. Although the event that brought the family to this point was sudden and unexpected, the patient is not yet dead. The disbelief usually experienced during this brief time is further complicated by the intense hope that the patient might recover. Over a period of a few hours or a few days, the patient's prognosis may vary, causing an intensely emotional roller-coaster effect for the family.

Unlike immediate sudden death, this situation creates some brief history leading up to the donor's death. Within the brief forewarning period, events are taking place. For instance, there are always valiant efforts to save the patient's life, decisions to be made concerning care, and usually time for family and friends to arrive at the hospital to offer support.

> *Anna Grace's mother and father arrived at the hospital first, followed by their twin sons. Three hours later their eldest son and his wife arrived. Family and friends began to come and go. "Each time someone new came into the waiting room," Anna Grace's mother noted, "I realized that this was not a bad dream. This was real. Every tear-stained face told me that Anna Grace was in serious trouble."*

Each time someone came to visit Anna Grace's family in the hospital, that reality broke through her mother's denial and facilitated her acceptance. Accepting the reality of loss or impending loss is something that every involved family member must do (Worden, 1991). Sooner or later, the family must realize that their loved one is dead (i.e., brain dead).

Brain Death

The second distinguishing feature of the donor family's experience is the issue of brain death.

"For a brief while I could speak to Anna Grace, and I felt certain she knew we were there beside her. The experience was bittersweet," stated Anna Grace's mother, "for although I knew about organ donation, no one had ever explained brain death to me before that night. And what I was told didn't make sense. She looked as though she were sleeping, her color was good, her chest moved as though she were breathing. It was hard to believe that she was truly gone."

It is extraordinarily difficult for a family to understand that the loved one has died. The inability to grasp this reality often persists regardless of the way the information is presented. However, when the family is confronted with brain death, this difficulty is compounded. According to many reports, when the patient is being supported by a ventilator, brain death is difficult to acknowledge because of the absence of external injuries and the signs of viability and normal body functions—the body is warm to the touch, the color is good, and there is urine output (Pelletier, 1992). The situation seems surreal; involved individuals may experience cognitive dissonance. Even when the family comprehends the concept of brain death on an intellectual level, there is often a gap between intellectual knowledge and emotional acceptance.

Prior understanding of the concept of brain death is as important as knowledge about the value of and the need for donated organs. This understanding would be particularly helpful in light of the fact that people generally "absorb information most effectively when it fits their existing view. Any information that requires radical reorientation and is, in addition, highly unpleasant, is apt to be distorted, suppressed, or exaggerated" (Parkes & Weiss, 1983, p. 232). Accepting a visual presentation of death that is contrary to lifelong views of death may well require radical reorientation.

Decisions Regarding Donation

During this abbreviated period when family members are facing the greatest stressor in their lives, when they are shocked, confused, disoriented, and vulnerable, they must make a number of critical decisions. One of those decisions is whether or not to donate their loved one's organs and tissues. If the question of donation has been discussed before the terminal event or if the patient has indicated his or her desire on the driver's license, this decision is considerably easier. The decision to donate is and must remain an individual matter. Neither the great need for organs nor the value of donation as perceived by other donor families should obscure the reality that donation is not the best option for some families.

Contrary to the opinions of some health care professionals and lay people, studies have indicated that most donor families do not perceive the process of requests for donation as an additional stressor or burden (Bartucci, 1987; Savaria, Rovell, & Schweizer, 1990). Because Rando (1984) asserts that bringing meaning out of suffering can be considered a useful strategy for dealing with loss, we should not be surprised that some families indicated that organ donation served as a coping strategy (Pelletier, 1992).

Anna's father describes his thoughts on this issue.

"The trauma unit was chaos, I was chaotic—crazy. When I was asked if I was willing for Anna Grace to be a donor, it was the only thing that night that had made any sense at all. The act of donation brought something of worth from absolute madness."

For many, the act of donating an organ that may save the life of another, thus preventing another family's loss, may bring a sense of meaning to an otherwise senseless reality. During this time of chaos, however, every effort must be made to reduce further stress on the family. Addressing their needs can be a way of preventing unnecessary stress. Because a donor family experiences some measure of anticipation of the loved one's death, it stands to reason that many of their needs can be met through anticipatory processes.

THERAPEUTIC POSSIBILITIES FOUND WITHIN ANTICIPATORY MOURNING

Even the professionals who challenge the concept of anticipatory mourning do not deny that there is value in a period of preparation preceding the death of a loved one (Parkes & Weiss, 1983). Several issues that emerge in that period present themselves as opportunities for the donor family (Rando, 1984). The brief preparation time provides opportunities to do the following:

• Absorb the news of the impending death gradually

• Finish unfinished business and say good-byes

• Do for or be involved with the patient

• Explore life assumptions and personal identities

• Come to terms with the impending loss

Absorbing the News Gradually

Absorbing the news of impending death over a period of time lessens the individual's chances of being overwhelmed. Learning that the death is a time-bound possibility rather than an abstract future event allows family members some time to absorb the information. This period, however brief, affords some time for reconciliation that is not available to loved ones of those who die suddenly.

Finishing Unfinished Business

Donor family members often have the chance to address unfinished business. Although communication with the donor patient is usually one sided, loved ones often speak with gratitude of the opportunity to say their good-byes and to express their regrets, joys, and affection.

Doing for or Being Involved with the Patient

For many potential donor families, participation in care is a major complicating problem. The nature of the injury and the presence of the medical equipment used to sustain life or maintain the viability of organs may deprive family members of "doing for" and "being with" their loved one. "There is a real danger that intensive care units and other inpatient facilities, to the extent that they take away from the family the opportunity to care for the individual, may create problems for the family in the future" (Parkes & Weiss, 1983, p. 96). This statement has particular significance for the donor family because most donors are generally cared for in trauma and critical care units.

Anna Grace's mother spoke to the importance of the family's participation in care.

> "When I first saw Anna Grace, she looked as though she were sleeping. I smoothed the sheets and stroked her hair while her father held her free hand. We just needed to be with her. We needed to do something, but couldn't think of what to do."

Exploring Life Assumptions and Identity

Many changes in assumptions about life and personal identity will take place after the loved one dies. When there is forewarning, some family members begin to make those changes prior to the death. In the brief time allowed a potential donor family, it is questionable whether any actual changes occur. However, glimpses of breached assumptions and altered senses of identity may transcend the shock and disbelief. Anna Grace's eldest brother spoke of just such glimpses.

"I never thought anything like this could happen to our family. Not to my baby sister. All her life I had protected her. I had been there for her all through school, and now I could do nothing to help her. I felt so confused I could scarcely think."

Coming to Terms with the Impending Loss

An observation by Stephenson evokes a strong association with the donor family experience: "Successful anticipatory grieving does not mean moving ahead to readjustment and recovery . . . but rather it means being aware of the disorganization that is taking place and living with it" (1985, p. 160). During the brief period of forewarning, the donor family has some opportunity to come to terms with the impending loss as family members begin to recognize the terrible disorganization that is taking place in their lives.

DONOR FAMILY NEEDS AND ANTICIPATORY MOURNING TECHNIQUES

According to knowledgeable sources (Holtkamp, 1997; National Kidney Foundation, 1994; Willis & Skelley, 1992), after the potential donor family reaches the hospital and before the death of the loved one is declared, family members have immediate and specific needs that may be categorized under the broad headings of support, information, access to the patient, and time for reconciliation. Anyone attempting to meet those needs can see that some of the principles and tasks involved in caring for families anticipating death in the more traditional manner also apply within this compressed setting.

Parkes and Weiss (1983) suggest, from their findings, that

> the impact of an unexpected and untimely bereavement can overwhelm a person's existing ability to cope with stress and trigger reactions that will lead to lasting problems. It follows that any action which reduces that impact could be expected to be of lasting benefit. (p. 239)

Paradoxically, many of the interventions suggested by Parkes and Weiss and others (Rando, 1984; Stephenson, 1985) to reduce the stress of people who are mourning a forewarned loss may also help reduce the *impact of the suddenness* of death and thus produce a lasting benefit. It must be clearly understood that interventions never change the reality of suffering. The purpose of intervening is to relieve the unnecessary stress associated with the situation and to improve the quality of the remaining time available. This reality presents both challenges and opportunities for health care professionals.

Being summoned to the hospital and learning that your loved one has experienced life-threatening trauma can be devastating. Sources (Holtkamp, 1997; National Kidney Foundation, 1994; Willis & Skelley, 1992) outline the immediate needs of a family that experiences such devastation as follows:

- Accurate information regarding the patient's trauma, current status, and prognosis
- Information about brain death and methods for its determination
- Empathy and sensitivity from both hospital and organ procurement organization staff
- Absolute assurance that everything was/is being done to save their loved one's life
- Access to the patient before and after brain-death determination
- Time for reconciliation to the loss of the loved one
- Time to say good-bye to the loved one
- The opportunity to donate the loved one's organs
- Time, privacy, confidentiality, and information to make the decision privately, within the family

In addition, Youngner (1992) and Holtkamp (1997) argue that another need pleads attention. When a patient is declared brain dead, the family needs an exact time of death, which must be given and recorded consistently.

The donor family's needs begin even before family members enter the hospital. Sensitivity in informing the family of the precipitating event is critical: "The way in which news is broken and support is given could be of crucial importance" (Parkes & Weiss, 1983, p. 239). The task of imparting this news has become increasingly problematic because of the level of sophistication on the part of the public. To the extent that the family of the patient have absorbed the process of death notification as shown in films and television, it may be difficult for professionals to wait for the appropriate time and place to reveal alarming news.

Refusal to answer the family's direct questions by phone is often perceived as an ominous sign and tends to make people anticipate the worst. However, in the case of a potential donor, the patient is usually still alive. This information may be all that is necessary to share in the initial contact; further details should wait until the family has arrived safely at the hospital.

Emotional support is essential and basically encompasses all other interventions. This support should be in place when the family reaches the hospital (Back, 1991; Johnson, 1992). Every effort made on behalf of the donor family should weave a safety net of emotional support that endures even when the family returns home.

FAMILY ADAPTATIONAL TASKS AND IMPLICATIONS FOR CAREGIVERS

Because the family's needs become manifest before the determination of death, they fall within the anticipation period. These needs—things that a family should *have*—bear considerable resemblance to the adaptational tasks—things that a family should *do*. Lebow (1976) lists the adaptational tasks that are inherent in the anticipatory mourning process:

- Remaining involved with the patient
- Remaining separate from the patient
- Adapting to role changes
- Bearing the affects of grief
- Coming to terms with the impending loss
- Saying good-bye

The ease with which the donor family's needs can be addressed within the set of tasks outlined for families who experience longer forewarning (Lebow, 1976; Rando, 1984) suggests that assistance with these tasks may be beneficial even within this abbreviated anticipation period. This assistance may come from a number of professionals—the nurse, the physician, the chaplain, the family representative, and, eventually, the staff person from the organ procurement organization. Although these people have distinct functions, each can and must provide empathic and sensitive care for the family (Swazey, 1986).

Remaining Involved with the Patient

Although there are many ways to ensure that the donor family remains involved with the dying patient, it would be difficult to find anything more effective than open and informative communication. Information is empowering; it offers family members a sense of participation in and control over a world that has ceased to make sense. Providing and receiving information is one of the primary ways for a donor family to remain involved with the patient. Doing something as routine as contributing information somewhat reduces feelings of helplessness.

Appropriate warnings can help people prepare themselves more effectively, but "it takes time to break bad news and the setting in which communication takes place will influence how it is received" (Parkes & Weiss, 1983, p. 231). Medical updates given over a period of time allow family members to absorb the reality of their loved one's condition in a piecemeal fashion that will reduce the risk of their being overwhelmed. All information must be offered in easily understood language, as free as possible of medical terms and repeated as often as necessary. Informants should periodically question the family members to determine what they know and how much they are comprehending. By staying close to the family, gently providing updates on the patient's condition, and confirming that those warnings are understood, the caring professional can assess the family's capacity to cope with the reality of the situation. Wright (1978) stresses the value of this approach:

> Families can be much less reactionary and uncooperative
> when they are kept informed, in terminology understand-
> able to them, of their significant other's progress. Even
> when a client's recovery seems very uncertain . . . taking a
> few moments to talk with the family and listen to their
> perceptions of what is happening can have a tremendous
> impact on the family's acceptance of the patient's status,
> [including] the inevitability of death. Though it is
> simplistic, it is most essential that families and patients
> know that they are truly cared about as people. (p. 978)

Almost without exception, donor families have reported that receiving information about the loved one's condition and prognosis was of vital importance (Back, 1991, Pelletier, 1993). Families resent any false hope offered in misguided attempts to assuage their suffering. The possibility of terminal outcome must be made known to the family as soon as it is medically recognized (Parkes & Weiss, 1983). Offering the family hope is laudable only when that hope is realistic.

From the moment the family members enter the hospital, they also must be assured that everything possible is being done to save the life of their loved one (Holtkamp, 1997; Willis & Skelley, 1992). All families deserve this assurance. However, in the case of a potential donor, the family needs absolute trust that everything medically possible was done for the loved one. There should never be the slightest suggestion that organ procurement took precedence over efforts to save the patient's life. Keeping family members continually informed during this period of uncertainty fosters trust that will serve the family well throughout the mourning process.

As noted earlier, that trust must extend to the determination of the exact time of the patient's death. Not only is it essential that family members be given an exact time of death, that time must be consistent with the time recorded by the coroner or whoever signs the death certificate. In theory this is a simple matter. The attending physician records the time of declaration of brain death, and that time should be accepted. However, life is not always so neat.

> *Anna Grace's mother sat in my office and almost apologized for her concerns. "I was told," she began, as she folded and unfolded a pleat in her skirt, "that Anna Grace died at 7:30 at night. But when we received our daughter's death certificate, the coroner had written the time of death as after midnight, when the surgery to remove the organs was completed. This is the date that was put on her headstone. It has haunted us ever since."*

Anna Grace's accident had been over 9 months ago. For the better part of a year, her parents had suffered unnecessarily.

There can be no equivocation regarding the time of death. Although on the surface this question may not seem to be part of the anticipation phase of mourning, it concerns the end result of an anticipated death related to organ donation. Also, caregivers must remember that the family is continuing to absorb what has happened: "Even though bereavement is an established reality, the bereaved still need time and the chance to talk through the implications of their loss and to react emotionally. They have to prepare themselves for an event that has already taken place" (Parkes & Weiss, 1983, p. 239).

Unique to the donor family's situation is the need for information about organ donation and brain death, including the criteria used to determine brain death. Family members may benefit from written information that they can refer to later. Because few laypersons have much understanding of brain anatomy, visuals accompanied by simple explanations might be especially helpful. According to the New York Regional Transplant Program (1990), communication about brain death should start when the patient is admitted to the hospital with a brain injury, rather than at the time of brain death. That communication should address (a) the cause of the injury, (b) the extent of brain damage, (c) the treatment plan, and (d) the probable outcomes.

Information about organ donation and the opportunity to donate must be offered for the family's consideration. This option should be presented only after the family has become reconciled to the declaration of brain death. The decision to say no to donation is as valid as the decision to say yes. The opportunity must be presented so that the family will not later have any regrets concerning this issue.

This option of donation must be offered in a sensitive, timely, and compassionate manner. The family members must be afforded time, privacy, freedom from coercion, and confidentiality so they can make an informed and free decision (Holtkamp, 1997; National Kidney Foundation, 1994; Willis & Skelley, 1992). It should be self-evident that the family's decision is to be accepted without question.

The hospital experience and all that transpires within that setting may contribute to and can help set the tone for the postdeath mourning experience. When family members become focused on poor treatment or lack of trust due to ineffective communication or support, they may become fixated on that point. Fixation on peripheral issues may delay, distort, or complicate the mourning process.

Facilitating access to the patient is one of the most effective ways to ensure that complications do not arise from the hospital experience. This access is particularly helpful in enabling the family to remain involved with the patient. Without question, one of the most supportive gestures that hospital staff can offer a potential donor family is frequent opportunities to visit (Back, 1991; National Kidney Foundation, 1990; Johnson, 1992; Willis & Skelley, 1992): "Restricting access of the family to the donor may serve to engender mistrust and bitterness toward the hospital and the staff" (Willis & Skelley, 1992, p. 71). Access to the patient also facilitates a number of anticipatory mourning tasks. As mentioned, family members benefit from "being with" and "doing for" the patient (Parkes & Weiss, 1983; Rando, 1984). The family's frustration over their inability to do something for Anna Grace was voiced by her father.

"The worst part of waiting was those times when we had absolutely nothing to do. And when we were not with our Anna Grace, the waiting until we could see her again was torture. If only there had been more that we could have done for her."

Doing for the patient is one of the essential and beneficial aspects of preparatory mourning (Parkes & Weiss, 1983; Rando, 1984). Being involved in the patient's care is so important that Parkes and Weiss determined that families experienced subsequent problems to the extent that the opportunity to do for the patients was denied.

A perception of being helpful or needed reduces family members' sense of helplessness. The sharing of information is helpful in that it gives the family "something to do." It also helps the medical staff by providing them time to assess the family's coping patterns, needs, and resources. This interaction with the family may also build trust between family and medical staff. This trust in turn enhances participation with professional staff in decision making and planning; this participation represents another form of caregiving that may reduce the family's feelings of helplessness. For example, at one point Anna Grace's mother was asked specific questions about her daughter's medical history that only she could answer. Simply answering those questions enabled her to feel needed, thereby reducing her anxiety. "Doing for" the patient may also take a more personal turn, encompassing the simplest forms of care: stroking her hair, smoothing his sheet, holding her hand.

Throughout the period of forewarning, the family has an opportunity to assess the lethality of the patient's injury and to begin gradually to absorb the reality of impending death. This slow realization that death will be the probable outcome is another beneficial result of anticipatory mourning that may be facilitated by access to the patient.

> *"The last image I had of Anna Grace," said her father, "was of her bounding down the stairs to leave for school. With car keys jingling in her hand and her laughter filling the room, she was full of life. Only when I saw her in the hospital could I realize how desperate the situation was."*

The opportunity to address unfinished business is yet another beneficial aspect of anticipatory mourning (Parkes & Weiss, 1983; Rando, 1984). Access to the patient increases the opportunity for family members to accomplish this task, to express regrets, affection, and appreciation. Although the patient cannot respond, his or her presence facilitates the communication process. Anna Grace's father expressed the value of this opportunity.

> *"I had often told her that I loved her. Yet I needed to tell her once again how she had graced my life. I needed to tell her how wonderful she was. I wanted her to feel that we were there. I will be forever grateful for those moments."*

Hospital policy that denies family members access to the patient suggests professional or administrative myopia. Potential donor family members—more specifically, those closest to the patient—need to see the patient as soon as medically possible. Hospital personnel do not always recognize how important family involvement is to ensure healthy mourning.

Implications for the Caregiver

Caregivers must recognize and provide adequate information about the trauma, the patient's status, and the prognosis. Information should be repeated as needed. Careful explanations concerning brain death are essential; they should be presented in terms suited to the family's level of understanding. Close family members should be included in the care of their loved one to the extent possible. This involvement is particularly important within the realm of decision making. Involving family members with the patient demands giving them access to the patient, and providing access should be a primary goal of intervention for the family's caregiver. Every effort to allow access to the dying or brain-dead patient serves the needs of the donor family. In the short term, this access facilitates healthy mourning; in the long term, it lessens some of the risks of complicated mourning. Creative solutions must be found to circumvent the problems, practical concerns, and other considerations that complicate accommodating family members within trauma and critical care units.

Remaining Separate from the Patient

On the surface, remaining separate from the patient seems contradictory to remaining involved with the patient. However, a closer look will reveal that this task is paradoxical rather than contradictory, with both being achieved at the same time.

To recognize that they are separate from the patient, family members must begin to realize that they will live whereas the patient will die. This realization is difficult but necessary. However, it does not preclude remaining involved with the patient. These two tasks are pursued in tandem as family members come to understand that their needs are different from the patient's and that taking care of their own needs serves the patient best.

Implications for the Caregiver

Caregivers should focus on supporting family members as they struggle to maintain their own identities and recognize their own needs. Family members may say, "I wish I could take her place" or "I can't eat when she is suffering." Gentle reminders that one cannot take another's place are supportive. When a caregiver urges the family to take time out to eat or get some rest or reminds family members that they will need their strength, he or she is assisting them in remembering their separateness. Indeed, during this abbreviated time of waiting, family members can be helped to reframe asserting their separateness and attending to their own needs as acts of love rather than of betrayal.

Adapting to Role Changes

When one person is removed from the family system, there are always changes for everyone else: "Anything that affects the system as a whole will affect the individual members while anything that affects the individual will necessarily affect the family as a whole" (Rando, 1984, p. 327). Understandably, much of this adaptation will take place over time in the future. The potential donor family may have scant opportunity to adapt to role changes and explore life assumptions and identities. Yet, even in the waiting room, new leaders may emerge within the family as individuals attempt to fill the role of the fallen patient. Although this jockeying for new positions within the family system can create some temporary discomfort and disorganization, it is preliminary to all the changes to come.

In addition to trying on new roles, family members may challenge old roles and deeply held assumptions. Anna Grace's father spoke to this issue.

> *"The very idea that my child might die before me had never entered my mind. Such an idea was unthinkable. Yet, here I was—her big, strong daddy—her protector—and I was totally helpless. I couldn't even find my way to the rest rooms."*

Anna Grace's father expressed a broken assumption—"My daughter will outlive me"—and an altered identity in relation to his role in the family system. No longer was he the strong protector. He was able to articulate all these changes in one brief conversation.

Implications for the Caregiver

Intervention should be directed toward helping family members realize that they can work together to reassign roles and to anticipate future, more permanent changes (Rando, 1984). Support should be offered, and the family should be encouraged to focus on what can be done now.

Acknowledging the assault on basic assumptions can offer some comfort to the mourning family. Accurate understanding validates the mourner and helps reduce feelings of unreality and isolation.

Bearing the Affects of Grief

Inability to grasp the reality of the situation is a hallmark of sudden trauma. To the extent that reality breaks through disbelief, family members may experience myriad feelings that may threaten to overwhelm them. These feelings may include intense sadness, anxiety, anger, and fear. When people are overwhelmed by emotions, they may even react with aggressive or demanding behavior to camouflage their feelings (Rando, 1984).

Although intense expressive grief is not unusual, neither is an absence of display of strong emotions. Shock, numbness, and disbelief may be so pervasive that family members may be unable to demonstrate their emotions. It is unwise to assume that a quiet, unexpressive family member needs less support.

Implications for the Caregiver

Rando (1984) suggests a number of points that caregivers should remember when dealing with expressive grief.

1. Help family members understand that intense feelings are appropriate in this situation.

2. Reframe terms such as *loss of control* as *emotional release*, and help the family understand that releasing the emotions a little at a time actually prevents loss of control.

3. Encourage the expression of feelings in a place that is comfortable and private.

4. Remain calm and reassuring. This doesn't mean that the caregiver should be stoic—tears may be a form of compassion. However, do not let the intensity of emotion cause you to become disorganized.

5. Gently facilitate closure, if necessary, when family members become overwhelmed by their emotions. This is particularly important when the family must address practical considerations.

6. Be especially mindful of family members who appear relatively unemotional. Do not assume they need less support. They may actually warrant closer attention than those who are able to engage in expressive grieving.

7. Take great care not to attempt to diminish the family's pain. Anything said or done that discounts the enormity of the pain or robs individuals of the experience can be harmful.

Coming to Terms with the Impending Loss

According to Rando (1984), "The family goes through a series of emotional reactions that lead them to the increased awareness and acceptance of the loved one's dying" (p. 341). With the anticipatory period so abbreviated, the donor family may experience heightened awareness of the impending death, but the acceptance that is observed is often superficial. Acceptance of any death comes on many levels and is aided by a number of events—for example, viewing the body, attending the funeral, seeing the empty chair at breakfast, and so on. When organ donation is involved, this acceptance may be reinforced when the family signs the "consent to donate" form.

"I knew my Anna Grace was gone. I knew she wanted to be a donor. I was the one who heard her say so. Yet when I reached for the pen to sign the consent form, I knew in a whole new way that my darling girl was never coming home."

Painful as this realization was for Anna Grace's father, it was pain in the service of facilitating his sorrow. He was a step closer to accepting the full reality of his daughter's death.

Some professionals have attempted to relate the Kübler-Ross (1969) stages to the donor family experience. There might be some merit to the suggestion that the family moves within this brief period of forewarning through denial, anger, bargaining, and depression and then to acceptance. However, individuals never move through their emotional responses in such an orderly, linear fashion, nor did Kübler-Ross intend to imply that they did. Given that people with many months of anticipation often never arrive at acceptance, it is improbable that anyone would reach that state within hours or days. What health care professionals are observing and are terming *acceptance* is more likely a bowing to the inevitable, a reconciliation that is brief, temporary, and necessary. Regardless of the terminology used, this period of reconciliation is vital to the process of requesting the family's consent for donation.

Those who work closely with donor families agree about the importance of a time for reconciliation (Holtkamp, 1997; National Kidney Foundation, 1994; Willis & Skelley, 1992). There are three distinct occasions when the donor family must be allowed time to get used to the idea of death. The first occurs as the family is realizing the gravity of the situation. The second occurs after the declaration of actual brain death. During either of these times, family members may react with shock or with intense expressive responses.

After brain death has been declared, and after family members have had some time to confront the meaning of that declaration to the patient and to themselves, the option of organ donation must be offered. Any benefit of forewarning may be lost if family members are approached for donation prior to this period of reconciliation. Never, under any circumstances, should the request for donation be made in tandem with the pronouncement of brain death. The third opportunity for reconciliation should come after the option of organ donation has been offered. Family members must be allowed time in private, free of coercion, to make the decision that is appropriate for them.

Implications for the Caregiver

The caregiver can assist the donor family in these three phases of reconciliation through reality testing and planning (Rando, 1984). This assistance may include serving as an interpreter of medical information and listening to determine whether the family understands what has been said. During the first phase of reconciliation, while family members are adjusting to the idea that their loved one is in a life-threatening crisis, it is often helpful if they can be guided in discussions about the events leading up to the trauma. This facilitates the family's gradual adaptation to the shock of the loss.

During the second phase, at the pronouncement of brain death, the family needs someone available to answer questions and offer support. Paradoxically, they may also need some time alone. After this reconciliation period, when the option of donation is introduced, there must be total reassurance and support of the family's decision. Family members must also know that they will have a contact person to speak with after donation. The exquisite balance of availability and almost intuitive recognition of the family's need for solitude is the caregiver's challenge during these times of reconciliation.

Saying Good-Bye

Being present with the patient provides further opportunity for the family to say good-bye. This opportunity is a feature of donor family grief that is not always available for those whose loved ones experience immediate, sudden death. The act of saying good-bye acknowledges that leave-taking is occurring. It is at once an act of love and an act of relinquishment, a reluctant farewell to the fortress that housed the essence of the beloved. This act may be verbal or nonverbal, concrete or symbolic, but it will always be meaningful to the family members who participate.

For the donor family there may be more than one good-bye as they visit the loved one after brain death and again after the surgical removal of organs. Each time, family members should be prepared for any visual changes they might see. Although Jones (1987) found that family expectations were usually worse than the reality, each family must be prepared in advance for bodily changes and for the presence of any medical equipment.

Good-byes are seldom without sorrow; final good-byes bring great, wrenching heartache. For donor family members who do not remain at the hospital for the extended time for the surgical removal of the organs to be completed, there may be the added perception that they are the ones who are leaving, rather than the patient's leaving them. This perception can be distinctly disconcerting.

Implications for the Caregiver

The role of the caregiver at the moment of good-byes is relatively simple. Helping family members recognize that the end is nearing and prompting them to say their good-byes is the primary goal (Rando, 1984). On occasion, the caregiver may model leave-taking; however, it is important for family members to be encouraged to say good-bye in their own unique, personal ways.

Often, when leaving someone, we take with us a reminder of the person. For a family saying the final good-bye, a lock of hair of an adult or the handprint of a child might be meaningful. It is important for the caregiver to offer such options.

It is also helpful for health care professionals to help family members reframe their leave-taking as "leaving the hospital experience" rather than leaving their loved one. A simple reminder that the essence of the loved one lives on forever in the hearts of the family may reduce the risk of the family's equating good-byes with abandonment.

THE HEALTH CARE PROFESSIONALS

In her work with dying children, Kupst (1986) found that, although absence of a prior relationship does not preclude effective emotional support for the family, "the caregiver who has not been fortunate enough to have had a pre-death involvement with the parents is at a relative disadvantage" (p. 196). The same may hold true for those attempting to intervene with donor families. Yet numerous health care professionals who come in contact with the families of potential donors have had no prior relationships with the patients or their families. The list of caregivers is lengthy, including the staff of the trauma unit, nurses in the critical care unit, chaplains, social workers, and family advocates. This situation sometimes makes it difficult for any one person to develop and maintain an ongoing supportive relationship with the family.

In a near-perfect world, one person would be attending family members from their arrival at the hospital throughout the patient's stay. This person would have time to establish a trusting relationship with the family. He or she would become familiar with family members' coping skills and would have opportunities to prepare them and be with them when death occurred (Kupst, 1986). He or she would also serve as a liaison between the family and the physician, filling the critical role of the intervenor. Familiarity with the potential donor family would allow this professional to strike a balance between providing support and allowing family members the solitude they needed to process what was happening (Kupst, 1986).

In reality, a different scenario unfolds. As the lethality of the trauma and the possibility of brain death become clear, hospital staff call in the transplant coordinator. This medical professional is drawn from nursing, emergency medical technology, social work, or another health-related background. He or she is usually employed by an organ procurement organization and is specifically trained to present the option of donation to the donor family, to answer questions, and to support the donor family in the decision. The transplant coordinator also assists with the medical management of the donor. Matching available organs with people who need them is another aspect of the coordinator's job.

Because the transplant coordinator is generally not involved in the unfolding medical drama until the lethality of the injury is established and, ideally, does not approach a family until brain death has been declared, his or her time with the family during the anticipatory mourning experience may be severely limited. Although the responsibility for addressing the family's anticipatory mourning needs often rests with various hospital staff members, the transplant coordinator may also minister to many of those needs. Meeting the donor family's needs can present both opportunity and challenge as family members begin to undertake the critical tasks that are part of the anticipatory mourning process.

SUMMARY

A curious study by Janis (1958), cited by both Rando (1984) and Parkes and Weiss (1983), speaks of the "work of worry." In his study of patients who faced major surgery, Janis and his associates discovered that when patients received realistic information, they responded with more worry and anxiety:

> But their initial distress appeared to be in the service of coming to terms with the experience they would undergo and proved in the final analysis to be of value. . . . The importance of forewarning suggest [sic] strongly that anticipatory guidance would be as valuable for men and women facing bereavement as for presurgical patients. (Parkes & Weiss, 1983, p. 233)

During the period of brief forewarning, caregivers have opportunities to assist donor families with their "work of worry." Yet we must bear in mind that the processing of anticipatory mourning varies from person to person, event to event. Even when the opportunity is present and caregivers do everything they can to optimize the quality of the time available, family members may be unable to address the tasks of anticipatory mourning. The caregivers' efforts may be therapeutic only in that family members can see that they are cared for. The value of this care alone should never be minimized, for accurate understanding and compassion are the deepest forms of human connection. Anna Grace's mother spoke eloquently of the care her family had received.

> *"It was important to know that Anna Grace had a wonderful doctor—a recognized specialist; it was essential that we knew everything possible was done to save her life. But oddly enough, when we think back over the hospital experience, that time of waiting, we don't focus on those things. Instead, we remember the tears in the social worker's eyes, the insistence of the nurse that we be allowed more time with Anna Grace. We often think of the transplant coordinator who reassured us and patiently explained things to us, who arranged for us to hold Anna Grace and helped us say good-bye, the chaplain who told us it was perfectly OK to ask God, 'Why?' When life was no longer an option for Anna Grace, those were the things that mattered. In the end, it was the compassionate care."*

Compassion is a form of advocacy. That advocacy must extend to the care of donor families. By utilizing anticipatory mourning techniques to intervene on behalf of donor families, we offer them compassion. Methods of intervention that facilitate the inherent tasks these families face may effectively set the tone and pattern for healthy mourning for people who find the courage to reach beyond their greatest suffering to think of others.

The trust that is built, the bonds that form during that period of brief forewarning can provide a safe place where donor families can freely begin their mourning, where they can voice both appreciation for the opportunity to find meaning within loss and the ambivalence involved in having to do so.

REFERENCES

Back, K. (1991). Sudden, unexpected pediatric death: Caring for the parents. *Pediatric Nursing, 17*, 30–41.

Bartucci, M. (1987). The meaning of organ donation to donor families. *Anna Journal, 14*, 369–371, 410.

Campbell, C. (1991). Physicians of no value. *Hastings Center Report, 21*(3), 32–33.

Cassell, E. (1991). Recognizing suffering. *Hastings Center Report, 21*(3), 24–31.

Fox, R., & Swazey, J. (1992). Spare parts: Organ replacement in American society. New York: Oxford University Press.

Holtkamp, S. C. (1997). The donor family experience: Sudden loss, brain death, organ donation, grief and recovery. In J. Chapman, M. Deierhoi, & C. Wight (Eds.), *Organ and tissue donation for transplantation*. London: Arnold.

Janis, I. (1958). *Psychological stress*. New York: Wiley.

Johnson, C. (1992). The nurse's role in organ donation from brain dead patients: Management of the family. *Intensive and Critical Care Nursing, 8,* 140–148.

Jones, W. (1987). Emergency room sudden death: What can be done for survivors? *Death Education, 2,* 231–245.

Kirste, G., Muthny, F., & Wilms, H. (1988). Psychological aspects of the approach to donor relatives. *Clinical Transplantation, 2,* 67–79.

Kübler-Ross, E. (1969). *On death and dying*. New York: Macmillan.

Kupst, M. (1986). Death of a child from a serious illness. In T. A. Rando (Ed.), *Parental loss of a child*. Champaign, IL: Research Press.

Lebow, G. (1976). Facilitating adaptation in anticipatory mourning. *Social Casework, 57,* 458–465.

Lindemann, E. (1944). Symptomatology and management of acute grief. *American Journal of Psychiatry, 101,* 141–148.

National Kidney Foundation. (1990). *Making the critical difference* ("Caring for donor families," M. Coolican, Segment Narrator)[Videotape]. New York: Author.

National Kidney Foundation. (1994). *Bill of rights for donor families* (Item #06–13). New York: Author.

New York Regional Transplant Program. (1990). NYRTP develops book to help doctors explain brain injury. *NY/RTP Review, 2,* 3.

Parkes, C. M., & Weiss, R. S. (1983). *Recovery from bereavement*. New York: Basic.

Pelletier, M. (1992). The organ donor family members' perception of stressful situations during organ donation experience. *Journal of Advanced Nursing, 17,* 90–97.

Pelletier, M. (1993). Emotions experienced and coping strategies used by family members of organ donors. *Canadian Journal of Nursing Research, 25,* 63–73.

Prottas, J. (1989). The organization of organ procurement. In J. Blumstein & F. Sloan (Eds.), *Organ transplantation policy: Issues and prospects*. Durham, NC: Duke University Press.

Rando, T. A. (1984). *Grief, dying, and death: Clinical interventions for caregivers*. Champaign, IL: Research Press.

Rando, T. A. (1993). *Treatment of complicated mourning*. Champaign, IL: Research Press.

Sanders, C. M. (1982–1983). Effects of sudden vs. chronic illness death in bereavement outcome. *Omega, 13,* 227–241.

Savaria, D., Rovell, M., & Schweizer, R. (1990). Donor family surveys provide useful information for organ procurement. *Transplant Proceedings, 22,* 316–317.

Silverman, P. (1974). Anticipatory grief from the perspective of widowhood. In B. Schoenberg, A. Carr, A. H. Kutscher, D. Peretz, & I. Goldberg (Eds.), *Anticipatory grief*. New York: Columbia University Press.

Stephenson, J. (1985). *Death, grief and mourning: Individual and social realities.* New York: Free Press.

Swazey, J. (1986, Summer). Transplants . . . the gift of life. *Wellesley,* p. 15.

Transplants in 1996 show little increase. (1997, May). *The UNOS Bulletin* (United Network for Organ Sharing), *2*(5).

Willis, R., & Skelley, L. (1992). Serving the needs of donor families: The role of the critical care nurse. *Critical Care Nursing Clinics of North America, 4,* 63–77.

Worden, J. W. (1991). *Grief counseling and grief therapy.* New York: Springer.

Wright, J. (1978). Toward a common goal. *Heart Lung, 7,* 978–979.

Youngner, S. (1992). Organ donation and procurement. In J. Craven and G. Rodin (Eds.), *Psychiatric aspects of organ transplantation.* Oxford, England: Oxford University Press.

CHAPTER 19
Anticipatory Mourning
and the Human-Animal Bond

Barbara Meyers

Human death and dying are all around us and, eventually, come to everyone. We are touched by them throughout our lives and finally are invited to them. But there are other deaths that wind themselves quietly into and around our lives, bringing all the accompaniments of loss, its anticipation, and its threat. Loss of innocence, extinction of ideals and dreams, loss of honor, family breakup, loss of occupation, and countless other psychosocial losses cause pain, confusion, anger, and the host of other emotions and consequent reactions. Among all the underrecognized deaths and losses, one of the most neglected remains the dying and death of animals.

Before examining techniques and interventions required in addressing the loss of a companion animal, we must first comprehend the extraordinary phenomenon that is the human-animal bond. Too many professionals attempt to intervene without understanding this relationship. In doing so, they abandon the central principle that should guide us all—First, do no harm! Worse yet are professionals who, often arrogantly, believe they know and understand and forge ahead, actually exacerbating the trauma.

THE MAGICAL LINK: THE HUMAN-ANIMAL BOND

The dictionary defines *bond* as a uniting force or influence: that which binds or holds together, often permanently. *Permanently* is a very odd word in the context of our culture, a culture which has, unfortunately, come to view most of life as transient and even disposable. Anyone

---

No one should have to cry alone. No one should have to die alone. This work (and my life) is dedicated to all those who have done both. Suffering unseen, crying unheard, lingering in agony and dying alone, they shall not be forgotten . . . and to Queenie, my cribmate and first animal friend who, through her invisible web of wisdom and love, bound me forever to the magic between humans and animals.

who has found his or her "permanent" porcelain crown in the salad will attest to the questionable permanence of any bond!

There is, however, a bond that I view as permanent: the human-animal bond. It is the magical link between the natural world and ourselves, the slender strand that binds us to other living beings who can provide us with all that we desperately want from one another but cannot find.

With hamster or horse, bunny or bison, the link between animals and people is vital. It is a relationship that can be traced back to ancient times. Archaeologists have unearthed prehistoric evidence of early humans and dogs, positioned so as to indicate that their lives were shared in a very special way.

The early Egyptians so loved and revered their cats that they would shave their eyebrows to indicate the death of a cat in the household. They cared for their dead feline companions in much the same ways they cared for them during life. Out of love and respect they mummified their cats, placed them in cat-shaped wooden or bronze caskets, and put them in the tombs of their people or in special cat cemeteries.

Recently, Harvard University archaeologist Lawrence Stager discovered a mysterious dog cemetery in the ancient city of Ashkelon in Israel. The burial ground holds several hundred mummified skeletons of adult dogs and puppies. All appear to be of a similar breed, which today would be called either greyhound or whippet. Each skeleton has an individual grave—proof that these animals were prized and, no doubt, beloved companions. Plans exist to continue excavations in order to peel away the mystery.

The most frequently occurring human-animal relationships are with cats and dogs. This is not to say that there are not equally treasured and rewarding bonds between people and other animals but, rather, that the human-canine or human-feline interaction is the most common.

The human-animal bond is available 24 hours a day, and the relationship thrives on that contact. It is strong and resilient enough to tolerate long separations without a hint of tarnish, and it is free of judgment. Our animal friends are tolerant of every life and personal defect, alteration, and failure. No paw has ever been jerked away from the deformed human hand that reached for it. Open display of physical affection has never been withdrawn because the object of that affection has become sick, old, or unattractive.

Companion Animal: It's More Than Just Semantics

Before we go any further, we must pause to examine the use of the word *pet*. Therapists as well as others would do well to look carefully at what this word means to them, means to others, and may mean to others. The use of the word is not necessarily offensive, but it may signal to the listener—in this case, the reader's client(s)—that the speaker is less than sensitive or sophisticated about the current view of the word. Therefore, I urge readers to consider carefully the following definition and decide for themselves how, or if, they want to add to, alter, or adjust their ways of thinking, their feelings, and their approaches. One dictionary definition of pet includes the following meanings: (a) a domesticated animal kept for pleasure or (b) kept or treated as a pet (dog).

At one time it was considered acceptable, even complimentary, to refer to women as "broads." That time has passed. Along the path to our present social stance on the word, many have defended its continued use with vigor. That defense appears to have failed. It is widely accepted that employment of the term is, at the very least, in poor taste. Similarly, for at least the last 17 years, there has been a growing impetus to abandon the word *pet*. For reasons not unlike those related to the use of the word *broad*, this is not simply about political correctness. It is about an honest and sincere attempt to improve the images conveyed through words and to do so in a manner that not only describes but honors.

The term that is currently most widely accepted is *companion animal*. Other terms in use include *animal companion, animal friend, animal member of the family,* and *animal family*. Entire departments of veterinary teaching institutions and hospitals have been set up or redefined in ways that reflect this change in language. For instance, there are the Department of Companion Animal Medicine, the Department of Companion Animal Health, and the like. In another lexical change, the relationship between animals and people has come to be known as the human-animal bond, and departments in veterinary teaching institutions focus on this relationship. Humane societies all over the world have adopted the terms *companion animals* to refer to what were previously known as pets and *human-animal bond* to refer to the relationship, the latter with a view toward eliminating the word *owner* as well. There is even a humane organization known as The Human-Animal Bond Association of Canada.

One of my preferred ways to refer to and talk about companion animals is much the same way as we might talk about any other beloved family member or friend—for instance, "my sister Janice," "my Aunt Rose," or "my friend Alan." We can easily transfer this titled status to animals—for instance, "my dog Bill," "my cat Sam," "your hamster Lulu," and so forth. Naturally, when talking with someone who knows one's family and friends, simply referring to animals by their names is sufficient.

Although the word *pet* does not do justice to the human-animal relationship, it doesn't have to become a dirty word, nor should the more enlightened feel obliged to assault those who continue to use it. Your repeated use of an alternate term is often enough to be noticed and to spark friendly discussion. It is useful to talk about why the word is being phased out and why you have chosen to adopt a different term. The last thing we would do is generate an issue or create discomfort so that others become defensive or unwilling to talk with you. We hope it will be enough to set a good example, plant the seeds, and let others take in the information without conveying disapproval or an unspoken demand for them to change.

What the Human-Animal Bond Is Not

Perhaps the most important thing to understand about the human-animal bond is what it is not. Contrary to widespread and mistaken belief, the human-animal bond is not a substitute or replacement for human companionship; rather, it is another instance of the many relationships each of us is capable of enjoying. The human-animal relationship stands on its own, possessing unique properties that distinguish it from the others. It is not more or less important than another relationship; it is simply different, valuable, and worthy of affirmation, validation, and respect.

People with strong animal relationships are frequently thought of as social misfits who can't find mates or friends. In the case of a couple, their animal friends may be perceived as poor substitutes for children. It is not unusual to hear statements like "If they had a child, they could get rid of that stupid cat!" Many people, professionals included, cannot refrain from placing human-animal relationships in competition with human-human relationships. They view the care of animals and animal charities as competing with human progress and are angered by generosity toward animals, believing that the money, love, and time would be better spent on people. They fail to see that, among the many choices available to people, are where, on whom, and how to spend their emotional and economic resources. In fact, the total of the aforementioned resources spent on humans far surpasses the amount spent on animals. Nonetheless, it is also true that those people who build animal sanctuaries are frequently the very same people who build wings on children's hospitals!

The Individual Human-Animal Bond

The human-animal relationship is a tapestry woven of many fine threads. Most of those threads are found woven into other relationships. Some are seen in a few special relationships between and among people; others exist nowhere but in the remarkable friendships between animals and people.

In the human-animal relationship, each participant can play multiple roles, which can be interchanged with great ease and adaptability. The significance and complexity of these roles might not be obvious to the casual observer. For instance, a person might tell about his large, dominant, and protective German shepherd, who has bitten someone in his defense or has jumped through a window to "save" him from a real or perceived threat. The person may even reveal that the dog's behavior has left him embroiled in a lawsuit and yet continue to narrate the events with great pride and pleasure. Why? What is this person recounting with such pride?

This person is, in fact, describing the roles that characterize the relationship he shares with his dog. This dog is not "just a dog" but his friend and champion—his hero! Who else would this person dare to have as a hero? Healthy independence frequently prevents such relationships from flourishing between people. With animals, however, it is possible to gratify delicate longings without the unhealthy complications that might arise from indulging them with other people—complications like destructive dominance, victimization, and/or dependent-codependent behavior. The human-animal relationship provides a safe setting for expression of this need.

The animal members of our families, in turn, offer unconditional love. They greet us every day with the love, respect, and honor afforded a returning warrior. Who among our family, friends, or peers can offer up that much consistently sincere recognition and affirmation?

Children and Animals

Children and animals are a winning combination—a perfect blend of energy, curiosity, trust, and wonder. How they tug at our heartstrings!

Children and animals have a great deal in common. They both call on our deepest emotional treasuries. They come to us manifesting all the qualities we yearn for in one another but find so difficult to share and maintain: total acceptance, unconditional love, and an unending capacity for nonjudgmental interaction.

"A boy and his dog" is an image more American than apple pie, Chevrolet, or Mom and is probably equally represented in many countries and cultures. How often have we purchased a greeting card or poster that was not exactly right in its message but bore a cover photo of a dirty-faced boy with a shaggy dog or a calico cat in a little girl's arms?

Children retain the ability to sustain satisfying and healthy relationships with animals long after relationships with particular people have changed in response to the demands of development and increasing maturity. They are, in fact, able to maintain the human-animal bond for a lifetime. The lesson that even Mother's love is not unconditional for very long usually comes as a painful, but necessary, fact of social development and is, in most cases, learned fairly quickly. Unconditional animal love persists unchanged and is a constant in the midst of other transitions.

As sociocultural demands increase and expand, the secure and unchanging human-animal bond becomes more apparent and more precious. Although I do not yet know of any empirical data to support the notion, I am confident that volumes could be filled on the subjects of children's thought processes and behavior if all the kittens, dogs, and goldfish would reveal the secrets told to them by children!

The First Good-Bye: The Impact of Animal Illness, Dying, and Death on Children

We adults must be aware of the pseudodeath, perideath, and death-like events to which we (and children) are all subject. Among the saddest for children is, perhaps, the loss of childhood and innocence. Sadder still is the unnecessary or premature loss of childhood to an event that could have been prevented or buffered through education.

Although it is well known that we cannot fool children for very long, adults often try to do just that. We have been attempting it for generations and still have not done it with any degree of success. In our feeble efforts to avoid addressing the subjects of catastrophic illness and death, we give children mixed and inappropriate signals that result in fear, rejection, confusion, and guilt. The wish to protect children from the harshness of serious injury, illness, or death is natural and good, but actualizing it is dangerous if that wish leads to isolating the child from reality. Measured and well-thought-through exposure to facts is more likely to produce children who can surmount personal history and learn to appreciate themselves and others—including animals—with whom they share the planet.

The hasty dispatch or euthanasia of a sick or injured animal who requires nursing care at home because "it would be too hard for the children to see" can, and often does, teach children that an animal's life is cheap, especially when it becomes inconvenient, expensive, or difficult. From that point, it is a relatively short leap for children to internalize that they, too, can be dispensed with if they are sick, misbehave, or cause displeasure.

When an animal is removed from the home and children are not involved in the process, they often feel that they have been excluded because of something they have done wrong, and they can bear the guilt of that perceived wrongdoing for years. Too many children experience "the case of the disappearing animal." The child arrives home from school, and the family companion animal is not there. The opening line of this mystery is usually "Where's Charlie?" . . . and then the mystery turns into a horror show of deceit, lies, and pain. "You know that Charlie was getting too old to walk up the stairs . . ." or "You know that Charlie could never learn not to wet the floor . . . so while you were at school, we gave him to a nice farmer where that won't be a problem." This scenario is often played out after an animal has been euthanized due to illness or given to a shelter because of a behavior problem that the family did not know how to remedy and was unable or unwilling to address through professional help. When, after much questioning—which always includes "When is he coming back?" and "When can I go to see him?"—the child knows that there is a finality over which he or she has no control, shock and sadness likely will be compounded with guilty thoughts: "I should have taken him for more walks like I was supposed to"; "Maybe he would have been able to walk better if I didn't play so hard with him. Then they wouldn't have sent him away."

Sadly, parents may think they have convinced the child of the veracity of the story when the sadness, anger, and pain are no longer apparent. They may even feel reassured that all is well, but typically they have fooled only themselves. In many cases, the child never believes the story and never will. The child instinctively understands that there is no farm or farmer, and a bond of trust between parent and child is broken. In other cases, the child believes the story temporarily, only to recognize the lie later on.

"The case of the disappearing animal" takes place in the school setting, too. It is similar in many ways, and the disappearance often takes place over a weekend or a holiday. Here, again, adults have an opportunity either to attempt to delude children in an effort to "protect" the children and themselves or to provide children an experience that can guide them from pain and bereavement into awareness and understanding.

A well-thought-out, responsible, and holistic approach that begins before the animal ever comes to the school or the home takes account of the mortality of the animal who is becoming a part of the classroom or the family. This is not to say that the joy of bringing an animal into the child's life should be overshadowed by "Death Education 101," but rather that all the matters that concern the animal and the children need to be included appropriately. By definition, this means that experiences of illness, disability, loss, and death be honestly dealt with at the children's developmental level and not swept under the psychological rug with lies and misinformation that obscure the reality of life—the very life we are striving to prepare our children to contend with effectively.

Animals, like people, can die suddenly or be killed accidentally. In such circumstances, children can experience appropriate witness to death and bereavement. Adults should address these situations with care, honesty, and compassion. The words *death* and *sleep* must never be interchanged. Adults must remember that this may be the first experience of bereavement. "But she looks like she's sleeping," the child says. This can be solved with a simple, direct explanation of the difference between being asleep and being dead: When you're sleeping, your body is moving and working and you will wake up; when you are dead, your body is not working and will not move and you will not wake up.

While helping parents and teachers to approach this matter honestly and to make children welcome in the process, we must also caution them against turning invitation and encouragement into force or coercion. This can be as traumatic and damaging as exclusion and deceit. The gentle and sincere opening of the door to discussion about loss, dying, or death is probably all that children require. They will walk through on their own if they so choose. The important thing is to open, invite, and be on the other side waiting for them.

Healing Wounds Inflicted through Inappropriate Management of Loss

How can the therapist help heal wounds already sustained by children where the loss of an animal friend has been less than desirably managed? Whenever possible, see the parent(s) alone first. You should do so without the child's knowledge to avoid creating unnecessary additional anxiety for him or her. The child, however, should be party to all information around his or her own sessions, with the first one perhaps including the parent. The child should be informed that the parent has talked briefly with the therapist about what has happened so he or she will not be puzzled by some familiarity the therapist already has about the child and the family. Naturally, age-appropriate guidelines should apply.

The initial meeting with the parent should focus on all the customary goals of obtaining a complete history of the current circumstance; learning the chief complaint or worry about the child; and hearing the parent's own complaints, worries, anxieties, and so on, but with two very important additional perspectives: (a) a highly detailed account of the parent's relationship with animals and (b) the parent's perceptions and understanding of the child's relationship with the dying or deceased animal. To achieve these goals, you should ask the following questions:

1. What is/was your companion animal's name? From this point forward, always refer to the animal by name. It often surprises people just how important this is to the bereaved person. Most anyone who shares life with an animal has had a lifetime full of people (including even those who know the animal's name!) who refer to the beloved as "the dog" or "the cat." Also, take this opportunity to talk about how this name was chosen. You may find that the animal was named after a deceased member of the human family, a celebrity or sports figure, an admired political or community leader, or a friend. Odd, interesting, and whimsical names often are likely to produce wonderful anecdotes, and the discussion of naming will invite the client to begin telling the personal story. The story cannot be told without your sincere inquiry and certainly will not be told if the client just fills out an information form.

2. Was this animal a part of the household before the child/children were born?

3. When, and under what conditions, was the animal brought into the family? For instance, was it in response to a child's request, a mutual family decision, or a parent's wish? This information exchange provides another opportunity to learn a great deal. For example, Thomas may have been Grandma's cat. Grandma may be dead, in a nursing home, or moved to a place where she could not take him, or she may have become unable to care for him for some other reason.

4. What were the circumstances of the illness or death? In the case of an animal with a catastrophic illness, learn as much as possible about the care and treatment as well as the prognosis. Do not hesitate to talk with the veterinarian (with the client's permission, of course).

5. What part has the child played in caring for the companion animal?

6. What has the child been told about his or her role in caring for the companion animal?

7. What are the parent's impressions concerning what the child is experiencing, asking about, not asking about, and so on?

8. Are there other children or animals in the household? What are their reactions both to the loss and to the child who seems to be having the most trouble around it?

When seeing the child for the first time, you should follow the sequence represented by the acronym GAMS: greet, affirm, make safe, (elicit) story. The following example illustrates this sequence.

Greet. "Hi, Jessica. I'm glad to see you."

Affirm. "Your mom/dad has told me that Sam (be sure to use the animal's name) has been sick (or died). I'm so sorry. This must be very hard for you." Try to avoid suggesting emotions like sad, confusing, and so on, even though they are all probably part of the mix. It is more useful to make way for the child to express any or all emotions he or she may be experiencing. A suggestion that "This must be a very sad time" or "You may feel very sad" may occur at a point where sadness is not the overriding condition. "Very hard for you" is helpful in that it covers all feelings without directing, or misdirecting, any single one.

Make safe. Use whatever methods have worked well for you before to ensure that the child receives the message "Nothing bad can happen when you're with me."

Elicit story. "Jessica, tell me about Sam, please. I'd love to hear about him." At this time, avoid asking what happened to Sam. That can come later. It is most important first to invite the child to tell his or her story. Details, specifics, photos, drawings, and so forth can be woven in as a safe, therapeutic relationship develops.

Do not hesitate to reach out for feedback from colleagues who may be more experienced in this area. When necessary, a second opinion or consult may prove useful.

BETWEEN FRIENDS: ANIMAL-ANIMAL BONDS

Animals have extraordinary relationships with one another. They share with humans the abilities to love, nurture, play, and protect as well as the need and capacity to grieve, mourn, and experience anticipatory grief. This can easily be seen in elephants, gorillas, dolphins, whales, cats, dogs, and horses, but it certainly exists within many other species.

Some folks still cling stubbornly to the archaic notion that it is only humans who are aware of their own mortality and death. This notion is quickly dispelled by the demonstrations of anticipatory and postdeath grief and mourning in animals. They will gather around the sick, injured, frail, and dying to support and protect emotionally and physically. For instance, mother dolphins and other cetaceans have been observed repeatedly bringing a member of their group up to the surface of the water to enable the individual to breathe when it is having difficulty. When a calf dies, a mother dolphin will support its body on her head at the surface for many days. Marine biologists have observed female beluga whales doing the same with logs and driftwood. It is believed that these are mothers whose calves have recently died. Washoe, the first chimpanzee who learned sign language, stopped signing upon the death of her baby and remained "silent" until she was presented with an orphan to foster and adopt (Masson & McCarthy, 1995). Many species bring food to those who need it. Mud and leaves are lovingly placed over wounds. Burial grounds are clearly defined, and the dead are watched over, often for many days.

Are the foregoing gestures the actions of some mere preprogrammed survival machines? I suggest that they are behaviors of sentimental, intelligent, compassionate, altruistic, and loving beings. . . . some of whom are steeped in the larger phenomenon of anticipatory mourning. As in humans, not all anticipatory mourning is displayed in such admirable examples. Animals are also known to avoid one another in these situations, and some, like us, are moved actively to assist the dying in their journeys.

Many forms of grief, bereavement, mourning, and threat of the unraveling of a relationship, as humans have known it, are shared by people and animals for, with, and about each other.

ANTICIPATORY MOURNING
AND THE HUMAN-ANIMAL BOND

Anticipatory grief—herein referred to as *anticipatory mourning*—has been defined by many clinicians. We struggle to understand its origins, manifestations, functions, directions, and outcomes. But what does it feel like? How does it taste, smell, look, sound? How does it persist and spill over onto the jagged shores of postdeath mourning?

For some it feels like running in quicksand. It may taste like Bitter Apple (a foul-tasting preparation used to discourage animals from biting at or licking wounds or certain objects). It might smell like the acrid breath associated with kidney failure. It can look like the frail frame of a once-powerful German shepherd or the faltering step of a cat who, only weeks ago, could leap from the floor to the narrowest window ledge with the precision of an Olympic athlete. It could sound like moaning, whimpering, coughing, gasping, or, worst of all, like nothing at all—nothing where there used to be something, nothing where there used to be so much.

For many people, anticipatory mourning is long term and chronic, as it concerns the mass anticipated loss associated with the millions of nameless animals sacrificed to biomedical research or slaughtered and rendered homeless through loss of habitat. Mass anticipatory mourning is also experienced by people who are aware of the horrendous conditions of animals in circuses, rodeos, some zoos, puppy and kitten mills, and wherever animals are consumed at the will and whim of people. This is a legitimate grief experience that can no longer be passed off as the ranting and raving of "humaniacs" or "those vegetarian nuts." Thus, when your client (or anyone) comes into your office one day with what you may be tempted to view as an inappropriate, exaggerated, or disproportionate response to a televised report of a farm fire that killed 23 horses, or a tornado that destroyed a bird sanctuary, or the anticipated loss of dozens of lives in a shelter that will close, it is important to pay attention.

One story, although it does not speak to anticipatory mourning per se, may be a worthy example of mass grief. In 1987, three boys under 12 scaled the fence at the Prospect Park Zoo in Brooklyn, New York, and entered into the enclave of two polar bears. One boy, Juan Perez, paid for the adventure with his life. The bears, Teddy and Lucy, were executed by local police. The tragedy gripped the hearts of the entire community and the city at large. People who experienced these multiple losses (the death of a child and the deaths of the bears) were able to speak of the tragedy of the bears' death only in selected circles, for those who spoke of it indiscriminately were bombarded with criticism—for example, "How can you speak of those bears when a child has died?"

Teddy and Lucy had lived most of their pathetic lives in a zoo so poorly designed and managed that it was closed for massive redesign shortly after the incident. Yet, in spite of their own misery, they had delighted many children and adults. They were the childhood friends of hundreds of visitors who came to see them regularly, calling on them immediately on arrival at the zoo and then going back to say good-bye before leaving. I myself was one of those visitors, so I can attest to this. We visitors knew their names, we knew who was who, we knew what and when they ate; a special treat would be to visit them during their lunchtime. The world is a different place because Juan Perez didn't get to grow up. It is also a different place without Teddy and Lucy. Each loss is great and everlasting. Each of the mourners deserves the right to mourn.

Anticipatory mourning as it relates to animals is rarely presented, observed, or recognized. As a result, it is not treated, even by the most seasoned therapists who may stumble upon it in the course of other therapies. Even when it is uncovered, it is too often ranked as a minor subtext to a larger issue. Many people with legitimate animal-related mourning struggles are inappropriately accused of transference and projection. This is largely due to the therapist's failure to understand and appreciate the human-animal bond as well as the failure to include the client's possible relationships with animals in the initial history and evaluation. It is fundamental and vital to ascertain in detail the role of animals in the initial history and evaluation. By doing so, the therapist can quickly learn a great deal about the client. It is not unusual to find out that though a client does not currently (or did not recently) have a companion animal, he or she had one or longed for one as a child. Learning what happened to that childhood friend or why the client was denied the opportunity to have that friend can spare dozens of hours of therapeutic "fishing expeditions." When asked about their first death experiences, people will not hesitate to report the deaths of grandparents, other family members, or even world figures. Because the loss of an animal often was not recognized in childhood and is a source of what is called "disenfranchised grief" (Doka, 1989), this traumatic event often remains suppressed until it is specifically elicited. Only then can the client feel safe to reveal what was his or her true first death experience. This revelation usually occurs with a great display of tears and emotion.

Anticipatory Mourning for the Dying Companion Animal

There is no formal way to recognize anticipatory mourning over the dying of a companion animal, even for the person experiencing it. Often, it is handled through premature euthanasia. Excruciating grief is quickly put to an end with logic, rationale, and the well-meaning advice of friends, family, and insensitive professionals, who make such comments as "Why put her through it?"; "He IS 14 years old, after all"; "This is not gonna have a good end, so . . ."; or "End it while it's good." When the mourner lacks knowledge of alternatives, an experienced and competent hand and heart, or a history of success in similar encounters, euthanasia easily meets the need or wish to prevent or relieve pain.

Pain Control

Although veterinary science has made great strides in pain control, practical application lags far behind for the average veterinarian. Many veterinarians still hold fast to the old beliefs and must be forcefully pressed into the service of their patients. The only one who can exert this pressure is the patient's representative—that is, his or her human family. However, people often are ignorant of available treatments or are worn down from the management of illness or dying. They are sometimes held back by fear—fear of insulting the vet, fear the vet will refuse to continue caring for the animal, fear of seeking a new vet at a difficult time, fear of recognizing that the vet has enjoyed a worn-out or misplaced confidence. All of these factors lead to complicated guilt at a time when the emotions cannot withstand it.

The good news is that many veterinarians can be pressed into service with less difficulty than expected. A well-informed animal advocate can be very effective. A therapist can arm the client with tools more powerful than support, sympathy, and hand-holding: information and choice! Doing so of course requires that the therapist be informed, and so it is important to remember that, historically, the road to recovery for animals has been a minefield of uncontrolled pain and suffering. A wide variety of veterinary mythologies have contributed to this situation. They include, but are not necessarily limited, to (a) the belief that animals need pain to limit activity that might interfere with healing; (b) the belief that animals experience pain in some different way than people do; and (c) least defensible, that complicated record keeping for narcotics is an unacceptable intrusion and that narcotics are too costly.

Current knowledge of pain physiology indicates that animals process pain through neurologic pathways equivalent to those in humans. Animals do not tolerate pain any better or any differently than do humans. Because we can describe pain (often in detail) and animals cannot, we rationalize that they don't experience it. Nothing could be further from the truth! Animals provide evidence of their pain and suffering through very distinct behaviors, and it is up to humans to recognize, understand, and respond to those behaviors.

If you are describing your animal with the following or similar words, you are probably describing pain:

- Lame
- Uncomfortable
- Unhappy
- Shaking
- Shivering
- Crying

- Whining
- Grumpy
- Whimpering
- Quiet
- Not him-/herself
- Depressed

Red flags following hospitalization for illness, injury, or surgery include the following behaviors:

- Refusal to eat for more than 12 hours
- Reluctance to move
- Crying
- Whining
- Inability to achieve a comfortable position
- Behavior changes
- Aggression
- Inappropriate urination or defecation
- Panting while at rest
- Excessive attention to the surgical site
- Quick movement toward the surgical site during routine activity

The use of uncontrolled pain to modify an animal's postoperative activity is no longer conscionable for the compassionate, ethical health care provider and should not be tolerated by a loving and responsible family or individual who has entrusted the well-being of a beloved companion to a veterinarian. Would you permit a dentist to remove your human child's wisdom teeth without administering proper anesthesia (not just sedation) and pain control? Would you leave your grandmother in a hospital that had a policy of not offering pain control? Would you have the cartilage in your knee removed by a surgeon who thought you'd be better off with pain so you wouldn't walk too soon or too much? Is it OK for your wife, sister, mother, or daughter to have a hysterectomy with no relief of pain and anxiety? Do you want to end your life because controllable pain has not been controlled? As Eeg and Johnson (1997) emphasize, the need for pain control should be anticipated and met before the pain is full blown; a "wait-and-see" attitude is unacceptable.

Considerations Surrounding Life-Threatening or Terminal Illness: Palliative Care and Anticipatory Mourning

In the serious illness of a companion animal, what can be tragically lost is the opportunity to make a well-thought-out, as well as heart-based, decision. That decision may indeed include euthanasia, but that is not the only option. Providing good, loving palliative care is no longer the exclusive domain of hospice for people. Modern veterinary medicine that extends its technology to embrace an integrative approach (holistic, alternative, complementary, oriental/eastern, massage and aquatherapy, acupuncture, and other bodywork) can offer a great deal more than is generally believed.

Although some dogs with lymphoma can live with active treatments that include chemotherapy, immuno-augmented therapy, and other integrative modalities for 3 or more years, most do not. In general, 6 to 18 months of combined aggressive, supportive, and palliative care is the time frame around catastrophic illness such as cancer, feline infectious peritonitis, feline leukemia, and the like. Chronic and recurrent life-threatening conditions (for instance, degenerative myelopathy, diabetes and other metabolic diseases, complicated seizure disorders, etc.) certainly can extend much longer and present other challenges, to be addressed later.

The 6- to 18-month time frame, when it is not interrupted by premature euthanasia, seems to make for the best-prepared mourner when death actually occurs. It is highly interesting to note a correlation with Rando's (1983) study revealing that parents whose children died from illness in the interim ranges (6 to 18 months) were most prepared at the time of death and adjusted most satisfactorily afterward.

A well-prepared mourner neither detaches too early or too late nor fails to detach, and actually benefits from the processes that include the caregiving that can have positive and healthy effects on both caregiver and care recipient. The opportunity to re-cement existing bonds is but one advantage; the chance to create new and deeper bonds is another. Often we know and are accustomed to one set of ways to relate to another. When that pattern is no longer available, we can become abruptly lost or disconnected. Unless a person has highly developed adaptive skills, he or she will need support and assistance, often of a professional nature, to learn new ways to relate with loved ones. Psychological support appears to be one of the most important factors related to the 6- to 18-month time frame.

Prior knowledge of diagnosis and prognosis does not necessarily equal or lead to a healthy state of anticipatory mourning. This healthy or productive state is one in which bonds are secured, new bonds are made, love is expressed in new ways, and preparedness for death is best accomplished. In Rando's (1983) study, a parent's anticipatory grief score was determined according to the reported occurrence of certain behaviors. These included (a) discussing with someone the possibility that the child would die, (b) thinking what the future would be like without the child, (c) acknowledging the fact that the child was going to die, (d) grieving in anticipation of the loss of the child, (e) discussing the child's dying with the child, (f) planning the type of death the parent wanted for the child, (g) making funeral preparations, and (h) beginning a partial emotional disengagement from the child.

Though all these anticipatory mourning behaviors are involved in the illness and death of an animal, typically there is poor involvement at best in the last three areas. Because our current sociocultural environment remains underdeveloped in these areas, there is little opportunity to make funeral preparations of the kind we know to be most beneficial and therapeutic. Yes, there are many animal cemeteries; however, they are more of the "box and bury" model.

Most "funerals" for animals are really burials, the difference being that a funeral is accompanied by ritual(s) whereas a burial is simply a bare functional activity. Even these funerals are attended only by the most significant people in the animals' lives. There is rarely a service or any other formal leave-taking or good-bye. There is no postinternment sharing of food, drink, time, and talk because there is no one to share with. This absence is sad and crucial for the mourners, who are then generally expected (by themselves as well) to go about their business as though nothing much had happened.

When anticipatory mourning is recognized, supported, and given the environment in which to develop, it can be both a facilitating and a healing experience. When it, as well as other states and events surrounding animal-related loss, death, grief, and mourning, is suppressed or denied, people are left with few coping choices. Except for highly adaptive individuals, most will disconnect in more or less permanent fashion. This decathexis can extend to non-animal-related loss. This is especially true if the first or early experience has established a tendency to freeze acute grief, and the mourner may be disabled from that point forward.

Anticipatory mourning does not have to be filled with dangerous psychological curves, roadblocks, and detours onto permanently damaged pathways. For some, it is a self-limiting, natural part of the journey. The danger increases markedly, however, when animals, animal illness, and death are involved. This is, again, the case because the human-animal relationship still remains largely disenfranchised, undervalued, misunderstood, and at times openly ridiculed.

Concerned caregivers must be mindful of this situation and take appropriate steps to (a) legitimize companion animal dying and death, (b) enfranchise the mourner and assist in securing needed social support, and (c) enable the mourner successfully to address the processes of anticipatory and postdeath mourning as delineated by Rando in chapter 2. Practically every concern relevant to those mourning human dying and death is directly relevant to someone mourning the dying or death of a beloved companion animal. Those concerns that do relate exclusively to humans have counterparts that can be extrapolated with relation to companion animals.

A person engaged in anticipatory mourning for a beloved animal can be encouraged actively to create loving memories and strengthen the bonds with the animal friend. Conscious memory making involves simple acts of mindfulness, presence in the moment, and loving thoughtfulness. Though often mistakenly perceived as such, it is not staged, phony, false, or propped. People are encouraged and supported to focus on and enhance activities that will have personal meaning to them in the present as well as to create warm, though initially bittersweet, memories.

Where the prognosis is a fatal outcome—but where energy and quality of life are still high—the person should be encouraged to plan car rides, afternoons in the park, or whatever the animal especially enjoys. As energy and ability decline, wellness-associated activities can replace the more challenging ones. The Saturday afternoon the answering machine was turned off and there were only the music and the smell of treats baking in the oven, the purposeful time together, will leave a warm memory that can be treasured forever. In addition, just as when a human loved one is dying, such shared activities can testify to the importance of the relationship, make a statement of the mourner's love, and counterbalance any guilt that may be present. Because memories of the painful and less attractive—even haunting—are in ready supply for almost everyone, it only makes sense to make way for the healing kind.

Anticipating the Death of the Service-Oriented Companion Animal

During the last decade, increasing amounts of attention, media coverage, and professional literature have focused on the human-animal bond. This attention, unfortunately, has been spawned by yet another narrow and, many believe, exploitative use of animals as assistants to the physically challenged and institutionalized (including prison inmates). These animals include but are not limited to guide dogs, hearing ear dogs, working companion dogs, social dogs, therapeutic riding horses, a variety of mammals for animal-facilitated therapy and visitation, and monkeys that aid quadraplegics. (Unfortunately, these monkeys have all their teeth extracted as a prerequisite for their work.)

People's relationships with guide and assistance animals (primarily dogs) provide a stunning example of anticipatory mourning that can be chronic, with acute-on-chronic episodes. Part of the background to this mourning may be an awareness that the animal's working life, as well as his or her life itself, is of naturally limited duration.

The service animal was, until recently, most often pictured as the beloved, faithful guiding eyes of the blind. Guide dogs have won a place in society and in the hearts of all who are acquainted with the service and companionship they offer. They have been joined by other, less widely known service animals: the monkey with its helping hands, the dog that assists a wheelchair user with its strength and mobility, and the extraordinary hearing ear dog. Service animals fulfill numerous functions in the lives of the people they live with and assist. They are willing helpers, loving companions, and the gatekeepers to freedom and independence.

The hearing ear dog program provides at least two types of canine helpers: hearing ear dogs and assistance dogs. The hearing ear dog is trained to respond to sounds, such as an alarm clock, a ringing telephone, a crying baby, and so forth. The dog goes back and forth from the sound to his or her person and leads the person to the source of the sound. If the sound emanates from a smoke alarm, the dog leads the person to an outside exit. The assistance dog is trained to be the extension of the person who uses a wheelchair. He or she picks up dropped articles, retrieves things off high shelves, turns light switches on and off, pulls the wheelchair, and carries articles in a specially designed pack.

These extraordinary dogs, in addition to the specialized training that enables them to provide valuable assistance in the quest for independence, bring with them a quality for which no training is required. That quality is as much a part of the dog as is hock, sinew, or blood; it is unconditional love, total acceptance, and a genuine desire to please the human animal. These are the qualities that we humans long for in one another but often cannot find, as they usually are not available at high levels or for extended periods in the human being.

People whose lives are shared with and changed by assistance animals share a unique bond, and when that bond is interrupted by illness, retirement, or death of the animal, the impact on the human survivor is as unique as the relationship itself. In the absence of preparation and a support system, the death of a service animal can so greatly affect a person that it may produce a stress-induced exacerbation of any illness or condition he or she has.

Preparation for this loss must be woven into the early strands of the relationship; it is best addressed during the introduction/training phase. Bereavement counseling and grief therapy are, of course, vital interventions following a loss, but a broad-based and comprehensive inclusion of death education in the initial training will better prepare everyone involved (staff and assistance animal recipients) for the impact of the retirement, catastrophic illness, or death of the beloved companion/assistant.

We have a natural resistance to the subject of dying and death. This resistance is not difficult to understand, but it remains a major obstacle to the acquisition of a full and realistic picture of ourselves and the world we share. Therefore, it is, in my opinion, the responsibility of every ethical assistance animal organization to take a hard look at the subject and begin to reevaluate its programs with a view toward including appropriate death education. Both staff and assistance animal users should receive ongoing education in the form of workshops and seminars conducted by experienced specialists in the field of grief therapy and the human-animal bond.

The older a program is, the more cumulative grief and mourning will be found among longtime staff members. Cumulative grief is often accompanied by chronic denial. For this reason, even when there is no outward sign of trouble, the topic must be addressed. Failure to address it only serves to complicate and postpone the inevitable. Service animals, like humans, will get sick, grow old, develop physical disabilities that interfere with their work (there is possibly no greater sadness or irony than the hearing ear dog who becomes deaf), become involved in vehicular accidents, retire, or even be murdered! (It's hard to believe that anyone would intentionally take the life of an assistance dog, but I have been involved in more than one such case.)

Simply having a "second dog policy" is not enough. That policy must be accompanied by a system for support and healing. It is a long and often rocky road from the death of a friend to a second dog. A dog cannot be "replaced" like rusty yard furniture. In fact, I suggest that the word *replaced* be eliminated entirely.

In order to address a loss, one must first recognize and understand what has been lost. Loss and death come in many forms; they wind themselves quietly into our lives, accompanied by pain, confusion, anger, and so forth. Among all those who incur unrecognized losses, the most disenfranchised mourner is the human survivor of companion animal death. After all, "It's only a dog!" Only a dog, indeed! Only the singular experience in life that offers what we all need and want—total acceptance and unconditional love. In that experience lies the beginning of the understanding of the human-animal bond.

The healthy human-animal bond is a relationship filled with mutual love, respect, pathos, and joy. Individual humans have their own special relationships with animals, and these relationships must be individually addressed. When they are properly addressed, it is easy to see the extra ingredient that is part of the bond between physically challenged people and their service animals is not present in any other human-animal relationships. It is freedom—and how we treasure our freedom! Few of us need to stop and think what life would be like were we not free to reach for the light switch or pick up a dropped item. Suppose that the dropped item was a mouth stick, the only mobility tool for a quadriplegic. Suppose that you could not hear the doorbell or a child calling your name. How small and unsafe the world would become!

Those whose service animals die lose their freedom, security, and independence in the same blow. Many report the brutalizing experience of becoming deaf, blind, or handicapped all over again! How does such a person approach grief and mourning? What does one mourn first? The death of a beloved friend and companion or one's own freedom?

The tasks of grief and mourning can be arduous, and they require time: time to get in touch with the pain, time to work through it, and time to regain the strength and the desire to reinvest in another relationship. Many service animal users are not given this gift of time. Often, the very nature of the person's circumstances demands that he or she have another animal right away. There is no time to mourn, no time to prepare for reinvestment. The survivor experiences the burden of reinvesting under the worst possible conditions. The new animal is burdened as well. He or she may have to perform for and bond to a naturally reluctant person and, for a long time, walk in the shadow of a ghost.

Some people will resist reinvestment for a time, and, although this is entirely appropriate, they will require the highest level of support for this decision as they temporarily relinquish some independence. Others may say "never again" and return to a limited life-style without an animal assistant. Proper counseling at the earliest possible time can bring palliation for the grief and shock and may eliminate the "never again" syndrome entirely. This is particularly true if the person has had the benefit of death education at the beginning of the pairing with the service animal.

It is possible that you will one day be faced with the unusual needs of a client with an assistance animal. This is particularly true in the current context of settings in which these relationships are increasingly common. Such settings include special education schools and programs, group homes for the developmentally challenged, prisons, senior citizen clubs, free-standing and home hospice care settings, and therapeutic horseback riding programs. Thus, it is important to recognize that service dogs and other animals are not just mobility tools. They are trusted, highly skilled members of the world family. When they die, they leave behind them not just broken hearts but their myriad gifts. Not the least of these are patience, compassion, and the gentle art of true giving.

Moreover, grief and bereavement not being the privileged experience of humans, animals also share in the shock of loss and the mourning of a significant other. Some service animals survive their people, and it is essential that their loss be recognized as well. Program directors, family, and friends must join with the assistance animal's person in planning for the care of the surviving animal.

FUNERALS AND THE HUMAN-ANIMAL BOND

It is important to take into account the human-animal bond when planning funerary rituals both for people and for the animals with whom they are connected.

When a Person Dies

When helping a family dealing with the loss of a loved one, therapists must inquire about the presence of companion animals in that person's life. Funeral directors and their staff also need to do so when taking a pychosocial history. More often than not, the funeral director is among the first contacts a family has following a death. He or she is also among the first to bring comfort while creating a therapeutic funeral. Funeral service professionals share the unique opportunity to recognize and include the human-animal relationship in their process. Along with the usual arrangement interview questions, such as "Did Mother have any special interests?" or "To which clubs or organizations did Dad belong?" questions about the deceased's companion animals should be included. Given that people have important relationships with animals other than their companions, the inquiry should extend to wildlife—in particular, backyard wildlife. Many people have deep attachments to birds, squirrels, opossums, and raccoons that are expressed not only in watching them but in actually providing food and shelter on a regular basis. Not everyone considers these glorious children of Mother Nature to be pests that must be eliminated!

I have been present at many arrangement interviews and often watched a family go from rigid, controlled, brief responses with down-turned mouths and downcast eyes to animated descriptions of Dad and his dog or Mother and her cats. The arrangement interview serves purposes other than the practical matters related to the funeral. It is also the time when the family can begin the mourning processes in the most healthy way.

I suspect that every funeral director has personally seen evidence of the powerful human-animal bond while attempting to remove the deceased from the home. Dogs howl, whimper, and are found guarding their dead humans. Many removers have been bitten; often, removal cannot be accomplished until someone takes the dog into another room.

One result of the inclusion of questions about animals in the arrangement interview has been the presence of more than a few companion animals at their humans' funerals and gravesites—a presence that has linked families together in a very special way.

One funeral home in Brooklyn, New York, has a resident cat. At the Daniel George and Son Funeral Home, "Momma's" presence has softened the mood, brought smiles, and encouraged memories of "Mom's dog," "Dad's cat," and so forth. By her mere presence, this animal has facilitated the healing properties of "telling the story," thus making it more possible to design a therapeutic funeral for the family. I am not suggesting that every funeral home take up a staff of feline therapists, but that the example of this funeral home illustrates the many important roles animals play in our lives.

When an Animal Dies

I know she's dying. She's been my best friend for over 15 years. I hate it that she's dying . . . anyway, she seems to be holding her own, this week. I feel guilty about planning her death or funeral or any of it, but I owe it to her. I actually want to do this right for her. She deserves it . And even when I feel I can, I can't bear to think of doing all the things I want to do for her and then have no one show up!

This statement conveys some sense of what it is like for someone to contemplate funeral rituals for a beloved companion animal. Though there are many beautiful animal cemeteries, lovely memorial parks, and exquisite caskets and cremation wares for animals, they are underused and largely unshared. One complication of anticipatory mourning surrounding the death of an animal is the expectation that one will say good-bye to the beloved friend alone.

Funerals, memorial services, and other rituals are designed to honor the bodies in which the beloved lived, to celebrate their lives, and to bring comfort to the bereaved. Almost none of these rituals is realistically available to the survivor of animal death. Only the rare individual, surrounded by even more rare friends and family, enjoys this deserved support.

As therapists, we have the opportunity and the obligation to offer other possibilities. Sometimes the mere exploration of choices is sufficient comfort to allow a person the needed measure of strength. For example, someone contemplating a ritual for a beloved animal can consider several options. Given that almost no one will take a day off from work to attend a funeral for an animal, a memorial luncheon could instead be held on a weekend date not too long into the future. Postponing the funeral to a weekend day is not a good option for several reasons. First, sophisticated preparation and care for deceased animals' bodies is not yet available, though I hope that will change in the future. Second, even if the funeral could be comfortably postponed, the bereaved person would risk being disappointed by meager attendance. This would be an unnecessary risk at a fragile time.

Given that a conventional funeral is not a likely option, there are other acts of love and sharing that can be accomplished and serve the mourner very well. Therapists should not instruct clients or imply that they must do something, but rather offer choices, along with the reassurance that it is also OK to choose to do nothing. One option that seems to have been very well received involves death announcements. We announce so much of our lives to one another for the purpose of sharing. Why not do so in this case, as well? The announcement can be a poem, a simple statement of facts, a passage from scripture, or anything that appeals to the individual or family. It can be accompanied by a small photograph of the animal friend and become a keepsake for the recipient. The announcement can be copied in any quantity and on any kind of paper. If a photo is chosen, it can be reproduced in wallet size. The following fragment of a poem movingly illustrates this concept:

Miss Pinky Lee
—1981–1996
. . . and she went, gently, into that good night
with all the dignity and grace with which she lived her life.

Dear Heart, Dear Girl, Dear Friend.

Some people find great comfort in preparing the announcement during the time of anticipation of the death; others prepare it shortly afterward. My own observation suggests that preparing the announcement prior to the death works best. This practice also serves another function. The announcement helps one avoid talking during a time when words may fail and, yet, when one most needs others to know. The mailed announcement informs people and gives them the opportunity to respond.

Remind your clients that if they cannot or prefer not to take a lot of phone calls but do want to hear from others, they can let their answering machines work for them. They might consider adding words such as the following to their recorded announcement: "I won't be coming to the phone for a while, but I would love to be able to listen to your message or receive a note from you. I'll be returning your call as soon as I'm able."

If you think this is straight grief work and not anticipatory mourning, please think again. As previously mentioned, anxiety, confusion, and empty space are significant elements of anticipatory grief. What I have just described are remedies for those elements that will allow clients to experience this difficult time without complications that interfere with the process. People should be encouraged and supported in the partaking or reinventing of any cultural or religious rituals that they would dedicate to any other family member. Prayers, altars, candle lighting, and saying of the kaddish need not be exclusively for humans.

A particularly useful, loving, and joyful tribute is a video production of the type produced by the National Music Service in Spokane, Washington. As part of their Tribute Program, this organization creates a video remembrance that blends personal photographs spanning the life of the deceased animal with exquisite live video scenery, to the accompaniment of beautiful background music. Numerous choices of background music and scenery are available. When longing and searching occupy much of the bereaved's time, he or she can satisfy at least some part of that need by looking no further than the VCR. It is reported consistently that in times when people have trouble remembering what the deceased looked like, a video serves better than a photo or a painting. Even though still photos are used in the composition of the video, the live background and the music lend life to the images.

ANTICIPATING THE DEATH OF A PERSON BONDED TO A COMPANION ANIMAL

Among the end-of-life issues that the dying and their families, friends, and significant others must address is the dying person's relationship with his or her animal friends. Following are some general guidelines for the therapist to follow:

1. Be sure to ask questions about the animals (name, breed, color, age, personality, special qualities, etc.). Inquire how long the person and the animals have been together, how they met, and so forth.

2. Ask these questions of all the people involved as you meet or come in contact with them.

3. Bear in mind that dying people are likely to be experiencing anticipatory mourning not only about their own ebbing lives but also about the lives of their animals.

4. To help alleviate the anxiety that can complicate this mourning, encourage the dying person to include his or her animals and, in the process, to create a care plan for the animals.

5. Ask what arrangements have been made for the animals and ensure that the arrangements are really satisfactory.

6. Verify that these arrangements cover temporary hospitalizations during the person's illness as well as permanent placement upon his or her death.

7. Do not blindly accept an arrangement such as "Oh, my sister will take care of him." Talk with the sister to ensure this is not an unwanted legacy that will end in the death of the animal, too.

8. Many people who have have chosen cremation for their previously deceased animals have the cremains in their homes. Find out what is to be done with the cremains. Remember that cremation is not final: Something must eventually be done with the cremains. Perhaps the person would like to scatter the cremains personally before dying. Perhaps you can do it for or with the person. Perhaps the person would like to have the cremains buried with him or her or, if cremation is planned, have all the cremains scattered or commingled and placed in the care of someone appropriate.

9. If animals are to be cared for by others who are very much willing, verify that financial support for that care will accompany the arrangements if at all possible. Veterinary insurance is available; prepaying a year's premium can assure the dying person that the animals' health needs will be taken care of for this period of time. (A local veterinarian will likely have the names of veterinary insurance providers.)

10. Where no family member or friend is willing or able to adopt the animal, be aware that long-term care facilities are an alternative. These must be researched very carefully and almost always require a bequest/fee or donation. Two examples are Last Post

Sanctuary for Cats in Falls Village, Connecticut, and Living Free in Mountain Center, California.

11. Euthanasia of animals is, yet, an option that people sometimes choose. In my own practice, I have worked with many people whose sole problem is the discomfort and guilt they feel about planning to have their animals euthanized following their own deaths. They have made their decisions because they believed that (perhaps correctly) no other option remained. In such cases, share some of the suggestions listed. If, after exploring alternatives, the person still considers euthanasia the best option, he or she will be more comfortable with the decision, and you will have made an enormous therapeutic and humane contribution. If euthanasia is the final decision, remember to work out the details. Who will take the animals to the veterinarian? Is the vet informed and willing? Who will pay the bill? What is to be done with the remains? This discussion will also cement your relationship with the dying person in a special way that many others do not understand. This closeness is more valuable than it may seem.

12. Do not allow family or friends to underestimate the importance of discussing the subject. In their own distress, they may falsely accuse you of "caring more about the nasty bird" than about their loved one. Proceed with caution, but proceed. Help them to understand the benefits that the loved one will reap when this very important matter has been addressed. Reassure them that the issues around the animals are not superseding any other but are part of the whole. Assure them that you are not sacrificing any of your role to this concern and that you remain fully available to them and their loved one on all matters.

13. If necessary, give dying persons the opportunity to have their animal with them (e.g., visit the hospital, sit on the bed). Comfort, joy, and the chance to say good-bye are but a few of the benefits. As life dwindles, touching one's animals can be very consoling.

Arranging for these and other kinds of comfort care are rewarding for the therapist, professional caregivers, and friends and family of the dying person. One's beloved animals can actively ease the transitions at the end of life; caregivers may even bring the gift of animal companionship to the dying person if animals are not a part of that person's family.

The human-animal bond is a magical connection among species, including humankind. It connects us to ourselves and to one another, doing so as little else can. We feel deeply the dying and deaths of the animals with whom we share this earth. As we ourselves draw nearer to death, our connections with animals are part of the anticipatory mourning process, and these losses must be acknowledged. Finally, the roots and footprints we leave behind are not only our own.

REFERENCES

Doka, K. J. (Ed.). (1989). *Disenfranchised grief: Recognizing hidden sorrow.* Lexington, MA: Lexington Books.

Eeg, P. H., & Johnson, J. (1997). *Compendium.* Trenton, NJ: Veterinary Learning Systems.

Masson, J., & McCarthy, S. (1995). *When elephants weep: The emotional lives of animals.* New York: Delacorte.

Rando, T. A. (1983). An investigation of grief and adaptation in parents whose children have died from cancer. *Journal of Pediatric Psychology, 8,* 3–20.

Name Index

Note: Figures are indicated by an italicized *f*.

Subject Index

Note: Tables are indicated by an italicized *t*; figures by an italicized *f*.

About the Editor

Therese A. Rando, Ph.D., is a clinical psychologist in Warwick, Rhode Island and Clinical Director of The Institute for the Study and Treatment of Loss, which provides advanced training, supervision, and consultation to professionals working with the dying and the bereaved, and offers selected clinical services directly to these populations. Since 1970, she has consulted, conducted research, provided therapy, written, and lectured internationally in areas related to loss, grief, and death. In recent years, she also has provided expert witness testimony in legal proceedings involving bereavement.

Dr. Rando has authored over 60 publications pertaining to the clinical aspects of thanatology, among them *Treatment of Complicated Mourning; How to Go On Living When Someone You Love Dies;* and *Grief, Dying, and Death: Clinical Interventions for Caregivers*. She is the editor of *Parental Loss of a Child*, as well as co-editor of the Trauma and Loss Book Series for Brunner/Mazel Publishers. Currently writing a book for the general public on coping with traumatic death, Dr. Rando also serves on the editorial boards of the journals *Death Studies* and *Omega*. She is a national media resource expert in dying, death, and loss for the American Psychological Association and a frequent consultant to the media.

Dr. Rando received the Association for Death Education and Counseling's 1987 award for Outstanding Contribution to the Study of Death, Dying, and Bereavement and its 1996 Clinical Practice Award. In 1997 she was among the initial group of international experts elected to membership in the Green Cross Foundation Academy of Traumatology. In 1999 she was accepted as a memer of the Academy of Experts in traumatic stress.

About the Contributors

Joyce Ashton, R.N., is a pediatric nurse, certified grief counselor, and RTS Bereavement Coordinator. She leads three support groups at Columbia Medical Center in Dallas for those experiencing neonatal loss, death of a child, and breast cancer. Dennis Ashton, L.M.S.W./A.C.P., D.A.P.A., is Assistant Commissioner of LDS Social Services for the State of Texas. He holds a master's degree in clinical social work and is a board certified licensed psychotherapist. The Ashtons speak on many topics: marriage and family issues, infertility/adoption/unplanned pregnancy, abuse, disabilities, illness, anxiety/depression, and death. They are the authors of *Loss and Grief Recovery: Caring for Children with Disabilities, Chronic and Terminal Illness* and are currently completing a book on general issues in loss and grief. They are the parents of six children, four of whom are living.

Thomas Attig, Ph.D., is Professor Emeritus and former Chair of the Philosophy Department at Bowling Green State University in Ohio. He is former President of the Association for Death Education and Counseling and currently Vice-Chair of the Board of the International Work Group on Death, Dying, and Bereavement. He is the author of *How We Grieve: Relearning the World* and *The Heart of Grief: The Desire for Lasting Love,* as well as numerous articles on death, dying, and grieving.

Stephen R. Connor, Ph.D., is Vice President and Director of Research and Professional Development at the National Hospice Organization in Arlington, Virginia. He has worked continuously in the hospice movement since 1975 as the CEO at four different hospice programs. In addition to being a hospice executive, he is a licensed clinical psychologist, a researcher, and a member of the International Work Group on Death, Dying, and Bereavement. He is the author of many articles and book chapters related to care of the dying and their families, as well as the recently published book *Hospice: Practice, Pitfalls, and Promise.*

Charles A. Corr, Ph.D., and Donna M. Corr, R.N., M.S.N., have been exploring issues associated with death, dying, and bereavement since 1975. Their publications include a dozen books and more than 60 articles and chapters. Among their books are *Hand-*

book of *Childhood Death and Bereavement, Handbook of Adolescent Death and Bereavement* (this last edited by Charles A. Corr and David E. Balk), and the third edition of their textbook *Death and Dying, Life and Living* (coauthored with Clyde M. Nabe). The Corrs live in St. Louis, Missouri, and St. Petersburg Beach, Florida. Recently, they each took early retirement from their respective academic positions in order to devote more time to writing and presenting.

Betty Davies, R.N., Ph.D., is a professor in the School of Nursing, University of British Columbia. She is a founding member of Canuck Place, North America's first freestanding hospice for children. She has served on the boards of both the International Work Group on Death, Dying, and Bereavement and the Association for Death Education and Counseling. She is the author of *Fading Away: The Experience of Transition in Families Facing Terminal Illness* and *Shadows in the Sun: Experiences of Sibling Bereavement in Childhood,* as well as over 100 articles and book chapters.

Kenneth J. Doka is a professor of gerontology at the College of New Rochelle, New York. Among Dr. Doka's many books are *Disenfranchised Grief; Living with Life-Threatening Illness; Death and Spirituality; AIDS, Fear, and Society;* and *Children Mourning, Mourning Children.* In addition, he has published over 60 articles and chapters. Dr. Doka is the editor of the journal *Omega* and *Journeys,* a newsletter for the bereaved. He has served as a consultant to medical, nursing, and hospice organizations, as well as to businesses and educational and social service organizations. As Senior Consultant to the Hospice Foundation of America, he assists in planning and participates in their annual teleconference. In 1988 he received the award for outstanding contributions to the field of death education from the Association for Death Education and Counseling and in 1993 was elected President of that organization. Elected in 1995 to the Board of the International Work Group on Dying, Death, and Bereavement, Dr. Doka was elected Chair in 1997. He is an ordained Lutheran minister.

Sue C. Holtkamp, Ph.D., is founder and director of Something More Grief Counseling and Bereavement Programs. Working almost exclusively with organ procurement programs since 1987, Dr. Holtkamp has interviewed over 2,000 donor family members, providing private therapeutic intervention for more than 500 of these individuals. She reaches a larger audience through the column "Bereavement and Organ Donation," which she edits for *Bereavement Magazine.* Since 1988, Dr. Holtkamp has presented and consulted nationally and internationally on donor family grief. She is author of the book *Grieving with Hope* and a contributor to the book *Organ and Tissue Donation for Transplantation,* an international effort published in London. The working title of Dr. Holtkamp's latest book is *Wrapped in Mourning: The Gift of Life and Donor Family Trauma.*

Sandra Jacoby Klein, M.A., M.F.T., is a marriage and family therapist in Los Angeles. Specializing in the emotional effects of illness and loss, she is known worldwide for her presentations on psychosocial issues in HIV/AIDS. She is a past chairperson of the Human Services Commission of the City of West Hollywood, California, and a clinical member of the American Association for Marriage and Family Therapy, the California Association of Marriage and Family Therapists, the International AIDS Society, and the Association for Death Education and Counseling.

William M. Lamers, Jr., M.D., began his practice in psychiatry in Marin County, California, in the 1960s. In the early 1970s, he established one of the earliest hospice programs in the United States. For several years he also served as Chairperson of the Standards and Accreditation Committee of the National Hospice Organization. He is a long-time member of the International Work Group on Dying, Death, and Bereavement, and served as President of the Board of Directors in 1983 and 1984. In 1981, Dr. Lamers accepted dual appointments as Associate Clinical Professor at the University of Calgary Medical School and the Tom Baker Cancer Centre, in Calgary, Alberta. Following his return in 1985 to Southern California, he helped develop the Chris Brownlie AIDS Hospice in Los Angeles and served as Medical Director of Hospice of the Canyon and Avalon Hospice. The author and coauthor of a number of books and papers in the fields of medicine, psychiatry, and hospice care, Dr. Lamers has lectured both nationally and internationally. He has received the Founder's Award of the National Hospice Association, the "Brother's Keeper" Award from the Los Angeles Clergy Relations Network, and a lifetime achievement award from the Marquette University Alumni Association. Dr. Lamers resides in Malibu, California, and works as a consultant in the areas of hospice, palliative care, and pain management.

Dale G. Larson, Ph.D., is Associate Professor of Counseling Psychology and Director of the Graduate Counseling Psychology Program at Santa Clara University in California. A clinician and researcher, Larson has published extensively in the areas of oncology and hospice. He has lectured and conducted research in Europe as a Fulbright Scholar and is the author of the much-acclaimed book *The Helper's Journey: Working with People Facing Grief, Loss, and Life-Threatening Illness.*

David K. Meagher, Ed.D., is a professor of health science and Coordinator of the thanatology master's degree concentration at Brooklyn College of CUNY. He is also the editor of *The Thanatology Newsletter* and *As It Is Written: A Selected Annotated Bibliography on Death and Dying.* He is on the advisory board of the Metropolitan Hospice of Greater New York and has also served as President of the Association for Death Education and Counseling.

Barbara Meyers is a human-animal bond consultant and certified grief therapist in private practice on Staten Island. A symposia lecturer at the Foundation of Thanatology at Columbia-Presbyterian Medical Center and a University Seminarian, she is also an associate faculty member in death studies at Columbia University in New York City. She has been certified in thanatology by the National Center for Death Education in Boston and has studied extensively in the area of animal behavior/ethnology. As an active member of many professional and humane organizations, she has appeared in the media and lectured internationally.

Donna Jeane Hitchcock Pappas, M.Ed., L.P.C., is Coordinator of Bereavement Services at Duke University Medical Center, where she oversees a hospital-wide bereavement program for patients, staff, and families. Previously, she provided counseling at the Department of Obstetrics and Gynecology at the University of North Carolina Medical School in Chapel Hill for families experiencing a crisis surrounding reproductive issues and coordinated the perinatal loss bereavement program there. She is a member of the Association for Death Education and Counseling, the North Carolina association of ADEC, and the Licensed Professional Counselors Association of North Carolina. She has presented on the state and national levels. Keeping life and work in balance comes with the help of her family, her husband, Jim, and her children, Josh, Michael, Cameron, and Peyton.

Marsha (Max) Quinn, J.D., is the Fellow in Pediatric Bioethics at Montefiore Medical Center, New York, where she also directs the Samuels Foundation Pediatric Palliative Care Initiative. She received her law degree from Yale Law College and is a candidate for the master's degree in the thanatology concentration at Brooklyn College of CUNY. In addition, she is a 1999 recipient of the Emily Davie and Joseph S. Kornfeld Foundation Fellowship.

J. William Worden, Ph.D. ABPP, is a Fellow of the American Psychological Association and holds academic appointments at Harvard Medical School and at the Rosemead School of Psychology in California. He is currently a codirector for Harvard's Child Bereavement Study, based at the Massachusetts General Hospital. His research and clinical work over 30 years has centered on issues of life-threatening illness and life-threatening behavior. Dr. Worden has lectured and written extensively on topics related to terminal illness, cancer care, and grief. He is the author of *Personal Death Awareness* and coauthor of *Helping Cancer Patients Cope*. His book *Grief Counseling and Grief Therapy*, now in its second edition, has been translated into seven foreign languages and is widely used around the world as the standard reference on the subject. His newest book, *Children and Grief: When a Parent Dies*, was published by Guilford Press. Dr. Worden's clinical practice is in Newport Beach, California.